THE
GREATNESS
OF GOD

THE
GREATNESS
OF GOD

How God Is the Foundation of All Reality,
Truth, Love, Goodness, Beauty, and Purpose

CHARLES FRANK THOMPSON

WESTBOW
PRESS®
A DIVISION OF THOMAS NELSON
& ZONDERVAN

WestBow Press books may be ordered through booksellers or by contacting:

WestBow Press
A Division of Thomas Nelson & Zondervan
1663 Liberty Drive
Bloomington, IN 47403
www.westbowpress.com
1 (866) 928-1240

ISBN: 978-1-5127-0177-7 (sc)
ISBN: 978-1-5127-0179-1 (hc)
ISBN: 978-1-5127-0178-4 (e)

Print information available on the last page.

WestBow Press rev. date: 02/08/2016

For Rev. C. Frank Thompson and Grace Thompson,
My Dad and Mother,
Who showed me the way.

CONTENTS

Chapter One. The Greatness of God: The Goodness, Beauty,
and Truth of the Created Natural World.....................................1

Chapter Two. The Greatness of God: Recently Discovered Wonders
of the Universe and the Natural World.....................................43

Chapter Three. The Supreme Intelligence of God: The Wonders
of Human Life 72

Chapter Four. God the Supreme Being, Creator, and Preserver
of All: The Being, Mind, and Ideas of God...........................101

Chapter Five. God the Foundation of Truth, Knowledge,
and Wisdom..126

Chapter Six. The Growing Rejection of God in Modern Thought...........150

Chapter Seven. The Rejection of God in Radical Twentieth-Century
Modern Art and Thought..186

Chapter Eight. The Absence of God in Later Twentieth-Century
Postmodern Art and Thought...210

Chapter Nine. God's Love, Goodness, and Sovereignty: Human
Responsibility, Love, Goodness, and Evil...............................246

Chapter Ten The Holiness and Justice of God: Sin, Punishment,
Death, War, And God's Plan for Human History 275

Chapter Eleven. God, the Maker of Ultimate Purpose and the
Providential Controller of History...310

Chapter Twelve. The Consummation of Creation: The Millennium
and the Eternal Kingdom of God...352

Bibliography 381
Glossary 394
Endnotes..410

List of Illustrations

Front Cover, Albrecht Dürer, *Adoration of the Trinity*, (detail of the Landauer Altar), 1511. Photo and permission by the Kunsthistorisches Museum, Vienna.

Fig. 1. *The Spearbearer (Doryphoros)*. Modern Bronze reconstruction by Georg Roemer of the Greek High Classical original of c. 440 BC by Polykleitos. 6'6". Formerly in Munich, destroyed in 1944. Foto Marburg/Art Resource, NY. 8

Fig. 2. *Christ Enthroned in Majesty, with the Twelve Apostles in the New Jerusalem (Heaven)*. c. AD 390. Apse mosaic in the Church of Sta. Pudenziana, Rome. Photo credit: Alinari/Art Resource, NY. 11

Fig. 3. Albrecht Dürer, *Adoration of the Trinity* (Landauer Altar), 1511. Oil on lime panel, 53 x 48½". Photo and permission by the Kunsthistorisches Museum, Vienna. 14

Fig. 4. Picasso, *Demoiselles d'Avignon (The Women of Avignon)*, 1907. 8' x 7' 8." Museum of Modern Art, NY. Photo credit: Digital Image The Museum of Modern Art/Licensed by Scala/Art Resource, NY. © 2011 Estate of Pablo Picasso / Artists Rights Society (ARS), New York ADAGP, Paris. 15

Fig. 5. Raphael, *The Triumph of Christian Religion* (*Disputà*, or *Disputation Over the Sacrament*), c. 1509. Fresco in the Stanza della Segnatura, Vatican Museums, Vatican State, Rome. Photo credit Erich Lessing / Art Resource, NY. 20

Fig. 6. Max Ernst, *The Virgin Spanking the Christ Child in Front of Three Witnesses, Breton, Eluard, Ernst*, 1926. Wallraff-Richartz Museum, Fondation Corboud., Cologne Germany. Photo Credit, Snark/Art Resource, NY. © 2011 Artists Rights Society (ARS), New York / ADAGP, Paris. 21

Fig. 7. Marcel Duchamp, *Bicycle Wheel*, original 1913, reconstructed 1964. Metal and painted wood. Musée National d'Art Moderne, Centre Georges Pompidou. Paris, France. Photo Philippe Migeat. Photo Credit: CNAC/MNAM/Dist. Reunion des Musée Nationaux / Art Resource, NY. 190

Fig. 8. Marcel Duchamp, *L.H.O.O.Q.*, 1919. "Rectified Readymade": pencil on reproduction of Leonardo da Vinci's Mona Lisa. 7¾ x 4¾. Private collection. Photo credit: Scala/White Images / Art Resource, NY. 191

Fig. 9. *Robert Rauschenberg, First Landing Jump*, 1961. Cloth, metal, leather, electrical fixture, cable, and oil paint on composition board, with automobile tire and wood plank, 7' 5" x 6' 8". Gift of Philip Johnson, The Museum of Modern Art, New York, NY. Photo credit: Digital Image © The Museum of Modern Art/Licensed by SCALA / Art Resource, NY. 215

Fig. 10. Roy Lichtenstein, *Artist's Studio "The Dance,"* 1974. © Estate of Roy Lichtenstein. Oil and Magna (synthetic polymer paint) on canvas. 8' x 10' 7." Gift of Mr. And Mrs. S. I. Newhouse, Jr. The Museum of Modern Art, New York, NY. Photo credit: Digital Image © Museum of Modern Art/Licensed by SCALA/ Art Resource, NY. 231

Fig. 11. David Salle, *Old Bottles*, 1995. Oil and acrylic on canvas. 8' ½" x 15' 6". The Saatchi Gallery, London. Art © David Salle/Licensed by VAGA, New York, NY. Courtesy of Mary Boone Gallery, New York., NY. 238

Fig. 12. *Profane Music and the Demon of Licentiousness* (Demon Of Impurity), c.1120-32. Nave capital, Church of Ste. Madelene, Vézelay, Burgundy, France. Detail of Romanesque capital in the nave of Vézelay Basilica, depicting the wickedness of non-sacred music. © Holly Hayes/Art History Images. 322

Fig. 13. *The Temptation of Eve*, c. 1130. Limestone sculpture by Gislebertus. Lintel of former north transept portal, Cathedral of St. Lazare, Autun, France. Now in the Musée Rolin, Autun, France. © Holly Hayes/Art History Images. 323

Chapter One

The Greatness of God
The Goodness, Beauty, and Truth of the Created Natural World

For the LORD your God is God of gods and Lord of lords, the great God, mighty and awesome, who shows no partiality and accepts no bribes. (Deuteronomy 10:17)[1]

"How great you are, Sovereign LORD! There is no one like you, and there is no God but you, as we have heard with our own ears. (2 Samuel 7:22)

God made the earth by his power; he founded the world by his wisdom and stretched out the heavens by his understanding. (Jeremiah 10:12)

O LORD, our Lord, how majestic is your name in all the earth! You have set your glory above the heavens. Great is the Lord, and greatly to be praised (Psalms 8:1).

When we come to know God, we are in awe, overwhelmed, we find in him a greatness that dwarfs all other actual and potential objects of knowledge.[2]

In Praise of Creation and Creator. The focus of the first three chapters will be largely on the order, structure, beauty, and wonders of the created natural world, seen in specific ways by writers through many centuries, and by various scientists, astronomers, biologists, and others. Shortcomings and evils found in nature and in human life will be dealt with more extensively in later chapters. Since so many traditional poems, songs, hymns, and art works have taken order, goodness, and beauty as themes, several will be included in this chapter, and some contrasts with modern art and thought will be made.

In the ancient world people were in many ways closer to nature than in the modern world. Most ancient people universally worked or interacted with nature on a daily basis. Their roles within the natural world strongly shaped their lives and were a primary stimulus to religious belief. They were highly aware of nature's cycles of creation and recession, and realized their close dependence on earth, water, and sun for their life, food, and security. While the pagan religions of the ancient world represented many gods of earth, sun, sky, waters, weather, crops, sex and fertility, Judeo-Christian revelation and tradition told of a uniquely transcendent God who designed, created, structured, and sustains all aspects of the natural world.

Today huge numbers of people live in large or colossal cities whose closely packed buildings, overpasses, streets, cars, planes, trains, buses, tunnels, goods, services, work, luxuries, and entertainments create an almost total artificial environment that sets the daily routine, establishes the yearly calendar, and constitutes a framework on which life and work depend. The result is that few vestiges of nature remain in many modern people's lives. No doubt this is one reason that a spate of books on the virtues of atheism—something largely unthinkable in ancient times, or at any time before the modern world—has risen to best-seller status in recent years. Another reason, of course, is the tradition of modernity itself, which since the "Enlightenment" has increasingly sought autonomy and liberation from Christian or any religious and philosophical traditions, seeing them as unsupportable, time-bound beliefs, and thought by some to be no more than harmful superstitions, fears, or lies. Modern philosophy, art, and sciences have largely developed out of the Enlightenment and Romantic revolutions, which essentially rejected traditional Christian beliefs (dealt with in Chapters Six, Seven, and Eight). But such radical views are quite recent and short in world history, and are sharply at odds with the far longer belief in the God of Judeo-Christianity, as well as with other beliefs, including pagan views of nature and fertility gods.

The ardent, poetic verses of the Psalms best express ancient biblical man's deep realization of nature as the creation of the Almighty God. Psalm 19 of David listens to the voice of nature telling of the glory and knowledge of their maker. Note the firm belief that nature directly *tells* one about God: various aspects of nature, especially the heavens, *declare*, *proclaim*, and *speak*, of God as their creator. The message runs throughout the entire world.

> The heavens declare the glory of God;
> the skies proclaim the work of his hands,
> Day after day they pour forth speech;
> Night after night they display knowledge.
> There is no speech or language
> Where their voice is not heard.
> Their voice goes out into all the earth,
> Their words to the ends of the world.

Similar thoughts are expressed again in the first century AD, and with an additional emphasis by Paul in a biblical verse of key importance concerning universal human knowledge of God from created nature. The verse, from Romans 1:20, serves as one theme of this book: "For since the creation of the world God's invisible qualities—his eternal power and divine nature—have been clearly seen, being understood from what has been made, so that men are without excuse."

These same beliefs were still proclaimed, even amplified in radiant poetic form in the early eighteenth century after Christ by Joseph Addison, English poet, essayist, and statesman. His poem, "The Heavens," focuses on the sky, sun, moon, stars, and planets as wondrous tidings of divine truth, speaking to "reason's ear," and proclaiming their Creator, "their great Original."

> The spacious firmament on high,
> With all the blue ethereal sky,
> And spangled heavens, a shining frame,
> Their great Original proclaim.
>
> The unwearied sun, from day to day,
> Does his Creator's power display,
> And publishes to every land
> The work of an Almighty hand.
>
> Soon as the evening shades prevail,
> The moon takes up the wondrous tale,
> and nightly to the listening earth
> Repeats the story of her birth;
> Whilst all the stars that round her burn,
> And all the planets in their turn,
> Confirm the tidings as they roll,
> And spread the truth from pole to pole.
>
> What though in solemn silence all
> Move round the dark terrestrial ball;
> What though no real voice or sound
> Amidst their radiant orbs be found;
> In reason's ear they all rejoice,
> And utter forth a glorious voice,
> Forever singing as they shine,
> "The hand that made us is divine."[3]

During the twentieth and twenty-first centuries we have become more aware than ever before, through the sciences, of the incredible vastness, the awesome sizes, spaces, and interrelationships of the heavens—the planets, stars, galaxies, and other features of the cosmos. To dwell on the seemingly infinite number of stars, and the superhuman distances between them, staggers the imagination and strikes awe in one's heart. When we gaze at the stars at night, we see only a small fraction of their total. The number of stars in our own galaxy, the Milky Way, is thought to be 100 billion. And it has been estimated that the total number of stars throughout the entire universe may be *70 billion trillion*, roughly comparable to the total number of grains of sand on all the beaches of the earth. And the unseen "dark matter" of space may constitute 87 percent of the known universe, while the planets, stars, and galaxies form only 13 percent. Such seemingly infinite numbers are magnified still further when we consider the vastness of space, and the great distances between each star. The star nearest to our sun, Proxima Centauri, is almost 25 trillion miles beyond it. The average distance between stars is 30 trillion miles. No human, or even a team over many centuries, can travel such a distance. Even at a space-ship speed of 5 miles per second it would take well over 200,000 *years* to travel from one star to another.[4] More than anything we know on the earth, the heavens speak of infinitude. In these newly discovered intimations of infinitude, for the Psalmist, and for Paul, as well as for Addison, "the heavens" would "declare the glory of God."

Psalm 104 is an extended hymn to God for the goodness of His creation. In a rapturously loving and poetic way it first praises the greatness, splendor, and majesty of God, then His work in the celestial realm, the secure laws and order of the earth, the luxurious proliferation of life on earth, the orderly cycles, the sea, and His continuing sustenance of all life:

	Praise the Lord, O my soul.
[addressing God]	O Lord my God, you are very great;
	you are clothed with splendor and majesty.
	He wraps himself in light as with a garment;
[the celestial realm]	he stretches out the heavens like a tent
	and lays the beams of his upper chambers on
	their waters.
	He makes the clouds his chariot
	and rides on the wings of the wind.
	He makes the winds his messengers,
	flames of fire his servants.
[the secure laws and order of earth]	He set the earth on its foundations;
	it can never be moved.
	You covered it with the deep as with a garment;

the waters stood above the mountains.
But at your rebuke the waters fled,
    at the sound of your thunder they
        took to flight;
they flowed over the mountains,
    they went down into the valleys,
    to the place you assigned for them.
You set a boundary they cannot cross;
    never again will they cover the earth.

[the luxurious proliferation of life]

He makes springs pour water into the ravines;
    it flows between the mountains.
They give water to all the beasts of the field;
    the wild donkeys quench their thirst.
The birds of the air nest by the waters;
    they sing among the branches.
He waters the mountains from his upper
        chambers;
    the earth is satisfied by the fruit of his work.
He makes grass grow for the cattle,
    and plants for man to cultivate—
    bringing forth food from the earth:
wine that gladdens the heart of man,
    oil to make his face shine,
    and bread that sustains his heart.
The trees of the Lord are well watered,
    the cedars of Lebanon that he planted.
There the birds make their nests;
    the stork has its home in the pine trees.
The high mountains belong to the wild goats;
    the crags are a refuge for the coneys.

[the orderly cycles of life on earth]

The moon marks off the seasons,
    and the sun knows when to go down.
You bring darkness, it becomes night,
    and all the beasts of the forests prowl.
The lions roar for their prey
    and seek their food from God.
The sun rises, and they steal away;
    they return and lie down in their dens.
Then man goes out to his work,
    to his labor until evening.
How many are your works, O Lord!
    In wisdom you made them all,
    the earth is full of your creatures.

[the wondrous sea]

There is the sea, vast and spacious,
    teeming with creatures beyond number—

5

living things both large and small.
There the ships go to and fro,
and the leviathan, which you
formed to frolic there.

[God sustains and
cares for his creatures]

These all look to you
to give them their food at the proper time.
When you give it to them,
they gather it up;
when you open your hand,
they are satisfied with good things.
When you hide your face,
they are terrified;
when you take away their breath,
they die and return to the dust.
When you send your Spirit,
they are created,
and you renew the face of the earth . . . .

The word, faithfulness, truth, and enduring laws of God are further praised in several other Psalms, as are His eternal plans and purpose in watching everything human beings do:

Your word, O Lord, is eternal;
it stands firm in the heavens.
Your faithfulness continues through all generations;
you established the earth, and it endures.
Your laws endure to this day,
for all things serve you."
(Psalm 119:89-91)

For the word of the Lord is right and true;
he is faithful in all he does . . . .
By the word of the Lord were the heavens made,
their starry host by the breath of his mouth.
He gathers the waters of the sea into jars;
he puts the deep into storehouses."
(Psalm 33:4-7)

For you created my inmost being;
you knit me together in my mother's womb.
I praise you because I am fearfully and wonderfully made;
your works are wonderful,
I know that full well.
My frame was not hidden from you

when I was made in the secret place.
When I was woven together in the depths of the earth,
    your eyes saw my unformed body.
All the days ordained for me
    were written in your book
    before one of them came to be."[5]
(Psalm 139:13-16)

But the plans of the Lord stand firm forever,
    the purposes of his heart through all generations.
....

    from his dwelling place he watches
    all who live on earth—
he who forms the hearts of all,
    who considers everything they do."
(Psalm 33:11-15)

Your word is a lamp to my feet
    and a light to my path.[6]
                                            (Psalm 119:105)

Prominently attributed to God's word and wisdom in these verses are the formal order and structure of all creation, from the heavens and earth to the embryo in the womb: the complex formation of the human body and the way it knits and holds together, structurally, causally; the organization of human life in work and rest; the number of days specifically allotted to one's life; the ordering of times, areas, and processes of nature—the waters, the regular procession of days, nights, months, and seasons; the structuring of animal instincts. In addition there is the rich plenitude and wonder of creation. All of this is recognized as part of God's eternal design, plan, and purpose. And God's word is also seen as the guiding and illuminating light for one's life.

Classical and Christian Beliefs and Art. Many of the Psalms are dated to the reign of King David during the eleventh and tenth centuries BC. Classical Greek culture flourished some five and six centuries later. Much Classical Greek thought and art essentially saw signs of mind, Idea, design, order, plan, goodness, and purpose in the nature of things. The art surpassed previous ancient art by achieving a new height of realism. The fifth century BC *Spearbearer (Doryphoros)* of Polykleitos (Fig. 1) epitomizes the new historical height of classical realism with its greater accuracy, definition, and fluid integration of flesh-and-bone body, achieved after only two centuries of progressive study. Muscular shape and structure are given new attention and detailed development. There is also a new sense of ease and rightness

7

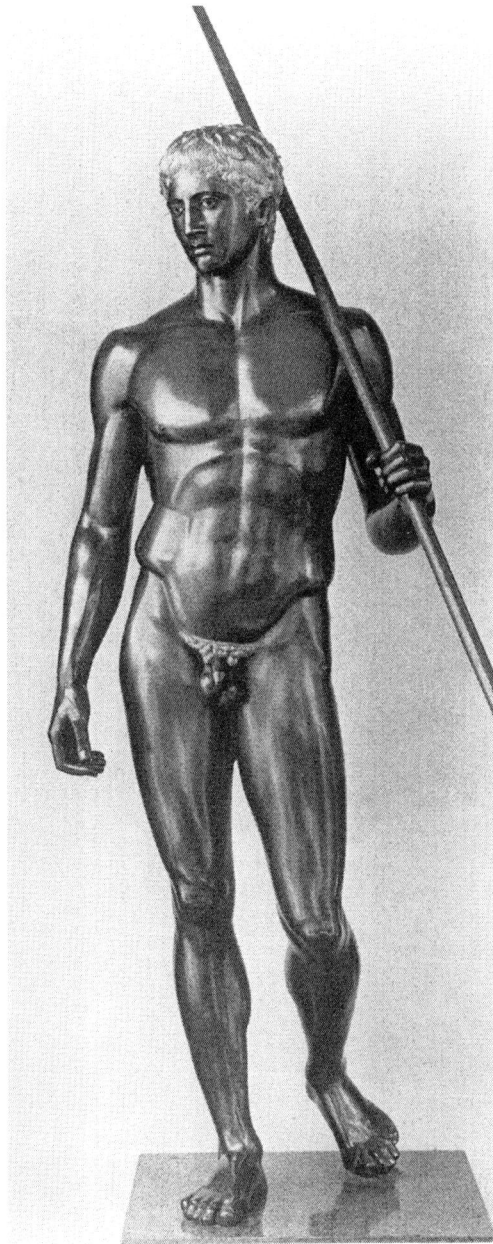

Fig. 1. ***The Spearbearer (Doryphoros)***. Modern Bronze reconstruction by Georg Roemer of the Greek High Classical original of c. 440 BC by Polykleitos. 6'6". Formerly in Munich, destroyed in 1944. Foto Marburg/Art Resource, NY.

of man being in the world, conveyed by the flexible, balanced, and graceful stance, the slight turn of his head, and the calm, surveying gaze.

In this Classical vision, man can be confident and calmly active in the world because of an essential rightness and goodness—a determining cosmic order that is divine. The fatalistic Homeric world of battle and death seems overcome by a higher, ideal realm of form, law, structure, purpose, and meaning. An ideal ordered cosmos is evoked and reflected by the structural canon and perfect harmony of the figure. For the Classical Greeks such ideal proportions, canons, and harmony were imitations of *objective, ideal cosmic form, order, laws, and patterns*, not simply formulated or invented by artists or thinkers. In Plato's time (c. 428-348 BC), the term *eidos* (Form, Idea) "meant something outside the mind, in the real world, and presented as such to the mind's gaze."[7] Classical art achieves, along with an unprecedented realism, a grand, transcendental dimension of *objective ideality*. The relative positions of the transcendental, the heroic, and man in Greek Classical art are summarized in key form in the Parthenon sculptures: the fully round, over-lifesize gods reign on high in the pediments; the smaller, high-relief heroes just below in the metopes, between ordinary man and gods; and the level of ordinary mortal citizen is less visible and in low-relief in the frieze behind the metopes.

From about 530-330 BC the strong Greek philosophical sense of the being, truth, and order of reality was developed in concepts and terms that were to be central to philosophy and theology for centuries. Although well outside of biblical belief in the One Creator God, the Greeks developed certain high understandings of transcendental reality, truth, and knowledge. Heracleitus named *logos* as the ordering principle underlying the changing appearances of things, and identified cosmic order with law (*nomos*), which he treated as divine. The Pythagoreans held that such order was mathematical, and applied to all existing things as a cosmic whole (*kosmos*). Xenophanes advanced the concept of God as divine mind (*nous*), the source of all movement in things. Anaxagoras treated *nous* as a purposeful intellectual principle and force that knows all things past, present, and future, and orders the universe. Plato recognized not only the *nous* immanent in the human soul (*psyche*), but cosmic *nous* (cosmic mind, reason) as the divine principle that orders the universe, rules everything, and leads toward the Good. In the order of true reality for Plato, however, the perfect, eternal Forms or Ideas (*eidos, eide*) that determine all existing forms, types, and categories of things, are distinct from his creator *demiourgos* who copies them, and from cosmic *nous*, ranking still higher. But the *eide*, and ultimately "the Good," are the cause of all sensible phenomena, giving them the form and reality they possess.[8]

Platonic thought emphasized the concepts of cosmic order, teleological purpose and goodness, including rewards and punishments in an afterlife, and developed more precise understandings of perfect, eternal Forms as the ultimate formative basis of the world, adding substantially to ways of thinking about transcendental reality, truth, and wisdom. Plato did not identify the Forms with the mind of a Supreme Being, the transcendent Creator, however, and there remained, along with eternal matter as "non-being," some final sense of plurality in his cosmology—an absence of absolute transcendence and personal Being. Aristotle indicated more specifically than before how Forms are actually determinative and causally connected with material things. He developed the sense of transcendental reason, cause, and purpose at work throughout the world, making things knowable and meaningful, thus extending and giving historically new means and capabilities to philosophical and theological thought. The Greeks were the first in history to differentiate and emphasize reason as a human faculty, as well as the structuring principle of the cosmos, making it a crucial factor in knowledge, an immense contribution to thought.[9] Later Christian thought from Philo through Augustine and Aquinas established that ultimately, reason must be traced to God. Since Christian thought holds God to be the ultimate source and ground of reason, reason in itself cannot be construed as bad or faulty, but only its improper use. Neither can reason be dismissed as a false transcendental established by the Enlightenment to ground universal knowledge, as postmodern thought suggests. The problem with Enlightenment reason is that its basis in God was abandoned, and recentered in the subject/self/mind.

One of the earliest and finest surviving Early Christian apse mosaics is in the Church of Sta. Pudenziana in Rome (Fig. 2). It dates around AD 390, and conveys a number of biblical doctrines that are the essence of Christian teachings and faith. The primary subject is *Christ Enthroned in Majesty with the Twelve Apostles in the New Jerusalem*, the spiritual center of Heaven after the end of this age and the final judgment.[10] The jeweled gold cross above and behind Christ's head is the Triumphal Cross, symbolizing Christ's victory over sin and death by means of his crucifixion and resurrection during his earthly life, making possible salvation and everlasting life in paradise for everone. Only the absolutely transcendent God could provide such substitutionary atonement for all humanity. The divine revelation of the scriptural message is thus recognized. Only the *Creator* God qualifies for such absolute transcendence. The symbolic figures on each side of the cross indicate the four Gospel writers. This is the first known use of these symbols, often used in early Christian and later medieval art: Matthew (a winged man), Mark (a winged lion), Luke (a winged ox), and John (a winged eagle). The gleaming buildings behind the figures evoke the eternal magnificence and beauty of the New Jerusalem in Heaven. The two female figures crowning Paul and Peter symbolize the Church of the Circumcision and the Church of the Gentiles. (Two Apostles were lost when the edges were cut shorter in later times.)

Fig. 2. *Christ Enthroned in Majesty, with the Twelve Apostles in the New Jerusalem (Heaven)*. c. AD 390. Apse mosaic in the Church of Sta. Pudenziana, Rome. Photo credit: Alinari/Art Resource, NY.

Catacomb paintings such as *The Good Shepherd* ceiling fresco in the Catacomb of Saints Peter and Marcellinus in Rome convey the same beliefs (image unavailable). The predominant theme of catacomb painting is salvation. In this one the encompassing circle is symbolic of the divine realm of Heaven, and the paradise of the redeemed after death. Another circle at the center shows Christ the Good Shepherd as the source of salvation. Jesus' crucial question in Matthew 15:16, "who do you say that I am?" is answered: He is the divine Savior who redeems and cares for His sheep.

Around thirteen centuries later, near the end of the seventeenth century, Richard Hooker, an influential clergyman and theologian of the Church of England, represents an important aspect of continuing Christian tradition of the Renaissance and Elizabethan age—Christian humanism. His theological writings are essentially based on Scripture as the final source of ultimate truths. They also appeal to reason and the light of nature as means of ascent to God through the classical "chain of being." In his treatise, *Of the Laws of Ecclesiastical Polity* (1593-1600), Hooker, often echoing or quoting verses of the Old and New Testaments, praises the wise, lawful, and purposeful work of the Trinity in Creation: "from the Father, by the Son, through the Spirit, all things are possible."[11]

For Hooker, it is clear that everything in creation has divine reason, purpose, and law: "God worketh nothing without cause. All those things which are done by him have some end for which they are done; and the end for which they are done is a reason of his will to do them." He writes that "a proper and certain reason there is of every finite work of God, inasmuch as there is a law imposed upon it." God "worketh all things . . . not only according to his own will, but 'the Counsel of his own will'. And whatsoever is done with counsel or wise resolution hath of necessity some reason why it should be done," although man may not always be able to know it. "This world's first creation, and the preservation since of things created, what is it but only so far forth a manifestation by execution, what the eternal law of God is concerning things natural?" The law of nature thus derives from the ultimate law of God. "See we not plainly that obedience of creatures unto the law of nature is the stay of the whole world."[12]

Hooker warns of the deadly consequences for mankind of loss of divine cosmic law and order. Strangely enough, the following passage from his *Laws of Ecclesiastical Polity* evokes, both literally and figuratively, aspects of twentieth and twenty-first-century arts in which disbelief in God and divine cosmic law and order predominates—this is the radical anti-Logos aspect of Modernism. We see it clearly in such art movements as Dada, Surrealism, arts of the Absurd, Pop, Neo-Pop, Process art, and subsequent Postmodernism.[13]

since the time that God did first proclaim the edicts of his law upon it, heaven and earth have hearkened unto his voice, and their labor hath been to do his will: He "made a law for the rain" [Job 28:26]; He gave his "decree unto the sea, that the waters should not pass his commandment" [Jeremiah 5:22]. Now if nature should intermit her course, and leave altogether though it were but for a while the observation of her own laws; if those principal and mother elements of the world, whereof all things in this lower world are made, should lose the qualities which now they have; if the frame of that heavenly arch erected over our heads should loosen and dissolve itself; if celestial spheres should forget their wonted motions, and by irregular volubility turn themselves any way as it might happen; if the prince of the lights of heaven, which now as a giant doth run his unwearied course [Psalm 19:5], should as it were though as languishing faintness begin to stand and rest himself; if the moon should wander from her way, the times and seasons of the year blend themselves by disordered and confused mixture, the winds breathe out their last gasp, the clouds yield no rain, the earth be defeated of heavenly influence, the fruits of the earth pine away as children at the withered breasts of their mother no longer able to yield them relief: what would become of man himself, whom these things now do all serve?[14]

Christian and Classical Traditions in Art. Two striking examples of modern art that almost literally seem to illustrate the disturbing changes that Hooker speaks of are Picasso's *Demoiselles d'Avignon* (Fig. 4) and Max Ernst's Surrealist collage books of the 1930s. The views behind these art works contrast diametrically and starkly with traditional type beliefs found in such paintings as Albrecht Dürer's *Adoration of the Trinity* and Raphael's frescoes in the *Stanza della Segnatura* (Figs. 3, 5), revealing the kind of paradigmatic changes that Modernism has brought with it.

The basic gospel message can be found in Christian art and doctrine down through the centuries. A radiant example is Albrecht Dürer's German Renaissance altarpiece painting of the *Adoration of the Trinity* (1511; Fig. 3, and detail on front cover). The meaning of the crucifixion of Christ is the central theme. Understandings of the Father, Son, and Holy Spirit of Scripture had been progressively developed into the doctrine of the Trinity since the Council of Nicaea, near the time of *The Good Shepherd* painting, and had already been a subject of art for centuries. As so often in Medieval, Renaissance, and Baroque art, this painting depicts the *two realms* of heaven and earth, the *transcendent divine* and the *human*, and the *interrelationship* of the two. The image of the Trinity is placed in a diamond formation at the top center. The structure of the painting as a whole shows that "the Trinity is the pivot to which everything is anchored."[15] God the Father is symbolized here as an Emperor, enthroned on a rainbow, with the symbolic Dove of the Holy Spirit above His head. This is the Throne of Mercy, for the Father

Fig. 3. Albrecht Dürer, *Adoration of the Trinity* (Landauer Altar), 1511. Oil on lime panel, 53 x 48½". Photo and permission by the Kunsthistorisches Museum, Vienna.

Fig. 4. Picasso, ***Demoiselles d'Avignon (The Women of Avignon)***, 1907. 8' x 7' 8." Museum of Modern Art, NY. Photo credit: Digital Image The Museum of Modern Art/Licensed by Scala/Art Resource, NY. © 2011 Estate of Pablo Picasso / Artists Rights Society (ARS), New York ADAGP, Paris.

holds and offers the cross with Christ on it, visibly expressing the central Christian message of John 3:16, "For God so loved the world that he gave his only begotten Son that whosoever believes in him should not perish but have everlasting life."

Four circles of figures revolve around the Trinity from top to bottom, their identity and purpose centrally determined by the divine. They include angels as well as the redeemed of past and present. In the first circle at the top are cherubim and seraphim, around the Dove. Next are larger angels who hold the instruments of the Passion and spread the green-lined, golden cloak of the Father. Third are the blessed of the past, including John the Baptist on the right, the precursor of the Savior, kneeling at the head of patriarchs and prophets of the Old Covenant. At the same level on the left is the Virgin Mother of God, with a group of female saints and martyrs. The fourth circle below includes living representatives of the church, with men and women of all walks. To left of center is the Pope, with cardinals, bishops, monks and nuns. To the right, the secular world is led by Emperor and King, with doges, princes, nobles, knights, burghers, and peasants. In the center, a mass of believers stretches out of sight. The carved wooden frame (not shown) represents the Last Judgment, with Christ as Judge. The comprehensive subject of this painting is thus the timeless adoration of the Trinity in Paradise, following the end of the temporal world. It presents the biblical understanding of reality and truth, which extends from the absolute transcendence of the Creator and Savior God, throughout the world to every believer, from beginning to end.

A small figure of Dürer himself stands on the earth at the bottom right holding a plaque that says "Albrecht Dürer of Nuremberg made this in the year 1511 after the Virgin gave birth." Evidence suggests that Dürer, who was a Catholic most of his life, became a Protestant by the 1520s. An entry in his journal of May 17, 1521, expressing great concern over the arrest of Martin Luther, also indicates the sincerity of Dürer's belief in God. Part of it is like a prayer addressed to God, speaking of "free Christians, ransomed by thy blood. O highest, heavenly Father, pour into our hearts, through Thy son Jesus Christ, such a light, that by it we may know what messenger we are bound to obey, so that with good conscience we may lay aside the burden of others and serve Thee, eternal, Heavenly Father, with light and joyful hearts."[16]

About the same time as Dürer's art, during the Italian High Renaissance, Raphael's highly classical art represents a world of transcendental ideals, rational order, harmony, purpose, and meaning. Idealism balanced by new levels of naturalism, are key bases of classicism as it developed from Greek art onward.[17] Raphael sought the ideal through artistic unity, harmony, and perfection of forms. Such ideals, of course, imply the existence of perfect, unchanging truth. Raphael's art, like so much Christian art of the Renaissance, has as its very basis a conviction of the reality of absolute truth and the possibility of perfect ideals based on it. Skepticism, uncertainty, indeterminacy, imperfection, vulgarity, and pornography in modern and postmodern art stand at the opposite pole to these perfections. Through artistic form and content, Raphael presents a model of a higher form of life for humankind in which universal truth, perfection, and ultimate purposes are determinative.

In dramatic contrast to the art of Dürer and Raphael, the growing modern turn away from belief in God and metaphysical absolutes since the Enlightenment has left twentieth and twenty-first century arts and thought without any basis in unchanging universal being, truth, and ideals. By comparing and contrasting the art of Dürer and Raphael with examples of twentieth-century Modernism, here and in Chapters Seven and Eight, we can clearly see the stark differences not only in form and appearance, but in underlying beliefs and ideas. By the twentieth century, genuine Christian beliefs had essentially vanished from modern art, and subsequently, in Postmodernism, and any sense of absolute truth and ideals of perfection have also declined and vanished. Instead of a secure conviction of absolute being, truth, goodness, unity, and beauty, what we largely find is relativism, difference, skepticism, absurdity, and nihilism. Relativism holds that there is no absolute truth: one religion, belief, or viewpoint is as good as another; knowledge is only relative to a person, culture, or time. In philosophy and the arts, this means that there is no Supreme God who is the source of eternal truth. Rather than a positive, ideal, and elevated view, relativism results in a sense of conflict, irony, cynicism, vulgarity, or comic-absurdity. Raphael's development of perfection, grandeur, and propriety banishes factors of lowliness, banality, and vulgarity, which are increasingly found in twentieth-century art from Cubism, Expressionism, Dada, and Surrealism through Pop, Neo-Pop, New Image, Neo-Expressionism, Porno, Graffiti, and Replication art.

Raphael's art also developed very high levels of pictorial unity and harmony in the organization of groups of figures and architecture, surpassing previous classical art in these ways, even that of Leonardo and Michelangelo. His high sense of the harmonious interrelatedness of all things stands in diametric contrast to characteristic twentieth-century developments of collage and assemblage, with their increasing celebration of fragmentation, disparity, and disjunction. The works of Raphael and Michelangelo show no inclination to relativism, cosmic irrationality, purposelessness, disunity, and chaos that increasingly prevail from twentieth-century Modernism into Postmodernism. In Raphael's art the harmonious interrelatedness of things implies not only an effective causality at work in the world, linking things together, but an ultimate rationality and guiding cause providing meaningful, purposeful goals.

In many ways the height of Raphael's classical art is in the *Stanza della Segnatura* frescoes (1509-1511). The essential thematic program of this room is *truth*. On the four walls and the ceiling Raphael painted subjects that show the primary ways, according to Renaissance Christian humanism, that man knows truth. The four principle themes reflect the major faculties of learning held at the time: *theology, philosophy, poetry,* and *law*. From this idealistic viewpoint, there is no essential conflict between these four ways of attaining knowledge. They are conceived and treated as interlinking and mutually complementary.

A general theme is the unity of all truth and knowledge. Christian and classical thought and art are treated as essentially compatible. The four major themes of the walls are interrelated by their placement across from, and next to each other. The first wall painting in order of execution is probably the *Disputà*, or *Disputation Over the Sacrament*—more accurately known as *The Triumph of Christian Religion* (detail in Fig. 5). Its general theme is the *revealed truth of Christianity*, specifically indicated by a ceiling tondo personifying *Theology*. This work essentially presents a grand and glowing image of the Trinity, the Eucharist, saints, angels, and church leaders, in a highly ordered, symmetrical arrangement in three curved tiers. While this painting is traditionally and powerfully Christian in its images, and its sense of rational order, unity, balance, harmony, purpose, and meaning, some of the humanistic implications behind it and its relation to the other walls are at odds with specific biblical teachings.[18] On the wall across from the *Disputà* is the *School of Athens*. Its assembly of various philosophers and intellects of the ancient world represents the human search for *rational or natural truth*, identified by the personification of *Philosophy* in a tondo above. To the left of the *School of Athens* is the slightly smaller painting of *Parnassus*, which treats the general theme of *truth and beauty in art (poetry)*, with its figure of *Poetry* in a tondo above. Again smaller, and to the right of the *School of Athens* is the last of these frescoes, with the general theme of the *truth and goodness of law or justice*, and its personification of *Justice* above. Altogether, these paintings emphasize the *truth* of revealed religion, rational thought, poetry, and law, while also affirming *beauty* in art, and *goodness* in law.[19]

A major aspect of Raphael's classicism in contrast to twentieth-century arts and thought is its highly developed sense of *order*. In addition to the stress on ideal content, classical art is characterized by a quest for perfect order and structure, reflecting its basis in idealism, and a strong belief in reason and rational cosmic order. Basically constitutive of classical order are the integrity provided by the highest levels of *harmony, unity in variety,* and *wholeness*. Equally important are the formal qualities of *simplicity, clarity, balance,* and *regularity*. Raphael developed all these factors to new historical levels and amplitudes, with the use of large numbers of figures in simulated pictorial space. For this, as well as his high sense of nobility, grace, and beauty, his paintings define one of the highest levels of classicism.

Representative of the highest levels of Renaissance art, Dürer, Raphael, and Michelangelo created some of the most developed and convincing representations of a real and solid material world of human beings, space, time, and history in world art. Their art also reflects worldviews essentially shaped by belief in a higher, perfect realm of truth, goodness, and beauty transcending the imperfection, fragmentation, flux, and senselessness of a world without divine sanction and purpose. Their art works tell us that the human and natural world are created and guided by the God of the Bible, the divine Creator, providential guide of creation, and savior of fallen humanity. These essential beliefs continued through the later Renaissance in England. And the flowering of literature in the Elizabethan (1558-1603) and Jacobean age (1603-1625) serves as a final monument to the dominance of Christianity in European culture before the acids of the Enlightenment and the rise of Modernism.

The Rejection of God, Being, and Absolute Truth in Twentieth-Century Art. The vast changes brought by Modernism from the seventeenth and eighteenth through the twentieth century are starkly emphasized by comparing the purposes of Dürer and Raphael with those of Picasso and Ernst. During the 1890s, on the threshold of Picasso's high-modern work, the French writer Alfred Jarry expressed some of the most radical, anti-traditional views to that time. They presented a world of comic absurdity and fantasy that matched or exceeded Nietzsche in all-devouring skepticism, ferocious destructiveness, and acceptance of irrationality, absurdity, and chaos as basic reality principles.[20] Picasso greatly admired Jarry's writing and his anarchic lifestyle. A friend of Picasso, writer and critic Guillaume Apollinaire, had met Jarry in 1903. The two poets found much in common in their "manic fantasy, anarchic wit and taste for the absurd." Jarry's "iconoclastic ideas would soon exert a formative influence on him and later, through him, on Picasso."[21] By 1907, the strongest and most revolutionary expression of avant-garde modern painting was Picasso's *Les Demoiselles d'Avignon* (*The Women of Avignon*, Fig. 5).[22] This work appears foremost as a proclamation of absolute freedom. It is a watershed declaration of the independence of the visual artist and of free pictorial form in the strongest terms to date. In line with Sade, Nietzsche, Jarry, and primitivist and anarchist thought, it is a subversion of traditional and existing orders and values, a Nietzschean "sounding out of idols" with a hammer. Like Jarry's "pataphysics" of the 1890s, it manages to "detonate all traditional canons of beauty, good taste, and propriety."[23]

Fig. 5. Raphael, *The Triumph of Christian Religion* (*Disputà*, or *Disputation Over the Sacrament*), c. 1509. Fresco in the Stanza della Segnatura, Vatican Museums, Vatican State, Rome. Photo credit Erich Lessing / Art Resource, NY.

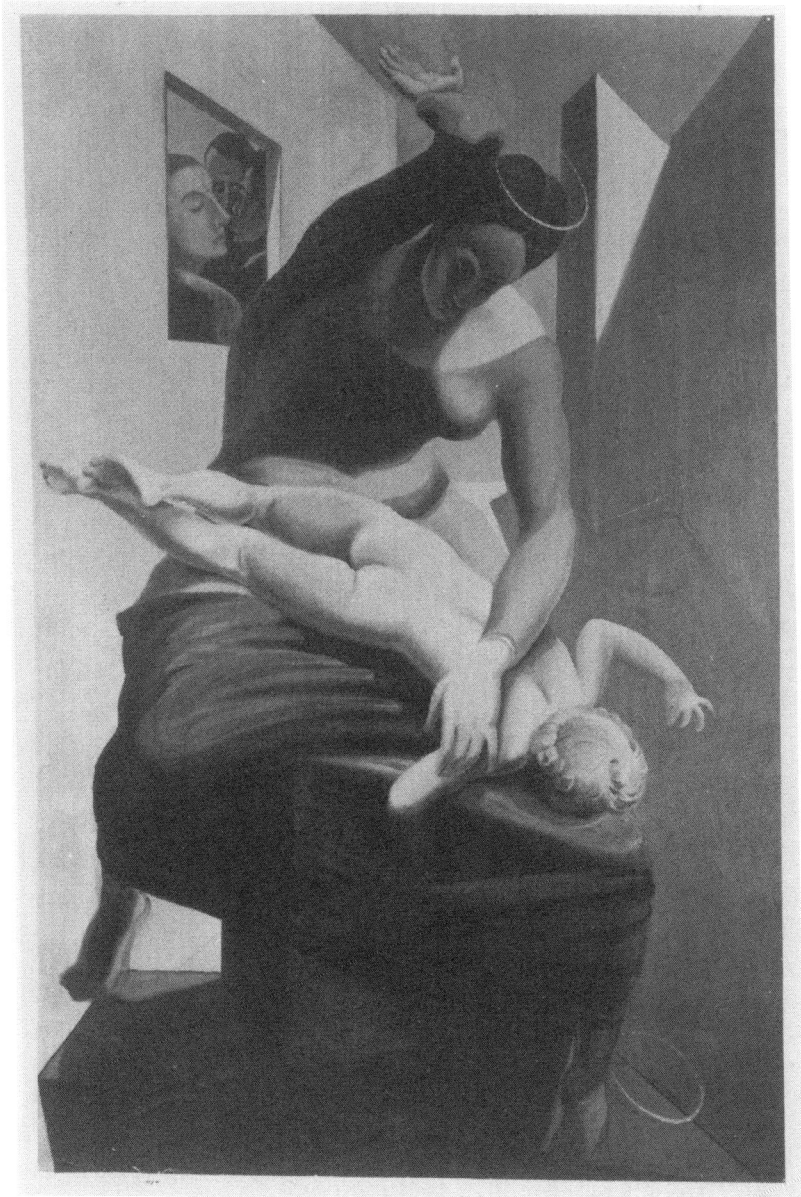

Fig. 6. Max Ernst, *The Virgin Spanking the Christ Child in Front of Three Witnesses, Breton, Eluard, Ernst*, 1926. Wallraff-Richartz Museum, Fondation Corboud., Cologne Germany. Photo Credit, Snark/Art Resource, NY. © 2011 Artists Rights Society (ARS), New York / ADAGP, Paris.

Like Jarry's work, and African Negro art, *Demoiselles* is shot through with raw, surging forces, creating a new, explosive dynamism. These things provide a more radical means of casting off centuries of Western tradition. There is an unparalleled sense in this painting of liberation of something unknown, irrational, and destructive. These factors, along with the new, crackling and bursting forms, are the reason *Demoiselles* is the atom-bomb blast of High Modernism.

One of the chief primitive influences on *Demoiselles* was Iberian sculpture, visible in the first three figures to the left. Iberians were the most ancient and primitive people in Spain, believed to have settled Picasso's native Andalusia by the fourth century BC. Picasso's turn to Iberian sculpture for inspiration and new forms is linked with modern theories of primitivism and anarchism. Like a modern primitive, he sought to return to his own "natural roots" in these primeval ancestors. Herder had been an original spokesman for primitivist views nearly a century and a half earlier: "Let us return to the oldest human nature and everything else will be all right." Romanticism had promoted certain currents of primitivism, exoticism, and orientalism. During the 1890s Paul Gauguin went much further toward rejecting Western tradition with his primitivism and orientalism. Then Picasso, by basing his approach on primitive Iberian and African art, pursued a still more revolutionary course as an adversary of traditional Western civilization with its basis in Christianity and classicism, and the fundamental beliefs and values associated with them.[24]

Such works challenged the very concept of the old order and announced its demise in the face of a full-scale revolt—a revolt in the name of those powerful, primitive forces of natural being that civilization, according to anarchists, had corrupted and suppressed for so long. . . . Picasso continued in this direction through 1907, increasing the violence of his departure from traditional canons and ending with the explosion that is *Les Demoiselles d'Avignon*.[25]

The two figures on the right side of *Demoiselles* are derived from African Negro sculpture. These images bring the demoniacal aspect of the painting to its most intense focus. Their grotesqueness and violence go well beyond that of the other three figures. They culminate the painting's sense of explosive, assaulting force—much like a hard slap in the face—and evoke mysterious psychic depths and forces that are terrible, threatening, and violent. It may be likened to the "id" set free—that dark, mysterious Freudian power discovered within individuals, which can either be suppressed in some way, or allowed its freedom to act with uncontrollable force—to grasp, take possession, devour, rape, maim, and kill. It suggests the primitive, irrational "unconscious," the old chaos, which breaks through all reason, restraints, bounds, and laws; the churning chaos of an overwhelming primeval force, both creative and destructive. And it stands in stark opposition to Christian ideas of the personal God, holiness, and morality. It is also antithetical to classical paradigms of being, rationality, propriety, moderation, and ethics.

Picasso's assault is not only on tradition, but on *nature* as a real, objective, divinely created, sustained, and ordered sphere. In this and other ways it is also an assault on woman.[26] Woman became for Picasso the chief representative of nature, to a great extent the image of nature as a whole—*woman-nature*. And with woman, as with nature, Picasso had to be the master controller—the real, liberated, divine creator—absorbing, decomposing, reordering and recomposing—recreating as he deemed fit. His view has more to do with usage than homage, more rape than love: woman, like nature, becomes the creator's clay—depersonalized matter. He increasingly concentrated in later years on images of bodies and sexual organs, rather than the whole person. From *Demoiselles* onward, man, woman, and nature are melted, dissolved, distilled in the alembic of his mind, recirculated and reconstituted anew in an endless variety of forms, proportions, combinations, and consistencies. Picasso was later heard to say what this meant: "God is really another artist . . . like me." "I am God, I am God, I am God."[27]

Some years after *Demoiselles*, Picasso was to call it his "first exorcism painting." In a talk with André Malraux he revealed the key to his worldview and his understanding of art—feelings and ideas that had been catalyzed before painting *Demoiselles*, by a powerful experience of African Negro art in the Trocadéro museum in Paris. He saw the Negro masks as "magic things":

The Negro pieces were *intercesseurs*, mediators; ever since then I've known the word in French. They were against everything—against unknown, threatening spirits. I always looked at fetishes. I understood; I too am against everything. I too believe that everything is unknown, that everything is an enemy! Everything! Not the details—women, children, babies, tobacco, playing—but the whole of it! I understood what the Negroes used their sculpture for . . . . It was clear that some guys had invented the models, and others had imitated them, right? Isn't that what we call tradition? But all the fetishes were used for the same thing. They were weapons. To help people avoid coming under the influence of spirits again, to help them become independent.[28]

Many of these ideas are closely related to those of Nietzsche, Jarry, and Apollinaire: *Everything is unknown*: there is no truth. *Men have invented the models* of truth, society, and art; others have imitated them. We must reject all such *traditions.* Our objective is to become *independent,* free, to escape all these threats and oppressions. The whole of nature is a threat. Picasso explicitly declared this: "Obviously, nature has to exist so that we may rape it."[29] Divine creation and the lawful created order of God is an intolerable threat to this view. Everything outside the individual *creative self* is a threat to its freedom and independence, as Rimbaud, a favorite poet of Picasso, had declared before Jarry and Apollinaire. Art is *a powerful weapon* to escape all these enemy influences, to be used against nature, and against the models of nature and truth that men create. Much like Apollinaire, Picasso claims that art is to be used *against* nature, to subdue it, as well as to break away from tradition. Destruction is thus as essential as creation—an increasingly potent idea from Romanticism onward, and brought to a fever pitch and activist dimension in anarchist thought. For Picasso, art becomes a potent magical weapon, an incendiary bomb, to be used to achieve freedom for the self.

The paradox of these claims, however, is that, while Picasso is rejecting tradition and all other men's models, he is accepting the ideas of Nietzsche, Jarry, and Apollinaire as if *they* are true. He abandons traditional doctrines for another set. But the doctrines of Rimbaud, Nietzsche, Jarry, and Apollinaire are radically different from pre-modern Western tradition: they make it possible for anything to be "true"—the divergent, the contradictory and the antithetical. These theories would allow one to proceed with freedom, from blasphemy to "spirituality"; from materialism to idealism; from cynicism and nihilism to "belief" and conviction; from naturalism to abstraction; from Cubism to Neo-Classicism; from whole figures to fragmented ones; from round to flat; from massive to linear form; from all soft to all hard images, etc. This is, in fact, the kind of zigzagging path that Picasso was to take during the course of his artistic life. And because of his skill, power, and imagination in doing it, he has been celebrated, lavished with wealth, and fêted as the ultimate master of art in the twentieth century—a century without certainty of God, Being, or Truth, without conviction, and open, more than previous centuries, to all manner of divergent and opposing ideas, beliefs, and directions. In this sense, Picasso (1881-1973), who spanned three-quarters of the century, encompasses and summarizes it more than any other artist.

Max Ernst (1891-1976) was active in both Dada and Surrealism. His Surrealist painting, *The Virgin Spanking the Christ Child in Front of Three Witnesses, Breton, Eluard, Ernst.,* done in 1926,[30] makes a bold and direct assault on traditional Christian beliefs, doctrines, and art. Playing on the image of the Madonna and Christ Child, Ernst mocks the central Christian doctrine of Christ's deity. The halo of Christ, symbolizing his divine, holy nature, has fallen to the floor. Having been very naughty in some way (lying?), he is being given a hard spanking by his mother. The three Surrealist leaders seen through a small open window, André Breton, Paul Éluard, and Ernst himself—assume the roles of the three wise men, witnessing the event. These ultra-moderns are pleased with what they see—a reversal of the traditional Adoration of the Magi theme—Christ's *fall* from divinity in modern views. If Christ had been guilty of some such sin, he would have been unable to save mankind from their sins.

This and many other of Ernst's art works also represent a critical assault on the belief-world of his authoritarian father, who was a devout Christian, and sought to raise little Max in Christian belief, even painting a portrait of him as the Christ Child in 1896. As a boy and young man Ernst increasingly revolted against his father and his beliefs, both in his art and ways of life. In his early teens he was deeply influenced by Max Stirner, who preached autonomy of the individual self, dissociation from all external authority, and complete freedom of action. Nietzsche was also a lifelong influence, with his praise of the higher man who was "above nationality, above religion, above law, above all the received ideas of the day, above the present and above the past."[31] This work is thus a key image of modern revolt against God and Christianity. It represents more directly what is expressed in various ways by other high-modern artists, and it stands in polar contrast to Raphael's *Triumph of Christian Religion* and Dürer's *Adoration of the Holy Trinity*, epitomizing the artistic expression of traditional Christian beliefs of pre-modern centuries.

In a series of collages grouped into "novel" form during the 1920s and '30s, Ernst began to interrelate images in ways that created new meanings and values. He clipped whole pictures and image parts from late nineteenth-century magazines, books, and novels, and then glued them together in strange new ways. He often began with whole pictures of street scenes, interiors, or landscapes, and then radically altered their character by adding other elements that contradicted expectations, known-laws, and understandings of nature, society, morality, and reality as a whole. The collage then served as a powerful instrument for undermining religious and philosophical beliefs, traditions, and knowledge, and for creating a macabre new reality.

The title of Ernst's major collage novel of 1929, *The Hundred Headless Woman* (*La femme 100 têtes*) reflects Surrealist belief in the constantly shifting identities of things due to the absence of any enduring being and essences. These collages reveal intricately thought out, destructive attacks on Christian theism and belief in divine creation. They depict a world in which God the Father and the Trinity are mocked and sardonically reduced to helpless jokes, while other Christian doctrines are vilified with black humor. God the Creator is mocked in one image labeled "The Eternal Father tries vainly to separate the light from the shadows." It shows the "Eternal Father" rushing down a flight of stairs, helplessly trying to separate a "lighter" woman below from a "darker" one above.[32] Another scene indicates that "Loplop" (a bird) instead of Christ the Logos has become flesh and dwells among us. Mockingly twisting a Bible verse ("the Word become flesh and dwelt among us," John 1:14), Ernst's title says "And Loplop, Bird Superior, has transformed himself into flesh without flesh and will dwell among us."[33] "Loplop" is a black humor pun on "Logos."

Other images show the world of creation undone: it is not only macabre and menacing, but existing contrary to known laws, structures, and causality. Descriptions of these pictures resemble Surrealist poetry. The sky opens up to disgorge stacked loads of logs sailing downward (p. 31), or a baby plummeting like a comet toward the sea, the top of its head flattened and glowing (p. 33). Giant hands grow out of a field of tall grass and pineapples, entwining around huge wine bottles (p. 23). The essential nature and identities of things are radically altered. Essences and transcendentals are destroyed. The principle of identity is subverted. The given world is effectively destroyed and a fantastic, ambiguous, new world of flux is activated. While Surrealism insists that true reality is a fusion of the demonic and the divine, evil and good,[34] the actual effect of Ernst's works is of an extreme sense of threat, violence, cruelty, and the demonic. It is no longer a stable creation guaranteed by God after the flood, but a world that has come unglued—dislocated and displaced, it is filled with darkening menace and constant flux. Little wonder that one of the last images has this sardonic caption: "Let us all thank Satan and be happy for the sympathy he has been pleased to show us."[35]

Ernst's largest, and most shocking collage novel, is entitled *A Week of Goodness or the Seven Deadly Elements* (*Une Semaine de bonté ou Les sept éléments capitaux*, 1933),[36] The title refers to the account in Genesis 1 of God's repeated declaration of each day of creation as "good." Since the book's basic premise is that there is no divine creator, and no enduring essences of individual things, flux (pervasive change) prevails in the images. Flux constitutes an essential meaning of Surrealist collage, and it wholly dominates these collage novels.[37] Such total prevalence of flux necessarily entails opposition to the Creator God who is Supreme Being, Truth, and Goodness, and who created objective world essences and structures. Ernst's "world" is thus a hodgepodge of constant metamorphosis, ungrounded by any individual essences.

The book makes destructive allusions to biblical creation while representing a very different kind of existence. The *Week of Goodness* of the title actually satirizes the account in Genesis 1 of God's declaration of the days of creation as "good." The 182 images of Ernst's book present a world that is radically destabilized, disrupted, and de-structured. There are also images of human-animal hybrid monsters, and escalating conflict and violence. In all these ways the book stands as a black-humor attack on, and reversal of Christian teachings of divine creation as real, lawful, and good, with all things having individual essences or natures according to distinct laws.

The subtitle, *the Seven Deadly Elements*, characterizes the very elements of creation as deadly, slyly comparing God's creative acts to the seven deadly sins (*les sept péches capitaux*). Instead of God's creation of light, one of the book's major "elements" is "blackness," listed for Thursday, the day corresponding to God's creation of the lights in the firmament.[38] Instead of God's orderly creation of the firmament and division of the waters, Ernst shows waters running rampant, infiltrating everywhere, through streets, walls, floors, etc., menacing and undermining everything, drowning and sweeping people away. These are waters of death rather than life.[39] Instead of God's separation of dry land from the waters, Ernst makes *mud* a major "element" of the book. (Mud later became a characteristic "element" of the absurd world of Samuel Beckett.)[40]

The essential identities of all things are intrinsically changed. They undergo, as Ernst wrote, "complete transmutation." Both Ernst and André Breton recognized this. Ernst quoted Breton: *"Who knows if we are not somehow preparing ourselves to escape from the principle of identity."*[41] Ernst had known Nietzsche's ideas since his student years. Nietzsche, who vehemently rejected ideas of God, being, and essence, claimed that the accepted identities of things, "their names, reputations, their place in hierarchy, and even their appearances" are only error and convention—standing as barriers to real creativity. They must be destroyed to permit the emergence of man the Creator. He proclaimed the core truth of the new view (much like Picasso): *"It is only as creators that we can annihilate!"*[42] He urged artists "to destroy this so-called 'real' world," of named, identified objects, and "create another, an alternative world."[43]

In annihilating the transcendentals (oneness, truth, goodness, beauty), essences, and named identities of the objective world, the artist, like Nietzsche, sees himself as destroying "its false absolute,"[44] and becoming the true ultimate Creator. Like the alchemist, the primary purpose of the collage artist is to realize his own "perfection and self-knowledge," rather than creating gold, or an artistic masterpiece.[45]

The Christian and Traditional European Sense of Law and Order in Creation. With such disturbing modern concepts and purposes in mind, further examination of traditional and Christian beliefs brings out more of their essential differences. Shakespeare, the great Elizabethan dramatist and poet, who preceded the Modernism of Enlightenment and its progeny by more than a century, has been very strongly associated with nature because of the range and richness of sensual nature imagery. His treatment reached its highest levels in expression of medieval-Renaissance views of universal cosmic order and degree-by-degree interrelatedness of nature. The *locus classicus* in his plays is in *Troilus and Cressida* (written c. 1601)—in the "degree" speech of Ulysses. It is one of the best known passages in Elizabethan literature, with its praise of harmonious cosmic order and function, and warnings of the disastrous consequences of its being shaken, choked, and lost.

> The heavens themselves, the planets, and this center
> Observe degree, priority, and place,
> Insisture course, proportion, season, form,
> Office, and custom, in all line of order.
> And therefore is the glorious planet Sol
> In noble eminence enthroned and sphered
> Amidst the other; whose med'cinable eye
> Corrects the ill aspects of planets evil,
> And posts, like the commandment of a king,
> Sans check, to good and bad. But when the planets
> In evil mixture to disorder wander,
> What plagues and what portents, what mutiny,
> What raging of the sea, shaking of earth,
> Commotion in the winds, frights, changes, horrors,
> Divert and crack, rend and deracinate
> The unity and married calm of states
> Quite from their fixure! O, when degree is shaked,
> Which is the ladder to all high designs,
> The enterprise is sick! How could communities,
> Degrees in schools, and brotherhoods in cities,
> Peaceful commerce from dividable shores,
> The primogenity and due of birth,
> Prerogative of age, crowns, sceptors, laurels,
> But by degree, stand in authentic place?
> Take but degree away, untune that string,
> And hark what discord follows. Each thing meets
> In mere oppugnancy. The bounded waters
> Should lift their bosoms higher than the shores
> And make a sop of all this solid globe;
> Strength should be lord of imbecility,
> And the rude son should strike his father dead;
> Force should be right, or rather right and wrong—
> *Between whose endless jar justice resides—
> Should lose their names, and so should justice too.
> Then everything include itself in power,
> Power into will, will into appetite,
> And appetite an universal wolf,

So doubly seconded with will and power,
Must make perforce an universal prey
And last eat up himself. Great Agamemnon,
This chaos, when degree is suffocate,
Follows the choking.   (I, iii, 85-126)

In the great chain of being moving link by link from the highest to the lowest, everything in creation is interrelated by orderly degree, and by correlation of lower planes to higher ones in the vertical hierarchy. In an idea common to Elizabethan and Jacobean culture, Shakespeare indicates that when the claim on this truth is weakened and lost, human society and institutions run amok, as do the orderly workings and sequences of nature and cosmos. Interestingly, Shakespeare lists as consequences certain factors which have actually become powerful influences in the modern world as belief in God, providence, and divine cosmic order and its hierarchies have been increasingly abandoned: philosophies of non-rational will and power (German voluntarism, Nietzsche, Foucault); philosophy and art that fuse good and evil (Romanticism, Late Romanticism, Symbolism, Jung, Surrealism, Postmodernism); abandonment to appetite; the discord of contradictory worldviews.

Edmund Spenser, one of the earliest great poets of the Elizabethan age, produced some of its most delightful, enchanting, and melodic poetry; but it is sweet poetry with a rich depth of ideas as well. Equipped with an extensive educational background in classical studies, Spenser wove idealistic Platonic and Neo-Platonic concepts and images with mythological elements, often fusing them into an overall Christian context. Although "his imagination dwelt in a realm of beauty and the noblest ideals," we are continually made aware of the links and parallels between two great realms in his poetry: the lower, created earthly realm of mankind and earth, which, although fallen, is still one of much goodness, love, beauty, and plenty; and the higher, perfect heavenly realm of Love and Beauty, and of God the Creator, the Trinity, the source and redeemer of everything good below.

The last of Spenser's *Fowre Hymn, An Hymne of Heavenly Beautie* (1596), is an exemplary, holistic expression of the Elizabethan worldview of the chain of being leading from the earth to the transcendent realm of God. Through forty-three stanzas of seven lines each the poet transports us upward stage by stage, to ever-higher degrees of beauty, culminating in the overpowering and humanly unbearable beauty and radiance of God. The poem is thus "an account of the ordered universe" which reaches its climax in "a vision of God's power and glory."[46]

The description of the solid, enduring structure of earth, "on adamantine pillars founded," "the Sea engirt with brasen bands," the moving air, the fixed stars—all ordered to their proper and harmonious places, echoes similar praises in the Psalms. It is a realm of plenty and beauty: within "the frame of this wyde universe" can be seen "endlesse kinds of creatures . . . made with wondrous wise respect, And all with admirable beautie deckt." As one rises from earth and water through air and heavenly fire, it becomes "still more cleare," "more pure and fayre." The "King and Queene" of the "Skye" are the sun and moon, "ruling night and day." Spenser then speaks of higher heavens: "farre above these heavens which here we see,/ Be others farre exceeding these in light,/ Not bounded, not corrupt, as these same bee,/ But infinite in largenesse and in hight, Untill they come to their first Movers bound," the *primum mobile*,

> Whence they doe still behold the glorious face
> Of the divine eternall Majestie;
> More faire is that, where those Idees on hie,
> Enraungéd be, which Plato so admyred,
> And pure Intelligences from God inspyred.

Nine orders of angels are found grouped in their proper hierarchy by their nearness to God.

The remaining two-thirds of the poem is given over to praises of the acts and attibutes of God, with much on his "Sapience" or Holy Wisdom. The poet tells of "His truth, his love, his wisedom, and his blis,/ His grace, his doome [judgment], his mercy and his might,/ By which he lends us of himselfe a sight." Since we cannot endure looking directly upon "The glory of that Majestie divine,"

> The meanes therefore which unto us is lent,
> Him to behold, is on his workes to looke,
> Which he hath made in beauty excellent,
> And in the same, as in a brasen booke,
> To reade enregistered in every nooke
> His goodnesse, which his beautie doth declare,
> For all thats good, is beautifull and faire.

God is eternal, unchanging: "His throne is built upon Eternity . . . . His scepter is the rod of Righteousnesse, . . . his judgement just; His seate is Truth, to which the faithfull trust;/ From which proceed her beames so pure and bright,/ That all about him sheddeth glorious light."

One-fourth of the poem is given over to God's "Sapience," his Holy Wisdom, praised in the Old Testament and in the Apocrypha. In keeping with these sources, and with the New Testament, where Christ is identified as "the power of God, and the wisdom of God" (I Cor. 1:22-24), Spenser is no doubt alluding to Christ, while using the feminine gender of Wisdom in the Old Testament.

> Both heaven and earth obey unto her will,
> And all the creatures which they both containe:
> For of her fulnesse which the world doth fill,
> They all partake, and do in state remaine,
> As their great maker did at first ordaine,
> Through observation of her high beheast,
> By which they first were made, and still increast.

For John Milton, as for Spenser and Elizabethan literature generally, God had created all things in an orderly and rational chain of being, proceeding from his throne downward through all creation, carefully linked, sphere by sphere, degree by degree. This continuous chain of being also reveals an inherent movement upward again from the lowest, inanimate sphere, through the increasingly higher vegetative, sensitive, and rational spheres of plants, animals, and men, respectively, to the spiritual sphere of angels, and ultimately to the divine Creator. Moving upward, man's bodily spirits are elevated to the sphere of the vital emotional spirits, and then to the intellectual (animal) spirits, enabling him to reason. Thus, intellect and reason find their properly high place and important role in this rational, ascending chain leading to God, and to man's final spiritual perfection.[47] Milton's *Paradise Lost* (1667, 1674) expresses many of these beliefs.

> One Almightie is, from whom
> All things proceed, and up to him return,
> If not deprav'd from good, created all
> Such to perfection, one first matter all,
> Indu'd with various forms, various degrees
> Of substance, and in things that live, of life;
> But more refin'd, more spiritous, and pure,
> As neerer to him plac'd or neerer tending
> Each in thir several active Sphears assign'd,
> Till body up to spirit work, in bounds
> Proportiond to each kind. So from the root
> Springs lighter the green stalk, from thence the leaves
> More aerie, last the bright consummate flowr
> Spirits odorous breathes: flowrs and thir fruit
> Mans nourishment, by gradual scale sublim'd
> To vital Spirits aspire, to animal,
> To intellectual, give both life and sense,
> Fansie and understanding, whence the Soul
> Reason receives, and reason is her being,

Discursive, or Intuitive; discourse
Is oftest yours, the latter most is ours,
Differing but in degree, of kind the same.
Wonder not then, what God for you saw good
If I refuse not, but convert, as you,
To proper substance; time may come when men
With Angels may participate, and find
No inconvenient Diet, nor too light Fare:
And from these corporal nutriments perhaps
Your bodies may at last turn all to Spirit,
Improv'd by tract of time, and wing'd ascend
Ethereal, as wee, or may at choice
Here or in Heav'nly Paradises dwell;
If ye be found obedient, and retain
Unalterably firm his love entire
Whose progenie you are.

(*Paradise Lost*, V, 469-503)

In absolute contrast, "Milton's hell is above all else a denial of order, a refusal of obedience, an establishment of chaos."[48] In Satan's words:

To do aught good never will be our task,
But ever to do ill our sole delight,
As being the contrary to his high will
Whom we resist. If then his Providence
Out of our evil seek to bring forth good,
Our labour must be to pervert that end.
(*Paradise Lost*, I, 159-64)

And "Satan is the personification of Reason denied, the embodiment of passionate disobedience, as God is the embodiment of Reason absolute. When he succeeds, Satan passes on his passionate disobedience to others."[49]

Upstart Passions catch the Government
From Reason, and to servitude reduce
Man till then free.
(*Paradise Lost*, XII, 88-90)

In the Elizabethan and Jacobean age, on the threshold of the modern era, belief in God, the Bible, and the upholding of orthodox doctrine was at high levels in English society and culture. Its influence permeated the literature and helped produce some of the greatest works of European history. But the "new philosophy" was on the rise, and its influence was being felt by more and more people. John Donne was shaken by prospects for the future. More informed about the new philosophy than others, he sensed a world beginning in which all degree would be suffocate, all ordered spheres shattered, hierarchies crumbled, and all beliefs cast in doubt. In retrospect, the individualism, autonomy, skepticism, disjunctions, and fragmentations of modernity are strongly suggested in Donne's *An Anatomie of the World: The First Anniversary*:

> And new Philosophy calls all in doubt,
> The element of fire is quite put out;
> The Sun is lost, and th'earth, and no mans wit
> Can well direct him where to looke for it.
> And freely men confesse that this world's spent,
> When in the Planets, and the Firmament
> They seeke so many new; they see that this
> Is crumbled out againe to his Atomies.
> 'Tis all in peeces, all cohaerence gone;
> All just supply, and all Relation:
> Prince, Subject, Father, Sonne, are things forgot,
> For every man alone thinkes he hath got
> To be a Phoenix and that then can bee
> None of that kinde, of which he is, but hee.[50]

But rather than turning to skepticism or atheism, Donne held more firmly to traditional orthodox beliefs of Christianity, and a continuing sense of cosmic order and divine purpose. By the 1660s Milton the Christian humanist was the last powerful literary exponent, before the outburst of Modernism, of older, beliefs in God, Creation, Providence, sin and salvation, and cosmic order.[51] In sum, the Elizabethan and Jacobean age, ending with its extension into Milton, was the last great and broad efflorescence of Christian belief in mainline European culture before the emergence of Modernism. The quite different philosophies of Bacon, Descartes, and Hobbes—the first great intellectual fathers of Modernism—were being written at the same time, during the first half of the seventeenth century, and represent the first major steps in a radically different direction. The arts modernity eventually produced would stand opposed to the old, traditional beliefs, even reversing their essential ideas, values, and worldview, especially those of God, creation, revelation, sin and salvation, world order, and purpose.

In 1730, nearly sixty years after Milton, and a century before the full bloom of modern romanticism, the Scottish poet James Thomson published a series of poems entitled *The Seasons*. They are remarkable for their reverent and sensitive listening to the voices of the natural world, and for hearing in them praises for their "Creator," the "Almighty Father," "the God of Seasons," and "the Great Shepherd." The following is a selection from "A Hymn on the Seasons."

His praise, ye brooks, attune, ye trembling rills;
And let me catch it as I muse along.
Ye headlong torrents, rapid and profound;
Ye softer floods, that lead the humid maze
Along the vale; and thou, majestic main,
A secret world of wonders in thyself,
Sound his stupendous praise, whose greater voice
Or bids you roar or bids your roarings fall.
Soft roll your incense, herbs, and fruits, and flowers,
In mingled clouds to him, whose sun exalts.
Whose breath perfumes you, and whose pencil paints.
Ye forests, bend; ye harvests, wave to him—
Breathe your still song into the reaper's heart
As home he goes beneath the joyous moon.
Ye that keep watch in heaven, as earth asleep
Unconscious lies, effuse your mildest beams,
Ye constellations! While your angels strike
Amid the spangled sky the silver lyre.
Great source of day! Best image here below
Of thy Creator, ever pouring wide
From world to world the vital ocean round!
On nature write with every beam his praise.
The thunder rolls: be hushed the prostrate world,
While cloud to cloud returns the solemn hymn.
Bleat out afresh, ye hills; ye mossy rocks,
Retain the sound, the broad responsive low,
Ye valleys, raise; for the Great Shepherd reigns,
And his unsuffering kingdom yet will come. . . .

The Beginnings of Modern Art in Romanticism. Romanticism (c. 1790-1830) represents the beginnings of Modernism in the arts, as the Enlightenment (eighteenth century) had just before it in thought. Byron, much like two other key figures of English romanticism, Shelley and Blake, was opposed to essential Christian beliefs, thinking of God as a cruel and limiting projection of the human mind. His free and rebellious way of living also reveals a stark opposition to Christian moral principles, although he claimed some belief in deistic views.[52] In this sense, verses of his poem, "Childe Harold's Pilgrimage" still express a sense of joy, and the beauty and limitlessness of the sea, where he could still sense "the Almighty's form," "the image of Eternity," and "the throne of the invisible."

There is a pleasure in the pathless woods,
There is a rapture on the lonely shore,
There is society where none intrudes,
By the deep Sea, and music in its roar . . . .

. . . .

Thou glorious mirror, where the Almighty's form
Glasses itself in tempests; in all time,
Calm or convulsed—in breeze, or gale, or storm,
Icing the pole, or in the torrid clime,
Dark-heaving; boundless, endless, and sublime—
The image of Eternity—the throne
Of the Invisible . . . .

. . . .

And I have loved thee, Ocean! And my joy
Of youthful sports was on thy breast to be
Borne, like thy bubbles, onward . . . .[53]

The "prime element" in the poetry of the young Romantic, John Keats, according to Harold Bloom, is his "thoroughgoing naturalistic humanism." From his "Ode to Psyche" onward, Keats "proclaims a more strenuously naturalistic confidence" than Wordsworth. There is an "uncompromising sense that we are completely physical in a physical world." More than any other poet since Shakespeare, Keats was "the one most able to grasp the individuality and reality of selves totally distinct from his own, and of an outward world that would survive his perception of it."[54] Nature, with its goodness and beauties, certainly played a primary role in Keats's poetry. And while Keats often refers to classical Greek gods, neither God the Father nor Christ play significant roles. In this sense too they are "naturalistic." Keats's observations, thoughts, and experiences of nature were often used to reflect on aspects of human life. Also central were transcendental concepts of art, beauty, truth, and imagination. Dreams, visions, memories, and fantasies played important roles as well.

Keats often used themes of nature as a springboard to flights of thought and imagination on the eternal in art, beauty, and truth. His poetry is characteristically charged with awareness of human consciousness, feelings, mortality, and an end in death. Beginning with the natural world, the poetic speaker often departs from it into a transcendental imaginative realm. In his mature work, there is a kind of replacement of human redemption and salvation through Christ, with romantic redemption from time, suffering, aging, and death by means of human transcendence through nature and art. Making lovely observations of nature, Keats constantly seeks the eternal *through* nature, imagination, poetry, art, and beauty. His two key themes, first of beauty in nature and the wonderful but mortal nature of human life, and second, of eternal transcendentals of beauty, truth, and art, are characteristically treated both in opposition to, and in some degree of harmony with each other. Thus, in his sonnet "Ode to a Nightingale" (1819), the natural art song of the bird, thought of as immortal, is contrasted with human suffering and mortality.

I

[The poet, mortally ill, and with deaths in family, hears the bird's beautiful song.] [55]

My heart aches, and a drowsy numbness pains
    My sense, as though of hemlock I had drunk,
Or emptied some dull opiate to the drains
    One minute past, and Lethe-wards had sunk:
'Tis not through envy of thy happy lot,
    But being too happy in thy happiness,—
    That thou, light-winged Dryad of the trees,
      In some melodious plot
    Of beechen green, and shadows numberless,
Singest of summer in full-throated ease.

II

[He longs for a carefree,] sensuous life.]

O, for a draught of vintage! That hath been
    Cooled a long age in the deep-delved earth,
Tasting of Flora and the country green,
    Dance, and Provencal song, and sunburnt mirth!
O for a beaker full of the warm South,
    Full of the true, the blushful Hippocrene,
    With beaded bubbles winking at the brim,
      And purple-stained mouth;
    That I might drink, and leave the world unseen,
    And with thee fade away into the forest dim:

III

[He returns to themes of sorrow, pain, and death.]

Fade far away, dissolve, and forget
    What thou among the leaves hast never known,
The weariness, the fever, and the fret
    Here, where men sit and hear each other groan;
Where palsy shakes a few, sad, last grey hairs,
Where youth grows pale, and spectre-thin, and dies;
      Where but to think is to be full of sorrow
    And leaden-eyed despairs,
    Where Beauty cannot keep her lustrous eyes,
Or new Love pine at them beyond tomorrow.

IV

[He begins a transcendent
flight, through poetry and
imagination.]

Away! Away! For I will fly to thee,
    Not charioted by Bacchus and his pards,
But on the viewless wings of Poesy,
    Though the dull brain perplexes and retards:
Already with thee! Tender is the night,
    And haply the Queen-Moon is on her throne,
        Clustered around by all her starry Fays;
        But here there is no light,
    Save what from heaven is with the breezes blown
Through verdurous glooms and winding mossy ways.

V

[He envisions a poetic paradise
where the sensuous beauty
of nature is perfected
in imagination.]

I cannot see what flowers are at my feet,
    Nor what soft incense hangs upon the boughs,
But in embalmed darkness, guess each sweet
    Wherewith the seasonable month endows
The grass, the thicket, and the fruit-tree wild;
    White hawthorn, and the pastoral eglantine;
        Fast fading violets covered up in leaves;
        And mid-May's eldest child,
    The coming musk-rose, full of dewy wine,
    The murmurous haunt of flies on summer eves.

VI

[Having witnessed a perfect
paradise, he reverts to
thoughts of death as a release
from the inadequacies of life.]

Darkling I listen; and, for many a time
    I have been half in love with easeful Death.
Called him soft names in many a mused rhyme,
    To take into the air my quiet breath;
    Now more than ever seems it rich to die,
    To cease upon the midnight with no pain,
        While thou art pouring forth thy soul abroad
            In such an ecstasy!
    Still wouldst thou sing, and I have ears in vain—
    To thy high requiem become a sod.

VII

[A lyric climax in the beauty
of nature and poetry is
reached, and contrasted
with the sadness of
actual existence.]

Thou wast not born for death, immortal Bird!
    No hungry generations tread thee down;
The voice I hear this passing night was heard
    In ancient days by emperor and clown:
Perhaps the self-same song that found a path
    Through the sad heart of Ruth, when, sick for home,
        She stood in tears amid the alien corn;
        The same that oft-times hath
    Charmed magic casements, opening on the foam

Of perilous seas, in faery lands forlorn.

VIII

[He returns to his mutable existence, uncertain whether his poetic vision is reality or delusion.]

Forlorn! the very word is like a bell
  To toll me back from thee to my sole self!
Adieu! the fancy cannot cheat so well
  As she is famed to do, deceiving elf.
Adieu! adieu! thy plaintive anthem fades
  Past the near meadows, over the still stream,
    Up the hill-side; and now 'tis buried deep
    In the next valley-glades:
  Was it a vision or a waking dream?
  Fled in that music:—Do I wake or sleep?

The Contrast of Hopkins' Christian Belief with Modernism. By the later nineteenth century Gerard Manley Hopkins turned essentially away from the dominant views of Modernism, back to central Christian ones. He transformed romanticism's focus on nature back to a Christian worship of God the Creator. Raised as an Anglican, and producing talented poetic writings in his youth, Hopkins converted to Roman Catholicism in 1866 at age 22. He reacted by ceasing to write, and burning his previous poems. He entered the Jesuit order two years later, and was subsequently ordained as a priest. During the later 1870s he began writing poetry again, developing a highly personal and innovative style. Sensitively attuned to the goodness, beauties, and truth of nature, his poems are meant to glorify and worship God, Jesus Christ, and the Holy Spirit as Creator of the wonders and endless diversity of the natural world. They are also intended to lead the reader into meditation, praise, and prayerful worship. The poem "Pied Beauty" emphasizes the endlessly subtle variations of color and surface of individual created things by using such words as "pied," "dappled," "couple-colored," "rose-moles," "stipple," "fresh-firecoal chestnut," "freckled," and "adazzle" —as much for their uniquely colorful evocativeness of *sound* as for their descriptive meanings. Alliteration, assonance, and euphony add their voices to the colorful panoply. Natural things are not only endlessly varied, but contrast ("counter") as unique and opposite beings. They reflect God in their manifoldness, but in contrast to their changing beauty, God's beauty is unchanging ("past change").

Glory be to God for dappled things—
  For skies of couple-colour as a brinded cow;
    For rose-moles all in stipple upon trout that swim;
Fresh-firecoal chestnut-falls; finches' wings;

Landscape plotted and pieced—fold, fallow, and plow;
And all trades, their gear and tackle and trim.

All things counter, original, spare, strange;
Whatever is fickle, freckled (who knows how?)
With swift, slow; sweet, sour; adazzle, dim;
He fathers-forth whose beauty is past change:
Praise him.

Like many romantics before, and later romantics during his time, Hopkins was acutely aware of the deleterious effects that rapidly advancing modern technology, industrialization, and urbanization were having on the world—on work, on cities, small towns, countryside, and on human relationship to nature. He was deeply distressed by all this, finding much that was repressive and destructive. In his poem "God's Grandeur," the realm of work now leads humans away from seeing and listening to nature, and thereby attuning themselves to God: "all is seared with trade; bleared, smeared with toil," infected by man ("wears man's smudge"), so that human beings are separated from the natural world as God created it ("nor can feel, being shod"). The sound and meaning of "shod" here evokes an appalling state, in which people have not only been separated from nature, but have thereby lost sight of their own spiritual nature, becoming increasingly animalistic, materialistic, mechanistic.

The World is charged with the grandeur of God.
It will flame out, like the shining from shook foil;
It gathers to a greatness, like the ooze of oil
Crushed. Why do men then now not reck his rod?
Generations have trod, have trod, have trod;
And all is seared with trade; bleared, smeared with toil;
And wears man's smudge and shares man's smell; the soil
Is bare now; nor can foot feel, being shod.
And for all this, nature is never spent;
There lives the dearest freshness deep down things;
And though the last lights off the black West went
Oh, morning, at the brown brink eastward, springs—
Because the Holy Ghost over the bent
World broods with warm breast and with ah! bright wings.

T. S. Eliot and the Modern Void. While Hopkins strongly sensed modern threats to nature, and the deterioration of human relationship with nature, T. S. Eliot, the major figure of American-British modern poetry, indicates a much more advanced condition about twenty-five or thirty years later. His first major poem, "The Lovesong of J. Alfred Prufrock" was completed in 1911, published in 1915, and again in 1917. Many of the general themes, views, and techniques of this poem had already been developing in modern visual arts a few years earlier—the sharp decline and virtual disappearance of nature as such, replaced by man-made images and surroundings; the loss of traditional senses of unity and harmony in what one sees and knows, resulting in pervasive fragmentation and disjunction. Such things can also be seen, for example in Analytical Cubism in Paris from 1907 through 1911, and a further sense of fragmentation in the sharp, sudden changes found in the collage effects of Synthetic Cubism beginning in 1912.

The modern sense of abandonment of believable, traditional truth had been broadening and growing stronger in the arts and thought from the last quarter of the nineteenth century onward. Nietzsche, with his fierce, all-out attacks on Christianity and classical metaphysics, is the key figure of modern doubt and opposition to tradition in philosophy in the 1870s and 80s. His writings were influential on many "high modern" artists and writers (c. 1905-1940), when modern thought and art reached its apogee. Results of his and related influences can be increasingly seen, for example, in German Expressionism from around 1905 onward, which essentially abandoned Christianity and western metaphysics of being with their claims of universal truths, turning instead to primitivism, or to assemblages of varied symbols and myths, and a sense of the crushing isolation of human beings in urban environments, a profound sense of alienation, and an exacerbated or paralyzed self-consciousness. The roots and early development of such views and themes can be traced back at least to the eighteenth-century Enlightenment as the early stage of modern thought, and to Romanticism (c. 1790-1830) as the first modern movement in the arts.

In "The Love Song of J. Alfred Prufrock," Eliot's version of these themes and techniques reached a maddening intensity. Nature, as traditionally known, is almost entirely gone, replaced by a swarm of artificial images such as meandering city streets, houses, window-panes, tables, coats, shawls, neckties, plates, spoons, toast, tea, and cakes. What remains of reality is the insistent tick-ticking of time. Transcendence has collapsed: the speaker finds himself surrounded and confined by mundane and lowly images, dropping to the lowest level in drain water and soot. Everything loses clarity and certainty in a pervasive yellow fog and yellow smoke. Human alienation and separation is evoked by "half-deserted streets," "lonely men in shirt-sleeves, leaning out of windows," and more intensely by "eyes that fix you . . . pinned and wriggling on the wall" (compare themes of alienation, separation, and self-fixation in Edvard Munch's paintings such as "Evening on Karl Johan Street" of 1894, carried further in pictures by Ludwig Kirchner.)

The speaker of "Prufrock" is hyper self-conscious: he is very disturbed and distanced by what those eyes think of his thin hair and bald spot, and the way they pin you on the wall with a "formulated phrase." There is only an uncertain, indistinct, and impersonal vestige of human relationship through sex. The poem's speaker has a limited focus—female arms. He claims, impersonally, to have "known them all," which (in his self-absorbed fantasy) suggests unlimited sexual freedom—a liberation from all limiting religious and metaphysical claims.

> Let us go then, you and I,
> When the evening is spread out against the sky
> Like a patient etherized upon a table;
> Let us go, through certain half-deserted streets,
> The muttering retreats
> Of restless nights in one-night cheap hotels
> And sawdust restaurants with oyster-shells:
> Streets that follow like a tedious argument
> Of insidious intent
> To lead you to an overwhelming question …
> Oh, do not ask, "What is it?"
> Let us go and make our visit.
> In the room the women come and go
> Talking of Michelangelo.
> The yellow fog that rubs its back upon the window-panes,
> The yellow smoke that rubs its muzzle on the window-panes,
> Licked its tongue into the corners of the evening,
> Lingered upon the pools that stand in drains,
> Let fall upon its back the soot that falls from chimneys,
> Slipped by the terrace, made a sudden leap,
> And seeing that it was a soft October night,
> Curled once about the house, and fell asleep.

Neither the objective reality of an external world nor any universal truth is securely known here, nor can they be known. The secure realities of God, nature, and universal beliefs are absent. Many of these poetic themes reflect Eliot's own views and experiences during the time. In his doctoral dissertation written between 1913 and 1916, Eliot denied the substantial reality of the material world, and claimed: "what is subjective is the whole world." "All significant truths are private truths." He "looked upon the world as a precarious, artificial construction . . . . It had no permanent substance: it was 'essentially vague, unprecise, swarming with insoluble contradictions'."

Any groupings of disparate images into a "world" quickly dissolved and fell apart.[56] Thus the speaker of "Prufrock" finds it impossible and hopeless to think well and to make any worthwhile decisions. Although the problem of Shakespeare's Hamlet is related, Hamlet in comparison still seems like a man of significant belief, decision, and action. Prufrock's speaker lacks *any* higher beliefs and principles that could lead him to decision and purposive action in a real world. Hopkins' most horrible fears have come to pass in the themes of this poem.

Eliot's dark views seem to have arisen from the depths of his being. But unlike most modernists, his agonies led him to religious belief. On June 29, 1927, Eliot was baptized and received into the Church of England in a secret ceremony. Although it is difficult to tell from biographies exactly what he believed, Eliot claimed to accept the official creed of the church. He expressed belief in life after death, and in the *Dial* of March 1927, "he affirmed that the chief distinction of Man is to glorify God." In 1928 he said that "Christianity reconciled him to human existence which otherwise seemed empty and distasteful." Peter Ackroyd has written of Eliot's sufferings, alienation, detachment, and aloofness. He says Eliot "was a writer who attempted to create order and coherence, and yet his central vision was of 'the Void'."[57]

Chapter Two

The Greatness of God
Recently Discovered Wonders of the Universe and the Natural World

"To whom will you compare me? Or who is my equal?" says the Holy One. Lift up your eyes and look to the heavens: Who created all these? He who brings out the starry host one by one and calls forth each of them by name. Because of his great power and mighty strength, not one of them is missing. (Isaiah 40:25-26, NIV)

Yours, O Lord, is the greatness and the power and the glory and the majesty and the splendor, for everything in heaven and earth is yours." (1 Chronicles 29:11)

God knows all processes and events of the universe not simply as unrelated facts but in their interrelationship with one another, and to all of reality.[1]

Only divine creation *guarantees the reality, reason, intelligence, order, law, design, and purpose of the universe, the Earth, mankind, and individual persons.*

A Vast, Well-Ordered Universe That Has a Beginning. Scientific discoveries in the twentieth and twenty-first centuries reveal in astonishing detail many new features of the universe, the Earth, and human beings. And like the earlier, divine creation beliefs seen in the previous chapter they indicate a universe that has not existed eternally, but has a specific point of origin—a definite beginning. Many scientists think that time itself began with that beginning, as well as space, matter and all the laws of the physical universe. These new discoveries reveal a universe so incredibly vast that it is far beyond anything else in human experience. Although it may not be absolutely infinite, its immense dimensions make it infinite relative to human life. These discoveries also reveal in the universe, from its beginnings to the present (in stark contrast to what radical modernist and postmodernist thinkers and artists claim), amazing degrees of order, precision, balances, and controls. These newly discovered, finely balanced aspects of the universe provide powerful evidence in support of the kind of order and purpose written about through the centuries from the Psalms up through Gerard Manley Hopkins in the late nineteenth century.

By finding strong and extensive evidence for a sudden beginning of the universe, modern scientific discoveries logically call for a "Beginner," that is, a Creator. How else could *anything* originate from *nothing*? Ancient cosmogonies often began with primordial waters of chaos, gods of heaven and Earth, stars, or at times an egg, womb, lotus, or turtle. But where did *they* come from? If the universe arose from an infinitely small and dense, hot primordial Big Bang, where did the dense hot energy come from, and why? Where did the *laws* of the universe come from? Without an eternal, *uncaused*, *super*natural Creator we are always left with another unanswered question for every answer concerning the origin of the universe. Atheists frequently show their ignorance by asking, "Who created God?" But that shows ignorance of the most basic lesson of Theology 101, that God is *eternal, uncreated Being.*[2]

Many scientists still cling to beliefs that all of these amazing characteristics and orderly features of the universe are the result of gradual self-development—of spontaneous self-generation and self-organization, with no transcendent or supernatural cause. As one flatly stated on television, "Life is not a miracle, it is a statistic." But as astronomer and Christian author Hugh Ross points out, *"not one example of significant self-generation or self-organization can be found in the entire realm of nature. In fact, nature shows us just the opposite."*[3] The number of those who believe in some ultimate supernatural cause has been increasing. A survey published in 1997 showed that of the thousand physicists, biologists, and mathematicians interviewed, 40% acknowledged belief in God—a God many thought of as a Supreme Being who operates in earthly affairs and hears prayers.[4] And there are numerous spokesmen in scientific fields today for a universe of "intelligent design" created by a super-intelligent God—a God of infinite knowledge, capable of creating such a huge, complex, "fine-tuned," and purposely ordered universe.

Origin of the Universe in the Big Bang. The present model for the origin of the universe accepted today by most scientists is the "big bang." It has been in gradual development for nearly a hundred years, since Einstein predicted an expanding universe in 1916. A long list of experimental evidence has been gathered to support it since then. Today there is telescopic and microwave radiation evidence reaching back through space-time to very early stages in the big bang. In 2004 the orbiting Hubble Space Telescope captured images of around 10,000 galaxies in the earliest periods of galaxy formation in the newly emerging universe—*actual images of the early universe in process of formation over 13 billion years ago.*[5] The oldest star yet discovered, HE 1523-0901, has an estimated age of 13.2 billion years.[6] And on July 11, 2007 six star-forming galaxies were found that are about 13.2 billion light years away.[7] (Looking back through the immense spatial distances of billions of light-years means that one is also *looking back in time* to the same extent—it is called "look-back time.") At present, with instruments now available, scientists can see 99.99972% of cosmic history—back very near the big bang. A recent calculation for the age of the universe following the big bang is 13.73 billion years.[8] The great blaze of radiation that arose from the big bang (Cosmic Microwave Background Radiation, or CMBR) has not only been predicted, but actually discovered and mapped in real images.[9]

In his revealing book, *The Creator and the Cosmos*, Hugh Ross lists 30 points of scientific evidence supporting the factual reality of the big bang creation event. Their substantiality can be seen by briefly restating 10 of them: (1) the current temperature of the CMBR has been proven to exist at the temperature expected to remain from the original big bang; (2) the current spectrum wavelength of CMBR closely fits that predicted to remain from the original big bang; (3) measured early temperatures of the CMBR fit those required, along with the expected cooling rate; (4) careful measurements of galaxy velocities show that the universe has been in process of expanding for over 13 billion years; (5) the existing stable orbits of planets about stars, and of stars about the nuclei of galaxies are only possible when there are three very large and rapidly expanding dimensions of space; (6) human and other life requires a stable solar-type star, which requires the carefully controlled expansion and cooling of the universe resulting from the hot big bang; (7) Einstein's theory of general relativity, which is the best proven scientific principle in physics, contains indications that the universe must be expanding from a finite beginning point; (8) Hawking and Penrose mathematically demonstrated in 1970 that for a universe containing mass and governed by the laws of general relativity, time itself must be finite and must have been created when the universe was created. Hawking later said, "Almost everyone now believes that the universe, and *time itself*, had a beginning in the big bang."[10] (9) the ages of stars, determined by their colors and surface temperatures, are consistent with the big bang model; (10) the known ages of galaxies are also consistent with it.[11]

What actually happened at the initial instant of the big bang, "time zero," from which the universe progressively emerged? Giles Sparrow gives a concise answer: "All the energy in the universe is created in the instant of the Big Bang itself." Then, within a split micro second (a hundred billionth of a yoctosecond) there is a rapid expansion ("inflation"), and energy dominates the universe. After only one millionth of a second all the matter of the universe is created. Over the next three minutes the first atomic nuclei are formed. The dense fog of created energy and matter clears. But it takes

300,000 years for the first atoms to form. Matter cools for over 100 million years, and after 200 million years the first giant stars are created and begin to enrich the universe with heavy elements. There is no visible light from the era before the first ignition of stars, although maps of prior Cosmic Microwave Background Radiation have been achieved. It is only after 400 or 500 million years that the first galaxies are formed.[12] But this is a short time in a universe that is now around 13.73 billion years old.

"Big bang" was coined as a depreciative term by astronomer-physicist Fred Hoyle around 1950, but has since stuck as a popular name. As understood by scientists, however, the actual event was not one of explosive destruction or chaotic disorder. "The universe was once infinitely small, dense, and hot. The big bang began a process of expansion and cooling that continues today." It was "not an explosion of matter into space, but an expansion of space itself, and in the beginning it brought time and space into existence."[13] The origin of the universe was not a random explosion ruled by chance, but an extremely rapid, orderly expansion from a tiny, incredibly dense and hot beginning state, through a controlled and orderly release of matter, energy, space, and time, with physical laws and constants regulating their behavior and interaction.

The Amazing Order of the Universe. The big bang had to be extraordinarily fine-tuned and ingeniously orchestrated in terms of the balance of energy with the amount of matter involved, or disaster would have occurred. A little too much energy or too little matter and the result would have been an explosion into bits and pieces—no stars, solar systems, and galaxies; inadequate chemical elements; and no complex life. Too little energy or too much matter and the big bang would have collapsed into a big heap. And this fine-tuned balance (the ratio of actual density of matter to the density for perfect balance in expansion) had to be controlled to one part in 10^{15} (1 with fifteen zeros after it) for complex life to result—*an incredibly micro-miniature difference.*[14] Such a precisely controlled and balanced beginning, as Ross indicates, points to a supernatural Agent, a Creator. It denies the notion of a self-existent universe. Instead, it suggests a purposive, personal Creator.[15]

Hoyle, an agnostic, was troubled by the theory of the big bang, *because* such a beginning implies a cause, a creator. Henry Margenau, the late, Professor Emeritus of Physics at Yale, has stated that the big-bang theory was "written and confirmed in the twentieth century," and that the universe and its laws were created by God: "A very small but extremely massive sphere of matter, in many respects similar to a black hole, could spring out of nothing without violating any known laws of nature. To be sure, it would be most unsatisfactory to regard this as an accident. God, however, created not only the physical universe but also the laws which it has to obey."[16]

Since the universe is now found by many astronomers, astro-physicists, theoretical physicists, and other scientists to have a definite origin, and an incredible array of orderly characteristics from its beginning onward, the ancient question, "why is there anything rather than nothing," takes on a new kind of urgency. And with it, a host of related questions arise: How could *order* arise from nothing? How could *intelligent design*, precision, and established control arise from nothing? How could the precisely controlled and sustained relationships of colossal heavenly bodies and of subatomic particles arise from nothing? How could energy, space, time, extreme heat and matter arise from nothing? How could any *life* arise from nothing? How could *mind* arise from nothing? *Why* does a universe that is billions of light-years across exist (one light-year is 5.88 trillion miles, the distance light travels in one year, at about 186,000 miles per second)? Responses that exclude God now appear at a great disadvantage from the outset. The new, twentieth and twenty-first-century model of the universe, and the large amount of evidence that supports it, seems to add new facts and strong scientific evidence to the focus of the biblical claim twenty centuries earlier, that "since the creation of the world God's invisible qualities—his eternal power and divine nature—have been clearly seen, being understood from what has been made, so that men are without excuse" (Romans 1:20).

Many astronomers, physicists, and astrophysicists have expressed their awe at the evidence of a high degree of orderly design in the universe, and the fine-tuning found in the anthropic principles that make human life possible. Hugh Ross has collected numerous examples in *The Creator and the Cosmos*. Paul Davies has written that the laws of physics seem to be "the product of exceedingly ingenious design." "It seems as though somebody has fine-tuned nature's numbers to make the universe."[17] Astronomer George Greenstein has written that "As we survey all the evidence, the thought insistently arises that some supernatural agency—or rather, Agency—must be involved. Is it possible that suddenly, without intending to, we have stumbled upon scientific proof of the existence of a Supreme Being. Was it God who stepped in and so providentially crafted the cosmos for our benefit?"[18] Tony Rothman, a theoretical physicist, has written: "when confronted with the order and beauty of the universe and the strange coincidences of nature, it's very tempting to take the leap of faith from science into religion. I am sure many physicists want to. I only wish they would admit it."[19] MIT physicist and Professor Emeritus Vera Kistiakowsky has said that "The exquisite order displayed by our scientific understanding of the physical world calls for the divine."[20] Arno Penzias, co-recipient of the Nobel Prize for physics, has said that "Astronomy leads us to a unique event, a universe which was created out of nothing, one with the very delicate balance needed to provide exactly the conditions required to permit life, and one which has an underlying (one might say 'supernatural') plan."[21] Chinese astrophysicist Fang Li Zhi and coauthor physicist Li Shu Xian have written: "A question that has always been considered a topic of metaphysics or theology the creation of the universe has now become an area of active research in physics."[22] Referring to the high degree of order in the universe, Alan Sandage, winner of the Crafoord prize in astronomy, has said: "I find it quite improbable that such order came out of chaos. There has to be some organizing principle. God to me is a mystery but is the explanation for the miracle of existence, why there is something instead of nothing."[23]

In his book *The Physics of Immortality*, mathematician and physicist Frank Tipler tells of his remarkable change from atheism to belief in God, and how scientific findings actually led him in that direction: "When I began my career as a cosmologist some twenty years ago, I was a convinced atheist. I never in my wildest dreams imagined that one day I would be writing a book purporting to show that the central claims of Judeo-Christian theology are in fact true, that these claims are straightforward deductions of the laws of physics as we now understand them. I have been forced into these conclusions by the inexorable logic of my own special branch of physics."[24]

The famous mathematician and theoretical physicist, Stephen Hawking, has indicated that the precise, controlled temperature and rate of expansion called for in the big bang points to the act of a Creator God. Writing about the hot big bang model of the universe, he points out that a very high degree of fine-tuned order would be necessary in such a process. He says that "the initial state of the universe would have to have had exactly the same temperature everywhere," and "the initial rate of expansion also would have had to be chosen very precisely for the rate of expansion still to be so close to the critical rate needed to avoid recollapse. This means that the initial state of the universe *must have been very carefully chosen* indeed if the hot big bang model was correct right back to the beginning of time. *It would be very difficult to explain why the universe should have begun in just this way, except as the act of a God who intended to create beings like us.*"[25] Despite all this, however, Hawking has claimed in a 2011 interview with the *Guardian* that belief in heaven or an afterlife is a "fairy story."

The Awe-Inspiring Nature of the Universe. Learning about the amazing features and characteristics of the universe immediately evokes awe and wonder. Times, sizes, and distances describing the universe are utterly incomprehensible in human and earthly terms. In the early twenty-first century astronomical observations indicate that the universe is 13.73 billion years old and at least 93 billion light years across.[26] Another estimate indicates it is 80 billion trillion miles in every direction.[27] Recent estimates indicate there are around 200 to 300 billion galaxies in the observable universe, and that each galaxy may contain an average of 200 billion stars. The total number of stars in the universe has been estimated at 10 to 50 billion trillion—truly staggering numbers.[28] But the Bible says that God "determines the number of the stars and calls them each by name" (Psalm 147:4).

In the New Testament Paul remarks on the differences in the "glory" or "splendor" of different stars. In the same verses he compares the moon, sun, and stars to our present earthly bodies and those of our future resurrected bodies: "There are also celestial bodies and terrestrial bodies; but the glory of the celestial one, and the glory of the terrestrial is another. There is one glory of the sun, another glory of the moon, and another glory of the stars; for *one star differs from another star in glory*. So also is the resurrection of the dead" (I Corinthians 15:40-42a, NKJV, emphasis added). Most stars last for billions of years, but the Bible and biblical theology teach that perfect, eternal, imperishable resurrection bodies will last forever.[29]

While our Sun is a medium-sized star, its diameter is about 109 times that of the Earth, and its mass is about 330,000 times greater. Some stars are smaller than the Earth. Neutron stars may have a diameter of only 3 to 12 miles. But the largest stars may have a diameter as much as 1000-2000 times that of the Sun! The luminosity of some stars is thousands of times greater than the Sun: Betelgeuse, which is 15 times more massive, is around 14,000 times brighter, and the supergiant star Eta Carinae, which is 100 times more massive, is 4-5.5 million times brighter.[30]

Nebulae are vast clouds of gas molecules (mostly hydrogen) and dust; they are not yet stars, but give birth to new generations of stars. Stars are born from nebulae through increasing gravitational attraction and compression. Hydrogen atoms at the core begin to change into helium atoms in a process of thermonuclear fusion that releases tremendous energy and light, similar in type to that of hydrogen bomb nuclear fusion. It has only been learned in the twentieth century that nuclear fusion is the real source of energy, heat, and light at the core of all stars. But the resulting stars may burn for billions of years. Some huge stars also end in spectacular explosions spreading new clouds of helium and heavier elements that mix with nebulae gases to become building materials for new stars and planets.[31]

The stars not only are pretty, poetic, and romantic lights in the sky, they are *intrinsically necessary* for all existing life in the universe. They precede the origin of our own Solar System, including the Earth and human beings, and have provided the material elements for their creation. Only four chemical elements existed when the first galaxies and stars were created–hydrogen, helium, lithium, and beryllium. Then other elements such as oxygen, silicon, and iron were created by processes of fusion within the stars. The very heaviest elements, such as lead, are created in the explosions of massive stars called supernovae, which distribute new elements throughout galaxies.[32] Thus, earth "dust" comes from star "dust," so human beings are not only made of earth "dust," or "clay," but of star dust (and according to the Bible, also created as beings of spirit and soul). Stars, including our Sun, also provide necessary energy, heat, and light for the universe, including planet Earth. Without the stars, we would be in the dark, frozen, and dead (or, more precisely, never existent at all).

The destiny of a star is determined early by its mass. "High-mass stars are brilliant and blue, while low-mass stars are dim and red." Most stars are stable at their determined level through most of their very long lives. But when their core nuclear fuel is eventually exhausted, they begin to draw on their outer layers for more. Their brightness rapidly increases, somewhat like a light bulb near its end. Radiation pressure causes their outer layers to balloon. This expanded star is called a "red giant." While it has become much larger and brighter, its surface is cooler. "Supergiant stars" also emerge from a similar process. They are "so brilliant that they can still keep their bloated surfaces hot, creating supergiant stars that can be orange, yellow, or even blue or white." Stars with more than eight times the mass of our Sun draw more and more rapidly on their core fuel, becoming increasingly brighter, and more unstable. "Eventually, the fuel runs out, and the star's sudden collapse triggers an enormous explosion—a supernova."[33]

A star that has largely run through its life as a bright burning star, and is growing smaller and dim, is known as a "white dwarf." Over billions of years a large star burns up its nuclear fusion material, sheds its outer layers, and grows cooler and weaker in intensity. These white dwarfs become more and more dense and faint. Being under extreme pressure, the carbon atoms at the center of the star begin to form crystals of diamonds. Finally the star gives off no light at all, and what remains is a *diamond* as large as a planet at the core of the resulting "black dwarf"[34]—in what seems like a miracle, *the star has become a planet-size diamond*!

The trillions of stars in the universe are clustered together in galaxies, like vast families or nations of people. A typical galaxy contains billions of stars. The Milky Way Galaxy, in which our solar system is located, exists as a colossal, slowly turning spiral-disk formation in space, and contains about 200 billion stars. The central star of our solar system, the Sun, is near one of the spiral arms of the Milky Way, about 26,000 light-years from the center, and turns around the galaxy's center every 230-250 million years. At the very center of the Milky Way is a colossal black hole, three million times as massive as the Sun. In a very large two-page image of the Milky Way our solar system looks like a very small o.[35] The Milky Way is between 100 and 130 thousand light-years in diameter. In miles that is some 600 to 780 thousand trillion miles. It has a glowing yellow core bulging from the center of its larger spiral-shaped disk. The core, 15 thousand light-years across, contains around 100 billion stars.

The nearest galaxy similar to the Milky Way is the Andromeda Galaxy. It is even larger than the Milky Way, being about twice its diameter (around 250,000 light-years), and containing perhaps as many as a trillion stars. While "nearer" to us than other galaxies, it is actually 2.1 million light-years distant (about 12 million trillion miles). Nevertheless, on a clear autumn evening it can be seen from Earth by the naked eye as a small hazy oval form. It is awe-inspiring to recall that the light we see as we gaze at it has been traveling for over two million years. The Milky Way, Andromeda, and Triangulum are the three major galaxies of a galaxy cluster known as the "Local Group," orbiting around a common center of gravity. And each of these galaxies is in turn orbited by "a swarm of smaller galaxies." Seeing such clusters, galaxies, and stars, especially in photographs and artist's renderings,[36] and thinking about their nearly endless numbers and colossal sizes and distances in the heavens, makes it all seem like an infinite, ingenious fireworks display, dwarfing and reducing to insignificance the biggest and best of human fireworks. And such a magnificent display really seems to be for human life and benefit, and ultimately to suggest the infinite nature and glory of God the Creator.

A 2010 date for the age of the universe is 13.75 billion years,[37] and the age of the oldest stars in our own galaxy has been calculated to be slightly more than 13 billion years. "The size of an average galaxy is 600 thousand trillion miles, and the average distance from one galaxy to another is 20 million trillion miles." Since a light-year is nearly six trillion miles, the average size of a galaxy is about one hundred thousand light-years, and the average distance between galaxies is over three million light-years.[38] How could such huge measures for time, seemingly infinite spaces, and colossal material things arise from nothing . . . and why?

As astronomers and scientists look deeper into the universe, they actually look farther and farther back in time toward its origin, since light from the greatest distances has been traveling for billions of light-years. This is "look-back" time. When using telescopes to study the features of the Orion Nebula, for example, it is actually seen as it was twelve hundred years ago, since the light we see from it has been traveling all that time to get to us. In observing the center of the Milky Way Galaxy, we see what was happening there 30,000 years ago, since it is that much farther away in light-years. When we examine the core of the next nearest one, the Andromeda Galaxy, we see it as it was 2.1 million years ago. And when light from the supernova SN

1994D reached Earth in March 1994, it was seen as it was 108 million years ago. For Galaxies NGC 6745A, NGC 1410, and UGC 10214 it is 200, 300, and 420 million years ago respectively. For the Ring Galaxy, "Hoag's Object," it is 600 million years ago.[39]

The billions of colossal galaxies in the universe are grouped into many even greater galaxy clusters, which may contain dozens or even hundreds of major and minor galaxies. Galaxy clusters and superclusters are *the largest discrete objects in the universe*, "spanning millions or hundreds of millions of light-years."[40] The galaxies within a cluster also display a system of order by orbiting an overall center of gravity. A supercluster is a group of galaxy clusters subject to the gravity of a more massive central galaxy cluster. And the still larger, orderly relation of galaxy superclusters to each other reveals a great chain-like pattern stretching through the universe. A map of the vast reaches around our Milky Way Galaxy reveals it as part of the "Local Group" Cluster, which is in turn part of the much greater Virgo Supercluster. And beyond the Virgo Supercluster, other Superclusters such as Centaurus, Perseus-Pisces, Coma, and Horologium reveal a great, orderly, chain-like interrelationship stretching on and on for a billion light-years and more.

Hubble Space Telescope's Ultra Deep Field images reveal young galaxies as much as 13 billion years ago, seen in various stages of merger and development.[41] And a recent infrared map of the "nearby" universe (2MASS Survey, 2 Micron All Sky Survey), although plotting only 1.6 million galaxies, clearly shows the regular, chain-like or "filamentary" structure of the universe in its spectacular scale. As Giles Sparrow poetically expresses it, "On the greatest scales of all, massive conglomerations of galaxies cluster like grains of dust to a celestial veil of cobwebs."[42] This infrared map recalls late 1940s paintings by Jackson Pollock. But the map conveys more powerfully the incredibly colossal, glowing, gossamer structure of the universe.

A phenomenon known as "gravitational lensing" has allowed astronomers to see some of the most distant objects visible in the universe. When the light from an extremely distant quasar or galaxy cluster passes close by another galaxy cluster nearer the Earth and more or less aligned with it, the gravitational field of the nearer cluster acts as a lens, bending and *magnifying* the light so that it comes into focus again on the Earth. The galaxy cluster known as Abell 1689, itself 2.2 billion light-years from the Earth, functions as such a gravitational lens, revealing and magnifying objects beyond it that date back to around 13 billion years ago, almost to the beginning of the universe.[43] As Ross says, "with recent technological advances, we can actually see all the way back to when light first separated from darkness, and even to a split second after the cosmic explosion with which all the universe's time, space, matter, and energy began."[44]

All the matter we know by direct observation—matter making up stars, planets, humans, animals, plants, rocks, and so on—is generally known as baryon matter. Since the 1930s, and especially since 1980, scientists have increasingly come to identify another type of matter in the universe—generally known as "dark matter." Unlike ordinary matter, dark matter interacts weakly or not at all with light and other forms of electromagnetic radiation, and so cannot be directly observed.[45] It can be detected, however, by its binding, gravitational field effects. The gravitational effects of visible material objects such as stars, galaxies, and galaxy clusters cannot by themselves explain the way galaxies and clusters hold together. Neither can they explain the exact rotation paths of stars in a galaxy. Recent studies have shown that the rotation speed across the entire disc of a galaxy such as our Milky Way is constant. "This can only mean that the entire disc of bright stars is embedded in a much bigger halo of dark material, which carries the bright Galaxy around in its gravitational grip." In addition, galaxies move too fast in their orbits within galaxy clusters to be held in place by the gravity of the visible matter. This also indicates the presence of non-visible dark matter. And studies of the larger universe show that "there is much more dark stuff in the depths of intergalactic space, holding galaxies together in clusters."[46]

Signs of Intelligence Establishing Precise Order and Balances. In recent years, because of rapidly advancing new evidence, many astronomers and other scientists have come to realize that the universe in its totality is very delicately balanced and interrelated in all its components. It has been documented from controlled observations that the universe's various components of matter, space, and energy are specifically *determined* and *balanced* relative to each other and to the universe as a whole. Without these many, controlled relationships, life would not be possible. Every component of the universe—the various forms of matter, space, and energy—has its determinate role and value for physical life to exist and be sustained.

Some have thought that such an awesomely spacious and massive universe so far outstrips human life that it is useless, and makes no sense. However, Hugh Ross maintains that "the universe *must* be as massive as it is or human life would not be possible." He gives two major reasons. The first is that if the cosmic mass or cosmic density were significantly lower, the density of protons and neutrons would be significantly lower, and incapable of converting 1% of the universe's mass into stars. Nuclear fusion would thus be lower and less efficient, and the universe would not produce enough of the heavy elements essential for any kind of physical life (carbon, oxygen, nitrogen, phosphorus, sodium, and potassium). But if the density of protons and neutrons were slightly higher, forming significantly more than 1% of cosmic mass into stars, nuclear fusion would be so high that all hydrogen would be too rapidly converted into elements as heavy or heavier than iron, and life-essential elements would again not exist.[47]

The second reason is that if cosmic mass density were significantly greater relative to total cosmic density, the effects of gravity would be stronger, and gas and dust would condense into more stars much larger than our Sun, creating too much radiation and heat (and too much fluctuation of both) for life to exist. In addition, if cosmic mass density were only a little greater, the universe would expand so slowly that all stars would rapidly become black holes and neutron stars. The densities near their surfaces would be so great that atoms and molecules could not exist, making life impossible. Thus, "the total quantity of protons and neutrons in the universe must be set at a precise value for the universe to produce the right kinds and quantities of life-essential elements at the right times in cosmic history . . . . Physical life cannot exist in a universe with a mass density any less or any more than the actual cosmic value."[48]

These facts show, as Ross emphasizes, that the universe reveals itself to be fine-tuned for physical life in at least two essential ways: "the just right amounts and diversity of elements," and "the just-right expansion rates throughout cosmic history so that certain types of stars and planets form at the just-right times and in the just-right locations."[49] It seems irrational and illogical to conclude, as non-theists do, that such astonishing precision on such an enormous scale of magnitude could be due to chance, "self-generation," and the absence of any plan and purpose. These and many other observed aspects of the universe logically suggest the prior existence of *superhuman* mind, ideas, power, and purpose.

Recent models of the various components of the universe have identified their proportionate cosmic densities relative to each other. One of the most recently studied cosmic components, directly identified in tests during 1998-99, is known as "dark energy." Another key component is dark matter. Dark energy and dark matter represent by far the greatest proportion of the energy and matter in the universe, and because they are not directly observable, they are fundamentally different from that observed on Earth.

While little is presently known about dark energy, it is believed to be an exotic form of "energy" that permeates and uniformly fills all space of the universe. The effect of dark energy is to promote and increase outward expansion of the universe, in a kind of slow, stretching effect. The expansionary effects of dark energy work in opposition to the gravitational effects of matter, which pulls matter together, compress, and has a braking effect on expansion. After the initial immense surge of the big bang, the universe expanded at a decelerating rate for its first 7 billion years. But during the subsequent 6.7 billion years it has been accelerating.[50] As the universe expands, the dark energy of space continues to increase the rate of expansion, slowly extending material bodies farther and farther apart.

Since the total space of the universe is much greater than the total mass (in itself incredibly immense), dark energy has been determined by recent tests to constitute 72-74% of the total cosmic density of the universe![51] In comparison, all the various forms of matter make up only about 26-28% of total cosmic density. Four general types of matter have been distinguished: first is the "exotic dark matter" ("cold dark matter") of particles that only interact weakly or not at all with ordinary matter and light. It constitutes by far the largest proportion of all matter, making up about 22-23.3 of the 26-28%; second is the "ordinary dark matter" of particles that interact strongly with light, forming about 4.35% of total cosmic density; third is the "ordinary bright matter" of light-producing stars and star remnants, which, despite the existence of about 50 billion trillion stars, makes up only 1% of all cosmic matter, and about 0.27% of total cosmic density (including dark energy); fourth is the matter of the planets (a sub-group of ordinary dark matter), making up only 0.0001% of total cosmic density. According to this data, exotic dark matter constitutes about 83.5% of the total matter in the universe. And when we add the percentages of all dark matter and dark energy we find that 99.73% of the universe is dark!

Dark energy has "a profound impact on the universe."[52] Its role and density is critical for life to exist in the universe. The cosmic density of dark energy must be extremely fine-tuned and balanced relative to the whole. Ross says, "If dark energy were changed by as little as one part in 10^{120}, the universe would be unable to support life."[53] One part in 10^{120} (1 with 120 zeros after it!) is an incredibly tiny, almost infinitesimal amount. Since there are 10^{65} atoms in our galaxy, one part in 10^{120} is roughly comparable to one atom in two galaxies the size of the Milky Way. Recent studies also indicate that dark energy density has remained "roughly constant throughout cosmic history, or at least all but its earliest moments."[54]

Since exotic dark matter does not appreciably interact with light and other electromagnetic radiation, it is not visible. Its presence is inferred from certain effects, such as gravity, on visible matter. It is believed to account for the vast majority of mass in the universe. Since dark matter gravitates as ordinary matter, it not only works to slow the expansion of the universe, but appears to help control the orbits of most stars in spiral galaxies, causing them to orbit at roughly the same speed. It is widely accepted today that as much as 95% of the matter gravitating around elliptical galaxies is dark matter. Our own Milky Way galaxy is believed to have roughly 10 times as much dark matter as ordinary matter.[55]

Ross emphasizes that physical life in the universe depends on precise balances and fine-tuning of numerous cosmic factors and components. One is that the combined matter (or mass) of stars and planets must be only about 1% of total cosmic matter of the universe. The amount must be "extraordinarily fine-tuned for life to exist." At certain early epochs in cosmic history, *if* no other density factors such as dark energy influenced expansion, the "mass density must have been as finely tuned as one part in 10^{60} to allow for the possible existence of physical life at any time or place within the entirety of the universe." In Ross's illustration, failure could result from adding to or subtracting only a dime's mass from the whole of the observable universe.[56]

Another example of precise balance involves the total quantity of protons and neutrons in the universe. Life requires a carefully fine-tuned proportion of bright matter (the protons and neutrons that form stars) to ordinary dark matter (the protons and neutrons that form gas, dust, rocks, and planets). For life to exist 5% of ordinary matter must be bright and 95% must be dark. Significantly more bright matter would cause too much heat, light, and radiation. A little less of bright matter would result in too little of these life-supporting essentials. Other essential elements for life, such as radioactive isotopes, can also be negatively affected by these changes.[57]

High degrees of stability and controlled distances apart are required for the existence of planets, stars, and galaxies, and thus for human life. Stars must orbit galaxy cores with stability, and they must burn with stability. Planets must also orbit with stability. Ross maintains that such stable orbits and stable stars "are possible *only* in a big bang universe." Also required is the kind of gravity of a rapidly expanding universe, with controlled spatial distances between galaxies and stars—those that are the result of the big-bang universe. A universe that expands faster than certain required limits would produce no stars, no planets, and no stable orbits. One that expands too slowly would produce only neutron stars and black holes. And if they are too close or too far apart, galaxies and stars tend to collide or fly apart.[58]

These are all signs of precise order, and of supremely intelligent mind establishing order with specific purposes. Such signs are found throughout the universe, the Earth, and the human body. To imagine that such precise controls, balances, and limits could arise by "self-generation" from nothing seems almost as irrational as the theory that a million monkeys pounding on typewriters for a million years would eventually type the complete works of Shakespeare.[59] Fred Hoyle, although an agnostic, came closer to the truth in saying that "A commonsense interpretation of the facts suggests that a super intellect has monkeyed with physics, as well as chemistry and biology, and that there are no blind forces worth speaking about in nature."[60]

The Milky Way. Our galaxy originated about 9-10 billion years ago. Specific design for life can be seen in the fact that it has a particular and exceptional location—in the "Local Group" on the outer edge of the Virgo supercluster of galaxies. In this protected location, Ross points out, it is not subject to frequent collisions and mergers with other galaxies, as the vast majority of galaxies are. Such collisions can be devastating for physical life. The structure of the Milky Way is also crucial for life. Its spiral structure made it possible for our Sun to form at the right time to support life, and for it to remain in a safe orbit about the center of the galaxy.[61]

The Milky Way Galaxy also has the right number and right kind of neighbor galaxies located at just the right distances to make life possible on a special planet with a special star. And the development of life on planet Earth took place within a time frame protected from destructive encounters with its neighbors. Significantly, a life-destroying merger with another galaxy (the Large Magellanic Cloud) has been predicted to take place four billion years in the future.[62]

The Sun. The powerful energy of the Sun is generated in its core by a continuing chain of thermonuclear reactions that convert hydrogen into helium. Like the billions and billions of other stars, our Sun is a giant nuclear power plant! But unlike man-made ones, it is 100% reliable, capable of operating for billions of years. While it has been in operation for 4.6 billion years, it is capable of lasting another 6 billion, even though it consumes 600 million tons of hydrogen every second. (Can human history last nearly so long, in view of receding glaciers and ice shelves, rising pollution, declining rainforests, species extinction, devastating world economic threats, catastrophic war potentials, and end-time prophesies?)

Forms of precise order and balanced controls exist in the structure and function of our Sun. Its light and heat is our ultimate source of light, warmth, energy, and food. It has taken several billion years for the Sun and Earth to be suitably prepared for physical life. The universe had been in development for about 9.13 to 9.2 billion years before the Sun was formed. Ross identifies 9.2 billion years as "the perfect time for a life-habitable solar system to form . . . no sooner, no later." The Sun is now about 4.6 billion years old. It has taken from 4.5-4.6 billion years for it to attain a proper level of brightness and for flaring activity to be reduced to a life-sustaining level. During that time, 3.8 billion years were also required to raise the free oxygen level of Earth's atmosphere from 1% up to the present life-supporting 21%.[63] Although the Sun's surface gravity is 28 times that of the Earth, there is a precise, orderly balance of gravity with outward pressure: the inner pull of gravity exactly compensates and balances the outward pressure of thermonuclear heat. This continuing balanced order is known as "hydrostatic equilibrium."[64] If this delicate balance were changed, the Sun would either collapse in on itself, or fly apart.

Our Sun reveals a proper balance of necessary elemental materials for life. It is neither *too* metal-rich nor metal-poor. If it had been overly metal-rich in its formation, it would have produced a chaotic grouping of planets and comets, causing them to collide or fall into life-denying zones. The Sun is just the right size for heating and lighting the Earth—"neither too big nor too small, neither too hot nor too cold." Its electromagnetic radiation is highly suitable for organic life. It provides us with an optimized range of electromagnetic radiation for life, vision, and scientific pursuits: "Unlike most other stars, our Sun emits 40% of its electromagnetic radiation in the visible range, peaking exactly in the middle of the visible spectrum."[65] Earth's atmosphere reveals a related delicate balance for life, transmitting most of the radiation that sustains life, and blocking out most of the deadly.

Ross has pointed out several other aspects of our Sun that show precise order and balance for the sustenance of life. It has a special and unique location in the Milky Way—between two spiral arms of the galaxy—that makes life possible and sustainable. The exceptional kind of rotation of the Sun within the galaxy makes it possible for it to maintain this location: it rotates at the same rate as the spiral arm structure, because it is at the same relative distance to the center of the galaxy (the "galactic corotation radius," or "corotation distance"). If it revolved at a different rate from the spiral arm structure, it would be "swept inside a spiral arm," disrupting the orbit of the Earth and exposing it to destructive radiation. The fact that the Sun does not deviate much from its nearly circular orbit about the center of our galaxy also prevents human exposure to deadly radiation from the galaxy's nucleus and from supernovae remnants.[66]

Ross also indicates that for a star such as our Sun to support life it must be a single star system. One or more extra stars will pull a planet out of its orbit, changing its temperature with deadly effects for life. A star that supports life must also be of a very specific mass. One more massive than our Sun will burn too quickly and erratically for life on a planet. Smaller stars have more numerous and dangerous flares. Smaller ones also require the planet to be closer, which drastically changes the planet's rotation period (Mercury and Venus are revealing examples). And only stars in the very middle part of their "middle-aged" phase have flaring subdued enough to sustain advanced life. Another remarkable kind of balanced relationship can be seen in the Sun's varying luminosity relative to the degree of greenhouse efficiency: the Sun's luminosity has increased 35% since life began on Earth. This would be fatal to life on Earth except for the fact that greenhouse efficiency has decreased enough to compensate for it.[67] Attempts to explain this and other aspects of design in the universe as natural self-developments are not convincing.

The Anthropic Principle. The fact that we know we exist as human beings, and can study and ask questions about the universe, proves that our place in the universe provides certain proper conditions for human life. Scientists refer to these required conditions as the "anthropic principle" (after the Greek word for man). They are part of the intricate design, the "fine-tuned" design, of the universe. Steven Hawking cites an obvious, primary example of an anthropic principle—three-dimensional space. Three-dimensions are required for human life, and even for the existence of matter. We continuously experience three-dimensional space, but *why is space three-dimensional?* Human beings could not possibly exist in a one- or two-dimensional space. And if space could be four-dimensional, gravitation would be increased and no planets would have stable orbits around the Sun. They would either fall into the Sun or fly off into cold, outer darkness. But before that could ever happen, electron orbits in atoms would not be stable, so no matter as we know it could exist.[68] Therefore planets, stars, galaxies, and the universe as we know them could not exist in a four-dimensional spatial universe.

Hawking cites another possible anthropic principle—the relationship in the universe between matter density and vacuum energy. In addition to matter, the universe contains "'vacuum energy' [space energy, dark energy], energy that is present even in apparently empty space." While the gravity effect of matter slows down the expansion of the universe, vacuum energy has the opposite effect, causing expansion to accelerate. For galaxies to form there must be a closely controlled relationship of matter and vacuum energy—of the slowing and expansion rates in the universe. Hawking notes that although the existing vacuum energy density is very nearly zero, if a higher percentage of it existed, galaxies could not have formed, and humans would not exist.[69] Similarly, Hugh Ross writes, "the expansion of the universe is governed by two factors, mass density and space energy [dark energy, vacuum energy] density." This "points to an astonishing degree of fine-tuning": "for life to be possible, that is, to obtain the stars and planets necessary for physical life, the value of the mass density must be fine-tuned to better than one part in 10^{60}, and the value of the space energy density must be fine-tuned to better than one part in 10^{120}." Ross quotes Lawrence Krauss, a physicist and self-declared atheist, who admits that the cosmological constant indicated, "would involve the most extreme fine-tuning problem known in physics."[70]

Ross has compiled a long list of anthropic principles required for human life to exist. "It is impossible," he writes, "to imagine a universe containing life in which any one of the fundamental constants of physics or any one of the fundamental parameters of the universe is different, even slightly so, in one way or another." He explains well over one hundred such constants or parameters on his web site and in his books. Ten examples selected from his web site provide clear evidence of design for life.[71] One such constant is that the gravitational force must be within a specific, limited range. If it were slightly stronger than it is, stars would be at least 1.4 times more massive than our Sun. These stars would still produce heavy elements for the formation of planets, but they would burn too rapidly and unevenly to support human life on surrounding planets. And "if the gravitational force were slightly weaker, all stars would be less than 0.8 times the mass of our Sun." Such stars would burn long and evenly enough for human life, but would produce no heavy elements needed to form planets on which life could exist.

A second anthropic principle is that the strong nuclear force holding together the particles in the nucleus of an atom must be of a particular, constant degree. "If the strong nuclear force were slightly weaker, multi-proton nuclei would not hold together. Hydrogen would be the only element in the universe." If it were slightly stronger, hydrogen and elements heavier than iron would be insufficient for human life.

A third anthropic principle involves the fact that stars must make a certain amount of heavy elements for life to be possible. For this to happen the weak nuclear force coupling constant must be the particular strength that it is. If it were slightly larger, neutrons would decay more readily, and less helium would be produced. "Without the necessary helium, heavy elements sufficient for the constructing of life would not be made by the nuclear furnaces inside stars. On the other hand, if this constant were slightly smaller, the big bang would burn most or all of the hydrogen into helium, with a subsequent over-abundance of heavy elements made by stars, and again life would not be possible." (Note in several of these principles the inescapable necessity of stars and their controlled functions for supporting human life!)

A fourth principle involves the electromagnetic coupling constant that binds electrons to protons in atoms. If it were slightly smaller than it is, "no electrons would be held in orbits about nuclei." And if it were slightly larger, "an atom could not 'share' an electron orbit with other atoms." Life would be impossible with either slight change.

A fifth one listed by Ross involves the ratio of electron to proton mass, which determines characteristics of the orbits of electrons about nuclei. "A proton is 1836 times more massive than an electron. If the electron to proton mass ratio were slightly larger or slightly smaller, again, molecules would not form, and life would be impossible."

The sixth one involves controlled limits on the time frame for the age of the universe. "The age of the universe governs what kinds of stars exist. It takes about three billion years for the first stars to form. It takes another ten or twelve billion years for supernovae to spew out enough heavy elements to make possible stars like our Sun, stars capable of spawning rocky planets. Yet another few billion years is necessary for solar-type stars to stabilize sufficiently to support advanced life on any of its planets. Hence, if the universe were just a couple of billion years younger, no environment suitable for life would exist. However, if the universe were about ten (or more) billion years older than it is, there would be no solar-type stars in a stable burning phase in the right part of a galaxy. In other words, the window of time during which life is possible in the universe is relatively narrow." (Again, stars are necessary for human life!)

The seventh of Ross's anthropic principles has to do with the rate of expansion of the universe. This expansion rate "determines what kinds of stars, if any, form in the universe. If the rate of expansion were slightly less, the whole universe would have recollapsed before any solar-type stars could have settled into a stable burning phase. If the universe were expanding slightly more rapidly, no galaxies (and hence no stars) would condense from the general expansion." The rate of controlled expansion must be fine-tuned to an extreme accuracy of one part in 10^{55}.

The eighth principle relates to the rate of entropy in the universe [entropy is "the degree to which energy in a closed system disperses, or radiates (as heat)"[72]]. This entropy rate must be at a highly controlled, limited level for life to exist. "If the entropy level for the universe were slightly larger, no galactic systems would form (and therefore no stars). If the entropy level were slightly smaller, the galactic systems that formed would effectively trap radiation and prevent any fragmentation of the Systems into stars. Either way the universe would be devoid of stars and, thus, of life." (Again, stars are necessary!)

The ninth of Ross's anthropic principles is an astonishing one. It requires a particular *size* for the entire universe, in terms of its *mass*—the colossal size that it is—for life to exist.

The mass of the universe (actually mass + energy, since $E = mc^2$) determines how much nuclear burning takes place as the universe cools from the hot big bang. If the mass were slightly larger, too much deuterium (hydrogen atoms with nuclei containing both a proton and a neutron) would form during the cooling of the big bang. Deuterium is a powerful catalyst for subsequent nuclear burning in stars. This extra deuterium would cause stars to burn much too rapidly to sustain life on any possible planet. On the other hand, if the mass of the universe were slightly smaller, no helium would be generated during the cooling of the big bang. Without helium, stars cannot produce the heavy elements necessary for life. Thus, we see a reason why the universe is as big as it is. If it were any smaller (or larger), not even one planet like the earth would be possible.

The tenth of Ross's anthropic principles emphasizes the high degree of uniformity, or smoothness, of the universe.

The uniformity of the universe determines its stellar components. Our universe has a high degree of uniformity. Such uniformity is considered to arise most probably from a brief period of inflationary expansion near the time of the origin of the universe. If the inflation (or some other mechanism) had not smoothed the universe to the degree we see, the universe would have developed into a plethora of black holes separated by virtually empty space. On the other hand, if the universe were smoothed beyond this degree, stars, star clusters, and galaxies may never have formed at all. Either way, the resultant universe would be incapable of supporting life.

Humankind appears to be at a specially advanced and revealing time in history. Astronomers, physicists, and mathematicians, for example, have seen and gained knowledge of the universe to very near the moment of its actual beginning. Increasingly massive and specific evidence shows us the nature of the beginnings of the universe as never before in history. There is extensive proof that the universe is not eternal, as many had thought in the past: it *did* have a moment of origin, which was also the beginning of energy, time, space, matter, atoms, and physical laws. The various bodies of the universe—stars, galaxies, supergalaxies, and other bodies and materials—have progressively appeared over very long periods of time, during the 13 billion plus years since the big bang. The star of our solar system, the Sun, came into existence only about 4.6 billion years ago, and the Earth about 4.57 billion.

The Order, Structure, and Design of the Earth. Life on Earth could not exist if our Sun were much larger or smaller than it is. It is the right size and distance from the Earth to support life. If it were not where it is relative to the Earth, no life on Earth could exist. A "change in the distance from the Sun as small as 2% would rid the planet of all life."[73] The Sun is the chief source of our light, warmth, and food supply. Plants store energy from the Sun in the process of photosynthesis. They take in water and carbon dioxide and release byproducts of water and oxygen necessary for human and animal life. Photosynthesis provides the source of energy that drives the metabolic processes of plants, animals, and humans. Humans and animals complete the cycle by producing carbon dioxide necessary for plants. Fossil fuels also get their stored energy from solar energy. The movements of air on Earth derive from convection currents created by solar heating. Solar radiation also determines the water cycle, including rainfall.

The Earth holds a special and privileged place in our Solar System and in the universe. The life-supporting structure and design of the Earth is so obvious that many such features are often taken for granted or overlooked.

In a universe of trillions upon trillions of stars, the Earth is the only known planet capable of supporting the complex life of human beings! To be aware of these things and not think of God as the omniscient and purposive Creator suggests illogical resistance to a logical conclusion. Unlike other planets the Earth has huge bodies of liquid water, the oceans, covering two-thirds of its surface, and these oceans support a rich and varied array of life, in addition to providing abundantly for life on all the continents.

The Earth itself, which is almost 8,000 miles in diameter (7,928), reveals intelligent, purposive design throughout, beginning in its essential structure and composition from the center outward. There are three basic parts: core, mantle, and crust. These are further differentiated into inner core, outer core, lower mantle, upper mantle, oceanic crust, and continental crust. Each layer shows regulated and balanced design functioning to sustain, provide materials for, renew, and enrich life on Earth. It is clearly designed for human life over extensive time periods. To think that it happened by self-generation according to physical laws ignores the obvious design and purposive factors. Why is there such intelligent design and purpose? How and why are there such supporting physical laws? How could design and purpose occur without mind? What mind?

Scientific evidence indicates that the innermost core of the Earth is composed largely of a solid iron-nickel alloy, possibly with some sulfur. This inner core is super-dense, as much as 12 grams per cubic centimeter—about twice as dense as the mantle above it, and five times as dense as the hard, surface rock we stand on. It is the hottest part of the Earth's cross-section (about 7200-8500 degrees F). It has been calculated at about 1,512 miles in diameter (2440 km). The outer core adds another, thicker layer all around (1,395 miles or 2,250 km thick). It is believed to be molten iron that is still extremely dense (about 10 grams per cubic centimeter) and very hot (6300-7200 degrees F). The core remains at such extreme temperatures even after 4.5 billion years of gradual cooling since the creation of the Earth. The inner and outer cores, which together are about 4,302 miles in diameter (6,940 km), are larger than the planet Mars (4,204 miles, 6,780 km), and constitute slightly more than one-half of the Earth's total diameter. They give the Earth's geoid form an extremely dense, hard, and hot inner foundation—very different from that of the stars![74]

The molten core is also the source of upward-moving magma, which, over long periods of time, provides various types of igneous rock, such as granite, basalt, gabbro (an important component of the oceanic crust), granodiorite (used for building facings, curbstones, and roads), kimberlite (kimberlite pipes are a primary source of diamonds), obsidian, and numerous other rocks.[75] The heat, which moves by convection outward from the cores through further layers, serves as another source of heat, supplementing that of the Sun. The Earth's magnetic field is also believed to be produced by the spinning molten iron of the outer core. The spinning motion is caused by the rotation of the Earth on its axis.

The inner and outer cores support a two-part mantle of rock, lower and upper, which in turn supports the crusts of the continents and the oceans. The mantle, being outside the core, and larger in expanse, actually constitutes 85% of the volume of the Earth. Lower and upper mantle together are about 1,797 miles thick (2,900 km). The lower mantle adds a layer around 1,382 miles thick (2,230 km) all around the core, and has a solid density of about 5.5 grams per cubic centimeter (twice the density of granite!), with very hot temperatures ranging from 1800 degrees F in the highest areas to 6300 in the lowest. The upper mantle adds a further layer about 415 miles thick (670km), with lesser temperatures (below 1800 degrees F). Remarkably, 99% of the Earth's interior remains over 1000 degrees F hot 4.5 billion years after its creation. The heat rising from the core causes the rocks of the mantle to move or churn very slowly in a rolling, convection movement. The result is that heat is transferred upward more efficiently, and tectonic plates near the surface are given slow, enduring mobility, permitting continuing renewal of Earth's surface and atmosphere. Both the heat from within the Earth and that coming from the Sun "confer enormous benefits on the Earth system and ensure its survival, probably for another 5 billion years."[76]

The crust of the Earth differs in thickness and materials according to whether it is the crust of the continents, or that of the oceans. Continental crusts generally vary in thickness from about 16 to 45 miles (25 to 70 km) and more. Although the crust thickness can be compared to the skin of an apple, drilling down into the earth has only penetrated to about 7.5 miles so far, well short of the full depth of just the skin. And even this distance into the crust has taken as much as 15 years. Thickness of the continental crust varies considerably, averaging about 18 miles (30 km), but it may be as thick as 40 to 62 miles (65 or 100 km) under large mountain ranges such as the Alps and the Sierra Nevada. The continental crust is rich in the elements of oxygen and silica, with lesser amounts of aluminum, iron, magnesium, calcium, potassium, and sodium. It has huge variations in kinds of rock, from sedimentary rocks such as sandstone, limestone, and coal, to metamorphic rocks like marble and slate, and igneous rocks such as granite and gabbro. Rocks such as andesite and granite, have an average density of 2.7 grams per cubic centimeter. Throughout geologic time new layers of rock have been added to continental surfaces, creating multi-layered strata. While a great variety of more than 4,000 minerals are known, only about 30 rock-forming minerals are common to the Earth's surface. Diamond, gold, and silver are among the richest gem minerals, while turquoise, topaz, emerald, ruby, and sapphire are among the most beautiful. Iron, copper, gypsum, and halite (rock salt) are among the highly useful ones.

A crucially important zone of rock, called the lithosphere, runs through the crust and uppermost part of the mantle. It varies from 31 to 93 miles thick, averaging at least 50 miles thick (80 km) over much of the Earth, although it is thinner under oceans and volcanically active continental areas. The rigid rock of the lithosphere is broken into a dozen or so huge, thick slabs, called tectonic plates, which support and contain the world's continents and oceans. These plates are brittle and can fracture. The lithosphere "floats," "rides," or slowly moves about on a narrower, more mobile zone below it, called the asthenosphere. This is possible because of the hotter, mobile nature of the semi-solid, partially molten material of the asthenosphere ("weak" sphere, lacking force). Asthenosphere rock becomes hot enough to stretch, fold, compress, or flow without fracturing. The resulting "floating" movement of the lithosphere upon the asthenosphere is crucial for the changing, self-renewing nature of the Earth's surface, slow changes in the growth and change of shapes of continents, and other processes crucial for sustaining animal and human life. This process is known as plate tectonics. No other planet or moon in our Solar System has such life-supporting plate tectonics, and no such process on any other planet in the universe has yet been discovered. That is why Mercury and Earth's Moon are both heavily pockmarked and rather dead looking—they do not have the self-renewing and life-supporting system of plate tectonics. In these and many other ways the Earth's processes are uniquely dynamic, interacting, balanced, and self-renewing rather than static and steadily deteriorating or stultifying, ultimately acting to support, sustain, and enrich life.

The oceanic crust, which covers over two-thirds of the Earth's surface, is considerably thinner than the continental crust, varying from 4 to 7 miles (6 to 11 km), and averaging 6 miles thick (10 km). It is composed largely of basalt lavas and rocks covered by a veneer of sediment. Since basalt forms much of the Earth's mantle as well, it is the most common rock on Earth. Remarkable renewal is evident in the fact that the oceanic crust is continuously formed and reformed out of material and processes from within the mantle moving upward through "spreading ridges." As tectonic plates move apart, basaltic magma from the mantle rises and erupts onto the sea floor, spreading and cooling in the seawater to form new crust. The process is repeated again and again, following the diverging movement of the plates. Such sea-floor spreading occurs at a rate of one or two inches a year. And in other areas called subduction zones, "the oceanic crust descends into the mantle at the same rate that it is created at the ridges." The subducted oceanic crust sinks back deep within the Earth's mantle and is re-melted to magma. As a result even the oldest known parts of the ocean floor are no more than 200 million years old.[77] Continual renewal is the rule of the oceanic crust.

Andesite and granite are the essential rocks, the real backbone, of the continental crust. These rocks are less dense than the basalt below them in the mantle. For this reason they "float" or "ride" over the more dense basalt and basaltic magma. Continents do not sink in subduction zones as oceanic crusts do. They can be split, or they can fragment and drift, but their basic volume cannot be reduced. They can be eroded, but not destroyed. In fact, continents actually enlarge through a process of producing new mountains and volcanoes along subduction zones and many continental edges where large quantities of granitic and andesitic magma rise from the mantle. Such continental growth has been estimated at between 650 and 1,300 cubic kilometers per year for recent times, and thought to be more rapid in early Earth history.[78]

In their important book, *Rare Earth*, Peter Ward and Donald Brownlee identify numerous ways that plate tectonics is crucially important for the support of ecosystems and thus for human and animal life. Continental growth is the result of plate tectonics, and as continents have grown over long periods of time, they have continued to have crucial effects on global climate and temperature, including how much the Earth retains or reflects sunlight (Earth's albedo), and thus stays warm or cool enough to support liquid water and the life that depends on it. Similarly affected are the incidence of glaciation, oceanic circulation patterns, and the amount of nutrients reaching the sea. Plate tectonics has changed and redefined continents over long periods of time, creating many new habitats for animals, thus stimulating biological productivity, promoting diversity, and protecting against extinction. Continental size and position, determined by plate tectonics, has strongly affected biodiversity. Continents with sizeable north-south coastlines have promoted species variation because of latitudinal temperature differences.

Plate tectonics has shaped a uniquely varied and diverse Earth, with mountain chains on continents, great, deep ocean basins with self-renewing floors, and with islands and volcanoes, quite unlike the structures of other known planets and moons (except for volcanoes). Earth displays an environmental complexity and biotic diversity unknown to any other sphere in the universe.[79] And all of this reflects ingenious, superhuman idea, design, and complex organization and interaction.

The necessity of plate tectonics for life can best be conveyed by an account of what would happen if it ceased. In such an event, crucial life-support systems of the Earth would be lost! Volcanic eruptions would stop with the end of plate tectonics, and so would the creation of new sea floor. Earth would eventually lose through erosion most or all of the continents which support terrestrial life. Carbon dioxide would be increasingly lost from the atmosphere, causing the Earth to freeze. Mountains and mountain chains would cease to rise, and erosion would eat away at existing ones, eventually reducing them to sea level. The mass of continents would gradually erode over tens of millions of years. And the eroding material of mountains and continents would wash into the seas, causing sea levels to rise, covering the entire planet with a shallower global ocean, returning the planet to its primordial state of 4 billion years ago, before the rise of continental land masses.[80] There would be a mass extinction of land life. Ocean life would also move toward extinction because most of its nutrients come from the land.

Earth's atmosphere contains greenhouse gases (water vapor, ozone, carbon dioxide, methane) critically important for maintaining a life-supporting temperature range averaging 59 degrees F (15 degrees C). The temperature range for liquid water to exist is between 32 and 212 degrees F (0 to 100 degrees C). The range for animal life is between 35.6 and about 113 degrees F (2 to 45 degrees C). "Greenhouse gases are keys to the presence of fresh water on this planet and thus are keys to the presence of animal life—and many scientists now believe that the balance of greenhouse gases in Earth's atmosphere is directly related to existence of plate tectonics." "Plate tectonics plays an important part—perhaps the most important part—in maintaining levels of greenhouse gases, and these in turn maintain the temperatures necessary for animal life." Greenhouse gases eventually break down or change and must be constantly replenished, or the Earth will grow colder, freeze, and then rapidly get colder. The most important provider of greenhouse gases is volcanoes and volcanic eruption. Even "dormant" volcanoes give off carbon dioxide.[81] (Even volcanoes have a crucial function for life!)

Also, because of plate tectonics many materials are recycled within the Earth. Limestone, for example, when subducted deep into the mantle, is transformed, and releases carbon dioxide into the atmosphere. But the amount of carbon dioxide in the atmosphere must be neither too much nor too little: too much and the planet would get too hot for life; too little and it would get too cold. Plate tectonics also figures importantly in the rate of weathering of certain minerals (silicates such as feldspar and mica, and materials that contain silicates, such as granite), creating reactions that function like a planetary thermostat. As the planet warms, the rate of weathering increases, making more silicate material available for reaction, and removing more carbon dioxide from the atmosphere, causing cooling. But as the rate of weathering decreases with cooling of the planet, the level of carbon dioxide increases, causing warming.

Calcium also figures into this thermostat-like balancing of carbon dioxide in the atmosphere. Calcium is made steadily available by plate tectonics for the formation of new mountains. The calcium can then draw carbon dioxide out of the atmosphere, reacting with it to form limestone, and thereby cool the planet. "The planetary thermostat requires a balance between the amount of CO_2 being pumped into the atmosphere through volcanic action and the amount being taken out through the formation of limestone." Ward and Brownlee maintain that plate tectonics plays an integral part in maintaining a stable global temperature, and it may be the key to fine-tuning the narrower range of temperature necessary for animal life to flourish (41-104 F; 5-40 degrees C).[82]

Plate tectonics is also believed to have an important effect on the Earth's magnetic field. As Earth spins on its axis, convective movement in the molten outer iron core "produces a giant magnetic field surrounding the entire planet. What produces the convection cells in the core is loss of heat. Heat must be exported out of the core, and this liberation of heat appears to be greatly influenced by Earth's plate tectonic regime." One researcher has suggested that without plate tectonics there would not be enough convection cells to generate Earth's magnetic field. What would the effect be if there was no magnetic field? Functions more critical than compass directions would be lost. The magnetic field deflects the vast majority of harmful cosmic rays that hurtle through space at near the speed of light. Cosmic rays include elementary particles such as electrons, protons, helium nuclei, and heavier nuclei coming from distant sources in the universe. If the Earth's magnetic field did not exist, life could be extinguished by cosmic rays within several generations. In addition, the magnetic field reduces the gradual loss of atmosphere into space by "sputtering."[83] These and many other aspects of the Earth's structure and workings provide excellent examples of intelligent design, "anthropic principles," "fine-tuning," and complex, interrelated functions.

The Mathematical Order of the Elements. Of many other features of the Earth revealing clear order, complex design, and purpose, a key one involves the essential *elements* of *all existing things* and their organization into the Periodic Table.[84] Answers to questions about what elements form the basis of all existing things have been sought since the ancient world. A clear definition of chemical "element" was not attained until the second half of the seventeenth century, by Robert Boyle, and the first true element, oxygen, was only isolated and named in the late eighteenth century, by Antoine Lavoisier. Lavoisier actually succeeded in correctly identifying 24 elements. By the mid-twentieth century, 75% of the elements were known. By 2006, 118 elements were listed in standard periodic tables. 92 of these occur naturally on

Earth, while the rest are synthetic elements produced in particle accelerators. Thus, in little over two centuries, extensive modern knowledge of chemical elements and their order and interrelationship has been gained.

The chemical elements are critically important for revealing a clear mathematical order lying at the heart of nature. Most basically, it has been learned that the elements are sequentially related by the number of protons that each has in its nucleus, beginning with the simplest one, hydrogen (H), which has one proton. The next element in number is helium (He), with 2 protons in its nucleus. Then follows lithium (Li) with 3 protons, beryllium (Be) with 4, boron (B) with 5, carbon (C) with 6, nitrogen (N) with 7, oxygen (O) with 8, fluorine (F) with 9, neon (Ne) with 10, and so on. These serve as the atomic numbers of each element. The first two elements, hydrogen and helium, make up the first horizontal row or "period" of the "periodic" table, forming only the two top corners. The next 8 elements form the second horizontal row or period, and the subsequent eight form the third period (with each grouped as 2 blocks, 10 open spaces, 6 blocks). Four more horizontal rows of eighteen elements each make up periods 4 through 7. There are a total of 7 such commonly accepted periods. For the two remaining rows, often called lanthanides and actinides, there are differing interpretations of the precise placement or group relationship.

There are numerous interrelationships between the elements of the periodic table. Most basic is the fact that the elements are perfectly sequential in the number of protons in the nucleus, beginning with 1 and continuing by whole numbers through 118. If this had been known early on, the existence and number of protons of certain undiscovered elements could have been predicted before their discovery (there was some prediction of undiscovered elements by Dmitri Mendeleev). We also know that each element has one electron for each proton in its nucleus, and that the electrons orbit the nucleus in precisely defined energy levels, or shells. The horizontal rows of elements are called periods because there are recurring patterns, or periodic relationships, of the top elements with other elements in a vertical line directly below them. The vertical line of elements down through the periods is called "groups" because they are related in particular ways. In groups with Roman numerals I-VIII, the group elements are related by the number of electrons orbiting the nucleus in the outermost energy level or shell of the atom. For example, in the first group (I), with hydrogen at the top, all 7 elements (H, Li, Na, K, Rb, Cs, Fr) have one electron in the outermost level, like hydrogen. In group II, topped by beryllium (Be), all 6 elements have two electrons in the outermost level, like beryllium. In group III, which is 11 spaces over horizontally to the right on the table and topped by boron, all elements have 3 electrons in the outermost level. This pattern continues in groups IV through VIII.[85]

The transition elements, or "transition metals," are those that form a kind of lower "bridge" extending between calcium (Ca) and gallium (Ga), three blocks below hydrogen. They establish a kind of gradual transition of qualities between the beryllium group, which has two electrons in the outer shell, and the boron group, which has three. The transition elements differ from groups I through VIII: they are interrelated because they build electrons in the inner shells rather than in the outer. They serve well as transition elements because their properties vary only slightly.[86]

There are other important patterns of relationship in the periodic table. For instance, there are *triads* of elements lined up within vertical groups. The relationship within triads is that the atomic weight of the middle element is approximately the mean between the other two elements. One such triad includes calcium, strontium, and barium, with strontium as the middle element. Three other such triads are lithium, sodium, and potassium; sulfur, selenium, and tellurium; and chlorine, bromine, and iodine. Each triad thus exhibits specific, controlled mathematical interrelationships.[87]

Certain mathematical patterns have also been discovered among four sequential elements in four different vertical groups of the table. For example, in the group sequence of nitrogen, phosphorous, arsenic, antimony, and bismuth, the pattern of electrons in the shells of each runs in the following consecutive order from nitrogen through bismuth: (N) $2 + 5$; (P) $2 + 8 + 5$; (As) $2 + 8 + 18 + 5$; (Sb) $2 + 8 + 18 + 18 + 5$; (Bi) $2 + 8 + 18 + 32 + 18 + 5$. This is obviously an exact and clearly defined mathematical pattern at the core of nature's essential structure. There are three other groups with clearly related mathematical patterns: magnesium through barium, oxygen through tellurium, and fluorine through iodine. In all these patterns we see a very deep, underlying order in nature that conforms to simple mathematical patterns![88]

Another key relationship is known as the "law of octaves." Beginning, for example, with lithium (Li) and counting the next eight elements according to increasing atomic weights, we end up with sodium (Na), which has chemical properties closely related to lithium. Doing the same beginning with beryllium, we end with one very similar to it, magnesium. In fact (setting aside the transitional elements from this relationship), such notably similar chemical properties run vertically down through all the elements listed in the eight groups with Roman numerals I through VIII. In these ways the law of octaves "defines the order of the periodic table."[89]

In scientific investigation, theory often precedes proven fact, and experimental evidence derived from nature is what proves or disproves the theory. This shows that "it is ultimately the order in nature that determines the accuracy of the theory."[90] As often happens, evidence emerges "pointing us away from the theory to the actual intricacies of nature before our eyes." Nature is our physical source and guide, and often leads as a patient teacher. As Wiker and Witt show and explain in a chapter filled with examples, "If we are not the creators of nature's intelligibility, if our intellect is indeed subordinate to that order, then we are obviously not the cause of nature's intelligibility any more than we are the cause of nature itself. That intelligibility is built into nature, and as we have noted at many points, built into nature in a tutorial way that seems to be ingeniously accommodated to human beings as students of nature."[91]

But who or what has established the kind of deep, underlying mathematical order in the elements, the order in the structure of the Earth, the balanced order and continual renewal seen in the workings of the tectonic plates, and the marvelous order and fine-tuned balances throughout the universe? Why do the beliefs, facts, and evidence reviewed in this and the previous chapter reveal such clear patterns of order, law, complex interrelationship, and purpose? The logical answer must be that *only divine creation guarantees the reality, reason, intelligence, order, law, design, and purpose of the universe, the Earth, mankind, and individual persons.* What is the origin of the universe? Physics scientist Henry Margenau has given a succinct, logical answer: "God created the universe out of nothing in an act that brought time into existence." And he has given a clear answer to the question of the origin of all the physical laws of nature: "They surely could not have been developed by chance or accident . . . . I know only one answer that is adequate to their universal validity: they were created by God . . . and God is omnipotent and omniscient." And a view of the origin of life itself that Margenau favorably quotes is "that life would not have started by chance," but "that a Creator beyond the cosmos is the most plausible explanation for life's origin."[92]

The Creator God is the only absolute, immediate, and continuing source of life and movement in all living things. The Bible tells us, "in Him all things consist" (Colossians 1:17); "in Him we live, and move, and have our being" (Acts 17:28). Since God is the Absolute Reality of living Spirit, the life, being, and substance he gives in creation is *real.* The name that God gave to Moses as his essential name, "I AM" and "I AM WHO I AM" (Exodus 3:14), reveals God's identity as Eternal Unchanging Being and Lord of Creation. Thus, for God to create means to bring things into being. Without the being given to all created things, nothing would exist or could exist. To claim that anything exists of and by itself is philosophically and theologically unsound, and scientifically unsupportable. As one writer recently expressed it, "God's reality has to be seen to lie at the source of any created object's reality . . . . insofar as any object or thing has reality, it only does so because all reality owes its origin not to itself but to God."[93]

Chapter Three

The Supreme Intelligence of God
The Wonders of Human Life

For you created my inmost being; you knit me together in my mother's womb. I praise you because I am fearfully and wonderfully made; your works are wonderful, I know that full well. (Psalm 139:13-14)

The Amazing Cells and DNA of the Human Body. In the last chapter we noted some of the miraculous features of the vast and awe-inspiring Universe, some of the wondrous structural features of the Earth, and important aspects of the intelligent design, structure, and purposeful functioning of both. The living human body is no less miraculous in its structure and functioning than the Earth and the Universe. How, for example, did the human body come to have the kind of structural features it has, and why does it function in the living way it does? Many of the specific answers to these questions have only become known within recent decades.

Key functions of a living cell are controlled or directed by the molecules known as DNA (deoxyribonucleic acid). The essential purpose and function of DNA is the long-term storage and supply of *information* for cell functions necessary for human life. DNA contains within it all the determining genetic instructions for the human body from birth and infancy through maturity and later years. Coiled inside the tiny nucleus of each human cell, the spiral "ladder" of DNA has "rungs" of *nucleotides*, and contains the structures of *genes* and *chromosomes*. The term *genome* is used to indicate the sum total of DNA in a cell—the total of all its genetic units, including chromosomes, genes, and nucleotides. Genes are strands of nucleotides that specify inheritance. Chromosomes are larger units that also bear much genetic information. Nucleotides are extremely small molecules serving as the basic structural unit of DNA and RNA. They carry most of the information in the genome. Each cell has 46 chromosomes, and perhaps as many as 20,000-30,000 genes.[1] The complete human genome of a cell may contain 1.6 - 6 *billion nucleotides*, the latter number nearly the same as the Earth's total human population! In the broadest sense, the genome is "the instruction manual which specifies life," "specifies human cells to be human cells, and specifies the human body to be the human body." *Miracle number one*: the complete human genome package of 46 chromosomes, 30,000 genes, and 6 billion nucleotides is contained inside each cell's nucleus, which is smaller than the smallest speck of dust. "No information system designed by man . . . can even begin to compare to it."[2]

The Super Information System. In his powerful book, *Genetic Entropy and the Mystery of the Genome*, geneticist J. C. Sanford explains why there is no information system designed by a human that can even begin to compare to that of the complete human genome. While the information contained within one of the simplest forms of life, a single-celled bacterium, is "arguably as great as that of a space shuttle," the great leap in amount and complexity of information from a bacterium up to a human being is analogous to the leap from a simple little red wagon all the way up to a complex space shuttle. Even so, "There is simply no human technology that can begin to serve as an adequate analogy for the complexity of human life." Roughly 100,000 different human proteins are encoded by the human genome, and an uncounted number of human RNA molecules. Each of these proteins and RNA are "essentially miniature machines" with hundreds of component parts. And each has "its own exquisite complexity, design, and function."[3]

But, Sanford adds that, even though the genome's *linear* information is equivalent to many complete sets of a large encyclopedia, it is not enough to explain the full complexity of life. The genome "actually embodies multiple linear codes which overlap and constitute an exceedingly sophisticated information system, embodying what is called 'data compression'." . . . The genome is also "full of countless loops and branches—like a computer program. It has genes that regulate genes that regulate genes. It has genes that sense changes in the environment, and then instruct other genes to react by setting in motion complex cascades of events that can then modify the environment. Some genes actively rearrange themselves, or modify and methylate other gene sequences—basically *changing* portions of the instruction manual!" And "there is good evidence that linear DNA can fold into two- and three-dimensional structures (as do proteins and RNAs), and that such folding probably encodes still higher levels of information. Within the typical non-dividing nucleus, there is reason to believe there may be fabulously complex arrays of DNA, whose 3-D architecture controls higher biological functions. The bottom line is this: the genome's set of instructions is not a simple, static, linear array of letters; but is dynamic, self-regulating, and multi-dimensional . . . . The genome's highest levels of complexity and interaction are probably beyond the reach of our understanding."[4]

In Sanford's evocative analogy, the information-rich genome "instruction manual" consists first of the *nucleotides*—the small molecules making up the "rungs" or "steps" of the spiral DNA ladder. These nucleotide molecules constitute the elementary "letters" of the genetic code, indicated symbolically as A, T, C, and G. They function literally as the letters of the genome instruction manual. These molecular letters are strung together in small clusters or motifs, forming the "words" of the genetic code. These word clusters are further combined to form *genes*, considered the "chapters" of the instruction manual. These chapters are further combined to form *chromosomes*, constituting the "volumes" of the manual. Altogether, they constitute the complete *genome*, the entire information "library" that specifies life.[5]

One key process of life, cell division, begins with the duplication or "replication" of the chromosomes. Chromatin proteins act within the chromosomes to compact and organize DNA, helping to control its interactions with other proteins, thus helping to control which genes are transcribed. The process of replication, a miraculous event in itself, will be described more below. DNA functions much like an instruction manual or set of blueprints, with information for construction of other components of cells, such as proteins and RNA molecules. DNA is thus the essential information center of living organisms.

Also to be discussed below, the vast and complex information encoded in DNA clearly points to an original source in super-human, intelligent *mind* having the original creative *ideas* that determine physical life—not only human life, but that of *all* living things. How did such information originate? How could it? How does it work? The very fact that DNA is able to do these things seems nothing less than miraculous. DNA works in cooperation with its messenger/partner, RNA (ribonucleic acid). But there is more to this story that vastly adds to the sense of the miraculous. Of primary importance is the place of residence of DNA—the cell.

Miracle number two: every human body is a kind of universe in itself—a universe of cells: from 75 to 100 trillion cells make up each adult human body.[6] This number is over 15,000 times greater than the entire human population of the Earth (about 6.6 billion people). Each cell is a microscopic unit, too minute to be seen by the naked eye, a micro-sphere 20 to 30 millionths of a meter (20-30 microns) in diameter. Each cell is a world in its own right—a microcosm comparable in complexity and quality of functions with the macrocosm of the universe.

The cell is the most basic unit of all known living organisms. All living things are composed of cells, which, although differing in numbers, have the same basic structure. Humans, animals, and plants have trillions of cells, while bacteria and protozoa have only one. Vital functions of all living organisms take place within these tiny cells, including hereditary information, regulation of cell functions, and the transmission of information. Each cell stores its own information for its functions, which include taking in nutrients, converting them into energy, conveying energy and nutrients, disposing of by-products, and reproducing.

All existing cells come from preexisting ones. But the questions which science has not been able to definitively answer are: how did living cells begin in the first place, and where did such determining information originate. We should not take living cells and their complex information as simple "givens." Their source must be thoughtfully questioned. Increasing evidence over recent decades indicates that living cells did not slowly "evolve" from non-living elements over billions of years, as older theory had it. One reason is, as Gerald Schroeder points out, the fossil record indicates that they appeared early and very rapidly in geological time, "almost simultaneously with the appearance of liquid water on Earth." Another is that there is a great gap, a qualitative leap, from non-living elements and existing physical laws to living, functioning cells, with their own built-in information system that provides the determining information for structuring and sustaining life, and for reproducing. "The laws of nature that govern interactions among atoms are simple and fixed . . . . They do not produce the complex, information-rich molecules we find in life. There is no clue in nature as to how these simple laws could induce the nonrepetitive, multi-faceted information we associate with the genetic code or the proteins made from the information stored in those genetic codes."[7] For these and many other reasons discussed below, materialist explanations of living cells evolving from non-living chemicals in "warm ponds" and "prebiotic soup" have no real, credible evidence of support.

Schroeder, a former professor of nuclear physics at MIT, indicates that cells work in amazing ways, and at an astonishing rate and capacity, to support and maintain life. Every cell in every human body makes about two thousand proteins every second of every minute of every day. Astronomical numbers of amino acids (about 150 thousand, thousand, thousand, thousand, thousand, thousand) are organized by every human body every second to carefully construct predetermined strings of proteins. The strings are checked to make sure they are folded into specific shapes. Then they are sent on specific routes, either inside or outside the cell, to "sites that somehow have signaled a need for these specific proteins."[8]

The information or ideas that control and direct these functions come from two types of molecules, DNA and RNA. They establish the patterns and processes of all life. In these ways they are the "superstars of all life."[9] DNA is nature's greatest source of encoded information. Protected like a wise mentor within the walls of the tiny, inner nucleus of the cell, DNA is the primary repository of the bio-information of the body. It remains constant and ready for use within the nucleus of the cell, where its crucial information can be read, copied, and transported. Its information is encoded using combinations of four base nucleotide molecules, (A) adenine, (G) guanine, (C) cytosine, and (T) thymine. These four letter-designated molecules are thus known as the alphabet of life. RNA is a copy of DNA information, and serves as its messenger in transporting it. RNA is clearly distinguished from DNA in the cell by having (U) uracil as a replacement for (T) thymine.[10]

Miracle number three: the miniscule size of DNA is another aspect of the miraculous in living things. While the diameter of a cell is a microscopic 20-30 millionths of a meter, the diameter of the nucleus within it is only about 10 millionths of a meter. Yet within the micro-miniature nucleus lies the DNA, which is about *6-7 feet* (around two meters) in its fully extended length, the height of a tall adult. The length of DNA is thus more than a million times longer than the cellular nucleus in which it is coiled. A strand of DNA can be thought of as a micro-miniature information tape, only two millionths of a millimeter thick, barely visible with an electron microscope. Two strands of DNA are twisted and folded into a supercoiled helix, or helix within a helix to fit within the tiny nucleus. The resulting ball of DNA is less than 5 millionths of a meter, or about one one hundred thousandth of an inch in diameter. Yet the helix of DNA must be rapidly opened to be read. In order for this to be done without damage, there must be a balanced *fine-tuning* of the strong and weak bonds—the strong bonds which maintain the basic molecular structure, and the weaker bonds which hold the strands in a helix. The miraculous micro-miniature scale of the nucleus and of DNA within it can be compared to the wonders of the huge scale of the Earth and its core, and the awe-inspiring macrocosmic scale of galaxies, supergalaxies, and intergalactic space. DNA also has a macro-dimension: if the entire DNA of all cells in one human body could be unwound and placed end to end, its continuous thread would extend to the Sun and back about one hundred times![11]

Miracle number four: the extreme density of components in a cell is also awe-inspiring. Drawings of a human cell give only a reduced and simplified diagram. If all the component organelles could be shown, the drawing would be densely covered with ink. And the extremely dense information capacity of DNA is quite miraculous. Werner Gitt indicates that the amount of information of a human DNA is so immense that, if typed on paper with standard letter sizes, "it would stretch from the North Pole to the equator."[12] And Schroeder points out that "If all the information in all the libraries in all languages were transcribed into the language of DNA, it could be recorded within a volume equivalent to 1 percent of the head of a pin." The stability of DNA is also remarkably impressive. It has been recovered from Neanderthal bones one hundred thousand years old. But the history goes back much further, since all life forms are essentially based on cells, DNA, and RNA, and evidence for the earliest life forms on Earth goes back nearly three billion years (3.8 billion for single-cells; 2.2-2.7 billion for multi-cells). Thus, the DNA and RNA "dream team" has been working a long time to support every known life form.[13]

Miracle number five: a principal function of DNA is the making of protein. The actual process is a long and complex one that is not easy for a non-expert to follow and understand. Nevertheless, a quick review is invaluable, because it reveals not only the speed, complexity, and precision of the process, but the amazing kinds of information involved. Many intricate steps make it appear as though it would be slow and difficult. However, it really takes place so easily and rapidly that each cell of the human body produces two thousand proteins every second. The essential process runs like this:[14] first a chemical messenger is sent from the outer part of a cell through a tiny pore in the wall of the nucleus to relay a need for a specific type of protein. How the messenger knows to go to the nucleus is only one part in the amazing sequence of informational ideas directing this fundamental working process of the cell. The messenger then travels along the DNA helix until it finds and selects the needed chromosome out of twenty-three available pairs. It locks onto that chromosome and moves along from one of its nucleotides to another until it finds the specific sequence of bases identifying the beginning of the gene that is the code for the needed protein.

An enzyme called RNA polymerase ("RNA-P") is then called on to activate further steps. It binds to the promoter region of the chromosome situated at the start of the gene, breaks the bonds holding the parallel strands of the DNA helix, and *pulls open* the rungs of the helix "ladder." With the helix open, the exposed nucleotide bases can be read by the messenger RNA-P. RNA-P then reads each nucleotide base and selects the correct complementary base from among the four available types. It also selects the molecules that make up the lengthening spine of mRNA (messenger RNA) being manufactured and trailing behind the RNA-P, and it joins the just-selected base to the spine. Then it reseals the strands of the portion of DNA that were just opened and read. It continues in this way to read the next required portion of DNA until it reaches an encoded order to stop. RNA-P accomplishes all this at the very rapid rate of fifty bases per second. As many as thirty RNA-P molecules can be working simultaneously along a single gene, forming multiple copies of mRNA.

More steps are required in this process to make a protein. Unneeded parts, introns, must be snipped out, and the needed sections, exons, must be spliced together. With that done the mRNA is ready to proceed. It is transported back out through a pore of the nucleus into the outer cell. Two parts of the cell's ribosome join together to clasp the mRNA, read the information it sequesters in groups of three bases, and call for another messenger, transfer RNA (tRNA). The tRNA brings the amino acid corresponding to the just-read three bases to the ribosome and then joins the amino acids one to another as the bases are read, finally forming the needed protein. The striking thing about this is the amazing complexity, precision, and speed of the process, and the fact that all of it depends on encoded information, which is to say (as we will see below), on precise knowledge based on *ideas*. The ideas involved here are intricate and complex ones.

All of our experience shows that ideas originate only in living minds. Only a mind is capable of ideas. In this case it cannot be the human mind, since cells and DNA preceded the origin of human beings and human mind. The most logical conclusion is that it must be the mind of the Creator God, the God who possesses super-mind, omniscient mind, and is super-capable of transforming his ideas into physical reality by his omnipotent power. It is neither rational, logical, nor satisfying to assume that the universe and the human mind have arisen in random, progressive, or *self*-developing stages from matter, non-mind, nothing, or chaos. All of our experience indicates that mind and ideas cannot come from non-mind or nothing. The same can be said for the origin of the big bang, matter, space, time, the physical laws of the universe, and for the Idea-controlled development and relationship of the universe, stars, galaxies, and supergalaxies: nothing "natural" *ultimately* necessitates the singularity of the Big Bang and the subsequent coming into existence of cosmic entities, the origin of the physical laws we know, the complex and orderly functional interrelationship of these things, and the origin of living cells, plants, animals, and humans.

Two related, modern "big guns" widely used to deny the existence of God are naturalist and materialist theories of the origin of life and evolution of species by natural means. If evolution of one species from another by natural means (for example, humans from apes) could be advanced to dominance in educational institutions and society, the idea of God could be more easily and widely rejected as false. This is in fact what has happened. Naturalist and materialist theories of origin and evolution of species have not been proven and cannot be proven.[15] Naturalism and materialism that go beyond the legitimate bounds of science are philosophical theories, not facts. But they have nevertheless been forced into public schools and universities as the only permissible answer to the questions of the origin of the universe and human life. This type of thought has evolved out of Modernism that, since the eighteenth-century Enlightenment, has more and more strongly rejected the God of the Bible, and turned to materialist and naturalist beliefs.[16] This direction grew into a major movement in the nineteenth century, the century of Darwin, Ernst Haeckel, Thomas Henry Huxley, and Nietzsche. And for decades now evolution has been taught and required universally. It has been developed by people who seek to discredit the idea of God's divine creation of all things.

If divine creation can be suppressed and outlawed, so can God. Without creation, God cannot be God, since all other things would be independent of Him. In such a case, God would be insignificant. He would have no power or authority, and all existing things would be independent and self-dependent. Divine creation of all things is thus required by a proper definition of God.

Evidence and arguments in this chapter will indicate, however, that such evolutionary theories are not only unfounded and unproven, but in fact are false and logically absurd. Thus, these modern big guns not only are not loaded, they do not even work.

Today the understanding of the myriad parts of a cell, and their precise and complex activities and interrelationship, renders incredible the claims of materialist theories of the gradual evolution of a living cell from non-living elements. In the time of Charles Darwin and his contemporaries, around a century and a half ago, a cell was thought of as a simple blob of protoplasm, and the primitive microscopes of the time seemed to support such an image. Today, however, and for several decades, the cell and its functions have been investigated in much greater depth and detail using much more advanced instruments and techniques. No one today understands the cell as such a simple blob. As Benjamin Wiker and Jonathan Witt state, the cell is widely recognized as "a world of complex circuits, miniaturized motors and digital code. We now know that even the simplest functional cell is almost unfathomably complex, containing at least 250 genes and their corresponding proteins, each one extraordinarily difficult to produce randomly and none of which can function apart from the intricate structure of the cell."[17]

Origin of life researchers holding to materialist assumptions have tried for decades to build a case based on the slow generation of significant chemical parts of the cell, with the theory that if certain parts could somehow arise, then other parts could somehow follow, and a whole cell would eventually develop. The problem with such views, as Wiker and Witt argue, is that a living cell has a thoroughly *integrated* nature that cannot be bypassed: "it depends on a multitude of parts for its existence; these parts are interdependent, so that if one did happen to arise (*per impossible*), it would stand as idle and functionless as a carburetor in a pile of scrap metal. It's not just a matter of getting all the necessary individual parts in one location—in itself, a potentially insurmountable difficulty, but, even more, a matter of explaining how they became functionally integrated according to blueprints that do not yet exist."[18]

Modern scientific research into the nature and function of living cells indicates that "such complex structures were not produced by an abiotic and purposeless shuffling of chemicals."[19] The statement made by H. P. Yockey over thirty years ago is still true today: "contrary to the established and current wisdom a scenario describing the genesis of life on Earth by chance and natural causes which can be accepted on the basis of fact and not faith has not yet been written."[20]. Wiker and Witt add that, even if the hypothetical "prebiotic soup rich in all the right chemical constituents" of materialist origin scenarios had been possible on early Earth (which evidence does not support), what would be "the probability of attaining a specific chain of one hundred amino acids by chance? As a purely mathematical exercise, we would say that, since there are twenty relevant amino acids then there are 20^{100} possible arrangements of the 100-amino-acid-long chain—about a probability of 1 in 10^{130} of getting the right sequence."[21] But such an abstract probability, virtually impossible or absurd in itself, is reduced to essentially nothing when factors of actual reality are taken into account.

The question of probability is abstracted from time and space, as if protein synthesis could occur *ex nihilo* and *de novo*—that is, *outside* the organization of time and space provided by the living cell, and as if no factors were necessary (such as cellular protection and direction), and as if no other factors existed to dramatically lower the probability (such as chemically interfering reactions). Actual (as opposed to abstract) protein synthesis depends on hundreds, if not thousands, of supporting activities and structures in the cell that are provided by a multitude of other proteins of even greater complexity than a mere 100-amino-acid chain. The cell is not simply some confined boundary where chemicals associate randomly in a kind of amorphous soup, but like Shakespeare's plays, it is tightly and elegantly organized drama in regard to time and place, where the intrinsic powers of the chemical elements are used with exquisite efficiency . . . . In a real cell, a specific chain of one hundred amino acids is generated with the help of a particular and highly complex ribosome translating a particular and highly complex strand of mRNA, with the help of highly complex tRNA . . . . the cells are not merely highly advanced robots but living things capable of reproducing living things. Materialism erases the distinction between nonliving and living things, and that misses the essential nature of the way proteins exist in cells. A functional protein structure depends on the *living* unity of the cell; that is, it is both built by the cell and built for the cell, so that its structure is specified by its function as a part in relation to the living whole, one whose particular, complex arrangement of parts is necessary to carry out its intricate function.[22]

Miracle number 6: reproduction is another essential and miraculous function of a cell.[23] Cell reproduction, known as mitosis, takes place at an amazingly rapid rate. At every second four to five million new cells are created by replication and division in the human body. In weight that amounts to an increase of 4 milligrams per second, 400 grams (14 ounces) a day, and 140 kilograms (300 pounds) a year. However the body sloughs off or discards old cells at almost the same rate. The replication of the cell's DNA begins the process. This replication process is very similar to the intricate and precise steps just described for the production of RNA in the making of protein. One difference is that while only one strand of DNA is copied in RNA transcription, both strands of the DNA double helix are copied in cell division, resulting in two complete sets of chromosomes (92 instead of the characteristic 46). Another difference is that each new strand winds helically with the parent strand, brilliantly permitting a double check of accuracy.

According to Schroeder, replication of the complete DNA in a human cell requires ten hours of precise, information-guided steps *before* the actual division of each parent cell into two daughter cells begins. In this process, six to seven billion nucleotides must be copied! Cells are able to accomplish this great feat in ten hours instead of a potential four years by having a few thousand DNA-P enzymes working simultaneously. Schroeder points out that, if humans were able to do this (which they are not), it would be comparable to a team of workers reading ten books, each four hundred pages long, every minute for ten hours, while at the same time organizing and coordinating the information into a single coherent text.[24]

The actual division of the replicated cell (mitosis) takes only about one hour. It is an hour filled with many incredibly knowledgeable and purposeful micro-miniature workings that seem like a "fantasy brought to life." The cell now contains two sets of chromosomes within its one nucleus. The cell progressively works to separate the two sets. Two organelles, or centrioles, move to opposite sides of the cell, beginning to establish opposing poles, with spindle fibers between them, as the nucleus membrane begins to disintegrate. Ninety-two jumbled chromatin strands are condensed into twenty-three pairs of pairs, or forty-six pairs of chromosomes, with each pair joined. "Each pair consists of two identical copies of a given DNA/chromosome." The spindle fibers now draw the chromosomes to the central "equator" of the cell. "And then, wonder of wonders, miracle of miracles, a motor protein associated with each chromosome grasps with its little molecular hands the associated spindle fiber, contracts pulling its particular chromosome pole-ward, releases, reextends its hand, grasps and contracts again in a manner similar to the functioning of muscle proteins, each stage pulling its burden a bit closer to the pole. Tugging, straining, reaching out again, and pulling some more until finally the single link at the point of constriction breaks and the sister chromosome pairs move apart, each toward its respective pole." With about forty minutes past, there is now a full set of chromosomes at each of the two opposing poles. New nuclear membranes form, safely sealing in the genetic material. A ring of muscle protein forms around the equatorial line of the cell, gradually and continuously tightening until ultimately the cell divides in two. An additional five or more hours are needed for the cell to produce more organelles and become full fledged and full sized. Having checked itself for proper size and DNA function before separation, the cell checks again after separation, and also monitors the spindle fiber network for any malfunctions. If there is a flaw that is not repairable, the cell programs for its own disintegration and recycling![25]

The entire working processes of cells and their DNA clearly resonates with intelligent ideas, design, and purpose. How were such intelligent and complex ideas of function and purpose ever initiated and encoded in living cells? Can such high intelligence, order, and purpose arise ultimately out of non-intelligence, nothingness, or chaos? The logical and rational answer must surely be no—such highly intelligent ideas, design, and purpose must come originally from a *mind*—a *great mind*, capable of *great ideas*. Plato was right about all things having their original source in Ideas (*Idea; eidos*, singular, *eide* plural) and intellect; he did not realize, however, that the Ideas must be in the mind of an omniscient and omnipotent, personal God. The Old Testament speaks often of God's *word* and "*wisdom*" in creation, and the New Testament announces Christ as the "*Logos*," the *Word*, who expresses and mediates the ideas and will of God the Father. Subsequently it was Augustine and Aquinas who developed these teachings further theologically, illuminating much of the role of divine Ideas in creation.[26]

Due to mounting scientific evidence about the nature of cells and DNA, and other evidence against naturalist and materialist evolutionary theories over several decades, some prestigious atheists and materialists have recently changed their minds or positions. One of the most notable is Antony Flew, acclaimed British philosopher and philosophical materialist, who professsed his "Pilgrimage from Atheism to Theism" in an interview of 2004. Flew stated in the interview that he thought the case for a God of power and intelligence was "much stronger than ever before," and that although he had not accepted the notion of theistic revelation, he was still open to it, and was "much impressed with physicist Gerald Schroeder's comments on Genesis 1" (in *Genesis and the Big Bang: The Discovery of Harmony Between Modern Science and the Bible*). "That this biblical account might be scientifically accurate raises the possibility that it is revelation."

But Flew remained in some ways a doubting Antony, demanding "proof," and seemed unwilling to risk the choice of *belief* and *faith*. While he expressed views rejecting many essential Christian doctrines (including revelation) he was willing to admit this: "It now seems to me that the findings of more than fifty years of DNA research have provided materials for a new and enormously powerful argument to design." Flew's stated position then and later seems somewhat uncertain and equivocal about several of the Big Questions of life. But at eighty-one in 2004, he also seemed fully convinced, and pleased, that he would not have to face an afterlife (he died April 8, 2010).[27] Another notable example of change is biophysicist Dean Kenyon, who led an effort during the 1960s seeking to give a materialist explanation for the origin of cellular life by purely undirected processes. "But Kenyon later concluded that the regularities of chemistry couldn't produce the information-rich structures essential to even the simplest life."[28]

In some ways a quite different contemporary example is that of Alister McGrath. While raised in a Christian home in Ireland, McGrath turned as a teenager to scientific pursuits in mathematics, chemistry, physics, and biology. He relates that out of an early indifference to Christianity, he "began to develop more definitely atheistic views." He "became deeply influenced by the spirit of scientific materialism, and felt that God had no useful place or purpose in the universe." Still in his teens, he added Marxism and Theodor Adorno to his influences. But by 1971, at age 18, he began having doubts about Marxism. After hearing a speaker, Michael Green, at the Oxford Christian Union, he made a decisive *choice*: he "knew that Christianity had something far more satisfactory—and far more moral—than Marxism to offer the world." He began to commit himself "to the living and loving God" and to study Christian theology.[29] He eventually became a strong proponent of the beneficial union of Christian theology and science in such books as *The Science of God: An Introduction to Scientific Theology* (2004) and his three volumes of *A Scientific Theology*. In these ways McGrath reversed his early stance, and came to take a strong position *against* reductive scientific materialism. He has also become a critic of one of the most visible contemporary exponents of Darwinian materialist evolution, Richard Dawkins. McGrath published *The Dawkins Delusion* in June of 2007 as a Christian response to Dawkins' atheistic manifesto, *The God Delusion* of September 2006.

Why Does Encoded Information Exist? Much of the debate during recent decades about the origin and ultimate nature of life, and about belief in God, focuses on the nature and role of information in living things, and intelligent design throughout the universe. Werner Gitt, an information specialist in Germany, has analyzed the nature and role of information in his seminal book, *In the Beginning Was Information*. Key points made throughout the book support and extend the logical understanding of information briefly indicated above. From beginning to end, Gitt emphasizes the point that appears most obvious and logical: "The essential aspect of each and every piece of information is its mental content . . . . The fundamental quantity information is a non-material (mental) entity. It is not a property of matter, so that purely material processes are fundamentally precluded as sources of information." In contrast to widely held materialist views, such as those of Dawkins, Gitt gives good reasons that information is not a material phenomenon. Information is one of four fundamental entities, the other three being will (volition), energy, and mass. Information, "being a fundamental entity, cannot be a property of matter, and its origin cannot be explained in terms of material processes." Information is not in itself material, although encoded information does require a supporting material basis.

Gitt quotes related statements by several scientists. American mathematician Norbert Wiener has written: "Information is information, neither matter nor energy." East German scientist J. Piel states: "Information is neither a physical nor a chemical principle like energy and matter, even though the latter are required as carriers." Werner Strombach, a German information scientist, indicates the nonmaterial nature of information, defining it as an "enfolding order at the level of contemplative cognition." Hans-Joachim Flechtner, a German cyberneticist, indicates the mental nature of information because of its contents and the encoding process: "When a message is composed, it involves the coding of its mental content . . . ." The mental nature of information is also indicated by its close link with volition. "Information is always based on the will of a sender who issues the information." "All created systems originate through information. A creative source of information is always linked to the volitional intent of a person; this fact demonstrates the nonmaterial nature of information."[30]

In Gitt's analysis of information there are five aspects or levels that must be considered for its complete characterization. The first, simplest, and lowest level is the *statistical*. This aspect shows no particular concern with any possible content or purpose of the information, but is focused on the number and frequency of letters, numbers, or words making up the information. These are quantitative properties of the language used, and depend on sequences and frequencies. Meaning and import are not significant considerations.[31]

At the second level of information, the linguistic or *syntax* level, *mental processes* are required to *encode* ideas as information. "Matter as such is unable to generate any code. All experiences indicate that a thinking being voluntarily exercising his own free will, cognition, and creativity is required." There are many different types of codes. But a "code system is always the result of a mental process . . . (it requires an intelligent origin or inventor)." "Devising a code is a creative mental process." The codes of living cells, including those of the human brain, are highly complex examples, reflecting highly complex mental processes in their formulation. "Matter can be a carrier of codes, but it cannot generate any codes."[32]

The third level of information is *semantics* or meaning: "Any entity, to be accepted as information, must entail semantics; it must be meaningful." "Meanings always represent mental concepts . . . [and] every piece of information leads to a mental source, the mind of the sender." "A sender and a recipient are always involved whenever and wherever information is concerned." Meaning is contained in the information, and that meaning reflects the sender's mind. Every communication process between a sender and a recipient requires an understanding through a specific language of signs, following certain rules. "In the formulation process, the information to be transmitted is generated in a suitable language in the mind of the sender. In the comprehension process, the symbol combinations are analyzed by the recipient and converted into the corresponding ideas." Gitt's meaning here may be slightly extended in the following way: meaning begins as ideas in the mind of the sender; these ideas are encoded as information, either to be decoded and used in cell functions, or at the human level to be subsequently decoded and converted again into ideas and responses by a recipient's mind.[33]

Gitt describes a fourth level of information, that of *pragmatics*, or the resulting action. "Information always leads to some action . . . . It "always entails a pragmatic aspect." Some result, whether strictly determined or allowing some latitude, is to be achieved in a receiving system. This is true for inanimate systems such as computers and automatic car washes, as well as for living organisms such as cell activities, and the actions of humans and animals.

The fifth and most important level of information described by Gitt is the one of *purpose*, which he calls the level of "apobetics." "Every piece of information is intentional (the teleological aspect)." It "comprises the intentions of the sender." The lower levels "are only a means for attaining the purpose . . . ." Theories of materialism and materialistic evolution deliberately deny such purposefulness, and deny any original mental and spiritual source of life. Gitt quotes an explicit statement of such a view by the highly influential American zoologist and paleontologist, George G. Simpson: "Man is the result of a materialistic process having no purpose or intent; he represents the highest fortuitous organizational form of matter and energy."[34] Richard Dawkins promotes a similar materialist, evolutionary view of the universe as indifferent and lacking purpose: "nature is not cruel, only pitilessly indifferent. This is one of the hardest lessons for humans to learn.

We cannot admit that things might be neither good nor evil, neither cruel nor kind, but simply callous—indifferent to all suffering, lacking all purpose."[35]

But Gitt correctly emphasizes [as have J. C. Sanford, Wiker and Witt, Gerald Schroeder, Jonathan Wells, Stephen C. Meyer, Jonathan Sarfati, and H. P. Yockey, among others] that **"There is no known natural law through which matter can give rise to information, neither is any physical process or material phenomenon known that can do this."** All five levels of his analysis of information indicate, **"It is impossible that information can exist without having had a mental source."** Information requires a code; it cannot be set up, stored, or transmitted without a code. Codes cannot originate in statistical processes. **Codes require an intelligent original source and sender.** Codes must be established by a free will. **Purpose is always involved, which indicates idea and purpose in a creative mind that originates the code for whatever the purpose may be.**[36]

Against such materialist and naturalist views, Gitt emphasizes *purpose* in a *holistic* view of information and life: "If one carefully considers living organisms in their entirety as well as in selected detail, the purposefulness is unmistakable. The apobetics aspect is thus obvious for anybody to see; this includes the observation that information never originates by chance, but is always conceived purposefully." **It is clear "that the information present in living organisms requires an intelligent source. Man could not have been this source, so the only remaining possibility is that there must have been a Creator."**[37]

Gitt identifies three forms or types of information: (1) constructional or creative, (2) operational, and (3) communicational. The creative form of information results in the production or invention of something new. This may occur in widely different degrees of creativity, from a new cake recipe to a technical drawing for a machine, the Sistine Ceiling, or the much more complex genetic information for the construction of a living cell. Operational information includes all systems or programs such as those of computers and robots, pheromone languages of animals, the hormonal system of the human body, and the information for the workings of the nervous system to and from the brain and the organs. Communicational information includes all other forms, such as letters, books, phone calls, radio, TV, and even bird songs.

Information, Mind, and Creative Purpose. Information reaches its very highest level in creativity. "Creative information . . . is the highest level of transmitted information: something new is produced. It does not involve copied or reproduced information. This kind of information always requires a personal mind exercising its own free will, as original source." "Creative information can always be linked to a person who has cognitive capabilities, and it represents something new." "Every piece of creative information represents some mental effort and can be traced to a personal idea-giver who exercised his own free will, and who is endowed with an intelligent mind."[38] Note the primary importance of *personal mind, intelligence, idea,* and *will* as the origin of creative information in these statements. And what could be more creative than the creation of the entire universe throughout both macrocosm and microcosm? What supreme greatness of mind, intelligence, idea, and power! Such a feat is unspeakably beyond all human creativity at its highest, and exposes the failure of notions of evolution from the slow workings in some lowly primeval soup. It also provides a simple, clear, beautiful, logical, and meaningful answer to the unanswered question of the origin of the universe.

It is difficult to understand how anyone can attribute the miraculous and mind-boggling creation of the universe, and the astonishing complexities of intelligence now evident in human life—how anyone can seriously attribute them to evolving matter, self-development, or random mutation and natural selection. Sadly, such views essentially reveal a determined *primary axiom* rejecting any possibility of a supreme, divine mind and power as original creative source.

The Failure of Evolutionary Models to Explain the Origin of Specified Genetic Information Necessary to Build a Living Cell. Geneticist John C. Sanford, in his impressive argument against materialist evolution, *Genetic Entropy and the Mystery of the Genome*, rightly points out that in Darwinian evolution, *no mind, Idea, intelligence, or purpose is involved*! Materialist evolution claims that all biological information began with "some simple 'first' genome," and subsequently evolved through a long series of random mutations and natural selection. Sanford compares "random mutations" to the workings of an imperfect "mechanical scribe," making continual errors in copying information over long periods of time, thereby producing increasingly different "copies" or mutations of the original. At some points in this process, "natural selection" is said to occur, functioning like a "judge, or quality control agent," determining which mutated copies are suitable for further copying. In this fashion, through error and selection, without intelligent mind or purpose, more and more complex, higher and higher life forms are supposedly evolved.[39]

In this evolutionary process, the "scribe and judge work entirely independently. The scribe is essentially blind, working on the level of molecules; and being extremely near-sighted, he can only see the individual letter which he is copying. The judge is also nearly blind, but he is extremely far-sighted." The judge never sees the letters or components of information, only the relative performance of the result. A popular recent promoter of such a blind, mindless, purposeless, evolutionary view is Richard Dawkins, who has stated it succinctly:

Natural selection, the blind, unconscious, automatic process which Darwin discovered, and which we now know is the explanation for the existence and apparently purposeful form of all life, has no purpose in mind. It has no mind and no mind's eye. It does not plan for the future. It has no vision, no foresight, no vision at all. If it can be said to play the role of watchmaker in nature, it is the *blind* watchmaker.[40]

Evolutionary theory further claims, Sanford continues, that certain harmless errors and duplications of letters by the mutation scribe can create new and useful information for new functional components of the living product. In this way, biological information is supposed not only to *improve*, but to greatly *expand*. By analogy, Sanford compares this process to beginning with a little red wagon, and gradually evolving it through blind copying, error, and selection of best results into an automobile, and then into a space shuttle.

Sanford extends this analogy still further: the information for the original little red wagon supposedly evolves into the information needed for creation of a "fanciful Star Ship Phenome," complete with 'warp-speed engines' and a 'holodeck'." Is it possible to proceed by error and selection from information for a simple little red wagon to that for such a complex Star Ship? Since the information needed for such a Star Ship must surely be enormous, it renders ridiculous the notion that it could evolve by error and selection from a little red wagon. And the actual information entailed in the complete human genome, including everything involved in cells, brain cells, nervous system, and the ability to self-reproduce, would no doubt exceed that for such a Star Ship![41]

In order for Darwinian evolutionary theory to work, the rate of beneficial mutations in an organism must be high enough and strong enough to produce the greater, more complex information of higher organisms. Sanford provides substantial evidence that this is not true at all. According to actual tests, the rate and strength of any possible *beneficial* mutations is so low, and so nearly neutral, that they "must be 'un-selectable'." Essentially the entire range of all hypothetical beneficial mutations falls within the "effectively neutral" zone indicated in studies by population geneticist Motoo Kimura. Such near-neutral nucleotide positions are *un-selectable* by natural selection. Thus, selection could never favor them. And this "makes progressive evolution, on the genomic level, virtually impossible." Sanford also cites studies by Bataillon and Elena et al showing that "the actual rate of beneficial mutations is so extremely low as to thwart any actual measurement . . . ." Further, the ratio of *deleterious* mutations to beneficial ones is enormous, at least one thousand to one, and more likely, according to a study by Gerrish and Lenski, *one million to one.*

In these ways the near-neutral quality of supposedly beneficial mutations, as well as the very strong predominance of deleterious mutations, "absolutely guarantees net loss of information," rather than any forward gain. For these and other reasons Sanford holds that "mutations cannot result in a net gain of information . . . . Everything about the true distribution of mutations argues against their possible role in forward evolution." Beneficial mutations "are exceedingly rare—much too rare for genome-building." Genomic mutations "appear to be overwhelmingly deleterious. And even when one may be classified as beneficial in some specific sense, it is still usually part of an over-all breakdown and erosion of information."[42]

Since random mutations fail to add significant higher information to make evolution possible, what role does natural selection actually play? Sanford allows that natural selection does work "on a limited level," and with a very limited range of operation. But "the most basic problem" is that natural selection never "sees" the individual nucleotides carrying parts of the information of a cell. It only sees the *whole organism*. It can never see or select any particular nucleotide. It only selects the whole organism. "The nucleotide and the organism are very literally worlds apart." There is a great gulf between *molecular mutation* ("genotypic change") and *a whole organism's reproduction* ("phenotypic selection"). Many different levels of complex organization stand between a nucleotide and an individual organism, with massive amounts of uncertainty and dilution added at each organizational level. "For example, a single nucleotide may affect a specific gene's transcription, which may then affect mRNA processing, which may then affect the abundance of a given enzyme, which may then affect a given metabolic pathway, which may then affect the division of a cell, which may then affect the division of a cell, which may then affect a certain tissue, which may then affect a whole organism, which may then affect the probability of reproduction, which may then affect the chance that specific mutation gets passed on to the next generation." Other important variables also widen the gap. There is "an incredibly complex network of sensors and regulators within each cell," self-adjusting to maintain a proper sameness of conditions while circumstances change ("*homeostasis*").[43]

Natural selection is very limited because it can only accept or reject the *complete organism, not individually selected parts.* Selection operates only on the level of the *whole organism*, not on the basis of selection of limited numbers of nucleotides, and the rejection of others: "selection is **never, ever** for individual nucleotides." It "acts on the level of the organism, not on the level of the nucleotides . . . . Human genes never exist in 'pools', they exist only in massive clusters, within real people. Each nucleotide exists intimately associated with all the other nucleotides within a given person, and they are only selected or rejected as a set of 6 billion. The phenomenon of linkage is profound and extensive . . . . No nucleotide is <u>ever</u> inherited independently. Each nucleotide is intimately connected to its surrounding nucleotides—even as each letter on this page is specifically associated with a specific word, sentence, paragraph, and chapter."

Human nucleotides "exist in large linked clusters or blocks, ranging in size from 10,000 to a million. These linkage blocks are inherited as a single unit, and never break apart. This totally negates one of the most fundamental assumptions of the theorists—that each nucleotide can be viewed as an individually selectable unit . . . . On a practical level—it means natural selection can never create, or even maintain, specific nucleotide sequences." The "Primary Axiom" of Neo-Darwinian evolution theory is that a limited amount of selection of individual nucleotide information is possible at the reproductive level for the whole organism. For these and other reasons Sanford presents, this is "totally impossible."[44]

To what extent then can natural selection actually advance the supposed evolution of species by effectively adding new and higher variations in successive individuals? In other words, how much possibility is there of progressive evolution of successive individual types ("additive phenotypic variation")? Sanford examines in some detail the amount of additive genetic variation possible when the various components affecting natural selection are fully considered. Among the seven components he examines, only a very tiny one, amounting to less than 1% of the total is found to have the potential of *additive genetic variation*! All of the rest, constituting more than 99% of the total, actually work very powerfully *against* effective selection. The first two components, (1) the environment (indicated by graph as about 50% of the total), and (2) the interaction of the environment with the genotype (about 25%), are non-genetic, non-heritable, and act as "noise" *working against* effective selection. The next three (indicated as constituting about 4-5 % each of the total), (3) epigenetics, (4) epistasis, and (5) dominance, are also genetic, but not heritable, and *interfere* with long-term selection. Factor (6), includes "other" genetic components (also indicated as about 4-5%), which would be selectable, but are "neutralized" in various ways, and also work *against* selection. Thus, (7) the only actual "additive genetic variation," constitutes less than 1% of the total, and so is "a relatively insignificant component of phenotypic variation . . . . All variation that is not due to additive genetic variation, actually works very powerfully *against* effective selection. It acts as noise, which obscures the actual effects of heritable genetic variations."[45]

Sanford asks, "'Could mutation/selection create even a single functional gene?' The answer is that it cannot—because of the enormous preponderance of deleterious mutations even within the context of a single gene. The net information must always still be declining, even within a single gene." In every way it is analyzed, "the genome must degenerate. This problem overrides all hope for the forward evolution of the whole genome." Even if we mentally set aside the overwhelming negative effects of deleterious mutations (which cannot actually be done), "mutation/selection cannot even create a single gene—not within the human evolutionary timescale." The billions of nucleotides forming the human genome are specifically interrelated in complex informational formations like the text of a book. They constitute a complex and integrated informational context with surrounding nucleotides and with the whole genome. Any changes would change the context. To create any new function, as a start toward forward evolution, a particular nucleotide would need to be selected as the first beneficial mutation. That presents a major problem in itself—how could such a "decision" be made without mind, intelligence, idea, or purpose? Furthermore, that first nucleotide's value could only be defined in relation to its neighbors. And most of the neighbors would also have to be changed to create any new function. This becomes a circular, self-destructive course, since the context being built upon is being destroyed in the same process.

Sanford finds that the inter-relational complex of nucleotides (called "epistasis"), which carries genetic information, constitutes "irreducible complexity at its most fundamental level." "True epistasis is essentially *infinitely* complex, and virtually impossible to analyze, which is why geneticists have always conveniently ignored it. Such bewildering complexity is exactly why language (including genetic language) can never be the product of chance, but requires intelligent design. The genome is literally a book, written in a language, and short sequences are literally sentences." Such information can never occur by random letters simply "falling into place," whether in the vast and complex information of the human genome, or in one single meaningful sentence. Linked sequences of functional nucleotides "*never* just 'fall into place'. This has been mathematically demonstrated repeatedly." But "neither can such a sequence arise randomly one nucleotide at a time. A pre-existing 'concept' is required as a framework upon which a sentence or a functional sequence must be built. Such a concept can only pre-exist within the 'mind of the author'."[46]

Can gene duplication be a cause of new information forwarding the evolution of species? The doubling of one chromosome is called *aneuploidy*. The doubling of all chromosomes is called *polyploidy*. Sanford asks, "Do such duplications create new information." Any doubling of the given "letters," "sentences" and "books" of genetic information is actually "deleterious." It does not increase communication, but obviously disrupts it, just as the doubling of letters and sentences on this page would disrupt without adding anything new.

Can natural selection come to the rescue? Sanford's evidence throughout this book shows that "while selection can slow mutational loss of information, it cannot stop it. Most emphatically selection can not reverse this loss." Much of the book shows "that nearly all duplications will be both deleterious and nearly-neutral—like all other classes of mutation. This means selection will only be able to eliminate the very worst duplications, the rest will relentlessly accumulate and gradually destroy the genome." "Are there any polyploidal humans? Of course not, duplicating all the human genome is absolutely lethal." And while aneuploidy is lethal for larger human chromosomes, genetic abnormalities can result from an extra copy of the smallest ones.[47]

Can new species actually originate from existing species ("speciation") through selection and variation, as Darwinian materialist evolution claims, and not only claims, but asserts as "fact"? Can "one species split into two that continue to diverge," as Darwinian theory requires? The fact is, as biologist and Discovery Institute researcher Jonathan Wells states, "no one has observed the origin of even *one* species by this process." Wells examines several claims of such observed speciation, and finds that, at times contrary to their claims, no such speciation actually occurred. Some evolutionary biologists, such as Lynn Margulis and Dorion Sagan, have stated that speciation "has never been directly traced." And although University of Bristol (England) bacteriologist Alan Linton searched for direct evidence of speciation, he found none, concluding that "throughout 150 years of the science of bacteriology, there is no evidence that one species of bacteria has changed into another . . . Since there is no evidence for species changes between the simplest forms of unicellular life, it is not surprising that there is no evidence for evolution from prokaryotic [i.e., bacterial] to eukaryotic [i.e., plant and animal] cells, let alone throughout the whole array of higher multicellular organisms." Wells adds, "Despite centuries of artificial breeding and decades of laboratory experiments, no one has ever observed speciation through variation and selection. What Darwin claimed is true for *all* species has not been demonstrated even for one."[48] Natural selection cannot create any new biological information.[49]

Charles Darwin used as one of his strongest pieces of "evidence" for evolution of one species from another the theory of descent with continuing modification of embryos of different species. He claimed that "the embryos of the most distinct species belonging to the same class are closely similar, but become, when fully developed, widely dissimilar." The means "that vertebrates start out looking very similar as early embryos, and then become progressively more different as they develop into adults." If this were true Darwin could claim that "various classess of vertbrates (i.e. fishes, amphibians, reptiles, birds, and mammals [placental mammals include rodents, cats, whales, bats, and humans]) were descended from a common ancestor." This seemed to strongly support the descent of one species from another. And drawings of embryos done by biologist Ernst Haeckel (who was an outspoken critic of organized religion) seemed to prove it. But some people even then, and ever since, have known that Haeckel's drawings were "doctored," purposely faked in order to support the theory of evolution. They were not science, just a fakery to support a theory. In 2000, even the evolutionary biologist, Stephen Jay Gould, called Haeckel's drawings "fraudulent." Nevertheless they have still been used recently in some biology books as evidence of evolution.[50]

The claims for natural evolution of all species are based on philosophical naturalism and materialism rather than scientific evidence. The evolutionary naturalism preached by Julian Huxley in 1959 has become a ruling dogma for many in the fifty-some years since then. Huxley claimed

that all aspects of reality are subject to evolution, from atoms and stars to fish and flowers, from fish and flowers to human societies and values—indeed, that all reality is a single process of evolution . . . . In the evolutionary pattern of thought, there is no longer either need or room for the supernatural. The earth was not created; it evolved. So did all the animals and plants that inhabit it, including our human selves, mind and soul as well as brain and body. So did religion.[51]

But this is itself a philosophical and religious claim (*scientism*) that cannot be supported by science *per se*. Naturalism and materialism are *theories*, not facts.

Meyer's Critique of Evolutionary Views. All of the above arguments and information concerning naturalistic and materialistic evolutionary origins and development seem to demolish such views, indicating that they are essentially unsupportable because they have no secure basis in biological life processes or in the nature and origin of information. Perhaps the most devastating critique of evolutionary views on the origin of life is in a sixty-three-page, moderate-toned, formal paper by Stephen C. Meyer, entitled "DNA and the Origin of Life: Information, Specification, and Explanation."[52]

The big question of the origin of life is now known to be intimately linked with the question of the origin of *information* in living cells: "The problem of the origin of life is clearly basically equivalent to the problem of the origin of biological information."[53] Meyer shows at some length that "molecular biologists have used the term *information* consistently to refer to the joint properties of *complexity* and functional *specificity* or *specification*" and that the term actually "refers to two real features of living systems, complexity and specification." "Molecular biologists routinely refer to DNA, RNA, and proteins as carriers or repositories of 'information.'"[54]

Late nineteenth-century work, such as that of Ernst Haeckel and Thomas Henry Huxley had treated the cell as "a chemically simple substance called 'protoplasm' that could easily be constructed by combining and recombining simple chemicals such as carbon dioxide, oxygen, and nitrogen." (Huxley was "agnostic"/atheist, and Haeckel sharply criticized organized religion, while developing his own brand of religious views based on natural evolution). In stark contrast to such early views, DNA, RNA, and proteins have been increasingly found, during the second half of the twentieth century, to be highly complex, and quite specific as to their various particular functions. By the 1950s it was determined that "The amino acid sequence in functional proteins generally defies expression by any simple rule and is characterized instead by aperiodicity or complexity." More studies revealed "an extraordinarily complex and irregular three-dimensional shape . . . a twisting, turning tangle of amino acids." "In addition to their complexity, proteins also exhibit specificity, both as one-dimensional arrays and three-dimensional structures."

While proteins are built from chemically rather simple amino acid building blocks, "their function (whether as enzymes, signal transducers, or structural components in the cell) depends crucially on a complex but specific arrangement of those building blocks." The specific sequence of amino acids in a chain and the resultant chemical interactions between them "largely determine the specific three-dimensional structure that the chain as a whole will adopt." These structures determine what function, if any, the chain can perform. The three-dimensional shape enables a protein to fit perfectly with other molecules, and "catalyze specific chemical reactions or to build specific structures within the cell." The three-dimensional structure enables a specific function, so that one protein cannot usually substitute for another.[55]

During the early twentieth century DNA was also understood in overly simple terms—as being so uninterestingly repetitive and invariant that many thought it "could play little if any role in the transmission of heredity." But by the 1940s DNA was identified as the key factor in certain heritable differences. And it was recognized that enormous numbers of variations in nucleotide sequence were possible—as many as 10^{1500} (1 with 1500 zeros after it!) in the length of a single long gene. By the 1950s the three-dimensional double helix structure of DNA was revealed, and it became clear that DNA could carry heredity information. The extreme length and molecular-weight of the large DNA molecule was indicated, as was its chemical and structural complexity, and its "impressive potential for variability and complexity." All this made it seem likely that "the precise sequence of bases is the code which carries genetic information."

Subsequent discoveries "soon showed that DNA sequences were not only complex but also highly specific relative to the requirements of biological function." The newly understood complexity of DNA "suggested a means by which information or 'specificity' might be encoded along the spine of DNA's sugar-phosphate backbone." It was proposed that "the specificity of arrangement of amino acids in proteins derives from the specific arrangement of the nucleotide bases on the DNA molecule." This further "suggested that the nucleotide bases in DNA functioned like letters in an alphabet or characters in a machine code." During the early 1960s and later, it became clearer that the sequential arrangement of the nucleotide bases in DNA largely determines the one-dimensional sequential arrangement of amino acids during protein synthesis. "Since protein function depends critically on amino acid sequence and amino acid sequence depends critically on DNA base sequence, the sequences in the coding regions of DNA themselves possess a high degree of specificity relative to the requirements of protein (and cellular) function."[56]

Meyer presents evidence and reasons showing that the nucleotide sequences in coding regions of DNA possess both syntactic information and specified information: "the sequence specificity of DNA occurs within a syntactic (or functionally alphabetic) domain. Thus DNA possesses both syntactic and specified information." The crucial biomolecular constituents of living organisms possess not only "syntactic information but also *'specified* information' or *'specified* complexity.' Biological information so defined, therefore, constitutes a salient feature of living systems that any origin-of-life scenario must explain 'the origin of.'" But Meyer goes on to show that "all naturalistic chemical evolutionary theories have encountered difficulty explaining the origin of such functionally 'specified' biological information."[57]

One by one Meyer critiques the three major types of naturalistic explanations of the origin of life—(1) chance, (2) necessity, and (3) a combination of these two factors—giving solid reasons and evidence that none of these three types actually reveal such capabilities, and in fact, the evidence indicates clear signs of *complete incapability* of causing the origin of life.

Although the most common and popular naturalistic view of the origin of life has been that it happened exclusively by chance, almost all serious origin-of-life researchers now consider 'chance' an inadequate causal explanation for the origin of biological information. The "probability of obtaining functionally sequenced biomacromolecules at random is, in [physicist Ilya] Prigogine's words 'vanishingly small . . . even on the scale of . . . billions of

95

years.'" For one thing, the requirements for chemical bonding are much too great: the probability of building a protein chain of just 100 amino acids in which all linkages involve peptide linkages is roughly 1 chance in 10^{30} (while typical protein chains consist of 300, and many are much longer). Second, the probability of attaining at random the required L-amino (left-handed version) acids in such a chain is again only 10^{30}. And in starting from mixtures of DL- (right-left-) forms, the probability plummets to 10^{60}. Third, functioning proteins also require "that their amino acids must link up in a specific sequential arrangement just as the letters in a meaningful sentence must. In some cases, changing even one amino acid at a given site results in loss of protein function." Since there are twenty biologically occurring amino acids, the probability of getting a specific one at a given site by chance can be as impossibly low as 10^{130}. And the probability of generating a moderately longer protein of 150 amino acids rockets to 1 chance in 10^{180}. Considering that there are 10^{65} atoms in our galaxy, such numbers exceed the probabilistic resources of the known universe and thus fall within the realm of absurdity or logical impossibility.[58]

"More realistic calculations (taking into account the probable presence of nonproteinous amino acids, the need for much longer proteins to perform specific functions such as polymerization, and the need for hundreds of proteins working in coordination to produce a functioning cell) only compound these improbabilities, almost beyond computability." Recent work seeking to determine the "minimal complexity required to sustain the simplest possible living organism suggests a lower bound of some 250 to 400 genes and their corresponding proteins. The nucleotide sequence-space corresponding to such a system of proteins exceeds $4^{300,000}$." This vastly exceeds the probabilistic resources of the entire universe. "When one considers the full complement of functional biomolecules required to maintain minimal cell function and vitality, one can see why chance-based theories of the origin of life have been abandoned."[59]

Meyer shows that natural selection theories concerning the origin of life have equally serious flaws. This section of the paper holds that "prebiotic natural selection" is "a contradiction in terms." An important example of early materialistic theories of the origin of living organisms from lifeless matter (known as "abiogenesis") is that of Soviet biochemist Alexander Oparin, sometimes called the "Darwin of the twentieth century." By the 1920s and 1930s Oparin invoked prebiotic natural selection as a complement to chance interactions. His theory "envisioned a series of chemical reactions that he thought would enable a complex cell to assemble itself gradually and naturalistically from simple chemical precursors." Simple gases such as ammonia, methane, water vapor, carbon dioxide, and hydrogen supposedly combined and interacted in stage after stage to produce hydrocarbon compounds, then amino acids, sugars, and other "building blocks" such as proteins. These products then arranged themselves by chance into primitive metabolic systems within simple cell-like enclosures. Oparin claimed that some cells grew more and more complex and efficient by chance, and thus survived, while less complex and efficient ones dissolved. In this way he invoked differential survival or natural selection.[60]

However, discoveries of the extreme complexity and specificity of even primitive cellular metabolism during the 1950s undermined the plausibility of Oparin's claims, forcing him to revise his theory. His new theory, published in 1968, attempted to establish natural selection earlier in the process, claiming that it acted on random polymers as they formed and changed within his protocells. "As more complex and efficient molecules accumulated, they would have survived and reproduced more prolifically." But this new theory remained problematic because "it seemed to presuppose a preexisting mechanism of self-replication. Yet self-replication in all extant cells depends on functional and, therefore, (to a high degree) sequence-specific proteins and nucleic acids. Yet the origin of specificity in these molecules is precisely what Oparin needed to explain. As [biochemist] Christian de Duve has stated, theories of prebiotic natural selection 'need information which implies they have to presuppose what is to be explained in the first place.'" Meyer indicates additional problems in Oparin's theory, including no account of "error catastrophe, in which small errors, or deviations from functionally necessary sequences, are quickly amplified in successive replications."[61]

In summary of the problems of Oparin's theories [and many related ones], Meyer writes, "the need to explain the origin of specified information created an intractable dilemma for Oparin. On the one hand, if he invoked natural selection late in his scenario, he would need to rely on chance alone to produce the highly complex and specified biomolecules necessary to self-replication. On the other hand, if Oparin invoked natural selection earlier in the process of chemical evolution, before functional specificity in biomacro-molecules would have arisen, he could give no account of how such prebiotic natural selection could even function (given the phenomenon of error-catastrophe). Natural selection presupposes a self-replication system, but self-replication requires functioning nucleic acids and proteins (or molecules approaching their complexity)—the very entities that Oparin needed to explain. Thus, [geneticist and evolutionary biologist Theodosius] Dobzhansky would insist that, 'prebiological natural selection is a contradiction in terms.'"[62]

Meyer also reveals flaws in the attempt during the 1980s by Richard Dawkins and Bernd-Olaf Kuppers to resuscitate prebiotic natural selection as an explanation for the origin of biological information.[63] These flaws include: (1) ways of using computers not found in natural processes; (2) supplying target sequences that do not exist in molecules; (3) making distinctions on the basis of function among sequences that have no function; and (4) the impossibility of non-functional polypeptides conferring selective advantage on a hypothetical protocell.[64]

Meyer further explains why natural selection is a contradiction in terms:

During the 1960s, [mathematician John] von Neumann showed that any system capable of self-replication would require subsystems that were functionally equivalent to the information storage, replicating, and processing systems found in extant cells. His calculations established a very high minimal threshold of biological function, as would later experimental work. These minimal-complexity requirements pose a fundamental difficulty for natural selection. Natural selection selects for functional advantage. It can play no role, therefore, until random variations produce some biologically advantageous arrangement of matter. Yet von Neumann's calculations and similar ones by Wigner, Landsberg, and Morowitz showed that in all probability (to understate the case) random fluctuations of molecules would not produce the minimal complexity needed for even a primitive replication system . . . . the improbability of developing a functionally integrated replication system vastly exceeds the improbability of developing the protein or DNA components of such a system.[65]

Because of such difficulties with theories based on chance, or chance and natural selection, researchers after the mid-1960s began to seek explanations in terms of chemical or physical necessity—on "self-organizational laws and properties of chemical attraction that might explain the origin of specified information in DNA and proteins." Some, such as Steinman and Cole, suggested that simple chemicals had self-ordering properties capable of forming the constituent parts of proteins, DNA, and RNA into their proper arrangements. By 1969 Kenyon and Steinman put forward the idea that life might have been "'biologically predestined' by the properties of attraction existing between its constituent parts, particularly among the amino acids in proteins." In 1977, another self-organizational theory was proposed by Prigogine and Nicolis. And in 1995 Kauffman and de Duve proposed further self-organizational theories.[66]

Many scientists now consider self-organizational models the most promising. However, one former proponent, Dean Kenyon, has since repudiated such theories as both incompatible with empirical findings and theoretically incoherent. Meyer brings devastating criticisms against them. In proteins, for example, "differing chemical affinities do not explain the multiplicity of amino acid sequences existing in naturally occurring proteins or the sequential arrangement of amino acids in any particular protein." And "self-organizing" principles also fail to work for DNA. It is precisely along the longitudinal axis of the DNA molecule that the genetic information in DNA is stored. "Self-organizing" bonding affinities cannot explain the sequentially specific arrangement of nucleotide bases in DNA. because (1) there are *no* bonds between bases along the information-bearing axis of the molecule, and (2) there are no *differential* affinities between the backbone and the specific bases that could account for variations in sequence." The same holds true for RNA.[67]

Meyer adds that "biochemistry and molecular biology make clear that forces of attraction between the constituents in DNA, RNA, and proteins do not explain the sequence specificity of these large, information-bearing biomolecules. The properties of the monomers [smaller molecules] constituting nucleic acids and proteins simply do not make a particular gene, let alone life as we know it, inevitable." Even if we imagine the most favorable conditions, such as "a pool of all four DNA bases and all necessary sugars and phosphates, would any particular genetic sequence inevitably arise? Given all necessary monomers, would any particular functional protein or gene, let alone a specific genetic code, replication system, or signal traduction circuitry, inevitably arise? Clearly not." "Functional genes or proteins are no more inevitable, given the properties of their 'building blocks,' than, for example, the Palace of Versailles was inevitable, given the properties of the stone blocks that were used to construct it."[68]

The base sequences in DNA possess not only information-carrying capacity (syntactic information), they also store functionally specified information—they are specified as well as complex. "Clearly, however, a sequence cannot be both specified and complex if it is not at least complex. Therefore, self-organizational forces of chemical necessity, which produce redundant order and *preclude* complexity, also preclude the generation of specified complexity (or specified information) as well. Chemical affinities do not generate complex sequences. Thus, they cannot be invoked to explain the origin of information, whether specified or otherwise."[69]

Meyer supports intelligent design as a more satisfactory explanation of the presence of complex, specified information in living organisms. "Experience affirms that specified complexity or information . . . routinely arises from the activity of intelligent agents." It comes "from a mental, rather than a strictly material, cause." Like computer or book information, it can be traced invariably to a mind. Systems with large amounts of specified complexity or information "*invariably* originate from an intelligent source— that is, from a mind or a personal agent." "During the last forty years, every naturalistic model proposed has failed to explain the origin of the specified genetic information required to build a living cell. Thus, mind or intelligence, or what philosophers call 'agent causation,' now stands as the only cause known to be capable of generating large amounts of information starting from a nonliving state. As a result, the presence of specified information-rich sequences in even the simplest living systems would seem to imply intelligent design."[70]

Do Naturalist and Materialist Theories of Origin and Evolution Prove the Non-Existence of God? The various reasons and evidence reviewed in this chapter thus expose many of the underlying inadequacies, failures, and fallacies of naturalist and materialist evolutionary theories, which are often artfully cloaked by their proponents, and have become the "Primary Axiom" of scientific understandings of life's origins and evolution of species for many decades. Such evolutionary views are not only unproven, and contrary to reason, but, in view of extensive evidence, futile and absurd. By eliminating from the outset the idea of God, including God as first cause, naturalist and materialist evolutionary theories have wound up in foolish positions. They ignore the biblical admonition in Romans 1:20, "For since the creation of the world God's invisible qualities—his eternal power and divine nature—have been clearly seen, being understood from what has been made, so that men are without excuse." This verse shows that God has revealed himself clearly through creation to every human being. Through this *natural revelation*, unbelievers actually *have* knowledge of God's existence even if they have no other human or biblical revelation. And in addition to this knowledge through the created world or universe, God has given another revelation of himself within every person: "what may be known of God is manifest in them, for God has shown it to them" (Romans 1:19) "That which may be intuitively known about God has been placed in the minds (heart, conscience . . .) of all men by God."[71]

No one is ever simply ignorant of God. Every one has an inner knowledge of Him, but many seek in various ways to "suppress the truth," distort it, and "exchange the truth of God for a lie" (Romans 1:18-32). But there remains in every one "a memory of that revelation. It is against this memory that he sins, and it is because of that memory that he is held responsible for those sins . . . . Every human being is surrounded by God's revelation, even within himself."[72] Those who repress, deny, and "exchange them for lies" are subject to the strong reproach of Psalm 14:1: "The fool says in his heart, there is no God." It is to the actuality of God's eternal, incomparable Reality, Being, Life, Mind and Ideas that we turn in the next chapter.

Chapter Four

God the Supreme Being, Creator, and Preserver of All
The Being, Mind, and Ideas of God

It seems preposterous to suppose a project including the galaxies in their motion and orbits, as well as the life-processes of a microbe; including objects as complicated as the solar system and as mysterious as light and human consciousness; including processes as closely harmonized as the electrical hook-up between the human brain and hands playing a violin could simply have occurred without an intelligent design formed by an intelligent designer.[1]

God the Supreme Being, Creator, and Truth must exist for there to be any real contingent beings, living and inanimate, and for the existence of reason and logic in the nature of things, making any truth and knowledge possible.[2]

The Universe Must Have a Cause. The Big Bang model of recent science indicates that nothing of the universe as we know it existed before that great "singularity." How did such an event originate? All experience and logic tell us that *nothing comes from nothing*. "Nothing" cannot serve as a cause. Furthermore, once something exists, it cannot continue to exist with nothing to support its existence. American philosopher and theologian William Lane Craig emphasizes that the atheist view of the universe coming from nothing by nothing in the Big Bang makes no sense: "Out of nothing, nothing comes." Even the skeptical David Hume deemed it "absurd" to assert that "anything might arise without a cause." The early twentieth-century astro-physicist Sir Arthur Eddington held that "The beginning seems to present insuperable difficulties unless we agree to look on it as supernatural."[3] (What caused the Big Bang? What caused time? What caused energy, atoms, molecules? What caused the fundamental laws of physics? What is the cause of these causes, and their causes, and so on?)

Causes cannot run on to "infinity." Craig explains that the infinite is *not actually found in nature*: in the real world "infinity is just an idea in one's mind, not something that exists in reality."[4] There must be a First Cause, an original source. Aristotle was right that there must be a First Cause, although his own identification of it was far inadequate. Plato was right that ideas are behind every existing thing, although he did not trace their source to the mind of the Personal Living Supreme Being, God. As Norman Geisler and Étienne Gilson point out, "no Greek philosopher ever identified his ultimate metaphysical principle with his God or gods."[5]

A Personal Creator As Cause. Recognizing the nature of the Big Bang, Craig develops and defends a three-point logical argument for a supernatural first cause that is the personal Creator of the universe: "1. Whatever begins to exist has a cause. 2. The universe began to exist. 3. Therefore, the universe has a cause." Such a cause must be uncaused because "there cannot be an infinite regress of causes. It must be timeless and changeless because it created time." It must be "immaterial, not physical" since it transcends space, which it also created. It must be a personal agent, "for how else could a timeless cause give rise to a temporal effect such as the universe?" "The only way for the cause to be timeless and the effect to begin in time is for the cause to be a personal agent who freely chooses to create an effect in time without any prior determining conditions. For example, a man sitting from eternity could freely will to stand up. Thus, we are brought not merely to a transcendent cause of the universe but to its personal Creator."[6]

Craig reveals the failure of arguments against premises one and two of his argument. There is no basis in subatomic physics (quantum theory) that the universe is uncaused, nor that it came into being uncaused from nothing. Premise one involves a metaphysical principle: "Being cannot come from nonbeing; something cannot come into existence uncaused from nothing. The principle therefore applies to all reality. It is thus metaphysically absurd that the universe should pop into being uncaused out of nothing." Even a prominent atheist of recent decades, J. L. Mackie, found such a notion incredible: "I myself find it hard to accept the notion of self-creation *from nothing*, even given unrestricted chance. And how *can* this be given, if there really is nothing?" Craig adds that in the atheistic view, "the *potentiality* of the universe's existence didn't even exist prior to the Big Bang. But then how could the universe become actual if there wasn't even the potentiality of its existence? It makes much more sense to say that the potentiality of the universe lay in the power of God to create it."

Craig gives several reasons that infinite set theory of mathematics does not disprove his second premise that the universe began to exist. Set theory does not prove that an infinite number of things can actually exist. Set theory is a *realm of discourse* with its own presupposed axioms and rules, which give no guarantee that "an infinite number of things can exist in the real world." Furthermore, "the real existence of an infinite number of things would violate the rules of infinite set theory." Moreover, premise two actually has the overwhelming support of the scientific community, since "no theory is more probable than the Big Bang theory." Steven Hawking has said that "Almost everyone now believes that the universe, and *time itself*, had a beginning in the Big Bang."[7]

For these and other reasons Craig gives, his premises one and two "seem more plausible than their denials. Hence, it is plausible that a transcendent Creator of the universe exists. An explanation of the first state of the universe *"cannot* be scientific," since, as Oxford philosopher Richard Swinburne points out, "there is nothing before it." Craig concludes that "if a personal explanation does not exist, then there is simply no explanation at all—which is metaphysically absurd, since on that account the universe just popped into being out of nothing . . . . In sum, we have a powerful reason based on the origin of the universe to believe that an uncaused, changeless, timeless, immaterial, personal Creator of the universe exists."[8]

Being, Power, and Intelligent Mind and Ideas Are Required. The material presented in the previous chapters (actually only a small fraction of what is available), indicates that naturalist and materialist theories about the origins and development of the universe and of all living things are unsatisfactory, essentially lacking in support, or even absurd. It also indicates that Mind, Idea, and Intelligence are actual factors needed to explain the origin of the universe and the complex and specified information at the core of all living things. Since living things originated after the origin of the universe, and, according to both science and the Bible, human beings originated some time after the origin of simpler life forms such as bacteria, protozoa, plants, and animals, some other great mind and power must be behind these origins. Whoever or whatever this mind and power is, is thus the biggest of the big questions of life. This chapter will seek to show further that that actual mind and power is the revealed God of the Bible and of classical orthodox Christian tradition.

Without presupposing a full, affirmative answer to begin with, the first questions a curious person might ask are: "Who is this God? What are this God's attributes? Answers to these questions may logically begin with the idea that such a God is a *Creator.* Since naturalist and materialist theories of origins and development are known to fail, and since the mind, intelligence, and power behind existing and living things is, as we have seen, wondrous and mind-boggling, greater than anything humans will ever do or have ever done, the universe and all living things surely must be the creative work of a *Supreme Being*—a Being of *supernatural life, mind, intelligence,* and *power.*

The Reality and Being of World and Creator. Despite the claims of certain skeptical philosophies of the ancient world, as well as some religious views that the world is an illusion, and the radical skepticism of so much "Postmodernism," our common experience and thought, as well as most science, tells us that the world and our selves are actually *real*. If this is so, self and world *must* have an essential basis in enduring or eternal *being* of some kind, as the Bible and Christian theology and metaphysics have maintained for many centuries, and as certain classical philosophies have proposed. These prospective answers—eternal being, mind, ideas, intelligence, power, and creativity, are actually some of the key attributes of God as taught by the Bible and Christian theology.

If God has in fact created the universe and all existing and living things, these attributes must surely be above anything else we know, greater than the wondrous universe itself, greater than all of the miraculous information behind all living things—in fact, fully superhuman and super-natural. This is, in fact, the way the Bible and Christian tradition describe God—eternal being and life, everlasting, unchanging, omniscient and omnipotent. How could anything less *be* God, or create the incredibly vast assembly of stars and light-year spaces, energy and materials, the inanimate and living things of the universe, and the miraculous workings of DNA that we are now aware of in more depth and detail than ever before? In these ways, certainly, God is *Great!* Just in terms of such life, intelligence, power, and creativity, God is Great! The word "Great" is actually inadequate to indicate the full extent and import of such transcendent personal being, power, and intelligence (and as we shall suggest later, God is Great in other ways.) In such ways God is Supreme, the Incomparable One of Personal Being, Life, Knowledge, Power, and Creativity, infinitely greater than anything else humans have ever known.

Several essential attributes of God's nature, which have secure biblical basis and a long history in classical Christian theology and metaphysics, are: Being or Pure Actuality, Life, immateriality or spirituality, personality, simplicity (indivisibility), aseity (not caused by another); necessity (His nonexistence is impossible), immutability, eternality, infinity, omnipotence, omniscience, and wisdom.[9] In the foreground of importance for the present discussion of the origin and nature of the universe and all life are God's Being, incomparable Life, omnipotence, omniscience, and wisdom. Other attributes will be discussed in later chapters.

In order to create anything real and living, God must be real and living Himself—He must possess *ultimate reality and life*. God must *be* real, eternal, living *Being* in and of Himself—the *Supreme, Living Personal Being* who can be the ultimate creative source and sustaining ground of all created things and living personal beings. God is the *only* real *Being* in the sense of possessing eternal, unchanging living Being within Himself. All other things, which are all created, only have *being* because of Him, and in continual dependence upon the Being of God, the Creator and preserver. Nothing besides God possesses eternal, self-existent life and *Being*. All existing things are ultimately contingent upon God for their moment-to-moment existence. As we shall see, numerous biblical and theological passages make these points.

A text of essential importance, and "the most profound and sublime of all biblical references to a 'name' for God,"[10] is Exodus 3:13-14, in which God speaks to Moses from a burning bush. When Moses asks His name, God replies: "I AM WHO I AM" (in Hebrew, "*'ehyeh 'aser 'ehyeh*"). God then tells Moses to tell the Israelites that "I AM [*'ehyeh*] has sent me to you." Exodus 3:14 in a primary sense expresses "God's real, perfect, unconditional, independent existence. God exists in a way that no one and nothing else does. He is without beginning or end. He is the only Being who is self-existent. All other existence is dependent upon His uncaused existence."[11] The Hebrew text of Exodus 3:14 places emphasis on "*'ehyeh*" ("Yehweh" or "Yahweh)," which is one of the most sacred and frequent names for God in the Old Testament, and is evidently derived from the archaic verb, *hâwâh*, meaning *to be*.[12] In the Greek Septuagint translation the text reads "*Ego eimi ho on*," "I am the one who is." Christian scholar Jaroslav Pelikan relates a key aspect of meaning offered by the great fourth century "Trinitarian Theologian," Gregory of Nazianzus: God possesses "'eternity and infinity in respect to being, making everything contemplated therein always the same, neither growing nor being consumed,' a divine quality symbolized by the burning bush, which was 'on fire but was not being burnt up.'"[13]

Theologian Norman Geisler writes that Exodus 3:14 describes "God as Pure Existence . . . . God is pure 'I AM'-ness; He is the self-existent One who depends on no one else for His being."[14] Geisler states that "God, then, *is* Pure Actuality. He is Being. Everything else merely *has* being. Most early and even later Fathers identified this with God's self-revelation to Moses . . . as the great I AM or self-existent One."[15] Geisler explains at some length why the passage indicates that "God really is the 'I AM,' namely, the eternal, self-existent One." Even "the very name Yahweh (YHWH), usually translated "Lord" in the Old Testament, is probably a contraction of 'I AM WHO I AM.'" And the name is believed to be derived from the root *hwy* [*hayah*], having as one meaning to "exist."[16] Historical theologian John D. Hannah writes that "'*Ehyeh* is probably a wordplay on Yahweh (Lord) in verse 15. Thus, the name Yahweh, related to the verb 'to be,' probably speaks of God's self-existence, but it means more than that. It usually speaks of His relationship to His people. For example, as Lord, He redeemed them (6:6), was faithful to them (34:5-7), and made a covenant with them (Gen. 15:18).[17]

John Frame emphasizes at length that "Yahweh" "asserts God's sovereign lordship" and "denotes him as Lord of the covenant."[18]

Closely related key passages using the Greek words *ho on* are in Revelation 1:4 and 8, where God is twice identified as "he-who-is, he-who-was, and he-who-is-to-come" (*ho on kai ho en kai ho erchomenos*). "*On*" is a Greek term for "being," used in an important, related sense in Greek Classical ontology. While there are critical differences from Greek philosophical usages to Christian meanings, both have been taken to refer to "continuity and eternity and transcendence over all marks of time."[19] Pelikan also states that throughout the Bible the use of the words "to be" for God, and "I am" by God, as in Isaiah 41:4 and 43:10, "ascribed being in the fullest sense to God, and to God alone." "Being" in the true sense of that word, was "the special distinction of the Godhead."[20] Being in these biblical contexts does not refer to some abstract, impersonal property or power, but to the real eternal existence or Being of the Living Personal God.

Another key verse is John 8:58, where Jesus deliberately echoes Exodus 3:14, saying "Most assuredly, I say to you, before Abraham was, I AM" (*ego eimi*). This verse, by which Jesus states His eternal Being as a Person of the Godhead, can be taken as the climactic declaration of this Gospel, and of the entire New Testament.[21] Geisler comments that the traditional understanding of Exodus 3:14 as indicating God's actuality, His Pure Existence, is "confirmed by Jesus' usage of it in John 8:58."[22] And in John 5:26, Jesus declares, "as the Father has life in Himself, so He has granted the Son to have life in Himself." John, echoing and amplifying Genesis 1:1, makes the grand declaration of the eternal Being of God the Father and of Jesus Christ, and of divine creation of all things in verses 1:1-4: "In the beginning was the Word [Greek, *Logos* = Christ as the Word], and the Word was with God, and the Word was God. He was in the beginning with God. All things were made through Him, and without Him nothing was made that was made. In Him was life, and the life was the light of men."[23]

God's Being or Existence is also expressed in metaphysical theological terms as His *actuality*. Geisler explains that "actuality" is that which is pure *act* or that which *is*, in contrast to "potentiality," that which has the potential for change and non-existence. Pure actuality is "that which *is* (existence) with *no possibility* to *not* exist or to be anything other than it is—existence pure and simple." God's actuality is pure actuality, or pure existence: it had no beginning and it has no potential for change or ceasing to exist. "God existed prior to and independently of anything else. All other things that exist depend on Him, while He depends on nothing else for His existence." As Geisler says, "God's pure actuality is fundamental to the classical orthodox view of God." "God was considered Pure Existence, without any possibility or potentiality for nonexistence, from the very beginning of the Christian faith." And in his chapters two and three he supplies quotations from Irenaeus through Augustine and Aquinas into recent times.[24] Thomas Aquinas showed the logic of the actuality of God: "the first being must of necessity be in act, and in no way in potentiality . . . . absolutely speaking, actuality is prior to potentiality; for whatever is in potentiality can be reduced into actuality only by some being in actuality . . . . God is the First Being. It is therefore impossible that in God there should be any potentiality."[25]

Along with the biblical texts discussed above, several others imply or point to God's pure actuality. Genesis 1:1 introduces God as the eternal Creator: "In the *beginning* God created the heavens and the earth." Psalm 90:2 praises God the eternal Creator: "Before the mountains were brought forth, or ever You had formed the earth and the world, even *from everlasting to everlasting, You are God*." Colossians 1:17 reveals God as the eternal Being and Creator on whom all things depend: "He is *before* all things, and *in Him all things consist* [or *hold together*]." Several verses in Revelation reveal God as the Eternal Living Being: "'I am the Alpha and the Omega, *the Beginning and the End*,' says the Lord, '*who is and who was and who is to come, the Almighty*'" (1:8). "I am *the Alpha and the Omega, the First and the Last*" (1:11, and see 1:17-18).[26]

John M. Frame's approach to theology gives primary place to God's lordship in creation, emphasizing God's control, authority, and presence. For this reason he does not give extensive development to the doctrine of the eternal Being of God, although he does solidly support it. He writes that "Aquinas argues well for the necessity of God's being." For Aquinas, God's Being carries a "more profound sense" than "being in general," "that of *esse*, sometimes translated *existence*." "To say that God is Being, then, is to say that God's essence is *esse*, that his very nature is to exist. Rather than identifying him with the world, the scholastics argue, *esse* underscores the Creator-creature distinction: for of all the beings in the universe, only God is identical with his own *esse*." Frame has "no problem affirming that God is necessary being," but he wants to do it "on the basis of Scripture . . . rather than on specifically Thomistic premises. If God necessarily exists, then it is not wrong to say that his *esse* is essential to his being," although he thinks it is "no more essential than his holiness, goodness, knowledge, wisdom, and so on." "I agree with Aquinas's view that God exists necessarily. He does not merely happen to exist; he must exist. His nonexistence is impossible."[27]

God is Living *Personal* Being. He is not some impersonal, abstract being or thing existing in a wholly different manner from the persons He creates. In order to create persons He must possess the quality that He creates. *Personal* being cannot arise from the impersonal or abstract. If God is the original creative source of mind, intelligence, ideas, will, and act, He must be personal and exemplify the highest order of mind, intelligence, ideas, and will. Throughout the Bible God is represented as an Incomparable Spiritual Person who creates, communicates, and leads in the lives and histories of the persons He creates. Only as Person can He exercise His knowledge, wisdom, ideas, holiness, goodness, justice, authority, will, and active power in personal relationships. Frame properly emphasizes the personal nature of God. God is Spirit, and "'Spirit' in Scripture is personal." As Spirit, God speaks, bears witness, helps, loves, and reveals. Secular and atheist thought generally assumes that persons are the product of impersonal structures or forces such as matter, motion, chance, time, and physical laws.[28] But how can the personal possibly arise from anything impersonal? The Bible and Christian tradition teach that all things come originally from a unique and incomparable Personal Being—the Living God.

Theologian Thomas C. Oden illuminates the doctrine of God's Being with the illustration of a scale of "participation in being." At the very bottom of the scale is nonbeing, "that which never has been or can be." Above it is "that which never has been." Then comes "lifeless, inorganic matter." Above it is plant life, and then animal life. Still higher is "human life, consciousness and freedom." And at the apex is "that which completely *is* and is aware that it is, transcending our capacity to understand how fully such a being could be." Some things participate in being at very low levels, like rocks. Plants participate at higher levels. And human intelligence is far more capable than instinctual animal consciousness. Such a scale of degrees of perfection requires the apex of that scale. It must have "nonbeing at one end and supreme being at another end; otherwise the scale itself is defective and incomplete."[29]

"By analogy," Oden writes, "one may posit another reality at the apex of the scale: One who insurmountably *is* more than anything else thinkable and more fully shares in being, grounds being, embraces all being; hence One who more fully *is*, and is conscious of fully being, than any other conceivable being. To posit that One who supremely *is*, by the way of heightening or eminent thinking, is to reliably know, learn, and affirm something about God, namely, that God supremely *is* (i.e., Supremely Being, or the Supreme Being)."

Oden strongly affirms the classic Christian doctrine of God's eternal, Supreme Being. God is "the One who supremely *is*," "the Supreme Being." He explains, persuasively I think, why "the word *being* (cognate with the direct name 'I AM') is a more intensive word than the flatter word *existence* (even in English, but moreso in its Latin and Greek roots). The word "existence" (from *ex*, and *sistere*) suggests a *"standing-out," "out-from."* But "one cannot exist (stand out) without something to stand upon (being), just as one cannot subsist (stand firm, from *sub* + *sistere*) without having something (being, *esse*) to support one's subsistence. Thus "*existing* seems a less full term than *being*, and 'merely to exist' less weighty than 'to be.'" "God indeed participates in natural and historical existence, but God *is* more fully, completely, awarely, and amply than any creature could be. Thus the term *existence* does not pertain to God in precisely the same way that it pertains to creatures. For God *is*—immeasurably, necessarily, and eternally—whereas creatures exist measurably, contingently, and temporarily . . . Hebrew Scriptures did not use Greco-Latin terms like God's *essence* or *substance*, but they did speak often of God as Yahweh (the incomparable 'I AM'), the One who insurmountably *is*."[30]

Oden describes the primary or essential attributes of God: "God is uncreated, necessary, one, infinite, immense, eternal being, the life of all that is." God is "the Uncreated One, the underived Source and End of all things . . . . The most penetrating Hebraic name for God, 'I AM' (Yahweh) suggests that God simply and incomparably *is* . . . . This uncreated cause of all things is addressed personally, unlike the 'other gods' . . . . To this independent, self-sufficient being 'everything is possible' (Mark 10:27) . . . . To affirm that God is independent and necessary means that God depends on no cause external to God. God's life is contingent upon nothing else . . . . To say that God is uncreated or self-existent (or self-subsistent) means simply that God is without origin, that God is the only ground of God's being, and that there is no cause prior to God . . . . This supreme being has not at some point in time *become* the Supreme Being, but simply *is*, and has never been otherwise. This underived being whose nature is to be, the Hebrews called Yahweh ('I am Who I am,' Exod. 3:14) and Teutonic languages have called God.

God has no cause external to God, and this is precisely what makes God God, and not something else . . . ." God's "being is eternally necessary and essential to God's nature and essence . . . . God is the one and only incomparable divine being." The triune teaching "strongly affirms the unity of God, for God is 'not three gods,' but Three-in-One . . . and indivisible, hence simple . . . . All attributes of this incomparable One are interfused and joined together in the one indivisible essence in a way that transcends partial human perception . . . . The essence of anything is that which makes a thing what it is, that to which its definition points. The essence of God is simply to exist in the way that only God can exist."[31]

According to Geisler, "all the basic metaphysical attributes of God follow logically from His pure actuality, and His pure actuality follows from His being the Uncaused First Cause of all else that exists." He discusses all these attributes. Only three more need be briefly developed in the present context—God's *life*, and His *knowledge* and *wisdom*, with the last two being different aspects of the same attribute.

God's Life, Activity, and Power. God's life and immortality are, as Geisler says, "tied together . . . . Since God is life intrinsically, it follows that He is immortal as well." "Life" means "alive," "active," "moving"; it "involves immanent self-activity." "Theologically, to speak of God as life is to say two basic things: God is alive, and He is the Source of all other life. He *is* life intrinsically, while all other things *have* life as a gift from Him." Life can only come from the living God. God created all living things; He puts to death and brings to life, He wounds and heals. (Deut. 32:39). He can raise the dead, and He is "the resurrection and the life" (John 11:25). Since God created each individual according to His divine ideas, He can also resurrect and restore the person according to those eternal ideas. Geisler quotes many Old and New Testament passages speaking of the "living God" in numerous ways, often contrasting God with pagan gods or idols, which are dead or inactive. "As life, God is the most active, dynamic, and moving Being in the universe." "Whatever reality God gives, He has; hence, God has life (i.e., God is life)." Since God is Pure Actuality, and life is a form of being or actuality, the Life God possesses is eternal, inexhaustible, and incomparable.

Only such a Supreme Being and source of Life can *create* life. Life cannot originate out of nothing, or out of lifeless atoms and molecules (and the Big Bang also denies the eternal existence of energy, atoms, and molecules). "There cannot be an infinite regress where everything is receiving life, but nothing is giving it." Ultimately there must be a Supreme *Living* Being to cause life. "While God is the Unmoved Mover, He is not the unmoving mover. He is immovable but not immobile. All motion and activity begin ultimately with Him as the Prime Mover."[32]

Oden also observes that the *living* God is the frequent subject of Scripture, and is often contrasted with "the immobility and impotence of 'the gods.'" "The life of God is the eternal, underived energy of his being, ever active within God himself, enabling movement and change in creation. Life is that which differentiates a plant, animal, or human being from something that is dead—inorganic, non-living matter. God's being is intrinsically characterized by life, by being alive." "The lives of plants, animals, and humans depend radically upon God, but the life of God does not depend on something external to God's life."

The bodily life of plants, animals, and humans ends in death. "From the moment of conception the processes of decay and death are at work in our bodies. Not so in God's life. God's life is eternal life. God's life is not only without end, but without beginning. For before anything was alive, God was alive . . . . God is known to be more alive than any imaginable living being. God has no trace of decay or death at work in himself." Furthermore, God is incomparably active and tireless. "It is an active, engaged God that is portrayed in Scripture, not quiescent, not merely letting creation be or leaving men and women to their own devices." God's activities are prodigious, multiple, and varied, which "suggest that God is *purus actus*, pure actuality, which means that the God who most *is* is eternally active, that God's willing is eternally operative, and that God's power is never static or latent but always completely present and active. Contrary to Aristotle's passive God, Yahweh is always working, ever doing, eternally in motion, never immobilized, never stalemated, never depressed."[33]

God's Knowledge and Wisdom. Concerning God's knowledge, His omniscience, Geisler writes, "All theists agree that God is infinite (without limits), and God's knowledge is identical to His nature, since He is simple [indivisible]. God must know according to His Being; therefore God must know infinitely . . . ." As a Being of Pure Actuality God has no potentiality, no limitation in Being. Since His knowledge is identical to His Being, His knowledge must also be without limitation. As an absolutely perfect Being, His knowledge must also be absolutely perfect. "God's infinite knowledge must include everything, including all future events." "God is the First Cause of all that exists or will ever exist; thus, the future (including all of its free actions) preexists in God. Therefore, by knowing Himself, God knows all future free actions." "All effects preexist in their efficient cause . . . since a cause cannot produce what it does not possess—it cannot give what it hasn't got to give." "The effect preexists in God (its Cause) in two ways. As efficient Cause, He cannot produce what He does not possess; He cannot share what He does not have to share. Further, *as the ultimate exemplar Cause of everything, God contains the idea or pattern of all that comes from Him. Thus, all of creation preexisted in the mind of the Creator before He made it.*"[34]

Theologian Herman Bavinck has written about God's knowledge and wisdom at some length in *The Doctrine of God*. He acknowledges, like many before him, that "God's knowledge is all-comprehensive, simultaneous, simple [indivisible], unchangeable, and eternal." And Bavinck elucidates the meaning of "light" in numerous Bible verses: "God is light; in him there is no darkness at all" (I John 1:5); God the Father is the "King of kings . . . who lives in unapproachable light, whom no one has seen or can see" (I Timothy 6:15-16); "in your light we see light"; "Send forth your light and your truth, let them guide me" (Psalm 36:9; 43:3); Christ the eternal Logos came as a witness to the light, and said of Himself, "I am the light of the world. Whoever follows me will never walk in darkness, but will have the light of life" (John 8:12). The symbolic meaning of "light," Bavinck writes, is that of "knowledge," since the main function of light is revealing what is hidden in darkness, making it manifest. When God is called "light" He is designated as "perfect in self-consciousness, perfect in the knowledge of his own being." "Light" is also symbolic in Scripture of "purity, chastity, holiness, and of joy, cheerfulness, blessedness," while darkness is symbolic of ignorance and error, unchastity and moral corruption.[35]

"Wisdom" is another perspective on God's incomparable knowledge and action. God's knowledge and wisdom work in many ways. Geisler writes of God's wisdom as "His unerring ability to choose the best means to accomplish the best ends." God's "omniscience provides the knowledge for His wise choices; His omnibenevolence assures that they will be good choices; and His omnipotence enables Him to achieve His ends by the means He chooses." As Oden states it, "The wisdom of God is God's incomparable ability to order all things in the light of the good, to adjust causes to effects, and means to ends, so that the divine purposes are ensured and never finally thwarted. Divine knowledge grasps things as they are. Divine wisdom grasps fitting means to good ends."[36]

Bavinck emphasizes, in addition to these aspects, that God's wisdom has been logically related to the "realization of God's ideas" in the work of creation. "Philo and especially Augustine connected the Scriptural doctrine of wisdom with Plato's 'ideas,'" Augustine's use of "idea" was as "the pattern of a thing in the creative mind of God, an archetype." "God is not an unconscious Creator, but he created all things with a purpose, after a pattern, an 'idea,' hence, with wisdom. Creation is the realization of these ideas. God is the great Architect. His ideas are: (1) absolutely original, (2) eternal, unchangeable, (3) manifold, yet unified, having as their ultimate purpose God's glorification."[37] These concepts will be developed further through the rest of this chapter.

Creation and Preservation. Geisler upholds the two orthodox Christian doctrines of God's original *creation*, and His continuing *preservation* of all things created. He holds that God is not only the First Cause, the originating source of all things, He is the necessary continuing sustenance and support for all existing things. As he states it, "Creation is utterly dependent on God; this dependence applies to creation's present status as well as to its past start. The universe and everything in it began as God's creation, and it continues to be God's creation. God is the *originating Cause* as well as the *sustaining Cause* of everything that exists." The logical reason is that creation is contingent. Any contingent being requires the act of a necessary Being both for its origin and its continuing existence. "Creation by nature is contingent; only God is a necessary Being . . . . a contingent being is one dependent on the necessary Being for its existence, and once a contingent being, always a contingent being. No contingent being can become a necessary Being, for a necessary

Being by its very nature cannot come to be or cease to be. If a necessary being exists, it must exist necessarily. However, if a contingent being is always contingent, then it is always dependent for its existence on a necessary Being; it can no more not be dependent for its existence at any time than it can cease being a contingent being. Dependent beings are not only dependent when they come to be; they are dependent whenever they are (exist). Hence, all of creation, being contingent (i.e., something that could not be), is dependent for its existence at all times."[38]

The Bible points in these directions, telling us that since God created the world, He has continued to sustain its very existence. He continues to preserve the world, maintaining and upholding the laws and workings of nature. Hebrews 1:3 says that God sustains creation: God the Second Person of the Trinity, Jesus Christ, through whom the Father made the worlds, is *"upholding all things* by the word of his power." Colossians 1:19, also speaking of Christ, says that "All things were created through Him and for Him," that "He is before all things, and *in Him all things consist* [or *hold together*]." Revelation 4:11 tells us that all things have their being from God: "you created all things, and *by your will they were created and have their being.*" Two key verses, Acts 17:24 and 28, tell us not only that God *"made* the world and everything in it," but that "In Him we live and move and *have our being.*"[39]

Geisler states the truth that God "is not simply the original Cause but also the continual Cause of its existence. He is Creator and Preserver; there would be no world, past or present, were it not for God." "He brought it from nothing in the past, and He also keeps it from returning to nothing in the present." "The Creator is the Cause, and the creature is the effect. An effect is not free-floating—it needs a cause as long as it is an effect, because if it ever ceased being an effect, then it would be uncaused. Only God the Creator is uncaused; hence, creation as an effect of God must be in a state of being effected at every moment of its existence. In brief, existence only comes one instant at a time; therefore, if one is a creature, then he is dependent on a Cause at each moment of His being."[40]

Frame also upholds the orthodox Christian doctrine of God's preservation of creation. He writes that "the world depends on God at every moment, not only at the moment of its origin." "At every moment, it is dependent on God, yet it operates out of its own God-given resources." "If God is to direct the creation toward his intended goal, he must, of course, preserve its existence until it reaches that goal. Preservation, therefore, is an aspect of God's government of the world and an expression of his lordship attribute of control." Pursuing his basic theology of God's lordship, Frame describes metaphysical preservation as "one of four ways in which God's work of preservation is evident in the world. *Metaphysical preservation* is God's act to keep the universe in being . . . . Without God, nothing would come into existence; that is the doctrine of creation. Without God, nothing would continue to exist; that is the doctrine of metaphysical preservation. The world continues to exist by God's permission. Were he to withdraw his permission, there would be no world." "To say that God metaphysically preserves the world is simply to say that the world is radically contingent. It depends on God for everything, and without his permission it could not continue to exist. To say this is merely to be consistent with our confession that the world is completely under the control of its sovereign Lord."[41]

God's Word and Wisdom. Original creation by God proceeded in an orderly fashion through the Word (*dabar, logos*) of God. As told in Genesis 1, "And God said" preceded each major stage, beginning with the creation of light, and continuing through the separation of the waters, the appearance of dry ground, vegetation, the lights of the heavenly bodies, the creatures of the waters and the birds, creatures of the land, and finally man in God's own image, male and female. "The Word spoken by God is not a mere sound but a power so great that the universe is thereby created and upheld." "The Word, which is spoken by God, proceeds from him, and is therefore distinct from him, is later on personified as Wisdom."[42] Job speaks of wisdom in terms of God's power, all-encompassing knowledge, law, and perfect ordering of creation: "for he views the ends of the earth and sees everything under the heavens. When he established the force of the wind and measured out the waters, when he made a decree for the rain and a path for the thunderstorm, then he saw *wisdom* and declared it; he confirmed it and tested it." Proverbs 8 and 3 then reveal more: the origin of Wisdom was in God, "from everlasting," and "before all things"; and "By wisdom the Lord laid the earth's foundations, by understanding he set the heavens in place; by his knowledge the deeps were divided, and the clouds let drop the dew." The excellence of wisdom is praised at length in Proverbs 8:22-30.[43] The lawful, regular order, structure, operation, and processes of created nature are indicated in these passages.

God's Word and Wisdom are identified in the New Testament as Christ. Christ the Creative Logos is not some abstract, impersonal, natural, or mechanical force or law, but "a living Being and the source of life; not a personification, but a Person and that Person divine."[44] In this sense, "Jesus is not to be interpreted by Logos; Logos is intelligible only as we think of Jesus."[45] Like the Father and the Holy Spirit He is God of infinite Being, Personality, Power, Life, and Wisdom, who will not tire or lose track of world-order, or run down entropically in sustaining creation. The revelation of Christ the Logos as Creator and structurer of the world, and as mediator and guarantor of human language, knowledge, and wisdom, as well as incarnate Redeemer, is the culmination of a tendency inherent in Christianity from the start. This revelation is in terms of the Word (*dabar*) and Wisdom (*hokmah*) of God in the Old Testament, and the *logos* and *sophia* of the New. All are designations for Christ, the eternally existent Son, and mediating Creator Word, Wisdom, Redeemer, Ruler, and Judge.[46]

Carl F. H. Henry emphasizes that Christ the Son and Logos is the express eternal Mind of God, his Being, Wisdom, Intelligence, and Archetypal Ideas at work in creating, forming, and structuring the entirety of nature, world, and cosmos. He is the "transcendent source of the orders and structures of being."[47] For Christian doctrine, as in the context of John, "The Logos is the eternal Reason or Mind of God."

Just as the eternal Logos (John 1:3) or the eternal Son (Col. 1:13-16, Heb. 1:2-3) is set forth in the New Testament as the divine agent in creation, so also the Logos is declared to be God's agent in all divine disclosure. In eternity past, before created reality existed, intelligible communication transpired even within the Godhead through the Logos. "In the beginning the Word was, and the Word was face to face with God, and the Word was God" (John 1:1, Montgomery). Greek philosophers at best represented reason as a principle immanent in man and/or the cosmos; the Bible declares the Word to be the personal organ and revelatory mediating agent of the transcendent God. The Johannine prologue affirms that the Logos functions both in a cosmic role (as creator-sustainer) and an epistemic role ("he is the true light," 1:9), as well as in a soteriological role; Hebrews 1:1-4 alludes to this same comprehensive activity.[48]

The Creator-Logos is the active personal, rational, and formal cause of world and cosmos. As the Logos of creation, Christ provides the archetypal ideas of creation from God the Father: through Him come the idea, reason, form, model, pattern, and unity, as well as life and purpose of the world and mankind. Without Him there would be no archetypal ideas, reason, universals, laws, causal connections, canons, models, and patterns—all of which were sought, praised, and emulated in different ways by ancient peoples in their arts. Without his work, cosmic order and operation would be non-existent, and nature at best would be uncreated and unreal, a flux of chaos arising from a void—as it has actually been evoked by Nietzsche, Heidegger, and Sartre, and has been increasingly depicted in twentieth-century art from Dada and Surrealism through Sartre's *Nausea*, Theater of the Absurd, novels of the absurd, and postmodern visual arts. In these ways it is Christ the creating and ordering "Logos who stands invisibly but identifiably as the true center of nature, history, ethics, philosophy, and religion."[49]

As Son and Mediator from God the Father, Christ the Living Word acts as the formal cause of all creation, creating and sustaining in all things the form according to the Idea or Archetype that He has in mind. He differs from

Aristotle's formal cause, however, by being the living, personal God, and not a passive, impersonal principle contained and limited by nature. Moreover, in sharp contrast to Aristotle's causes, He acts in fulfilling all other aspects of divine design and decrees for creation, redemption, and judgment. Christ came from His eternal Father, freely creating and ordering according to His Father's will. Divine idea and plan preceded the creation. "In a perfect manner, everything in this world has been made according to certain ideas existing in the Mind of God from all eternity. God, being Perfect Intelligence, must be, therefore, possessed of the models, ideas, or representations of all the things He wishes to call into the light of day. Every tree, every flower, every bird, every thing has had its spiritual model in the Divine Mind . . . . These ideas, which from our point of view are multiple but really are one in the Divine Mind and identical with his Being, are called Archetypal Ideas."[50]

Bavinck emphasizes the difference between modern meanings of the word "idea," and its former theological-metaphysical meaning. "Formerly an 'idea' was considered to be the pattern of a thing in the creative mind of God."[51] But with the increasing prevalence through modern [and postmodern] thought of antimetaphysical, antitheological premises, it has been reinterpreted in changing *human terms* to merely denote a concept or notion of the human mind, the result of abstract thinking, a concept of "pure reason," or something even less credible [e.g., see Descartes's notion of "idea", pp. 147-48]. Traditional Platonic and Christian theological uses of "idea" have been increasingly disparaged, attacked, and abandoned in modern thought and arts.

Bavinck writes that God "creates all things in accordance with the ideas which he himself has formed. The universe is God's masterpiece. God is the Architect and Maker of the entire universe. He is not an unconscious Creator; on the contrary, in all his works he is guided by wisdom, by his idea. Nevertheless there are also differences between God and the human artificer. God's ideas are absolutely original; they arise out of his own being, and are eternal and immutable; indeed, they are one with his own being. The ideas in God themselves constitute the 'essence of God' insofar as this is the pattern of created things and can be expressed and reflected in finite creatures. Every creature is a revelation of the Deity, and partakes of God's being. The character of this participation is not such that a creature is a modification of God's being or that it has in reality received into itself the divine essence, but every creature has its own essence because in its existence it is an ectype [image, likeness] of the divine essence."[52]

God's Archetypal Ideas are said by Thomas Aquinas to be present in things as "exemplars." Fulton J. Sheen has explained that "these Divine Archetypal Ideas reflected in things, as well as the very rational plan of their being, are called forms, as in the mind they are called ideas (and sometimes forms). Everything in the world has its form, which is the reason for its intelligibility, and makes it what it is. A tree is a tree in virtue of its form (not external shape, but internal participation or reflection of the Archetypal Ideas) and for that reason differs from a camel which has a different form." "Not only is God present in things as the Wisdom which planned them, but in the richness and variety of His Wisdom. Being infinite, His Wisdom reaches to the abyss of all things that are known and can be known. Quite naturally, no created thing could perfectly express the depth and variety of His knowledge, only an uncreated and single Word can express it, and that is the Logos or the Son. It was fitting that God became present by His Wisdom, not only in one thing, but in many. What one created thing failed to reveal, the other might disclose. Thus creation became like a great orchestra, with thousands of instruments blending their various notes, and yet all cooperating to produce the beautiful harmony in which Heaven and earth declare forth the Wisdom of their Omnipotent Creator."[53]

In the New Testament, all of these things are attributed to God's Word and Wisdom, the Logos, now specifically identified as Christ. Paul identifies the preexistent Christ as God's "own son," the "firstborn," by whom "all things were created," and says that since the creation of the world, "in him all things hold together." He links Christ with wisdom themes of the Old Testament by identifying Him as "wisdom from God," as "Christ the power and the wisdom of God," who was "the hidden wisdom" before the incarnation.[54] Christ is described by John as the "only begotten Son of God," and identified as the divine "word," the "logos," affirming that "all things were made through him," and adding that after creation "he was in the world." John also spoke of Christ the Logos as "the true light that gives light to every man." Jesus Christ Himself confirmed it: "I am the light of the world. Whoever follows me will never walk in darkness, but will have the light of life."[55]

Mankind and world have come into being from the Mind, Being, Will, and Power of God, powerfully expressed and enacted through Christ the divine Creator-Logos. God's Mind is the very fount of truth, reason, and logic, the source of all meaning and purpose in mankind and the world. His Mind is the ultimate source of the forms and identities of all things that exist. The only reason the world is an orderly, related cosmos instead of nothing, or chaos, and amenable to reason at all, is that the rational will of the Creator is realized in it. With this in mind we can understand why worldviews that reject the Personal Creator tend to see the world as irrational and/or chaotic.

The universe, according to Christian faith, does not arise by a timeless necessity from an impersonal Logos. However, it is only through him who is the Logos that the will of the Creator has been actualized in creation. All things, we are told, were made through the Logos (Jn. 1:3). Hence the will of the Creator is an intelligent will and the world he has made is a world amenable to reason: a cosmos, not a chaos . . . . The theologian, therefore, should gladly acknowledge the insights into the nature of this world that philosophy and science have afforded . . . . The doctrine that all things were created through the Logos implies that the creation has a structure that is ordered and accessible to the mind through rational analysis. While it is only by observation that we can learn what the world is like in particular, we can know a priori that it will reflect the intelligent will (wisdom) of its Maker . . . . In fact, the Christian doctrine of creation helps one understand why mathematics, a product of pure intellect, applies so universally in the natural order . . . . To acknowledge the rational character of the natural order is not to affirm that the universe will finally prove to be self-explanatory. Such a conclusion would be the denial of the doctrine of creation. In fact, the more the universe is understood, the more mysterious it becomes.[56]

If God created the universe, nothing exists but that which was created by Him. This means that not only do all things owe their *existence* totally to Him, but that *all the ideas, forms, structures, patterns, and types of existing natural things have their only origin and source in God*, making them essentially dependent upon Him. These are the understandings of nature's being, law, and order, and the broader meanings of Christ as the Word and Wisdom of God, as described in the Old and New Testament. In this way one can speak of the *mind* and *wisdom* of God, and of the *ideas* of God, as the *intelligible world* from which all created things have come.

The Teachings of Augustine and Aquinas. Augustine (354-430), Church Father and one of the greatest of early Christian intellects, developed concepts of an intelligible world related to the thought of Plato, Philo, Plotinus, and Porphyry, interpreting them in the light of Johannine and other scriptural revelations about Christ, Logos, and Wisdom. For him the intelligible world is "the eternal and unchangeable reason (*rationem*) by which He [God] made the world." And the reason by which God made the world is within Him. Thus, the "Platonic ideas in their totality, described by the Philonic and Plotinian term 'intelligible world' are taken to exist *only as thoughts of God* . . . . This 'intelligible world' is identified with 'that eternal and unchangeable reason (*ratio*) by which [God] made the world,' that is to say, it is identified with the Logos who 'was with God' and who 'was God' and by whom 'all things were made.' Thus the Platonic intelligible world of ideas and the Christian Logos are identified and both of them are said to be in God."[57] Augustine wrote: "Ideas are the primary forms, or the permanent and immutable reasons of real things, and they are not themselves formed; so they are, as a consequence, eternal and ever the same in themselves, and they are contained in the divine intelligence." Everything that comes into being and goes out of it is "formed in accord with them." Thus, the ideas behind creation are divine, eternal, and unchanging, and are in the divine mind, so that God did not look to any paradigm outside Himself.[58] For Augustine the existence of such an intelligible world and its ideas is implied in the Christian belief in the Logos: "For the world which [Plato] called by the name 'intelligible' is that eternal and unchangeable reason (*rationem*) by which He [God] made the world. Any man who denies that such a reason exists will find himself compelled to say either that God made what He made without reason or that He did not know what He made either while He made it or before He made it . . . ."[59]

Augustine indicates that the Platonic intelligible ideas on which the universe is modeled exist in the "eternal intelligence" of God, not independently.[60] He says that although "Plato was the first to describe his pattern of things by the term ideas, the existence of such patterns was known before him" by "sages" of "other nations," (no doubt including Moses and the prophets). Augustine identifies these patterns by the term *rationes*, "reasons," which stands for the Greek term *logoi*, rather than the Latinized Greek term *ideae* or its Latin equivalents *formae* or *species*. He thus emphasizes that creation is the work of divine reason and intelligence. He defines the ideas as "certain principal forms or certain fixed and immutable reasons of things, which have not been formed and hence are eternal and always in the same state of existence, and are contained in the divine intelligence."[61] And for Augustine the created universe "is organized entirely on the model of the divine ideas. Its entire order, form, and productivity come from them, so that the fundamental tie linking the world to God is a relationship of similarity." Without this relationship "the universe would immediately cease to be intelligible and even to exist."[62]

Much like Augustine on these matters, and often quoting him, Thomas Aquinas (1225-1274) maintains conceptions of ideas in the mind of God, in the Word (Logos) generated by Him, and serving as the innermost basis of existence of all created things: "God is above all things by the excellence of His nature; nevertheless, He is in all things as the cause of the being of all things." "God is in all things; not, indeed, as part of their essence, nor as an accident; but as an agent is present to that upon which it works." Since God is the very agent of a thing's being, He is innermost in all things.[63] "Augustine says (*De Trin.* vii), 'In God to be is the same as to be wise. But to be wise is the same thing as to understand. Therefore in God to be is the same thing as to understand. But God's existence is His substance, . . . therefore the act of God's intellect is His substance'." Being, wisdom, intellect, and understanding are thus the very essence and substance of God. "Word" (Logos) "is the proper name of the person of the Son. For it signifies an emanation of the intellect: and the person Who proceeds in God, by way of emanation of the intellect, is called the Son; and this procession is called generation." In God "*to be* and *to understand* are one and the same: hence the Word of God is not an accident in Him, or an effect of His; but belongs to His very nature." "To be intelligent belongs to the Son, in the same way as it belongs to Him to be God, since to understand is said of God essentially." "Because God by one act understands Himself and all things, His one only Word is expressive not only of the Father, but of all creatures."[64]

"The knowledge of God is the cause of things. For the knowledge of God is to all creatures what the knowledge of the artificer is to things made by his art." "The knowledge of the artificer is the cause of the things made by his art from the fact that the artificer works by his intellect. Hence the form of the intellect must be the principle of action." "God causes things by His intellect, since His being is His act of understanding; and hence His knowledge must be the cause of things, in so far as His will is joined to it." "It is necessary to suppose ideas in the divine mind. For the Greek word *Idea* is in Latin *Forma*. Hence by ideas are understood the forms of things, existing apart from the things themselves." "As then the world was not made by chance, but by God acting by His intellect . . . . there must exist in the divine mind a form to the likeness of which the world was made." An idea in God is not only "identical with His essence," but "is the principle of knowing and operating." Aquinas approvingly quotes Augustine's statement that "Ideas are certain principal forms, or permanent and immutable types of things, they themselves not being formed. Thus they are eternal, and existing always in the same manner, as being contained in the divine intelligence." While they "neither come into being nor decay, yet we say that in accordance with them everything is formed that can arise or decay, and all that actually does so." It is evident, as Aquinas says, that "things made by nature receive determinate forms. This determination of forms must be reduced to the divine wisdom as its first principle, for divine wisdom devised the order of the universe, which order consists in the variety of things. And therefore we must say that in the divine wisdom are the types of all things, which types we have called ideas—i.e., exemplar forms existing in the divine mind."[65]

Aquinas does not begin his philosophy with and base it on a theory of knowledge, as modern post-Cartesian and Kantian thought does. Instead, he bases it on the reality of *being* (*esse*), which in his metaphysical terms, is the reality of God—of God the Supreme Being, and the contingent reality of all beings created by God. His theory of knowledge is secondary to belief in Being and beings, act and potency, form and matter. Because God is ultimate reality and truth, all created beings are real, have real existence, and can be apprehended in knowledge. Aquinas "set being at the very core of his metaphysical system. His metaphysical inquiry always centers around being:

it starts from the intuition of the supreme value of being; then it moves on to discover the existence of being itself, and it concludes with the explanation of the participation of the perfection of being by creatures."[66]

In Thomistic thought being is "that whose act is to exist." God is infinite, unlimited *esse*. *Esse* is "the highest of all perfections," "unlimited perfection." It is "more fundamental and perfect than the very fine perfections of life, knowledge, justice and beauty: it is what counts most in every thing, since it is the principle that confers reality to a thing: *esse est actus entis*" (being is the act of the thing). In God, *esse* is "the receptacle of all perfections." The unique dispenser of *esse* is God: "it is He who gives being (*esse*) to creatures." The absolute being of God is *esse* itself—the *esse divinum*. Thus, "*esse* constitutes the very essence of God." The divine being is singular and exclusive—"the only one in which an identity between *esse* and essence takes place: 'Since only in God is his being (*esse*) the same as his quidiity' [nature, essence]." *Esse* is the essence of God, but not of creatures. With any creature *esse* does not constitute its essence, or better, its essence is not *esse*. Utterly dependent upon God for its being, its degree of *esse* is finite, contingent, and perishable. *Esse* "belongs to creatures only by participation." There is a hierarchy of degrees of *esse*: (1) *esse absolutum*—the divine being, with no limitation at all; (2) *esse* limited only by form—in angelic creatures, whose essence is pure form; and (3) *esse* in creatures whose *essence* is both *matter* and *form*—as in human beings, animals, plants. All creatures are composed of two elements, *esse* and essence. The essence is the individual nature or quiddity, that which restricts and limits *esse* in particular things.[67]

Being is the first *transcendental* in Thomistic thought, and the first of all concepts, necessarily implied in all others. Being-as-such, or *that which is*, is prior to that which is material, changeable, quantifiable, or perceptible. Being-as-such is immaterial. Being is "the primary and most fundamental object of thought, the object without which no other object can be thought." Relative to the intellect and knowledge, "being alone makes anything intelligible; being alone can affect the intellect; being is the proper object of the intellect, the only stuff on which it feeds." *Essence* is also a transcendental. It indicates the definite nature of a thing: "whatever is is some definite thing." It has an essence. This is a universal predication. The term *res* is used to indicate the thing as a definite individual. *Res* expresses the quiddity (*quod quid est*) or essence of a being, while *ens* expresses its very act of being.

The other Thomistic transcendentals or transcendental attributes of being—the three classic ones, the one, the true, the good—are "not divisions of being, but transcend all divisions." Each is equivalent to being itself. *Unity* (*unum*) or indivision is a primary transcendental. Every being is said to be *one* insofar as it is undivided in itself. "Thus, a man has an essence (*res*), he is undivided in Himself (*unum*); and he is distinct from anything else (*aliquid*)." "Every being is divided off from, or is not, something else (*aliud quid*)." A man cannot become a shark or a bird, as Lautréamont and the Surrealists thought. *Truth*, defined as "the conformity of being and intellect," follows unity as a transcendental. The cognitive power is "that by which the soul knows being, and since by its intellect the soul is capable of apprehending being as such, every being, in so far as it is being, is conformed to the intellect. This conformity of being to the intellect is called truth; and consequently, every being, inasmuch as it is related to intellect, is true (*verum*)." The third classic transcendental is *good*. "Being in so far as it is desirable is called good (*bonum*), for 'the good is what all things desire,' as Aristotle says." Desire is "the act of appetite, and consequently it is by virtue of its relation to appetite that anything is good."[68]

Besides the transcendental modes, the Thomistic "predicaments" (cf. predication), are his "categories," the essential divisions or highest genera of being. *Substance* is the most important of these, signifying the subject as to its essence. Substance is the subject of the accidents, the remaining nine predicaments.[69] These understandings of being, with its transcendentals and categories, are core aspects of the realism of Thomistic metaphysics. They express his most fundamental understandings of reality. While much more developed than commonsense realism, they remain essentially compatible with it.

The traditional understanding of God's creation of all things according to divine ideas serving as exemplars is a logical and powerful one still upheld by some today. Linda Zagzebski writes of exemplarism as "a brilliant attempt to explain both how the creation comes to be and how God knows created things."

Exemplarism is the theory that the ideas of all possible created beings exist eternally in God's mind and act as models or exemplars for those among them that God chooses to create. The explanation of how it comes to be that these ideas are in God's mind is very interesting. The Father knows himself and this act of knowledge is the perfect image of himself. It is the Word, the second Person of the Trinity. As proceeding from the Father, the Son is divine, and as representing the Father, all that the Father can effect is expressed in the Son. If anyone could know the Word he would know all objects, says Bonaventure. All that the Father could create, then, is represented in the Son; that is, all possible beings represent ideas contained in the Son. These ideas are not only of all possible individuals, but also of universals. They are infinite in number since they are the infinitely many ways the Father can be imperfectly imitated.[70]

"The view that exemplars are ideas of the ways in which God's essence can be mirrored externally links God's knowledge of himself to finite beings in a way that shows how the creation is both nonarbitrary and non-necessitated. Exemplarism, then, has great explanatory force in the understanding of the creation." Zagzebski holds that each individual person or thing has "a set of properties that is essential to it," an "individual essence composed of purely qualitative properties." "There are then individual qualitative essences (IQEs)." She then identifies exemplars in the traditional theory with IQEs. "Since these essences include only purely conceptual properties, they are knowable prior to their exemplification in an actual being . . . . And they are sufficient to differentiate one possible object from another. So there is no problem about God having the idea of an object prior to its becoming actual." Since there are an infinite number of exemplars or IQEs in the mind of God, he chooses those he wishes to exemplify. "There are no possible but nonactual individuals, but there are unexemplified IQEs."

One of the most interesting features of exemplars is the way in which they connect God's essence with that of creatures. Each created thing imitates the divine essence, but no created thing does so fully. If it did, there would be only one such imitation. There is, in fact, one image of the Father that does perfectly imitate him, and that is the Son. There are infinitely many ways, though, of imperfectly imitating him, and this is what we and all other possible creatures do. According to Aquinas, God's essence is the intelligible character of each and every possible being. It is the proper intelligible character of every creature in that each thing imitates the divine essence in a different way, and it is the common intelligible character of every creature in that each imitates the same divine essence. The exemplar of a thing is just what makes it intelligible. It is each object's way of imitating the divine essence. The conceptual or intelligible character of the exemplar is crucial for the theory, then, and it should be apparent that an individual qualitative essence does have such a character.[71]

In His role as Creator-Logos, Christ is the divine mediative and executive Creator of everything that exists. All things are made by the Father through Him, and without Him nothing is made or exists. In Him is the eternal Being, Life, Mind, Ideas, and Power of the Father, and He gives being, life, mind, ideas, and power to the human individuals He creates. He is not simply the instrumental cause of all things for the Father, but is fully God and Creator with the Father and the Holy Spirit. As Creator-Logos He acts in part as the divine, personal, formal cause of creation, since He mediates and executes the form, order, and purpose of creation. He is the eternal Word, Wisdom, and Law of the Old Testament, as well as Messiah, and the Word (Logos), Wisdom, and Truth of the New, and the Redeemer and post-incarnate Ruler of the universe and universal Judge. As divine Creator-

Logos, Christ mediates and executes the idea, plan, decree, design, form, law, order structure, and pattern of creation. Because He was, is, and will be Creator, He is the Redeeming Creator of new life, and Creator and Ruler of the new heavenly world to come. He acts as the mediating formal cause of the wisdom, reason, and intelligence in creation, which have their ultimate origin in the Father who is in Him and in whom He is. All law, order, form, pattern, and structure in the natural world are due to His execution of the Father's divine idea, plan, and will for creation, and without Him none exists. All truth, wisdom, reason, logic, and knowledge in the world are due to His creative activities, fulfilling His Father's idea, plan, and will, and without Him none exists.

Modern Disbelief. The more belief in God has declined in the modern world, the more philosophies of change and flux (becoming) have risen to dominance. For over fifteen centuries the concept of Being was paramount in classical philosophy. For around twenty centuries belief in God as the ultimate source of life and being has been central to biblical teachings and traditional Christian theology. It has only come into disrepute in modern thought and arts, increasingly since the "Age of Reason" (seventeenth century) the "Enlightenment" (eighteenth century). These developments served as the basic origins of "modern" thought and arts by raising serious doubts and objections, among other things, to Christian teachings of God, and classical teachings of being and logos. From the Enlightenment into the twentieth century, concepts of being and logos have been progressively deemphasized, criticized, and redefined, while the opposite notions of "becoming," change, and flux have been increasingly elevated. As a result, the twentieth century has been identified as an age of "triumph of becoming."[72]

In one of the great books of the twentieth century (although without a specifically Christian basis), historian Franklin L. Baumer has traced in detail the increasing "loss of belief in transcendence" and "eclipse of God" in the modern world, and the progressive rise of philosophies of becoming. He finds in the seventeenth century still a sense of the prevalence of "being over becoming." With the eighteenth century there is some degree of balance of "being and becoming." By the nineteenth century there is a dominance of "becoming over being." And by the twentieth century he documents "the triumph of becoming."[73] By the 1880s Nietzsche became the prime figure to declare in the strongest terms the falsity and evils of concepts of God and Being. Leading twentieth-century modern philosophers—Husserl, Heidegger, Wittgenstein, and Sartre—have been shaped by these radical modern directions, and have taken philosophical positions essentially opposed to the Christian understanding of God as Being, Logos, and ground of existing things, and as the crucial link between self and world. Modern arts from Cubism (c. 1907-1920) on have increasingly emphasized becoming, change, and flux. Dada art (c. 1915-1920) expressed a radical Nietzschean skepticism concerning Being, God, truth, and knowledge. Dadaists essentially treated the world and man in radical flux, with no essential reality or truth, and did things to art that even Nietzsche would have deplored. Postmodern philosophies and art since around 1970 have given full place to becoming or change, and have sought to attack and "deconstruct" concepts of Being, God, and Logos, which they consider false, misleading, and destructive.

Without Being, however, there could be no God. If God exists, He is Personal Being, the eternal, unchanging, Living One, the essential and continuing source and ground of all existence and life, and the Incomparable Intelligence whose ideas are essential to all existing things. Only God could possibly be Ultimate Personal Being and Life. In comparison to world religious beliefs, only the Bible and Christian tradition testify to such a Triune Creative God. In comparison, Platonic and Neo-Platonic philosophies, which bear certain key resemblances, are revealed as abstract thought constructions with numerous faults. If God as Being did not exist, nothing would exist. Postmodernists find that since, in their view, neither God nor Being exists, all is change and flux; there is no universal truth, no universals, essences, reason, or lasting knowledge. But if God did not exist, there would be no human beings and no change and flux to know. Nothing would exist. Many other consequences flow from such an absence, including the lack of any eternal, transcendental ground for self, world, truth, logic, morality, and historical purpose (much explored by Nietzsche and subsequent twentieth-century followers, and in the arts of Dada and Postmodernism). The next chapter will take up the question of truth and knowledge relative to the eternal Being or non-existence of God. Subsequent ones will deal with the questions of love, morality, evil, and historical purpose.

Chapter Five

God the Foundation of Truth, Knowledge, and Wisdom

The metaphysical ultimacy of God's Personal Spiritual Being intrinsically involves the ultimacy of his truth, indivisible from his Being.

God *must* exist if there is to be any meaning to the world. In a biblical worldview, God is the basis for all reality, and therefore for all rationality, truth, goodness, and beauty.[1]

Everything in this world is true inasmuch as it corresponds with the idea that God had in mind in making it. In this sense there is absolute truth.[2]

God as the Foundation of Truth. Just as God is the Supreme Being who is the ground of all being, so He is the Supreme Truth who is the ground of all truth, reason, logic, and knowledge. All that is true has its ultimate source in the Person, Mind, and Wisdom of God, for He knows all things and determines all that is true. God not only creates the being of all existing things in the universe, He establishes the very structures of truth, rationality, and logic in creation and in the human mind. It is through these structures that we are able to know anything, instead of chaos and confusion, or more precisely, nothing at all.

The Truth of God in the metaphysical sense must be fully united with His Absolute Being. Without Absolute Being there would be no real ground for Absolute Truth. In such a hypothetical case, Truth would have no true being. Truth cannot *be* without *Being.* Conversely, *Being* cannot be *true* without *Truth*: the existence of Being would not be *true.* And since the Supreme Being would be incomprehensibly *limited* without Truth, God would not exist without Absolute Truth. Absolute Being and Truth are intimately connected. Without God the Supreme Being, there can be no absolute truth. And without absolute truth, all we know would be relative, and ultimately meaningless and purposeless. But even prior to such a case, without the Supreme Being of Truth who not only creates all things, but creates the intelligible, interrelated ideas, forms, and codes of all things, there would be no *possibility* of truth or knowledge at all. The existence of the Supreme Being is necessary for all these forms and patterns, and for any knowledge of truth at all. (So by denying God, Modernism-Postmodernism denies truth.)

Logically elucidating the biblical teaching that not only is truth *in* God, but God Himself *is* truth, Thomas Aquinas says that *the true* and *being* are "convertible terms." This means that truth is one of the transcendentals, coequal with being, the good, unity, and the beautiful: "the divine substance is truth itself"; "being is included in the idea of the true"; "being cannot be understood, unless being is intelligible." Etienne Gilson explains that for Aquinas, God "Himself is His own act of being and of understanding. In this perfect coincidence of a being, of its knowledge, and of the object of its knowledge, is found the identity of absolute being with its own truth."[3] The belief is expressed in another way by Augustus Strong: "God's being and God's knowledge eternally conform to each other." Jesus' claim in John 14:6, "I am . . . the truth," refers to his "truth of being, not merely truth of expression." God's truth is ultimately the conformity of his essence with his intellect. Since He knows all things, and self-knowing is identical with his being, God is Absolute Truth. His Absolute Truth is his knowledge that corresponds to his being, and his being that corresponds to his knowledge.[4] **Understood in this light, denial of the existence of absolute truth, as in the widespread relativism today, and in Postmodernism, involves denial of the Supreme Being of God.** Relativism holds that there is no absolute truth: one religion, belief, or viewpoint is as good as another; knowledge is only relative to a person, culture, or the time. In philosophy and the arts, this means that there is no Supreme God who is the source of eternal truth and knowledge.

Truth in knowledge of things or of states of existence involves the true correspondence of one's knowledge with the actual nature of the thing or state. But it is the Creator God who has created the actual natures of all things and set the conditions for all existing states. God established the actual forms, patterns, laws, and codes that determine the nature of all things. Thus, in order to accurately know those things, our knowledge must not only conform to the things, but to the ideas or forms God employed to create them.

In his *Doctrine of God*, John Frame expresses the biblical and classical Christian teaching that "God *must* exist if there is to be any meaning to the world. In a biblical worldview, God is the basis for all reality, and therefore for all rationality, truth, goodness, and beauty. Logic itself is based on his nature, and the logical structure of the world and the human mind is based on the fact that God's rationality, his wisdom, is reflected in creation. Without him, therefore, we could not even speak rationally. Therefore, we must presuppose his existence in all rational thought and action . . . . God's existence is necessary to the very existence of logic, for he is the very source of logical truth . . . . For human knowledge to be possible, certain metaphysical conditions (including the existence of God) must be satisfied. We have the option, of course, of denying that human knowledge is possible. But such radical skepticism cannot be advanced in a rational view. On any rational view of the matter, therefore, God exists, and exists necessarily."[5]

Frame emphasizes the importance of the biblical teaching that God is truth and expresses truth: "your word is truth" (John 17:17); "Your words are true" (2 Samuel 7:28); "the word of the Lord in your mouth *is* the truth" (1 Kings 17:24); "Your law is truth" (Psalm 119:142); "Your commandments are truth" (Psalm 119:151). The essential meaning is, as Frame writes, that "truth is the internal standard that governs God's speech." "Like goodness and righteousness, . . . truth is what God is, and therefore what he says. There is no higher standard than God against which his truth may be measured." Those who have abandoned God's natural revelation in creation and in their own minds, have "exchanged the truth of God for the lie" (Romans 1:25). God does not only *reveal* truth, He *is* the Truth. The Bible associates truth with God's essential nature—this is absolute, metaphysical truth. For Thomas Aquinas "being, unity, truth, beauty, and goodness . . . are all ultimately the same, both in God and in the creation."[6] The metaphysical ultimacy of God's Personal Spiritual Being intrinsically involves the metaphysical ultimacy of His Truth, indivisible from His Being.

Absolute metaphysical truth is the attribute not only of God the Father, but of the second Person of the Trinity, Jesus Christ, and of the third Person, the Holy Spirit. Several verses in the book of John confirm this. Jesus stated His eternal Being: "before Abraham was, I AM" (8:58); and His divine oneness and equality with God the Father: "I and my Father are one" (10:30); "I am in the Father and the Father in Me" (14:11); "All things that the Father has are Mine" (16:15). And He confirmed His absolute Truth with a saying to His disciples that can be taken as a summary of the gospel, and the central message of Christianity: "I am the way, the truth, and the life. No one comes to the Father except through me" (14:6). Jesus Christ "does not simply show the way; He is *the* Way. He does not simply reveal truth, He is *the* Truth. He does not simply give life, He is *the* Life."[7] That is also the closely related meaning of 12:46: "I have come as a light into the world, that whoever believes in Me should not abide in darkness." His "light" is His Truth, which brings real knowledge of ultimate truth to the believer, and deliverance from the darkness of error, deception, and evil.

The Person of the Holy Spirit is equal in Being and Truth with the Father and the Son. Thus, "the Spirit is truth" (I John 5:6). In the gospel of John, Jesus spoke often of the Spirit of "truth" as the "Helper" who would come after him: "when the Helper comes, whom I shall send to you from the Father, the Spirit of truth who proceeds from the Father, He will testify of Me" (15:26). Jesus said that, for believers, the invisible Spirit "dwells with you and will be in you" (14:17, 23); and He would lead the disciples and future believers in knowledge of truth: "He will teach you all things, and bring to your remembrance all things that I said to you." "When He, the Spirit of truth, has come, He will guide you into all truth (16:13). The Holy Spirit, who had worked in many ways in earlier times, came to begin this work at Pentecost, after the death and resurrection of Christ (Acts 2:1-4). The Spirit works in many ways—in convicting, regenerating, and cleansing the sinner, and in guiding, teaching, inspiring, and empowering the believer. In earlier times He had inspired the prophets and writers of Scriptures. He guides the believer internally to true belief and knowledge of God. "His presence in the believer constitutes a seal, a guarantee of salvation"[8] (Ephesians 1:13).

The Truth of Scripture. If the universe has a beginning, and that beginning can only be by a Creator who is the Supreme Being, and the Creator of humankind, then divine revelations from the invisible, transcendent Creator are necessary for humans to know him, his laws, and his purposes in fuller measure. Besides God's self-revelation within each person, in created nature, in the physical life and acts of Jesus Christ, and in the work of the Holy Spirit, there is another crucially important manifestation of God's truth available to humankind. As one would logically think, if God wanted to reveal Himself to more and more people down through the centuries, in more extensive ways and explicit terms, He would no doubt choose to provide written documents. The authenticity of these documents would depend on several things. They would not be written by only one person at one particular time, but would be recorded during many centuries by actual living persons who were key witnesses to the unfolding of God's acts and revelations to mankind in history. They would not be written exclusively from the limited knowledge and viewpoints of these persons (although those would be real factors), but would have their essential source in God Himself. God would be the necessary source, the *divine inspiration* for such writings directly through each writer. To be fully truthful, as God Himself is fully and necessarily truthful, the writings would have to originate with God, and faithfully and exactly record His messages.

And it is true that the Bible and traditional Christian theology maintain that the Bible is the Word of God in the form of written Scripture. It is divinely inspired, or more precisely, "God-breathed." There are many claims in the Bible, supported for centuries by Christian tradition, that all the words of Scripture are God's words in written form. Jesus spoke of the written word of Scripture as that which "comes out of the mouth of God" (Matthew 4:4). Paul says in 2 Timothy 3:16 that "All Scripture is God-breathed" [Greek, *theopneustos*], indicating God's direct, powerful, and pervasive involvement in the writings, making them fully authoritative and infallible. "God-breathed" or "breathed-out by God" is to be understood as a metaphor for God speaking the words of Scripture:[9] the words of Scripture are from God Himself. The logical conclusion is that "Since the words of the Bible are God's words, and since God cannot lie or speak falsely, . . . there is no untruthfulness or error in any part of the words of the Scripture."[10] The penetrating power of Scripture is indicated in Hebrews 4:12: "For the word of God is living and active. Sharper than any double-edged sword."

According to 2 Peter 1:20, "no prophecy of Scripture is of any private interpretation, for prophecy never came by the will of man, but holy men of God spoke as they were moved by the Holy Spirit." The words of Scripture are not set forth simply by the minds of the men who wrote them; they are *inspired* or *breathed* through the human writers by the Holy Spirit, who conveys the message of God the Father. As Geisler says, it is not just God's message set in men's words: "the very choice of words was from God." "If God cannot err and the Bible is the Word of God, then it follows necessarily that the Bible cannot err."[11] But it is also in the light and understanding that comes through the Holy Spirit that the writings must be received and understood.[12] Although the Bible possesses directness, clarity, power, and amazing interconnectedness through its sixty-six books, it can be seriously misunderstood, and frequently is, by anyone who does not read it in the light of the Holy Spirit. (We will see in the next chapter how a great modern philosopher, Hegel, completely misinterpreted the essential message of the Bible. There are many such examples.)

Since God is holy, and the words and message of the Bible are from God, the Bible is also holy. Holy means pure, righteous, true, perfectly good, and sacred. As the word of God, the Bible is like God because it is unlike anything else in its sacredness, perfect truthfulness, and its teaching of absolute truth and moral uprightness. It is "set apart from other things, to be sacred, to be exalted . . . . God's Word is not only holy itself, but it is able to make us holy. Jesus prayed, 'Sanctify them by the truth; your word is truth' (John 17:17) . . . . The Bible is set apart above all other books in the world, since it alone is able to save (Romans 1:16; Peter 1:23) and sanctify."[13] Jesus spoke of the Scriptures not simply as "true," but as "truth." Since "God's Word is itself *truth*, . . . the ultimate definition of what is true and what is not true," it is proper to think of the Bible as "the final standard of truth."[14]

In one important sense "it can be argued that the Bible is necessary for certain knowledge about anything." Often in daily life, as well as in scientific knowledge, some new "fact" can turn up that "disproves" previous understandings. No doubt no one, whether scientist, philosopher, historian, theologian, or ordinary person, would claim to know all facts about everything. Theologian Wayne Grudem poses this question: "If we do not know *all* facts in the universe, past, present, and future, how can we ever attain *certainty* that we have correct information about any one fact?" However, "God knows all facts that ever have been or ever will be. And this God who is omniscient (all-knowing) has absolutely certain knowledge: there can never be any fact that he does not already know; thus, there can never be any fact that would prove that something God thinks is actually false."[15]

Many have tried to find errors or self-contradictions in the Bible. Recently a confident young religion professor spoke on TV claiming such a clear self-contradiction in the Bible about the killer of the giant Goliath: while the young David is said to kill him in 1 Samuel 17: 48-51, the professor said that a later verse [2 Samuel 21:19] contradicted this by telling that Elhanan killed Goliath. The professor did not mention, however, that an early copiest had misread and miscopied the text which originally said that Elhanan killed "Lahmi the brother of Goliath." The latter meaning is confirmed in 1 Chronicles 20:5-8, with the further mention that Jonathan killed a third giant.[16] There are many misunderstandings and misinterpretations of the Bible, however. Just to mention two: the Bible does not say that the Earth was created in 4004 BC (there are gaps in genealogies); it does not teach as a scientific fact that the sun goes around the Earth (but only gives a description of appearances from a human viewpoint).[17]

There are a number of difficult questions about certain passages. The precise meaning of the "six days" of creation is still much debated, and no universally accepted answer has been achieved. Interpretations differ about who Adam and Eve were.[18] These are questions that seem to relate to historical and scientific knowledge. But despite our desire to know, and God's knowledge of everything, the Bible does not claim to give all answers to all possible questions, or to provide all knowledge about everything. What it does present is immense, authoritative, and trustworthy. Most importantly, it provides the ultimate answers to the big questions in human life, and gives reliable teachings about what we need, how to live, and what to expect in the future. In these and many ways the Bible is truth—divine, theological, and metaphysical truth.

Metaphysical truth, as theologian John Murray has written, denotes what is absolute, ultimate, and eternal: "It is the absolute as contrasted with the relative, the ultimate as contrasted with the derived, the eternal as contrasted with the temporal, the permanent as contrasted with the temporary, the complete in contrast with the partial, the substantial in contrast with the shadowy."[19] The teaching of God's absolute Truth has been at the heart of biblical meaning and Christian theology through the centuries. There is absolute truth! It rests ultimately in God. God is Living, Personal Being and Truth—these truths are eternal and inseparable. The Bible and classic Christian theology make it clear that absolute Truth exists and that knowledge of truth is possible and actual in human life.

Rational Mind, Forms, Ideas, Order, and Knowledge. The divine creation of the being and integrity of things includes the establishment of their rational order, structure, pattern, and intelligibility. Christ the Logos is the active agent, the living formal cause, in the structuring of the world, so that it is characterized by rational, intelligible order rather than irrationality, unintelligibility, formlessness, or chaos. The work of the Logos makes possible the ideas and categories in human minds, and their correspondence with forms and structures of the created world. Rational ideas of the human mind can correspond with rational forms of things because they all have the same divine source. This makes possible the truth function and sense of words—to conceptually link mind and ideas with specific objects and events. Thus the work of the Logos makes possible the representational accuracy and fidelity of words. In these ways too Christ is the Ruler of the universe—the Creator and Revealer of universal rational structures, faithful correspondences, and meanings. To deny the Logos is to fall into the hole of chaos with Nietsche.

"All Truth is God's Truth,"[20] and eternally so, since Christ the Logos is the eternal, unchanging, unifying center of creation from the beginning, and of all human knowledge, language, and art. He is truth in creating ideas, forms, and structures in nature, and making possible those of the human mind, which correspond with the Archetypal Ideas of God the Father; and in the highest sense He is the living Truth itself, being the true *image of God*, essentially embodying, reflecting, and corresponding in perfect unity to the Being, Mind, and Power of the Father. Christ the Logos mediates and links the eternal Mind and Truth of God with the faithful believer, God's general revelational truth with rational humans, and rational, knowing mind with rationally structured nature. He is the center of truth, the structurer and mediator of all existing truth, and the living Truth itself. All truth that humanity knows corresponds with logos-structured truth in nature, and with eternal ideas in the Mind of

God. Human wisdom must include the harmonious spiritual, mental, and physical reception through some degree of belief or faith in self, world, and God, of these unified aspects of truth.

Pagan and non-Christian societies have not failed to appropriate many aspects of general knowledge, truth, wisdom, and skill in everyday life and culture from the endless wealth of God's revelation in created nature, mind, and conscience. The history of art and culture bears witness. Much knowledge, truth, wisdom, beauty, and skill runs through the history of culture from prehistory through ancient Egypt, Greece, Rome, the Middle Ages, and even within the modern culture of revolt against God. The failure that characterizes them is not total ignorance and incapability, but the ultimate foolishness of refusing to believe in the living Reality and Truth of the one Creator God and His revelation. Paul himself was well educated and knowledgeable; he highly valued mind and reason. Thus he did not intend to suggest in I Corinthians 3:19 and 1:20 that all human wisdom and knowledge are foolish in themselves.[21] They only become so when people *reject* God's revelation, and take their own differing thoughts and beliefs as truth or "wisdom of this world" instead. To call all knowledge foolishness would be to label as foolish the God who is omniscient, and Christ who is the Truth and light of all illumination and knowledge. All true knowledge and wisdom is good; it is *false* knowledge, or error, that is foolish—and that is not real knowledge at all. Even Christian tradition has at times dismissed genuine truth in non-Christian cultures or individuals in the effort to cast out all error and paganism. And at other times it has appropriated error. But the task is by no means simple or easy, and is properly guarded.

Non-Christian truth and error in knowledge of aspects of God's natural revelation from the beginnings can be seen throughout human cultural history. This shows the universality and power of God's general revelation, the extensive human knowledge and utilization of it, and the wrongful rejection of its ultimate content, resulting in distortions and errors. Any real truth should not be overlooked. And when Hebrews and Christians have conveyed aspects of God's revealed truth at a time later than another culture, it does not mean that they simply appropriated it in a derivative, naturalistic sense, as both some supporters and detractors have claimed. Since God's general revelation has been available in creation *from the beginning*, many aspects of it have been recognized and utilized outside Hebrew and Christian societies from the beginning, both in truth and in error. Examples within worldwide pagan and non-Christian religions can be seen in the passionate and intelligent response to nature, worship of limited creator gods, the flood, many triadic deities (but not the Trinitarian God), salvific divine deaths and resurrections, gods of wisdom, epiphanies, belief in life after death, spiritual wonders and miracles, divine models and patterns for art and life, literature of quest for truth, salvation, and self-perfection, and the scrupulous quest for perfection of design, form, law and order in society and in the arts and sciences. All human society and culture constantly testify to the Reality and Truth of God, either positively or negatively, in truth or in willful error and foolishness.

Examples of development of wisdom, knowledge, law, and order are widespread throughout ancient cultures, especially prominent from Egyptian through classical Greco-Roman civilization. Egyptian art is amazing for its very high sense of order—structured in clear, geometric forms, and related to the cosmos, which was divinely ordered, in their view, by gods—creator gods such as Atum, Ra, Amun, and Ptah—and with order, truth, learning, and wisdom patronized by Maat and Thoth. Outstanding among Greek philosophical concepts of transcendental mind, idea, and order are *nous* (the mind, intelligence, reason that orders the universe), *logos* (the ordering word, law, reason), *eidos* (the ordering idea or form), and *kosmos* (cosmos, the whole ordered universe). By identifying Christ as *logos*, John not only echoed and amplified the Old Testament on creation, word, wisdom, and law, but recognized and accepted the truth-content within non-Christian Judaic and Hellenistic religious doctrines of his time, while rejecting the error-content by recognizing Christ as the Eternal Son, Word, and Redeemer, the Logos who had become flesh. It has also been pointed out that "the main stem of New Testament usage of Logos is not Greek but the ancient Hebraic *dabar Yahweh* ("Word of God") by which the world was made and the prophets inspired."[22]

Aristotelian Forms. For Aristotle (384-322 BC), the universe is ruled by *Forms*, which indicate divine *Mind (nous)*, *Ideas (eide)*, and *reason*. Related to Plato, and to later Christian theology, *Mind rules a real universe for a good purpose*. Aristotle found man and cosmos essentially permeated by *reason, design, structure, meaning, purpose*, and *goodness*. The same basic types of forms that determine physical nature, also determine human concepts, language and logic. Rational "categories" constitute the most fundamental forms of physical reality itself—the basic nature, structures, and patterns of all things. They also constitute the fundamental forms of language and logic, the primary subject of Aristotle's *Categories*. "The categories are the fundamental and indivisible concepts of thought; they are at the same time basic features of the real."[23]

The existence of forms and rational categories in the world and their appropriation by the mind makes rational knowledge possible. In Aristotle's view, the *form* of a natural thing is separated and abstracted from its material conditions and received in the soul. It is through the immaterial form received in the sense or the intellect that we are able to know that same form in the external object. The intellect is "completely open to any and all forms" and is "capable of apprehending anything and everything in whatever category." Knowledge is possible by *rational intuition,* with the cognitive intellect apprehending the forms of things. The *"agent intellect"* abstracts the forms and impresses them upon the *potential or receptive intellect.*[24]

Language is able to link rational concepts of the mind with the rational forms of real things because it is structured by the same categories. "The general ways of designating things, or the parts of discourse (the *categories* of language and of grammar), correspond to the different forms according to which we conceive them, or to the *categories* of the understanding, . . . and these *categories* of the understanding in their turn signify the modes of being of things themselves." Aristotle attributed to man a secure power of knowledge: "man alone is endowed with speech. By means of language, we designate . . . things as we conceive them; by *reason* we conceive them as they are." This is *rational intuition.* But Aristotle saw it as reaching all the way to God, with no need for active divine illumination or revelation: "man is the only being who partakes of the active intellect, that is, of God Himself, and through him of the knowledge of the absolute."[25]

Aristotle's ten categories are essential to natural things and to human knowledge: *substance, quality, quantity, relation, place (space), time, position, state (mode of being), activity, and passivity.* "Substance" is primary: it constitutes the most basic nature of all things—their concrete individual reality, unity, and independence. Together, these categories determine the concrete nature, structure, relationship, and motion of things in space and time. They assure us that "the objects of our experience exist in time and place, can be measured and counted, are related to other things, act and are acted on, have essential and accidental qualities."[26] Thus, there was no doubt for Aristotle about the possibility of real human knowledge of truth.

Divine Logos. Like some other Greek philosophers Aristotle saw "evidence of divine existence and action almost exclusively in the order and regularity of nature." This was specifically identified by many Greeks and by later Christians as *logos.* The idea of the ordering of the world by a divine intelligence underwent much development in the Greek world from the end of the sixth century BC onward, beginning with Xenophanes and Heracleitus. With Anaxagoras in the fifth century BC "intelligence not only directs but forms the world and pre-existing matter." "Plato developed the idea that is central to his philosophical religion, of a divine intelligence which forms and rules the world, ordering everything for the best. This divine intelligence is symbolized by the great Craftsman, the Demiurge, of the *Timaeus.*"[27] Heracleitus had treated *logos* as the rational element in nature, giving rational, intelligible, ordered process to "what would otherwise be a confusing and chaotic flux."

The *Logos*, moreover, is associated with human intelligence and its power to think soundly and give to life the guidance of reason. Anaxagoras (d. *circa* 428 BC) employed the synonym *Nous*, or Mind, in related ways. It too is a rational principle at work in nature, holding things together which otherwise would fall apart, and making them intelligible to man. The term *Logos* appears similarly in the Stoics for an active and rational force that controls the material elements and gives to nature its ordered unity. The *Logos* is a life-giving principle diffused throughout nature, and a seminal deposit of it comprises each man's soul. The Alexandrian Jew, Philo (d. AD 50), viewed the *Logos* as the sum of all the intermediary beings emanating from God, as the shaper of the universe, the divine reason diffused among men.[28]

We recognize a number of concepts in this that are partly related to the Bible and Christian theology: the Word or Logos as life-giving; (but through divine creation, not emanation); the shaping of the universe; controlling Mind at work in nature; the idea of a rational, ordering cause that makes nature orderly and intelligible in structure and process; the idea of a cause holding things together and creating unity; and the same power at work among men in the human soul, mind, and reason, making sound thought possible, and making the things of nature intelligible.

But "the Biblical usage goes further. It presents the *Logos* as coeternal and coequal with God, and as the personal Creator who transcends the world he makes from nothing." "John's *Logos* also recalls the personified wisdom who governs the nations, rewards the just," and lives from eternity.

He who finds such wisdom finds life (Prov. 8:35). John therefore declares that the *Logos* is personal, and one with God; he is creator of all, and he gives life and light to men. By incarnating himself, he revealed both grace and truth (John 1:1-14). John's *Logos*, and the Biblical world-view of which John's *Logos* is the focus, thereby stand in marked contrast to their extra-Biblical parallels.[29]

Carl F. H. Henry on Logos and Reason. In recent times, Henry has emphasized the work of the Logos. "John's Gospel declares the eternality of the Logos who grounds the meaning and purposes of created reality and becomes flesh. The eternal divine Word is at one and the same time the ultimately personal and rational." Thus we are able to speak of "the inherent rationality of the Logos." "The reality of the transcendent Logos of the Bible" creates and guarantees the reality and rational order and correspondence of the natural world. "As the source of created existence, the Logos of God grounded the meaning and purpose of man and the world, and objective reality was held to be divinely structured by complex formal patterns. Endowed with more than animal perception, gifted in fact with a mode of cognition not to be confused with sensation, man was therefore able to intuit intelligible universals; as a divinely intended knower, he was able to cognize, within limits, the nature and structure of the externally real world."[30]

Henry supports and develops the classical Augustinian Christian position that "without the antecedent activity of the Logos neither human knowledge of God nor human knowledge of cosmic and ordinary reality would be possible. All human experience presupposes the divine Logos and involves intuitive reception of divine revelation. As the light 'which lighteth every man' (John 1:9), the eternal Logos is the source of all intelligible, moral and spiritual illumination."[31] "Christian theology insists that God maintains the logical rationality of his creation and rules the universe as an intelligible order. The divine Logos is the norm and measure of reality and of truth."[32] "God as the creator and sustainer of man and the world constitutes the bond of union between man's mind and the world as an object of man's knowledge." "A rational God, who constitutes the ground of man's existence and of the existence of the world, by his immanence in both man and the world constitutes the possibility of man's knowledge of the world. Such a God desires to bring man into 'intelligent communion with himself'."[33] "Christianity affirms that this world is a rational universe, that it is God's world; knowability of the universe is grounded in God's creation of man as a rational creature whose forms of thought correspond to the laws of logic subsisting in the mind of God, as well as to the rational character of the world as God's creation."[34]

The ground of all truth, rationality, logic, and meaningful propositions is in God, mediated and revealed by the divine Logos. "Truth is truth because God thinks and wills it; in other words, truth depends on the sovereignty of God. God sovereignly upholds the truth; he establishes and preserves whatever is true. As creative, the Word of God is the ground of existence; as revelatory, it is the ground of all human knowledge." "Since God is the source and ground of all truth, all truth is in some sense dependent upon divine disclosure and therefore 'revelational'." If God is the ultimate source of truth, he must also be the source and ground of true reason and logic. "Reason is a divine attribute and the laws of reason are definitive of God's nature and descriptive of his will." "The laws of logic are the 'architecture' or organization of the divine mind. They are the systematic arrangement of God's mind or the way God thinks. The laws of logic, therefore, have an ultimately ontological reality."

From the human side of the God-man relationship, however, the understanding of perfect divine truth, reason, and logic, tends to be incomplete, distorted, or corrupted in various degrees by cultures and individuals in different stages of development, and in different states of relationship to world, history, and God. But ultimately, "God is the author of all meaning, the foundation of all facts; his thought is ultimately decisive for all predication. Without the very God who in revelation speaks in Christ through the Bible, nothing has eternally durable meaning." "God is the God of intelligible order, not of irrationality, self-contradiction or paradox. Scripture speaks of him as *Logos* or *Wisdom*, not as the Irrational or Paradoxical." "Truth consists of cognitively meaningful propositions; the totality of these propositions constitutes the mind of God." "Truth is the conformity of our propositions to what God knows to be the case; insofar as we know anything we know God's mind, that is, we think God's thoughts after him." Henry concurs with William Temple's statement that "The truth of things is what they are in the mind of God, and it is only when we act according to the mind of God that we are acting in accordance with reality."[35]

"The Old Testament asserts that 'In thy light shall we see light' (Psalms 36:9). It is only because of this hinterland relationship to the divine mind that humans know the truth about anything. The *nous* of God is not a mental faculty wholly different in kind from the *nous* of mankind in its content. Man not merely has the image of God but *is* the image of God."[36] Christianity affirms that ideas are "a rational activity gifted by the Logos to humans who bear the divine image by creation, and who are thus enabled to think God's thoughts after him". They are not "simply psychological reflexes of our sense experience." And they are not "an activity of supernatural mind of which man *immediately* partakes as a spiritual being." "The fact that human minds and God's mind—or Christian minds and the mind of Christ—coincide in the knowledge of certain propositions does not, of course, equate God and mankind either pantheistically or existentially."[37] Propositional truth and knowledge are made possible through the Logos: "the Bible encompasses the Logos as the divine agent in all revelation, the incarnation of the Logos in Jesus of Nazareth, and the intelligible verbal nature of God's epistemic disclosure." "The fourth Gospel affirms that the Logos—not the Irrational or the Paradoxical—became flesh." "Gordon Clark pointedly comments that in the New Testament understanding, the Word of God has in view not simply the personal but the propositional as well: . . . 'what became flesh was the Word, the Logos, the Ratio or Verbum. Such a Logos cannot be restricted to one proposition.'"[38]

Henry rightly points out that "loss of the self-revealed Logos of God as an ontological reality and epistemic presupposition led Western philosophy to an intellectual aporia, a skeptical predicament beyond which it has been unable to find passage. This skepticism has eroded all confident ontological affirmation—whether about God, or about nature or man objectively considered." This has led in Wittgenstein to "a death-rattle for metaphysical inquiry." Likewise, we find in Dada and Surrealist art, and in postmodern art and thought, the radical sense of absence of divine and metaphysical truth, reason, logic, and order, indicating the disappearance of belief in God and the Scriptures. "In a day when modern wisdom considers the cosmos devoid of teleology and derives man from purposeless nature, *the reality of the self-revealed Logos towers anew as the only intelligible ground and sustaining source of meaning, value and purpose.* Contemporary philosophy is presiding over a secular emptying of the Logos by the total negation of transcendence, and a resignation to dynamic processes lacking all final and definitive form." The inevitable fruit must be nihilism.[39]

Sheen on Logos. Fulton Sheen has addressed many of these matters from a Thomistic perspective. It is God's Wisdom, Logos, participating in the things of creation that "explains our own intelligibility." "We know, not because we invent, but because we discover—discover the Wisdom of God hidden in the things which He has made." "Knowledge is spiritual." The human mind has been given a power above that of the animal and beyond mere sense perception, to penetrate beyond surfaces to the very essence, the rational inner idea or form of a thing or object, and apprehend it mentally, spiritually. "The power Almighty God has given to the human mind is what has been called the 'active intellect,' which has the power, once it enters into sensible contact with things, to grasp their essence, or the form which makes them what they are. But since the form is the participation of the Archetypal Idea of that thing in the Divine Mind—as the cathedral is the participation of the idea in the mind of the architect—it follows that in knowing the essence or nature of things, the mind knows the likeness of the Divine ideas existing in things. Thus, in an indirect way, the Wisdom of God becomes immanent in our own minds through the intermediary of things." "Everything in this world is true inasmuch as it corresponds with the idea that God had in mind in making it. In this sense there is absolute truth." "If things are true because they correspond to the Divine Mind, likewise in a derived sense, our minds enjoy truth when they correspond to the things made according to the Ideas of God immanent in them by participation, thanks to the Creative Act."[40]

Augustine on Divine Ideas and Knowledge. Related understandings of truth and knowledge are part of a long, rich tradition in Christian spiritual and intellectual history, intimated and implied in the Bible and thoughtfully developed from Augustine through Anselm and Aquinas, Luther and Calvin, and still part of Christian thought and doctrine today.[41] Augustine is the early and "unrivaled exponent" of the view that man's primary, creaturely relationship to God and the spiritual realm sustains him in intuitive correlation with God, the world, and other persons, making genuine knowledge possible. God, creation, revelation, and faith are determinative for human knowledge of truth. "That man has valid knowledge at all is explained by Augustine on the ground of his creation-link to the supernatural world. Never is human knowledge adequately described as an achievement of human factors operating wholly in isolation from divine activity." Divine revelation is the precondition of any human knowledge at all. "Man's knowledge is set continually and always in a context of revelation and faith."

Certain knowledge of an objectively real, natural world is thus possible through the senses, and confident and certain metaphysical knowledge of the supernatural world is possible through faith, obedience, and the intellect. The Creator sustains this relationship: "The Creator's determination constantly maintains man in this joint relationship to the rational and phenomenal worlds, and to the Creator himself as decisive for all." Man is not abandoned in an unknown world by an unrevealing, unknowable, irrational God, nonexistent Being, unrelieved natural process, primal chaos, or a void. God is the ultimate, active source of the truths and laws found in the human intellect. The human mind cannot be sovereignly creative, but is in some respects passive: "man creates neither the intelligible world nor the sense world."[42]

For Augustine the structure, rationality, and knowability of all existing things are due to their rational patterns, which come from the original, eternal ideas of God. Augustine referred to the eternal ideas in the mind of God as *rationes aeternae*. These eternal reasons or ideas serve as the "principal forms or stable and unchangeable essences of things."[43] Ronald Nash explains that "these forms or divine ideas are archetypal forms of created reality." "Since they subsist in God's intellect, they share God's essential attributes and thus are eternal, necessary, and unchangeable." And since they are eternal and unchanging, always in the same state, they can serve as the stable basis for patterns of all particular, changing things.[44]

Augustine also referred to certain ideas, reasons, or forms created in nature as *rationes seminales* the "seed-like principles that exist in the nature of the world's elements. When God created the world, He embedded in the creation principles that guide its development." Like an architect, God had a plan before He created the universe. "His creation is patterned or copied after the divine ideas [*rationes aeternae*]. Therefore because the divine forms are the exemplary cause of everything that exists, they are *the basic foundation of all created reality*. Moreover, because the judgments men make must accord with the eternal forms, they are an indispensable element in human knowledge." But "Augustine makes it clear that man can know this present temporal, corporeal world only because he first knows the eternal, incorporeal, intelligible world of ideas that exist in the mind of God."[45]

"Just as all of God's creation is good, so all of reality partakes of truth in varying degrees. Inasmuch as creatures embody or exemplify the form or pattern in the mind of God, they possess ontological truth." Ontological truth thus actually resides in created reality (in contrast to Kantian and post-Kantian modern thought, which tend to relate "truths" to a quality of propositions and categories of human intellect—i.e., to *human* mind or subjectivity). In Augustine's view of reality and knowledge there is a "close relationship between intellectual and ontological truth," and no room for any unknowable Kantian thing-in-itself. For Augustine, "reality is knowable because it was created by God after the pattern of the divine ideas."[46]

God created the human mind so that one may know both the eternal reasons or forms in the mind of God and the physical world patterned after these forms. Knowledge of the eternal, divine forms or universals is, for Augustine, in contrast to Thomas Aquinas, always prior to sense experience, *a priori*, since sense experience is always changing. Our knowledge of eternal, unchanging divine ideas is absolutely independent of sense experience, made available to our mind by God, as we are prepared for it through properly directed attention, and through faith. These universals or divine forms are not given to a person in a once-and-for-all manner and in fully conscious form, but are described by Augustine as latent or virtual in an individual's mind or "memory." Thus, "the truth is always available to us in the sense that Christ will make it available if we are attentive to it." "Man does not remember truths learned in some previous existence [as in Platonic recollection, *anamnesis*] but actualizes latent or virtual knowledge of necessary truth that has been stored in what Augustine calls the memory."[47]

Man's possession of the forms of thought is something natural, inasmuch as he possesses them from the time his life begins. They are part of the rational structure of his mind and are his by virtue of his creation in the image of God. However, we must not think of the forms as having been given to man once-and-for-all. Augustine is clear in stating that the soul never ceases to be dependent upon God for its knowledge. "God, having so made man, has not left him deistically, to himself, but continually reflects into his soul the contents of His own eternal and immutable mind—which are precisely those eternal and immutable truths which constitute the intelligible world. The soul is therefore in unbroken communion with God, and in the body of intelligible truths reflected into it from God, sees God." Thus, knowledge is possible because God has created man after His own image as a rational soul and because God continually sustains and aids the soul in its quest for knowledge.[48]

As in Augustine's theology, *a Christian understanding of the experience of knowledge requires the doctrines of creation, preservation, revelation and illumination.*

Only with divine creation are rational forms given structure in nature. And only if man is created in the image of God can he possess the spirit, mind, reason, and intellect needed to understand and appropriate rational truths and ideas that come from and correspond with rational truths in the Mind of God, and with rationally articulated forms in nature. According to Augustine this consists in the continual impressing of God's truths as ideas upon the human mind, and thus requires God's continuing preservation of creation. Revelation as the revealing activity of the divine Logos, and illumination by His divine light is also required, since not only knowledge of the ultimate truths of God cannot be reached by human reason alone, but even knowledge of objective things external to the knowing self would be impossible, as Kant, then Nietzsche, other modernists, and postmodernists, who rejected Christ the Logos or any ontological source as a basis for philosophy, would later hold.

Truth for Aquinas. According to Aquinas, knowledge provides truth about the actual being of the world: he grants to human knowledge the property of objectivity on the ground of the intentional character of our ideas. As a result, he says, "the consideration of the intellect does not stop before the idea *(species)*, but through the idea moves toward the thing of which it is a reproduction *(similitudo)*; in the same way as the eye, through the species that is in the pupil, sees the stone itself."[49] In Battista Mondin's analysis, "man does not create the objects he knows but merely represents them." "This means that our mind acquires knowledge only when it is actualized by the form of the object." H. D. Gardeil writes that for Aquinas "truth always implies a relation between being and intellect. But the relation can be considered from either of its terms, either as based in the intellect, or as grounded in being. Truth is in the intellect, or an intellect is true when its act (of knowledge) conforms with being, with what is."[50]

"True knowledge, then, is knowledge which bears a relation of conformity with its object, with reality. Thus understood, truth is defined as the conformity of intellect to thing: *adaequatio intellectus ad rem*; which, by common accord, is the definition of *logical truth*. Conversely, from the objective point of view, truth is in things or a thing is true in proportion to its conformity with the intellect. This is *ontological truth*, the conformity of thing to intellect: *adaequation rei ad intellectum*."[51] Aquinas's primary definition is in terms of *logical* or *formal* truth: "all knowledge is produced by the assimilation of the knower to the thing known. Therefore, the primary relation of being to intellect consists in the one's corresponding to the other. This correspondence is called the equation [*adequation*] of the thing and the intellect. In this conformity the notion of truth is realized formally. It is this that truth adds to being: conformity or equation [*adequation*] of thing and intellect. The consequence of this conformity is the knowledge of a thing. Thus the being of the thing precedes formal truth, although knowledge is a certain effect of truth."[52]

A formal definition of truth is also indicated by Augustine: "truth takes place when a thing is represented in the same way as it is." And Anselm states, "truth is rightness perceptible to the mind alone." According to Hilary, "truth is that which declares and manifests being." Aquinas also supports *ontological truth*, seen primarily in the conformity of created things to the divine intellect, and secondarily in the conformity of a created work to the mind of an artist.[53] Augustine expressed another ontological view: "the true is that which is." Anselm wrote, "truth is the indivision of being and of what is." And Avicenna said, "the truth of each thing is the property of the being that is assigned to it." Another concept of truth focuses on the *revelatory effects of being*. As Augustine said, "truth is that by which that which is, is shown forth." And for Hilary, "truth is manifestive and declarative being."[54]

All truth is ultimately from the first truth of God. As Benignus writes in his study of Thomistic thought, "both the truth of things and the truth of human intellects are from and depend upon the first truth, that is to say, the truth of the divine intellect upon which things depend for their being. This intellect measures or determines the truth of things, since it gives them their being and the relation of that being to itself. It gives them also their truth in reference to human intellects, since in this respect they are true in so far as they are knowable, and they are knowable by virtue of their forms; and these forms, which are the principles by which things are what they are, are from the divine intellect, the Creator, who is the exemplary and efficient cause of all things. Finally, since human intellects are true in so far as they are in conformity with things and since they are in such conformity only in so far as they possess the forms of things and predicate these of the things, it is manifest that their truth is from that intellect whence these forms are, and whence their own nature, power, and operation are—the creative intellect of God. Hence the divine intellect is the first truth and the source of all truth."[55]

A brief summary of the actual process of human cognition in Thomistic philosophy reveals its strong sense of the realism and fidelity of knowledge: (1) The corporeal substance of an existing thing determines the *sense impression* in the corporeal sense organ of the knower. (2) The internal sense determination is known as the *phantasm*, a material image that also embodies the immaterial *form* of the thing to be known. The phantasm is a mental image, appearance, or percept—a sensible representation of the thing to be known, still concrete and particular. (3) A *sensible species* is abstracted from the phantasm by the *active* or *agent intellect*. This is now the *universal idea* of the thing to be known. (4) An *intelligible species*, which is immaterial and universal, is then impressed in the *possible intellect*. This is the *universal* or *intelligible form* of the thing to be known, which is received by the possible intellect, thereby actualizing and determining it; (5) A mental *representation*—the *concept* or *idea*—of the thing apprehended is then produced. It is something other than the intelligible species, being the conscious, intelligible idea and likeness of the thing apprehended. Faithful knowledge of the external thing is thus attained. "The concept, therefore, is a conscious likeness of the external thing, produced within itself by the intellect; *it must be a faithful likeness of the thing*, because it is determined in its intelligible content *by the very form of the thing* informing the intellect and determining it to the production of this concept; the intellect is incapable of producing anything but a likeness of the thing whose form is at the moment its own form. And, of course, the intellect actually knows the thing by means of the concept, because to have consciously or cognitively in itself the likeness of something is nothing else than to know that something."[56]

Aquinas wrote, "Since in every thing quiddity [the essence or individual nature of a thing] and its act of being are present, truth is founded on the act of being rather than on quiddity; and it is the operation of the intellect that receives the being of the thing (*esse rei*), by way of some sort of reproduction of it, that the relation of correspondence, which makes up the notion of truth, takes place." What is received by the intellect is the *actual form* of the external thing, reproduced as a *mental concept or idea*. In this way "truth consists in some correspondence of the intellect or speech to reality. And since correspondence *(aequalitas)* is something intermediate between the more and the less, it befits that the good of intellectual virtue lies in the middle, namely that what may be said of the object is what the object really is. Therefore if what is said exceeds either by way of addition or of subtraction, it will be false." Judgment, not the senses, is the proper seat of truth. It is judgment that makes the final determination of truth or untruth. Blame for error falls on the intellect, not on the senses.[57]

Common Understandings. The views of both Augustine and Aquinas support major claims of this book concerning the reality and knowability of God and world, and the truth of divine creation, revelation, and salvation. While similar in these essential respects, there are also some important differences between them. Most important for this book, both held, in harmony with Scripture, that the reality, truth, rationality, structure, purpose, end, and knowability of all created things depend on the eternal Being of God and Ideas in the Mind, Word, and Wisdom of God. Reality, truth, and knowledge for both depend on God's eternal Being, Mind, Ideas, and plan, and the rational formation of His ideas and plan in creation. God is absolutely real, while creation is contingently real. Individual spiritual souls, spirits, and bodies are real, and created things of the world are real and structured. God is the absolute source of the transcendentals of oneness, truth, goodness, and beauty. Contrary to subjectivism, relativism, skepticism, and Postmodernism, things have truth by reflecting the Truth of the ideas of God. True knowledge of the nature of the world is possible. Knowledge of universal, metaphysical, theological, and moral truth is possible. These basic understandings, common to Augustine and Aquinas, and to many other Christian thinkers, are based on the Bible and on doctrines of God, creation, and revelation.

The chief difference between Augustine and Aquinas on these issues has to do with *how* and *in what priority* human beings know universal ideas or essences. Augustine maintains that individuals receive *all* universal ideas from God *a priori*, impressed on the mind in unconscious form *prior to sense experience*, to be activated under proper conditions in the light of God's illumination, thus recognizing determinative place for continual divine revelation in the process. In contrast, Aquinas, similar to Aristotle, holds that individuals grasp universal ideas or essences *through sense experience of things* by the "active intellect," reaching as far as the idea of God, thus allowing a greater role for divinely created human intellect and reason, and a lesser role for divine revelation in this process, although some of those ideas can come only through divine revelation.[58]

Like Aquinas, the general trend of medieval philosophy was "realist": the mind was seen as "ruled by a world of objects that exist apart from it and govern its content." "Being, or reality, came first; thought, corresponding to reality, came second. Interpreted, this means that what the mind knows directly is reality; then, upon reflection, its thoughts of reality. Transposed to sense it means that when I look at a thing, what I see is the thing and not my sight of the thing. This is the attitude of common sense, and both the ancients and medievals as a whole, accepted it on that basis." The modern "inversion" began with Descartes: instead of external reality, "thought, or the activity of thought, is adjudged the more immediate experience." The effect was "to leave the mind cut off from reality."[59]

Intuitive Reason and Knowledge. It is the God-given spiritual capacity of the human mind to comprehend the rational forms of created things and the divine, universal ideas of God at their basis. Henry points out that "what had distinguished man's reason in the classical ancient and medieval outlooks was especially its comprehension of intelligible universals." From Aristotle through the medieval era onward, this capacity of the mind has been known as "intuitive reason." Francis Parker affirms this essential function of *rational intuition*: "The conception of intuitive reason involves the idea of a bond of intelligibility between the mind of man and the structure of nature, a rational pattern in which both nature and the human mind participate." He rightly points out

145

"the replacement of intuitive reason by constructive reason" in the modern world, and finds it to be "a fundamental theme of the rise and development of modern philosophy." He adds that "the late medieval and early modern loss of intuitive reason as man's definitive in-betweenness also meant, I believe, the loss of God as rational mediator between man and nature . . . . Without a source and home for those intelligible forms which mediated between the mind of man and the structure of nature, man's bond with nature was broken. Thus, arose the subjectivism, *apriorism*, and constructivism definitive of modernity."[60]

Modern-Postmodern Losses. The material presented in the next three chapters indicates that the modern rejection of God the Creator, and the Bible as the word of God, has been accompanied by a progressive sense of loss of the ontological and metaphysical reality of the world and the self. The classic belief in truth as correspondence has declined, and then disappeared in Postmodernism. There has been a recession of metaphysics, and the elevation of subjective constructions of "reality" as a central preoccupation in modern philosophy, literature, and the arts. By rejecting one area of God's revelation that is centered and unified in Christ the Word, the others are progressively lost, commensurate with the degree of revolt. Modernity began by rejecting aspects of God's revelation in the Bible. As it has expanded it has turned to a more radical assault on the core of God's revelation—divine Creation, Wisdom, Word, and Logos (modern *anti-Logos*), so that all avenues of God's revelation have radically receded or vanished, not only in special, but in general revelation—in nature, self, conscience, history, and language, as well as the ultimate reality of unity, truth, goodness, beauty, and purpose.

Not only the biblical revelation of Logos, but the related concepts in Greek culture and classical tradition have been increasingly criticized and destructively attacked by the leading edge of modern thought from Kant through Hegel, Nietzsche, Wittgenstein, Heidegger, Sartre, into the Postmodernism of Foucault, Derrida, Baudrillard, and others. The core direction has been one of anti-Theos, anti-Logos, anti-Being, anti-metaphysics, and anti-Form. This has led to the contemporary scene in which leading theoretical talk revolves around "deconstruction" of all previous theological and metaphysical treatises and doctrines as artificial "master narratives," and the devising of new "strategies" for "construction" of contemporary religion, philosophy, literature, morality, sexuality, and the arts.

Traditional metaphysics and ontology are thus officially dead for modernity and postmodernity. The rule of modern constructive reason renders them impossible. Henry points out that without intuitive reason "ontology is impossible. For only if the intelligible forms are expressive of external reality can human knowledge contain propositions that are necessarily and factually true, that is, convey authentic metaphysical knowledge. Ontology is precluded if no completely universal data are given to the human mind. The view that human reason is wholly constructive rules out such data. Whoever lays claim to metaphysical knowledge must transcend the notion of constructive reason and insist that human knowledge includes rational intuition."[61]

Men and women persuaded and guided by the radical thought and art of modernity have lost secure knowledge or hope of universal truth. They even admit, like Wittgenger, Heidegger, Foucault, Derrida, and Rorty, that they are "always learning and never able to come to the knowledge of the truth."[62] As God, the revealed Word of God, and the very image of His Father, Christ the Son and Logos is absolute Truth in person: as He declared, "I am the way, the truth, and the life."[63] He mediates the truth, and the Holy Spirit leads individuals to the truth. As the divine cosmic Logos creating all forms and structures of nature, their causal connection, and epistemological correspondence, He provides the only available revelation and knowledge of general truth within nature and the human mind. And as incarnate Redeemer, He provides the only real and true means of salvation and reconciling knowledge of God.

Absolute truth comes *only* through God's Son the Logos—through His creation-revelation in nature, and His special revelation through incarnation, redemption, and the word of Scripture. To revolt against Christ the Word is to lose all these avenues of access to absolute truth. As for general truth in knowledge of nature, individuals gain truth when their ideas faithfully match or correspond to the forms of nature, and thereby to the ideas of the Creator and Mediator of those forms and ideas that they reflect.

Just as the nature of the Trinity is the most intimate and faithful unity, harmony, and correspondence, the nature of God's revelation through the Word is communication and correspondence—a linking and binding together in harmonious love and fellowship—this is the rich and multiple meaning of biblical "knowledge" and "wisdom." And knowledge for man, made in the image of God, is a faithful communicative linking of the human spiritual and mental self with what would otherwise be separate and unknown, made possible by the universal agency of the Logos. Perfect knowledge is characteristic only of the Trinity. The relationship of God the Father to His Son, and Son and Spirit to Father, epitomizes it. And in biblical terms, the word *knowledge* is also used for the most intimate union of marriage; and the relationship of Christ to the church of believers is described as that of the bridegroom to His bride.

This faithful personal correspondence and oneness is characteristic first and foremost of the unity and harmony of the Trinity. It is also characteristic of the work of the Trinity in creation. And from this, it is characteristic of

the entire network of rational and logical structures and relationships constituting the perfect harmonious unity of God's creation itself. (Needless to
say, that perfection has been tainted since mankind's first disobedience, and
subjected to corruptions and disruptions. Next, as the Old Testament testifies,
it is characteristic of human *knowledge* and *wisdom*, which at the highest level
is the faithful submission of oneself to the universal Wisdom, Truth, and
Law of God. And at ordinary levels, knowledge is faithful submission and
correspondence to the structures, orders, and relationships within nature.
General knowledge thus consists of the correspondence or communicative
linking together of mind and external object, idea and objective reality and
truth. Language [logos] plays an integral role in knowledge: the human word
is the communicative medium, whether spoken or written, that links together
mind and world, idea and objective reality in intimate union, again through
the agency of the universal Divine Word.

He binds together man and nature in one organic whole, so that we can speak of a
"universe." Without him there would be no intellectual bond, no uniformity of law,
no unity of truth. He is the principle of induction that enables us to argue from one
thing to another. The medium of interaction between things is also the medium
of intercommunication between minds. It is fitting that he who draws and holds
together the physical and intellectual, should also draw and hold together the moral
universe, drawing all men to himself (John 12:32) and so to God, and reconciling
all things in heaven and earth. (Col. 1:20). In Christ "the law appears, Drawn out in
living characters," because he is the ground and source of all law, both in nature and
in humanity.[64]

The same holds true for the visual arts, where the *visual form or image* functions
like the corresponding word, linking together the mind and the thing that
it represents. And similarly, but at the highest level, and with a most costly
price, redemption is the restoration of the intimate union, communication,
and correspondence of human beings—separated from God by revolt against
God's Word and law—to God's presence and favor.

As it has more intensively and essentially revolted against God and
His Word, and therefore become increasingly impoverished of the bounty
of God's Logos and Spirit, modern anti-Logos thought, art, and culture
has increasingly reflected and celebrated fragmentation, disjunction, and
anti-form, rather than the ordering gifts of the Word in creation. Even in
the late medieval world, when theologians first began to seriously doubt
the validity of God's Word in certain ways, the doctrine of nominalism
began to emerge, claiming that all things are separate and discrete, having
no objective universal link or cause. The Renaissance and Baroque periods
still strongly preserved traditional forms of unity and integrity in the arts,

however. Fragmentation and disjunction, still not prominent or disturbing in the eighteenth century, have characterized the development of modernity in increasing degrees since Romanticism.

Fragmentation, disjunction, and displacement, have become key theoretical concepts and practices in modern art since Cubism, and in Postmodernism. The "collage aesthetic," invented in Cubism and developed further in Dada and Surrealism, is a milestone in the development of modern anti-form: it provided the visual means par excellence for rendering fragmentation and disjunction. It has been further developed as a primary means in post-World-War-II arts, where forms such as "assemblage," "combines," "multimedia," and performance arts often combine almost anything in any way (except in unity, rational order, and harmony)—the more disjunctive and disparate the better, since in these ways they better reflect modern and postmodern views about "reality," "truth," "knowledge," and the "human condition." Recent novels (e.g. Barth, Pynchon) also openly attack God's "Word," "the Father," Christ, and divine authority, while extolling multiplicity, pluralism, ambiguity, paradox, contradiction, and endless change.

Chapter Six

The Growing Rejection of God in Modern Thought

For the wisdom of this world is foolishness in God's sight. As it is written: "He catches the wise in their craftiness;" and again, "The Lord knows that the thoughts of the wise are futile" (I Cor. 3:19-20, NIV).

Descartes' foundation of modernity began with doubt, radical criticism, dismissal of past and present foundations, and a turn to the interiority of the pure thinking subject, its ideas, and reason.

Kant's *Critique of Pure Reason* essentially shifted the basis of philosophy further in the direction modern philosophy had been moving since Descartes: from a primary basis in God, Being, Logos, *eide*, *nous*, cosmos, and world, to one in the conscious subject and its experiences, forms, ideas, reason, knowledge, will, and practical actions.

"When philosophy posits self-consciousness as its starting point, however, we have entered a new stage of human history."[1]

Modern Relativism and Skepticism Reject Belief in God. We do not live in a world of no absolutes, as modern relativism and skepticism claim. Relativism is rampant today, however, not only as prevailing "scholarly" or "philosophical" positions, but as ways of understanding the world for millions of people. It is very common to think that there are no absolute truths or moral laws—no universal and necessary ones, only those beliefs or values that pertain to different societies, groups, or individuals.[2] This is especially apparent in twentieth-century art where purposes and "meanings" are almost totally determined or "constructed" by the individual artist (by the *subject/self*) and have become increasingly unusual and idiosyncratic in movements from Cubism through Dada, Surrealism, and Abstract Expressionism, into the fast flurry of Pop, Minimal, Color-Field, Conceptual, Neo-Pop, Graffiti, etc., and on into "Postmodernism." As a result, art has grown more hybrid and strange looking, more weird and disturbing, often even looking psychotic, starkly contrasting with earlier art. Such relativism and skepticism are so pervasive, and taken for granted that it is difficult to sway many people to consider that there may be absolutes, and to entertain the idea that there may be a God of Absolute Being and Truth. In society at large, knowledge of the Bible and the history of theology and pre-modern philosophy is often so low and so seldom considered important, that current mass opinions can be widely swayed by movies, magazines, and TV talk shows. And more thoughtful approaches are often influenced by liberal and radical professors and modern or postmodern writers.

The essential, underlying reason for the pervasiveness of modern relativism and skepticism in our time is that the prevailing directions of modern thought have gradually and increasingly rejected belief in the Living God of Being and Truth.[3] Since Nietzsche's direct and vicious assault on these beliefs in the late-nineteenth century, it has become increasingly difficult for modern and postmodern thinkers and artists to find any substantial basis for absolute being and truth. The opposites—becoming, change, difference, relativism—have become the new keys to thought. Before Nietzsche there had been a slowly growing, then intensifying direction since the "Age of Reason" and "Enlightenment" to increasingly modify, doubt, attack, and eliminate biblical, theological, and metaphysical concepts of God, Being, and Truth as untenable in modern philosophical thought.[4]

The emphasis has progressively shifted away from God and Being to "man," the "human," and more narrowly to "social," "group," "self" or "individual" requirements and determinations. In these limited categories no real absolutes can be logically or philosophically sustained. That direction, beginning to emerge in the Renaissance, then formally inaugurated by Descartes in philosophy, and progressively expanded by Hume, Kant, Hegel, Nietzsche, and Heideggger, has reached its broadest and fullest expression to date in "Postmodernism," which has widespread influence in philosophy, theology, literature, the other arts, and thus in university studies. As Richard Swinburne, former professor at the University of Oxford, writes, "both among professional philosopher and outside their narrow circle, there is today deep skepticism about the power of reason to reach a justified conclusion about the existence of God."[5]

Descartes and the Beginnings of Modern Thought. René Descartes (1596-1650), writing in the 1630s and 40s, is the first great philosopher to put forward some essential purposes and goals of Modernism. In books and articles on Descartes and Locke, Peter Schouls shows that the fundamental concepts of the Enlightenment, "freedom, mastery, and progress," were originally those of Descartes, a century before Enlightenment thinkers.

Descartes' method and these three concepts essentially speak of the modern ideal of autonomy—the freedom of radical self-determination. "The ideal expressed through this triad of concepts may well be called that of autonomy. This ideal of autonomy reveals the mainstream of Enlightenment thought." Schouls demonstrates that Descartes' method and triad of concepts call not simply for a reformation, but for *revolt*, a *revolution*—a complete sweeping away of past beliefs and principles, and the substitution of new ones to replace them. "Descartes' position may be called that of a revolutionary because his method dictates that if we are to obtain knowledge we must begin by *rejecting all beliefs and opinions* which we have absorbed from the contexts in which we live."[6]

Descartes did not found his philosophy on God the Creator, or the Bible, but on his own isolated, thinking self. His primary thought is not "God has created all things including me, therefore I exist and think," but the very different "*I* think, therefore *I* am—"*Cogito, ergo sum.*" "I," the thinking self, dominates this philosophical foundation.[7] The traditional priority of relationship of God and man is thus overthrown from the very start, establishing the thinking subject as the new ground and center of existence and certainty. As Jacques Maritain analyzes it, "thought directly attains only itself." The thinking self is not primarily and ultimately determined and conditioned by God the Supreme Being, Creator, and structurer of all things that exist, but by its own thought, ideas, and reason. Beginning with Descartes modern thought and reason are self-determining, autonomous. The thinking subject is conceived as self-enclosed, absolute, possessing existence and thought by itself alone. It is "a human knowledge like divine knowledge, a knowledge which depends only upon itself."[8] Modern subjectivity is initiated with this thought, and the way leading to Locke, Hume, Kant, Hegel, and beyond, is laid.

Despite Descartes' often avowed belief in God (which is highly questionable[9]), his philosophical method, epistemology, and view of reason stand in essential conflict with biblical and Christian theological teachings about God. "Descartes' position tends towards making God irrelevant for philosophizing."[10] This can be seen in his argument concerning the truth of his own reason relative to a veracious or deceiver God or demon. As Hiram Caton and Gerhard Krüger write, "By bringing reason to consciousness of its inner nature . . . the Cogito ["I think"] emancipates reason from all restraints of piety: it empowers a self-consciously secular reason . . . . An unshakable and immutable will is the basis of the autonomy of reason. 'Self consciousness constitutes itself in defiance of all omnipotence.'"[11] Descartes thus sets reason up as secular, autonomous, and infallible. And Peter Schouls states: "This 'rebellion against Christianity' which here 'begins in philosophy as such' is neither timid nor half-hearted, for it is unequivocally reason's unilateral declaration of independence." Pascal also saw that Descartes' position essentially made God irrelevant for philosophy: "I cannot forgive Descartes. In all his philosophy he would have been quite willing to dispense with God. But he could not help granting him a flick of the forefinger to start the world in motion; beyond this he has no further need of God." Schouls also supports Maritain's assessment of Descartes' philosophy—"the profound incompatibility of his philosophy with the whole authentic tradition of Christian wisdom."[12]

As yet with no knowledge of world or God, it is only in the second step of his thought that Descartes turns to God. It is not God himself, however, but the *idea* of God in the *thinking self.* The self finds certainty in this "clear and distinct idea." From the certainty of the idea of God in the *cogito,* Descartes makes the great leap to the existence of God (a leap that subsequent modernists would increasingly reject as unsupportable and unnecessary). The existence of God for Descartes is thus erected on a foundation of *ideas* in the thinking *subject*—a second major reversal of traditional Christian and classical thought. It is only then that God is said to be the veridical guarantee of the thinking subject's ideas and knowledge of things of the world. In this third step, God becomes a *secondary support,* a *bridge,* a *means* for Descartes—a *tool* to guarantee the certainty of his scientific knowledge. After this assurance, Descartes "loses interest in God" and turns to the material world.

But this third step is actually unnecessary and superfluous. If thought, ideas, certainty, and existence can *be* and *be known* before and outside of God at all, then God is unnecessary for any further step. If one can actually be and think and have ideas without God, then God must be unnecessary for all existence, thought, and ideas. All existence must logically be self-existence, and all thought and ideas must be self-originating. If thought can know the existence of the self, it can know the existence of the world just as well. In the Cartesian foundation, as Maritain says, "thought is a god who unfolds himself," and "things either conform to it, or do not even exist apart from it." "Either there is no being to set off against thought, or there is only being completely docile to thought." Objects revolve around human thought. This Cartesian foundation [and subsequent modern subjectivism] "presupposes a rupture with being."[13]

Maritain point out that Descartes' position indicates a philosophical rupture with *being*: "in spite of Descartes' personal intentions and in spite of the efforts of his immediate successors, it supposes an *eviction of the ontological.* There we have the primordial Cartesian break. Man shut up within himself is condemned to sterility, because his thought lives and is nourished only upon the things that God has made. Man the center of an intelligible universe which he has created in his own image, himself loses his center of gravity and his own consistence, for his consistence is to be the image of God. He is in the middle of a desert."[14] More fully realizing this rupture, postmodern thinkers have found that if we cannot know the world, neither can we know the self or subject, and reason. They realize that, if all this is true, we certainly do not know God, being, or truth. In contrast to Christianity, however, radical postmodernists conclude that there is no God, being, and truth.

Descartes also radically transforms the meaning of "idea." Previously the term had been used to describe the Ideas of Plato, and Christian tradition from Augustine through Aquinas. With Descartes "idea" takes on a revolutionary new philosophical meaning. Descartes acknowledges that he is taking the term previously used to refer to God's ideas, and specifically states that he is using it for "everything which is in our mind when we conceive something, no matter how we conceive it."[15] In traditional Christian thought ideas are acknowledged to be located originally and primarily in the mind of God, and to serve as exemplars for divine creation of things. The exemplars or forms of created things then make possible human knowledge of things, and serve artists as models to imitate for their own creations (e.g portraits of existing individuals). "God makes things that imitate His ideas, and the artist in turn makes imitations of those created realities." But with Descartes ideas are treated in terms of all particular mental acts or explicit concepts of thinking human subjects. In the *Meditations* "clear and distinct ideas" become "the units of Cartesian knowledge." An idea becomes "as it were an image, expressive of something, something which the mind contemplates." Descartes gives a new emphasis to the idea as an image in the human mind. He seeks to separate human ideas from sense perception: "Ideas are intelligible and other than what is sensed." "The act of the maker (in Descartes's case, thinker) is itself representative: it is *of* something reflected in the mind, and in this sense objective." "The reality of a Cartesian idea though it is *of* something, is itself a mental existent and not tied to an external reality."[16]

Descartes actually abandons the use of the term "exemplar," associated with traditional Platonic and Christian creation contexts. And with it he drops the entire view of God creating by exemplars, and of the human artist as imitator of those forms or exemplars. In general, "Idea as model for creation, whether divine or human, is left aside in the Cartesian texts. What is retained is the notion of a mental act that is also (as we would say) intentional." In exemplary causality of Platonic and Christian tradition "it is things that must conform to the idea in the mind of the maker, divine or human." Descartes thus inaugurates a great reversal that sets precedent for Kant and modern subjective thought. First, he undermines traditional doctrines of reality: he cancels out "the major context of the traditional doctrine of ideas: the context of archetype or model, in which the idea informs its imitations and gives them, or their 'images,' such reality as they have." And second, he undermines traditional doctrines of truth: he inverts the traditional view in which "truth consists in the conformity of the thing to the exemplar. For Descartes the truth of clear and distinct ideas will run in the other direction, from ideas to things." And these determinative ideas are associated with the pure, bodiless, worldless, thinking subject.[17] Descartes' foundation of modernity began with doubt, radical criticism, dismissal of past and present foundations, and a turn to the interiority of the pure thinking subject, its ideas, and reason. Such a revolutionary move—an inversion of the dominant bases of previous Western theology and philosophy—had radical consequences that have been increasingly realized through succeeding centuries. As William Barrett has written, it resulted in a bifurcation into two worlds, a dualism of subject and object, self and world. "The ego is the subject, essentially a thinking substance; nature is the world of objects, extended substances. Modern philosophy thus begins with a radical subjectivism." "Man is locked up in his own ego. Outside him is the doubtful world of things." "When philosophy posits self-consciousness as its starting point . . . we have entered a new stage of human history." "The exaltation of self-consciousness . . . splits the mind off from a realm of objects, which it proceeds now to understand in quantitative terms very different from those of everyday life." "The object which has been detached from the enveloping ground of Being can be measured and calculated, but the essence of the object—the thing-in-itself—becomes more and more remote from man." Freedom and the will begin to assert themselves in new ways. "The will in its freedom chooses to go against nature and natural impulse in order to conquer nature and its secrets. Here is the first step toward the metaphysics of power that will dominate the modern age . . . . There is left to man nothing but his Will to Power over objects." Technological man is "the final descendant of Cartesian man."[18] And accompanying the mechanization and technicization of all possible areas of life is "a consumer crowned by science."[19]

The evolving Cartesian-modern voyage into the interior of the thinking self results in a progressive reduction, differentiation, and distancing of the world as its object. Things are increasingly alienated from reason, knowability, and relatedness, and reduced to mindless, mechanical matter, energy, or some neutral stuff that is unrelated to the human and the divine. And in the more skeptical stages of subsequent radical empiricism and radical idealism, material things are reduced merely to subjective sensations and/or ideas (Berkeley, Hume, Fichte, Hegel). Such a voyage into the self is profoundly and essentially non-biblical, non-Christian, and non-human in a number of ways. Most importantly it rejects *relatedness* to the Personal Living God as its primary and most basic center and foundation. Implicitly, and then explicitly, it denies divine creation, in which *real* matter and substance are created and sustained by God, and given specific shape, order, life, and humanness by divine *ideas* or *forms*. In creation, divine archetypal ideas give preformed, potential ideas not only to the human mind, but corresponding rational structures to real material things of the world. Thus, nature is not "pure raw matter" or "mere stuff," utterly divorced from "pure mind." Mind and matter are *interrelated* by the fact that matter bears the indelible imprint of the divine mind and ideas that shape it, while human mind is, so to speak, indelibly stamped into matter. To divorce them, as Descartes began to do, and as Locke, Berkeley, Hume, Kant, and Hegel carried further, is to attempt to disassociate what God associates, and to unravel his creation, recentering it in "pure subjectivity." It is an anti-theistic, anti-logos project, since it opposes the work of the divine Logos in creation. Modern subjectivity and autonomy are required by their own philosophical foundations to reject divine creation.

From Descartes onward, modern self or subject-centeredness leads to the loss of relatedness to the world and to God, including the commonly and traditionally known essential realities of the material world—substance, integrity, causality, and even of one's own self. With Descartes the journey begins with a primary commitment to the pure thinking subject, and a resulting radical alienation and reduction of the material world. By 1690, Locke proceeds more fully into the sensing, thinking subject, with the result that substances of the world recede much further from knowability. By 1710, Berkeley moves almost exclusively into mental sensations and ideas, resulting in the complete denial of substance and matter. By 1740 Hume radicalized the direction he felt that Berkeley had not pursued to final conclusions. Hume saw that full commitment to mental sensations and ideas requires the rejection not only of substance and material things as fictions, but also of any real causality and continuity, including the real existence of an integral, substantial self (hello Postmodernism). Thus, with Hume, substantial self and world disappear, and the concept of God is reduced to natural generation and to a debilitating fiction arising from fear and superstition.

With Descartes, reason also loses its secure, ancient and medieval divine, cosmic, and objective status, and appears assimilated to the thinking subject, the "I think," or *cogito*. In this sense reason is subjectivized, and identified with each individual. The subjective path leading to Locke, Kant, and Hegel is further strengthened. Reason is no longer treated as an objective, universal form in nature, as in classical tradition, or as created in nature by the Supreme God, as in biblical and Christian theology.

Enlightenment Modernism. The group of eighteenth-century thinkers and writers known as the "philosophes"—Voltaire, Hume, Diderot, d'Alembert, Condillac, Condorcet, Helvétius, La Mettrie, Holbach, Kant, and others—formed the intellectual core of the Enlightenment. They helped to further establish the major early foundations, goals, and criteria of Modernism. In the assessment of Peter Gay, a leading historian of the Enlightenment, for Voltaire and other philosophes, "Submission to organized religion is a betrayal of man's true estate, hope for eternal salvation is a childish dream. Man, dreadful though this may often appear, is on his own. This rebellious pagan spirit dominates the philosophes' proud declarations of man's dignity." The fundamental opposition of the Enlightenment view of man to that of traditional Christianity is central to understanding it and the modern world. According to Peter Gay, "the point of view of Christian anthropology was that man is a son, dependent on God," while "the point of the Enlightenment's anthropology was that man is an adult, dependent upon himself." For Enlightenment thought, "the myths of God's fatherhood and man's fall from grace were so much nonsense."[20] Gay touches here on the most crucial issue of Enlightenment, and of modernity as a whole, that of *autonomy*—the freedom first of all from subjection to a divine Creator and Lord, and second, from all other external authority, all seen as deceptive and debilitating.

Autonomy became the cornerstone of the foundation of modernity. It was given its most extensive and authoritative philosophical formulations by Kant, and later by Hegel. Such autonomy requires *criticism*—the "rational" criticism developing ultimately into critical rejection of God, divine revelation, and related tradition in order to achieve freedom. *Criticism* is thought to increasingly yield *autonomy*, which gives *freedom*, and leads to *mastery* and *progress* toward a new and better future. By means of "rational" and "scientific" criticism, and through the benefits of the developing sciences, it was thought, mankind would be able to achieve new advances and unparalleled progress, knowledge, and happiness. But all of this depended on rejection of the idea of a Creator God, to whom one is intrinsically subject as dependent creature, ontologically, epistemologically, morally, and teleologically.[21]

The philosophes as a whole rejected the idea of original sin. Their "insistence on man's original innocence was a decisive break with Christian anthropology." "Both Christians and philosophes recognized that the Enlightenment anthropology was revolutionary."[22] The new anthropocentric idea, common to the philosophes, and expressive of autonomy, was precisely stated by Diderot: "For man is the unique starting point, and the end to which everything must be related."[23] This view inverts a key biblical theme by asserting that man, not Christ, is "the Alpha and the Omega, the Beginning and the End." Hume believed this no less strongly than Diderot, holding that human nature is "the capital or center" of the sciences, and that "the science of man is the only foundation for the other sciences."[24]

Hume: the Fiction of World, Substance, Self, and Soul. In David Hume's (1711-1776) radically empirical view the world, self, and soul vanish as substantial, integral, knowable realities. Developing further the direction established from Descartes through Locke, and pressing Locke's sensationalism to radical ends, Hume claims that sensations and the ideas derived from them are *all* we can know. Even more exclusively than in Locke, ideas in the mind, rather than actual things of the world become the sole objects of our knowledge. Following the lead of Berkeley, Hume also does away with Locke's notion of *abstraction* from the ideas of sense experience, and identifies the sense image with the idea. A kind of nominalism results in which "every distinct perception is a distinct existence, and is different, distinguishable and separable from every other perception." "The understanding never observes any real connection among objects."[25] As Hume wrote in *A Treatise of Human Nature* (1739-40), "all ideas are derived from impressions, and are nothing but copies and representations of them." "Impressions and ideas differ only in their strength and vivacity."[26]

All of reality for Hume becomes only perceptions (sense impressions plus the ideas derived from them). We cannot even proceed from our perceptions to objects of the external world that we imagine cause them. There is no evidence that sensations are caused by supposed external objects, substance, or God. "We can never hope to attain any satisfactory knowledge with regard to the origin of our impressions or the ultimate constitution of a universe behind our impressions and ideas."[27] These concepts lead Hume to a skeptical denial of any existence external to the perceptions: "For as to the notion of external existence, when taken for something specifically different from our perceptions, we have already shown its *absurdity*." He even refers to it as a "*fiction*," and indicates nature and reason as "*two enemies*."[28]

With perception as the exclusive basis of knowledge, Hume rejects the reality of substance: "We have no perfect idea of any thing but of a perception. A substance is entirely different from a perception. We have, therefore, no idea of substance." The argument also extends to mind, self, and soul. Mind can be nothing more than a grouping of perceptions for Hume: "what we call mind is nothing but a heap or collection of perceptions" that "exist separately."[29] If substance is a fiction, so is "soul." We have no idea of any integral substance of soul, mind, or self. Thus, Hume sails deeper than Descartes and Locke into subjectivity. He "does away with both mind and matter, knowing subject and external objects, and reduces all to perceptions which are both knower and known."[30] With Hume there is already a radical modern subjectivity in which objective self, world, and God vanish.

In his *Natural History of Religion* (1755), Hume claims that religion has purely natural rather than divine origins, attributing it not even to essential aspects of human nature, but to lesser, derivative aspects—especially to primitive fear and superstition in the face of the hardships and vagaries of life. In this sense religion for Hume had a "natural history" which he traced back to "ignorance and fear" in early primitive peoples. J. C. A. Gaskin indicates that in numerous writings on religion Hume put together a "comprehensive critique" of religion, attempting to philosophically crush all reasons why anyone should believe in a God or gods. He attacked and undermined the major supports for religious belief as they were understood in his time, including claims of divine revelation, prophecy, miracles, the existence and immortality of the soul, and arguments for the existence of God from design in the world. In this way he sought to methodically annihilate the essential bases of religious belief in God or gods. Hume anticipated Kant by seeking to destroy ontological, cosmological, and teleological proofs for the existence of God. Essentially for Hume, "all religious belief appears to derive from fear and ignorance." But because of the dangers of prosecution or strong social penalties for making such claims during his time, he often made short covering statements that conflict with his main arguments against religion and reasons for belief in God, and seem to present him as a supporter of faith, and of God. These tactics fooled few, however, and by 1745 he "had been branded as a religious skeptic with atheistic tendencies."[31] Peter Gay designates Hume "the complete modern pagan." For him, "religion has lost all specificity and all authority; it is no more than a dim, meaningless, and unwelcome shadow on the face of reason." The tension of his philosophy with Christianity is "wholly unappeasable at all points." "He was willing to live with uncertainty, with no supernatural justifications . . . . Hume makes plain that since God is silent, man is his own master: he must live in a disenchanted world, submit everything to criticism, and make his own way."[32]

The Subjective Modernism of Kant. Most influential in the early foundation of modern thought was the German philosopher Immanuel Kant (1724-1804). Essential to his writings is the concept that the autonomous self replaces the Sovereign Creator God as authority. Kant "destroys the traditional arguments in defense of morality and Christianity" and "culminates the Enlightenment ideal of the rational autonomy of the individual."[33] He named and defined the modern concept of "autonomy," which Robert Pippin says is "the great, single modernity problem in the German tradition," and "the deepest assumption in modernity's self-understanding."[34] "Kant finally inaugurates in a radical and consistent way the modern idea of a new, self-determining beginning." His Modernism "is more consistent than any other with modernity's general self-understanding as an origination in history, a beginning not bounded or conditioned by tradition or religious authority, finally free and independent, and so fully self-conscious about its own possibility."[35]

Descartes had paved the way for "making the relevance of the knowing self the center of thought." With his *Cogito, ergo sum*, Descartes "initiated all the movements which find their point of departure in the I as the subject of experience and understanding," thus creating a "cleavage in intellectual history." "Kant works out the principle programmatically in his great *Critiques*. The I is always present now as an autonomous theme."[36] The thinking subject is seen as more independent, more self-dependent, than ever before in history—the formulator of all experience and knowledge, the legislator of morality, the formulator of beauty and purpose in art, and thus the creator of its own world out of the meaningless flux of experience.

As Kant formulated it, the thinking subject is *self-grounded* in its own determinative sense experience, reason, mental categories, ideas, will, and aesthetic and teleological judgment. This philosophy rejects belief in a real Creator God as its basis, a God to whom each person is subject as dependent creature—subject to his truth, law, authority, divine revelation, and entirely dependent upon for redemption. As Cornelius Van Til has written:

Though Kant disclaims knowledge of the supersensible realm, he nonetheless makes, to all effects, a universal negative statement about it. He is certain that the God who lives in that realm cannot be man's creator and law-giver. To hold to such a God would be against the principles of theoretical reason. Thus theoretical reason, while with seeming humility abstains from making any pronouncements about the realm of the practical reason, nevertheless makes sure for itself that only a certain kind of God *can* exist there. It is a God who makes no demands on man. It is a God against whom man could not sin and therefore has not sinned. Accordingly, man's radical evil is not so radical as to need atonement by any sacrifice provided by God himself. Salvation is a matter of character. After making sure that no Creator-redeemer God in the biblical sense of the term can exist in the realm of practical reason, Kant projects into this realm a God who is good by human standards. And this good God is then said, somehow, to cause the good to prevail even in the natural realm.[37]

Leonhard Stählin emphasizes that the "underlying principle" of Kant's entire Critical System is "the principle of the spontaneity and autonomy of the human mind." In so doing, "Kant isolates the subject from all real being"—from things in themselves, and from God; "the original connection between [the subject] and God is completely severed." The outcome is that "we are logically driven to deny, not only the real existence of things, but also the existence of God," and "it becomes impossible to retain our hold on any reality at all."[38] Kant also "conceived the moral being of each man to be centered in himself and to exist in a self-determined inward realm (autonomy) that bars the entrance of another . . . . The kind of autonomy for which Kant stood unflinchingly was for Paul the very source of man's sinful predicament, namely: unbelief, in which one removes the center of his being from the divine center to which it belongs; and *hubris*, the act by which one makes himself the center of himself and his world."[39] "The age had now dawned in which the dominant vision was of a world which man creates for himself scientifically, artistically, and philosophically."[40]

There is no possibility of the biblical God still being the origin and center—the Supreme Being and Creator, and source of being, ultimate truth, law, authority, and redemption in Kant's philosophy. Instead, God and the world are conceptually transformed into "rational ideas," ideals, or essential postulates of the human mind—the formative ideas of "pure reason," the implications of "practical reason," the "moral imperative," and the representations of "aesthetic ideas" and experience in art. Kant thus reverses Christian and classical positions in which anthropology, epistemology, ethics, and aesthetics are subordinate to and dependent upon religion and theology and centered in God (Christian), and metaphysics-ontology (classical): he makes religion, theology, and metaphysics wholly dependent upon anthropology, epistemology, ethics, and aesthetics, centering them in man.

In his first major work, the *Critique of Pure Reason*, Kant attacks the arguments of natural theology and metaphysics, attempting to destroy rational grounds for the existence of God. He repeatedly stresses the difference between God as actual highest intelligence and real cause of the world, and "God" as an idea of "pure reason":

It makes a great difference whether something is represented to our reason as an *object absolutely*, or merely as an *object in the idea*. In the former case my concepts are meant to determine the object, in the latter *there is only a schema to which no object, not even a hypothetical one, corresponds directly*, but which only serves to represent to ourselves indirectly other objects through their relation to that idea, and according to their systematical unity. *Thus I say that the concept of a highest intelligence is a mere idea . . . .*[41]

161

Here, typical of this *Critique*, "God" is represented as "only a schema," "a mere idea." And our notion "that the things of the world" somehow "owe their existence to some supreme intelligence" is "heuristic only," representing no real Being corresponding to the idea, and indicating no "constitution and connection of the objects of experience in general." "We have not the slightest ground," Kant claims, "to admit absolutely the object" of the "hypothesis of a Being which is the only and all-sufficient cause of all cosmological series [cosmos, world, universal laws as known by experience and reason], . . . the idea of God."[42] "God" is interpreted as a formative, regulative idea of pure reason, not a real, knowable, living Being—an idea serving to unify and systematize human experience and thought. Kant's "theory of knowledge wholly disallows the objective existence of God. While Kant holds that the idea of God is a necessary conception of reason, he rules out any conclusion that God actually exists as an external metaphysical reality."[43] "God is here no longer, as in the seventeenth century, the experienceable and knowable *ground* of finite being, human autonomy, moral experience, and future hope; for Kant, the idea of God is rather (in part) the implication of an unknowable ideal of pure reason, supplementing an autonomously studied nature, and (much more surely) the consequence and so the postulate of autonomously acting moral reason." This is truly a "radically transformed status for the idea of God."[44]

Ernst Cassirer has written that Kant's "transcendental analogue to the metaphysical concept of God as the 'most real being' . . . [is] not the totality of absolute existence [as in traditional theology and metaphysics], but only the expression of a definite epistemological postulate." More simply expressed, in the *Critique of Pure Reason* Kant's concept of God is not of a real existing Being, but of a postulate of human thought—a basic but unknowable and unprovable human idea. Kant holds that what is involved in rational claims that God is real is an "illusion of the understanding," "an intellectual fraud," a "false dialectical reification," "by which we attribute objective reality to an Idea that functions solely as a rule." And in Kant's practical, moral philosophy, God is thought of "not as Creator, not as the explanation of the genesis of the world, but as the guarantee of its moral goal and end." "This assumption is in no way necessary *for* morality, but rather is necessitated *by* it." Similarly, in the *Critique of Judgment*, "the aim is definitely not to comprehend God in the metaphysical sense as the infinite substance with attributes and properties, but to try to determine ourselves and our wills appropriately. The concept of God is the concrete form under which we think our intelligible moral task and its progressive empirical fulfillment."[45]

In such ways Kant philosophically rejected the primary, foundational belief and doctrine of Judeo-Christianity—that of the actual living Reality,

Being, and Sovereignty of God, the self-existent creative source of all life. It is not surprising then to find that in some way or degree he opposed all major aspects of historical Christian belief and doctrine—divine creation, revelation, the fall, grace, judgment, the incarnate divinity of Christ, divine redemption and salvation through Christ, the indwelling Holy Spirit, miracles, worship, ceremonial praise of God, prayer, and the church. "The only really acceptable religion for Kant is a religion of pure reason." He only condoned special divine revelation when it accorded with precepts naturally revealed to everyone through reason. "He regarded creeds as unconscionable impositions on our inner freedom of thought."[46]

He revealed many of his views in *Religion within the Boundaries of Mere Reason Alone* (1793). Historical and supernatural events of the Bible are symbolically reinterpreted as inner spiritual and mental ones. The idea of God reflects genuine human inner moral disposition, but to attribute objective reality to "God" is illusory. "To believe in Christ" means to strive to realize the ideal of human nature within one's own self; the incarnation of God in Christ is rejected. The only foundation for the church is the "pure faith of reason." To subordinate human reason to biblical and church doctrine, creed, and dogma constitutes "false service." Mankind is duty bound to serve in the transition from historical orthodox tradition to the new religious faith of reason, helping humanity to "come of age."[47]

Since Kant rejected belief in the actual Being and historical revelation of God known to Hebrew-Christian tradition, his own alternative conception of God could only lead away from it. Rather than reaffirming God and Christianity in a new, modern context after the atheism of the later Enlightenment, as has sometimes been suggested, it proves to be one of Christianity's most insidious and subversive opponents. In *Religion within the Boundaries of Mere Reason Alone* he *redefined* the central doctrines of Christianity in terms of reason and humanity, inverting their orthodox meanings. His philosophy became "the basis of liberal Protestantism,"[48] and predecessor of many nineteenth and twentieth-century "spiritual beliefs" that went still further by absolutizing or deifying the subject or self, giving it the name of "God," "Absolute Ego," "Absolute Reason," "Absolute Spirit," "World Soul," "the Numinous," or "the Collective Unconscious." Like Kant's philosophy, spiritual views such as those of Fichte, Schelling, Hegel, Rudolf Otto, and Carl Jung reject orthodox doctrine as repressive and destructive, and reassign the effective center of reality, power, and causality—the religious a priori—to human thought, experience, and praxis.

In Kant's philosophy human self-consciousness takes itself to be central, self-dependent, and determinative: by its own rational perception, intuitional forms, categories, and ideas, it gives form, unity, structure, law, and system to an otherwise raw and formless manifold of sense-impressions—it creates the entire formal structure and systematic meaning of knowledge by itself: first, rational intuition imparts the formal structures of space and time to the flux of sense impressions; second, rational judgment (*Verstand*) connects and relates the resulting phenomena by means of twelve innate "categories," giving lawful structure to what we know as "nature"; and third, "reason" (*Vernunft*), the highest faculty, gives systematic organization to the judgments by structuring them according to a series of innate universal ideas of the mind—self, world (nature, cosmos), and God. Thus, human reason structures its own understandings of knowledge; it erects its own rational ideas of self and world; it determines and projects a rational idea of God suitable to the demands of pure and practical reason and morality; it creates a sense of form, goal, and ultimacy through art; and it creates its own religious ideals and the means of their realization.

Kant's Reversal of Traditional Views of Reality and Truth. Kant's "Copernican revolution" is first presented in his theory of knowledge expounded in the *Critique of Pure Reason*. This work essentially shifted the basis of philosophy further in the direction modern philosophy had been moving since Descartes: from a primary basis in God, Being, Logos, *eide*, *nous*, cosmos, and world, to one in the conscious subject and its experiences, forms, ideas, reason, knowledge, will, and practical actions. Kant first fully asserted the primacy of the formative, legislative, and creative capabilities of the human mind in knowledge in the *Critique of Pure Reason* (1781). In the next two, the *Critique of Practical Reason* (1788), and the *Critique of Judgment* (1790), he did something similar for moral will and art. In these works all knowable reality is referred to the knowing subject rather than to God's Living Being, Mind, Ideas, and their guarantee that created things are real and knowable. "There is here a complete shifting of the center to which all is referred, but in other respects all that was previously said of *being* has now to be said of *knowing*."[49]

Prior to modern subjectivism and its pivotal formulations in Kant, Western philosophy, as well as ordinary experience, had held that *our knowledge must conform to objects*. Kant's revolution was to reverse these views, maintaining that "*objects must conform to our knowledge.*" This meant that Kant attributed to human thought, and to nothing else—not to God or to things themselves—the all-important principles and laws of reality and knowledge: *space, time, unity, substance, existence, causality, self, world,* and *God*—now conceived as purely subjective mental forms, categories, and ideas, not as objective, external realities. *This epochal reversal—from a basis in the reality of logos-structured creation and the reality of God's Being and Truth, to one in human-centered and determined reality, knowledge, and meaning—was to prove determinative for modernity.*

Where common sense and previous philosophy saw the mind circling around and conforming to its objects, just as common sense and Ptolemaic astronomy saw the sun circling around the earth, Kant postulates that the objects of knowledge conform to the knowing mind, just as Copernicus postulated that the earth circles around the sun. Hume had seen that sense experience presents only discrete, unconnected particulars and that their necessary connection into universal causal laws is the work of the mind by means of its principle of habit or custom . . . . Kant extended this organizing power of the mind to all knowledge whatsoever, and his 'Copernican' revolution is thus a generalization of Hume's principle of habit. *More broadly speaking, Kant's "Copernican" revolution is the logical outcome of the drive toward subjectivism which can be seen all through modern philosophy.* If modern philosophers of quite different approaches are all forced to conclude that the mind can know only its own ideas, this must be because the objects of human knowledge conform to the knowing mind.[50]

Kant's entire philosophy is built on the foundational claims of the pure subjectivity of the *forms, categories,* and *ideas.* The two *forms* of sensory experience are *space* and *time*; the twelve *categories* of the understanding are: quantity—*unity, plurality, totality*; quality—*reality, negation, limitation*; relation—*substance, causation, reciprocity*; modality—*possibility and impossibility, existence and non-existence, necessity and contingency*; the three *transcendental ideas* of pure reason are *self, world,* and *God.* Outside of sense experience, none of these have any guaranteed objective reality.[51] Anything else Kant says in trying to establish some form of "realism" to save his philosophy from charges of pure subjective idealism, illusion, or atheism, cannot deny this basic foundation without self-destruction.

The unprecedented extent of human autonomy and subjectivity established in Kant's philosophy provided widely respected, influential, and authoritative grounds for historically new, human-centered philosophies, religions, and aesthetics—for the *philosophies of subject* and *Humanity* that were developed during the 1770s, '80s, and '90s by Herder, Fichte, Schelling, Schleiermacher, and Novalis. Hegel and Schopenhauer carried these ideas to apparent limits by about 1820. But by pressing the direction to further ends, Strauss, Feuerbach, and Marx constructed more radical philosophies of total, atheistic humanism during the 1830s, '40s, and '50s. With them, theology became wholly anthropology. And by the 1840s and '50s August Comte began to establish his "Religion of Humanity," renaming Humanity "the Great Being," and making it the center of worship in his "Church of Humanity." Helmut Thielicke describes this as the "Dawn of the New Age: Emancipation of Adult Man," in which "man has learned to see himself as adult and this has made him his own theme." **"Once he gets the idea he can comprehend humanity apart from God and must respect its autonomous dignity as an end in itself, *there is no going back.*"**[52]

The Revolutionary Views of Romanticism. William Blake (1757-1827), older than other Romantics, but living through the heart of the Romantic movement, was the quintessential radical Romantic and "arch-non-conformist, a private rebel who wished to reject virtually the entire system of art, society, and religion into which he was born in the mid-eighteenth century in favor of a grandiose private structure of new myths, new moral truths, even new visual vocabularies that might provide vehicles for the eradication of what he saw as the corrupt status quo (hello twentieth-century Modernism/Post-modernism).[53]

Blake created his own personal reinterpretation of religion, life, art, and the Bible. His painting of the *Ancient of Days* and his *Book of Urizen* (both 1794) are major examples of his own "private interpretations of the origins of the universe" and passionate efforts "to rewrite the Book of Genesis" for a world in need of revisions. Blake treats the "Creator" in these works as the evil "Urizen" ("Your Reason"), who delimits man's freedom and divides his infinite nature by means of abstraction, reason, geometry, and fixed laws.[54] According to Blake, "The evil that is in this world must be due to the Creator of the world. . . . the Creator of this world is a very cruel Being."[55] His attribution of evil to the Creator amounts to a blasphemous rejection of the Hebrew-Christian God. Similar thoughts are found among negative and late Romantics. Blake tended to reverse the attributes of God and Satan, making God evil and Satan a symbol of the forces of life, energy, and goodness (hello Nietzsche).

In *The Book of Urizen* Blake created a personal, mythical account of the origin of "natural" existence. As Leslie Tannenbaum writes, he "inverts the entire book of Genesis," and by satirizing it, "attacks orthodox theology and philosophy, which he believes to be the true cause of the Fall." *The Book of Urizen* serves as the Genesis of "The Bible of Hell" that Blake had promised in *The Marriage of Heaven and Hell* (1790-91). His imaginative, mythical account of creation as Fall cannot be divine creation, however, because there is no transcendent Creator, and the actual result is a dividing and limiting "fall" from an original, infinite, and eternal state into a horribly confined temporal existence and death. The two separate masculine agents behind this fallen existence, Urizen and Los, are Blake's satirical play on the two creation accounts in Genesis that identify "Elohim" and "Jahweh" (Jehovah) as Creator. They are Blake's way of suggesting that "the God of creation is self-divided." Both actually represent "fragmented parts of fallen or natural man." Thus, "creation" to Blake is the most evil event, since it represents the fall of man from his eternal and infinite "real" state of Oneness into the divisions, conflicts, confusions, and limitations of existence.

Urizen represents all that Blake hated about "one-eyed Reason"—its abstract universal laws, "mind-forged manacles," materialism, narrowness, divisions, fragmentation, conflicts, and jealousies. The laws of good and evil, including the Ten Commandments and all universal moral laws, are fundamental aspects of this abstract division of infinite Reality into polar opposites by Urizen in the Creation-Fall. With this division and the triumph of Urizen-Elohim's Law and "Justice" over the "Mercy" of Los-Jehovah, and with reference to God's foreknowledge of the Fall, "Blake is asserting that the world was created by a fragmented, imperfect being for the sole purpose of accusing man of sin." In these ways, Blake sees the creator as "arbitrary and perverse."[56]

For Blake existence is not a moral fall through disobedience of divine laws, but a fall from imagination, creativity, and ultimately from the original unity and Oneness that he referred to as "the infinite," "the Eternal." God is not the good and holy Creator, with man his dutiful creature. The divine is found only in Man and imagination: "Throughout Blake's work, the true world-ruler is 'Jesus, the Imagination', the 'God within', whose mystical marriage with the soul is celebrated in the last plate of *Jerusalem*." Blake was interested in "'the religions of all nations' as an expression of the one Imagination."[57] He thought of Jesus and the Apostles as artists, and considered the Virgin birth an act of free love, adultery with an unidentified father, making Christ illegitimate.[58] He thought that Christ's "real message lay in his challenge to authority."[59]

Penetrating the colorful and complex, personally invented myths, symbols, allegories, and proverbs of his writings (no short or simple task), we find that ultimately Blake did not believe in a transcendent God, or in divine creation, revelation, a moral fall, sin, or divine redemption. Such a God represents Evil to Blake, because he stands for confining reason, fixed laws, human limitation, division, and enslavement, and denial of the ultimate Oneness that Blake philosophically placed above all things. Humanity could not imaginatively and creatively expand to rightful *infinity*, *Eternity*, and *Oneness* in the face of an independent, Sovereign Creator God.

While the Bible was Blake's central reading and material source, he essentially disbelieved it, satirized, denied it, and constantly inverted its contents, while imitating its structural and thematic types, word-use, and sound. In *The Marriage of Heaven and Hell*, he writes of speaking and dining with the Old Testament prophets Isaiah and Ezekiel, who renounce and invert their biblical messages: Isaiah says, "I saw no God, nor heard any, . . .

but my senses discover'd the infinite in every thing . . . ."; Ezekiel now says that for Israel "the Poetic Genius (as you now call it)" was God, the "first principle," and "origin." Blake then has his "particular friend," the Devil, state his own view that there is no God except Man: "The worship of God is: Honouring his gifts in other men, each according to his genius, and loving the greatest men best: those who envy or calumniate great men hate God; for there is no other God." Much like Enlightenment philosophes, Blake briefly explains how ancient Poets had invented "Gods and Geniuses" to identify objects and places, "till a system was formed, which took some advantage of and enslav'd the vulgar by attempting to realize or abstract the deities from their objects: thus began Priesthood." "Thus men forgot that All deities reside in the human breast."[60]

Although Blake used religious myth and idiom to convey his revolutionary views, "all that is most incisive and creative in his thought or expression is directed towards life on earth, towards society and the individuals composing it, and not to other-worldly spheres."[61]

Many Romantics, like Blake, Shelley, and Byron, were hostile to the Christian doctrine of God. They rejected belief in such a living Supreme Being, and any revealed absolute truths and laws, seeing them as *projected human concepts*[62] serving only to enslave man and thwart the realization of inner powers of Nature through imaginative creativity and self-development in the arts. Such an artificial God also limits freedom, preventing proper enjoyment of beauty, pleasure, love, and sex. In treating the Christian conception of God as an illusory human projection, many Romantics rejected biblical revelation and traditional knowledge of God, substituting Romantic concepts of *Nature*, *Man*, and *Art*, which assumed much of the ultimacy and attributes of God.

In England, Shelley (1790-1822) prophesied "a new religion 'antithetical' to Christianity," turning to pre-Christian Greek paganism for inspiration, and identifying with the forces of nature, intrinsically associated with eros and sex. It is in such Romantic thought that we find the ancestry of modern neo-paganism, which centralizes and glorifies natural forces from below as the "dark gods" of eros and sex. Something similar existed with Blake, Byron, and Novalis, and was developed further by late Romantics and High Moderns such as Yeats, D. H. Lawrence, and Joyce.

In Shelley's poetic masterpiece, *Prometheus Unbound* (1818-19, published 1820), Jupiter represents a tyrannical, human-projected God like those of Blake's Urizen and Nobodaddy, while Prometheus, who finally triumphs over Jupiter, symbolizes creative mind and imagination, so beloved by Romantics, and associated with mankind. Prometheus's victory is "a victory over the kind of religion now associated with the names of Jehovah and Jesus" and a restoration of pre-Christian paganism. For Shelley, who had argued early on for the "necessity of atheism," "God, if he exists at all, can exist only as existence, as an aspect of our own identity."[63]

Shelley's Jupiter stands for the Christian God, and other "false and oppressive human mental fabrications"—religious, moral, or political—God, priest, church, cleric, king, or despot. All are phantom human constructs, reified and established as ruling powers that cruelly subjugate humanity. Thus Shelley characterizes Jupiter as "the Oppressor of mankind." He is "the principle of disunion," representing human mind and spirit separated from, and opposed by its own creations. As in the Enlightenment, the factors that sustain this self-imposed servitude are "hypocrisy, custom, hatred, fear, and contempt." Jupiter will vanish if only they are withdrawn.

Although Shelley highly admired Jesus in the context of morality, he considered the doctrine of his divinity to be sheer imposture. So is all divine revelation. "Moses' claim that he heard the voice of God was a fraud designed to enforce his new code on the people," as Michael Ferber writes. In "Hymn to Intellectual Beauty" Shelley specifically rejected divine revelation: "No voice from some sublimer world hath ever/ To sage or poet these responses given/ Therefore the name of God and ghosts and Heaven,/ Remain the record of their vain endeavor . . . ." It is only our own voice that we vainly hear in all quests for transcendent religious certainty. Queen Mab, in the poem of that title (1812-13, pub. 1821), is Shelley's educative voice to the British people, teaching them "cosmic self-sufficiency against the dogmas of creation, incarnation, resurrection, and the like." She teaches that "God, Hell, and Heaven," are foisted on us by hypocritical clerics.[64] According to Shelley, a destructive revolt against Christianity is at the generative center of modern thought and literature: "We owe the great writers of the golden age of our literature to that fervid awakening of the public mind which shook to dust the oldest and most oppressive form of the Christian religion."[65]

Lord Byron (1788-1824) opposed essential Christian doctrines, most importantly that of the Trinity, as "superstitions." As Jerome McGann points out, Byron denied the divinity of Jesus Christ, although he too upheld the exemplary value of his life as worthy of imitation. He also denied the Virgin Birth, and constantly opposed the doctrine of the eternity of hell, seeing these doctrines as un-biblical. He rejected the doctrine of original sin and flatly denied the doctrine of the Atonement, or salvation through Christ.

Byron certainly recognized "the wickedness and depravity of human nature," the cruelty and evil of human acts, but he did not see them as sins against God. Evil for him was an ethical, not a theological matter; it is between human beings, not between man and God. The Genesis themes of a paradisal Garden of Eden and an original unity and goodness broken by the fall, are central ones in his poetry, but he interprets them allegorically, giving them meanings far different from those of the Bible.

He spoke of the biblical story of creation and the fall as "an allegory."[66] He criticized those who upheld biblical doctrines of sin and judgment. In his view they obsessively focus on evil and unforgiving judgment, setting them in opposition to his strong belief in freedom and charity. Other results of such "superstitions" for Byron are ignorance and sectarian dogmatism, which render people unable to "think for themselves"—"a key Byronic idea." In fundamental opposition to such dogmas, Byron maintained two constant themes: "a determined intellectual freedom" accompanied by tolerance and mutual sympathy.[67]

Byron's own religious beliefs consisted of a "loose set of principles," prominently displaying deistic and liberal Socinian concepts, although "his own vigorous skepticism . . . made it difficult for him to affirm or deny anything categorically." He expressed belief in a single reigning deity, "the Almighty God of Deism, the First Principle and Cause of all," "the energic source of the universe," apart from man as well as Christ.[68]

Despite his constant stress on intellectual freedom, Byron was a fatalist, but not a predestinarian. He saw history as "a blind series of cycles, totally without morality as such." While rejecting the key doctrines of Christianity, Byron was partly attracted to Italian Catholicism, especially to what he perceived as its elegant, sensuous, and materialistic aspects. He saw it as a "tangible religion" with "something sensible to grasp at"— "incense, pictures, statues, altars, shrines, relics, and the real presence, confession, absolution," as well as the thought that "it leaves no possibility of doubt."[69]

In his late drama *Cain* (1821), as McGann indicates, Byron treats the Hebrew-Christian God Jehovah as an evil, cruel, and bloodthirsty tyrant. Although he is supposedly the creator of all corporeal existence, he has no love or sympathy for humanity. He fosters strife through the doctrines of election and sinfulness, and brutalizes creation with his demand for blood sacrifice. Jehovah, the God of Adam and Abel in *Cain*, is not really the eternal Creator however, but merely an interloper, entirely historical and circumstantial in nature. Only "Life" has existed from the beginning. "The world that Cain sees is the latest form that Life has urged upon matter through the agency of the god Jehovah." Jehovah is "a temporary power—very like Shelley's Jupiter." He "has formed the present state of the world," but Byron does not indicate when he will be superseded.

In contrast, Byron's deistic "One True God is the source of life, a totally amoral Entity which presides over and perdures through the various convulsions that the earth and its inhabitants suffer." The other principal figure in *Cain* is Lucifer, who reigns together with and in opposition to Jehovah. "Their opposition is the allegorical representation of man's dual nature (mind and body)." "Lucifer is the intellectual power of man's world," while Jehovah, although immaterial, rules over matter. "Being a composite of these two powers, man alone has the power to love truly (Lucifer cannot love, and Jehovah can only establish restricted, codified, and unfree relationships)." Both Lucifer and Jehovah desire absolute power, but neither is able to love. "Lucifer reigns over a confederacy of anarchists bent upon hatred and opposition only, while Jehovah reigns over a union of ignorant worshippers."[70]

Hegel's Radical Redefinition of God: Mankind Progressively Actualizes Subjective Spirit. Subjectivism in nineteenth-century modern philosophy reached a kind of ultimate with Georg Wilhelm Friedrich Hegel (1770-1831). Although the chief German "Idealist," he is closely related to Romanticism in several key ways. All his major theories were devised to explain how reality is a whole, a unity, and precisely how finite things constitute the infinite in a total, unified system. "God" had to be completely redefined for such a monistic system. He is no longer the eternally complete and perfect living Spiritual Being, the One who lives in eternal wholeness and unity, but the growing, changing, dialectical evolution and realization of "Spirit" in and through time, process, and human thought in a comprehensive unity of all concepts and things. For Hegel, like many Romantics, the one reality that could so comprehend, resolve, and unify *all* contradictory things into a unified whole, is Spirit or Mind (*Geist*). "Mind" may be somewhat closer to Hegel's meaning of *Geist* than "Spirit," since he traces the process of the gradually, historically evolving whole to mind, thought, reason, and ultimately to *"the Idea," "the concept" (der Begriff)* indicating the most decisive categories that humanity adopts for the nature and structure of things. The categories were centrally important for reality in the philosophy of Kant, before him in Aristotle, and in the related, reality-determining Ideas of Plato. But they were shifted by Kant to the subjective human mind. Hegel radicalizes the subjectivity of the categories, and embeds them in dialectically developing history.[71]

In traditional Christian terms the categories have been identified with the Archetypal Ideas of God that are determinative for creation—its nature, structure, relationships, and purposes. The Archetypal Ideas are not only in the mind of God the Father, but in the mind of Christ the *Logos*, through whom the Father accomplishes creation. For Hegel, however, there is no longer an objective, eternal, Supreme Being, whether triune or not, in whom the Ideas or categories have their origin. Instead it is the naked, "abstract" mind, reason, concept, *the Idea* alone, which Hegel declares as the first, original source of all nature, things, and reality. Spirit, thought, and Idea are then identified as "the subject" that is the general source of all things that exist, *positing things, all phenomena, and ultimately producing the comprehensive whole, which is Reality or Being.* In this sense "the subject" is reinterpreted by Hegel as *God or Being itself.* The "subject," though theoretically Spirit, Mind, and "Idea," achieves actuality and development only through human activity, however. In this sense mankind actualizes and produces Being or God by progressively manifesting and realizing through "adequate concepts" the full, comprehensive reality of Spirit. Not the biblical God, but *fully developed subjective thought,* with its actual locus in mankind, is reinterpreted as *Being, substance,* as *Reality* itself. *Subjectivity* thus becomes "the only basic of this reality,"[72] "self-determining," free, and absolute. All the fundamental categories of Christian and classical thought are redefined and inverted in this system!

The interpretations of Christ and Christianity by Hegel show just how far a great modern thinker can go in distorting the nature and teachings of both. His fantasies are related to those of the Enlightenment before, and then to Nietzsche, Freud, and Heidegger after him. For Hegel the notion of Jesus as Messiah was only a myth. And Christianity was a failed religion, especially because, in his way of thinking, Jesus had to die because the world was not prepared to receive his message. That message, according to Hegel, was the modern one of *autonomy*! Jesus had renounced the Jewish morality of law grounded on external authority and turned instead to teachings based on reason and the heart (Hegel's own philosophical grounds). Such "alien" law is an imposition on our "natural" inner self. Jesus tried to replace external authority and laws with inner reason and feeling—to exchange "heteronomy" for "autonomy." Hegel criticized Jewish religious belief and Christianity as dreaded forms of "positive" religion, meaning that they were based on external authority and a system of religious propositions upheld as truth, rather than on our natural inner reason supplemented by our feeling response to reason.

Because Jesus' contemporaries, including his disciples, failed to understand his message, they fell back on a false worship of Christ himself, and empty belief in an afterlife. Abraham, Father of the Jewish nation, had broken with nature and with his tribe at the very beginning, thereby initiating loss of an original oneness and unity with nature, resulting in a separation from nature and others, and an "unhappy consciousness." With nature externalized, so was God, according to Hegel. This projected deity was made into a God of *Heerschaft* (domination), with human beings as his slaves. Judeo-Christianity thus became one of the primary and most destructive forms of the master-slave mentality [cf. Nietzsche later]. Christ tried to recall people to their lost unity with nature, reason, and the heart, but when that message was misunderstood, he was forced to fall back on the Messiah myth. In *Phenomenology of Spirit* Hegel reinterprets the Incarnation, Crucifixion, and Pentecost as successive steps in the history of God-Spirit-Nature moving toward greater realization in mankind—God must live his life through man.[73]

With its intensifying exclusion of the biblical God, modern philosophy from Kant through German Idealism, culminating in Hegel, represents the primary expression of the so-called "death of God." God is excluded and replaced in these key modern philosophies by humanity, or more precisely, *the conscious, thinking subject*. German Idealism thus provides philosophical sanction to its twin sister, Romanticism, for the death of God, cited by Octavio Paz as the beginning of the theme in modern literature. This momentous historical change must also be associated with another one linked with Kant and German Idealism—the end of metaphysics in modern philosophy. Present-day thinkers such as Jürgen Habermas find an end of the force of modern metaphysical thinking with Hegel. Richard Rorty associated himself with Hegel, Nietzsche, Heidegger, and Derrida in "jostling for the position of history's first really radical anti-Platonist." And Andrew Bowie cites the "failure of totalizing projects like Hegel's" as a key point for contemporary discussions of the "end of metaphysics" and "end of philosophy."[74] Logic suggests, however, that these momentous historical "endings" follow from the exclusion of the objective, transcendent reality of God.

Nietzsche's Assault on God and Metaphysics. Sixty years after Hegel, Friedrich Nietzsche (1844-1900) drew more radical consequences from these developments in modern thought. He not only saw and described the breakdown of European beliefs and values, but sought to take the necessary last step of philosophically crushing the remaining "vestiges" of belief in God, Being, divine and metaphysical Truth, Reason, the Good, world order, moral world order, and related categories and values. He sought to establish a New Gospel of the superman or overman (*Übermensch*) who could live and flourish with power and creativity in such a groundless, structureless, valueless, and purposeless world.

"No thinker in the history of modern philosophy has made such a radical attack on Western values as Friedrich Nietzsche. His importance as a philosopher lies precisely in the challenge he threw down to the religio-moral and intellectual foundations of Western society."[75] Sensing the rising skepticism and nihilism of his age, he believed he had discovered the root cause—the "life-denying" "lies" and "fictions" of Christianity, theism, Platonism, metaphysics, and all other transcendental beliefs. He sought to philosophically destroy these beliefs and values, and open up a "healthier" way beyond them—to a future Godless world in which human-surpassing creativity in art, philosophy, and science, driven by the "will to power," or "Dionysian life force" and passions, would raise cultural achievements to new, "superhuman" heights.

Largely ignored during his writing lifetime, Nietzsche's works quickly achieved a highly regarded and very influential position in the development of modern thought and arts during the early decades of the twentieth century. Writing during the 1870s and '80s, at the time of the rise to dominance of the avant-garde, with its anti-traditionalism, anti-Christianity, anti-Classicism, futurism, and search for new languages, values, and goals for art, Nietzsche himself expressed these and other modern concepts in their most advanced and radical form in philosophy and literature to that time. By 1900 his reputation and influence was rising rapidly. Since then he has influenced nearly every major modernist, including Freud, Jung, Mann, Rilke, Scheler, Apollinaire, Gide, Joyce, Kafka, the German Expressionists, Futurists, Dadaists and Surrealists, German and French Existentialism, and Abstract Expressionism. In recent years he has been cited as the "linchpin of early Modernism," the "pivotal Modernist," who "hailed the new and decadent as a means of cleaning out the corruption of former cultures."[76] With good reason it has been maintained that in many ways he "set the agenda . . . for the whole of modernist and postmodernist art and thought."[77] And at present, his influence continues to grow.

Nietzsche developed the most radical, most complete anti-traditionalism to his time. In his book *Joyful Wisdom* (*Die Fröhliche Wissenschaft*, 1882; also translated as *The Gay Science*), he claimed: "Over immense periods of time the intellect produces nothing but errors."[78] He continued and augmented his attacks in later books. In *Twilight of the Idols* (*Die Götzen-Dämmerung*, written 1888, published 1889), subtitled *How to Philosophize with a Hammer*, he declared his objective of sounding out the hollowness of previous forms of thought with the hammer of his criticism, declaring "there are more idols in the world than there are realities."[79]

Nietzsche attacked and maligned all transcendental and metaphysical philosophies and religions as forms of devitalizing fiction, error, lies, weakness, and slavish self-deception—including the centuries-long Platonic, Neo-Platonic, and Aristotelian traditions, and especially Christianity. He maintained that they all promoted an "unreal" absolute realm in contrast to the real, here-and-now world.

Nietzsche usually links together "Platonic metaphysics, "the Christian notion of God, and the ideal of an absolute truth, as containing variations on a common theme. They agree in sponsoring belief in a "beyond, "a "really real" world, which stands in noticeable contrast with the here-and-now "apparent" world, emptying the latter of all significance and value for men. There is supposed to be a transcendent realm of absolute truth, eternal values, and perfect being, which provides a standard for our knowledge and conduct. But this leads to a flight from the real world of becoming. Hence a philosophy of pure becoming must eliminate the absolute truth, along with the idea of God.[80]

His destructive attacks extend not only to all forms of theism, idealism, and essentialism, ancient and modern, but to the central concepts of metaphysics (self, Being, Logos, Reason, truth, form, substance, causality, identity, unity) and logic. Nietzsche, along with Freud, Wittgenstein, and Heidegger, has been cited as a "great destroyer" of Western metaphysics.[81] He attacked the Christian tradition with great intensity: "I regard Christianity as the most fatal seductive lie that has yet existed . . . ."[82] Christianity is "a form of mortal hostility against reality as yet unsurpassed,"[83] and a fatal illness from which mankind, and modern Europe, has never fully recovered.[84] He sought to completely destroy and pass beyond Christian theism and classical metaphysics (hello Postmodernism).

Nietzsche's assault on Christianity, theism, and any sense of transcendent being and morality, is contained in essence in his most famous remark, "God is dead." Although the same expression had been used by Diderot in the eighteenth, and Hegel in the early nineteenth century, Nietzsche made it well known to the world, and extended its meaning for the modern world. In a major sense Nietzsche used "God is dead" to indicate the steep decline of belief in the Christian God in the modern world, especially in the nineteenth century, and its significance. But it also expresses his own radical philosophical anti-theism, anti-Christianity, and anti-metaphysical animus.

Nietzsche's "God is dead" refers not only to the Christian God, but to all claims of transcendental realities. It "is intended to include everything that has ever been subsumed in the concept of 'God': other worlds, ultimate realities, 'things in themselves' . . . ."[85] Because of this loss of secure belief and moral value Europe was faced with the specter of *nihilism*.

For Nietzsche, the problem of nihilism arose out of the discovery that "God is dead." "God" here means the historical God of the Christian faith. But in a wider philosophical sense it means also the whole realm of supersensible reality—Platonic ideas, the Absolute, or what not—that philosophy has traditionally posited beyond the sensible realm, and in which it has located man's highest values. Now that this other, higher, eternal realm is gone, Nietzsche declared, man's highest values lose their value. If man has lost this anchor to which he has hitherto been moored, Nietzsche asks, will he not drift in an infinite void? The only value Nietzsche can set up to take the place of these highest values that have lost their value for contemporary man is: Power.[86]

More than anyone, Nietzsche was awed by the depths of nihilism beginning to emerge in the wake of Europe's increasing rejection of traditional Western beliefs and values. In retrospect, he appears to have seen much of the terrible significance and envisioned the catastrophic consequences to follow from the loss of belief in God and the consequent collapse of Christian values due to loss of metaphysical ground:

One basic thought, intended to answer the question: What is going on today "when everything is shaking and the whole earth is trembling"? gives depth and unity to these alarming descriptions of the age: *Unbelief has become a reality.* The fundamental fact of the age is becoming evident: "God is Dead." . . . "The loss of faith is notorious, . . . and now follows the cessation of fear, of authority, and of trust." Nothing remains but "living according to the moment, for the coarsest aims . . . ."[87] Nietzsche took the step that others resisted or refused to face—he directly confronted the devastating questions of ultimate disbelief and meaninglessness. His own response to this cosmic nihilism was his philosophy of the world as nothing but *becoming, will to power,* and the *superman,* who could make positive use of the will to power, through creative art, in a passionate defiance of cosmic meaninglessness and valuelessness (hello Existentialism).

But Nietzsche's own response to God was radical disbelief, revulsion, and revolt. The trouble was not just that "God is dead," but that modern man had only partially "killed him": while sliding into unbelief, he still clung to "shadows of God," afraid to finally be done with them and face the great void. For Nietzsche, the crucial question no longer concerned the reality of God, but *how to face* a Godless, Being-less, world—a world with no universals of being, truth, morality, or unity; a groundless world of change—*a world of becoming.* This is the most essential way that Nietzsche prefigures twentieth-century Modern culture. He believed that modern man must recognize this crisis of nihilism and move *beyond* it, to new, boldly affirmative, atheistic visions of reality. At the same time that he wrote of the terrible, nihilistic consequences of loss of belief in God, and suffered it deeply within himself,[88] he aggressively asserted the idea of God to be false, self-deceptive, and most destructive. The essential thrust of his philosophy was to *destroy* this belief, along with all the key doctrines and categories that accompanied it, and establish a new philosophy that totally eliminated them.

His new philosophy so radically redefined the real "that a transcendent, immutable God could not figure as a real principle in any inquiry."[89] In *Twilight of the Idols* he mocked the "stupendous concept 'God'" as "the last, thinnest, emptiest" one of human thought, central to "the brainsick fancies of morbid cobweb spinners," for which mankind "has paid dearly." "The concept 'God' has hitherto been the greatest objection to existence . . . . We deny God; in denying God, we deny accountability: only by doing *that* do we redeem the world."[90] In *Beyond Good and Evil* (1886) he tried to justify contemporary atheism, mockingly asserting that "'The father' in God has been thoroughly refuted: ditto, 'the judge,' 'the rewarder'. Also his 'free will' . . . ." Sarcastically he adds, "he does not hear—and if he heard he still would not know how to help. Worst of all: he seems incapable of clear communication."

Nietzsche's primary response to the idea of God is that it is antithetical to, and hostile to, "life," the "Dionysian," and the "will to power." Thus he can claim in *The Antichrist* (written 1888, published 1895) that "the Christian conception of God" had "degenerated to the *contradiction of life*, instead of being its transfiguration and eternal *Yes!*" "In God a declaration of hostility towards life, nature, the will to life! God the formula for every calumny of 'this world', for every lie about 'the next world'! In God nothingness deified, the will to nothingness sanctified! . . ."[91] "I call Christianity the *one* great curse, the *one* great intrinsic depravity, the *one* great instinct for revenge for which no expedient is sufficiently poisonous, secret, subterranean, *petty*—I call it the *one* immortal blemish of mankind." For him the whole of Christian theology is unreal, a "purely fictitious world" which "has its roots in hatred of the natural":

In Christianity neither morality nor religion come into contact with reality at any point. Nothing but imaginary *causes* ("God," "soul," "ego," "spirit," "free will"—or "unfree will"): nothing but imaginary *effects* ("sin," "redemption," "grace," "punishment," "forgiveness of sins"). A traffic between imaginary beings ("God," "spirits," "souls"); . . . an imaginary *teleology* ("the kingdom of God," "the Last Judgment," "eternal life").[92]

Nietzsche furiously attacked Christian doctrines of a moral God, and that "*one has need of a savior*": "The concept of guilt and punishment, including the doctrine of 'grace,' of 'redemption,' of 'forgiveness'—*lies* through and through and without any psychological reality—were invented to destroy the *causal sense* of man: they are an outrage on the concept cause and effect!" They are an outrage "from the most cowardly, cunning, lowest instincts! An *outrage of the priest*! An *outrage of the parasite*! A vampirism of pale subterranean bloodsuckers!"[93]

Nietzsche attacked metaphysics with equal fury. He sought to annihilate all transcendental and ontological bases and categories of metaphysics. In *Twilight of the Idols* he wrote, "being is an empty fiction. The 'apparent' world is the only one: the 'real' world has only been *lyingly added* . . ."[94] He intends to "eradicate and abolish" all metaphysical oppositions or contradistinctions, such as a real, unified "self" and "world," and the ultimate opposition of a Platonic or Christian "true world" with the "apparent world." "Without doubt, the strictly Platonic structure of metaphysics (based on the separation of true being and lesser being) is abolished, and not just overturned."[95] Philosophers, he claims, have created the "lie" of being, by "rejecting the evidence of the senses." "In so far as the senses show becoming, passing away, change, they do not lie."

Nietzsche recognized that great consequences follow for the world and mankind from the "death of God." Central to his philosophy is the notion that the world is totally groundless—without God, Being, essence, substance, thing in itself: there is no divine Being, guiding Spirit, Mind, Logos, Reason, or Good that creates or brings the world into being, sustains it, guides it, and gives it form, law, structural and moral order, purpose, and *telos*. His new view of the world without God actually lacks, as it logically should, all the major structures, reason, and purpose that the divinely created cosmos enjoys. He gets to the core of this in *Joyful Wisdom*:

The total character of the world . . . is in all eternity chaos—in the sense not of a lack of necessity but of a lack of order, arrangement, form, beauty, wisdom, and whatever other names there are for our aesthetic anthropomorphisms . . . . [The universe] is neither perfect nor beautiful, nor noble, nor does it wish to become any of these things; it does not by any means strive to imitate man. None of our aesthetic and moral judgments apply to it. Nor does it have any instinct for self-preservation or any other instinct; and it does not observe any laws either. Let us beware of saying that there are laws in nature. There are only necessities: there is nobody who commands, nobody who obeys, nobody who trespasses. Once you know that there are no purposes, you also know that there is no accident; for it is only beside a world of purposes that the word "accident" has meaning . . . . Let us beware of thinking that the world eternally creates new things. There are no eternally enduring substances. But when shall we ever be done with our caution and care? When will all these shadows of God cease to darken our minds?[96]

For Nietzsche, the world without God is a *primal chaos* in which there is no mental structuring, directing, and commanding agency; no legislator and providential provider; no given form and order, no substances, no moral order; and no purpose and goal. All these "shadows of God," he realizes, are ultimately dependent upon the idea of God. In his view, they must all be annihilated if one is to finally get rid of the idea of God.

For Nietzsche the only given reality is the ceaseless flux of *becoming* (groundless change). Our constantly shifting sensations are taken as true indications of the one thing he admits as given reality—*the will to power*, a dynamic, primal flux. This must be described largely in negative terms. It is mindless, unconscious, formless, multiple, chaotic *impulses, drives,* or *forces.* There are no formal structures; primal flux is amorphous, indeterminate, boundless. *There is no identity and unity,* only primal *difference and chaos.* "[Sensation] may be regarded as a true sampling of the original flux of the cosmos. This flux is a chaotic and completely unorganized becoming, not containing any permanent, essential structures."[97] The world, instead of being created by God, and reflecting the activity of divine mind, reason, and ideas (*nous, logos, eide, rationes aeternae* and *seminales*) within its holistic order (*kosmos*),[98] is organized and projected as human concepts onto the boundless, non-mental, non-rational dynamic force of will to power, which Nietzsche describes as "terrible," "ugly," "horrible," "frightening," as well as natural and life-giving.

"Nietzsche explicitly underscores and affirms in various ways that everything that exists is, at bottom and in its totality, Will to Power: 'The essence of the world is Will to Power'. 'The essence of life is Will to Power'. 'The most intimate essence of being is Will to Power'. World, Life, Being, these are not ultimate things, but only formations of the Will to Power: herein we find the 'ultimate face'." Even more radically than Hegel, Nietzsche annihilates Being and redefines it as becoming. Heidegger would develop the direction further in the next century. In Will to Power "there is no fixed and defining center (the center is always shifting and it cannot be grasped), but rather a plurality of elementary 'wills,' i.e., unconscious impulses, forever in conflict, alternately imposing themselves and subordinating themselves."[99] The attributes of will to power—continuous change, difference, plurality, multiplicity; the unconscious, mindless chaos and contradiction of all possible forces and impulses—stand in complete antithesis to those of God, who is absolute in Being, Person, Mind, Reason, Unity, Constancy, and Purpose. But in Nietzsche's philosophy, the dynamic life-force of will to power determines the nature of reality as utterly groundless and changing *becoming,* without being, essence, identity, unity, or universal truth, and necessitates constant change and "revaluation of all values" in human society and culture. Human "will to power"

has its metaphysical basis in the cosmic becoming itself, which produces all the forms of life. The first resonance of will in the specifically human sphere is felt in the unconscious life of the impulses and desires. But will also manifests itself in the senses and thinking: knowledge and reason are its tools for gaining foresight and control. Nietzsche thinks that the dynamic aspects of psychic life are of the same stuff as the cosmic becoming, and that therefore the universal force is a will to the increase of power.[100]

In this way the Dionysian life force and its existence as human will to power became Nietzsche's substitute for the Christian God. He pleaded not to be misunderstood, that he stood for *"Dionysos versus the Crucified."*[101] His description of the Dionysian in his first major book, *The Birth of Tragedy* (*Die Geburt der Tragödie*, 1871), bears some resemblance to the unconscious of von Hartmann and Freud. It is "the eternal and original artistic power that first calls the whole world of phenomena into existence." It is the "foundation of all existence—the Dionysian basic ground of the world."[102] It is "a most destructive fever" and "the symbol of that drunken frenzy which threatens to destroy all forms and codes; the ceaseless striving which apparently defies all limitations; the ultimate abandonment we sometimes sense in music."[103]

Since Nietzsche's given reality, the Dionysian life force, is in constant change, flux, chaos, nothing but change can arise from it. Nietzsche's philosophy is thus one of total becoming. We already see in his philosophy of the 1880s the "triumph of becoming,"[104] which will broadly and increasingly characterize twentieth-century High Modern and postmodern culture from Cubism and Futurism onward. "Even more than Bergson, Nietzsche stands out as the philosopher of becoming."[105] Pursuing modern critical method to much more extreme ends, he radicalizes Hegel's world of becoming by eliminating its quasi-metaphysical Absolute Spirit, Reason, and Concept.

Nietzsche proposed to substitute sovereign becoming for Hegel's sovereign reason. His metaphysical option or (as he himself called it) "preference" was to take the description of finite reality-in-process as a definitive and ultimate account, beyond which philosophical investigation is forbidden to move. He converted the *description* of the world as the region of constant becoming, into a *demonstration* that this world is self-sufficient and in no need of causal explanation. The ultimacy of becoming, as a character or descriptive fact of the world, was converted into an ontological ultimacy, belonging to an autonomous dynamic principle.[106]

For Nietzsche, "being is an empty fiction. The 'apparent' world is the only one: the 'real' world has only been lyingly added."[107] "There is no 'other,' no 'true,' no essential being"[108] Nietzsche's backwards philosophy radically reverses Plato, as well as Christianity. And his reversals are more extreme and extensive than Kant's, Hegel's, and Schopenhauer's.

Nietzsche sought to draw the ultimate conclusions for his philosophy of primal reality as dynamic flux—a world of becoming, existing altogether without God, Being, essence, substance, and matter. Through the 1880s he increasingly came to realize that it demanded a world without objectively real and substantial "things" or "things in themselves." This means, of course, that there is no real, objective "world" at all. In *Beyond Good and Evil* he pays tribute to the eighteenth-century philosopher, Boscovich, who "taught us to abjure belief in the last part of the earth that 'stood fast'—the belief in 'substance,' in 'matter,' in the earth-residuum and particle-atom." On this view there are no "things" or real substances. Nietzsche saw this as "the greatest triumph over the senses that has been gained on earth so far."[109] Many sections of *The Will to Power* then develop these matters further:

The world with which we are concerned is false, i.e., is not a fact but a fable and approximation on the basis of a meager sum of observations; it is "in flux," as something in a state of becoming, as a falsehood always changing but never getting near the truth: for—there is no "truth" . . . *there are no facts*, everything is in flux, incomprehensible, elusive; what is relatively most enduring is—our opinions . . . . *there are no things (—they are fictions invented by us)* . . . the essence of a thing is only an *opinion* about the "thing." . . . behold, *there are no things-in-themselves!* . . . The "thing-in-itself" is nonsensical. If I remove all the relationships, all the "properties," all the "activities" of a thing, the thing does not remain over; because thingness has only been invented by us owing to the requirements of logic, thus with the aim of defining, communication (to bind together the multiplicity of relationships, properties, activities) . . . . *That things possess a constitution in themselves quite apart from interpretation and subjectivity, is quite idle hypothesis* . . . . [110]

The real, solid, objective world of common experience and knowledge, of traditional thought and art, thus completely vanishes, replaced by the dynamic actions of many surging forces—many "centers of force," eternally, continuously, acting and reacting. Nietzsche's view of "the world" is of "a monster of energy, without beginning, without end; . . . a sea of forces flowing and rushing together, eternally changing, . . . with tremendous years of recurrence," and "enclosed by 'nothingness'."[111]

This philosophy radically denies a world of independently real *things*, including human beings of flesh and blood, created and sustained by God, and given objective, material reality and substantial being that is dependent upon and supported by *His* divine Being and power. The philosopher of the strong and healthy body and sex thus even admits the *body* to be a fiction! The body is not an objective material thing, but a constantly shifting interplay of myriad "impulses," "forces," which we ourselves mentally constitute as a "body." In that sense it is only a subjective construct that we create and recreate, invent and reinvent, over and over ourselves—a work of creative art. "At the deepest level, man is a nothing that must be constituted and reconstituted as a work of art, a notion that is nothing but an advanced form of the modern antinature animus." For Nietzsche "the great problem is that there is no underlying natural [or divinely created and supported] substratum to human existence [or to self, things, or world]. *Nietzsche clearly takes over and radicalizes modernity's antinature animus.*"[112]

Nietzsche hoped to help liberate modern man from the modern antinature drive with his appeals to the body, instinct, sex, nature, and the natural. But "nature" and all of these concepts have degenerated in his thought beyond recognition in premodern senses, even into reversals of Christian and Classical understandings. "Nature," "world," and "body" are at base no more or less than the will to power—innumerable impulses, and without any substance, unity, identity, or material reality. The other side of the modern bifurcation and antagonism of self and nature is the self, subject, or man. Nietzsche also "hoped to emancipate man from the [modern] nihilistic hypertrophy of self-consciousness which manifests itself in the hegemony of the self-grounding, self-legislating ego qua Will, which ultimately will accept nothing else in reality but itself."[113] But again, Nietzsche actually extended and further radicalized the modern "philosophy of the subject," by making man or ego as will to power the only source of any reason, logic, form, unity, identity, law, and order in the creation of a "knowable world." The modern self or subject is now so alienated from any real "world" and "body" that all it can know are its own fictions, whether believable or not. And it is so separated from being that it no longer has any substance, unity, or identity.

Nietzsche's constant charge that Christianity creates "despisers of the body," and "ascetic, otherworldly," "life-denying" views, is turned back upon him by his own philosophy. His charge is not only false, but obtuse and mean-spirited: the doctrines of creation, revelation, incarnation, and salvation *absolutely affirm* material body and world as real, valuable, good, and purposeful things. God's Absolute Being and Power *sustain* the reality of world. *Man's place and role in the world is crucially important*; redemption through Christ makes the body *the temple of the eternal Holy Spirit*, not only for saintly life in the hereafter, but *for abundant life and service here*. But because he radically denies God, Being, substance, and matter, Nietzsche's self-proclaimed philosophy of the "body" and "this world" necessarily ends in the self-contradictory and absurd position of denying the reality of both.

Nietzsche's philosophy denies that there are any spiritual substances, including not only the Trinity, but the spirit and soul of man. It denies that there are any divinely created, objective laws, forms, and structures given to the world by God the Logos; and it denies that there is any actual reason and logic operative in "nature." It is thus not only a radical denial of common human experience, but of God, Logos, and creation (see Chapters 3-5). With Nietzsche, reason and logic, major traditional attributes of spirit, are reduced to necessary and useful *human fictions* (hello Postmodernism) that are *projected* on the totally incompatible, irrational, illogical impulses of the will to power.

Reason and logic—*logos*—are no longer divine, or present in "nature," but arise only in "man" as a *counter to reality*, the will to power. *Logos* is now so far removed from reality that it is only a fictional human construct, although still necessary and useful for any sense of world, individual things, self, form, law, and order at all! This is the lowest level for reason/*logos* in Western intellectual history to that time—lower than Kant, Hegel, and even lower than in Schopenhauer's philosophy (where "eternal Ideas" were still posited), although Nietzsche's "reality" most resembles his. *Logos* now only creates fiction, lies. In this sense *logos* is demonized. Christ the Logos appears as Anti-logos. But the question still arises, that if reason and logic are only operative in man, how could they possibly originate from Nietzsche's only core of reality, the mindless, irrational, alogical chaos of will to power?

The Rejection of God and Being and the Triumph of Becoming. Not only are there no real "things" in a real "world" in Nietzsche's philosophy, *there is no real, substantial "subject," "ego," "self," or "soul"* that perceives, projects, or produces those concepts, "things," or "objects"! "Self," "soul," and "subject," as well as "object," "thing," "world," "causality," and all moral systems, are simply human "fictions," "semiotic fictions." Belief in the soul is an age-old "superstition." Without substance neither "subject" nor "object" can exist as real, unified entities. There is, as Nietzsche writes, "no subject but an action." There are, he claims, many such "centers of force," each of which "has its perspective for the rest of the world, i.e., its quite definite valuation and way of acting and resisting. The 'apparent world' reduces itself to specific sorts of action proceeding from such centers. The 'world' is only a word for the total play of such actions." Such is Nietzsche's vision of a "world" of total becoming.

Former Yale historian Franklin Baumer states in his chapter on "The Triumph of Becoming" in the twentieth century, "The first half of the twentieth century, especially after 1914, marked a revolution in European thinking almost beyond compare." This revolution "destroyed, in a comparatively short period of time, nearly all of the 'idols' [Nietzsche's term] that had been so painstakingly constructed, not merely by the Middle Ages but by 'modern' times as well." One kind of modernity gave way to another: The old Enlightenment modernity had made "profound changes in world-outlook, but left important bastions of being virtually intact. The 'new' modernity, however, dispensed with being, leaving men without landmarks, casting them adrift on an endless sea of becoming." "Time-mind," where reality was seen as "a becoming, a history, an unending dialectical process," was now seen as dominant. Ortega y Gasset analyzed such viewpoints as "'scandalously provisional,' not merely changing, but without standards or roots." The twentieth century was to him, "the first period in history that recognized nothing in the past as a standard. It had broken even with 'modern culture, or at least refused to recognize it as definitive." In Baumer's analysis, this "revolution, or crisis, as contemporaries more often called it, had been coming for a long time . . . . It might be likened to a tidal wave, generated by underground earthquakes over a period of time, which at last had a cumulative effect. By the end of the nineteenth century, becoming was already a major category of thinking . . . and Nietzsche was not alone in seeing the advent of a new sort of age, characterized by a transvaluation of values, and a new, and dangerous, openness of thought and culture."[114]

Baumer sees "a sense in which the revolution was not normal." "Man became problematic . . . . The universe became mysterious . . . and nature became remote. For the first time, theological questions began to seem, not merely controversial, but meaningless, to a significant number of people." The sense of the substantial reality of the world and its objects began to fade and disappear. In fields of psychoanalysis, Surrealism, and Existentialism, Cyril Joad found a "dropping of the object," which meant on the one hand, subjectivism, or going inward toward the self (or Self, as in Jung), and on the other hand, "disbelief in any sort of transcendence." Art movements from Cubism, through Dada and Surrealism reveal increasing movement into the self and away from the sense of any substantial, objective reality of the world. The world as previously known became less and less visible and less securely known or desirable in art. Joad complained about "the nonknowability of 'objects' other than mental states." In Baumer's analysis, neither psychologism nor skepticism "fully describes the new mentality. More than anything else, it was conscious of loss, loss of belief in transcendence."

Baumer notes that three key concepts of Existentialism during the early to mid decades of the twentieth century were the "Absurd, anxiety, and alienation." The Absurd signified a universe "devoid of meaning, at least for man; lacking being or essence; in any case, irrational and incomprehensible." A powerful sense of the Absurd, the irrational, and unknowable emerged in Dada art with Duchamp and others during World War I. And as early as 1926 characters in Andre Malraux's writings spoke of "an essential absurdity . . . in the depths of European man," where nothing is permanent, values have disappeared, and he is left face to face with the Absurd. The Absurd was the key to the nausea of one of the fictional characters of the atheist philosopher and writer, Jean-Paul Sartre, in his novel, *Nausea (La Nausée)* of 1938. Anxiety and alienation were caused by the Absurd, and in 1952 Paul Tillich wrote of our time as an "age of anxiety," which he attributed to "the contemporary sense of the meaninglessness of life." In all this there was "a new 'cosmic alienation,'" dooming one to "live like a stranger in an indifferent universe ... a fate from which there was no escape. These words signified, not merely the toppling, but the abandonment, of absolutes. *This* was what was new, above everything else: not iconoclasm *per se*, which is characteristic of every revolution of the mind, but the realization, widespread in the twentieth century as never before, that icons were always changing and would continue to change." This is what Baumer refers to as the sense of becoming, and its triumph in the twentieth century.[115]

Chapter Seven

The Rejection of God in Radical Twentieth-Century Modern Art and Thought

Duchamp's disinterest in concepts of God is well known. He is said to have been "alien to all forms of transcendence."[1]

For Heidegger, Being depends on existence, rather than existence depending on Being. Human life comes from Nothingness, is suspended over Nothingness, and penetrated by Nothingness.

For Wittgenstein, language can express "nothing that is higher" in propositions of metaphysics, theology, philosophy, ethics, and aesthetics. All such statements are literally "nonsensical."

The Skepticism and Nihilism of Dada Art.[2] The individualistic movement in art, literature, and theater known as Dada (c. 1912-1923), reaching its height during World War I, was the most extreme form of cultural expression in world history to its time. It produced insane-looking artworks, irrationalist and nonsense writings, and cynical rejections of the bases of Western tradition. The views and art of Dada represent forms of radical skepticism and subjectivism, culminating modern critical rejection of the past since the Enlightenment. Briefly and essentially stated, Dada stood opposed to: belief in God or any transcendent reality; the substantial reality of a world of things; universal truth, beauty, and goodness; reason, logic, and systematic thought; any absolute or universal source of authority, law, rules, and morality; any objective correspondence of word and image to thing represented; and any unitary or sequential development in history. In all these negative views Dada is the predecessor of "Postmodernism" of the past four decades.[3]

Nietzsche's radically critical and destructive views of traditional beliefs can be compared in essential ways with Dada and later Postmodernism.

Many Dada artists and writers were influenced either directly or indirectly by Nietzsche, especially Hugo Ball, Picabia, Ernst, and Benjamin De Casseres. Most importantly, for Nietzsche and the Dadaists, the world is totally groundless—without God, Being, or essence. There is no eternal, unchanging Being, no thing-in-itself, no divine Spirit serving as Creator or unchanging source of the world, sustaining and guiding it, and giving form, structure, law, and purpose. While Nietzsche launched fierce philosophical assaults on Christian theism and the classical metaphysical tradition with their doctrines of the eternal reality of God, Mind, and Ideas, the Dadaists attacked all traditional and conventional beliefs in radical ways through their "anti-art" and "anti-literature." In these and other ways, Dada is nihilistic.

For Nietzsche and the Dadaists, the given world presents only the ceaseless flux of becoming (groundless change). As for supposed objective "things," there is nothing enduring—no essence behind appearance, no noumena behind phenomena. The status of "world" and "things" becomes highly problematic in these views. There is no objective or universal law and order, including moral order. There is no divine or universal truth which knowledge mediates; there are only innumerable subjective "perspectives." These are the underlying philosophical reasons for the radical sense of indeterminacy, formlessness, and change in Dada arts.

In their various ways, Nietzsche and then the Dadaists attacked and sought to undermine all previous philosophies, theologies, and metaphysics, hoping to destroy them. The Dadaists added updated attacks on current and previous art, aesthetics, and social and political traditions. They both claimed *freedom* for thoroughly new ways of life, thought, and art, with the Dadaists outstripping their predecessor (Nietzsche would no doubt have been horrified by Dada arts).

The Irrational, Absurd, and Nihilistic World of Duchamp. Marcel Duchamp (1887-1968) exemplifies major aspects of Dada in their most extreme forms, during the movement and afterwards until his death in 1968. "Duchamp seems to have resolved to play the role of a modern Descartes and doubt the validity of everything but his own consciousness of ironic disillusionment with the certitudes of the past and the dogmas of the present, including those of his enthusiastic contemporaries whether laymen or artists."[4] While Duchamp did not try to logically critique traditional beliefs and doctrines, his artwork emphatically confronts and rejects, either directly or implicitly, all ideas of reality, truth, and knowledge of Christian and classical traditions. In their place cynicism, irony, paradox, ambiguity, enigma, indeterminacy, eroticism and sexuality permeate his artworks and notes, spiced with dry wit, humor, puns, and cryptic allusions.

According to Hans Richter, one of the Dadaists who knew him, "Duchamp's attitude is that life is a melancholy joke, an indecipherable nonsense, not worth the trouble of investigating. To his superior intelligence the total absurdity of life, the contingent nature of a world denuded of all values, are logical consequences of Descartes' *Cogito ergo sum.* His total detachment from what goes on around him (*'ego cogito'*) places him safely in the 'beyond' without the need to kill himself . . . He approaches life as he does the chessboard; the gambits fascinate him without leading him to imagine that there is a meaning behind it all which might make it necessary for him to believe in something."[5]

Duchamp's method was not the traditional one of creating by painting or sculpting new, personal, and expressive artworks, but simply by giving new titles, "identities," and "meanings" to objects that he bought, found, or had made. He called these works "readymades," which he often "modified" or "assisted." More than anyone else Duchamp is the father of this method, which has been increasingly adopted in certain ways in twentieth-century art from Surrealism on through Rauschenberg, Johns, Assemblage, Happenings, Pop, Performance, and Postmodernism. Such new methods, so different from traditional art, reflect dramatically changed views of art, the artist, and concepts of reality, truth, and creativity. Duchamp's method served primarily to *distance* his work from traditional beliefs—to set forth his skepticism and comic-nihilistic destruction of previous beliefs.

Dada art and poetry evokes a radical world of becoming, without unchanging being or essence. Throughout his oeuvre, Duchamp stressed dynamic movement and change. In his key early work, *Bicycle Wheel* (Fig. 7), originally of 1913, actual movement (the wheel to be turned by the viewer) is central. The wheel's movement is now meaningless and purposeless, since it is divorced from its previous function. Motion is used or indicated in much of Duchamp's art, suggesting a view of the world as universal dynamism. Duchamp spoke of such a force in an interview with Lawrence Steefel in 1956: "Duchamp says that he considers a force he calls 'eros' to be a universal force of creative energy and potency . . . . Eros seems to be a kind of *elan vital* or life force inherent in the universe which manifests itself in human eroticism, as a sublimated stimulus for art, and as a kind of attraction-repulsion dynamic in the mysterious flow of things."[6] "Duchamp . . . does not speak of a personal God, however hidden, but rather implies the existence of an occult impersonal dynamism in the universe which is ultimately inscrutable, and apparently without personal attributes."[7] Duchamp carried movement further with his continuously moving *Rotary* objects of the 1920's (e.g., *Rotary Demisphere*, 1925). The *Bicycle Wheel* and these works are the predecessors of Kinetic, Assemblage, Performance, and other forms of subsequent art emphasizing movement, change, and process.

Duchamp was also influenced by concepts of a fourth dimension, and by occult ideas associated with alchemy. He read Gaston de Pawlowski's 1912 book on the fourth dimension.[8] Some think his artworks are intended to evoke a greater fourth dimensional realm beyond the ordinary three-dimensional world. To Duchamp this realm is an invisible one of universal dynamism, eros, chance, and the unconscious. "As intended epiphanies of irrational and even extra-sensory experience the readymades presuppose the existence of a 'meta-world,' which Duchamp has described as 'fourth-dimensional'."[9]

Bicycle Wheel also reflects the Dada "collage aesthetic," with its elements put together, but more essentially separate and different. Lucy Lippard has described the collage aesthetic as "totally incongruous and unrelated realities (images, words, sounds, actions) brought together to form either no sense at all or a new and unexpected sense, a harshly critical commentary."[10] Forms of collage aesthetic are ubiquitous in postmodern art of recent decades.

The work by Duchamp that most reflects his cynical and humorous rejection of Western tradition is the small but powerful one of 1919 entitled *L. H. O. O. Q.* (Fig. 8).[11] Of the type Duchamp called "rectified readymade," it consists of a cheap reproduction of Leonardo's Mona Lisa (*La Gioconda*), bought by Duchamp, given a penciled mustache and goatee, and a new title. With these simple acts Duchamp laughingly mocks and dismisses essential aspects of Western tradition in art and thought. Leonardo's Mona Lisa is one of the most valued art masterpieces of the Western world, and represents an idealistic Renaissance view of art, life, truth, and beauty. By defacing and mocking it, Duchamp asserts his own radically skeptical view that none of these beliefs has universal or necessary truth. He defaces it by adding the mustache and goatee, a favorite trick of children and graffiti amateurs for deflating and making fun of public images and beauty. But this is carried to comic-absurd and vulgar extremes by giving it a new title. The letters L. H. O. O. Q., when pronounced rapidly in French, sound like the vulgar French expression, "*Elle a chaud au cul!*"[12] Thus, the noble humanity, femininity, dignity, and divine grace of Leonardo's painting are verbally reduced by Duchamp to the level of bathroom humor. Moral standards concerning sexuality are satirized. The complex and mysterious inner spirit and humanity of Leonardo's portrait are reduced to a coarse, one-dimensional level. Duchamp implicitly affirms the absence of universal moral standards, and any necessity of propriety, decorum, and decency. These expressed views may be identified as nihilism, defined as "a viewpoint that traditional values and beliefs are unfounded and that existence is senseless and useless," and "a doctrine that denies any objective ground of truth and especially of moral truths."[13]

Any truth of the image and what it stands for are mockingly rejected. No other beliefs and values are put in their place except vulgar humor and mocking laughter. With this as a guide for life, one could well mock not only Renaissance beliefs and values, but any others. By devaluing the forms and values of this work Duchamp slyly asserts that there can be no ideals or canons for an artist to believe in and express in art, whether of truth, beauty, humanity, form, proportion, or technique. As in all of Duchamp's work, even the concept of "aesthetic appeal" is undermined. No actual painting or drawing is done, except for the few pencil strokes for mustache and goatee.

Fig. 7. Marcel Duchamp, *Bicycle Wheel*, original 1913, reconstructed 1964. Metal and painted wood. Musée National d'Art Moderne, Centre Georges Pompidou. Paris, France. Photo Philippe Migeat. Photo Credit: CNAC/MNAM/Dist. Reunion des Musée Nationaux / Art Resource, NY.

Fig. 8. Marcel Duchamp, *L.H.O.O.Q.*, 1919. "Rectified Readymade": pencil on reproduction of Leonardo da Vinci's Mona Lisa. 7¾ x 4¾. Private collection. Photo credit: Scala/White Images / Art Resource, NY.

Duchamp often shifted his method, materials, and determining idea from work to work. Traditional canons of unity, consistency, and development are thus overturned. In a traditional sense *L. H. O. O. Q.* is not an original work, but a modified reproduction of another artist's work. Traditional criteria of creativity, uniqueness, and masterpiece are scrapped. Duchamp stressed the importance of his *ideas* and *decisions* as the real basis of his artworks, in contrast to actual personal form and execution. But we may well question the value of his ideas, driven by skepticism, cynicism, and nihilism, no matter how cleverly put.

By Duchamp's actions, Leonardo's rich and densely meaningful painting is reduced to the sham surface of a mediocre mechanical copy, divested of its original beliefs, values, and depth, and by implication, so is the whole of Western tradition. Finally, so are all concepts of universal truth, morality, and goodness. Such broad nihilism inevitably takes the form of cynicism. Duchamp's nihilism is made appealing to some, however, by its cleverness, wit, humor, and wide-ranging allusions. His art is not only "anti-art," but art as *anti-belief.* In Duchamp's art no God of Being, Truth, Goodness, Love, Holiness, and Judgment can possibly exist.

Another work that reveals many of Duchamp's views is the "assisted readymade" of 1921 with the comic-absurd title of *Why not Sneeze Rose Sélavy?* (not shown).[14] It consists of a small, dented birdcage bought in a flea market, containing marble cubes made to look like sugar lumps, a large piece of cuttlebone, and a thermometer. Through the combination of different and unrelated objects, and an apparently absurd and disjunctive title, the work presents a situation in which perception, knowledge, and truth appear radically problematic, even impossible. Everything seems to be deadlocked in enigma and indeterminacy. Each object is so different that nothing seems related to the others. Identities of objects seem to be suddenly erased by these strange new combinations and title. All their former purposes and uses vanish. Reason, logic, and relationships seem so absent that the work might have been done by a demented person. Instead of fluttering birds the cage contains heavy, earth-bound blocks of marble. The marble cubes, which appear magically transformed by Duchamp into sugar lumps, lose even this new identity when one lifts the cage and feels its heaviness. All objects are metamorphosed into strange things lacking known identities and purposes. "Reality" and "truth" in terms of the essential nature and purpose of things seem destroyed. Instead, we are left with the blank, hollow shells of things, suggesting that they are not real, that we have no true knowledge of them, and they have no purpose.

In this artwork all rational truth, knowledge, and purpose appear to be illusions established by convention and tradition. They have now been properly destroyed (or to use a postmodernist term, "deconstructed"), leaving us with a groundless and irrational assemblage. The result is an "anti-art" object, fundamentally different from traditional artworks. It seems to have no real purpose, beauty, or aesthetic appeal. Reality and truth in rational, classical, and Christian senses are cynically dismissed, as are goodness and beauty.

Duchamp's disinterest in concepts of God is well known. He is said to have been "alien to all forms of transcendence."[15] Calvin Tomkins relates that "so far as Duchamp was concerned, atheism and belief in God were simply opposite sides of the same issue, an issue that did not interest him at all. The older he became, in fact, the less interest he took in religious questions. 'For me,' as he wrote to [André] Breton, 'there is something other than *yes*, *no*, and *indifferent*—it is for example the *absence of investigations of this kind*'." Somewhat like Wittgenstein Duchamp saw such matters as part of a language game: "All this twaddle—the existence of God, atheism, determinism, free will, societies, death, etc., are the pieces of a chess game called language, and they are only amusing if one does not preoccupy oneself with 'winning or losing this game of chess'."

Among Greek philosophers, the one who interested Duchamp most during his crucially formative year of 1913 was Pyrrho of Elis (c. 365-275 BC), the founder, immediately after Plato and Aristotle, of the skeptical tradition. The basic views of Pyrrho, as described by Tomkins, also identify essential factors in Duchamp's lifelong outlook and art, especially concerning absolutes, truth and falsehood, "this and that" [identity], and indifference:

Disputing Plato's theory of ideal forms, Pyrrho denied the existence of absolutes. There was no possibility of arriving at an objective truth, he said, because "nothing is in itself more this than that." Since nothing was either wholly true or false, one should cultivate an attitude of 'indifference' and 'imperturbability' toward life, according to Pyrrho, avoiding judgments and opinions but keeping oneself in a state of alertness to each passing moment. Pyrrho's thinking was very close in some ways to the central tenets of Zen Buddhism. It was of more than passing importance to Duchamp, who began at this time to make references in his notes to the "beauty of indifference."[16]

With Duchamp there is extreme distrust of reason, and his artwork reflects lack of confidence in sensory knowledge. A sense of slippery, changing, and lost identities of things is centrally characteristic of his art, much other Dada, and especially of Surrealism. It has also been increasingly characteristic of art from Rauschenberg and Johns from the mid 1950s and '60s, into Postmodernism.

The Destruction of Metaphysics and Theology, and End of Transcendence in the Philosophy of Heidegger. Born in the same year as Wittgenstein, and in the midst of many High Modern thinkers, writers, and artists, Martin Heidegger (1889-1976) became one of the most radical, and influential of modern philosophical thinkers from the late 1920s onward. In many ways his thought carried High Modernity to its most extreme philosophical form, and became the immediate predecessor of Post-modernism, emerging during his last years. Many postmodern concepts are already well developed in Heidegger. Sartre was heavily influenced by him, and no doubt did more than anyone to spread and popularize related ideas. For Heidegger the very basis of existence is radically different from Christian and classical views, even antithetical: he quietly propounded revolutionary new conceptions of "Being," "Logos," "man," "nature," and history, finding it necessary to construct strange new word-concepts to accomplish his goal.

For Heidegger, as for Nietzsche, collapsing belief in God was the primary fact of the modern world. It gave shape to the philosophies of both men. Of course, neither Nietzsche nor Heidegger believed in the God of Christianity. The claims that Heidegger's philosophy is neither theistic nor atheistic,[17] and that it does not oppose Christianity or proclaim slogans against the Christian God as supernatural reality,[18] are grossly misleading, since Heidegger's major tenets seek to eliminate any credibility for essential Christian beliefs and doctrines, with claims that are antithetical to them, and are intent on destroying their foundations.

Like Nietzsche, Heidegger thought of Christian theology and classical metaphysics as essentially the same, even though there are fundamental differences as well as similarities. Christian metaphysical realism recognizes the primacy of divine revelation, and such revealed doctrines as the aseity, personality, and Triune nature of the Creator God. But in certain essential philosophical terms, Christian theology is clearly related to classical metaphysics. James Perotti writes,

Metaphysics is not only ontology, it is also theology. According to Heidegger, it is both at once. The ontology of essences is ultimately grounded in god. The *Nous* of Anaxagoras, the Divine Maker in Plato's *Republic*, the Prime Mover of Aristotle, the medieval god and creator, are all conceptions of god thoroughly entwined with an essentialistic metaphysics . . . . Metaphysics has ascribed to god the structuring and ordering of the eternally existing universe. The Medieval philosophers carried this Greek insight to its completion; god the creator pre-planned all by deciding the nature of things in advance, and then created accordingly. For this reason the essences of things are discoverable by man. The structure and order are also there awaiting man's knowledge. This guarantees the possibility of the truth of man's knowledge as Augustine, Anselm, and Descartes saw so well. The ultimate correctness of man's grasping the essence of things is rooted in the god's having placed those essences there to be grasped.[19]

Heidegger set himself the task of correcting this "error" and "failure" by "overcoming" traditional Western metaphysics and theology. In the process, he *redefined* Being in a manner antithetical to traditional metaphysics. Traditional thought affirms that man has a "'transcendental need' for metaphysics." In the classical tradition this takes the form of a need and quest for the unity, eternity, universality, perfection, and truth of substantial Being. In Christianity it is found in man's inherent need for the Creator God. "The overcoming of metaphysics implies an overcoming of what was originally considered essential to man—metaphysics. Therefore, the overcoming of metaphysics necessitates a change in the conception of the essence of man; it implies a growing-up, a self-overcoming."[20] According to Heidegger, man must no longer conceive himself as a "rational animal": "As long as man understands himself as the rational animal, metaphysics belongs, as Kant said, to the nature of man."[21] More basically, man must *reconceive* metaphysics, ontology, Being, and theology.

Heidegger set out not only to "overcome" metaphysics and theology,[22] but to "destroy" them. His destructive method consisted in: (1) finding their ultimate principles; (2) discovering what made them possible; (3) indicating the disparity between these principles and his own concepts of Being, man, and world.[23] There is much similarity in this to the subsequent postmodernist "end of metaphysics," and "deconstruction," with its strategies of critical subversion and destruction of traditional texts, concepts, and "master narratives." The idea is to destroy your enemies by submitting them to the meat-grinder of your own conceptual system, while grooming your own views to win adherents. Whatever is to be destroyed is effectively "shown," within the destroyer's conceptual system, to be misconceived, illusory, harmful, and failed. Heidegger claimed that he wanted to renew metaphysics in the light of its "true," "original" source in pre-Socratic Greek thought, especially Heracleitus and Parmenides, before classical metaphysics and Christianity "led the Western world away from 'true Being' and 'truth'," eventually culminating in the present age of darkness and the "death of God." In this way, "Heidegger understands his own philosophy as an attempt to remove all the *concealments* imposed by traditional philosophy which obscured the *primary, authentic* thought of the early Greek thinkers."[24]

Heidegger also sought "the 'destruction' of traditional theology."[25] He "questions the basis of a belief in a divine creator which makes possible a comprehension of everything: God, world (creation), and man."[26]

The notion of creation makes possible the accurate representation of the divinity of god—not to mention the contingency of creatures. Thus, *what is at stake is the divinity of god*, which has a tradition of being stated in terms of creation and which dates back, according to theologians, to the first words of Genesis. Yet this key conception of creation is antithetical to Heidegger's thinking; it is this conception of the divine which is at the center of the metaphysics which he "destroyed," at the center of the metaphysical theologic which he overcame.[27]

Heidegger did not merely deny the Reality of God: he established the foundations of his philosophy to eliminate the very concept of God. He made the claim, in step with Hegel and Nietzsche, that the ideas of Being and God constitute the crucial "error" that has increasingly debilitated Western civilization since Plato and the rise of Christianity, and he set out to illuminate the proper understanding of "Being," "Logos," "man," and "world".

Heidegger also asserted, contrary to biblical Christian tradition, but consistent with post-Kantian modernist philosophy, that experience of God is impossible.[28] He demeaned faith as nothing more than "convenience" and "indifference," in the interest of our reason and security, or our unthinking adherence to traditional doctrine, which prevents us from asking the all-important ground-question he poses, *"why is there anything at all, rather than nothing?"*[29] He rejected the biblical and theological answer as repugnant and repressive. In his view "the theological affirmation of god stands in the way of the question of Being."[30]

Heidegger confronts this theological affirmation of a divine ground for all Beings with his ground-question. It is posed in a different fashion with a penetration that "destroys" the theological ground by breaking through to the abyss below [the abyss of *Nothing*]. The abyss discloses the precariousness of beings, the possibility of non-being, the utter strangeness of all beings at all, our own finitude and thrownness.[31]

And the "answers" that Heidegger conceived—*Nichts* (Nothing, "non-Being"), *Sein* ("Being"), and *Dasein* (the "essential" existence of man as "being-there")—are, in fundamental ways, *opposites of traditional* theological and metaphysical answers. The two are mutually exclusive. Only in this way can it be claimed that Heidegger "overcomes the god of theology":

The overcoming of metaphysics as theology, then, is more than the "destruction" of ancient ontology. The "destruction," in service of metaphysics, brackets the question of god for a time and proceeds with "fundamental ontology". The overcoming of metaphysics does more than that in its attempt to recall Being itself; it completely leaves behind the representation of beings in the light of a first ground. Since the way of representation excludes the *Andenken des Seins* [Heidegger's new manner of thinking about Being], the way of metaphysical theology is not the way along which the *Andenken* proceeds. The opposition is clear and fundamental: *Heidegger has overcome the god of theology*. . . . It might be said that metaphysics as theologic was long "destroyed" before it was overcome. But the overcoming, the "getting over it" (*Verwindung*), occurs after a much more serious confrontation and has a more permanent outcome.[32]

That "permanent outcome" can perhaps be seen from the time of the "death of God" theology movement that emerged in the 1960s, hard on the heels of Heidegger's late writings. The movement was still small and relatively short. But radical Nietzschean and Heideggerian themes have been extended in theology and philosophy since the 1960s and 70s. Theologies of "shifted paradigms" have increasingly proliferated, and come to dominate since then, much like the innumerable individual directions in the visual arts, with their own radically shifted paradigms. The proliferation of diverse and antithetical directions in philosophy, with a critical absence of common language and communication, has been characterized as "a second Babel,"[33] and "the end of philosophy."[34] The postmodern, neo-Nietzschean French philosophers, Foucault and Derrida, increasingly influential on philosophy, literary theory and criticism, and the arts since the late 1960s, have called for replacing philosophy with an entirely new discipline, "the archeology of knowledge" (Foucault), and "de-constituting the founding concepts of the history of philosophy" in favor of the "freeplay" that comes with "dancing outside the house of Being" (Derrida). These philosophies of Heidegger, Derrida, Foucault, and other postmodernists have been increasingly taught in American universities since the 1970s, and often touted as "truth."

Heidegger's non-transcendent, "earthly" agenda can be seen throughout his philosophy, particularly in his conceptions of "Being" (*Sein*), "man" or "the essence of man's existence" (*Dasein*), and the "earth and the gods," representing "a new dawn of Being." With Heidegger, as with Nietzsche, and Existentialism generally, what fundamentally determines his philosophy, his conception of "Being," is his conviction that there are no essences in the senses of traditional metaphysics and Christian theology—no permanent structure of the cosmos; no enduring substance, soul, or nature of man, or of things, and no divine or cosmic Logos. Traditional metaphysics and theology represent a great error, a fall. There is no absolute, eternal God, who is the supreme Creator of essences and souls. Nietzsche, Heidegger, Sartre, and Camus all drew these conclusions, and attempted to establish the ultimate inferences in their first principles. While Nietzsche chose the subjective route of will-to-power, Heidegger surpassed him at his own game by affirming *a new "Being" that is antithetical to traditional Being.* Somewhat after Heidegger, from 1938 through the 1940s, Sartre did much the same thing—redefining Being in terms antithetical to Christian and classical traditions—but heavily flavored with absurdity and "nausea." Camus renounced God, Being, universal truth and reason, while emphasizing the absurdity of man's situation, apotheosizing moment-to-moment existence, and claiming a "horizontal transcendence" from one person to another.

Heidegger's concepts of "Being," and "essence" are in fact opposite traditional ones. Although his complex new concepts and terms are designed to stand largely outside of Western tradition and avoid their sanction, the traditional terms closest to them are those of *appearance, becoming,* and *existence,* the very opposites of traditional substance, Being and essence! Many elemental inversions result. Heidegger's "Being" is not eternal, unchanging, and perfect, like the Christian God, and Platonic Ideas, but finite, constantly changing. It is not eternally self-existent and perfect, but must be "uncovered," "shepherded," and "cared for" by man, and is in constant peril of recession and extinction [man becomes the Good Shepherd of Being!]. In Heidegger's view, nothing is unchanging. "Being" is not the source and ground of man and world, but is itself contingent upon man as "*Dasein*" ("being there," man as self-world, a "field" of activity) for its very "appearance," development, and continuation. "Being" arises out of human existence, rather than human existence being created and grounded by God the Supreme Being.[35] There can be no "Being" without human existence (*Dasein*). Being depends on existence, rather than existence depending on Being. As Heidegger wrote, "The essence of *Dasein* lies in its existence."[36] This is true of both his early and late work: he took it for granted that *existence* defines the human condition; *everything* is conceived to be relative to *human* existence.[37]

For Heidegger ultimate reality is Nothingness, "Non-Being." "Being" (*Sein*) and human existence (*Dasein*) are not created and sustained by God the Supreme Being, but arise from "*Nothingness*" (*Nichts*) or "*Non-Being.*" Man is "thrown" into the world, and continues to be pervaded and threatened by Nothingness.

Human existence is related to nothingness as follows: first, human existence has no ground, it originates in the abyss of nothingness; second, it culminates in death, which is another abyss of nothingness; third, the very being of human existence is an anticipation of death, of nothingness: it is intrinsically void.[38]

Human life comes from Nothingness, is suspended over Nothingness, and penetrated by Nothingness. Heidegger, and Sartre after him, gave central importance to a "notion of nonbeing as a kind of circumambient medium in which being is contingently suspended."[39] Thus, "the essential finitude of man" is experienced "at the very center of his Being. He is finite because his Being is penetrated by non-Being."[40] Some of the strongest images in art of men and women seeming to emerge from nothingness and remain surrounded and penetrated by it are in the ravaged, toothpick-thin sculptures of Giacometti during the 1950s and 60s.

Rather than God creating beings out of nothing and, as Supreme Being, grounding them, Heidegger's "*Nothingness*" produces "Being" and beings by "nihilating itself." To rational and commonsense thought, this is patently absurd. The idea of Nothing nihilating itself has been the butt of many jokes from his critics. While for Heidegger "*Nothingness*" replaces God as ultimate "ground" of "Being," for Sartre "*Nothingness*" becomes the "ground" of "man" by making consciousness possible in contrast to a totally unconscious world. Heidegger concluded that, once we see the errors of traditional metaphysics and Christian dogma, we will understand that "Nothing ceases to be the vague opposite of what-is: it now reveals itself as *integral to the Being of what-is.* '*Pure Being and Pure Nothing are thus one and the same*'."[41] Thus his philosophy, from traditional and commonsense viewpoints, ends in an absurd paradox.

Heidegger's question of the ground of beings leads not to God who creates out of nothing; completely dismissing such a Supreme Being as Creator, it leads only to "Nothing," or "Being as Nothing," as the ultimate "Reality."

Heidegger's ground-question originates from and leads back to Nothing (Being) as the ground of beings. Nothing nihilating itself (*Nichts selbst nichtet*) reveals beings as "grounded" in nothingness and yet as other than Nothing . . . . Thus, anything that is must be thought of as coming from Nothing: '*ex nihilo omne ens qua ens fit*'. [Out of nothing come all beings as beings.] Only because Nothing nihilates itself, in some way overcomes itself, is every being able to be.[42]

In his reach into the foundations of beings, Heidegger comes up with Being which is not a being or the "beingness" of beings, but completely "opposite" in respect to beings. It is nothingness.[43]

Heidegger's considered answer to the questions of origins and ground, instead of God, was "Nothingness." The resulting philosophy is one of the most striking pieces of complex doubletalk, or "newspeak," to that point in history.

Traditional meanings of transcendence "fail" with Heidegger,[44] as they do with Sartre and Camus. No traditional Christian or theological, metaphysical meanings remain. Heidegger stands as a central figure, after Nietzsche, in what has been called "post-Christian" culture. He redefined transcendence in terms of *Nothing* or "*Non-Being*," rather than God and eternal, substantial Being. Human existence as *Dasein* now projects into *Nothing*, rather than being drawn toward God and elevated toward Being. Heidegger wrote: "*Dasein* means *being projected into Nothing.* Projected into

Nothing, *Dasein* is already beyond what-is-in-totality. This 'being beyond' what-is we call Transcendence."[45] "Transcendence" for Heidegger further indicates: (1) direct, active participation of "self" *in the world*, instead of a subject-object dichotomy; (2) direct, active participation with other "selves"; (3) overcoming of momentary temporal existence through anxiety, dread, and care for the future, and preoccupation with death. None of these relate to a Supreme Being, but are completely bound to the "self-as-field" within a world-dimension.

The end of transcendence in Heidegger, Sartre, and Camus, and the great influence they have had on subsequent thought and culture, as well as the radical effects of Surrealism, Positivism, Wittgenstein, and language philosophies, mark a crucial turn in modern thought and culture during the middle decades of the twentieth century. This phenomenon can also be seen in some of the most advanced art works of the 1950s and 60s (De Kooning, Dubuffet, Giacometti, Bacon, Beckett, Ionesco, Johns, Rauschenberg, Happenings), and becomes pervasive in art from around 1970 onward. During the 1960s and 70s there emerged Assemblage and Junk art, the coolness, irony, and mockery of urban Pop media images, the massive, brute presence of Minimal art, the autonomous color presence of Color-field and Hard-edge painting, the documentary and language games of Photo-Realism, and the beginnings of more radical language games in Conceptual art. By the end of the 1960s through the 1970s all known ideals, norms, forms, and categories of art had essentially broken down, and strange new things, endlessly odd and different, were proliferating.

Heidegger pressed Kantian skepticism about the "thing-in-itself" to a new modern level of rejection, surpassing it with his concept of a new "Being" which reveals itself as groundless existence or becoming (*Sein*, "beingness"; *Dasein*, man as "being-there").

For Heidegger, beings are not regarded in the light of their permanent essences, but rather in the light of their *existences* which participate in the *happening* of history. The uniqueness of each individual contributes to the *on-going newness* characteristic of history.[46]

The absence of permanent cosmic structures and human essences or souls is required by the absence of the eternal Creator God, who not only creates, but sustains, coordinates, and providentially guides creation, making eternal essence and life possible.

Heidegger's "Being" is no longer timeless, eternal, and unchanging like the Creator God, and the concept of Being in Christian metaphysics, but is *intrinsically temporal, dynamic, and "historical" in character.* It is ever emerging "appearance," "presence," or "beingness," rather than God the supreme, eternal Spiritual Being. For Heidegger, "Being" is an ongoing, non-substantial *Happening* (as it may be called), rather than Absolute Being and eternal Spirit. His "Being" is "constantly coming out of itself into revelation or openness. This coming out of Being from concealment into revelation gives birth to time; it *is* time. Being cannot be thought of as separate from time; time is Being's coming to openness."[47] For Heidegger, "Being" is essentially temporal, in contrast to the unchanging, eternal nature and perfection of the Creator God (who also grounds and participates in the changing reality of the world). Related views prevailed among other existentialists: "Being as understood by the existentialists was not a static but a dynamic concept.... Thus, to think of *man as being* really meant to think of him as *potencia*, or becoming."[48]

Thus, Heidegger's new concept of "Being" is *Happening, Appearance, Being-there, Being-in-the-world*, without essence, substance, or rational, logical sense, structure, or pattern, and without any transcendence in traditional senses. Of a related nature in art are *Happenings*, Kinetic art, Environmental and Process art, and Performance art. The first known Happening was staged by John Cage in 1952. Happenings were then popularized from the late 1950s onward by Alan Kaprow; at the same time there emerged some of the new, continuously moving (*becoming*) kinetic art works of the post-war period. Process art, beginning in the late 1960s, frequently involves an object in which some change is continuously in process of happening. *Happenings* (partly descended from anti-rational Dada events) are the predecessors of the free-form, little-or-non-structured temporal events known as Performance art, which has achieved increasing prominence in art since the 1980s. Such things have been taught in universities for decades.

For Heidegger, "Being" only appears in human *Dasein*, and he writes, "*Dasein* is historical in its Being."[49] Thus, "in the final analysis, it is the human individual who actuates and energizes history, both the historical reality itself (*Geschichte*) and the scientific study of it (*Historie*)."[50] This also means that all responsibility for "Being" itself, and for history, is thrown to man. Heidegger begins to treat "Being" as history in *Being and Time*; the concept is more fully developed in later works, *The Question of Being*, and *Letter on Humanism*.[51]

The purely dynamic, temporal, and "historical" character of "Being" and "*Dasein*" is one of the most telling contrasts with Christian and classical tradition: modern emphasis on time and change (becoming) had been gradually increasing, rising to dominance since the seventeenth century. "This sense of becoming is at the heart of what we mean by modernity, or 'the modern mind'."[52] Romanticism had already seen the world as essentially dynamic. Heidegger not only sees all things as thoroughly dynamic and temporal, but attributes it to the very core of reality, "Being," in *Sein* and *Dasein*. There is no longer any possibility of anything being sustained and redeemed by the eternal and the unchanging. The world and human existence appear permeated by time, change, and finitude as never before in history.

But Heidegger's philosophy, like Existentialism generally, also adds impetus to the modern *disrealization* of time and history. Neither time nor history any longer has an absolute source of sustenance and continuity, or the reason, meaning, and goal formerly provided by the Creator. History is no longer governed by the Creator, or guided by Absolute Mind or Reason. Outside of *Dasein's* efforts, there is no determination or direction whatsoever. And according to Heidegger, Western man has miserably failed in his "shepherding of Being" for twenty-five hundred years, bringing us to our dark age of the "death of God." For Heidegger, "history" can only emerge moment by moment, under the unique, uncertain guidance of *Dasein*. This moment-to-moment emergence, without given plan, direction, goal, or known outcome, is something fundamentally different from Christian conceptions of history, and even different from modern views of history up through the nineteenth and early twentieth centuries: it lacks any certainty of connection, direction, and outcome. According to Heidegger it has been going very badly, and may even end catastrophically. Furthermore, in being shepherded by *Dasein*, there is no longer a substantial being we can call "man" or "self" who is responsible.

For Heidegger, "Being is expressed in terms of time and history and not in terms of an eternally structured universe."

The permanent structure of the cosmos is antithetical to his notion of history in which there is no eternal intelligent plan at work and in which Being does fatefully alter itself. . . . Within the perspective of traditional metaphysics, god caused all beings to exist and placed them in the eternal structure and order of his universe. By viewing things in history, the permanence of things disappears, and no eternal order or structure is apparent. This does not mean that all is chaotic, but that there is nothing permanent, even the order of nature and the structure of institutions can and do change. The postulate of a divine creator fixing all things eternally to their essences is irreconcilable with Heidegger's historical point of view. [53]

In these senses, all is change. For Heidegger, in a Godless world, whatever *is*, appears somehow out of *Nothing* and continues to be penetrated by Nothing. Without eternal essence or *Logos* everything is *"uncanny,"* unspeakably strange and mysterious, always "emerging" anew, impermanent, finite, bound for death, guided by dread or anxiety (*Angst*) and guilt, and undergoing constant change.[54]

Heidegger tells us that it is through the "desirable" moods of anxiety and dread that we can feel "uncanny." "Uncanny," he tells us, means "unhomelike" (*unheimlich*), "not-at-home." Anxiety brings *Dasein* "back from its absorption in the 'world'. *Everyday familiarity collapses.*"[55] This requires the abandonment of any certainty about the "nature" of all things: with the realization that things have no nature or essence, we are thrust toward "Nothingness," or "Being," which is no longer the substance and Reality behind appearance, but only the non-substantial *appearance, emergence, happening.* Heidegger's uncanny world in which man is no longer at home, evoked by dread, eliminating known and named essences, and pointing to Nothingness, recalls the strange, de-structured, anti-rational, unnamable, objects of Dada art (e.g., Duchamp's *Bicycle Wheel*), and the sense of anti-rational, anti-logical "displacement" (*depaysement*) and the "marvelous" (*merveilleux*) of Surrealism. And Sartre's related "Nausea" is the feeling of sickness, ugliness, and revulsion upon realization of the radically groundless, thingless, nameless, antirational, "thereness" of a "world" that is Godless.

Anti-Logos Given Philosophical Sanction by Heidegger. The absence of essence, cosmic structure, soul, and eternal life in Heidegger's world means that there is no *Logos*, no divine or cosmic mind, word, reason, or truth, as in Christian and classical traditions. Not only are there no enduring essences or truth in the world, there are no corresponding rational ideas in the human mind by which those essences can be grasped. No God has created essences in things of the world so that they match or correspond to rational ideas and categories in the mind, making representational knowledge possible. Heidegger and Wittgenstein "constitute the dual-headed Zeus from whom postmodernity springs," and central to their influence is the notion that "truth is entirely mediated by historical flux, societal norms, cultural warrants" in "an ever-mutable humanity and society."[56] [Heidegger's thought is thus a radical philosophical form of today's widespread relativism] Heidegger rejects traditional metaphysics, which affirms that God structures and orders the universe he creates:

God the creator pre-planned all by deciding the nature of things in advance, and then created accordingly. For this reason the essences of things are discoverable by man. The structure and order are also there awaiting man's knowledge. This guarantees the possibility of the truth of man's knowledge as Augustine, Anselm, and Descartes saw so well. The ultimate correctness of man's grasping the essence of things is rooted in the god's having placed those essences there to be grasped . . . . Human nature, created by god and evident to man, is rational, i.e., capable of discerning the truth of what things are. God endowed man with essence-knowing reason; god structured the universe with essences whose intelligibility is directly suited to man's intelligence. Thus truth is assured.[57]

Heidegger's philosophy, along with that of Sartre, Camus, and other Existentialists, contributes to another major aspect of the modern revolution, developing since the time of Hume and Kant—the anti-*Logos* revolution. In this revolution lies the fundamental irrationalism, anti-rationalism, and nihilism of modernity, which has been expanding more rapidly since Nietzsche, Dada, and Surrealism. For Heidegger, reason is incapable of grasping "Being," since no traditional essences, structures, ideas, or universals exist in "mind, world, or Being." "Being" is indefinable;[58] it cannot be clearly formulated or expressed in terms of rational concepts and categories. To Heidegger "Being" remains a kind of elemental mystery or enigma that *appears* in experience of existence, and can only be pointed to, hinted at, felt as "presence" and possibility, and may be magically evoked in poetry or art. It cannot be *represented* in conceptual categories.[59] *Heidegger's philosophy attacks and undermines representational thinking, knowledge, and art in this sense.* Rational, logical knowledge is seen as fundamentally flawed with respect to "the truth of Being." Heidegger tells us that "thinking only begins at the point where we have come to know that *Reason, glorified for centuries, is the most obstinate adversary of thinking.*"[60]

All this indicates the necessary absence of *Logos*, essences, and universsals in both Christian and classical metaphysical senses, including the absence of any rational, propositional divine revelation. There is no God who has revealed himself through nature, human beings, history, and in the culminative sense, through Jesus Christ the divine *Logos*. If this were true, Heidegger would be right in indicating that there can be no propositional or categorical knowledge about Reality. This idea of course constitutes another crucial aspect of the growing modern revolutionary turn away from the core beliefs of centuries of Western tradition. The radical rejection of *Logos* entails the loss of rational, categorical knowledge of ultimate Reality, world, and self—necessitating various forms of intellectual and cultural irrationalism and anti-rationalism—already widely present and recognized in modern culture.

Just as Heidegger re-defines Being as purely temporal, worldly *appearance* of "Being," so he also re-defines *Logos* in terms of his concept of "Being." His "*Logos*" is the primordial oneness of all things in "Being," the "original togetherness of beings," and the "voice" of "Being" speaking to us in human language.[61] Since "*Logos* is the Being of beings," and "Being" only appears in human existence, "*Logos*" is identified with non-essential existence, like his "Being."[62] Instead of the voice and Word of the eternal, personal God, Heidegger's "*Logos*" is the "voice" of a changing, impersonal field or "open potential" of "Being," contingent upon human awareness, dread (*Angst*), care (*Sorge*) and "shepherding." The Christian biblical and metaphysical concept of Jesus Christ the divine *Logos*, the Word of God and coordinating Reality who holds everything together, is reversed by Heidegger, transformed into a naturally existing, impersonal, anti-rational, temporal, constantly changing, "human"-dependent ultimate reality.

In the anti-traditional context of modernity, Heidegger's attempt to preserve concepts of "Being" and "*Logos*" might possibly be considered conservative. But the radical nature of his new definitions, with their antithesis to traditional concepts, especially to Christ as the Creator, Mediator, and coordinator *Logos*, must be considered radically modern. Just as his new concept of "Being" may be called "anti-Being" because it is antithetical to traditional Being and essence, so his concept of "*Logos*" may be designated "anti-*Logos*." Anti-*Logos* is thus given major philosophical sanction. However, after Heidegger's work of the 1950s, the anti-*Logos* direction of modern thought and art has proceeded in a more direct and blunt fashion, and at a rapidly expanding pace. In Christian terms this not only means a destructive assault on given world structure, law, order, morality, and on reason in the full sense, but on the idea of Christ as divine *Logos*, the eternal Word of God, structurer and coordinator of creation, Mediator, and guarantor of representational truth and knowledge through reason and logic in language forms.

In these essential ways Nietzschean, Heideggerian, post-Heideggerian, post-Existentialist, and postmodern thought and art represent a growing destructive assault on reality, truth, goodness, morality, beauty, structure, law, order, language, and art. The increasing effects of this and related forms of thought on law, morality, and society from the 1960s onward has drawn considerable notice. And the effects in contemporary art since the late 1960s and 70s have become so omnipresent and evident that they have become virtually invisible—like the Emperor with no clothes. But that invisibility is also shielded and supported by contemporary theory and criticism.

Sartre's catchphrase for Existentialism, "existence precedes essence," is actually deceptive, since in terms of the Christian and classical Western tradition, Existentialism rejects and "destroys" Being and essence in favor of ever-newly-emerging-*existence*, understood in terms of "appearance," "presence," and potentiality as the *all-in-all*. Similar to Nietzsche there is no objective, transcendent Being, only appearance. Traditional essence is seen as only a human projection, like "God," traditional theology, and metaphysics. There is no substantial, integral reality of either self or world. Existentialism pursues the central modern path of the "triumph of becoming," the "death of God," "death of transcendence," "death of man," and "death of nature," to unprecedented reaches. Thus, a better catchphrase would be, "appearance determines reality," since there is no substantial "thing" or "self" to actually "exist," and no substantial world in which it may exist. "Appearance determines reality" inverts traditional beliefs, which hold that "Reality determines appearance."

The result of Heidegger's "destruction" and revision of Western philosophy and metaphysics is a world radically denuded of the major beliefs of Western tradition—God, Being, *Logos, Nous*, transcendence, essence, everlastingness, holiness, personality, divine and natural cosmic law and order, and of the substantial reality and independence of world, man, and self. With Heidegger's transvaluation of the basic ideas of Being, God, and *Logos*, combined with the fact that his philosophy pointedly restricts itself to "the earth and the gods," "the god of the world" claims the throne of the Most High within one of the most influential philosophical systems of the mid-twentieth century. Transcendence radically fails, man is confined to the earth with its "gods" and constant change, and to underlying, omnipresent, imminent Nothingness. There could hardly be a more significant moment in the ongoing "triumph of becoming." In these ways Heidegger's philosophy, and Existentialism more generally—along with the philosophies of Wittgenstein and Positivism in different ways—establish new milestones in modern thought, and in human spiritual history, surpassing Kant's Copernican revolution, and even Nietzsche's self-designation as "Antichrist" with the will to power.

The Anti-Metaphysical and Anti-Logos Thought of Ludwig Wittgenstein. While focusing basically on the nature and function of language and logic, the influential philosophy of Wittgenstein (1889-1951), works in a larger sense to undermine and destroy the Western metaphysics of Logos that underlies traditional beliefs and thought about language, knowledge, truth, and reality. Although Wittgenstein's assault is not in the form of a direct and sustained argument against Logos, it accomplishes that end as a cumulative result of philosophical claims about language and logic, and the larger implications of those claims. The resulting destructive effects on traditional concepts of Logos are so great that his philosophy stands as a new and radical form of anti-Logos thought in history. Wittgenstein's implicit "argument against the metaphysics of Logos," with its goal of "destroying the Logos," and the nightmarish effect of "a philosophical Walpurgisnacht," has been elucidated in more explicit form by Harry Redner in twenty pages on the core of Wittgenstein's thought.[63]

In a broad sense, Wittgenstein's argument hinges on the conviction that "there is no getting above, beyond or beneath language."[64] Even in the first phase of his thought, represented by the *Tractatus Logico-Philosophicus* (1918, 1921), language can express "nothing that is higher" in propositions of metaphysics, theology, philosophy, ethics, and aesthetics. All such statements are literally "nonsensical" for Wittgenstein, and cannot be talked about, because they attempt to transcend the limits of language. Wittgenstein's final conclusion in the book is that "what we cannot talk about we pass over in silence." Such views, which Wittgenstein claims to be "unassailable and definitive," indicate his "positive anti-metaphysical stance."[65]

In the second phase of his thought, represented by *Philosophical Investigations* (1953), Wittgenstein goes further in ascribing primacy, and even ultimacy, to language. Language is now seen to totally enclose human beings, like a "fly [trapped in a] fly-bottle," so that we are incapable of grasping anything higher or beyond it. In this sense *language* constitutes and formulates all that we know. "Words" are "what I have to talk about." Along with this, Wittgenstein emphasizes that the "*forms of life*," "the given," "must be accepted."[66] The flow of life in Wittgenstein's sense is found exclusively in human experience, and is constantly changing. Thus, all we can ever know is within changing language in changing human life—language beyond which it is impossible to reach in order to know any reality or meaning in propositions about Logos, God, or Being. We inhabit a world of *absence* of the eternal and unchanging—a world of fragmented *becoming*. The claim to ground all we know in immediate life and experience is typically modern. But Wittgenstein's primary claim to ground all that we know in *language*, goes well beyond earlier (pre-Nietzschean) modern views, to a more skeptical, *less metaphysical* level—to a primary basis in language. Language is conceived to be exclusively based and grounded in given human usage. It is a purely "natural" human phenomenon. An elementary assumption of Wittgenstein, and of contemporary Postmodernism, is that language has no higher or deeper ground or basis than human usage, in the given languages of communities. On this assumption the possible presence and activity of divine or universal Logos is completely dismissed.

Because of its apparent immediacy and historicity, language is assumed to be a credible, concrete reality. It is thought of as less metaphysical than "*ideas* in the *mind* of a thinking *subject*," and in particular, of the modern Kantian subject that is unified, transcendental, and rational. The Cartesian-Kantian concept of the conscious, thinking subject, which was at the time considered more immediate and credible than traditional grounds of belief in God, Being, archetypal Forms or Ideas, a substantially real and ordered world, etc., has been seen by radical modern thought from Nietzsche onward as unacceptably metaphysical and incredible, considered as substance and unity. Wittgenstein's thought, although not essentially and directly dealing with the great metaphysical claims about self, world, and God or Being, is fundamentally shaped by the highly skeptical, post-Nietzschean climate of thought concerning them. And his thought is related by its radical nature to Heidegger's.

Wittgenstein's implied argument against the existence of Logos rests more specifically on the notion that, if Logos did exist, it could not be experienced or known, and could have no effect on human affairs.[67] It is easier, of course (and often more effective as propaganda), to treat such matters as if they are so incredible that they do not merit close examination and reasoned argument. There are "echoes" in Wittgenstein of the ancient skeptical view of Gorgias that "if there is being, it is inaccessible and unknowable; if it is knowable it is inexpressible and incommunicable." Gorgias's claim that "speech can never transcend itself to apprehend something 'other,' standing over against it, that is to apprehend 'being' and truth," becomes a determining, foundational concept with Wittgenstein, and subsequently with Postmodernism.[68] And there are echoes of Wilhelm Dilthey's modern empirical rejection of transcendence through arguments such as, if there were "a timeless reality" behind the flow of life, we could not "directly experience" it, and it could only be "a realm of shadows."[69]

Wittgenstein's primary argument against metaphysical Logos, according to Redner, is that it would need to be understood to be followed, and that it could not be understood because of the inherent ambiguity or equivocation of language. But such a view of language as so deceptively ambiguous is completely inconsistent with Christian metaphysics of Logos, in which it is possible to a determined extent for human ideas and language to faithfully correspond with created structures of things, and with ideas in the mind of God, since they have the same origin and ground in the mind of God. In this sense, Wittgenstein's argument is non-applicable.

The notion of the ambiguity of language in Wittgensteinian and postmodern thought arises from radical disbelief in, and dismissal of divine Mind and Logos, and is arbitrarily and illogically injected into the argument against Logos. The argument ultimately rests on the absurd circular logic that there is no Logos since it cannot be understood because there is no Logos. Wittgenstein abandons Christian and classical doctrines that there are rational structures of the world implanted by God, and that language participates in their reality. The argument that Logos, if it existed, would not be accessible and experienceable, and would have no effect on human affairs, completely ignores Christian doctrine, and is specifically refuted by: (1) divine creation through the Logos; (2) divine immanence and acts within creation; (3) divine revelation of God's word (Logos); (4) the incarnation and mission of the Logos in Jesus Christ; (5) individual confirmation in divine salvation and the indwelling power and guidance of the Holy Spirit.

While Kant had held that empirically ungrounded reason leads us to unrealities, Wittgenstein claimed it is language that leads us into the "illusions" of metaphysics and theology. The notion that words and concepts lead us to metaphysical illusions had become a prominent feature in Nietzsche's thought (e.g., the "illusions" of "I," "self," "being"). Wittgenstein, like the primitivizing German Expressionists, depreciated rational mind, concepts and doctrines, emphasizing instead immediate experience, instinctual behavior, ceremony, ritual, and gesture. We allow ourselves to be "bewitched" by language, he thought. We tend to use it beyond ordinary circumstances as a kind of "magic" to call concepts of higher things into existence. Wittgenstein saw no genuine reality in concepts such as "spirit," "soul," or "Incarnation"—they are merely linguistic creations. He detested theology, interpreting doctrine as no more than fanciful theory and nonsense. His own "personal lack of faith" emerges from several of his statements. He considered religion acceptable if kept to the level of immediate experience, emotion, aesthetics, and ceremonial ritual, but to formulate any doctrinal propositions is to use language to create false myths and illusions.[70]

Chapter Eight

The Absence of God in Later Twentieth-Century Postmodern Art and Thought

For Derrida, all metaphysical and religious statements about God, Being, and universals are intrinsically imaginary.

There are no more fundamental rules, no more criteria of judgment or of pleasure. In the aesthetic realm of today there is no longer any God to recognize his own . . . . No matter how marginal, or banal, or even obscene it may be, everything is subject to aestheticization, culturalization, museumification. — Baudrillard.[1]

The experience and ground of "the real" disappears in Lichtenstein's art. The previous metaphysical era in which images referred to and corresponded with something real has come to an end. Images no longer refer to substantial things.

Salle's work, like Postmodernism generally, shows signs of skepticism about objective and universal truth and substantial reality. No clear sense of expressed or supporting universal and necessary truth or purposeful meaning emerges.

The Skepticism of Late Twentieth-Century Thought and Art. The concepts of Nietzsche, Saussure, Husserl, Heidegger, and Wittgenstein have led, in Structuralism, Poststructuralism, and postmodern[2] thought and arts, and much of the rest of contemporary art, to more intensive and pervasive views that human language, no longer conceived as grounded by God, being, reason, or truth, is the only source of "knowledge" we have. Philosophical thought from Wittgenstein into Postmodernism is much more skeptical and reductive concerning knowledge and its limits than with Kant two centuries earlier. It is no longer Kantian universal, rational *ideas*, but our more immediate, diverse, and changing *languages* that determine all conceptual thought. Existing languages are thought to determine all mental concepts and organized thinking, rather than transcendent mind and ideas rationally ordering things and thought, and determining effectiveness of linguistic concepts. Related views have been widely developed in recent art.[3]

The Anti-Metaphysical, Anti-Foundational Thought of Rorty. The recent American postmodernist philosopher and teacher, Richard Rorty (1931-2007) claimed that from the age of three or four we begin to internalize a particular community of language.[4] Language is the product of specific cultures and communities. Communities vary and are in the process of changing over time. Thus, language and conceptual thinking vary from one community to another. Influenced by Heidegger and Wittgenstein, among others, Rorty held that there is no truth in the sense of unchanging divine Ideas, universals, and accurate representations of essences or nature of things. Eternal, unchanging Platonic Ideas and the Christian Logos are rejected. According to Rorty, there is no reason to take the concept of truth seriously. There is no divine or unchanging ground for language. One cannot get "back behind language to something that 'grounds' it or that it 'expresses,' or to which it might hope to be adequate." "Language goes all the way down" and is "ubiquitous." "Persons and cultures are, for us, incarnated vocabularies," and "there is nothing beyond vocabularies which serves as a criterion of choice between them."[5] Human beings cannot reach beyond their own language constructs, but are forever confined to them. As in Wittgenstein's metaphor, they are trapped like a fly in a bottle [an appropriate image of humanity for such views of truth and knowledge]. Rorty advises the complete abandonment of search for such traditional concepts of truth, as well as modern Cartesian and Kantian revisions of them.

Rorty specifically rejects the traditional correspondence theory of truth and knowledge, discussing it as the view of the mind as a "mirror of nature." Words and sentences do not link with objects in one-to-one correspondences.[6] He writes that "our sense of objectivity is not a matter of corresponding to objects, but of getting together with other subjects . . . there is nothing to objectivity except intersubjectivity."[7] He disparages the theory of the mind as a mirror of nature. By abandoning this illusory view, we will no longer be tempted to think it possible to achieve accurate representations of nature. Since language is a human construct, we can never expect it to truthfully correspond to a nature we did not make. And in any case we can never go beyond language to verify objective truth. Rorty's response to traditional views of truth is that "we should drop the topic."[8] There is no necessary, demonstrable, or incontrovertible truth; we should give up on the quest for such apodictic and final claims. Similarly, one can never identify an essential or "true self." The chasm between language and the inner world is as unbridgeable as the one between language and the outer world.

We should abandon all foundational philosophies as misguided and misleading. The traditional concepts of divine Logos, Ideas, and Reason as source and ground of essential structures and ideas in mind and nature, and the bases for their correspondence, are abandoned by Rorty. Only by completely abandoning them can he make plausible his case for language as the source of all mental concepts. But the existence of divine ideas and structures is actually as logical as it is well attested by centuries of doctrine on God, Logos, creation, and revelation. Thus, Rorty's case, much like those of Nietzsche and Wittgenstein, rests on a basis of rejection of all that. Rorty recommends becoming, like himself, a "liberal ironist," an ironist being "one who faces up to the contingency of his or her own most central beliefs and desires." Like others who have rejected concepts of universal truth, from the Sophists through Hume and modern pragmatists like Dewey, Rorty turns to more immediate, pragmatic goals and solutions. Since language is not a true picture of the world or anything perfect or eternal, it should be used as a practical tool for solving problems, following our own personal desires and fantasies, and for continually re-creating ourselves by "redescription" (hello postmodern thought and art).[9]

Rorty thinks that post-Nietzschean philosophers such as Heidegger, Foucault, and Derrida have much in common with American pragmatists because they reject traditional metaphysics and ontology, as well as the correspondence theory of truth. He appreciates the funny, comic aspect of Derrida's *différence* writings, which Derrida employs as a means of discrediting previous concepts of truth and meaning, and discrediting Western philosophical and theological traditions.

Rorty has also referred to Christianity in insulting terms, slyly reducing it to "fundamentalism," and making accusations of "primitive fear, hatreds, and superstition," and references to "bigots" (he is not the only one). He has been forthright in stating the liberal and radical agendas in university teaching for him and many colleagues, showing us what much university education has become: "we try to arrange things so that students who enter as bigoted, homophobic, religious fundamentalists will leave college with views like our own . . . we do our best to convince these students of the benefits of secularization. We assign first-person accounts of growing up homosexual to our homophobic students for the same reasons that German schoolteachers in the postwar period assigned *The Diary of Anne Frank* . . . ."[10] In these allegations we see the trendy use of an illogical neologism, "homophobia" (literally, "fear of man"), that is meant to sound like a disease, with the illogical argument that moral condemnation of homosexuality can be equated with racial prejudice.

In contrast to such forms of anti-metaphysical, anti-foundational thought, Michael Devitt, (b. 1938) one of the smaller number of contemporary philosophers who support realist metaphysics and epistemology (his is based on naturalism and physicalism), emphasizes that "Kantian anti-realism" is behind various forms of anti-realism and constructivism from the nineteenth century into the present. "Kant's idea that we make the known world was dominant in the nineteenth century. In its relativistic form the idea is ubiquitous in the twentieth century." Two key influences of Kantian anti-realism are "the idea of an unknowable, noumenal world independent of us; and the idea of the known, phenomenal world as partly our creation through the imposition of concepts." A third one, relativism, was "alien to Kant," but has since become ubiquitous. Recent Constructivists like Nelson Goodman talk of "making worlds" by the imposition of human concepts. For Realism, in sharp contrast, the world is independent of our mentality, and not made by our concepts. "According to Constructivism, the known world is determined by our thought, which is constrained by a noumenal world in ways that are in principle unknowable." Devitt finds this "mysterious to the point of incoherence." "Constructivists blur the crucial distinction between theories and the world." "Relativistic Kantian anti-realism" or Constructivism has become influential in many areas of contemporary thought and art.

In recent years Michael Dummett and related figures in the British School have been very influential as anti-Realists. And the promotion of anti-Realism by "the radical philosophers of science," such as Thomas Kuhn, Paul Feyerabend, and others, as well as in the epistemologies of Hilary Putnam (recently) and Goodman, is "just the tip of the iceberg." "Particularly obscure versions of it pervade Structuralism,[11] Poststructuralism, and French thought in general. It is common in literature departments around the world. It is to be found in all the social sciences and in 'the sociology of knowledge'. It is the underlying metaphysics of various political movements including that in the universities against the 'canon' and for 'PC' ('political correctness'). Not even feminism has been left untouched." Devitt finds these various forms of Constructivism to be "*the* most dangerous contemporary intellectual tendency." "Constructivism has led to a veritable epidemic of 'worldmaking'. It attacks the immune system that saves us from silliness."[12]

The Development of Radical Skepticism in American Art by Rauschenberg. Duchamp was still alive and active when Robert Rauschenberg (1925-2008) was doing his first original art works during the 1950s. An admirer of Duchamp and his work, many of Rauschenberg's guiding beliefs are related to those of his art, and to those of their common friend, John Cage. Art critic and historian Irving Sandler has written about the "Duchamp-Cage aesthetic" which influenced Rauschenberg's art. A major concept of this aesthetic is that one thing in the world is as good as another.[13] This means that there are no higher or lower things, objects, or people. Philosophically it implies that there is no hierarchical order. And this further indicates that there can be no ultimate God or Being on whom such hierarchies are based. Thus, like Duchamp, both Cage and Rauschenberg held to worldviews that eliminated any kind of ultimate, rationally ordering Supreme Being. Like Duchamp, their views and art are in these senses, atheistic. For Cage, the musician, it meant that anything could be music, any kind of noise, or even silence. For Rauschenberg it meant that art could be made from anything at all.

In Rauschenberg's work, almost any combination of objects and materials can be found. During the 1950s and 60s he often used trash and discarded objects he picked up on the streets of New York City, reflecting the Duchamp-Cage aesthetic that art can be found anywhere at any time, especially in "lowly" materials. In doing so he created what is called Assemblage (or "Combines"), which became a stimulus to Junk and Pop art movements. Rauschenberg's *First Landing Jump* of 1961 (Fig. 9) combines cloth, metal can, leather, an electrical fixture, cable, pale image transfers, and oil paint on composition board, with a car tire and wood plank. As in Duchamp's work (though somewhat less radically), these things have lost most of their identities and usual connections, and convey a strange sense of disjunction, while retaining enigmatic allusions to the city, streets, and cars.

Rauschenberg's *Odalisk*[14] of 1955-58 is a mixed media "combine" that puts together oil paints, watercolor, pencil, crayon, paper, fabric, photographs, printed reproductions, miniature blueprint, newspaper, metal, glass, dried grass, hanging whiskey bottles, an old tie, and steel wool with a pillow, a wood post, electric lights, and a stuffed rooster at the very top. Traditional senses of hierarchy are mocked in this work by placing a stuffed rooster at the top center, the position traditionally reserved for God, pagan gods, kings, or heroic leaders. This work is nearly seven feet tall, so we are obliged to look up to a chicken. Since *Odalisk* includes naked photographic reproductions from a girlie magazine, the title becomes a satirical demolition of classical and neo-classical nudes emphasizing ideal beauty and propriety. This is a form of parody, practiced by Duchamp, Rauschenberg, and by much recent Postmodernism. Parody implies "a mocking, burlesque version which ridicules by exaggerating qualities in the original which it distorts."[15]

Another work of the same time, *Monogram*, has a life-size stuffed goat (at top center again) standing upright on a board that suggests a painting, but is now lying flat on the floor rather than on a wall, dissociated from its usual place, role, and meanings. The goat also has a tire encircling its mid-section, and a darkened tennis ball lying behind its rear end.

Fig. 9. ***Robert Rauschenberg, First Landing Jump***, 1961. Cloth, metal, leather, electrical fixture, cable, and oil paint on composition board, with automobile tire and wood plank, 7' 5" x 6' 8". Gift of Philip Johnson, The Museum of Modern Art, New York, NY. Photo credit: Digital Image © The Museum of Modern Art/Licensed by SCALA / Art Resource, NY.

Also similar to Duchamp and Cage, and to recent Postmodernism, is the strong sense of discontinuity and dissociation in Rauschenberg's work. In contrast to traditional art, both Christian and classical, which stressed unity, continuity, and harmony, pointing to a higher, ultimate and unifying reality and reason, Rauschenberg expressed radical skepticism by combining diverse things in separation from one another, and not parts of any greater whole.[16] This suggests an anti-world of fundamental *difference* or *heterogeneity*, often referred to as "difference" or "*differance*" by Derrida and some other postmodernists. Different things in different forms are pervasive, with no transcendent dimension depicted or symbolized. For them there is nothing higher to depict or symbolize. In both Duchamp and Rauschenberg there is a strong sense of the separateness and disconnectedness that would become a hallmark of Postmodernism. In *Odalisk* not only are there sudden changes from one technique, material, object, and mode of representation to another, but abrupt jumps, overlaps, and cut-offs from one image to another, creating a fragmented concatenation.

These works could almost have been made by Duchamp, except that they do more with color combinations and painterly effects of drips, smears, calligraphic brushstrokes, and translucencies. Rauschenberg continued to develop effects of color and paint—more aesthetic throughout his later work. These direct effects of paint and color, so appealing to modern sensibilities, as well as a kind of disjunctive allusiveness to modern life and the city, and the surprise of unexpected objects included—no doubt have much to do with his long-term fame and fortune. Duchamp did not permit so much aesthetic pleasure in his own anti-art.

Duchamp, Rauschenberg, and Postmodernism do not simply represent modern changes in style or form, like previous historical changes in style. They represent revolutionary changes in *beliefs* or *worldviews*. They differ essentially from the beliefs of both Christian and classical art. Classicism dominated from Greece through Rome, Renaissance, and the Baroque age, weakening through Rococo, Neo-Classicism, and modern realism. Before Modernism, classical art and thought had been influential for twenty-four centuries or so. Classical art emphasized belief in a real world that could be objectively represented, and the belief in ideals. Hebrew-Christian belief has been widely influential for twenty centuries, or forty if we add the time from God's covenant with Abraham onward. And there has been knowledge of God from the very beginning of human life. But such radical skepticism as that of Duchamp had played a minor role in art and thought up until recently. While Duchamp and Dada still represent the relatively limited role of radical skepticism in modern art of the early twentieth century, the extreme skepticism of Postmodernism in its many forms is now widespread. It dominates the international art world, and is highly influential in intellectual circles and in universities. Modern philosophical thought has led in this direction, with its progressive rejection of the revealed God of creation and the Bible, from Descartes and Kant through Hegel and Nietzsche. That line has continued in the twentieth century into Heidegger, Sartre, and Wittgenstein, and risen to cultural dominance with postmodernists such as Lyotard, Foucault, Derrida, Baudrillard, and Rorty.

The Abandonment of Universals, and Truth as Fiction in the Thought of Foucault. For Michel Foucault (1926-1984), human thought and science are not capable of attaining any universal or absolute truth. There is a resounding absence of universals in his viewpoint (the same can be said of Rauschenberg). He thinks that only certain limited *understandings* of truth and meaning can be established through the underlying paradigms and ideologies of different epochs of history. They arise only in human society; there is no God or transcendent source. Such ideologies are limited and changing, having no unchanging ground, and no ultimacy. They are supported in language and art by the power of social institutions and traditions of the time, and by repetition and reinforcement. For Foucault, much like Nietzsche, "Universal truth was just another name for power disguised as the criterion of all knowledge."[17] In his view, societies search for knowledge and meaning in order to establish social power and dominance.

There is an "abandonment of the principle of a universal reason" in Foucault, as well as in Heidegger's earlier ontology.[18] Like radical postmodern thought generally, rational knowledge of universals is rejected, and the traditional Christian ideas of divine revelation, and of God creating corresponding rational structures of thought and things, making real knowledge possible, are no longer even considered.

Modern philosophy since Kant, but especially since the destructive assaults by Schopenhauer, Hegel, Marx, Nietzsche, Husserl, Heidegger, Wittgenstein, and Sartre, no longer allows any place for the Creator God of the Bible, self-existent Being, and universal reason. Heidegger and Wittgenstein established the context in which anti-theistic, anti-essentialist, anti-universal postmodern thought and art could flourish. They have given rise to the thought of Foucault, Derrida, Baudrillard, Rorty, and others. The varied views of these radical postmodernists commonly include rejection of all types of foundationalism and totalizing understandings of reality. All forms of metaphysics and ontology are viewed as untenable. Their philosophies operate within "horizons of finitude, sociocultural embeddedness, and contextualized reason."[19]

In a key book, *The Order of Things* (1970; French, 1966), Foucault sought to analyze concepts of knowledge and truth by examining historical eras from Renaissance to Modern. His study assumes that no universality of truth or transcendent basis of knowledge and certainty is available. History is characterized by a succession of radically different and separate modes of understanding that he calls *epistemes*. An *episteme* is the underlying conceptual framework that serves as the basis for the various fields of knowledge of an epoch. It is "a mental infrastructure underlying all strands of knowledge (on man) at a given age, a conceptual 'grid'." It is the "historical *a priori*" of a time period, establishing the structure and limits for knowledge, and serving to determine the nature of things known within those structures. It is broader than a worldview, since it functions at unconscious levels, below those of conscious theory and method. Foucault's *epistemes* are "fundamental codes" giving form to cognitive language and thought.[20]

For Foucault all such *epistemes* are radically different and divergent. Thus, they are incompatible with each other. The result is that history is separated into discontinuous epochs or blocks. [But if different epochs have incompatible *epistemes*, wouldn't it make it impossible to understand another epoch?] In *The Order of Things* Foucault focuses on describing *mutations* between the *epistemes* he deals with, rather than seeking answers to questions about sources and causes. He sees these mutations as arbitrary. As J. G. Merquior writes, "Epistemes succeed one another without any inner logic. Moreover they tend to constitute radically heterogeneous blocks of knowledge: absolute discontinuity is the supreme interepistemic law."[21]

But Foucault proceeds with the very objective of analyzing the three epochal *epistemes* he has identified as incompatible, and unrelated to his own [postmodern] era—Renaissance, classical, and post-classical or modern. If they are radically discontinuous, how is it possible for him to identify and analyze them? Merquior supports David Leary's question about this: "if one denies any kind of continuity in history—and it is Foucault's avowed task to demonstrate the radical discontinuity in history—then how is one to explain the possibility of doing history?" And Merquior adds, "How, unless we introduce some degree of historical continuity, can we ever begin to understand the past?" This historical disconnectedness, along with the absence of universals and any secure and enduring knowledge, indicates the anti-rationalism of Foucault's thought. But very similar views dominate much of visual arts of the past thirty or forty years. It is clear that such views have completely dismissed the rational structuring of creation and the providential control of history by the omniscient, omnipotent God.

In a later book, *The Archaeology of Knowledge* (1972; French 1969), he developed further the view that knowledge is without any transcendent ground. He held that his "essential task was to free the history of thought from its subjection to transcendence."[22] A key thought of the book is closely related to Nietzsche: "there are no facts, only interpretations."[23] Foucault develops a novel terminology for expressing this, however. All ideas of *presence* are devaluated. He seeks to "dispense with 'things.'" And "'*depresentify*' them." His aim is to "substitute for the enigmatic treasure of 'things' anterior to discourse, the regular formation of objects that emerge only in discourse."[24] Expressed in simpler terms, this means that it is only through our language that we establish all we think we know. All supposed new understandings of language and "knowledge" have no real, objective basis, but are merely *reinterpretations* of existing *interpretations*. Words "do not indicate a signified but rather impose an interpretation." Discourse does not lead us beyond itself to a real referent, but actually creates its own objects. For Foucault, "there is no solid or objective truth that can serve as a point of termination, no final signified in which all signifiers find their culmination."[25] In his term, this means there is no "exteriority." Language or discourse has no reference to anything real or in depth external to it. "Foucault is engaged in undermining a whole structure of thinking, a whole approach toward 'reality' that he sees as oppressively uncreative. By focusing on 'discourse' as the final end of his analysis, he aims to bypass this rigidifying mind-set, much as Nietzsche sought to do in declaring reality itself to be a human creation."[26]

Another important aspect of *The Archaeology of Knowledge* is the use of parody. Allan Megill points out ways that the book is a "parodic repetition" of Descartes' *Discourse on Method*, a founding monument of modern thought. Foucault uses parody to undercut these foundational modern views and seek liberation from "oppressive" modern tradition. Nietzsche had used parody in his own drive to liberate his thought from previous traditions. He presciently claimed historical beginnings of such parody in the preface to one of his books of 1887: "Parody begins" ("*Incipit parodia*"). Megill observes that "this could well stand as a motto for the writings not only of Nietzsche but of Foucault and Derrida as well."[27] Parody could also stand as a motto for much postmodern art. As Nigel Wheale writes, parody usually implies "a mocking, burlesque version which ridicules by exaggerating qualities in the original which it distorts, producing a pastiche, or a patching together of pieces."[28] Thus, it becomes a key method for advancing the radically skeptical postmodern view that there is no objective truth available in historical art or thought of any epoch, and that any claims to such knowledge or exemplary style in art, are "oppressive" and should be exposed as misleading or oppressive.

For Foucault, "knowledge" is only a "perspective," without objective truth. There is no final authority for truth. All discourse is "fiction," "discursive strategies" that purport to be knowledge or truth. Foucault even recognizes his own writing about history as fiction. Its purpose is to oppose the current perspective of order and meaning.[29] He writes that it is "parodic, directed against reality, dissociative, directed against identity, . . . sacrificial, directed against truth."[30] Foucault's thought after 1970 pursues a course of "radical activism": he gives more emphasis to power-attacks on previous perspectives. Since "discourse" without any final object is all there is, the ruling present form of discourse is open to discursive attack. When it has been replaced, the discourse that replaces it and comes to rule, will itself be open to attack. For these reasons Megill describes Foucault as a "thinker of crisis."[31] Others have referred to Foucault and Derrida as "masters of suspicion."

The history of modern and postmodern thought and art exhibits a related development: one form of discourse has ruled for a time, and then been replaced by another, another, and another. These replacements have become faster and faster during the twentieth century. But with radical Postmodernism, not only all preceding perspectives, but all replacements are seen as "fictions." However, the Christian belief in the ultimate Reality and Truth of God, and the authority of Scripture, still holds firm for millions, twenty centuries after Christ, and forty centuries after God's covenant with Abraham.

Radical postmodern views about the absence of universals, and truth as fiction, have served as a basis for much postmodern art of the past three decades, like that of Rauschenberg and Lichtenstein, using pervasive parody or combining many different images and fragments of images in different modes and styles. Much Postmodernism, like Foucault, conveys the sense that there is no truth or depth, only "strategic discourses." There is a "widely diffused postmodernist notion of the superficiality of art" that is related to Foucault. "Postmodernism teaches us to look at the work of art not in order to discern a meaning that lies beneath it but rather to enjoy it for what it is, with nothing concealed, no intention to be discovered, only the infinite play of the work itself."[32]

The Radical Postmodern Thought of Derrida. With modern critical attacks on metaphysics and ontology, there has been a progressive reduction of the role and nature of reason and rationality in much leading modern philosophy (e.g., Schopenhauer, Nietzsche, Heidegger, Sartre, and postmodernists such as Derrida, Foucault, Baudrillard). By divorcing them from God, reason and logic they have come to appear highly problematic, misleading, and even oppressive. Thinking appears split into two opposed camps, or two cultures, the aesthetic or artistic, and the scientific or analytical. The aesthetic side reduces reason and rationality to virtual helplessness or pure deception, incapable of grasping any universal truth. While the scientific disposition treats it as capable only of limited fact, and incapable of religious, theological, and metaphysical content. Harry Redner thinks we live in "an age when rationality has been almost completely appropriated by the sciences," leaving philosophy "threatened with exclusion."[33]

The most intense attacks against rationality in recent decades have come from neo-Nietzschean poststructuralists and postmodernists such as Derrida and Foucault. Jacques Derrida (1930-2004) has been one of the leading anti-rationalists among them. He treats all language, including philosophic and religious texts, as inherently "metaphoric." He understands "metaphor as the very structure or possibility of all language and concepts."[34] This indicates that all forms of language are metaphorical, not only philosophy, but even the sciences and logic: there is never a one-to-one correspondence or identity between a word or text and the thing it signifies. Language consists of tropes—inherently figurative and suggestive, rather than authoritatively defining. Derrida thus essentially ties language to human imagination. "Logic is only slavery within the bounds of language. Language has within it, however, an illogical element, the metaphor. Its principal force brings about an identification of the non-identical; it is thus an operation of the imagination. It is on this that the existence of concepts, forms, etc. rests."[35] Thus, all metaphysical and religious statements about God, Being, and universals are intrinsically *imaginary*. [Such views about language are widely taught in universities today as leading forms of thought for our era.]

For Derrida, in central ways, language is all in all—all there is in order to know anything and make decisions. One of his most famous statements is "there is nothing outside the text." But even this statement in the original French has an intentional ambiguity and Dada-like comic-absurd quality about it, since it can also be translated as "there is no inset plate."[36] The problem for Derrida is that language is arbitrary and unstable, and has no objective connection with external things or any supposed objective truth. At the core of his writing is his view of the intrinsic instability and undecidability of language, meaning, and truth. For him all writing consists of texts that refer to other texts that refer to other texts, and so on ad infinitum. No text even corresponds accurately or truthfully with any external object of the world, or to any objective or universal truth. The traditional correspondence theory of truth is essentially rejected. The sense that we can know *any* universal or logical truth is lost. Texts are "liberated" from Truth or any transcendental signified. They now become "originary," imaginative works. Instead of relating or discovering truth, they operate by invention.[37]

These basic views set Derrida in fundamental opposition not only to Enlightenment modernity, but to centuries of Western philosophy since Plato and Aristotle, and to the Bible and centuries of Christian theology. His view that there is no stable truth or meaning contradicts all essential teachings of the Bible. Most obviously it contradicts the teachings about the Holy Trinity: that God the Trinity is the eternal, supreme Being who created all things and gave all rational structures to the world; that Jesus Christ is eternal, unchanging deity ("Jesus Christ is the same yesterday and today and forever," Hebrews 13:8); that Christ proclaimed himself to be the truth ("I am the way, the truth, and the life. No one comes to the Father except through Me," John 14:6); and that the gospel message is eternal and unchanging (Galatians 1:8-9). It is not surprising to find that Derrida did not believe in life after death. In one of his most forthright statements he said: "I do not believe that one lives on post-mortem."[38] This contradicts the central message of Christianity of the death and resurrection of Christ, with the purpose that all who believe in Him might have eternal life.[39]

Moving forward on paths opened by Nietzsche, Heidegger, and Husserl, Derrida sets his thought in opposition to Western metaphysics since Plato and Aristotle. This tradition held that *meaning* is essentially stable and determinate and can be perceived, understood, and comprehended. Derrida rejects this central belief of metaphysics (and of ordinary belief), disparaging it as the "metaphysics of presence." He employs novel terms of *difference* and *logocentrism* in his quest to destabilize traditional metaphysical concepts of being and certainty ("presence") and the univocity of meaning. Western metaphysics and theology have been centered on Being as "presence"—in such foundational terms as God, being, substance, and essence (*ousia*), mind (*nous*), reason (*logos*) idea (*eidos*), origin (*arche*), and end or goal (*telos*). Throughout his writings Derrida sought to avoid making decisions about meaning and truth in terms of "presence."[40] The recent term, *presence* (from Heidegger), is adopted to indicate the central belief in traditional Western metaphysics, and in the Bible, of the actual, objective existence of rational and divine truth and meaning, and of it being accessible either through rational thought (classical), everyday knowledge, and divine revelation (Christian). As skeptical and atheistic postmodern thought has it, Western metaphysics or ontotheology was built around the *privileging of presence over absence*. As radical Postmodernism (which is generally atheistic) sees it, truth and meaning in any final or ultimate terms is never "present." Derrida set a course to deconstruct (to expose the weaknesses and failures) of these metaphysical and Christian views, but in the guise of strange, new terms.

Similarly, Derrida criticizes the central view of Western philosophy that we are capable of receiving, discovering, and communicating real truth and meaning in and through words, disparagingly characterizing the view as "logocentrism" [logos-centered]. While the Greek word *logos* at simpler levels means *word, reason,* or *spirit,* in classical metaphysics it is extended to mean reason, logic, and order in words and things, to the capacity of words to name and identify things, and to ultimate meanings of truth, reason, and order at cosmic and divine levels. Derrida saw in Nietzsche's writings an important "liberation from logos" and "closure of metaphysics" that supported his own enterprise. This liberation from logos meant that linguistic signs (texts, concepts) could no longer be authoritatively understood to signify a fully present meaning or truth (i.e., a signified that is grounded in being, logos).

In early Greek metaphysics it was Heracleitus who first emphasized the reality of cosmic Logos giving order and intelligibility to the world, and of analogous reason in man, making real knowledge possible. And in the Bible and Christian theology, Christ is specifically identified as the Logos, the supreme, divine embodiment of Truth, and Creator of the world and its rational structures, making them knowable.[41] In Christian theology these concepts were highly developed in the writings of Augustine and Aquinas, among others (see Chapters Four and Five). Thus, for Derrida to attempt to "deconstruct" Logos, is a sly attempt to undermine belief in Christ, as well as any certainty of final truth and meaning, through linguistic shrewdness and circumvention.

Beginning with such forms of thought, rather than with belief in God as uncreated Creator and Supreme Being, Derrida also rejects the metaphysical and theological polarities of Western thought, such as good/evil. Instead of the eternal God who is all good, opposed by the subordinate, created Satan who rebelled against God and is evil, Derrida rejects the "conceptual oppositions" of good/evil, as well as transcendental/ empirical, universal/ particular, original/derivative, internal/external, in which the first concept is "privileged" over the second. In the Bible and Christian theology God is certainly "privileged" since He is the eternal, self-sufficient Personal Spiritual Being who created everything else. But since Derrida's thought arises from assumptions *against* belief in God, it follows that he will reject any "privileging" of God, Being, Logos, and the good, transcendental, universal, and original. Derrida's complex rhetoric, studded with privileged neologisms, leads his readers to be favorably disposed to his way of thinking, draws them away from truths of Christian theology and Western metaphysics, and leaves them largely ignorant of them. His subtle but destructive depreciation of traditional theological and metaphysical concepts seems to reinforce modern and postmodern views that ancient and medieval fathers, prophets, and philosophers were ignorant, deluded, and superstitious, while postmodernists [although they can possess no truth] know so much better the way things really are—no real God, Logos, being, essential reality, and no life after death. It is to such teachings as these that large numbers of students in American universities have been exposed in recent decades.

223

For Derrida all meaning is characterized by the continual play of *difference*. A key term Derrida employs is *"différance,"* which sound like both *différence* (difference) and *différance* (deferral). He uses it to indicate the continuously changing and "undecidable" nature of meaning, and the endless deferral of meaning from one text to another and another. Derrida claims that *différance* is "older" than Being: *"différance*, in a certain and very strange way, (is) 'older' than the ontological difference or than the truth of Being."[42] For Derrida, all linguistic signs are arbitrary, rather than decidable or determinate. Linguistic meanings and identifications of objects are thus indeterminate. These views even seem to undermine the very basic universal law of identity, which holds that an object is the same as itself. For him the "undecidability" of texts is a kind of "negativity" or "nothingness," making any completeness or "totalization" of meaning impossible. As he writes, "no completeness is possible for undecidability."[43] All of his writings are attempts to critically undermine, or "deconstruct" the logocentric bases of traditional philosophical and theological discourse. Besides Nietzsche, Heidegger was a major influence on the development of Derrida's thought, especially for the concept of deconstruction.

In pursuing his view that "there is nothing outside of the text," Derrida's writings seem to destroy the very notion of sense. They appear to have no "thesis," no "position" at all. "Distinctions are grandly postulated, yet simultaneously undermined . . . all positions seem to be wiped away as soon as they become visible. One is left with a structure of words haunted by the merest ghost of meaning . . . Every stance that Derrida articulates has both its 'pro' and its 'anti' aspects; every position that he adopts is immediately rendered nugatory." He "seems intent on destroying the very notion of sense."[44] Throughout all this, much like Marcel Duchamp and James Joyce earlier, there is a pervasive sense of irony, parody, and much of the comic or comic-absurd in his writing. Megill finds that Derrida is "a supreme ironist . . . undoubtedly the most accomplished ironist of our age," as well as a parodist. His irony is "far more radical" than that of Nietzsche, Heidegger, and Foucault. His sense of "ironic seriousness" brings to the foreground and makes explicit "an attitude pervasive in modernist and especially in postmodernist art."[45]

For Baudrillard, Reality and Truth Vanish into Simulacra and Hyperreality. In his early writings of the late 1960s and early 70s Jean Baudrillard (1929-2007) sought to analyze how linguistic signs and symbols are used as systems of encoded meanings that affect and change daily life in societies today dominated by consumerism and pervasive media. Partly influenced by neo-Marxist thought, he analyzed the rising power of monopoly capitalism in terms of manipulative control of the "sign-value" of commodities to increase and control consumer demand and consumption. As a result, commodities are represented not simply in terms of use-value and exchange value, but as primarily promoting "sign-value" such as style, prestige, power, sexuality, and luxury, and thereby establishing one's social standing.[46] In such societies he finds pervasive "commodification" dominating people's thinking and actions. He indicates the serious results in *The Consumer Society* (1970, English tr. 1998): in a society where everything is treated as commodity, alienation is rampant, and Baudrillard detects "the end of transcendence," with individuals losing sight of any other way of life.[47]

In another book, *Symbolic Exchange and Death* (French 1976, English 1993), Baudrillard advocates resistance and a break with capitalist values of production, utility, and profit. To accomplish this he hints at various types of creative cultural activities, which he refers to as "symbolic exchange." Tactics include defiance (*le defi*) and cultural ridicule, as well as use of linguistic forms that oppose capitalist values. He also advocates the free expenditure of energy in work in place of the demands of slavish production and the profit motive of capitalism. He thinks that adopting such cultural values can resist and provide an alternative to the capitalist economic system with its "unnatural" and "inhuman" modes of production, utility, and reduction of life and work to instrumental rationality. In another work of 1987, Baudrillard speaks in favor of free expenditure of human energy in work, which he sees as a fundamental human principle, like the solar principle of expenditure. He advances a kind of Nietzschean "master morality" in which "superior individuals create their own values and their life articulates an excess, overflow, and intensification of creative and erotic energies."[48]

Baudrillard's *Symbolic Exchange and Death* (1976, tr. 1993) and *Simulation and Simulacra* (1981, tr. 1994) both point to an essential break of postmodern societies from modern. He finds that modern societies were organized on the basis of production and consumption of commodities. But postmodern societies, he claims, revolve on what he calls "simulation" and the "play of images and signs." Signs, codes, and models are the new organizing forms for this new social order of simulation. There is continuous proliferation and dissemination of signs and images. As Baudrillard scholar, Douglas Kellner analyzes it, "In the society of simulation, identities are constructed by the appropriation of images, and codes and models determine how individuals perceive themselves and relate to other people. Economics, politics, social life, and culture are all governed by the mode of simulation, whereby codes and models determine how goods are consumed and used, politics unfold, culture is produced and consumed, and everyday life is lived."[49]

For Baudrillard this means more than the end of the modern; it is a fundamental break in history. In a paragraph citing key endings, he lists not only "the end of production" and "the end of political economy," but "the end of the signifier/signified dialectic which facilitates the accumulation of knowledge and meaning," "the end of the linear dimension of discourse," and "*the end of the classical era of the sign.*"[50] We are now in a new era of *simulation* in which information processing, communication, and knowledge industries replace production as the organizing form of society. People now "live in the 'hyperreality' of simulations in which images, spectacles, and the play of signs replace the concepts of production and class conflict as key constituents of contemporary societies . . . Henceforth, signs and codes proliferate and produce other signs and new sign machines in ever-expanding and spiraling cycles." Baudrillard's "postmodern turn is thus connected to a form of technological determinism."[51]

Related references to capitalism, mass production and consumption, monetary exchange, globalization, the profit motive, cybernetics and media imagery, have increasingly appeared in much art since Pop art of the 1960s. Clearly there are many things to criticize in such economic practices, marketing strategies, emphasis on profits, repetitive and reductive imaging, and the manipulations of advertising and social codes. A number of critical points in Baudrillard's writings, as well as those in recent art, seem to have substantial value and have attracted a worldwide audience. But perhaps the most important response to these critical analyses is that they tend to turn the economic system or advanced technology and image and code-making into a kind of ultimate—the ultimate cause of the ills of society. So capitalism or technology, cybernetics, and media imaging become the *bêtes noires* of our times, a kind of substitute Satan. And criticism, defiance, and dissent become the new social gospel, the only kind of "truth" remaining for a radically skeptical society that can no longer believe in the transcendent reality of God, Being, and ultimate truth, including the moral truth of the Bible. It is more logical to say that radical disbelief in the Supreme God of Being, Truth, and Purpose has brought about these conditions of loss of reality, truth, and meaning.

In this new postmodern world Baudrillard also claims the disappearance of distinctions and boundaries that were important in previous eras, such as those between social classes, political parties, and genders. He uses the term "implosion" to identify this complete collapse of distinctions. The previously different realms of politics, economics, culture, and sexuality all implode into each other. Implosion affects everything, even eroding distinctions between words, signs, images, and the real. Kellner indicates the immense significance of this: "the boundary between representation and reality implodes" with the result that "the very experience and ground of 'the real' disappears." The previous metaphysical era in which words identified things, and representations referred to and corresponded with something real has come to an end. Signs no longer refer to substantial things. Thought and discourse can no longer be grounded in a priori or necessary structures of the real.[52]

As Baudrillard writes, the new postmodern era is one of "total relativity, of generalized commutation, which is combinatory and simulatory. This means simulation in the sense that from now on signs will exchange among themselves exclusively, without interacting with the real . . . . The emancipation of the sign: released from that 'archaic' obligation that it might have to designate something, the sign is at last free for a structural or combinatory play according to indifference and a total indetermination which succeeds the previous role of determinate equivalence."[53]

There is an important similarity to Derrida in Baudrillard's view that signs and images do not signify substantially real things in determinate ways. Both writers represent radical change, not only from modern views, but from classic Western metaphysics and Christian theology. For Baudrillard, Kellner says, "signs and modes of representation come to *constitute* 'reality', and signs gain autonomy and, in interaction with other signs, come to *constitute* a new type of social order in which it is signs and codes that *constitute* the 'real.'"[54]

The result is that we now live in a world that Baudrillard characterizes by the neologism *hyperreality*. We are inundated by *simulations* by which signs, images, and constructed codes replace reality as previously known. These simulations have taken control of the limited range of options and choices people now have. People have less and less relationship to a substantial, external reality. *Simulacra* are the artificial reproductions or images of things or events, without ground in "the real." Commodity signs, images, media spectacles and codes that appear more real than the formerly "real" now have a commanding hold on society. We have experienced "cyberblitz." Society has been "cyberneticized." Cybernetic order is moving toward total control. "Signifying culture" has triumphed over nature. Nature and things that appeared real in previous eras have been replaced by the more impressive and commanding images and signs we experience in cybernetics, computer simulations, TV images, artificial models [and we may add postmodern art], so that we no longer experience substantially real things and events.

Baudrillard's "postmodern universe is one of *hyperreality* in which entertainment, information, and communication technologies provide experiences more intense and involving than the scenes of banal everyday life. "The realm of the hyperreal (e.g., media simulations of reality, Disneyland and amusement parks, malls and consumer fantasylands, TV sports, and other excursions into ideal worlds) is more real than the real, whereby the models, images, and codes of the hyperreal come to control thought and behavior."[55] The result is a radically self-enclosed, relativistic and imaginary universe. Former metaphysical and Christian standards of morality, aesthetics, and epistemic truth are wiped out by the omnipresence of constructed signs that create the artificial situation of *hyperreality*. "All dichotomies between appearance and reality, surface and depth, life and art, subject and object, collapse into a functionalized, integrated, and self-reproducing universe of 'simulacra' controlled by 'simulation' models and codes."[56]

In *Fatal Strategies* (French 1983, English 1990) Baudrillard sees our recent world characterized by the ever growing "excretion" of more and more goods, services, information, images, and controlling models. This "excrescence" has surpassed all rational ends and become a spiral of uncontrolled growth and replication. Its "objects" triumph over the human subject in what he refers to as an "obscene" proliferation beyond all attempts to understand and control it. But this "ecstasy of excrescence" has expanded so far that it is accompanied by "inertia." The excreted objects have come to dominate the exhausted human subject to the extent that previous "play" with them has led to apathy, stupefaction, and inertia.[57]

Kellner's assessment of these views is that "Baudrillard's is a totally absurd universe where objects rule in mysterious ways, and people and events are governed by absurd and ultimately unknowable interconnections and predestination." He finds that Baudrillard's thought has been "deeply inspired by the pataphysics of Alfred Jarry." A century earlier, Jarry had put forward a kind of comic-absurd "metaphysics" of wild imagination and defiance of accepted standards of truth and morality. "Like Jarry's pataphysics, Baudrillard's universe is ruled by surprise, reversal, hallucination, blasphemy, obscenity, and a desire to shock and outrage."[58]

In the context of these views of our world, Baudrillard wrote some biting criticisms of contemporary art. In *The Transparency of Evil* (French 1990, English 1993), he characterized our time in a way that seems to fit art in increasing degrees from Pop to Postmodernism. He labels our present era a "fractal stage" in which "there is now no law of value, merely a sort of *epidemic of value*, a sort of general metastasis of value, a haphazard proliferation and dispersal of value . . . . it is impossible to make estimations between beautiful and ugly, true and false, or good and evil . . . . Good is no longer the opposite of evil . . . ." Signs and images have been freed from their ideas, essences, and values. Cut loose from their origins and points of reference, they fall into "an endless process of self-reproduction." Disorder and "metastasis" sets in, a "cancerous proliferation."[59]

As a result, aesthetics, as well as economics, and sexuality have been radically transformed: "they lose their specificity and partake of a process of confusion and contagion—a viral loss of determinacy." Aesthetics has become what he calls *transaesthetics*. There is a "contamination," a "virulence" in every area from this "haphazard and senseless proliferation and metastasis." All fields of activity are affected—art (aesthetics), economics, politics, media and communications, sports, sexuality. All categories are confused: "everything is now aestheticized." "When everything is aesthetic, nothing is beautiful or ugly anymore, and art itself disappears . . . . The glorious march of modernity has not led to the transformation of all values, as we once dreamed it would, but instead to a dispersal and involution of value whose upshot for us is total confusion—the impossibility of apprehending any determining principle, whether of an aesthetic, a sexual or a political kind."[60]

Art has likewise failed to realize the utopian aesthetic of modern times, to transcend itself and become an ideal form of life. (In earlier times, of course, art had no need of self-transcendence, no need to become a totality, for such a totality already existed—in the shape of religion.) Instead of being subsumed in a transcendent ideality, art has been dissolved within a general aestheticization of everyday life, giving way to a pure circulation of images, a transaethetics of banality . . . . The crucial moment for art was undoubtedly that of Dada and Duchamp, that moment when art, by renouncing its own aesthetic rules of the game, debouched into the transaethetic era of the banality of the image . . . . **There are no more fundamental rules, no more criteria of judgment or of pleasure. In the aesthetic realm of today there is no longer any God to recognize his own** . . . . Behind the whole convulsive movement of modern art lies a kind of inertia, something that can no longer transcend itself and has therefore turned in upon itself, merely repeating itself at a faster and faster rate . . . . **No matter how marginal, or banal, or even obscene it may be, everything is subject to aestheticization, culturalization, museumification.**[61]

Many of these observations about art and aesthetics could be used to accurately describe and analyze art from Pop art onward. And Baudrillard comes close to pointing out the underlying situation of our world today, but because of his own ultimate skepticism, he misses the essential point. He attributes the "cancerous" evils he describes to expansion and proliferation of capitalism, technology, and media imagery, which have lost their fundamental ground or essences and are running completely wild. In his view, religion in earlier centuries was only a transcendent prop for art, and is now defunct. And so, he is accurate in saying that we can find *anything* in art today, "no matter how marginal, or banal, or even obscene." Today we can see sculpted toilets with their contents included. In 1993 a three-foot high pile of matter, identified as "doodoo," was exhibited in a major New York museum. In 1996 an exhibition of cut-up parts of dead cows in formaldehyde became an important New York artistic event, and in 1998 bulls were intended to be slaughtered in front of an audience, to make art from their blood and entrails. A few decades ago one artist sold his fecal matter in small capsules as art. Why is it that intelligent people support such things?

The most logical explanation that fits the conditions Baudrillard points out in art and in every area of contemporary life is *the modern-postmodern rejection of God* that has been "expanding and proliferating" since the seventeenth and eighteenth centuries, and has reached increasingly critical stages since Nietzsche, Dada, and Heidegger. It is the rejection of the true, living God who is the Supreme Being and Divine Creator, the God who has established the very basis and structures of "the real," and the only secure standards of truth, beauty, goodness, and morality that Baudrillard finds so radically missing in art and life today. God is the *Transcendent One* who is responsible for all sense of transcendence, apodictic truth, and reality that we know and seek in life. And it is He who has been the subject of art in its greatest epochs in history.

The Images of Images in Lichtenstein's Art.[62] Roy Lichtenstein (1923-1997) began his rise to fame as a Pop artist at the beginning of the 1960s. Even then his paintings exhibited certain characteristics related to postmodern thought, which became more pronounced during subsequent decades. He began with images of images—his own selective and slightly altered images of cartoon images from comic books like Mickey Mouse and Donald Duck, from adventure and romance cartoon comics, and from advertising art. From the 1970s through the 1990s, he added images from many earlier artists and art movements. He did images of images from ancient Greek art, Baroque art, Synthetic Cubism, Purism, Futurism, Art Deco, Surrealism, German Expressionism, and Abstract Expressionism. The artists he did take-offs on are almost all modern: Monet, Van Gogh, Cézanne, Picasso, Matisse, Léger, Dali, Ernst, Magritte, Mondrian, and De Kooning. Baudrillard's concept of "simulations," or better still, "ironic simulations," can be used to characterize much of Lichtenstein's work. They reiterate other images with a comic and ironic twist. Some are closer to the originals, while others are more improvisational. The example shown here, *Artist's Studio "The Dance"* (1974; Fig. 10) is based on a Matisse painting but with several changes.

Lichtenstein's choice to use images of images corresponds to a central postmodern dictum: texts only refer to other texts, images to other images. A second postmodern view related to this one is that there is no universal

Fig. 10. Roy Lichtenstein, *Artist's Studio "The Dance,"* 1974. © Estate of Roy Lichtenstein. Oil and Magna (synthetic polymer paint) on canvas. 8' x 10' 7." Gift of Mr. And Mrs. S. I. Newhouse, Jr. The Museum of Modern Art, New York, NY. Photo credit: Digital Image © Museum of Modern Art/ Licensed by SCALA/ Art Resource, NY.

truth, only texts and images that are limited to the time period or culture in which they arise. Lichtenstein has taken images from many different time periods and subtly revamped them, with irony and humor to suggest many different allusions, attitudes, and techniques behind them.

His art works have a subtle and limited type of content—often with some ironic criticism—found in the relation of his form, style, and image context to the type of art, techniques, values, and narrative of the image they are derived from: for example, allusions to sentimental and cliché dreams of romance and heartbreak; the macho male in comic-book war scenes; stereotypes of gender roles; light and reflections from mirrors; notions of intuition, chance, and randomness in expressionist brushstroke paintings; and a parody of the rational design formulas used to insure "art" in Art Deco.[63]

Lichtenstein was intrigued by a "mechanical method of drawing beautiful women that was part of the process of comic-book reproduction, which made the images seem so far removed from a real person or a photograph that they were almost an abstraction." According to Lichtenstein, "even the way they looked was a function of the printing process." And Diane Waldman adds that this mechanical look "removes them from any semblance of reality."[64] Thus, major concerns of Lichtenstein for his art were: (1) an exclusive commitment to making images of other images; (2) that his images should be "far removed from a real person"; (3) interest in the *pictorial process* involved in making comic images; and (4) a mechanical look that "removes them from any semblance of reality." Removal from reality somehow becomes a virtue. It allows irony and criticism of the images, outlooks, and values behind the images he uses, while turning away from the actual reality of the world. In this sense it is a form of critical deconstruction.

Lichtenstein's paintings are powerfully done, on a very large scale (often four or five to ten feet or more in length), with expansive areas of intense primary colors of yellow, red, and blue, and with black lines (compare Mondrian!). The early, romance-comic type painting, *Hopeless* (1963), contains a comic-stereotypical tearful face and head of a broken-hearted woman filling almost all of the 44" height of the canvas. Lichtenstein intensified the comic-book colors by changing them to light blue, bright red, and blazing yellow, and adding many bold, wavy, black lines. We can see the great advances he has made in form, color, composition, and overall power of image by comparing *Hopeless* with *The Kiss* of the previous year.[65]

In a series of landscapes painted in the mid 1960s, Lichtenstein used even more minimal formal means with cliché and stereotypical images. Waldman observes that, while previous artists had changed certain conventions in landscape painting, "without undermining its fundamental verity, . . . Lichtenstein denies that reality altogether, asking us to recall landscape through its reproduction in the mass media."[66] Denying the reality of the objective, external world suggests the postmodern view that words and images do not correspond objectively and accurately to any "natural things," which may not even have an essential and substantial form and nature. Waldman says that "when we accept the fact that the image has little relation to reality, we are faced with the realization that the image as a representation of reality is only one of many fictions."[67]

In another series of paintings of the early 1970s Lichtenstein turned to the traditional subject of still life. But he continued to use the mechanical forms and colors of printing processes, adding green (good-bye Mondrian). The dazzling color and optical effects are even heightened in some of these paintings. Works such as *Still Life with Silver Pitcher* (1972) and *Still Life with Crystal Bowl* (1973)[68] rival the optical effects of Op art in their brilliant dazzle. Lichtenstein's colors are not essentially derived from nature either, but from the "artificial-looking process colors used in mechanical reproduction."[69] Their large size, combined with the blazing intensity of the colors and black lines, creates an overpowering effect on a viewer standing in front of one.

Lichtenstein's painting of 1974, *Artist's Studio, "The Dance"* (Fig. 10), shows more invention of forms and colors in comparison to his paintings of ten or twelve years before.[70] Both artists represent some degrees of abstraction, with Lichtenstein's work being much more abstract in its extreme flatness, and big bold forms. Lichtenstein eliminates the partial sense of space still remaining in Matisse's work by pulling the still life forward and making it much larger, bolder, and flatter, and by using the very flat forms and colors of his previous work. The still life objects are considerably changed, and several new objects are introduced. The oriental influence in Matisse's art is gone, as well as the lyrical color and delicate, felt drawing. The female dancers are also considerably changed, and a comparison of Lichtenstein's with Matisse's dancers shows that the images have been somewhat more stylized and further removed from actual reality than those in Matisse's work (although they are more related to Matisse's later, larger work, *The Dance*). The colors and lines are less severe, more pleasing than many of his previous works. Three softened, light blues are introduced, and the linear movements throughout the painting are very rhythmical and dance-like. There is some humor in this, and in the use of musical notes on the right side of the painting.

All of the things discussed above reveal a contrast of Lichtenstein's work with Christian theological and metaphysical teachings (discussed in Chapters Four and Five) that the world has been created by God, insuring its objective reality, rational forms, and its knowability, guaranteed by God's Being, ideas, reason, knowledge, and power. Lichtenstein has moved away from these understandings of reality, knowledge, and truth by developing a kind of involuted art based on other art works—images of images—not on the actual world, and making them critically allude to certain cultural, social, and art issues. The actual nature and forms of the world and human beings are not freshly seen and renewed, but are left behind, and even become "fictions." It may seem superfluous and silly to ask about Lichtenstein's art, and other art of the last fifty or more years, "where is God, or where are His attributes and gifts in creation." Obviously, God is absent. He is not represented in any way, and neither are any biblical characters or saints. But in addition, there is no sense of an objectively created real world that is substantial, and has rational and logical forms corresponding to human intellect and ideas. Those kind of meanings are also absent.

Epistemic logic and ultimate truth are notably absent in Lichtenstein's work (and in other postmodern art and thought). The unspoken but unavoidable implication is that the God of Being and Truth who creates real, substantial beings and makes objective, rational truth possible, is absent. A third major postmodern implication is that there is no sense of ontological reality in the images—no substantial being and essence ground the images of images. "Reality" is only an illusion, a bold and impressive fiction. In the early paintings, cliché images of sham, comic-beautiful women and comic-handsome men saying cliché things in cartoon blurbs inhabit a flat, comic-absurd anti-world. And the later subjects of Lichtenstein's art also exhibit various types of fictional treatments.

Related implications come from the type of form and style employed. From the beginning, Lichtenstein deliberately accentuated an ultra-flat surface by means of thick black lines and very flat colors. Enlarged Benday dots and heavy, repeated diagonal shading lines used in some paintings also emphasize flatness and unreality. Dots and repeated shading lines in comics were meant to suggest some roundness, depth, and tonal range, but by being enlarged and exaggerated in Lichtenstein's work, they radically deny depth (as well as ironically refer to their artificial source). What little depth that remained in the art he mimicked has been humorously eliminated. What was meant to suggest strong emotions, actions, and feelings in original cartoon images has been countermanded by the cool, impersonal forms and the high-art context, and is now unemotional, unmoving and incredible.

The result is that Lichtenstein's work (like most postmodern thought and art) does not state or reflect important universal truths, objective reality, and genuine expression of feeling or emotion as seen, for example, in medieval, Renaisance, and Baroque art, but avoids such depth and density. It is all cool, ironic surface that seems to reflect a shallow, mediocre, mechanized, and dehumanized culture and society. Sheer surface with no depth is the major effect. No depth of purpose of life can be couched in these terms. The paintings put forward no substantial concepts or beliefs on which we can base our lives. Among other things, the irony and flatness preclude it. What the paintings largely evoke is sardonic criticism of certain social and cultural notions of heroism, romance, and criticism of the *illusion* of ideological, grand, or totalizing aims in previous art.

Much of Baudrillard's critical analysis of recent society and art seems to relate to Lichtenstein's work. Lichtenstein takes as his subject some of the images and signs used as systems of encoded meanings that affect daily life in recent society dominated by pervasive media and consumerism. The mani-pulative power of "sign-value" in media and advertising, especially those promoting art, luxury, power, and romance, often with implications of social standing, is subverted. There is the suggestion of advanced commodification, in "an endless flow of products and reproductions,"[71] resulting in the suppression of human qualities and a cool intensification of alienation. And it seems clear that there is an "end of transcendence," not only for the stereotype society implied, but for Lichtenstein's art as a whole.

Lichtenstein's art is fully one of *simulation* and the play of images. Images and signs rule completely. As Baudrillard said of technological society, there is an "end of the signifier/signified dialectic which facilitates the accumulation of knowledge and meaning," "the end of the linear dimension of discourse," and "the end of the classical era of the sign." Images of images replace traditional images with one-to-one correspondences to real people and things, communicating substantial truth, including knowledge of how to live, who we are, where we came from, and where we are going. Lichtenstein's art suggests that we now live in the "hyperreality" of simulations where images and their interplay replace such considerations.

The experience and ground of "the real" disappears in Lichtenstein's art. The previous metaphysical era in which images referred to and corresponded with something real has come to an end. Images no longer refer to substantial things. This is advanced *simulation* in the sense that images of images exchange among themselves exclusively, with no determinate link to objects in a one-to-one correspondence. Images are "emancipated" from the obligation to designate something real, and now are "free" for structural and combinatory *play*. In these ways Lichtenstein's art is one of *hyperreality*. We are presented with *simulations* in which powerful images of images replace objective reality as traditionally known.

There is no clear sense of relationship to a substantial, external world. There are only *simulacra*, fictional images of images with no ultimate ground. Lichtenstein's images have subverted the reality of the images he uses, and portray "nature as artificial."[72] Nature and things that appeared real in previous eras have been replaced by large, dazzling images of images, so that we no longer experience substantially real things and events. With reality and truth absent, what remains is the indirect suggestion through the art work that no absolute being, reality, truth, and meaning exist. More obviously, the artworks function to entertain. On the other hand, we are led away from the truths of Christian and classical beliefs into a form of skeptical Postmodernism. Powerful visual images entertain, give pleasure, and seemingly criticize, providing more lively experiences than scenes of banal everyday life. The fictional realm of the hyperreal seems more real than the real. The result is a radically self-enclosed, relativistic and imaginary realm. Former metaphysical, and Christian canons of ontological reality, epistemic truth, morality, and aesthetics are eliminated by the omnipresence of fabricated images that create an artificial situation of *hyperreality.*

Lichtenstein's art has especially focused on images of the art of other artists. In this way he also has been able to implicitly reject traditional views about originality, creativity, style, and the artist as a great master or genius. Although his works do have a kind of originality and a kind of personal form and recognizable style, they are more obviously framed in terms of the non-original, non-creative, and non-stylistic. But even more important in these works is the implicit view, contrary to classical and Christian art and thought, that no artwork has the important mission of conveying substantial reality, objective truth, and meaningful purposes. Like Baudrillard's postmodern world of simulation and hyperreality, the ubiquitous "play" of images results in "total relativity," and fades into "total indetermination."[73] Because he conveys such views on a large scale, in dazzling, and powerful form and color, this writer sees Lichtenstein as the outstanding artist of the late-twentieth century, the representative artist of postmodern views of the time.

The Postmodern Art of David Salle. While painting—a traditional form of art from the beginning of the human race—has often been declared dead over the past four decades, it is still around—in greatly modified forms. Traditionally, painting, as well as sculpture, was a vehicle for truth. In today's climate of skepticism, it is often a vehicle for views of the uncertainty or unreality of the objective world and truth, or for trendy criticism of capitalism, consumerism, the grand pretensions of art, themes of gender and identity, cultural globalization, reductions of personal freedom, or other aspects of our modern-postmodern world. Painting continues despite the fact that so much recent art consists of assemblages or conglomerations of objects that look like scattered remains from a remodeling project, expansive stage-sets done by someone under panic attack, or the nightmare of a scientist, biologist, cartoonist, or engineer with severe gastric distress. Much of what has been created as advanced or postmodern art over the past thirty or forty years ranks as the weirdest, silliest, ugliest, and most vulgar art in world history.[74] Its stark separation as a whole from previous art is striking. One has the impression from this that art *is* dead, and artists have been desperately trying to revive it.

The paintings of David Salle (b. 1952) are outstanding among contemporary attempts to revive painting, and the representation of the human figure. His paintings are big, bold, and challenging, and they exude a strong sense of the contemporary world. The extreme number, variety, and diversity of images he puts into just one painting, or into a series of paintings, is mind-boggling, and suggests the diversity of possible modes of represen-ation, and the multiplicity, speed, abruptness, and fragmentation of changing forms of life and perceptions. Looking at dozens of his paintings, one is also struck by the importance of color in many of them.[75] His color has more appeal as color than many other contemporary artists, at times with much of the harmonic, then suddenly changing into one totally different color system after another in several smaller image panels popping up in various places in the same painting.

Some of his paintings are divided into two or three large panels about the same size (for example, *Old Bottles*, 1995 [Fig. 11] and *Muscular Paper*, 1985),[76] often with one of those panels again divided into a series of smaller panels, some equal, some not. *Old Bottles* has an especially appealing coloristic effect, with its dominant orange-sienna and browns played against blues, pinks, and reds. The large right-hand panel is a flat orange-sienna color throughout, with a large-scale, snapshot-type image of two dressed women, seen from behind, painted in grisaille technique over it. They are walking through a wide colonnade toward a doorway. The women are painted in a kind of plain, photographic realism. But the strangeness of the view of their backs, walking in-step, and frozen-in-time positions, and the flat, unrealistic all-over orange color creates a kind of unreal or surrealistic effect. The large left panel has about fifteen or more different images in different techniques, some in rectangular panels, others dropping behind them, and more images, done in painted line drawings hovering transparently in front of them. It has been aptly observed that these fragmentary images, framed within rectangles and squares reflect the screen world of movies, computers, and television. There are a multitude of suggestive allusions running through these smaller panels and images, which different people might interpret in different ways.

The two large-scale, dressed women in the right panel are treated with much aesthetic awareness of the abstract patterns of the dark shadows on their dresses. Other aesthetic patterns appear as a feature in many of Salle's

Fig. 11. David Salle, *Old Bottles*, 1995. Oil and acrylic on canvas. 8' ½" x 15' 6". The Saatchi Gallery, London. Art © David Salle/Licensed by VAGA, New York, NY. Courtesy of Mary Boone Gallery, New York., NY.

paintings. These patterns, as well as the emphasis on "singing" colors, create a pleasing aesthetic appeal that is not common in art today.

There are also sexual images and references in his work. In *Old Bottles* there is a small inset panel with an image of two longneck bottles placed over the backside of one woman, perhaps or perhaps not carrying a phallic symbolism. A similar, small panel on the left side of the painting shows two more longneck bottles and several small cup-like glasses, suggesting both male and female symbols. Such sexual content is more obvious and direct in his paintings of naked and partly undressed women, described below.

In these ways Salle uses a greater number of images, and in more varied ways, than many other artists. And the manner of combining all the images is a modern-postmodern one of collage, or pastiche, generally seen before in Cubism, Dada, Surrealism, and Rauschenberg. These images seem to evoke some kind of meaning, although it is very elusive and enigmatic.

The multiple images in Salle's paintings, with their contrasting appearances and multiple techniques suggests that there is no one way of seeing and understanding images, and their relationship or non-relationship to real things, and seemingly no objective external world that we can know in any determinate way. There is a skepticism about the world and any certain, objective knowledge of it, which runs through postmodern thought and runs counter to the beliefs of Christian theology and metaphysics based on divine creation, discussed before in this chapter, and in Chapters Four and Five. Quoting Salle, a Museum of Modern Art statement says that "Salle has claimed independence for his art from the system of logic that governs the real: 'I do think that there are things that exist in the world that relate to one another. And then there are things in my paintings that relate to one another. And I think what matters to me is that these are not the same.'"[77]

Three separate panels fastened together make up Salle's huge painting (over fifteen feet long) entitled *Muscular Paper* (1985). Another part of the enigma of a Salle painting is the title (a rather common aspect of art in recent decades). The Museum of Modern Art, which owns this painting, provides a basic identification of images in the three panels: "The left panel of *Muscular Paper* depicts a photograph by Brassaï of Pablo Picasso's 1931 sculpture Bather. The center panel includes a doubled likeness of a head from the painting *The Club-Footed Boy* (1642) by Jusepe de Ribera, and the right panel replicates a bridge from a print by the German Expressionist artist Max Beckmann. Superimposed on these explicit references are nonspecific and seemingly unrelated images and patterns, which compete for prominence and suggest multiple and shifting meanings."[78]

Two large, naked women holding hands and skipping one rope fill most of the space of the center panel of the work's three parts. Naked women skipping rope in itself seems strange. And they are another instance of doubled figures that look almost the same in Salle's work. Such doubled figures create a surrealistic or eerie feeling that can be disturbing (remember the two look-alike little girls in front of the elevator in *The Shining*, just before a river of blood rushed out?). The doubled, blue faces of the club-footed boy with a harsh smile, placed over the backsides of the young women, create a strange, menacing, quality. A large strip of bacon, half as tall as the young women appears next to the woman on the left, adding to the sense of disjunction. And in the center, overlapping the two young women is a ragged brush sketch of two more women: an old, emaciated one who seems to suggest death, and another on her hands and knees. But these are subjective interpretions, and could be seen in different ways.

Salle's paintings reveal several postmodern views. He is probably best known for paintings of females, mostly naked or with underclothes half off, or others totally naked and shown from the rear, bending over, or in high-arched back-bends, with graphic private parts turned toward the viewer.[79] Such works, which have been called "soft porn," surely have a shock effect on many viewers. Some, like Salle's *Saltimbanques* of 1986, include a large image of an eye looking back at the viewer, suggesting more than the visual nature of art. While other images in each painting utilize a form of collage aesthetic to sharply interrupt, or contradict, real, literal, or narrative aspects of these figures, the graphic sexual aspect remains inescapable. These images of bodies in strange or artificial positions, with emphasis on private parts, place them in a new category in the history of art. Heads and faces are sometimes not shown, or are minimized. The human figure is not treated with the understandings of either classical propriety or Christian morality. Some of Salle's diverse imagery is taken from pornography. There is neither the sense of human dignity and value found in the Greek *Spearbearer* and *Aphrodite of Melos*, nor the high spirituality, personality, and humanity of medieval sculpture, the figures of Michelangelo, Raphael, El Greco, and Rembrandt. Indications of such religious and transcendental realities do not appear. Like most art and movies today, Salle's art is an icon for an iconoclastic age—a postmodern, post-metaphysical, and "post-Christian" age of becoming.

Salle's naked figures are not solitary phenomena in art today, however. While nudity has been common in art in various forms since its beginnings, stark nakedness and raw sexual images by artists have increasingly become a calling card of twentieth and twenty-first century artists since the 1960s.[80] A famous early one is the performance work by Carolee Schneemann in 1975, entitled *Interior Scroll*. While standing naked in front of an audience and being photographed, she slowly pulled a long, thin scroll from her vagina, reading a feminist speech from it.[81] Schneemann had participated in a 1964 performance work, entitled *Meat Joy*, in which eight partially nude people danced and played with sausage, raw fish, raw chickens, and paint. It was filmed at ultra-liberal Judson Memorial Church in New York City. Schneemann described it as an "erotic rite" and an indulgent Dionysian "celebration of flesh as material."[82] Many recent artists have either painted or sculpted themselves or others graphically naked in works later placed in public museums, often staring back at the viewer, or they have appeared naked in photographs, or executed public performance works while naked. Graphic nakedness and sexuality in the arts, liberated from traditional classical propriety and Christian moral considerations is a sign of our times.

In these figure paintings by Salle, as well as in his other works, such as *Picture Builder* (1993) and *Bigger Rack* (1997-98), we can identify further aspects of a "post-Christian" and "postmodern" world. Salle's work, like Postmodernism generally, shows signs of skepticism about objective and universal truth and substantial reality. No clear sense of expressed or supporting universal and necessary truth or purposeful meaning emerges. The viewer is left to his own thoughts about any meaning. Difference, disjunction, and dissociation rule. Diverse images are gathered from very different sources and assembled in disjunctive ways. Salle typically employs second-hand images from photography, advertising art, kitsch, schlock, old engravings, painting and drawings from masterworks to calendar art, each with different styles and color contexts. There is often no logical sequence, no up or down, no beginning or end to them. They appear abruptly, as full images or fragments. There is no hierarchy, no high or low, no graduated inter-relationships. Smaller rectangular images overlay, interrupt, and partially obliterate one or more larger ones. Fragmentary words and typeface appear above or underneath images. Sketchy line drawings or diagrams float across others. Lines of pure paint at times flow over parts in arbitrary lengths and directions.

There is no clear affirmation of a real world in Salle's art: "everything in the picture is a mere sign—a substitute for reality." All signs are different. Images are juxtaposed or layered "in ways that invite interpretation but ultimately deny it."[83] Images seem stripped of potential meaning and value. As in much other art of recent decades, diverse combinations "jostle together in a way that simultaneously encourages and undermines the viewer's efforts to create meaningful associations."[84] It seems that, much like Foucault's views, human thought is not capable of attaining any universal or absolute truth. Foundational universals that give unity are absent. Totalizing understandings of reality, seem to have no sway. Knowledge seems without any transcendent, unifying ground. Thought and knowledge are freed from subjection to transcendence. There is no final authority for truth, with the result that "there are no facts, only interpretations."[85] The result is that all discourse and use of images are "fictions," without any objective ground, knowledge, or truth.[86]

Like much postmodern thought and art, all this suggests the absence of a transcendental ground for a logical, rational, intelligently structured and interrelated world. The absence of hierarchy and universal, rational order and meaning essentially eliminate belief in such an absolute ground of reality and truth, and ultimate source of law and order. Many postmodern artists have been influenced, often through teachers and friends, by the thought of poststructuralists and postmodernists such as Michel Foucault, Roland Barthes, Jean Baudrillard, Jean-Francois Lyotard, Jacques Derrida, and others, which is essentially anti-theistic and anti-metaphysical. Their thought argues against all foundational, metaphysical and ontological forms—against all universal, unified, and totalizing understandings of life and world, instead emphasizing languages and *difference*. For them there is no absolute Being and Truth—no ultimate source and ground for real substances and essences of things, on which universal truth and knowledge can be founded. There is no transcendent reason that guarantees reason in things, and valid correspondences between words, images and things. Thus, all we can "know" is images or texts arising from different subjective and cultural values and interpretations. "Reality" and "truth" are only cultural or personal constructs.

Daniel Wheeler briefly notes the difference of Salle's art with that of artists of previous centuries, some of whose images Salle appropriates: their worlds were "perhaps less chaotic or spiritually bankrupt times and worlds." By vividly appropriating and deconstructing their images, however, Salle's art works seem to strive to "illuminate a meretricious age."[87]

The Postmodern Art of Jeff Koons. Another contemporary artist who reflects the postmodern, and "post-Christian" character of our times is Jeff Koons (b. 1955). His art has also at times included graphic displays of nakedness and sex. The first of his own six tenets for his work that reveals much of his attitude to life and art is that "sex is not embarrassing, private, illicit, or sinful." In 1992 Koons organized an exhibit of billboard-size photographic images, airbrushed into technicolor fantasies, of him and his then wife, Ilona Staller, an international porn star, "copulating in missionary and devilish positions."[88] Art works graphically depicting their sexual relations were given the ironic, pseudo-naïve title, "Made in Heaven." Linda Weintraub claims that "the artist displayed their nudity freed of sin and their erotic encounters without a trace of shame. Koons and Staller were less the Ken and Barbie of the art world than the Adam and Eve of a pop religion. In states of poised rapture staged in a plastic, candy-colored paradise, they displayed their sex freed of the disgrace of the expulsion and the moral conflict that followed. In some of the images from this series, Koons even invited the serpent to be their witness." Weintraub offers the liberal opinion that Koons' "depiction of fornication is not pornography if it thwarts the shame connected to titillation instead of arousing it."[89] And Koons goes further in his own assessment: "Through our union, we're aligned once again with nature, I mean we've become God. That's the bottom line—we've become God." (However, the marriage "made in heaven" ended not very long after the exhibit.) Koons claims that he seeks to carry his message of liberation, freedom, pleasure, and happiness to all of society: "I am interested in love and being beneficial to the rest of humankind."[90]

In 1992 Koons displayed an "adorable," forty-foot high *Puppy*[91] supported by a steel and wood frame, covered all over with living flowers set in earth. Children's toys and cuddly, stuffed, cartoon animals are other subjects of his art. There is a series of the type of entertaining images of rabbits and dogs made with balloons, which Koons has had replicated, but in the very different material of stainless steel (he frequently employs assistants or skilled craftsmen to fabricate works). There is a life-size porcelain sculpture of *Michael Jackson and Bubbles* (1988) in full entertainment garb, seated on a floor strewn with flowers, with the pet chimp on his lap. In another porcelain work, a cartoon-like, semi-nude blond clasps a large *Pink Panther* to her chest.

Koons denies irony and hidden meanings in his art: "a viewer might at first see irony in my work . . . but I see none at all. Irony causes too much critical contemplation."[92] But while he speaks of these and other works much like a social messiah, their irony and sense of kitsch or schlock seems inescapable. His art contains its own brand of postmodern irony, difference, and self-contradiction: it shows a kind of feigned naiveté that is ultra sophisticated—a pseudo-childlike sweetness and rosiness that has an underlying bite. Another sculpture, *Popples* (1988), is a replication of a cuddly stuffed cartoon animal with soft, short tufts of hair all over, but remade in prickly and non-cuddly porcelain. It has bright primary colors—red, heart-shaped hands, round, red cheeks, and a blue muzzle and tummy that seem happy enough. But the sense of irony and the incredibility of the image in art makes us suspect that Chucky lurks behind.

These subjects and their treatment also make us think they may be another of the many critiques of capitalist consumer society that recent artists have made. But Koons' fourth tenet is that "kitsch is captivating . . . . I try not to use it in any cynical manner. I use it to penetrate mass consciousness—to communicate to people." And what is his mission? It is "to treat viewers to pleasurable sensations." Since "some of his viewers enjoy kitsch." He thinks his art will lead the lower and middle class to "an ultimate state of rest," and the upper class to "an unprecedented state of confidence." In his unabashed egoism and exhibitionism (tenet 2), Koons "compares himself to the Messiah, to the acclaimed artist Michelangelo, and to the celebrated pop star Elvis Presley." He also treats art as a highly commercial enterprise (tenet 3), and sets very high prices, claiming that "price determines desire and merit" (tenet 5). Art is a high-priced luxury item (tenet 6), and Koons exploits it to the hilt. But he thinks his art combines satisfaction of the desires of the lower and middle classes for mass-produced knick-knacks, and for the wealthy who find it in buying luxury art objects they hope will increase in value (the *Michael Jackson* porcelain was sold in 1991 by Sotheby's for $5.6 million dollars).[93] This price was surpassed in 2008 when Koons' *Balloon flower (Magenta)* sold for 25.76 million dollars at Christie's London).

For Koons, art today becomes a catering to the tastes of different social classes in order to make them happy, restful, and satisfy their desires. Money and fame are at the core of his purpose. Subjects of cuddly dogs, stuffed animals, pop figures, and graphic sexual themes seem to suggest a Paradise Island, but with an ironic twist. Such subjects also challenge and break with classical views of decorum and hierarchies of cultural value.[94] Style varies from one work to another depending on the subject chosen. His choice to replicate lowly artificial objects and to use photographic reproductions suggests that no substantial reality is available. Second-hand objects and replicated photographic images carry a sense of artificial images of images. As much postmodernist thought declares, all is simulacra—images of images of images. There is no transcendent Being and Truth to lead one toward a credible, higher belief and destiny. There is no religious or metaphysical message, unless one can take the suggestion to be happy, relax, and have fun and pleasure as a "pop religion." (Or how about "eat, drink, and be merry.")

The Anti-Theistic Direction of Modern and Postmodern Thought. Chapters Six, Seven, and Eight show that thought and art since the seventeenth and eighteenth centuries have led increasingly away from belief in God, and to indifference or antagonism toward it. While there were still many great Christian leaders and theologians during the nineteenth century, the most influential modern philosophical thinkers either were atheistic or attempted to redefine God and religion in non-biblical terms. The most prominent were anti-theists with respect to the biblical God—Schopenhauer, Hegel, Marx, Nietzsche. By the late nineteenth century, Nietzsche stood out as a shrill and violent voice railing against God and Being (labeling himself the "Antichrist") in a Western world where intellectual leaders, writers, and artists were increasingly turning away from Christianity, becoming more secular and irreligious, or adopting other religious views.

Christianity has grown and spread in some ways during the twentieth century, and has produced some of the finest biblical theologians in history.

But genuine belief in Christianity has not only been totally abandoned by modern, twentieth-century philosophical thought and art, its theological foundations have been broadly attacked with the intent of undermining and destroying them in one way or another. If Picasso and Matisse are the outstanding, characteristic artists of the twentieth century (at least until about 1960), Heidegger and Wittgenstein are the characteristic philosophers. The later twentieth century (since about 1960 or 1970) has seen the widespread influence of various kinds of anti-theistic or non-theistic movements in thought and art—"Death of God" theology, "Negative Theology," Neo-Marxism, Poststructuralism, Postmodernism, and others. People who dedicate themselves to modern or postmodern thought and art are led ineluctably away from belief in God, and perpetuate and extend those views.

While God is very much alive and still the source of all life, reason, order, truth, and purpose in history, various thinkers and artists of the twentieth century have declared the death of God, the death of man, the death of art, the death of painting, the death of the author, the death of history, and death of various other things. Why has there been this widespread sense of end or death? The most logical answer must be that modern and postmodern thought and art have increasingly turned against and away from the very ground and source of all life, truth, hope, and inspiration—the Supreme God who has declared himself in His Word, Jesus Christ, in Creation, and in the Bible.

Chapter Nine

God's Love, Goodness, and Sovereignty
Human Responsibility, Love, Goodness, and Evil

Give thanks to the Lord, for he is good; his love endures forever. (Psalm 107:1)

The sheer greatness of God, and of all his qualities, greatly exceeds our power to understand. His love is beyond measure (Eph. 3:17-19), as are his wisdom, grace, power, and eternity.[1]

God's absolute control and authority over his creation is indicated by several things: (1) he is the creator of all things that exist, making him the sole owner and Lord of all creation; (2) he is infinitely greater and superior in all respects to his creation; (3) he has by his divine ideas, purpose, will, and fore-ordination determined the being, nature, structure, functions, and ultimate purposes of all individual things; (4) he is infinite being, power, goodness, love, and holiness, and so is the fount and standard of all that is good, holy, and lawful for creation; (5) created things have no other true source of being, continuing sustenance, function, morality, purpose, or law and authority than God. God is thus *Supreme Lord* of all creation.

God, Atheists, Suffering, and Evil. One of the most common claims of atheists is that there cannot be a God of love because there is so much evil, suffering, disease, violence, and death. No God of love would permit such senseless suffering and atrocities. In his book, *god is Not Great; How Religion Poisons Everything* [note his use of the small g for God], Christopher Hitchens devotes Chapter Two to "Religion Kills." Hitchens moves his readers through use of clever and entertaining journalistic word selection and colorful phrase turning, with a generous amount of sarcasm, all of which tends to prevent consideration of deeper distinctions and reasons for the situations he describes. But since he is so thoroughly committed, much like Nietzsche, to an anti-theological, anti-metaphysical viewpoint, he is self-prohibited from considering higher or deeper causes and judgments than the limited and conflicting ones running across the surface. For him, one religion—Muslim, Jew, Christian, Hindu, etc.—is much like another, "wholly man-made," since what they all worship is nothing but a deceptive fiction.[2]

In Hitchens' view, a principal aim of religions is "bloodlust" in aggressive pursuit of their faiths. In Belfast, many were "kidnapped and killed or tortured by rival religious death squads, often for no other reason than membership of another confession." Beirut, because it had a "surplus of religions," is described as "infested with a wide variety of serpents," resulting in a horrible massacre and the introduction of "the beauties of suicide bombing." In Bombay, when the leader of a Hindu nationalist movement gained power, he "loosed a tide of goons and thugs onto the streets." In 1940s Croatia, "a Nazi puppet state . . . enjoying the patronage of the Vatican . . . naturally sought to exterminate all the Jews." And in another campaign of conversion, "tens of thousands of Orthodox Christians were either slaughtered or deported." By the 1990s Milosevic's "anti-Muslim crusade, which was a cover for the annexation of Bosnia to a 'Greater Serbia,' was largely carried out by "gangs made up of religious bigots, often blessed by Orthodox priests and bishops." In Bethlehem constant conflicts are driven, says Hitchens, by "messianic rabbis and mullahs and priests," who have "put the whole of humanity in the position of hostage to a quarrel that now features the threat of nuclear war." On Baghdad, Hitchens lists several of the atrocities during and since the regime of Saddam Hussein (which he suggests was religious): hangings, mutilations, sexual assaults, sabotage, bombings, murderous attacks of Sunnis on Shiites, and Shiites on Sunnis. With no belief in any faith or any God, Hitchens casts all of these atrocities into the same pot of stew, that of the evils of "religion," and ends each litany with his own bigoted refrain, "religion poisons everything."[3] He conveniently ignores the fact that the Bible and Christianity strongly condemn hatred, violence, and murder, and instead teach loving God and loving your neighbor as yourself.

In his Chapter entitled "The Metaphysical Claims of Religion Are False" (only nine pages are needed!), Hitchens reveals his utter failure to examine and deal with Christian metaphysics, and the biblical and theological bases of Christianity. While he claims to highly value reason and human intellectual accomplishments, his own rantings are depressingly irrational and anti-intellectual. He makes such grossly incorrect statements as: "Religion comes from the period of human prehistory where nobody . . . had the smallest idea of what was going on. It comes from the bawling and fearful infancy of our species" and is the result of fear of "the weather, the dark, the plague, the eclipse, and all manner of other things now easily explicable."[4]

In Augustine and Aquinas, two of the greatest, proven intellects of early Christianity, who used reason in *great* ways to elucidate biblical theology,[5] Hitchens finds nothing rational at all: "Augustine was a self-centered fantasist and an earth-centered ignoramus"; "Aquinas half-believed in astrology" and thought the fully formed nucleus of a human being was in each individual sperm. "The scholastic obsessives of the Middle Ages were doing the best they could," he condescendingly allows, "on the basis of the hopelessly limited information, ever-present fear of death and judgment, very low life expectancy, and an audience of illiterates."[6]

On the one metaphysical principle he briefly mentions, God as the first cause, he does not even know the correct Christian metaphysical teaching, but concludes that "the postulate of a designer or creator only raises the unanswerable question of who designed the designer or created the creator." It is absurd for Hitchens to say that God the Creator must have a cause: to be God, God must be *necessary Being*, uncaused and eternal. If caused, God would be contingent, and therefore not God. Hitchens cites the time of the Enlightenment [when, as Peter Gay says, "the myths of God's fatherhood and man's fall from grace were so much nonsense."][7] as the time when "humanity began to grow up a little," and applauds Laplace for saying that he had no need for the "hypothesis" of God in his explanation of the solar system. Hitchens concludes, "And neither do we."[8]

The Disturbing Problems and Evils of Life. Besides the horrible events of murder and war that Hitchens mentions, even simple rudeness is a frequent problem in life. It can cause a person to feel upset or angry, and can start a quarrel or a fight. Recently an eighteen-year-old girl pulled her car out of a side exit directly into the front side of my vehicle. She was apologetic, however, admitting that she had been looking backwards and waving at someone. I helped her to back her car out of my crumpled fender, and pulled her fender out enough so it would not cut her tire. Around two months later a male driver broke the law by running a red light into moving traffic, forcing me to swerve aside. I blew my horn as I swerved. When he pulled around me he blew his horn in defiance. Although a small event, how is one supposed to deal with such behaviour? A more antagonistic person might have chased him down and started a fight, or even shot him. Some time ago a driver in my home town (a relatively safe place) was shot in the head with a shotgun by a man who said he had tried to "cut him off." And there are reports elsewhere of motorists being shot for no more than blowing their horns at other motorists. While such initial acts are often relatively small, we can see the kind of extreme feelings and harsh reactions they can elicit.

We read in newspapers, books, and on the Internet of many horrible things. Suicide bombers have killed thousands of men, women, and children.

Roadside bombs or car bombs kill scores or hundreds. The world Trade Center is destroyed by planes and thousands die horribly, some leaping to their death. Saddam Hussein tortured and killed thousands, dropping some of his victims into acid vats. Hitler, Stalin, and Pol Pot were responsible for the deaths of millions upon millions of people. Newspapers and TV tell us of many horrible things. A political leader is murdered by a shooter-bomber. A thief or killer breaks into a home and kills the whole family, or kills a daughter and granddaughter, or kills a football star. A drug-user takes a rifle into a mall and kills many people at random, then kills himself. A pig-farmer kills many prostitutes and drug addicts, cuts up their remains and feeds them to his pigs. A young man kills his girlfriend, then fillets and cooks parts of her body. A woman chemist knocks out her husband with a stun gun and stuffs him head first into a barrel of hydrochloric acid, dissolving his flesh. A mother murders all of her children by drowning them. Another woman kills a pregnant woman and cuts her belly open to get the baby. Jealous and disconsolate ex-husbands often kill their ex-wives and their children. School children and young adults are shot down in scores by others their age. A serial killer rapes and kills many young women. And what about the many deaths caused by epidemics, earthquakes, tsunamis, cyclones, hurricanes, tornados, mine explosions, ship and ferry sinkings, plane and car crashes, bridge collapses?

Can such things be by the will of the all-good, all-loving God who created all people? Can God commit immoral acts or command them? Does God sanction or command torture, rape, or murder? Does God *force* anyone to believe in Him, or to believe in a particular way? The questions of suffering, death, conflict, killings, and wars, whether "religious" or not, *is* a big, perplexing, and disturbing one. It is paraded by Hitchens, but not probed and analyzed. If there is no God and no true religious belief, as he claims, then killings and wars prompted by religions beliefs could, in truth, be interpreted as utterly absurd and inhuman. But if one posits the non-existence of God, there is also very good reason for the non-existence of any beings and truth at all, or of any good and evil. Nietzsche, a better thinker than Hitchens, could at least see that without God there is only a "dynamic, primal flux," mindless, formless, and chaotic—no identity and unity, only primal difference and chaos. He described it as "terrible," "ugly," "horrible," and "frightening." In such a view without God, one might expect endless chaos and violence.

But the evidence, reason, and logic of preceding chapters indicate that the most logical metaphysical argument is that God the Supreme Being, Creator, and Truth must exist for there to be any real contingent beings, living and inanimate, and for the existence of reason and logic in the nature of things, making any truth and knowledge possible. How are we to understand why there are such horrible events as those described above, considering the belief that a Supreme Being exists, who is not only the fount of Being, Truth, Reason, and Logic, but is also Supreme *Love* and *Goodness.*

God is Love. In order to deal with this question properly, it is important to understand what is meant by "God is Love" and "God is Supreme Goodness." God's Love is an active concern and caring for all things that He has created, especially for human beings, whom He has created in His own image. It involves willing and doing good, and achieving what is best and right for His creatures. God is "goodness itself; God, truly, is *all-good* (or 'omnibenevolent'). Biblically, the basic Hebrew term for 'love' (*chesed*), used of God, means 'lovingkindness' or 'tender lovingkindness.' The Greek word *agape,* used of God's love, means 'selfless' or 'sacrificial' love."[9] God's love and goodness (benevolence) are inseparably related in his essence. Because 1 John 4:16 tells us that "God is love," we know that love is of God's very essence. "His love can no more be limited than His nature, and His nature is unlimited." "God must be wholly and completely Love" since He is simple in essence (without parts or divisions). He is not partly this or that, but is wholly whatever He is. Love and Goodness are Supreme and Perfect in God, as are his Being, Truth, Knowledge, and Power.[10]

By his very nature God is all-loving and all-benevolent. "God, in His very essence, is all-goodness, and, therefore, He can only *do* good, being subject to His own nature."[11] Since his nature or essence is *necessary*, "He cannot not love. God by His very nature must love."[12] This also means that evil and sin cannot be any part of God, for God is entirely and perfectly Good, Loving, and Moral. "God cannot even be tempted to sin (James 1:13)—He is absolutely impervious to evil."[13] God alone is Perfect Goodness in essence—the Supreme Good. To attribute any evil or wrongdoing to God is to misrepresent His very nature and essence; it is to speak of something that God is not and cannot be. While God is all-loving and all-benevolent, He cannot do what is immoral, since He is also completely moral and righteous. Thus, to attribute any immoral or unethical acts to God is to misrepresent His essence. Among other things this means that God will not force anyone to love Him, or to do moral things against their will: "an omnibenevolent God will only do what is moral. And it is not morally right to force moral beings against their will." Since God is supremely Moral, He cannot love immorality. Since He is Just, He cannot love injustice. Since He is Love and Goodness, He cannot love violence, murder, and war. He is not *forced* to do so, but acts freely, in harmony with his very essence. "Nothing forces God to be loving; it comes naturally to Him."[14]

God exists as three Persons in one substantial Being, the Divine Trinity. Three Persons is essential to God's nature—as three, and as Persons. "And since God does not exist without his three persons, the love among those persons is *necessary* to his nature."[15] The love that bonds the Father with the Son, the Son with the Father, and both with the Holy Spirit is eternal. It has no beginning and no end. Since there is nothing higher or greater than the Being of God, theirs is the supreme and incomparable essence of Love, the source of all love, and the ultimate example for humankind. If God were not three Persons, the nature of Love would be different—not ultimately inter-personal. If God were not one substantial Being, love would not have one absolute source. Jesus told of his love for the Father and his oneness with him (John 14:31; 10:30; 17:11, 21). Speaking to God the Father, Jesus said "you loved Me before the foundation of the world"; and he prayed on behalf of all believers "that the love with which you loved Me may be in them, and I in them" (John 17:24, 26). The three Persons are in one accord and in perfect unity and harmony. There is perfect agreement, fidelity, and mutual support: "each person of the Trinity embraces the others and glorifies the others."[16] Envy, jealousy, disagreement, conflict, hate, and violence have no place in the Trinity. In all these ways they are the highest ideal for all human relationships—in common courtesy, friendship, marriage, and in all societal forms.

God's Goodness. What is God's goodness? John Frame's response emphasizes the simplicity, or wholeness and unity of God's *personal* nature: divine goodness is not something part of him, other than him, or less than him, it is "really a way of referring to everything God is. For everything God does is good, and everything he is is good. All his attributes are good. All his decrees are good. All his actions are good. There is nothing in God that is not good." In praising God's goodness we praise *him*, not some abstract property. In the same sense, "Our moral standard is not an impersonal, abstract property. It is a person, the living God." "God relates to us as a whole person, not as a collection of attributes. The attributes merely describe different things about him. They are a kind of shorthand for talking about that person. Everything he says and does is good, right, true, eternal, wise, and so on . . . . God's relationship with us is fully personal . . . . The Christian is not devoted to some abstract philosophical goodness, but to the living Lord of heaven and earth." The triunity of God does not conflict with this wholeness or simplicity, since each person is "in" the other two, and includes the whole divine nature.[17]

Frame discusses many divine attributes linked with goodness: "goodness, perfection, love, grace, patience, faithfulness, mercy, justice, righteousness, jealousy, wrath, beauty, joy, and blessedness." God's perfection lies in the fact

251

that He is the only Being in whom love, goodness, morality, justice, etc., are eternally and supremely actualized. Since God is a person, and perfect in all these ways, he *is* the true, living, personal standard for all. In contrast to the views of Plato and many other philosophers, "goodness is the behavior and self-revelation of a person, not a general or abstract concept."[18] Goodness and moral perfection in humans is only relative, not absolute: no one is without sin; all must seek forgiveness (1 John 1:8-9), and strive to be perfect like God. Benevolence, the most common meaning of goodness in Scripture, is acting to benefit others, with God as the leading example.[19] As Psalm 145 says, God is good, not simply to believers, but to all: "The Lord is good to all; he has compassion on all he has made . . . . The Lord is faithful to all his promises and loving toward all he has made. The Lord upholds all those who fall and lifts up all who are bowed down . . . . The Lord watches over all who love him, but all the wicked he will destroy." (The role of divine destruction will be discussed further in the next chapter.)

God's Love Is Personal. "God's love is at the heart of the biblical story." Since love is before anything else the relationship between the Persons of the Trinity, it is ultimately and fundamentally *personal*—a relationship between persons. God's love for all creation "is motivated by a self-giving affection and concern for his creatures' well-being." God not only loves those who love Him, but also loves his enemies, and tells us to do the same. God's love does not rule out His wrath, however, because He is also supremely righteous and just. While he loves his enemies, those who continue to refuse His love and grace, and oppose his works, encounter various degrees of judgment in life, and will ultimately face his wrath, judgments in life, and final judgment after death. Even believers are under his wrath before they come to belief and faith.[20] The ultimate example of God's love for all human beings is that "He sent his one and only Son into the world that we might live through him. This is love: not that we loved God, but that he loved us and sent his Son as an atoning sacrifice for our sins" (1 John 4:9-10).

By examining scriptural passages John Frame arrives at a theological definition of God's grace as his "sovereign unmerited favor, given to those who deserve his wrath." God's grace was unmerited by Noah, then by Abraham, Isaac, Jacob, Benjamin, and Moses. It was also unmerited by Israel, described as a "stiff-necked" nation. Nevertheless God initiated a historically decisive covenant with Israel based on his own divine decision to favor the nation, and to historically introduce expanding knowledge of Himself, His word, and his will for the guidance and salvation of Israel, and eventually of the whole world. God thus established a personal, loving, covenantal relationship with Israel, through his own "attitude of favor toward his people." His grace, like his love and goodness, is "utterly *personal*." With the New Testament "grace is not only God's favor, and not only God's power to change hearts, but also the gift of salvation apart from the works of the law." It is only by God's grace, through faith, that anyone is saved, not by deserving it, not by any good works.[21]

Frame finds key meanings of God's love, goodness, and grace in scriptural passages using the Hebrew word *hesed* (variously translated as "love," "steadfast love," "kindness," "goodness," mercy). "Loyalty" and "faithfulness" also add important meanings. "*Hesed* represents one of the most important divine attributes" because the key to its meaning is the concept of covenant. Covenant loyalty in Scripture refers to God's self-commitment to relationships between himself and humans, and to relationships on the human level. It has a rich, fully personal and emotional meaning: "when we are covenantally loyal to God, we consecrate to him everything we are, loving him with heart, soul, strength, and mind . . . including, of course, all our emotions. It is not surprising, then, that Scripture regards marriage as a covenant . . . and that marriage is an image of the relationship between God and his people." "*Hesed* is God's faithfulness to his covenant promise, his truthfulness to his word, the fact that he will bless his people as he says he will."[22]

Frame gives good reasons why God has emotions. Numerous biblical passages refer to "God's compassion, tender mercy, patience, rejoicing, delight, pleasure, pity, love, wrath, and jealousy." He is also "grieved" by many things human do. But theologians have "sometimes thought that emotions are unworthy of God," and contradict his unchangeableness and self-sufficiency. The reason seems to be the influence of Greek metaphysical thought, which treated emotions as misleading and dangerous—in contrast to reason, which is superior and must overcome them. But Frame points out that "Scripture does not distinguish 'the emotions' as a part of the mind that is radically different from the intellect and will." It doesn't specify any metaphysical or categorical difference between God's emotions and his thoughts and decisions. Frame points to "a kind of coalescence between emotion and intellect." He concludes that "without emotions, God would lack intellectual capacity, and he would be unable to speak the full truth about himself and the world."[23] Norman Geisler writes that "The Bible makes it evident that God has feelings: God's Spirit is grieved at sin (Eph. 4:30); God hates evil (Ps. 45:7); God's jealousy burns with anger against sin (Deut. 29:20)."[24] It seems clear that, since God is a person, and has created us as persons, he must have emotions. Wayne Grudem gives a basic reason: "God, who is the origin of our emotions and who created our emotions, certainly does feel emotions." "Of course, God does not have *sinful* passions or emotions."[25]

253

There are innumerable ways in which we see or experience God's goodness. Some of these have been dealt with in previous chapters. There are the impressive marvels of the universe and the earth that make them so suitable for human life in many ingenious ways; the intricate working of the human body with its trillions of cells functioning rapidly and exactly to support human life; the existence and functional interrelationships of the very elements that make up the real world. The nature of the human brain and mind is a marvel and great example of God's goodness (which I have not been able to address in this book). Chapter 1 described many of the good and beautiful ordinary aspects of the world and human life. Chapters 4 and 5 described the reality of created beings grounded in the eternal and necessary Being of God, and the existence of divinely created structures of reason and logic throughout the natural world, making reason, logic, truth, and knowledge possible in human life. "We are literally surrounded by evidence of God's goodness . . . . All creation presents to us his actions and his love . . . . God reveals his goodness through his actions in the course of nature and history, both in the experience of the biblical writers and in our own."[26] God the Word actually came in the flesh to tell of the Father and the Spirit, and to give his life to save those who will believe. And God has given human beings his word of truth in two divinely inspired Testaments.

God Creates with Reason and Purpose. Atheistic thought tends to find the world not only without given order, reason, and logic, but essentially accidental, meaningless, purposeless, and ending with extinction in death. This view was characteristically expressed by Bertrand Russell, one of the leading mathematical and philosophical minds of the twentieth century (Russell also stated that religion was based on fear, and Christ probably never existed):[27]

That mankind is the product of causes which had no prevision of the end they were achieving, that its origin, growth, hopes, fears, loves, beliefs are but the outcome of the accidental collocation of atoms; that there is no fire, no heroism, no intensity of thought and feeling which can preserve the individual life beyond the grave; that all the labor of the ages, all the devotion, all the inspiration, all the noonday brightness of the human race are destined to extinction in the vast death of the solar system; that the whole temple of man's achievement must inevitably be buried beneath the debris of a universe in ruins—all these things, if not quite beyond dispute, are yet so nearly so that no philosophy which rejects them can hope to stand. Only within the scaffolding of these truths, only on the firm foundation of unyielding despair can the soul's habitation henceforth be safely built.[28]

Any meaning must be added by humans. But since humans are contingent and very limited, such meaning can only be limited and temporal, grounded by nothing. Belief in the true God, however, confirms that the created world, and human life are securely grounded in God and his attributes—Being, absolute truth, and meaning—and so are essentially good and meaningful, have real purpose, and do not simply end in death, but guarantee eternal life and happiness for those who believe in, know, and obey God. To obey God is not slavery, it is to pursue the good.

Hate, Cruelty, and Murder Are Not Divine Purposes For Creation. *This* is the God who created all human beings: He did not create them to take advantage of each other, and certainly not to hate, maim, and destroy his work by torturing and killing each other. Humans are created as *individuals*. Individuals are, in essential ways separate and different, and have attributes, needs, and desires that are often different. This is the problem of *individuation* that exists in the human realm: human beings do not exist as one harmonious and perfect Being, as does God, but as innumerable separate and different units, with different desires, choices, inheritances, backgrounds, abilities, advantages and disadvantages. Individuation fosters situations of difference and conflict. Hate, violence, and murder work against harmony and can destroy it. For a good society to exist there must be suitable degrees of caring, cooperation, and harmony. The same holds true for individual differences in race, religion, and nationality. Disagreements can lead to conflicts, which can lead further to violence and killing. Arguments, lying, stealing, fighting, raping, and killing not only reduce society and individual rights, but cause pain and death. Fighting (as well as heavy drinking) is often portrayed in films as a manly thing. But it is essentially a failure of proper individual, group, or national relationship in some way. Lying creates a wall of separation and deception between persons, or between nations, and especially in a marriage, and it can harm both, as well as degrade the character of the liar. Stealing from anyone harms them by taking away their rightful property, and it harms the thief by corrupting his character, and can lead to prison or death. Adultery constitutes a breaking of the marriage vow, and seriously harms both persons.

Love and Goodness Are Required By God. More important than these pragmatic reasons, however, all such acts by humans are antithetical to the essential nature of the Holy God, and are condemned by Him. God has created humans, world, and cosmos according to His essential nature and ideas. Goodness and love are "built into" the very structure of reality. They are thus required for human life. The very nature of creation not only *reflects* His love and goodness, but requires them for proper human living and functioning. The cosmos is a reflection or image of God according to His nature and ideas. (Although both nature and man are fallen since the first sins, and show aspects that are bad, harmful, and destructive.) Individual

255

human beings and societies must seek this created, natural basis of love and goodness in order to function properly. At the divine level, God's essence of Love and Goodness are perfect, establishing the ideal model for humanity. The love of Jesus Christ in self-sacrifice for all humankind is the paradigm for human life. His love for his disciples and for all believers is their model for each other: "Love one another. As I have loved you, so you must love one another. By this all men will know that you are my disciples, if you love one another" (John 13:34-35). God requires the love, trust, and moral perfection of humans to be at one with Him. At the human level, there must be a proper degree of courtesy, love, and goodness (as part of the necessary structures of divine creation) in all relationships. Without them relationships suffer and fail.

God is Love, gives His love, requires love of human beings, and has established love as part of the necessary structure of created nature—these are reasons for the "greatest commandment," given by Christ in the New Testament: "Love the Lord your God with all your heart and with all your soul and with all your mind. This is the first and greatest commandment. And the second is like it: Love your neighbor as yourself. All the Law and the Prophets hang on these two commandments" (Matthew 22:37-40).[29] This is the "law of love" or "royal law" that sums up both the Old and New Testaments. Your neighbor is anyone with whom you have any kind of relationship. The Old Testament commandments are "summed up in this one rule, 'Love your neighbor as yourself.' Love does no harm to its neighbor. Therefore love is the fulfillment of the law" (Romans 13:9-10). The results of failure to do this are serious: "whoever hates his brother is in the darkness and walks around in the darkness; he does not know where he is going, because the darkness has blinded him" (I John 2:11); "If you keep on biting and devouring each other, watch out or you will be destroyed by each other" (Galatians 5:15). If we show favoritism or discrimination for rich over poor [and other forms of discrimination], we violate the royal law of love, and will be judged by God (James 2:1-9). It is clear that most ill effects in society and in "religious beliefs" result from common violations of these teachings.

Jesus' teachings in the Sermon on the Mount and the Beatitudes (Matthew 5-7) deal with key aspects of goodness and evil. One needs to be guided by the Spirit to properly understand these tersely worded statements. Many of them have been misinterpreted by those who have their own interests in mind. Throughout these teachings Jesus calls for the highest standards of conduct from believers, with the guidance of the Holy Spirit. He stresses the sinfulness of anger: "anyone who is angry with his brother will be subject to judgment" (5:22). Jesus does not forbid righteous or just anger per se, but condemns anger without just cause or proper measure, because it involves malicious intentions of the heart and will. It is insulting and degrading; it hurts people and sows discord. It often leads to untrue and abusive name calling, such as "fool," "moron," "idiot" [coupled with vulgar cursing]. And it is a predecessor of murder, which begins in the heart (5:21-22). But Jesus could justly call those people fools, like the Pharisees, who concentrated on external acts and appearances while ignoring wicked inner intentions (Luke 11:37-41). And Psalm 14:1 judges as "fools" those who reject belief in God. But love and grace must rule by far; judgment should be kept to minimal necessity.

Inner intentions are also emphasized when Jesus says that "anyone who looks at a woman lustfully has already committed adultery with her in his heart" (5:28). Sex is intended by God only for marriage, and a man and a woman are meant to be united in marriage for life. Thus, "anyone who divorces his wife, except for marital unfaithfulness, causes her to become an adulteress, and anyone who marries the divorced woman commits adultery" (5:33, cf. 19:9). To be righteous, one must also tell the truth: lying or intentionally false testimony is evil and despicable. The truth needs only the telling, with no added swearing upon anything (5:33-37).

The "law of retaliation" of the Old Testament—"eye for eye, tooth for tooth, hand for hand, foot for foot" (Exodus 21:24)—was intended "to insure that the punishment in civil cases fit the crime. It was never meant to sanction acts of personal retaliation."[30] Jesus did not alter this law, but corrected misinterpretations of it by stressing the law of love:[31] a spirit of loving care and concern must prevail, rather than a spirit of meanness, revenge, or retaliation—don't resist an evil person, turn the other cheek, be charitable, go the extra mile (Matthew 5:38-42). These are "examples of the general principles of non-retaliation, impartiality, generosity, and graciousness." Jesus calls believers to a higher level of love and concern for all, even their enemies. But he sometimes uses hyperbole to emphasize such a loving attitude; the explicit recommendations were not intended to be used unthinkingly or foolishly.[32]

Being able to forgive those who wrong you is often difficult. But it is necessary for the righteous believer, and should be for all: "For if you forgive men when they sin against you, your heavenly Father will also forgive you. But if you do not forgive men their sins, your Father will not forgive your sins" (Matthew 6:14-15). Lack of forgiveness can fester and become malignant in a person, causing all sorts of ill effects, doing as much or more harm than the original wrong. It can foster permanent attitudes of coldness, hatefulness, meanness, and vindictiveness, not divinely intended for human society. This is closely interrelated with another aspect of Jesus' teaching: "Do not judge, or you too will be judged. For in the same way you judge others, you will be judged, and with the measure you use, it will be measured to you" (7:1-2). In these ways the person who judges others is himself judged both in life and death. Jesus does not prohibit any proper and suitable judgment and legal punishments at all, however. He balances love with judgment in Matthew 7:6 by using metaphor and hyperbole to indicate response to those who persistently reject and ridicule the word and grace of God: "Do not give what is holy to the dogs; nor cast your pearls before swine, lest they trample them under their feet, and turn and tear you in pieces." And in 1 Corinthians 5:5, "'judging'—even excommunicating—is required in the light of a church member's shameless sexual misconduct."[33]

There must be a balance of love and forgiveness with judgment and justice. Liars, thieves, and murderers break the law, and should be properly judged by the authorities of civil government. If someone steals your property, or substantially harms you with lies or slander, it may be suitable at times to seek legal redress, but litigiousness is forbidden, and seeking loving solutions is advocated. The degree of seriousness of a wrongdoing may have much to do with it. In daily life we often meet with rudeness, personal slights, and affronts that hurt feelings or even become harmful in nature. One should be able to face them with equanimity, forgiveness, and composure, rather than return rudeness for rudeness, evil for evil. In some situations one may not be able to do much to right a wrong. God must be the final Judge. In all situations believers must place love and forgiveness before judgment. Jesus taught that we should love not only the poor and needy, but even those who do not deserve it, those who do not love you, and those who work against you: "love your enemies, bless those who curse you, do good to those who hate you, and pray for those who spitefully use you and persecute you" (5:44). Nowhere does Jesus Christ call for hatred or persecution of non-believers, or for killing them because of their unbelief. Nowhere does the Bible call for killing infidels in order to forcefully spread the gospel (although God sometimes punishes or kills disbelievers who staunchly oppose his good purposes). Christ calls believers to strive to be perfect, like the Father: "Be perfect, therefore, as your heavenly Father is perfect." The results and rewards are great: "The fruit of the Spirit is love, joy, peace, patience, kindness, goodness, faithfulness, gentleness, and self-control" (Galatians 5:22-23).

In the Sermon on the Mount Jesus taught that believers should not be primarily occupied with seeking money, wealth, and possessions (Matthew 6:19-34). We should not become slaves to them: "No one can be a slave of two masters . . . . You cannot be slaves of God and of money [mammon]." Primary love of wealth and property leads one away from God. Primary commitment to acquisition of money and possessions erodes a person's commitment to God and a righteous way of life. A paramount concern for one's life, food, and clothing does the same. We often see this clearly in professions where looks, clothes, possessions, and money are all-important indicators of success or failure, as in the star business—actors, models, pop musicians, sports stars, etc. All such primary commitments can produce disturbing degrees of anxiety and worry, sometimes leading to drug abuse and health problems. Righteous believers can live without such fear, anxiety, and worry, however, because a paramount love and trust in God frees them from slavery to never-secure, never-satisfied earthly treasures.

Believers should not be troubled by fear and worry. 1 John 4:18 assures us that "There is no fear in love. But perfect love drives out fear.") "Do not store up for yourselves treasures on earth, where moth and rust destroy, and where thieves break in and steal. But store up for yourselves treasures in heaven, where moth and rust do not destroy, and where thieves do not break in and steal. For where your treasure is, there your heart will be also" (Matthew 6:19-21). Believers should "seek first the kingdom of God and His righteousness, and all these things shall be added to you." These teachings certainly do not tell us to totally ignore our bodies, clothes, food, money, and property, however. That would be foolish and irresponsible. Such matters should also be carried out with due care and responsibility, but should be fully subordinate to love of God and neighbor. Believers are called to a *loving*, *caring*, and *responsible* way of life in this world in preparation for eternal life, not to ignoring this life because of a totally "otherworldly" perspective.

The Beatitudes of Matthew 5:3-11 describe the constant, day-by-day outlooks and ways of living for the believer, the one who is to inherit the kingdom of God. They all reflect ways of loving and honoring God and willing the good for others. These ways taught by Jesus are revolutionary— antithetical to common, "worldly" views of goodness, purpose, and happiness. It is not riches, possessions, pleasure, and self-sufficiency that bring well-being, peace, and true joy, but quite different virtues. "Blessed are the poor in spirit"—those who are not driven by pride and self-sufficiency, but who humbly serve God and look to Him for spiritual guidance and purpose in their lives. "Blessed are those who mourn"—those who are not self-satisfied, but regret their disobedience to God, as well as that of others, and seek to change. "Blessed are the meek"—those who are not arrogant, essentially self-directing, or autonomous, but have controlled strength and purpose through submission to guidance by the goodness and power of the Holy Spirit. "Blessed are those who hunger and thirst after righteousness"— those who are not motivated by self-righteousness, selfishness, lust, greed, or hatred, but who love and obey God, and will the good for their brothers and sisters. "Blessed are the merciful"—those who are not angry, mean, and harshly judgmental, but act with graciousness, love, and mercy. "Blessed are the pure in heart"—those who do not rely on insincere acts and outer show, but who pursue righteousness from the center of their being. "Blessed are the peacemakers"—those who are not angry, hateful, violent, and murderous, but who work for the well-being of others, and the harmony of all. And finally, "Blessed are those who are persecuted because of righteousness"—those who do not give in to worldly pressures, but who love and obey God despite all hardships.

Addressing believers in 1 Corinthians 13, Paul beautifully describes the nature and necessity of love for human life and relationships. Even if we have and do all other things, without love we are barren:

Though I speak with the tongues of men and of angels, but have not love, I have become sounding brass or a clanging cymbal. And though I have the gift of prophecy, and understand all mysteries and all knowledge, and though I have all faith, so that I could remove mountains, but have not love, I am nothing. And though I bestow all my goods to feed the poor, and though I give my body to be burned, but have not love, it profits me nothing. Love suffers long and is kind; love does not envy; love does not parade itself, is not puffed up; does not behave rudely, does not seek its own, is not provoked, thinks no evil; does not rejoice in iniquity, but rejoices in the truth; bears all things, believes all things, hopes all things, endures all things. Love never fails . . . . And now abide faith, hope, love, these three; but the greatest of these is love.

Love will endure forever, even after the gifts and achievements that Paul mentions are fulfilled and complete. Love is never rude, selfish, or mean. Love means a genuine caring for others, an active willing to do good and right for all.

In Philippians 4:6-8 Paul gives wonderful advice for a positive outlook on life that promotes high-mindedness, peace, and joy by not allowing the false, unjust, vulgar, corrupt, and ugly to dominate one's mind: "whatever things are true, whatever things are noble, whatever things are just, whatever things are pure, whatever things are lovely, whatever things are of good report, if there is any virtue and if there is anything praiseworthy—meditate on these things." Although he is addressing the Philippian church, the advice is good for everyone: "Be anxious about nothing, but in everything by prayer and supplication, with thanksgiving, let your requests be made known to God." This stands in contrast to unbelievers, who tend to gravitate to essentially negative outlooks (without God what is left—no ultimate ground, reason, purpose, meaning, or truth, no life after death, and no ultimate justification for good or evil).

God is the Sovereign Lord Who Guides All Things. The Bible also teaches throughout that God is the *Sovereign* Creator. If God created all things, and is all-powerful, all-knowing, all-good, and all-loving, he must be in full control of his creation.[34] The Westminster Confession of Faith supports the biblical teaching that "God the great Creator of all things doth uphold, direct, dispose, and govern all creatures, actions, and things, from the greatest to the least, by His most wise and holy providence, according to His infallible foreknowledge, and the free and immutable counsel of His own will, to the praise of the glory of His wisdom, power, justice, goodness, and mercy" (V.I). God thus directs and governs all things. Individuals, the world, and history do not simply move along "on their own," or drift along naturally, randomly, or accidentally, as so much modern thought contends, but are under the guidance and control of the Sovereign Creator.

All things are guided by God for his ultimately grand and good purposes. The world and history are moving with direction and purpose, toward the goal determined and predestined before creation by the Creator. Frame points out that in Hebrews 1:3, which speaks of Christ "sustaining all things by his powerful word," the verb in Greek is *pherō* (to bear, carry). The meaning is thus a dynamic one, indicating that Christ is the Lord of history, sustaining and carrying the world through time toward a predetermined destination.[35]

One meaning of the name Yahweh (Lord, King), so often used in Scripture, is that God rules all of creation, fully controlling both nature and history. "God exercises such control over everything that happens in the world." The natural world is not controlled by impersonal, natural forces, but by God. Theories that the universe is governed by an "impersonal mechanism called 'nature' or 'natural law'" are incompatible with the Bible and true Christian belief in God the Creator. Since God is the personal creator and providential controller, the proper view of the natural world is, like that of the Bible, "intensely personal."[36] Neither are events in creation determined by impersonal fate, chance, or accident. Fatalistic views deny benevolent control of the world, and even see evil as dominant. Views supporting randomness or chance deny any intelligent control. But in the biblical Christian view, "Even those events that appear to be most random are under God's sovereign control." The throw of dice, casting of lots, or drawing of straws are decided by God. Even "'accidents' come from the Lord."[37]

Norman Geisler supports the scriptural teaching of God's sovereign dominion over all his creation: "since God is before all things, created all things, upholds all things, is above all things, and owns all things, He is the rightful ruler of all things." God is in control of all created things: "nothing happens apart from God's will." As Job confessed to God, "no plan of yours can be thwarted" (Job 42:2). And as the Psalmist knew, "The LORD does whatever pleases him, in the heavens and on the earth, in the seas and all their depths" (Psalm 135:6). Earthly rulers are under God's control (Proverbs

21:1; Revelation 19:16). Geisler concludes that *"There is nothing any human power does that is not done under God's power."* "Human events are under God's control. God not only controls the hearts of kings, He ordains the course of history before it occurs." Good angels, Satan, and evil angels are also under God's control: "God's sovereign domain includes not only the good angels but also the free choices of evil ones (Eph. 1:21)." "In summary, the Bible declares that God is in complete control of everything that happens in the whole course of history. This includes even free choices, both good and evil, which He ordained from all eternity."[38]

Scripture makes many statements indicating that *no event* in creation occurs outside of God's providential control—either in the natural world or in human history.[39] Having made the natural world according to his wisdom, ideas, and plan, God knows it completely and thoroughly. He has created the structures and operations of everything that exists. He created the very laws and structures of the universe, nature, and the human body and mind. He knows everything about them, inside and out, and he is the mind, power, and will that controls them. Job 38-40 and Psalms 104 and 147:15-18 relate much of this: God created both light and darkness; he founded the earth and brought forth the seas, setting their measures and boundaries. He controls the stars and constellations, the laws of the heavens, and the regular appearances of morning and night. "The moon marks off the seasons, and the sun knows when to go down." He creates storms and perils at sea, and then calms the waters; he turns rivers into a desert, and the desert into pools of water (Psalm 107). God ultimately controls all the workings of nature, including rain, the watering or dryness of the land, the growth of crops, existence of deserts, the actions of wind, clouds, thunderstorms, lightening, hail, dew, frost, snow, ice, and the many processes of the earth. He provides food for the birds and animals. He gives the horse its strength, beauty, and fighting courage. The hawk takes flight by God's wisdom, knowing which direction to fly, and the eagle soars at God's command, knowing where to make its stronghold. And when God takes away the breath of the creatures, "they die and return to the dust." All the regularities of the earth and the universe depend on the control of God (Genesis 8:22).

According to Jesus in the book of Matthew, God's control of creation encompasses the greatest of things, as well as the smallest of details. God's kingdom will come; his will *will* be done on earth as it is in heaven. God controls the movements of the sun, and the fall of rain. Being the second Person of the Trinity and having the full power of God, Jesus is able to raise the dead, heal the sick, the blind, and the lame. He commands Satan and demons and they obey his will. He walks on water, and calms the sea by his word. He has power over space and time. He gave to his disciples the "authority to drive out evil spirits and to heal every disease and sickness." He even empowered them to "raise the dead, cleanse those who have leprosy, drive out demons." Jesus predicted his own death, and his resurrection three days later. He revealed his divine glory to disciples in his glowing transfiguration, with Moses and Elijah appearing and talking with him, and the voice of God the Father from a cloud identifying Jesus as his Son. He foreknew and predicted that the Jews would reject him at his appearance on earth. He foreknew and predicted the destruction of the temple in Jerusalem. He foreknew and predicted many signs of the end of the human historical age—wars and rumors of wars, earthquakes, famines, many turning away from the faith, many false prophets, an increase of wickedness and suffering. He foreknew and predicted the afterlife in heaven "at the renewal of all things," when his disciples would sit on thrones "judging the twelve tribes of Israel." But he could also tell us that such a slight thing as the fall of a tiny sparrow is known and controlled by the will of God. And still more amazing, "even the very hairs of your head are numbered."[40]

God's absolute control and authority over his creation is indicated by several things: (1) he is the creator of all things that exist, making him the sole owner and Lord of all creation; (2) he is infinitely greater and superior in all respects to his creation; (3) he has by his divine ideas, purpose, will, and fore-ordination determined the being, nature, structure, functions, and ultimate purposes of all individual things; (4) he is infinite being, power, goodness, love, and holiness, and so is the fount and standard of all that is good, holy, and lawful for creation; (5) created things have no other true source of being, continuing sustenance, function, morality, purpose, or law and authority than God. God is thus *Supreme Lord* of all creation. How could it be otherwise? He knows, makes, shapes, supports, and determines all aspects of creation. If this were not so, creation would be out of his control. The notion that God creates the universe then leaves it to run on its own, as deism, contends, is really illogical and foolish. The Enlightenment-modern scenario of human autonomy and the final authority of human reason and science are just as short-sighted and foolish. Considering all these things, if God allowed creation to proceed by its own determination, as limited and fallible as it is, and considering human propensities to self-centeredness, greed, intolerance, hate, violence, murder, and war, it no doubt would end in total futility, unspeakable suffering, chaos, and death.

God Controls Individual Lives. Scripture also tells us that God controls the course of individual human lives and history. What else could be expected from the almighty Creator who determines the very structures, laws, and modes of operation of all natural things, and controls all natural events in detail, including apparently random and accidental ones? God's predetermined control of individual lives begins before we are conceived and born. Speaking to God in Psalm 139 David said, "you created my inmost being; you knit me together in my mother's womb," determining "all the days ordained for me."

Jeremiah is a clear example of God's foreknowledge of him, and of decreeing his purpose. The Lord said to Jeremiah: "Before I formed you in the womb I knew you, before you were born I set you apart; I appointed you as a prophet to the nations" (Jeremiah 1:5-6). From this passage Frame concludes that "If God knew Jeremiah before his conception, then he must have arranged for each of Jeremiah's ancestors to be born, and then Jeremiah himself. So God is in control of all the 'accidents' of history to create the precise person he seeks to employ as his prophet. God's foreknowledge of one individual implies comprehensive control over the entire human family."[41] The Jeremiah passage and a number of others indicate that "the whole history of human procreation is under God's control, as he acts intentionally to bring about the conception of each one of us."[42] God also revealed His knowledge and control of nations to Jeremiah, telling him that He puts His word that will make and break the destinies of nations and kingdoms into the prophet's mouth. He appointed Jeremiah "over nations and kingdoms to uproot and tear down, to destroy and overthrow, to build and to plant" (1:9-10)

There are several New Testament passages that tell of God's predestination or foreordination to salvation from sins. A key one is in Ephesians 1:4-8 (emphases added): "he *chose* us in him before the creation of the world to be holy and blameless in his sight. In love he *predestined* us to be adopted as his sons through Jesus Christ, *in accordance with his pleasure and will*—to the praise of his glorious *grace*, which he has freely given us in the One he loves. In him we have redemption through his blood, the forgiveness of sins, in accordance with the riches of God's grace that he lavished on us *with all wisdom and understanding*." So we learn that God's predestination of us to salvation takes place before the creation of the world. In verse 11 predestined salvation is also taught as part of God's *plan* that includes *everything*: "In him we were also *chosen*, having been *predestined* according to the *plan* of him who works out everything in conformity with the *purpose of his will* . . . ."[43] Romans 8:28-30 summarizes all these aspects of salvation: "For those God *foreknew* he also *predestined* to be conformed to the likeness of his son, that he might be the firstborn among many brothers. And those he predestined, he also *called*, he also *justified*; those he justified, he also *glorified*." But in doing this, God also permits human free will to choose to accept or reject salvation (discussed below).

God's Providential Covenants With Israel. The covenants, in fact, have as their ultimate purpose, shaping the Jewish leaders and all the people through the centuries not only to be obedient servants of God themselves, but to be a priesthood, an instrument of ministry and salvation to all of the world; the covenants thus lead progressively through the patriarchs and kings of Israel to the birth, ministry, crucifixion and resurrection of Jesus Christ, "the son of David, the son of Abraham,"[44] as the divine culmination of these purposes. Thus we are told that Jesus was *preordained* by God's will and purpose before the creation of the world to go to the cross in God's plan of salvation (Acts 2:23; 4:27-28).

We find primary examples of God's foreknowledge, foreordination, and control of individual human and historical events in the lives and history of the founding patriarchs of Israel—Abraham, Isaac, Jacob, then in Joseph, and later in Moses. God's foreordained plan for humanity and history is evident from the very beginning in his successive covenants, leading from Abraham to the promised blessings for all people on earth, eventually through Jesus Christ.[45] Covenant is a key mode of God's *self-presentation* and *relationship* with created humanity. Covenant in the Old Testament is different in important respects from that of the New Testament, due to the saving work of Christ. In the Old Testament, by God's determination, a binding agreement of divine legal nature was initiated by God, and agreed to by the human recipient. God essentially made a promise or promises of benefits to the recipient, with the provision that the recipient must be faithful and obedient. Since God is Supreme Lord of creation, it is a Lord and vassal, or master and servant relationship. While this may sound abhorrent to the modern mind, with its predilection for autonomous freedom and individual rights, it is essentially a *good* arrangement, because what the human recipient actually becomes servant to is truth, goodness, and love in the person of the living God. So serving God faithfully means seeking all that is good, and refusing everything that is bad, harmful, and evil. It sets one on the path of truth and life. The best expression of the relationship is that used throughout the Scriptures of the Father and his children. God's motive in establishing covenant is grace, and "lovingkindness" or "covenant love" (*hesed*).

It was with Abram (Abraham) that God initiated special early covenants that would be a blessing to him and his descendants, the future nation of Israel, and promised eventual blessings for all people on earth through Abram. God said: "I will make you into a great nation and I will bless you" (Genesis 12:1-3) By God's command, faithfully followed by Abram, he was led out of his pagan homeland, with its worship of nature and fertility deities (generally characteristic of the entire populated world of the time) and led ultimately into Canaan, the future homeland of Israel. Terah, Abram's father, was thoroughly pagan, and he died at Haran, not included in God's plan for those entering Canaan. For Abram and the people with him it became a fresh, new start in a new land for a new people of God. God revealed to Abram his foreordained will that the Hebrews would be in bondage in Egypt for 400 years, an event that would actually take place centuries later (Genesis 15:13; Exodus 12:31-42). And in a covenantal promise to Abram, God revealed his providential plan that Abram's descendants would inherit the entire land from the Nile east to the Euphrates River (15:18). Then, when Abram was 99 years old, God again showed his foreordination, through his covenant, that Abram would be "the father of many nations" (the Israelites, and many Arabic nations).[46]

God had predetermined that the first child in the Hebrew lineage would be by the body of Abram and his wife Sarai. But Sarai remained barren well into old age. Abram was a man of exceptional and enduring faith, but he began to have doubts about his and Sarai's age for childbearing. Sarai told Abram to sleep with her Egyptian maidservant, Hagar, so she could bear him a child, and Abram did. In so doing, Abram "violated God's basic ordinance for marriage, which dates back to creation," and in that sense committed adultery.[47] When Hagar became pregnant, a conflict arose immediately, causing Hagar to flee. Hagar was to become the mother of Ishmael, who is the ancestor of Arabian tribes. This was no "accident;" it is part of the predetermined plan of God. The "angel of the Lord"[48] appeared to Hagar, telling her to return and submit to her mistress. Significantly, the "angel" added, "I will so increase your descendants that they will be too numerous to count."

The angel of the Lord also predicted that Ishmael would be "a wild donkey of a man; his hand will be against everyone and everyone's hand against him, and he will live in hostility toward all his brothers" (Genesis 16:12). Kenneth Mathews writes that this is a picture of "Ishmael as antagonist whose hostilities are indiscriminate and without restraint. Hostility toward one's 'brother' characterized the nonelect line in Genesis, beginning with Cain (4:8, 23-24); Esau, like Ishmael, is portrayed as a wild belligerent (27:39-40)."[49] Such belligerence was repeated in Genesis 25:13-18, describing Ishmael's descendants living from Havilah to Shur near the border of Egypt: "they lived in hostility toward all their brothers."

Thirteen years after Ishmael's birth, when Abram was 99 "the Lord appeared to him, saying 'I am God Almighty'." God confirmed his covenant with Abram, promising that he would be "the father of many nations," and changed his name to Abraham. God promised the whole land of Canaan to Abraham and his descendents, and required circumcision of every male as a sign of the covenant. He also promised Abraham a son through Sarai—whose name he now changed to Sarah—by the same time next year. God commanded that this son through Sarah, who would be giving birth at 90, was to be called Isaac, and said: "I will establish my covenant with him as an everlasting covenant for his descendants after him." It was to be a miraculous birth, predestined for the covenant line.

God also promised to bless Ishmael, to "make him fruitful," "greatly increase his numbers," make him "the father of twelve rulers," and "make him into a great nation." But Ishmael's blessing was not in perpetuity.[50] After Isaac was born and weaned, Abraham held a great feast, but Ishmael stood by mocking. Sarah told Abraham "Get rid of that slave woman and her son, for that slave woman's son will never share in the inheritance with my son Isaac." God then came to Hagar and Ishmael in the desert, saving them from death. They lived in the desert, and when Ishmael grew up, his Egyptian mother "got a wife for him from Egypt" (Genesis 21).

Thus it is by God's predetermined plan that Isaac, the divinely promised son of Abraham and ancestor of the Hebrew-Christian tradition, and Ishmael, the ancestor of Arabic tribes, are both sons of Abraham. However, although Ishmael was fathered by Abraham, and could have been his heir according to customs of Abraham's time, he was illegitimate according to God's law for marriage beginning with creation, because Abraham was not married to Hagar. While Ishmael was about 14 years older than Isaac, he did not become his father's heir and did not inherit his property. More importantly for providential salvation history, according to God's decree given in Genesis 17:19-21, it was Isaac, not Ishmael, who inherited the Hebrew line of covenant with God. Since Hagar was Egyptian, Ishmael's bloodline was not pure Hebrew. Muslim Arabs have claimed descent from Ishmael. Arabian tribes descended from Ishmael have lived throughout the Arabian peninsula and Israel's Promised Land for centuries. The centuries-long conflicts between Arab Muslims and Hebrew-Christian tradition must surely have their roots in these troubling differences between Ishmael and Isaac. The immediate cause seems to have been Abraham's quest to fulfill, by his own efforts, God's prediction of a son and heir, and in the process, committing adultery according to God's creation standards. But, since all things are preordained by God, the ultimate source must be in God's predetermined plan.

When Isaac was grown, Abraham, insisting that no Canaanite woman should marry him, sent his servant back to his homeland to find a suitable wife, telling him that God's angel would lead the way. The servant, probably Eliezer, journeyed to the town of Nahor in northern Mesopotamia. There he prayed that God would give him a sign when "the one you have chosen" comes to the well. God's providential plan for Isaac is clearly evident in the quick and successful meeting of Eliezer with the beautiful maiden Rebekah at the town well (Genesis 24). Rebekah returned with Eliezer and married Isaac. After nearly twenty years there were no children and the covenant line seemed endangered again. But when Isaac prayed to God asking that Rebekah have a child, she became pregnant. Thus a second covenantal birth was due to an act of God. Rebekah then asked God why there was such a jostling inside her. God knew and told her not only that she would have twins, but what their future history would be: "Two nations are in your womb, and two peoples from within you will be separated; one people will be stronger than the other, and the older will serve the younger" (25:21-23). So the struggle between the twins Jacob and Esau began in the womb. It led to separation years after birth, and the propagation of different nations (Jew and Arab), at odds with each other. God's statement that the older son would serve the younger also set his decree in place of the human law of primogeniture.

A paramount example of God's control of the future of his covenant people can be found in the life of Joseph, son of Jacob. God not only allowed, but actually planned and sent the seventeen-year-old Joseph into slavery in Egypt for his preordained reasons. Joseph, who lived for God, knew that God had controlled the wicked deeds of his half-brothers who had sold him into slavery (perhaps 1898 BC),[51] and had turned their evil into an event of goodness and great historical importance ("it was not you who sent me here, but God . . . . "God intended it for good, . . . the saving of many lives" Genesis 45:5-8; 50:20). Twenty-two years later, Jacob, with his sons and their families (a small group of around 70), followed Joseph into Egypt. In this manner God saved the small covenantal group from starvation during a time of famine by sending them into bondage in Egypt for 430 years. The sufferings of Joseph strengthened his spiritual discipline, and carried him to a place of leadership in Egypt. And for Jacob and his descendants, although the stay in Egypt also involved subjugation and oppression, it had the ultimately good purpose of preserving Israel's national and spiritual identity, and allowing time for the few to grow into a great multitude.

Egyptian fears about the growth of Hebrew population are reflected in Pharaoh's edict requiring the killing of infant boys. Moses, who eventually led the Israelites out of Egyptian bondage, was born in Egypt probably in 1526 BC, at the beginning of the reign of the Pharaoh Thutmose I, while this law was in effect. God's providential planning and control of events is clearly evident in the birth and upbringing of Moses under such threatening circumstances, on through the exodus, 80 years later. Moses' mother hid the three-months-old boy in a floating papyrus basket among the reeds of the Nile. Pharaoh's daughter soon spotted the basket and felt compassion for the beautiful, crying infant. Moses' sister, Miriam, who had been watching nearby, came to Pharaoh's daughter and offered to find a nurse for the baby among the Hebrew women. "In a vivid display of God's control over events, Moses' mother was reunited with her child—which was legally sanctioned in the home despite Pharaoh's edict . . . and she was even remunerated for her services!"[52] As a child Moses was returned to Pharaoh's daughter, to grow up as her son, a member of the royal household, and receive a good education. For 40 years in Egypt, God providentially prepared Moses for the role of a strong leader.

Subsequent events further prepared Moses for this great role. Since the Bible says that God plans and controls all events that take place in the world, both good and evil ones, it would be true of the one which caused Moses to leave Egypt for the next forty years. He killed an Egyptian who was beating a Hebrew man, and hid the body in the sand. As word got around, Moses became afraid of retribution from Pharaoh, and left Egypt to live in Midian, a dry and desolate area to the northeast, near the Red Sea. Here Moses found a young woman, Zipporah ("little bird") to be his wife, one of seven daughters of the priest Reuel (Jethro). During his forty years in Midian as a shepherd, Moses developed into mature manhood as husband and father, learning patience, and developing endurance in the hard, dry surroundings, as he gained valuable knowledge of the land that would be the future route of the exodus. One day he came upon a burning bush on Mount Horeb (Mount Sinai). The bush was on fire but did not burn up. God's preparations for Moses were coming to a culmination here. As the covenantal Lord of history had previously manifested himself directly to Abraham, and then to Isaac and Jacob, he now revealed himself to Moses in a fire and a voice from a burning bush, saying that he was concerned for his people suffering in Egypt, and telling Moses, "bring my people the Israelites out of Egypt." It was then that God revealed his mysterious name to Moses, "I AM WHO I AM."

God Judged Egypt. God had promised Jacob earlier that he would bring his descendants out of Egypt again into the Promised Land. And with momentous significance, he changed Jacob's name to Israel.[53] When the time of exodus (perhaps 1446 BC) drew near, God "hardened the heart of the Pharaoh" (perhaps Amenhotep II)[54] so he would not let the Israelites go. Hardening of the heart (the center of a person's being, intellect, will, emotion) is often spoken of in Scripture as one of God's ways of controlling the thoughts and actions of disbelievers in order to confirm them in their disbelief, or to chastise the disobedient, and to carry out his plans.[55] (As it might be said today, a person can become hardened in his ways through stubborn perseverance, going from bad to worse.) God then brought down ten destructive evils, the plagues, on Egypt.

God did not bring the Hebrew people out of Egypt in one sudden and mighty act. Moses spent considerable, frustrating time, at God's command, trying to convince the Pharaoh to let the people go, with no success, and even with negative results. As the creator and planner of all things, God must have planned all of this in detail, including all the resistance, the failures and frustrations. Then God took more time (perhaps nine months) to make each of the ten plagues a judgment on Egypt and its gods, clearly revealing his power over the false gods.[56] The many gods of Egypt represented aspects of nature—the sun (Amon, Re), the Nile (Osiris, Isis), the sky (Nut, Hathor), the earth (Geb), vegetation and crops (Osiris), various animals, and other gods representing human life, health, fertility, and so on. The ten plagues brought by God on the Egyptians also served as attacks on, and humiliating defeat of all the gods of Egypt. With the seventh plague, God sent a message to Pharaoh that he could have wiped all the Egyptians off the face of the earth: "But I have raised you up for this purpose, that I might show you my power, and that my name might be proclaimed in all the earth."[57] "Raised you up for this purpose" indicates that God foreordained what had taken place in Egypt so that the power, truth, and glory of the real God might be revealed, in contrast to the falsity of the Egyptian gods.

In the first plague, God turned the Nile to blood, denying the life-giving power of Osiris and Isis. In the second, frogs multiplied everywhere, covering land, courtyards, and houses, becoming a curse on the Egyptians rather than an aid to birth by Heqet the frog-headed goddess. In order to get relief from a plague, Pharaoh at times lied to Moses and Aaron. When God caused the frogs to die, Pharaoh hardened his heart again. In the third plague, insects such as gnats, mosquitoes, or sand fleas covered the land, the people and the animals, driving them wild. Then came a plague of flies (perhaps biting ones), covering the ground, filling houses, and swarming all over the Egyptians. The fifth plague was the death of livestock in the fields—cattle, sheep, goats, horses, camels, and donkeys—revealing the powerlessness of the animal and half-animal-half-human gods of Egypt. Then came a plague of boils and sores on the people and animals, showing the powerlessness of Egyptian gods such as the lion-headed goddess Sekhmet to prevent disease, and Isis to heal. The worst hailstorm ever seen on earth came as the seventh plague, revealing the helplessness of Nut the sky goddess, as well as Osiris the god of crops. The eighth plague was locusts, covering the earth and eating whatever was left of ground vegetation and on trees, again showing the impotence of Osiris and Nut the sky goddess. Pharaoh finally acknowledged God, saying "I have sinned against the Lord your God and against you." He now seemed willing to let them go, but "the Lord hardened Pharaoh's heart" again, and brought the ninth plague. "Thick darkness" covered Egypt for three days. This time Pharaoh said he would let the Hebrews go, but they must leave their animals. Moses rejected this reservation. God again hardened Pharaoh's heart, and Pharaoh threatened to kill Moses if he ever saw him again.[58]

God then sent the final plague of death on every firstborn of the Egyptians, including the Pharaoh's son, because of their wicked treatment of God's own "firstborn," his covenant people. This plague showed that Isis could not protect children. God had known beforehand that Pharaoh would then let his people go. He had even told Moses before any of the pleas and plagues that when the time came to go, he would soften the hearts of the Egyptians and change their dispositions, so that when the Hebrew women asked their neighbors for articles of silver, gold, and clothing, they would be given whatever they wanted, leaving the Egyptians "plundered."[59]

These plagues reveal the mighty Creator's full control of all creation, the natural world, natural laws, and his control of human beings and history. While all this may sound incredible to the modern mind, such things were widely credible in the ancient world, before the pervasive, reductive influence of naturalistic and non-theistic views in the modern world. However, it should not be difficult for anyone to understand that a God who could create everything that exists, in its nearly infinite variety, wondrous complexity, and design, could also plan and preordain what is to transpire in his creation throughout its history. At God's will Abraham was given a divine covenant. Events in his life were preordained for this purpose. The covenant was passed on to Isaac and then Jacob. Joseph was sent to Egypt, and the Hebrew remnant followed. Then at God's will Moses was born, his life saved, and he was raised as a leader. At God's will and word, water changed to blood, calamitous masses of frogs, flies, and locusts appeared and disappeared. Darkness came and went. Animals and infants died. People prospered or lost goods, became sick or well. People's hearts were hardened or softened, and their minds were changed. For all these things to be known beforehand by God, they had to be planned, foreknown, and preordained before the beginning of the world by the sovereign God who created it.

God's Providential Plan of Covenant with David. David was chosen by God to be his anointed future covenant king when he was just a young boy—a lowly shepherd. Since David was to be the first king of Israel to be fully sanctioned and approved by God, he is the one who truly initiated covenant kingship in Israel. God had permitted Saul to rule for a time before David, due to impatient demands of Hebrew people for a king, but Saul was not from the chosen covenant tribe of Judah. Saul even ordered the killing of 85 priests of God, and their whole town of men, women, children, and animals.[60] Saul grievously disobeyed God in other ways. God removed his supporting power from Saul before the end of his reign, and Saul later died in ignominy. David's kingship was to be of a very different order and significance to that of Saul. David the divinely led warrior captured Jerusalem, and then was able to return the Ark of the Covenant, the holy seat of God, back to the city. Actually, only God had the authority and power to return the Ark, leading David as his powerful agent, just as it had been by God's authority that the Ark had been previously captured from the Jews. God was now making his presence known in the national life of Israel in a closer and stronger way. If Israel had remained faithful and devoted, Jerusalem and the Promised Land could have become a kind of new and impregnable Eden, with the Almighty God at its center.[61]

God made an important new covenant with David, making him king and unconditionally promising a dynasty of kings descending from him. The actual rise of kings in Israel clearly fulfilled part of the centuries-old Abrahamic covenant promise that the patriarchs would be fathers of kings.[62] It was to lead ultimately, many centuries after David, to "the son of David, the son of Abraham," Jesus Christ, the one promised to reign *forever* with a permanent throne and kingdom. God's covenants thus reached a kind of Old Testament fruition in the kingship of David: much of the land promised in the Abrahamic covenant was won by David; more importantly, kingship was historically instituted in Israel, setting the precedent for a future king who was to rule eternally over all nations, defeat all evil, including the evil one, and bring ultimate peace.[63]

God Controls Evil in the World. During the lives of the covenant patriarchs and kings, and throughout the Old Testament history of the Jews, there were many instances of disobedience, unfaithfulness, resulting punishments, and various evils brought down on individuals and on Israel as a whole. The Bible reveals a God who not only loves and blesses, but punishes, and actually brings forth evil for his own good purposes.

If evil in the world actually arose contrary to all of God's intentions and purposes, it would indicate that he did not have full control of the world he created. Evil in the world must be under God's sovereign control and work ultimately for good, otherwise he would not have complete control and authority over his own creation: "if we maintain that God does not use evil to fulfill his purposes, then we would have to admit that there is evil in the universe that God did not intend, is not under his control, and might not fulfill his purposes."[64] In such a case, God would not be omnipotent; evil could continually escalate and become overwhelmingly negative and destructive, ending in total chaos and annihilation.

In contrast to this, Scripture indicates in many places that God does bring forth evil in the world, controls it, and uses it for his own good purposes. In Isaiah 45:6-7 God speaks of himself as the fully sovereign Lord of creation who brings forth all things, both good and evil: "I am the Lord, and there is no other. I form the light and create darkness, I bring prosperity and create evil." Grudem points out that the Hebrew word *rā'*, used for evil here, and translated as "disaster" in the NIV, is a common one used for evil in general senses. A similar meaning is found in Lamentations 3:38, using a closely related Hebrew expression for evil, *rā 'ah*: "Is it not from the mouth of the Most High that good and evil come?" The same word is used in Amos 3:6: "When evil [disaster] comes to a city, has not the Lord caused it?"[65]

To be omnipotent, God must be in control of both good and evil. In his discussion of the problem of evil, John Frame holds to Scriptural teachings: "Somehow, we must confess both that God has a role in bringing evil about, and that in doing so he is holy and blameless . . . . God does bring sins about, but always for his own good purposes. So in bringing sin to pass, he himself does not commit sin."[66] Clear Scriptural statement that God brings forth evil and uses it for a greater good purpose is found in "the most evil deed of all history, the crucifixion of Christ." God predestined this event, which in some ways of looking at it is unthinkable, an ultimate horror—that the eternal God would be put to death, and would give Himself up to death for the sake of human beings. But more than anything else it shows God's infinite love: in order to save humans from their own folly, God willingly *died*. More strongly than any, this great, *predestined* event shows us that God brings about evil for his own good purposes—in this case, an infinitely wonderful good.[67] "It is essential to realize that even though God does bring evil into the world, he does it for a good reason. Therefore, he does not *do* evil in bringing evil to pass."[68]

God created the earth and human beings, and he loves his creation, but he also placed a curse on the earth and on humans at the start. Since God is the sole and supreme Creator of all that exists, he has complete sovereignty over his creation. His goodness, holiness, and will are supreme and authoritative, and his word is law. But from the beginning there has been disobedience and revolt against his authority and law. Lucifer's (Satan's) self-centered rebellion against God came first, followed by his temptation of Adam and Eve, and their disobedience. Disobedience of God, or *moral evil*, is the breaking of God's laws or commands. With Adam and Eve it resulted in the Fall of the human race. A consequence of the Fall has been *natural evil*: God cursed the ground [earth], and cursed humans with struggles, pain, injuries, "accidents," suffering, sickness, and death. Natural evil also includes all disasters such as earthquakes, hurricanes, and tornadoes. *"Natural evil is a curse brought upon the world because of moral evil. It functions as punishment to the wicked and as a means of discipline for those who are righteous by God's grace. It also reminds us of the cosmic dimensions of sin and redemption.* Sin brought death to the human race but also to the world over which man was to rule. God has ordained that the universe resist its human ruler until that ruler stops resisting God."[69] Because evil continues, divine wrath will continue until the time of final judgment of evil, and establishment of a new heaven and new earth in which there will be no pain, suffering, and death.

Whether in daily life or in covenant, God not only blesses, but disciplines and punishes. He blesses those who love and follow him. But those who grow proud and turn their backs on him are "humbled by oppression, calamity, and sorrow" (Psalm 107:39). "The Lord is righteous in all his ways and loving toward all he has made" (Psalm 145: 17). The same Psalm tells us that "The Lord watches over all who love him, but the wicked he will destroy" (v. 20). Many Scriptural passages tell of God's providential control and disciplining of his people, control of historical events, and punishment of nations and individuals for their resistance and evil deeds.

Individuals have a choice to believe or not believe in God. They may choose to believe in "other gods" or "no god." But sustained disbelief in the one true God comes at a severe price—the loss of truth, degradation of knowledge and character, and eventual punishment or death. While God is slow to anger and judgment, those who turn against him, especially against his decrees, covenants, and acts for creation, encounter his wrath, depending on the degree and kind of their opposition. Human beings always have a choice, to believe or not believe in God the sovereign Creator and Savior, to obey him or disobey, to serve or oppose him. Notwithstanding God's full sovereign control of creation, human beings do have decisions and choices that bring about real results. Geisler is in harmony with the Bible in saying that "human beings are totally depraved," that "sin extends to the whole person, 'spirit, soul, and body.'" But while total depravity is extensive, it is not intensive: it does not destroy a person's ability to know good from evil and to choose the good over the evil, otherwise "it would have destroyed man's ability to sin." Total depravity "does not destroy a person's humanness," his ability to think, feel, and choose; "without rational and volitional capability, a person would not be able to sin."[70]

Geisler is also in harmony with the Bible in holding that God did not foreknow a person's actions as *necessary*, but as *free*. We have a free choice to believe or disbelieve, to do good or evil. Geisler supports Calvinist Stephen Charnock's statement that God not only foreknew that we would do the actions we do, He knew that we would do them *freely*. God foresaw that a person's will would freely determine to do this or that. Human free choice is in this way established rather than removed. While God "*prompts* our act of faith, He does not *perform* it—it is, after all, our act. While God aids our choice, He does not choose for us. He provides the impetus and assistance, but we must make the decision to believe."[71] The next chapter will explore these matters further.

Chapter Ten

The Holiness and Justice of God
Sin, Punishment, Death, War, And God's Plan for Human History

The earth is the Lord's, and everything in it, the world, and all who live in it. (Psalm 24:1)

There is no god besides me. I put to death and I bring to life, I have wounded and I will heal. (Deuteronomy 32:39)

Since God is before all things, created all things, upholds all things, is above all things, and owns all things, He is the rightful ruler of all things.[1]

The god of this age has blinded the minds of unbelievers, so that they cannot see the light of the gospel of the glory of Christ, who is the image of God. (2 Corinthians 4:4)

For the wages of sin is death, but the gift of God is eternal life in Christ Jesus our Lord. (Romans 6:23)

Why Evil? What are the explanations for evil in the world? It is a very difficult question to deal with. Many answers can and have been given. Biblical answers can be given to some of the most troubling matters. While the Bible tells us much about God, his plan, laws, commands, and covenants it does not answer every question we may have. The Bible indicates that neither humans nor angels know all the answers. We know that the Almighty Creator God is in control of creation and history. But the mind and will of God, in some matters, remains unknown to us.

The first step in dealing with the question of good and evil is acknowledgment of God as the Supreme Being, Sovereign Creator, and Lord of His Creation (discussed in chapters 1-5, 9). Without this basis the answer remains elusive. But if God is the Creator of all things, all things belong to Him. God is thus the Sovereign Lord of His creation and can do with it as He pleases (Isaiah 46:9-10). What He wills conforms to His nature—always good, loving, holy, and just. As Sovereign Lord, God's decrees, laws, commands, and covenants are of crucial importance for answering questions about the reasons for evil in the world.

At the very beginning God created the universe by his word, bringing existing things out of nothing, creating matter, energy, time, light in darkness and giving the heavenly bodies their laws to obey. This authoritative establishment of order in creation shows God's relationship as Sovereign Lord to his creation: the world began by God's word of command; the universe, with the stars, sun, moon, and all other things, obeyed by coming into existence, and continued to obey God's commands and laws. Day and night were given appointed times of arrival by the Lord. God's creation also included the creation of the first man and woman, and establishment of laws for their behavior. Made in the image of God, they were required to worship and obey their Creator, permanently united as man and wife (a covenant relationship), create families and human society, and rule over creation as God's image-bearing regents.

The creation of the universe and the first human beings exhibits features like those of binding divine covenants:[2] God ordains, creation obeys. Obedience to God is good, rather than oppressive, because God always leads and directs to the good. Human disobedience of God is always movement away from truth and goodness. Rights and benefits are promised, but without obedience humans can be punished, and much can be lost. God's sovereign relationship as Lord of creation is eternal. And God has made some modifications in ways of dealing with human beings as they have grown, expanded, learned . . . and disobeyed.

Lucifer's Rebellion. At some point in creation, God the eternal, uncreated Spirit created a multitude of spirit beings known as angels. The Bible indicates that evil first entered creation by the acts of Lucifer (Satan) and one-third of all the angels, with their rebellion against God at some time before Adam and Eve sinned. Led by Lucifer, they apparently attempted to rise above God's dominion and establish their own self-rule, with Lucifer as their new prince, "like the Most High."[3] This primal sin essentially arose from pride, disregard of God's sovereign rule, and the desire to be fully self-directed (autonomous). Sin and evil thus originated with Lucifer, who disobeyed God before Adam and Eve did. Lucifer was good, beautiful, and wise when created, but with his rebellion and fall, his wisdom was distorted, and he became corrupted with a multitude of iniquities. Since Lucifer and the other angels were created as spirit beings, it was impossible for their corrupted natures to be changed and redeemed after their sins. They were forever fixed in the resulting evil natures. Lucifer was thereafter known as Satan, the devil, the great dragon, and other names. The angels who followed him became known as evil spirits or demons. The subsequent role of Satan, with the help of his demons, was to try to establish his own kingdom apart from God by tempting and deceiving human beings to follow him in disobedience of God's word, law, commands, and covenants, and thereby disrupt God's creation. The first man and woman were his first victims.

The revolt of Lucifer constitutes the origin of evil in creation. For the first time a clear contrast and opposition between the good of God and the evil of Satan existed. Before, there had only been good, the goodness of God. There is no cosmic dualism in this, however: while Satan is powerful, he is merely a created being; his existence is dependent upon God, and his power is miniscule in comparison to the Almighty Creator.

A Moral Choice. God must have had a good purpose in permitting Lucifer to rebel and establish evil. He must have known and foreordained Lucifer's revolt and fall. Otherwise He would have been ignorant of it, and his creation would have been to that extent out of his control. Furthermore, He foreordained the solution to sin and death in the work of Christ. The key result was that when humans were created, they did not simply have the goodness of God as the only possibility for their life; they could choose to follow the trickery, lies, and deceits of Satan. The ultimate significance was that they were forced to make a *choice* between good and evil. Without the existence of an evil principle (a real, spirit being) there would have been no such choice, only a blind following of the good.

Humans were thus required by God's foreordained plan to make a choice between good and evil; it is intrinsically a moral choice, and a moral test. God required humans to define themselves, to *prove* themselves, by making a moral choice between good and evil. This is a major reason there is evil in the world: by its contrast and opposition to good, it is meant to define and magnify the good, holy nature of God, glorify Him, and require a moral choice that determines human destinies. "God sets morally and spiritually responsible alternatives before human beings, leaving the *choice* and *responsibility* to them."[4] A second major reason is that God "chose to permit evil in order to defeat it, thus bringing about a greater good." His permission of evil in the world would eventually lead to its ultimate, total defeat, and the final establishment of God's Kingdom as eternal, holy, and perfectly good.[5]

Before their temptation and sin Adam and Eve knew nothing of evil, and the difference between good and evil. When Satan, in the form of a serpent, told Eve to eat the forbidden fruit, he slandered God by telling a lie: "You will not surely die." But he also told a partial truth: "For God knows that when you eat of it your eyes will be opened, and you will be like God, knowing good and evil." By disobeying God and eating the fruit, "the eyes of both of them were opened," and they came to realize they were "naked"—they knew they had done something *wrong* and *shameful*: for the first time they knew the difference between good and evil (Gen. 3:1-11).

Satan has the power of a powerful angel. Another result of his foreordained revolt against God is his ongoing struggle against God, creating a continuing spiritual warfare—a conflict and warfare of Satan and his followers against God and his followers. Satan is capable of great depths of evil, as great as anyone can imagine, by influencing those who follow his deceitful and corrupting influences. By his rebellion against God and deceit of the first humans he is the father of death. The Bible calls him "a liar and the father of lies," and a murderer.[6] Liars, murderers, and warmongers are among his boldest followers. History shows us to what depths it has led. Can there be anything *worse* than the worst things we have witnessed in our era—the brutal torturing, maiming, and killing of millions upon millions during World War II: the horrific and inhuman ways of Hitler and Stalin; the later evil deeds of Saddam Hussein, with the name of "Allah" constantly on his lips; suicide bombers blowing themselves and scores of civilians up almost daily, again in the name of "Allah." What can be more evil? But the Bible promises a final reckoning with Satan and with all evil, a final end to evil, and the establishment of God's eternal holy kingdom. (This will be the subject of the next two chapters of this book.)

Without God there is no ultimate basis for identification of moral good.[7] Since God is Supremely Good, he is that real basis. Since original creation was good, and Adam and Eve were created good, it seems that without the presence of the tree of knowledge of good and evil in Eden, and the presence of temptation and deception in the form of Satan, there would have been no basis for distinction of evil from good, and no temptation for them to do evil. And considering the fact that God fully plans and controls what is to happen in creation, as well as the fact that before creation He decreed the work of Christ on the cross to save people from their sins,[8] the rebellion of these angels must have been part of God's prior decree for permitting evil to exist so that human's could be tempted and make a choice between good and evil. But everyone since the beginning has sinned.[9] Christ's sacrifice then served as a gift of free redemption from sin, requiring only belief and trust in God. In these ways human beings could be tested and proven fit or unfit for the consummation of creation in eternal Paradise with God.

Disobedience Brings Punishment. Under the creation covenant,[10] Adam and Eve were being tested by God for their obedience. They were prohibited from eating the fruit of the tree of the knowledge of good and evil. Letting themselves be deceived by Satan, in the form of a serpent, they doubted God's word, and disobeyed his command not to eat the fruit. By their disobedience, they, who had been created good, came to do and know evil, and to be punished with many ill effects for their act. Just to encounter evil is bad. Experiencing it within your self is worse. They began to *see* evil for the first time—in their nakedness. They felt shame and guilt, and then tried to shift the blame for their disobedience. Having been created pure and innocent by God, they became sinful by disobedience. This fall into sin was not limited to them, it also brought condemnation on the entire human race: "the result of one trespass was condemnation for all men."[11] Their sin also brought the punishment of death for them and for all humankind after them, instead of the eternal life for which they had been created. Covenants usually come with warnings and some description of punishment or curses for disobedience. In this case, God had previously warned Adam that if this command was disobeyed, he would "surely die."[12] Why does evil exist in the world? Why do humans die? Sin is the key biblical answer—disobedience of the Holy God. Lucifer disobeyed first. Then Adam's sin caused the fall from original, created goodness of humankind, and involved all of his descendants in sin, condemnation, and death.

The paradisiacal created state in the Garden of Eden was lost. Human lives were greatly changed. Human character was broadly corrupted by the entrance of sin. All future human offspring came under the dominion of sin and death through the sin of the first man.[13] Unlike before, woman would now live with trouble and conflict with her husband, with much pain in childbirth, and man would have conflicts with his wife. Both would be subject to pain, suffering, sickness, and death. Nature had fallen as well as humans. God cursed the ground (the earth) so that it produced "thorns and thistles" to resist humans and cause pain and struggle. Later Scripture tells us that the whole of creation was placed "in bondage to decay" and "has been groaning as in the pains of childbirth right up to the present time" (Romans 8:20-23). These verses indicate that "the entire material universe languishes in a state of dysfunction."[14] Originally peaceful animals became wild and carnivorous. Instead of eternal life in a beautiful and harmonious garden, the world now brought forth resistance, pain, suffering, and death.[15]

The original creation of the Garden of Eden was perfect. Scripture tells us that God is perfect and that his works and way are perfect.[16] Since God is perfect, it follows that his original creation was perfect: "*Nothing less than perfect can come from an absolutely perfect Being.*"[17] Thus, the imperfect and evil effects we know in created nature—all those that resist, threaten, and cause pain or death to humans, such as lightening, earthquakes, tsunamis, cyclones, hurricanes, tornados, volcanoes, poisonous plants and snakes, and dangerous animals—must surely be the result of the Fall, the effects of sin, and the continued workings of Satan and his demons. But the Bible says that with the removal of the curse from nature in the future Millennium reign of Christ, snakes and animals will no longer be dangerous, and there will be no diseases or birth defects.[18] All such evils, including death, will be absent in the Eternal Kingdom of God. Adam and Eve were created to live eternally in perfect goodness, health, and harmony, if they remained in faithful obedience and communion with God. But they failed the first test. Their disobedience resulted in a multitude of evils. Scripture tells us that God has graciously provided a remedy and restoration since then. Evil will be defeated. The restoration and highest state of Paradise for the redeemed after the end of human history is promised to be free of all such evils. In this way God's original plan for creation will be fully and perfectly achieved.

The Effects of Sin. Considering the many evils and glaring sinfulness of human history, it now seems inevitable that the first humans would sin. God knew that this would happen, because the Bible tells us that He foreordained the remedy for it *before* creation—the birth, ministry, and work of the divine Savior.[19] The work of Jesus Christ fulfilled the New Covenant, which was preceded by the Old Testaments covenants from creation, Eden, and Adam, through Noah, Abraham, Moses, and David. God must have preordained all of these covenants, since they are closely interrelated, and they predict and lead progressively to the appearance and work of Jesus Christ. The work of Jesus Christ, related in the Bible, is the culmination of God's plan to offer salvation and redemption from sins to all people, so that a Paradise of eternal life and happiness, greater than that of Eden, is made possible through belief and faith in Christ.

Further consideration of the results and effects of the sins of the first humans help us to understand and answer the question of why there is evil in the world. Grudem presents the matter of sin inherited from Adam in a clear way. God "regards the human race as an organic whole, a unity, represented by Adam as its head . . . . As our representative, Adam sinned, and God counted us guilty as well as Adam." This is the meaning of the theological expression, "Adam's sin is *imputed* to all humanity." Grudem prefers the term "inherited sin" over the traditional "original sin" because it clearly refers to "the guilt and tendency to sin with which we are born."[20]

All human beings inherit a sinful nature because of Adam's sin. Grudem thinks that "inherited corruption" expresses this more clearly than the traditional "original sin" or "original pollution." David, a man of great faith from his youth onward, humbly acknowledged his own inherent sinful nature after being confronted by the prophet Nathan for his adultery with Bathsheba: "Have mercy on me, O God . . . wash away all my iniquity and cleanse me from my sin . . . . Surely I was sinful at birth, sinful from the time my mother conceived me."[21] This is a "strong statement of the inherent tendency to sin that attaches to our lives from the very beginning," even from conception.[22] Another Psalm expresses the same, innate sinful nature: "The wicked go astray from the womb, they err from their birth, speaking lies."[23] Paul affirms that before being saved, we all lived in the ways of the world, among the disobedient, "gratifying the cravings of our sinful nature and following its desires and thoughts. Like the rest, we were by nature children of wrath."[24]

Not all human beings are as bad as they could be, however. Family, society, and law create restraints. And there has been much good from individuals, societies, and cultures down through history, due to "God's common grace."[25] As we well know from experience, some people go much further in evil ways than others. The many moral evils that we see throughout history, and in recent abundance, stem essentially from sinful human nature, a nature that can be further expanded and distorted to incredible depths of depravity and horror.

Because of original or inherited sin, Geisler writes, "Human beings are totally depraved; that is, sin extends to every part of human nature, including body and soul, mind, will, and emotion. No facet of our being is immune to sin's pervasive influence. However, while total depravity is extensive, extending to every part of a human being, nonetheless, it is not intensive." This does not mean that fallen humans are as sinful as they could be, but that they are not as good as they must be in God's sight. Total depravity does not totally destroy a person's humanness; nor does it totally destroy the image of God in which human beings are created. It mars and corrupts, but does not totally destroy. If it did, a person "would not be able to think, feel, or choose; without rational and volitional capacity, a person would not be able to sin."

While humans are totally incapable of initiating or attaining salvation by their own power, they *are* capable of receiving or rejecting it. Every human being born since Adam is "spiritually dead," spiritually separated from God and totally unable to achieve or obtain salvation by his or her own efforts. No one can please God or come to God by his own power.[26] As Jesus said, "No one can come to me unless the Father who sent me draws him."[27] However, this does not mean that fallen humans are so depraved that they have no capacity to understand and respond to God's message. The context of Ephesians 2:8-9 shows that "salvation from spiritual death comes 'through faith.'" Despite original sin, humans still have the capability of believing and accepting the grace of God for salvation. If this were not true, the Bible could not justly call every person to believe in God and be saved. Without this capability there would be no free choice to believe or not to believe.[28]

Geisler points out that the effect of inherited sin on all human beings is so great that human life and society would be devastated if it were not for God's "common grace" (God's non-saving grace available to all living persons). Without it, the blinding effects of sin "would make it impossible for us to recognize evil as such"; the deceiving effects of sin "would make rational thought and action virtually impossible"; the debasing effects "would be destructive of self and others"; the corrupting effects "would produce moral decay that would dominate society"; the debilitating effects "would make the performance of social good unachievable"; and the judicial effects "would produce overwhelming guilt."[29]

Inherited sin leaves one without the proper guidance of God's Spirit of love and goodness. This makes a person naturally capable of committing sins by his own thoughts and actions. Even a very "good" person living with inherited sin is bound to commit additional sins of some degree. Some people go further than others. Then there are those who go to greater and greater extremes of evil, not always in their own view, but certainly by the laws of God, and often by those of society as well. All sins to a greater or lesser degree ignore or break the new commandment to love God with all one's heart and love one's neighbor as one's self.

Salvation Through Belief, Faith, and Grace. The relationship of God's divine sovereignty and human freedom is one of the most difficult questions of Christian theology. Modern Calvinism tends to emphasize God's sovereignty to the point that human freedom of choice remains unexplainable, or is essentially lost. On the other hand, Arminianism tends to emphasize human freedom to the point that God's sovereignty and grace is reduced or lost.[30] Contrary to such views, a proper understanding of God's full sovereignty and human freedom should not diminish the proper role of either: God's complete sovereignty as Creator must be understood even though He gives human beings the freedom to choose between good and evil, belief and disbelief. Throughout the Old and New Testaments people are constantly required to make decisions, choose what they will do, and act. They are urged and commanded to choose to believe in God, trust Him, and follow His laws and commandments. But one can only *choose* if one has the freedom to choose—if one's "choices" are not unilaterally or coercively predetermined or forced by God. "Forced freedom, whether of good or evil, is contrary to the nature of God as love and contrary to the God-given nature of human beings as free. Forced freedom is a contradiction in terms."[31]

Norman Geisler has put forward an answer to the very difficult question of God's total sovereignty and predetermination relative to human free will and responsibility on matters of moral choice and salvation. It is an answer that is in harmony with biblical teachings. A key biblical verse is 1 Peter

1:2, which says that we are "elect according to the foreknowledge of God the Father, in sanctification of the Spirit, for obedience and sprinkling of the blood of Jesus Christ" (NKJV). This verse indicates that "there is no chronological or logical priority of election and foreknowledge [of salvation]." Geisler quotes Walvoord who says the verse indicates that election and foreknowledge are "coextensive." Geisler explains that since God is the eternal, simple (fully unified in essence and attributes) Being, and since His thoughts must be eternally unified and coordinate, what He foreknows and what He forechooses are "simultaneous, eternal, and coordinate acts." Both foreknowledge and predetermination are one and eternal in God. "Whatever God knows, He determines. And whatever He determines, He knows." We may thus say that God *knowingly determines* and *determinately knows* "from all eternity everything that happens, including all free acts." It follows that "whatever God forechooses cannot be based on what He foreknows. Nor can what he foreknows be based on what He forechose. Thus, our moral actions are truly free, and God determined that they would be such. God is totally sovereign in the sense of actually determining what occurs, and yet man is completely free and responsible for what he does."[32]

Geisler supports Stephen Charnock's statement that God not only foreknew that we would do the things we do, He knew that we would do them *freely*. God foresaw that a person's will would freely determine to do one thing or the other. Human free choice is in this way established rather than removed. The *Westminster Confession of Faith* holds that while all things come to pass through God's foreknowledge and decree as first cause, he orders them to take place according to second causes, "either necessarily, freely, or contingently." And concerning free will, it states: "God hath endued the will of man with that natural liberty, that is neither forced, nor by any absolute necessity of nature determined to good or evil."[33]

Geisler identifies his "balanced view" as "moderate Calvinism," and clearly distinguishes it from "strong or extreme" Calvinism and from Arminianism. Simply expressed, moderate Calvinism holds that God's predetermination is *in accord with* or *coextensive* with His foreknowledge, thereby accommodating God's total sovereignty and human freedom of choice (the power of contrary choice). In a quite different view, extreme Calvinism holds that "predetermination is *independent of* foreknowledge." Among its problems is a loss or denial of human free choice that points to the use of divine force or coercion in election and damnation. And the extreme Calvinist claim of "limited atonement" suggests that God loves only the limited elect, and "does not really love all sinners and desire them to be saved." Such Calvinism tips the balance of freedom and choice heavily to the divine sphere. Arminianism, on the other hand, claims that "God's predetermination is *based on* His foreknowledge." A problem with this view is that God's choice or election of people to salvation would be based on human decisions rather than divine grace.[34] Arminianism thus tips the balance heavily into the human sphere.

The sins of Lucifer and Adam were not unilaterally *caused* by God, but were *self-caused* by those created beings. Nevertheless, their situations, decisions, and choices were still part of the eternal, sovereign plan of the omniscient, omnipotent Creator. God is never the efficient cause of sin and evil. Self-caused human *actions*, as everyday life constantly shows, are clearly possible, although self-caused *beings* are not possible. We do not cause ourselves, but we have a *choice* in causing our actions.[35] God, who by His holy nature is unable to sin, did not efficiently *cause* either Satan or Adam to sin. Being all-loving and omnibenevolent, God does not cause anyone to sin and be dammed for eternity; nor does He force anyone to believe and be saved. That would be an unjust act of coercion. It must be by a person's own freely chosen acts.

The original situations with Satan and Adam show that self-caused actions by angels and humans are possible. "Self-caused" means caused by an individual self or person (my *self*, I, or another self).[36] The Garden of Eden narrative shows that God creates and makes possible situations in which choices between good and evil are not only possible, but *required*. He does not coercively determine that anyone must commit evil or must do good, however. Adam was *free* to eat any fruit in the garden, but he was warned *not* to *choose* to eat the fruit of one particular tree.[37] He had the *option* of doing so, but was warned against it and promised dire consequences by God if he did. That was a situation requiring a *choice*. God allows each and every person to make his or her own choice. God does not force anyone to do good or do evil. Moral decisions are by nature not matters of force, but of choice. There must be personal choice in order to establish personal lawfulness or guilt, righteousness or sin.

Romans 1:18-21 indicates that humans since Adam's fall still have important knowledge of God and of right choices, but *suppress* it and turn away from it by *choice*:

The wrath of God is being revealed from heaven against all the godlessness and wickedness of men who suppress the truth by their wickedness, since what may be known about God is plain to them, because God has made it plain to them. For since the creation of the world God's invisible qualities—his eternal power and divine nature—have been clearly seen, being understood from what has been made, so that men are without excuse. For although they knew God, they neither glorified him as God nor gave thanks to him, but their thinking became futile and their foolish hearts were darkened.

In these ways people know God and his "righteous decree," but choose to deny them as worthless, and do the opposite. They "invent [that is, personally *choose*] ways of doing evil." As a result, they become more and more degraded, corrupted, and trapped by their own evil *choices*:

since they did not think it worthwhile to retain the knowledge of God, he gave them over to a depraved mind, to do what ought not to be done. They have become filled with every kind of wickedness, evil, greed and depravity. They are full of envy, murder, strife, deceit and malice. They are gossips, slanderers, God-haters, insolent, arrogant and boastful; they invent ways of doing evil; they disobey their parents; they are senseless, faithless, heartless, ruthless. Although they know God's righteous decree that those who do such things deserve death, they not only continue to do these very things but also approve of those who practice them [Romans 1: 28-32].

God's sovereignty does not mean that He unilaterally determines, forces, or coerces some to be saved and others to be damned. God wants *everyone* to *choose* not to sin, but instead to believe, have faith, and live moral and holy lives. Not just some, but "all people" are called on by God to believe in Him and to repent: "he commands *all* people everywhere to repent" (Acts 17:30). God our Savior, "wants *all* men to be saved and to come to a knowledge of the truth. For there is one God and one mediator between God and men, the man Christ Jesus, who gave himself as a ransom for *all* men" (1 Timothy 2:3-6). "He is the atoning sacrifice for our sins, and not only for ours but also for the sins of the *whole world*" (1 John 2:2). The Lord "is patient with you, not wanting anyone to perish, but *everyone* to come to repentance" (2 Peter 3:9).[38]

It is through the choice to believe and the act of faith that people are saved. The message of Romans 10:9-13 is clear and to the point: "if you confess with your mouth, 'Jesus is Lord,' and *believe* in your heart that God raised him from the dead, you will be saved. For it is with your heart that you believe and are justified, and it is with your mouth that you confess and are saved." *All* who do this will be saved: "Everyone who calls on the name of the Lord will be saved" (Romans 10:9-13; cf. Joel 2:32). Similarly, John tells us, "to all who received him, to those who *believed* in his name, he gave the right to become children of God." All who choose to believe are saved by grace through faith: "For it is by grace you have been saved, through faith—and this not from yourselves, it is the gift of God—not by works, so that no one can boast" (Ephesians 2:8-9). These verses mean that *salvation* is not from ourselves, but *belief and faith* are.[39] Romans 10:16 says, "faith *comes* by hearing, and hearing by the word of God (NKJV)."

Explicating over two dozen verses pertaining to belief, faith, grace, and salvation, Geisler concludes that "the uniform presentation of Scripture is that faith is something unbelievers are to exercise to receive salvation . . . and not something they must wait upon God to give them . . . . Everywhere the Bible assumes that anyone who wills to be saved can exercise saving faith . . . . The Bible describes faith as *ours* and not God's. It speaks of '*your* faith' (Luke 7:50), '*his* faith' (Rom. 4:5), and '*their* faith' (Matt. 9:2), but never of '*God's* faith.'"[40] Such exercise of belief and faith is possible for a relatively good unsaved person as well as for a bad sinner (e.g., the thief on the cross). Even liars, alcoholics, and murderers sometimes repent, believe, and are saved. But as a person goes further and further into sin, their character changes, darkens, and hardens. Not all turn to belief and faith and are saved by God's grace. Many choose to resist and turn away.[41] Some proceed ever deeper into evil ways.

The Degrees and Depths of Evil. Simple lack of caring and lack of courtesy and consideration, ranging further to coldness, rudeness, and hatefulness, are common, lower-degree forms of sin in comparison to murder. Nevertheless, they are sins that reveal lack of proper love for one's fellow human being. And God's standards for creation are the highest: we must treat others in the best ways we would treat ourselves. How else can separate and different individuals get along in good or perfect harmony? How else can we avoid making another person feel bad, slighted, hurt, depressed, or angry? Some people develop emotional problems because of such treatment. And they often provoke a worse sin in retaliation. The villain in films and dramas is usually cold or harsh, distorted by his own self-interest (and modern novels and films often emphasize repulsive forms in oppressive "religious" leaders, such as Mr. Brocklehurst in *Jane Eyre*, the self-interest, social climbing, and animalistic appetites of Vicar Collins in *Pride and Prejudice*, or the lusty appetites of a charismatic Elmer Gantry).

Many people go several steps further away from love of their fellow man. Prevailing self-interest leads them to take advantage of others through high financial charges in order to gain wealth. Cheating, lying, and manipulation can become part of this pursuit, adding further degrees of guilt. Lying for various reasons is a common sin, often in attempt to cover up another sin (prominent examples being the Watergate burglary, and more recent corporate abuse of loans or finances). Such things often wreck reputations, lives, and careers. Lies are often used in attempts to conceal theft, illicit sex, marital infidelity, and physical abuse. False testimony is a sin as repulsive to most people as it is odious to God. Vulgar language and cursing is also a repulsive sin that can be carried to greater and greater degrees. The impulses behind it—anger, hatred, foul feelings and behavior, self-assertion, and aggressive violence—are contrary to decency, love, and respect for others. Vulgar and suggestive ways of talking—often encountered in society and on

TV today—and foul curse words—especially heard in films, for so-called expressive and entertainment value—indicate a broad deterioration of public moral sensibility.

Developing tendencies of inherited sin further are examples of various kinds of drug abuse. Abuse of alcohol can be deteriorating and deadly for anyone, and equally harmful for family and friends. Many people of high social or cultural standing have sought treatment for abuse of alcohol in America. Many others have failed to curb it—one could make a long list of stars of film and music. Tragically, the use of various drugs, such as amphetamines, marijuana, cocaine, and heroin, has risen to public prominence in America. The demand and the high-money stakes involved, along with inadequate moral conviction, seem to keep it from being stopped, or to prevent its growth and spread, even to schools, teenagers, and younger children. Use of drugs grievously deteriorates a person spiritually, morally, and physically. It can rob a person of mentality, self-respect, and self-control. It often demands other evils—robbery, assault, prostitution, murder. At its worst drug abuse can destroy a person's moral sensibility, and can finally cost their life. Drug abuse is a horrendous sin, and an abomination to God and to human society. The widespread existence of it in America in recent years indicates a morally deteriorating society.

Sexual immorality is another sin of increasing degrees of seriousness. In God's creation covenant, laws, and throughout the Old and New Testaments, sex is strictly limited to marriage between a man and a woman.[42] Sex outside of marriage is a sin. Adultery is a sin by not only being outside of marriage, but by the lie involved in breaking the marriage vow, and the gross mistreatment of the marriage partner. Divorce is also sinful as a breaking of the marriage vow or covenant. Sexual immorality is one of the most common sins of human beings throughout history. Many people have engaged in sex with numerous partners within and without marriage, and in adultery. Prostitution has existed from ancient times. In ancient pagan societies it was regarded not only as right, but even as a religious pursuit. Jewish and Christian teachings during the eras of Greece and Rome, contrasted sharply with such pagan ways. Secular and libertarian views of sex have risen to high levels of popularity and acceptance in America over the past sixty or seventy years. Today public films regularly show naked bodies, caressing, fondling, and explicit sexual intercourse, often of unmarried partners, or of adulterous relationships. TV soap operas deal incessantly with these themes, and only a little less explicitly. TV commercials use sexual appeal, suggestive language, and bumps and grinds, to advertise almost anything as part of the good life of freedom, fun, and pleasure. One gets the impression that the life of complete freedom and pleasure is the right way for any normal, red-blooded American.

I am worth it—I deserve it—I need it—all we need is good looks, a cool car, the right clothes, fun, pleasure, good food and drinks, health-aids, and the liberating advice of Dr. DiddleDum.

Newspapers every day carry accounts of sexual assault, battery, or rape. Rape is a horrible sin and crime. Just short of murder, it is one of the blackest, most despicable violations of a person's rights and sanctity as a human being. Often the motive is just selfish lust. At other times it is predominantly aggressive violence or hatred. In all cases sex is being twisted to exactly the opposite of what God intended. Instead of the most intimate, loving communion of devoted husband and wife, it becomes self-centered, brutal violation of a person's selfhood. Victims usually feel horribly violated and dirty, beyond cleansing. It often affects their mental and emotional life badly, sometimes for years, or a lifetime. Rapists are often men who have some serious character flaws or a series of crimes in their past, and are already morally stunted and warped as a result. Some of the lowest and most despicable reprobates among them are the pedophiles who rape, and at times kidnap and kill children. As bad or worse are the examples of priests who rape or entice children to sex. But there are also women who entice men into such lustful, uncommitted sexual relations. And we have read about some women teachers who entice underage boys into sex with them.

Murder is in many ways the ultimate crime among human beings. The life that God created is snuffed out by another creature. What is behind it? What are the motives? Taking examples of some of the murders cited in the last chapter, it will help to suggest some possible motives and background (possible motives, rather than specific detective work). Theft is the primary cause for many murders, as in the case of a football star, and the murder of whole families or children. In the times in which we live, drug-use often requires theft. To serious drug addicts, human life means little or nothing. Uncounted numbers of jealous and disconsolate husbands have killed their separated or divorced wives, and at times all their children. The reasons usually seem clear. The breakup of marriage causes great pain, anxiety, and depression, mixed with surges of jealousy, hatred, and rage. Real bonds were snapped that were not meant to be. The pain and sense of loss are nearly impossible to suppress. Jealousy rages and can consume a person's thoughts. It can drive a person to depression and near madness, so that the only way to end it appears to be murder and suicide. How did the breakup come about? Often it begins with inconsiderateness, selfishness, rudeness, and hatefulness that lead to heated arguments, verbal abuse, swearing, and even beatings; further possible reasons include gross neglect, drinking, drugs, and unfaithfulness—all ways of breaking God's laws for marriage and for society. The lack of love—rudeness, anger, meanness, selfishness—can lead to worse things, even murder.

Why did the woman chemist knock out her husband with a stun gun and stuff him head first into a barrel of acid, dissolving his flesh? No doubt it included some of the above reasons. Intense hatred seems to have been involved, possibly arising from heated arguments or physical abuse. Unfaithfulness on the part of the woman (and perhaps the man) also appears likely. Why did the young man kill his girlfriend, then fillet and cook parts of her body? They had broken up and he seems to have been consumed by jealousy because she had another boyfriend. But the filleting and cooking suggests a twisted mentality that may have grown out of the breakup, or resulted from use of drugs or other previous sins in his life. Why did the pig farmer kill many prostitutes and drug addicts, cut up their remains and feed them to his pigs? That may result from intense hatred, or deranged mentality, the causes of which are impossible to trace unless one knows in detail the history of the man. Some kind of pseudo-religious mania may have been involved. Or it may have been from some serious sins of the farmer himself, and his attempts to suppress them and assuage his own guilt by killing prostitutes and drug addicts. Evil does not cancel out evil, however. And God neither calls for the killing of other sinners, nor tolerates murder and atrocities. The sixth commandment says: "You shall not murder" (Exodus 20). But long before that, in the time of Noah, God had said: "Whoever sheds the blood of man, by man shall his blood be shed; for in the image of God has God made man" (Genesis 9:6). One could go on and on with such cases of murder as these.

Why do such evils exist? They are certainly not the fault or responsibility of God. God is perfect and morally pure. The Bible repeatedly makes it clear that all the sins discussed above are *against* God's basic laws; they are forbidden and condemned by God, and are destined to be punished to the same degree as the offense. The Bible extensively discusses examples of sins, and often reveals the consequences or punishments. It constantly warns us *not* to commit these sins. That means that, if we will heed God's word, and seek to do right, God will help us avoid what is wrong, and do what is right. That is not easy, however, since we are born in inherited sin, with a tendency not to consider God and his word worthwhile. The more we emphasize such tendencies, the more we will proceed to sins like those described above. While God controls and determines all events that occur in the world, humans do have the right, if they choose to heed God's commands, and the societal laws based on them, to choose between right and wrong. It is the human beings who choose to do such sinful acts that are fully responsible for them.

While some people turn to God early in life, others do not. They may begin with a simple lack of interest in God and the Bible. As time goes on they make choices—decisions that can continue to lead away from God and his laws for human life. By continuing this direction the sinful life accumulates and solidifies, causing the person to be less and less amenable to consideration of God. Many people continue to lead essentially respectable lives in this way, abiding by accepted social laws and ethical guidelines and making contributions to society and culture. They may take a naturalistic view of life, reducing or eliminating belief in the divine and supernatural. Some go further, becoming so incredulous of anything not experienced as part of their daily life that they end as extreme skeptics or atheists, determined to attack theistic and metaphysical beliefs. Many others develop habitual or lifelong ways of essential self-interest, or selfishness and coldness. Financial and other material interests become paramount for many. Or achievement and success in business, science, politics, or the arts may serve as their answer to the purpose of life. Sexual excitement and pleasure become a primary goal for many. Then there are those who go still further, developing contempt for societal laws, and turn to forms of cheating, fraud, stealing, violence, rape, murder, and incredible atrocities.

At some point along the way, however, some people find that the direction they are traveling is disturbing, dissatisfying, and empty. They search for deeper understandings of life. Some seek answers in various religions or philosophies. But since there are so many differing answers, how are we to know what is true, or whether there is such a thing as ultimate truth? A prevailing relativism in America today holds the opinion that one religion is as good as another, and 70% of Americans with any religious affiliation say they believe many religions can lead to eternal life, including 57% of evangelicals and 83% of mainline church members.[43] But that is completely contrary to God's word in the Bible. Salvation and Heaven come only from God the Father through his Son Jesus Christ, and in the Holy Spirit. *No other religion teaches this.*

Five biblical teachings are pertinent for this quest for truth. One is that we all have some innate knowledge of God within ourselves and as seen in nature.[44] But the second is that because of inherited sin we cannot bring ourselves to God and truth by our own thought or efforts.[45] Inherited sin can actually lead us away from knowledge of God, and suppress it, or replace it with something false. The third is that it is only by the grace of God that we can come to him.[46] Since the Bible exhorts us to turn to God in belief and faith, God must respond in certain ways to our own attitude and the inclination of our hearts. Are our hearts open to God, or do we remain stand-offish and resistant? The fourth biblical teaching is that we can be led to God through the power of the word of God in the Scriptures or in some written or spoken form.[47] The fifth teaching is that the only way we can know God with complete assurance is through belief and faith in Jesus Christ as our divine Savior, resulting in the Holy Spirit dwelling within our hearts.[48] It is only in this way that we can have ultimate certainty of the reality and truth of God, and come to trust him and trust his word, which is in the Bible.

Disobedience, Punishment, Wars, and Religious Wars. Another group of key questions about evil and the existence of God revolves around the matter of killings in wars, especially of wars of religious beliefs. An important place to start dealing with these questions is the wars of the Israelites described in the Old Testament. Examining the history of the Israelites in this way equally involves study of the will of Yahweh, the Lord God of Israel, his divine Covenants, laws, and of obedience and rewards, disobedience and punishments.

The Israelites were delivered from Egypt probably in 1446 BC[49] by Yahweh's mighty acts in fulfillment of his predetermined plan for Israel as a nation. Israel could have enjoyed all the wonderful benefits of the covenants, including the full Promised Land in perpetuity, and could have constantly served as a blessed priest and guiding light to all future nations of the world, if she had remained faithful and obedient to God.

God intended that the nation Israel demonstrate to all people how glorious it can be to live under the government of God (Exodus 4:6). God chose Abraham to be the father of a family that would become a nation and be a blessing to the whole world (Genesis 12:1-3). This blessing would come to all mankind as Israel would allow the light of God's presence to dwell within her, transform her, and shine out from her as a light to the nations (Isaiah 42:6).[50]

But Israel as a nation was to slide into idolatry, immorality, and violence many times over the next eight centuries. She was to be constantly rebuked and warned by God for her disobedience. Her worst evil was infidelity to the true God who had showed her the favor of his covenant choice, had dwelt among them, and delivered them miraculously from Egypt. From Moses through Joshua, Samuel, David, and Solomon, God allowed Israel to grow and prosper into a strong nation, a nation of great kings, even though there were many serious forms of disobedience and unfaithfulness along the way, and with each bringing its form of discipline and punishment. Serious disobedience even began shortly after the deliverance from Egypt, in the Sinai, before entrance into the Promised Land. It would be about 435 years until David became king in 1011 B.C. Israel's time of greatest strength and prosperity lasted during the reigns of David and Solomon, a period of about

80 years. But with the death of Solomon in 931 BC, signs of trouble began with the division of the kingdom into two parts, the northern nation of Israel, and the southern one of Judah, which was to continue the covenant line. There were many evil rulers among the nineteen kings of the Davidic dynasty who followed Solomon, and God finally brought an end to them in 605 BC, 841 years after the exodus. It was Jesus Christ who came six centuries later to fulfill the covenant promise of a great king of the Davidic seed, who would rule forever. This New Covenant promised grace and salvation to all who would believe.[51]

This history of Israel tells us first about the covenants, the love and grace of God in providing for the people, the fortunes of the people and the nation, and how and to what degrees they were punished for disbelief and disobedience. But it also tells us much about the nature of belief, faith, and obedience to God for all of God's creatures, and about the kinds and degrees of discipline and punishment that God brings about because of human disobedience and disbelief.

Shortly after the exodus, while wandering in the wilderness of Sinai, the people began to engage in certain acts of disobedience, which soon escalated into outright idolatry and immorality. They began with grumblings about the lack of water and food. God graciously and miraculously provided water, meat, and bread ("manna") for them. Even in the face of these miracles, with bread appearing on the ground around them six days a week (for forty years!), the people still showed their lack of faith that Yahweh would provide, by trying to save bread for the next day, and disobeying God's command not to keep it overnight. For this disobedience, maggots appeared in the kept bread, and it began to smell (Exodus 15:22-16:35).

Only three months after the exodus, God came down on Mount Sinai in the sight of the Israelites in an epiphany of fire, smoke, lightening and thunder, with the whole mountain trembling violently. It was here that God first gave Moses the Ten Commandments. The first two forbade belief in any other gods, and commanded the people not to make any idols for worship. These two commandments came with an ominous warning of severe punishment for disobedience: "I, the Lord your God, am a jealous God, punishing the children for the sins of the fathers to the third and fourth generation of those who hate me, but showing love to a thousand generations of those who love me and keep my commandments" (Exodus 20:5-6).

God is "jealous" and will not tolerate unfaithfulness. Such acts bring forth terrible punishments or abandonment. The covenants are a close personal relationship, analogous to love in marriage, and "jealousy is part of the vocabulary of love."[52] The worship of false gods was *the* great temptation for the Israelites, since it was all around them through their biblical history.

It carries such extreme penalties because it is one of the worst possible sins, and it works exactly opposite to the purpose of God in the covenants. The covenantal acts of God came in the face of worldwide opposition. Atheistic disbelief was uncommon then, nothing like it has become in modern and postmodern culture. But atheism should fall under the same ominous warnings as belief in other gods. Those who turn their backs on God hate him, and work against him. And atheists and general nonbelievers often worship "other gods" as well, either the usual power, riches, success, fame, pleasure, and sex, or more elegantly, great human achievements in some field—politics, business, arts, theater, film, great literature, scholarship, or science.

God then gave to the Israelites, through Moses, a long series of requirements for worship, and the Law for their theocratic state under his rule. He also gave lengthy, detailed instructions for designing and making the Ark of the Covenant, the Tabernacle, Lampstand, and other sacred objects for worship services, including priestly garments. Moses was on the mountain receiving these laws and instructions for forty days and nights. During this time, the Israelites, who had just recently agreed to obey God's commands, *and had just seen his overwhelming epiphany*, fell quickly back into former pagan ways. They demanded that Aaron, the brother of Moses, make an idol of worship for them, which he did. They engaged in pagan rituals and revelry, probably including sexual-fertility rites around the golden calf. In so doing they turned their backs on God, and grievously violated the two primary commandments recently given them. One of the laws God had just given Moses required death ("destruction") as punishment for such idolatry. God was fiercely angry with the people, and disowned them. He told Moses to leave him so that He might destroy them. Moses pleaded with God, however, causing him to relent. But when Moses came down and saw the people in pagan revelry, he too became extremely angry. He called the faithful Levites to his side, and they went through the camp killing 3000 of the idolaters. Following this, the journey to the Promised Land, which should have taken no more than two weeks, actually took forty years. And because of their disobedience, none of the Israelites of the exodus, except those under 20, were allowed to cross the Jordan to enter the covenant land.[53]

While Moses was still head of the Israelites, they fought an early, successful battle in the south at Arad in the Negev, with God himself delivering the Canaanites to them for complete destruction along with their towns. Then they traveled on northeast and defeated Sihon, king of the Amorites. God again led and delivered the enemy to them, and they killed the king, his sons, and his whole army, took all his towns, and "completely destroyed them— men, women and children."[54] They left "no survivors." Then Og, the king of

Bashan, came out with his whole army to fight them. God told Moses: "Do to him what you did to Sihon." So the Israelites "struck him down, together with his sons and his whole army, leaving them no survivors. And they took possession of his land." They took all sixty of Og's cities, and "completely destroyed them, . . . destroying every city—men, women, and children"[55] and divided the land among themselves. These were powerful, sweeping victories that cast great fear into surrounding Canaanite towns. It was after this that God told Moses he could not enter the Promised Land east of the Jordan because of his own earlier disobedience. Moses died about 1406 BC at the age of 120. Joshua, about 83 at the time, succeeded Moses, grew as a great man of faith in God, and a powerful warrior leader of the Israelites during the seven years of battle for the Promised Land.

In human perspective, the killing of the entire population of many towns—all the men, women, and children—is a terrible thing. But in this particular situation, God's law requiring the destruction of idolaters was to be carried out again and again with the total destruction of town after town of Canaanites. It must also be realized that such acts were critical during these crucial times when God was working to establish enduring covenant and true belief in the teeth of omnipresent paganism.

The killing of the idolatrous Israelites at Sinai is another instance of terrible bloodshed, showing that God brings forth death in the world, but uses it for a good purpose. The Israelites had many *direct* demonstrations of God's real presence and power, and knew and vowed to obey his commandments, but they again and again reverted to disbelief and disobedience, sliding finally into depravity. Their actions showed that there was no hope for them. They became a cancer in the body of the covenant people. Thus, the Creator Lord who had given them life and lovingly guided and cared for them, took away the lives He had given.

The Canaanites, on the other hand, had been completely entrenched in paganism for many centuries. Their religion included prostitution and infant sacrifice.[56] God patiently waited for them to repent, but they did not. They stood in stubborn opposition to God's will and actions through his covenant people, which was to lead ultimately to provision for salvation for all through Christ. The time of the entrance of the people of Israel into the area of the Promised Land was a *unique*, early time in the history of God's relationship to the world, and his plan for covenant and salvation. God was beginning to reveal himself, his divine nature, and his will for human life in powerfully new and expanding ways. Here again, in the massive killings of the Canaanites, clearly commanded by God, it could be said that God brought forth "evil" by their total destruction. But it was according to his divine law for idolaters, and God is the ultimate source of law. And it was for the ultimately good purpose of bringing the truth of his nature, will, and salvation into the world. Without the achievement of this purpose, the entire world and its inhabitants would remain utterly lost, like the Canaanites. But the Bible tells us that God's purposes have been and will always be achieved.

It was Joshua who led the people and the army after Moses. He was chosen by Yahweh to lead the Israelites westward, across the Jordan, into the Promised Land. In great secrecy, Joshua sent two spies into Jericho, the gateway to rest of the land, to gain information for the coming battle. What they found reveals God's workings in one obvious way, and in one surprising and mysterious way. The surprising aspect is that the two agents came to a particular house in Jericho and entered, seeking information. We saw in the last chapter that God controls all events in the world, and that surely must be the case here—in this critical situation in which God is clearly leading the people into a key battle with Jericho—that He led the two men to this particular place—the house of a prostitute named Rahab. Why would God lead them to the house of a prostitute? As it turned out, Rahab was very helpful, telling them that Jericho and all of Canaan had heard about the miraculous exploits of the Israelites in crossing the Red Sea, and completely destroying two Amorite kingdoms. As a result they were all "melting in fear." Their hearts had sunk and their courage failed. Even more surprising is the fact that Rahab expressed belief in the God of the Israelites, referring to him as "Lord": "the Lord your God is God in heaven above and on earth below." The important lesson from Rahab is that, because of her belief, she was saved, spiritually as well as physically. Here was one woman living in a completely pagan environment, who believed in the living God. God knew her heart, as He knows all hearts, and allowed her and her family to be saved from the total destruction that was to befall Jericho. The agreed sign to save her was a scarlet cord hung from her window where the Israelites could see it.[57]

God then made it possible for about two million Israelites to cross the Jordan River (at flood stage!), much as He had done at the Red Sea forty years before. That Yahweh, the Lord of Israel was leading them was made clear by his command that Levite priests must carry the Ark of the Covenant, God's own seat, leading the way. When they first stepped into the Jordan, the waters would stop and part for them, creating a dry pathway for the people to follow, 3000 feet behind. God's absolute control of his creation is shown in this mighty act preceding the battle. God commanded that the Levites carrying the Ark remain at the center of the riverbed while the people completed the crossing, and 12 men gathered twelve large stones from the riverbed to erect a memorial of the crossing on the western side. As soon as all this was accomplished, the Levites were ordered to come out with the Ark, and immediately the Jordan resumed its flood-tide flow. For the Israelites, there was no turning back now.[58]

Before God would lead the Israelites into battle, however, He required three acts of consecration from them. The first was circumcision, which had been initiated with the Abrahamic covenant, and had not been done during the years of wanderings. Circumcision not only signified "the everlasting continuation of Abraham's seed and their everlasting possession of the land," but "symbolized a complete separation from the widely prevalent sins of the flesh: adultery, fornication, and sodomy." It had "spiritual overtones not only in relation to sexual conduct but in every phase of life. 'Circumcise your hearts, therefore, and do not be stiff-necked any longer.'" In this we again see that God was working to bring true, growing knowledge of himself and his will into a world that had been universally given over to various gods and rituals of nature, sex, and fertility. This specific mark in men's bodies served as a consecrated sign and reminder of the situation, and of the covenantal relationship with their holy God and Lord, requiring them to live in faithful, obedient, and holy ways.[59]

The second required consecration was the celebration of the Passover. This was only the third Passover celebration for the Israelites. The first had been the night before the exodus, and the second was at Mount Sinai. The Israelites were to reverently recall the way in which Yahweh had spared them from the plague of universal deaths of first-born infants in Egypt. By God's command, each Israelite father had sprinkled the blood of a lamb on their doorpost and lintel, and the death sentence decreed by God had passed over them. As in the former victory over Egyptian tyranny, the Israelites now prepared for victory over Jericho and Canaan. The third requirement of the Israelites was that they begin gathering the produce of the new land. They had relied on manna from heaven for 40 years. Now they began to eat the produce of the land, and the manna stopped the next day.[60]

When Joshua went out toward Jericho to observe its defenses, he "saw a man standing in front of him with a drawn sword," It was a heavenly figure who identified himself as "commander of the army of the Lord." Realizing immediately that he was of God, Joshua "fell facedown to the ground in reverence, asking, 'What message does my Lord have for his servant?'" This "Commander of the army of the Lord" may have been, as some think, one of several appearances in the Old Testament of "the Angel of the Lord"— God in human form, a theophany of Jesus Christ. The fact that He is twice referred to as "Lord," and He told Joshua to take off his sandals because he was standing in a holy place, seems to indicate the divine presence.[61] Then the "Lord" and "Commander" gave unusual and exciting orders to Joshua:

See, I have delivered Jericho into your hands, along with its king and its fighting men. March around the city once with all the armed men. Do this for six days. Have seven priests carry trumpets of rams' horns in front of the ark. On the seventh day, march around the city seven times, with the priests blowing the trumpets. When you hear them sound a long blast on the trumpets, have all the people give a loud shout; then the wall of the city will collapse and the people will go up, every man straight in.

These strange actions, which seem to put the marching people at risk, must also have cast fear and wonder into the enemy. They also served both as a test of faith and obedience for the Israelites, and as evidence of the mighty leadership by the covenant Lord. Joshua instructed the people as he was told, and when the last round was made, and the people shouted at the long blast of trumpets, "the wall collapsed; so every man charged straight in, and they took the city. They devoted the city to the Lord and destroyed with the sword every living thing in it—men and women, young and old, cattle, sheep and donkeys." They saved Rahab and her family, leading them outside the city, then "they burned the whole city and everything in it, but they put the silver and gold and the articles of bronze and iron into the treasury of the Lord's house."[62] This great victory came because Joshua and the Israelites trusted God and obeyed his commands.

For the purpose of this chapter, only one of the many other battles must be included. It not only shows the decisive leadership of God, but reveals more clearly the condition of strict obedience for God to continue leading them, and the disastrous results of disobedience. The battle was for the strategic town of Ai northwest of Jericho. The Israelites looked to Ai with too much *self*-confidence. Following the report of his spies, Joshua sent only 3000 soldiers to the battle. This was not the main difficulty, however. Before the battle of Jericho, God had commanded the Israelites to destroy and burn all the people, animals, and things of Jericho (the *herem* holy war ban), except for valuable items of gold, silver, and bronze to be devoted to the Lord's treasury. Nothing was to be taken for themselves. He warned them that they all would be liable to this same destruction ban if they disobeyed (Joshua 6:18-19). One man among the Israelites, Achan, deliberately disobeyed this command. God then brought about the rout of the 3000 Israelites sent to Ai, and the death of 36 of them. This was the only defeat of the Israelites in the seven-year war to win the Promised Land. Joshua was stunned and the elders were shocked and dismayed. God then told Joshua that He would not be with the Israelites any longer unless this sin was punished and the devoted things destroyed. Achan was discovered as the thief of the valuable objects. Because his disobedience was a breaking of the covenant with God, Achan and his family fell under the same destruction ban (*herem*) commanded by God for Jericho, and they were stoned to death, and then burned.[63]

God commanded that the Israelites consecrate themselves once again. He then gave Joshua a new strategy for the defeat of Ai, assuring him victory. A large army of 30,000 Israelites was to hide in ambush behind Ai to the west, a second group led by Joshua was stationed north of Ai to initiate a decoy attack, while a third group waited to block the entrance of any help for the soldiers of Ai. When the king of Ai saw Joshua and his smaller army, they all charged out to rout them as they had easily done before. As Joshua and his men retreated to draw the enemy into their trap, God told him to hold out his javelin toward Ai and He would deliver it into his hands. As Joshua did so, the large ambush army rushed into the defenseless city, quickly took it and set it on fire. God not only gave the Israelites a brilliant strategy for victory, He also turned the evil of the previous rout into a good purpose as part of that plan. God had also placed Ai under his destruction ban (*herem*), so that all 12,000 men, women, and children of Ai were killed. But since this was the second victory in the western land, God allowed the Israelites to take the livestock and plunder for themselves.

It is crucially important to realize that the divine covenants, which brought both good and bad experiences into Israelite history, were by the decree and act of the Almighty Creator and Lord God of history. Israel's history was essentially determined by God—the covenants with Abraham, Isaac, and Jacob, the bondage in Egypt, the exodus, the battles in Canaan, the monarchy, the Davidic covenant, Babylonian captivity, and subsequent events. Without God, the Jews would not have been in Egypt or Canaan. Without God there would not have been a Jewish nation. The battles in Canaan were led and determined by God. The destruction of scores of Canaanite towns and cities and many thousands of men, women, children, animals, and property was not the self-determined work of the Israelites, but came out of the plan and power of God. Since the Israelite covenants lead ultimately into the New Covenant in Jesus Christ as Davidic King, Priest, and Savior, and since the New Covenant and salvific mission of Christ was planned before the beginning of the world, all of these events in the history of Israel had to be planned and decreed by God before the beginning of the world.

One possible response to all this is an atheistic one. Atheists today, like Hitchens and Dawkins, could argue that these are examples of the "evils of religion." If there were no God, as atheists maintain, then that would seem to be true: these killings would seem as delusional, pointless, horrible, and evil as any in history. But God has presented his revelation through covenants with the Israelites, culminating in Christ, in the Scriptures, and in the faith and testimonies of millions down through the centuries. It is the burden of disbelievers to prove that all this is not true, and that the Bible is not the word of God. And that is impossible. A second possible response is from a competing religious viewpoint, such as that of Islam. Islam can claim that Allah has called for a kind of holy war (*jihad*) against infidels, and Muslims could claim to justify their destruction and the spread of Islam by terrorist killings, torture, suicide bombings, roadside bombings, and other such acts that kill men, women, and children.

The Claims of Islam. The main thing that would support or undermine this Islamic call to *jihad* is whether Allah is truly God, and thus, whether the call is legitimate or not. It is certainly not true that the deity of Islam is the same as the God of Judeo-Christianity, as some have said, including an American President, and as has been suggested on TV by some newscasters and Islamic spokesmen. All dedicated Muslims know this. The Judeo-Christian God is triune—three persons in one divine substance—Father, Son, Holy Spirit.[64] Muslims erroneously call this "polygamy," and claim that those who believe it are infidels. For Muslims the most crucial belief is that the deity of Islam is *one and only one*. Allah is *One* only. "To believe that there is more than one person in God is an idolatry and blasphemy called *shirk*." This *shirk* is considered an unpardonable sin.[65] Thus, to believe that Jesus is God, the Son of God, dooms one to Islamic hell forever.

For Islam, Jesus could not possibly be "the only begotten Son of God," and triune equal of Father and Holy Spirit, as the Bible and Christian theology teach,[66] because the Koran (Qur'an) states that Allah "begot none," or "begetteth not," and "None is equal to Him."[67] This Sura (Chapter), 112 of the Koran, which denies any begotten Son of God, is considered most valuable in Islam, worth a third of the whole Koran. The Koran even claims that saying Jesus Christ is the Son of God is a lie.[68] It exclaims: "God forbid that He should have a son!"[69] It declares it blasphemous to say that Jesus Christ is God: "They do blaspheme who declare: 'God is the Messiah, the son of Mary.'"[70] To speak of a Trinity is blasphemous.[71] Jesus is said to be an apostle, a prophet, but not God. Sura 43 claims that Jesus "was but a mortal whom [Allah] favored and made an example to the Israelites." The Koran even "quotes" Jesus as denying his divinity, and saying "I am the servant of Allah."[72] It claims that Jesus did not die on the cross for our sins, and did not rise from the grave three days later. The Koran declares the story of Christ's death on the cross a "monstrous falsehood."[73]

These denials show that one of the most prominent goals of the Koran is to prohibit anyone from believing that Jesus Christ is God, and that salvation is available through belief in Him. This *most important* teaching of the Bible and Christianity is thus called a "lie," and anyone who believes it blasphemes and will go to hell. According to Islam, Muhammad was the last and greatest of all prophets, greater than Jesus, and the one who superseded all prophets.[74]

But basic questions about these denials of the divinity of Christ in the Koran are: according to the Bible, *who* is most anxious to deny the deity of Jesus Christ and salvation available through belief in Him, and spread such beliefs throughout human society? Who was the very first to rebel against the Sovereign God? Who set out to establish his own kingdom apart from God?[75] Who advocates murder to his followers? Who "loves bitterness and hatred, war and revenge."[76]

We know that these Koranic denials of the divinity of Christ come from Muhammad in the seventh century. He claimed they came through the inspiration of the Angel Gabriel. We know, however, that he had some doubts about this. The Caner brothers (former Muslims converted to Christianity) write, "How can we trust his revelations and visions when he expressed doubt that they were revelations and sometimes thought himself to be demon-possessed? Muhammad's own foster mother, Halima, admitted that she thought he was possessed by the devil."[77]

It is well known that the Bible and Christianity teach as the central truth that Jesus Christ is God, the Son of God, the second Person of the Trinity, the reason for, and the fulfillment of the historically crucial successive covenants of the Old Testament, culminating in the New Covenant of the New Testament, and issuing in the Bible. Christ is the Mediator of God the Father, the one and only Son and Savior who gave his life as a ransom to make salvation possible for all of us.[78] One of the best known verses of the New Testament gives a beautiful statement of this core teaching: "For God so loved the world that He gave His only begotten Son, that whoever believes in Him should not perish but have everlasting life" (John 3:16). To deny Christ is to deny the Father who sent him on this mission of divine grace and salvation.

The book of 1 John is strongly explicit about this, linking the Father, Son, and Holy Spirit: "Who is the liar? It is the man who denies that Jesus is the Christ. Such a man is the antichrist—he denies the Father and the Son. No one who denies the Son has the Father; whoever acknowledges the Son has the Father also" (3:22-23). "And we have seen and testify that the Father has sent his Son to be the Savior of the world. If anyone acknowledges that Jesus is the Son of God, God lives in him and he in God" (4:14-15). "And this is the testimony: God has given us eternal life, and this life is in his Son. He who has the Son has life; he who does not have the Son of God does not have life" (5:11-12). "And this is his [God's] command: to believe in the name of his Son, Jesus Christ, and to love one another as He commanded us. Those who obey his commands live in him, and he in them. And this is how we know that he lives in us: We know it by the Spirit he gave us" (3:23-24). "Dear friends, do not believe every spirit, but test the spirits to see whether they are from God, because many false prophets have gone out into the world. This is how you can recognize the Spirit of God: Every spirit that acknowledges that Jesus Christ has come in the flesh is from God, but every spirit that does not acknowledge Jesus is not from God. This is the spirit of the antichrist, which you have heard is coming, and even now is in the world" (4:1-3).

These most crucial teachings of the Bible and Christianity are denied by Muhammad, the Koran, and Islam. Allah cannot possibly be the God of the Bible. Since Muhammad and his "recitations" in the Koran deny that Jesus Christ is God, the Son of God, and the Savior who died on the cross for our sins, he is, according to 1 John and the New Testament, a "false prophet," and one who opposed Christ—an "antichrist." 1 John also tells us that anyone who denies that Jesus is the Son of God, also denies God the Father and God the Holy Spirit.

While denying the essential content of the Bible, Islam attempts to appropriate parts of the Bible and reinterpret them in very different ways. It seeks to appropriate biblical fathers and prophets—Adam, Noah, Abraham, Moses, prophets, and Jesus, reinterpreting them as "apostles" or prophets who sought to teach the true Islamic religion, but whose revealed messages from Allah were distorted and corrupted by Jews and Christians. Muhammad is presented as the final prophet of Allah in this line, and he has given the final, true revelation of Allah to replace the "distorted and corrupted" Bible. Muhammad's Koran is said to surpass and complete all previous revelations as the verbally inspired word of God dictated to Muhammad by the angel Gabriel. Such claims contradict the biblical Christian doctrine that the Bible is the inerrant, everlasting Word of God. They are also completely incredible to anyone who knows the Bible well—the roles of Israel's fathers, kings, and prophets in the covenants, and the way they lead to Jesus Christ as God-man and divine Savior. The messianic mission of Jesus, as well as his teachings, stand in essential and unalterable contrast and conflict with such Islamic alterations.

Theologian John Frame thus identifies Islam as one of several Christian heresies. "Christian heresies are religions influenced by the Bible, but which deny the central biblical gospel. Among the Christian heresies are not only those designated as such in history (Arianism, Gnosticism, Sabellianism, Docetism, Eutychianism, etc.), but also the historic rivals of Christianity, namely Judaism and Islam. Also among the Christian heresies are the modern cults and denials of the gospel: Jehovah's Witnesses, Mormonism, liberalism, etc." No Christian heresy or liberalism "offers any solution to human sin . . . no free gift of divine forgiveness through the sacrifice of Jesus." They are all "religions of works righteousness, which is self-righteousness. They offer only the hollow advice to try harder, or the false and morally destructive claim that God will forgive without demanding anything."[79]

Mainstream Judaism, claiming belief in a Supreme Creator God, has continued to deny the deity of Jesus Christ and His divine mission of salvation for mankind. Judaism claims that Jesus is not the Messiah (*Mosiach*) announced in the Old Testament and confirmed in the New. The biblical and Christian teaching of Jesus as the divine Person who sacrificed Himself for the salvation of mankind has no place in Judaism. The Messiah has not yet come, but will appear as a future leader. He will not be divine, however, just a great human being, a righteous judge, and a great military leader who will win great battles for Israel.[80] Buddhism is still more extreme, denying even more of the basic teachings of the Bible and Christian theology. For Buddhism there is no Almighty God who created all things and rules and guides his creation. There is no divine Savior who died for the sins of human beings, and there will be no Judgment Day in which a just God gives rewards and punishments. Although some forms of Buddhism admit multiple divine beings, there is no Creator God to whom one must be united in faith and obedience.[81]

The Influence of Satan. During the earthly life of Jesus, it was the Pharisees who boldly challenged his claims to be the Son of God, sent by his Father, accusing him of being a liar and blasphemer. In John 8 Jesus told them, "I know where I came from and where I am going. But you have no idea where I come from or where I am going . . . . I stand with the Father who sent me . . . . My other witness is the Father who sent me." They asked, "Where is your father?" His reply—closely related to the verses previously quoted from 1 John—applies not only to the Pharisees, but to anyone who does not believe in him: "You do not know me or my Father . . . . If you knew me, you would know my Father also."

Jesus knew that some of the Jews, while claiming to be descendants of Abraham, and claiming God as their Father, were determined to kill him. His response shows who their real father was, and why they did not believe in him: "If God were your Father, you would love me, for I came from God and now am here. I have not come on my own; but he sent me. You are of your father the devil, and your will is to do your father's desires. He was a murderer from the beginning, and has nothing to do with the truth, because there is no truth in him. When he lies, he speaks according to his own nature, for he is a liar and the father of lies."[82]

Jesus thus explicitly said it is the influence of Satan the liar that led the Pharisees to deny him, and by implication, that it is Satan who influences *all* those who deny Christ's deity, his truth, and his being sent by God. "The tactics of Satan and his demons are to use lies (John 8:44), deception

(Revelation 12:9), murder (Ps. 106:37; John 8:44), and every other kind of destructive activity to attempt to cause people to turn away from God and destroy themselves." Like a thief, Satan "comes only to steal and kill and destroy."[83] These verses clearly indicate that it is Satan who stands behind the false religions denying the deity of Christ. Paul warned the Corinthians that pagan idolatry is actually a worship of demons, Satan's helpers: "The sacrifices of pagans are offered to demons, not to God, and I do not want you to be participants with demons" (1 Corinthians 10:20). He gave the example of Israelites of the Old Testament who participated in pagan worship and revelry, and 23,000 of them died in one day.

All beliefs that deny Christ and promote opposing goals or doctrines must be influenced by the great "adversary," Satan, and his demons.[84] In 2 Timothy Paul indicates that those who follow such false doctrines are caught in "the trap of the devil, who has taken them captive to do his will" (2:26). Paul teaches a proper Christian response to such cases, however, which is not to quarrel or be resentful, but to "be kind" and "gently instruct, in the hope that God will grant them repentance leading to a knowledge of the truth." In 1 Timothy 4:1-2 Paul goes further, with the ominous prediction of a great apostasy due to demonic influence in latter times: "Now the Spirit expressly says that in latter times some will depart from the faith, giving heed to deceiving spirits and doctrines of demons, speaking lies in hypocrisy, having their own conscience seared with a hot iron."

Spiritual Warfare, Satan, and the End of This Age. With the rebellion of the angel Lucifer and other evil angels against God, there was a war between them and the good angels led by the Archangel Michael. This was the beginning of a spiritual warfare between God and the powers of evil that has continued to the present. Some of the evil angels (demons) were cast down to hell and bound in chains of darkness (2 Peter 2:4). But Lucifer (Satan) and many of his followers were "cast to the earth" (Revelation 12:7-9). They were left free by God to roam the earth and heavens, where they have been pursuing their objective of engaging in evil works, and corrupting and destroying as much of God's creation as they can, before the time of their own final damnation.

Lucifer as he was created was second only to God in power! He was created immensely powerful, morally perfect, and beautiful. Perhaps it was just because he had so much, that he wanted it all. He became proud because of his "splendor." And such pride is the first of seven sins that are an abomination to God. Pride and the other six describe the devil and his effects on humans: lies, murder, wicked plans, quickness to evil, false witness, and discord (Proverbs 6:16-19). They all lead rapidly away from God. Lucifer

303

had enough pride, power, and freedom to choose to rebel against his Creator, and he did so.

All this must have been part of God's plan of creation, and for a good reason. *Evil had not existed before.* At the entrance of evil into creation with the rebellion of Lucifer, there arose a previously nonexistent separation and distinction between the Good (the Triune God) and evil (Satan and followers). Many angels chose to follow Lucifer in his rebellion against God, which was essentially and unavoidably a choice against goodness and truth. Since God is Goodness and Truth in essence, any revolt against him is a fall into evil and loss of truth. Many other angels chose to remain loyal to God their Creator. And subsequently, for human beings, this emergence of evil established the possibility, and the necessity, of choice between good and evil.

Knowing all things, God the Creator must have known that rebellion against his Sovereignty and Goodness would arise, and many forms and depths of evil would result. The teaching of the Bible is consistent: there is one supreme source of all that is—the triune Creator God. Without God willing it, nothing could be. "Satan is God's creature: for everything springs from God in the first instance."[85] God has controlled and limited the activities of Satan since then, as the book of Job and the Gospels show; and God's plan includes the eventual total isolation of Satan, his demons, and their unsaved human followers from Himself and saved humanity. Thus, God not only allowed the rebellion, but planned it from the start. This must surely be the reason that God allowed evil to arise and spread: with intelligent and powerful angels who had sufficient freedom of will to choose, evil first emerged in creation; human beings then were required to choose between good and evil.

The sin of Adam and Eve involved the choice between believing and trusting the truth and goodness of God the Creator, or taking the word of a strange creature who told them not to believe God. God placed in the Garden of Eden both the tree of life and the tree of the knowledge of good and evil. He allowed them the *opportunity* to eat from the latter, but commanded them *not* to eat or touch it, or else they would die. Satan's reason in tempting Eve was much like the one for his own revolt, "you will be like God." He coupled this with the partial truth that she would then know good and evil, making it sound like something wonderful.

Satan and demons play intrinsic parts in the accounts of Scriptures from Genesis on through the Old Testament, the Gospels, the Epistles, and the book of Revelation. They have been undeniable aspects of Christian belief from the time of the Bible onward. To doubt their existence is to doubt God's word. Modern acids of naturalism, scientism, skepticism, and atheism, however, have made them seem utterly incredible to vast numbers of people in our era. Nevertheless there is the authority of the Bible as God's unfailing word, and the testimony of millions. And logically, "the existence of wicked characteristics which are the very opposite of beauty, truth and goodness point beyond our world to an evil source for these things." "There cannot be power apart from an originating intelligence, planning it, calling it into being, using it." Evil is not merely the absence of good, there must be "a supernatural center and embodiment of evil who fouls all he touches." It is this that also ultimately explains the many threats to human life and to the Earth in our times—the satanic greed, lust for wealth and power, and lack of love or even caring. Satanic temptation has always been present in history, and never more so than in our era. There are also signs and outbreaks of the pagan and demonic occult in many places in America and the rest of the world that reflect "the existence of a concentrated power of evil to which men's lives can become prey." Examples of demonic possession have been recorded, not only in the Bible, but also by modern researchers.[86]

Jesus certainly knew that Satan and demons are real. To doubt this is to doubt the life and word of Jesus Christ. He knew that they had powerful influences and effects on people. He fought against them continually during his time of ministry on earth. He cast demons out of people who were afflicted or possessed by them. He healed those who had been made sick, diseased, lame, and blind, some through demonic influences and effects. He was assailed by the temptations of Satan himself for forty days in the wilderness, always rebuffing and rebuking him. The devil was able to offer Jesus all the kingdoms of the world with all their power, wealth, and glory if He would fall down and worship him. Jesus knew that the devil had great powers over the earth, and was actually able to give wealth, power, and glory to his followers. But He also knew that the final outcome of following the devil was death and eternal loss of God.

Jesus refuted the Jewish scribes who accused him of using the power of the devil to cast out demons: "How can Satan cast out Satan?"[87] He gave his disciples the power to cast out demons, heal all kinds of sickness and disease, and even raise the dead.[88] He "saw the whole of his ministry as a conflict with Satan. He saw his death as the supreme battle with the evil one. ... His teaching is bound up with it. His healing is bound up with it. His exorcisms are bound up with it. His death is bound up with it. At all the major points in his life and ministry the conflict with Satan is of cardinal importance."[89]

After his rebellion and fall to earth, Satan, with his demon followers, began their monomaniacal activity of roaming back and forth through the earth deceiving and luring as many as they could away from God, spreading harm, disease, and death, and leading many toward their own eventual damnation. Satan and demons were given audience by God. As the great "accuser," Satan spoke to God, saying Job would curse God if his possessions and family were taken away. God gave Satan permission to do it. The powers Satan used were permitted by God, and included destructive forces of nature and influencing acts of human beings: bringing in bands of thieves and murderers to kill Job's servants and steal his oxen; causing fire to fall from the sky killing his sheep and the servants who watched them; causing a mighty wind to destroy the house of a son, killing all of Job's children. Disease was included among Satan's powers, so that Job was afflicted with painful sores all over his body. Thus we learn from the Bible that, with God's permission, the devil can make use of many things to afflict, torture, and even kill human beings, including thieves, murderers, fires, hurricane or tornado type winds, and diseases.

Job was a man of faith and obedience, saved from death by God. What about unbelievers, or those who work determinedly against God? "A man lies under the power of Satan if he does not turn to God. Satan assails mankind assiduously"—"Satan attacks the minds of men with doubts, fears, and propaganda. Satan assails the spirits of men with lust, pride and hatred. Satan assaults the bodies of men with disease, torture, and death. Satan assails the institutions of men (which he seeks to impregnate) with structural evil."[90] He manipulates nations, city councils, rioting mobs, and the elements of nature.[91] He is "filled with violence" and "great wrath" (Ezekiel 28:15; Revelation 12:12) He is the "adversary" who "prowls around like a roaring lion, seeking someone to devour" (1 Peter 5:8-9). "He loves bitterness and hatred, war and revenge."[92] With God's permission, he can cause death. "Satan is the most powerful person in the universe after God." He "exerts dominion over the fallen human race. As men open the door to him by sin and rebellion against God, he enters to dominate and enslave."[93] His work is widespread and destructive. "The unsaved are largely under Satan's authority and he rules them through the evil world system over which he is the head and of which the unregenerate are a part."[94]

There are times and situations when God sends evil spirits on missions of judgment or punishment for a city, a person, or both. After the death of Joshua about 1375 BC, there was a period of over 300 years in which the Israelites were led by Judges. During that time they repeatedly disobeyed God, intermarried with pagans, turned to worship of pagan Canaanite gods, and paid severely for their disobedience and idolatry. Gideon arose as a strong military leader by listening to God and following his will. With God leading, he brought the Israelites out of severe oppression and restored some obedience and peace for 40 years. But as soon as he died, the people turned once again to idolatry, worshipping Baal-Berith, whose shrine was at the city of Shechem.

Gideon, later known as Jerubbaal (Jerub-Baal), had fathered seventy sons by his many wives, and another son, Abimelech, by a Canaanite concubine living in Shechem. Abimelech, treacherously pursuing his desire to be king, and stirring up the people of Shechem to support him, caused the murder of all seventy of Gideon's sons, his own brothers, except for one who hid. After Abimelech had reigned only three years, God sent an evil spirit (a demon) to Shechem, turning the townsmen against him. Abimelech came with his troops, destroyed Shechem, killed all the people, and salted the ruins. Then he burned its tower and the temple stronghold of Baal-Berith, killing another thousand men and women there. While attacking the nearby city of Thebez, Abimelech started to set fire to its tower, but a woman dropped a millstone from the tower, cracking his skull. Abimelech called his armor bearer to finish him with his sword so that no one could say a woman killed him. Thus, by sending an evil spirit to sow discord and revolt, God caused the pagan city of Shechem and its temple to be destroyed, and brought the penalty of death upon Abimelech, the mass murderer of Gideon's sons.[95]

Another example of God sending an evil spirit on a mission of punishment is in the reign of King Saul. Saul was the first king of Israel that God permitted, with some reluctance, in response to the request of the people. Saul was given divine support by the Spirit of God, and had some successes in battle, but he flagrantly disobeyed God's word in the Law of Moses concerning community sacrifice, disobeyed the word of God through the prophet Samuel calling for a total-destruction ban (*herem*) on the Amalekites, and disobeyed again by seeking to draw honors upon himself. As a result, the Spirit of God left Saul, and Samuel informed him that since he had rejected the word of the Lord, the Lord had rejected him as king, and he would be replaced. God sent an evil spirit to torment Saul, inducing him to try to kill David by hurling a spear at him while David was playing a harp to soothe him. Saul pursued David for many years, still trying to kill him. Saul later grievously disobeyed God again by seeking the advice of a spirit medium who claimed to draw on demonic power. Turning irrevocably away from God by directly consulting demonic powers, Saul and his three sons soon met their end in a crushing defeat. Saul had a humiliating death—beheaded, with his body fixed to a Philistine wall.[96]

Another instance of God sending a demonic spirit to do his bidding involved King Ahab, who ruled Israel for 22 years in the ninth century BC. Ahab was the most wicked king Israel had ever known, even worse than his father, Omri. He built a temple and sacrificial altar for the Canaanite rain and fertility god, Baal, in Samaria, the capital of Israel, and erected Asherah poles representing Baal's female consort and mother-goddess. Ahab's wife, Jezebel, who was even more wicked than Ahab, is known as one of the most evil women of the Bible, being a zealous promoter of the pagan religion of Baal, and the real force behind Ahab's temple building. She was also responsible for the murder of many of the prophets of Yahweh, the Lord of Israel.[97]

The Israelites were suffering under this evil pair because of a 3½-year drought and famine, with many hungry and dying. God had brought the drought on them, because of their apostasy—forsaking God and turning to Baal. But the rain god proved utterly unable to bring rain. Ahab continued in his self-centered ways. When he could not get a vineyard from its owner, Naboth, he sulked in despair; but Jezebel acted, setting up a false accusation of blasphemy and treason against Naboth, and having him stoned to death. Thus the man was murdered so that Ahab could have a nearby vegetable garden! The fearless prophet Elijah confronted Ahab with his evil deed, and prophesied that Ahab's blood would be licked up by dogs in the same place Naboth's had been. He added that dogs would also eat Jezebel by the wall of Jezreel.

Elijah called for a test between the Lord, represented only by himself, and all the prophets of Baal and Asherah in the employ of Jezebel (450 prophets of the male god Baal and 400 of his female consort Asherah!). They all gathered on Mount Carmel for the test. A bull was cut up ready for sacrifice as a burnt offering to Baal—if Baal could send down fire to consume it (lightening and fire were also believed to be among Baal's powers). Despite six hours of chanting, rituals, and bloody self-mutilation by the pagan prophets, nothing happened. Elijah then prepared his altar, wood, and bull for sacrifice, even having it thoroughly soaked with water. When he prayed, lightening immediately set fire to the sacrifice, burning up everything, including the altar, the water, and the surrounding soil. God's living reality and power were thus demonstrated in a miraculous fashion at a crucial time in the historical development of covenantal relationship. The Israelites who saw and believed, then put the false prophets of Baal and Asherah to the sword, following God's command given through Moses and Elijah. Elijah then prayed for rain, and a torrential downpour came, forcing him to run about 25 miles back to the city. He outran the chariot of Ahab, which had a head start![98]

In the last major event of his reign, Ahab entreated Jehoshaphat, the king of Judah to join him in attacking Ramoth-Gilead to gain that territory, Jehoshaphat advised him to first seek the counsel of the Lord. By this time Ahab had gathered 400 of his own prophets. They were not true prophets of God, but men who had been hired by Ahab to advise and predict outcomes of future events, especially wars. It was at this time that God chose and sent a lying evil spirit, a demon, to influence the false prophets to give Ahab advice that would send him to his death. So the prophets told Ahab, "Go up to Ramoth-Gilead and prosper, for the Lord will deliver it into the king's hand." Because there was still some doubt, a true prophet of God, Micaiah, was called in. Micaiah told Ahab exactly what God had done to put a lying spirit in the mouth of his prophets, and that God had declared disaster against him.

Having no faith in Yahweh, Ahab did not realize the full import of Micaiah's prophecy, because he went on into battle, taking only the precaution of disguising himself. Ahab must have thought that if there was any truth to Micaiah's prophecy, he could avoid it by going in disguise. During the battle, however, when an enemy arrow was shot *at random*, God directed it into a tiny joint in Ahab's armor, fatally wounding him, and his blood filled the floor of his chariot. His body was returned to Samaria for burial, and when the chariot was washed out at a pool, "the dogs licked up his blood while the harlots bathed," as Elijah had prophesied years earlier.[99]

Later, God selected and anointed a new king of Israel, Jehu, the son of Jehoshaphat, and told him through a prophet, to destroy the whole house of Ahab, including "every last male." When Jehu went to Jezreel, he saw Jezebel, with her face painted and hair carefully arranged looking down from a high window and hurling insults at him. He called to her servants to join him, and two or three eunuchs did so, throwing Jezebel down to the street and spattering her blood on the wall and on horses as they trampled her. Before she could be buried, her body was eaten by dogs, as had prophesied, until there was nothing left but her skull, hands, and feet.[100]

Satan and the Origins of Evil. This chapter has traced the origins of evil to Lucifer/Satan, and then to the sin of the first human beings, to be inherited by all the descendants of Adam. All evil is due, not to God, or "religion" in general, but to the rebellion of Satan, and to all those people who have followed his deceitful influence, or by their own free will have chosen to do selfish, unloving, and evil acts. The original separation between the infinite goodness of God, and the evil actions and workings of Satan on earth brought with it a necessary moral choice for people. It also brought a continuing spiritual warfare in history of Satan and his followers against God and his angels and saints. The next chapter will trace biblical predictions of the final outcome of the spiritual warfare between good and evil, leading to the Millennium and the Eternal Kingdom of God.

Chapter Eleven

God, the Maker of Ultimate Purpose and the Providential Controller of History

I am God and there is no other; I am God and there is none like me. I make known the end from the beginning, from ancient times, what is still to come. I say: My purpose will stand, and I will do all that I please. (Isaiah 46:9-10)

God from all eternity did by the most wise and holy counsel of his own will, freely and unchangeably ordain whatsoever comes to pass; yet so as thereby neither is God the author of sin; nor is violence offered to the will of the creatures. (Westminster Confession of Faith, III.1)

God Determines History. A central message running through the Bible is that God is not only the creator of all things that exist, but he is in sovereign control of all events that take place. To assume that history proceeds by a series of accidents, unguided actions, or happenings, as so much modern thought does, is completely contrary to belief in God the creator and providential ruler and guide of his creation. God guides the course of events toward the ends and purposes he has decreed.[1] Isaiah grandly describes God's sovereignty over people and world rulers: "He sits enthroned above the circle of the earth, and its people are like grasshoppers. He stretches out the heavens like a canopy, and spreads them out like a tent to live in. He brings princes to naught and reduces the rulers of this world to nothing" (40:22-23). God never fails in what he proposes to do. Because he planned and decreed acts and events in creation, those things will surely take place.

God's original intent was not that human beings die and disappear forever after a brief life, but that they would live on forever. The first humans *were* created to live forever, but they broke God's laws, thereby inheriting death for themselves and the entire human race. God's original purpose of everlasting life for humans has not been abandoned, however; it will be fully achieved in the final establishment of God's Eternal Kingdom on earth. In this and other ways God's purpose in creation and history cannot fail. The first humans (like everyone since) were required to prove themselves by a choice for or against God. God knew that the first humans would sin when given a choice between good and evil. We know this because he decreed a remedy for their failure, and for that of everyone, *before* the beginning of the world.[2]

Satan and Evil. God has planned the course of world history from before it began. Although history often seems like "a tale told by an idiot," and includes so much suffering and so many horrible, and seemingly unconnected and meaningless events, it is fully guided by God. God has allowed and permitted evil to exist from the revolt of Satan and the sin of Adam on down through all of human history. The evil that human beings have brought about throughout history, influenced in varying degrees by Satan and his demonic crew, has reached monumental proportions and staggering depths. Who can doubt that such people as Hitler, Stalin, and Mao were under heavy evil (i.e., satanic) influence. Their depths of evil stand out among all the evil deeds of history. But there are innumerable other horrifying examples. The depths of evil are truly frightening and revolting. But as bad as it has been, we can see how it could have been even worse. And the Bible prophesies that it *will* be worse, much worse, in the end times of history.

The evil that exists in the world cannot be explained without the actual existence and work of Satan. Purely rational and abstract metaphysical answers differ radically from each other, and fail to yield universal and necessary truth. Evil can only be defined in opposition to the good. But one can only know the good relative to knowing God, who is the essence and source of all truth and goodness. Evil must be identified not as an absence of the good, but as an aggressive, existing reality that stands in opposition to God, his laws, and thus to his love and goodness. To whatever extent a person disbelieves in the true living God, he or she is unable to properly identify or explain good and evil. A prominent example today is "political correctness," which is a form of human relativism. In such views one religion is supposedly as valid (or invalid) as another. Neither PC, atheism, nor secularism can securely identify the critical difference, for example, between Islam and Christianity, and the ultimate significance of that difference.

The Historical Roles of Israel, Jerusalem, the Jews, and the Church. By the plan and decree of God the Creator, the land of Israel is the center of the world. It has been central to his self-revelation to humankind through the Jews. It is central in covenant and prophecy. It is the eternal Promised Land of the Jews, even though they never obtained all of it, and were even cast out of it for much of history because of disbelief and disobedience. It was the place of the birth, ministry, crucifixion, and resurrection of Jesus Christ the Savior and Messiah, who has made salvation and eternal life possible for everyone. And very significantly, Israel will be central to events of the end times of world history. Israel will be the focus of the final great battles of history. It will be the place of the Millennial Temple of God. And it will be the primary reason for the Tribulation, and the center of the Millennium and the Eternal Kingdom of God.

According to the Bible, human history and the world as we know it will come to an end at some time in the future. Bible prophecy has much of great importance to say about the final stages of human history. It identifies signs of the end, and much about the great final events that take place. Simply expresed, among the most outstanding final events are: (1) the supernatural occurence known as the Rapture; (2) the emergence of the Antichrist in the complex seven-year period of sufferings and death called the Tribulation; (3) a great, multi-national coalition force attacks Israel in the battle of Gog and Magog; (4) the great final battle known as Armageddon; (5) the second coming of Christ and establishment of his Millennial Kingdom; (6) the Last Judgment and final defeat of Satan; and (7) the Eternal Kingdom of God begins—a New Heaven and New Earth—Paradise, with the New Jerusalem as capital.

Much of the prophetic language used in the Bible to describe apocalyptic events is figurative (symbolic, allegorical, or metaphorical). A huge statue seen by Daniel is used to symbolize successive empires; a great stone that breaks it sybolizes Christ's Kingdom; a ferocious beast symbolizes the powerful, evil ruler of end-times; a woman with a crown of twelve stars symbolizes the nation of Israel and its twelve tribes. Apocalyptic narratives, while often allegorical in form, require literal interpretations for actual future events.[3] Such language must be correctly interpreted to understand meanings. Intense study of various prophecies is required to relate, arrange, and interpret them. Different interpretations of cetain passages often appear possible. Apparently God meant it to be so for his own reasons. Specific meanings of some events sometimes only become clear well after the event has taken place. In other cases, they only become clearer as the prophesied event draws closer and closer. The Book of Revelation and other passages in the New and Old Testaments give us a vivid and compelling picture of what end-times will actually be like, but often without the kind of explicitness we want concerning the exact order of events, specific identities of figures, and the actual times. It seems that God may be allowing us to know what we need to know, without knowing every detail.[4]

A significant characteristic of biblical prophecies concerning Israel, including those about final events, involves clear distinctions between

"Israel" and the "church," despite much they have in common spiritually. The nation of Israel originated with Abraham, was originally led by Moses, and was, during Old Testament times, governed by the divine laws given to Moses by God. Membership in the body of Israel is by physical birth as a Jew. In the broadest sense "Israel" refers to the entire history of the Jewish people as an earthly, political body from the time of the covenants, through deliverance, conquests, disobedience, exile, restoration, rejection of Christ, loss of nation, centuries of dispersion, and the regathering as a nation since 1948, as well as the future history of the nation.[5] Some Jews have accepted Christ as Messiah and Savior from his time onward and have become part of the church (most notably, the apostles), but most have not. Israel as a majority group has rejected Christ as Messiah and Savior from his lifetime onward, and as a divine judgment, lost possession of the Promised Land and Temple.

On the other hand, one key meaning of the "church" is a reference to all true believers, both Gentile and Jew, who have accepted Christ as Messiah and Savior and received the gift of the Holy Spirit from the time of Pentecost (several weeks after the death and resurrection of Christ) onward. The church is non-ethnic, a *spiritual* rather than a national body, with no particular land, nationality, or race, united in Christ by the indwelling of the Holy Spirit. In 1 Corinthians 10:32 "Paul clearly distinguished" between Israel and the church. And in Romans 11:25-27 he spoke of Israel's restoration after the church age is completed: "Israel has experienced a hardening in part until the full number of the Gentiles has come in. And so all Israel will be saved, as it is written: 'The deliverer will come from Zion; he will turn godlessness away from Jacob. And this is my covenant with them when I take away their sins.'"[6]

Further differences between Israel and the church include the everlasting covenants that God made with Israel, which have not yet been completely fulfilled. "Emphatically declared in the Abrahamic covenant is the promise of the Holy Land to Abraham's physical descendants. The church received no such promise . . . . The New Testament nowhere switches over the Abrahamic promise from Israel to the church . . . ." This land-promise from God to Israel was unconditional and intended to be eternal. It includes what is now Israel, Jordan, Lebanon, Syria, on up to northern Iraq. Although it has been partly, but never completely fulfilled, it "must have a future literal fulfilment." Another divine covenant, not yet fulfilled, also distinguishes Israel significantly from the church: the Davidic covenant, which guarantees that a descendant of David will forever reign on his throne in Jerusalem, was made with Israel, with no part of the covenant promised to the church.[7] The New Testament makes it clear that the descendant of King David identified is Jesus Christ, "the son of David, the son of Abraham,"[8]

Jesus foreold his future literal reign over Israel at his Second Coming, served by his twelve apostles: "I tell you the truth, at the renewal of things, when the Son of Man sits on his glorious throne, you who have followed me will also sit on twelve thrones, judging the twelve tribes of Israel" (Matthew 19:28; cf. 24:30).[9] The Bible indicates, as Geisler writes, "the Second Coming is a literal physical return in a literal physical body. Jesus left physically and visibly, and He will return in the same manner, as Zechariah and John foresaw."[10] "Both He and His apostles will be in physical resurrection bodies. The reign after Christ's return can be no less literal and physical than the body in which He comes to reign; *a denial of Christ's literal reign is, in effect, a denial of His literal resurrection body.*"[11]

In the ancient world the Jews largely rejected Jesus as the Messiah, thus dismissing the possibility of his earthly Kingdom. John the Baptist exorted them to repent, and receive the coming Kingdom of God. And even after the church began, Peter called on the men of Israel and their leaders to repent, accept Jesus as Messiah, and receive his Kingdom. But, as God foreknew, they would not. And so, God initiated the time of the church, or "times of the Gentiles," to last for an undisclosed, intervening time period.[12] Because Israel did not repent, she in large part became hardened against faith in Christ. God did not totally and finally reject Israel as his chosen people for this, however, or for killing his prophets in previous centuries. Instead he brought judgment on them through dispersion and "hardening of the heart."[13] That would not essentially change until God's mission with the Gentiles was accomplished.

Since Israel did not repent when she had the chance, it can only occur at a future time following the time of the Gentiles—at the Second Coming: "the nation as a whole will be converted when their Messiah returns."[14] "The church and Israel are two distinct groups with whom God has a divine plan. The church is a mystery, unrevealed in the Old Testament. This present mystery age intervenes within the program of God for Israel because of Israel's rejection of the Messiah at His first advent. This mystery program must be completed before God can resume His program with Israel and bring it to completion."[15]

There must be a literal fulfillment of God's unconditional covenants with Israel. Geisler states that "The only way to deny Israel's literal national future is to deny literal interpretations of all covenants with Israel." But as he further shows, "denial of the literal hermeneutic is both self-defeating *and* undermining of the Christian faith." The literal hermeneutic, along with theology based on the biblical attributes of God, makes such a national future *certain* for Israel. As divine Creator, sovereign Lord and providential controller of history, God willed and decreed his plan and purpose for Israel from all eternity. Since God has infallible foreknowledge, what he willed in the covenants must surely come to pass. His eternal decrees and unconditional covenants will be accomplished by his immutable will and omnipotent power. It is by his omnisapience that God planned Israel's unconditional election, dispersion, and ultimate restoration.[16]

By divine covenant the people of Israel are thus especially favored and loved by God. "God has not, will not, and cannot cast them away."[17] God has specifically declared to the people of Israel that they are "his people, his treasured possession" and "he will set [them] in praise, fame and honor high above all the nations he has made and that [they] will be a people holy to the Lord [their] God, as he promised."[18] "They have been entrusted with the very words of God."[19] "Theirs is the adoption as sons; theirs is the divine glory, the covenants, the receiving of the law, the temple worship and the promises. Theirs are the patriarchs, and from them is traced the human ancestry of Christ, who is God over all . . . ."[20]

The official reestablishment of Israel as a nation in 1948 is a towering landmark in the fulfillment of covenant and prophecy. In spite of her infidelities, the power that ultimately stands behind Israel is God the Lord of creation and history. Israel continues to endure serious opposition and suffering, however, which is consistent with the history of her punishment for disobedience of God and rejection of Jesus Christ as Messiah. But an even greater time of suffering is prophesied for Israel in the future (the Tribulation period), to be followed by a final reconciliation with God in Jesus Christ, and the salvation of Israel.[21] Israel will have a *"functionally superior place* . . . in the future messianic kingdom."[22]

The Central Importance of Israel and Jerusalem. Much about the central importance of Israel and Jerusalem in God's final Kingdom was revealed to the prophet Isaiah long before the time of Christ: "In the last days the mountain [Mount Zion] of the Lord's temple will be established as chief among the mountains; it will be raised above the hills, and all nations will stream to it. Many peoples will come and say, 'Come, let us go up to the mountain of the Lord, to the house of the God of Jacob. He will teach us his ways, so that we may walk in his paths.' The law will go out from Zion, the word of the Lord from Jerusalem." Isaiah further declared that unbelieving neighbor nations who hate and oppress Israel would at a future time "come over to you and will be yours; they will trudge behind you, coming over to you in chains. They will bow down before you and plead with you, saying, 'Surely God is with you, and there is no other; there is no other god.'"[23] Fulfillment of this prophecy remains in the future.

The city of Jerusalem itself is central to God's eternal plan for creation. God the Sovereign Lord declared: "This is Jerusalem, which I have set in the center of the nations, with countries all around her."[24] It is divinely predestined to be the key city of the world and of the Eternal Kingdom of God—the city beloved by Jews and Christians through the centuries, and the final Holy City of God—the *New Jerusalem.* Jerusalem is "the apple of God's eye,"[25] and the eternal capital of the nation of Israel. King David established Jerusalem as the capital of Israel about 1004 BC. David brought the Ark of the Covenant to Jerusalem, but was not allowed to build the Temple. God's presence was manifested between the wings of the cherubs on top of the Ark.[26] The Ark and the divine presence spiritually established Jerusalem as the City of God.

Just as Israel and Jerusalem are central, not only to Jews, but to world history, including future events, so is the Temple of God originally located in Jerusalem. David's son Solomon built the First Temple on a sacred site in Jerusalem. It was on Mount Moriah, on a threshing floor where David had previously erected his altar, and where Abraham had started to sacrifice his son Isaac, as God had commanded. The Temple was completed about 959 BC, after seven years work. God told Solomon: "I have chosen and consecrated this temple so that my name may be there *forever.* My eyes and my heart will *always* be there."[27] A divine promise of "forever" and "always" from God cannot fail to come to pass.

It was in Jerusalem that Jesus Christ was later crucified, taking upon himself all the sins of mankind. And it was in Jerusalem that Jesus arose from the dead to make eternal life available to all who would believe in him. At a special time in the future, Jerusalem will become "The Throne of the Lord, and all nations will gather in Jerusalem to honor the name of the Lord."[28] God has made an enduring promise of great portent for the future of Israel: "I will return to Zion and dwell in Jerusalem. Then Jerusalem will be called the City of Truth, and the mountain of the Lord Almighty will be called the Holy Mountain."[29]

God's Warnings to Israel, and Punishments. At the time Solomon built the Temple, God gave a warning to him and to Israel, and he foretold exactly what would happen if the people did not remain faithful and obedient: "As for you, if you walk before me as David your father did, and do all I command, and observe my decrees and laws, I will establish your royal throne, as I covenanted with David your father when I said, 'You shall never fail to have a man to rule over Israel.' But if you turn away and forsake the decrees and commands I have given you and go off to serve other gods and worship them, *then I will uproot Israel from my land, which I have given them, and will reject this temple I have consecrated for my Name.* I will make it a byword and an object of ridicule among all peoples. And though this temple is now so imposing, all who pass by will be appalled and say, 'Why has the Lord done such a thing to this land and to this temple?' People will answer, 'Because they have forsaken the Lord, the God of their fathers, who brought them out of Egypt, and have embraced other gods, worshiping and serving them—that is why he brought all this disaster on them'."[30]

But Solomon, influenced by his 700 wives and 300 concubines, many of whom were foreign, increasingly included pagan gods in his worship, and built religious structures for Ashtoreth, Molech, and Chemosh. Ashtoreth was a goddess of sex and fertility, involving licentious sexual rites and worship of the stars. Molech worship included human sacrifices, especially of children. The worship of Chemosh also included child sacrifice and sexual licentiousness. Solomon moved further away from the God of his father David as he grew older.[31] For such extreme disobedience, God took away most of the kingdom from Solomon at his death, and split it into two parts, Israel and Judah.

Israel became progressively worse during the centuries following Solomon's death in 930 BC. God did exactly as he had foretold. The steep nature of the spiritual decline during the next three centuries is traced in Kings 1 and 2. The wickedest king Israel ever had, Ahab, ruled for about 22 years (874-853 BC) with his evil wife Jezebel. Pagan worship became widespread, and many of God's prophets were killed. During subsequent decades the people broke all the commands of God, worshiping calf idols, Asherah poles, Baal, and the "starry hosts." They even sacrificed their sons and daughters to Molech in fire. And they practiced divination and sorcery, provoking the wrath of God. God then caused the northern kingdom of Israel to be conquered and the people taken into captivity into Assyria in 722 BC.[32]

King Manassah, who ruled Judah for 55 years from 697 to 642, built altars to the pagan gods Baal and Asherah, the sun, and starry hosts. He sacrificed his own son in fire to Molech; he practiced sorcery and divination, and consulted mediums and spiritists. The holy places of the Jews were filled with pagan practices hateful to God. There were child sacrifices and shrines of prostitution in the temples.[33] Manassah's son, Amon, continued his evil practices until he was assassinated in 640 BC. God said of Manasseh through his prophets: "He has done more evil than the Amorites who preceded him and has led Judah into sin with his idols .... I am going to bring such disaster on Jerusalem and Judah that the ears of everyone who hears of it will tingle .... I will wipe out Jerusalem as one wipes a dish, wiping it and turning it upside down."[34]

A godly king, Josiah, changed the situation for a while during his reign (640-609 BC), having pagan sites and articles destroyed. But the people's hearts remained unfaithful after his death, and God's "fierce anger" still burned against Judah for all that Manasseh had done. God declared: "I will remove Judah also from my presence as I removed Israel, and I will reject

Jerusalem, the city I chose, and this temple, about which I said, 'There shall my Name be.'"[35] In 605 BC, after 325 years of growing defiance, God permitted the Babylonians under Nebuchadnezzar to enter the land and conquer Judah, the southern kingdom. Thousands were taken off into captivity in Babylon, including the faithful Daniel. Most of the treasures were taken from the Temple.[36]

Eight years later in 597 BC, God sent another message through his prophet Jeremiah, revealing his supreme control of empires and events as divine Creator and what was to happen to Judah because of her unfaithfulness: "This is what the Lord Almighty, the God of Israel, says: 'Tell this to your masters: With my great power and outstretched arm I made the earth and its people and the animals that are on it, and I give it to anyone I please. Now I will hand all your countries over to my servant Nebuchadnezzar king of Babylon; I will make even the wild animals subject to him. All nations will serve him and his son and his grandson until the time for his land comes; then many nations and great kings will subjugate him.'" Nebuchadnezzar's army then returned for the second time to defeat Jerusalem, loot it, and replace the king.[37]

After many warnings from God, and two devastating defeats within eight years, Israel had not learned her lesson. God the Lord of nations and history then sent this message through Jeremiah: "I am about to hand this city over to the Babylonians and to Nebuchadnezzar king of Babylon, who will capture it. The Babylonians who are attacking this city will come in and set it on fire; they will burn it down, along with the houses where the people provoked me to anger by burning incense on the roofs to Baal and by pouring out drink offerings to other gods."[38]

And so, in 586 BC, God permitted Nebuchadnezzar's army to return and completely destroy Jerusalem and the Temple built by Solomon. The walls of the city were knocked down and all important buildings were razed. This was a momentous destruction. The last evil king, Zedekiah, was captured. "They killed the sons of Zedekiah before his eyes. Then they put out his eyes, bound him with bronze shackles and took him to Babylon."[39] In this violent and ignominious manner the monarchy in Israel, which had held such a great future if Israel had remained faithful to God, was ended, and it has not yet been restored. But God revealed to Daniel that he had a greater, future plan for his people, the Jews, that would be fulfilled in a special place, Jerusalem: "Seventy 'sevens' are decreed for your people and your holy city to finish transgression, to put an end to sin, to atone for wickedness, to bring in everlasting righteousness, to seal up vision and prophecy and to anoint the most holy."[40]

After seventy years in captivity in Babylon, however, 50,000 Israelites of Judah were allowed to return to Jerusalem. Consistent work on rebuilding the Second Temple, under the leadership of Zerubbabel, began in 520 BC and it was completed and rededicated in 515 BC. By 170 BC, during Hellenistic times, this Second Temple was plundered and many Jews were killed during an ivasion. The ruler, Antiochus IV, desecrated the Temple in 168 BC, by placing a statue of Zeus in the Holy of Holies, and sacrificing a pig (an unclean animal) on the Temple altar. As Randall Price writes, "This action had been predicted by the prophet Daniel . . . and served as a partial fulfillment of the type of destruction the Temple would one day suffer under the Antichrist. . . ."[41] Another desecration occurred in 63 BC when the Jews were defeated by a Roman army led by Pompey. Pompey tore away the veil and walked into the Holy of Holies, thinking he would find valuables there, including a sculpture of a god. He was surprised to find it "empty" and "dark."[42]

Beginning in 19 BC Herod began a massive reconstruction and enlargement of the Second Temple. While the main part of the sacrificial area was completed in seven years, the remaining work went on for decades until about AD 63. In 67 the Roman army was sent to crush a full-scale Jewish rebellion. In April of 70 the Romans, led by Vespasian's son Titus, began a seige of Jerusalem that went on for months. Starvation became so bad for the Israelites that tens of thousands of them died, and some turned to cannibalism.

Amazingly, this seige, suffering, starvation, and cannibalism had been prophesied by Moses *over fourteen centuries earlier* in a startling passage in Deuteronomy! "The Lord will bring a nation against you from far away, from the ends of the earth, like an eagle swooping down." (The emblem of the Roman Empire was the eagle! And an image of the Roman eagle had been fixed over the Temple door in 4 BC, defiling the Temple and provoking a riot.) "They will lay siege to all the cities throughout your land until the high fortified walls in which you trust fall down . . . . Because of the suffering that your enemy will inflict on you during the siege, you will eat the fruit of the womb, the flesh of the sons and daughters the Lord your God has given you. Even the most gentle and sensitive man among you will have no compassion on his own brother or the wife he loves or his surviving children, and he will not give to one of them any of the flesh of his children that he is eating." The same was prophesied of the women.[43]

Later in AD 70 the Romans took Jerusalem and slaughtered the Israelite priests and people until blood ran through the streets. According to secular Jewish historian Josephus, who lived during the time, 1.1 million died and 97,000 were taken prisoner.[44] The Romans tore down the city defense walls, and sacked the city and the Temple. Then they completely destroyed the Temple until not one stone was left upon another, as Jesus Christ had predicted about 37 years earlier.[45] Many prisoners were exiled, or sold into slavery. Others were taken to Rome, led in chains in a triumphal procession, or sent to their deaths by lions or gladiators in the Colosseum. The triumph of Titus is commemorated in sculptures on the famous Arch of Titus, which still stands in Rome today.

The great Diaspora had begun—the Jews were cast out of their homeland. Their Temple and their beautiful, beloved Jerusalem were destroyed. While Jerusalem has been rebuilt, the Temple, as prophecy also indicates, has not. Interestingly, Titus, who had led the siege and destruction of Jerusalem and the Temple, and the parading of prisoners and spoils, died of a fever 11 years later, not quite 42.

In brief, these are some of the key historical facts of early Jewish history as the chosen people of God. Old Testament books not only recorded many of their actual divine punishments, but warned against them well in advance, time after time, and with the consequences accurately foretold decades or centuries before they happened, along with the reasons. These biblical prophecies have been proven true and accurate, in startling fashion, down to specific details.

Jerusalem has been a city of great conflict and battles, and has continued to survive threats, attacks, and battles since 1948. The greatest and most essential opposition and conflict of all in the world and in Israel must surely be that of Satan and his evil forces against God and his angels and saints.

Spiritual Warfare. The warfare between God and the Devil, and between humans, the Devil and his demons, was well understood during the Middle Ages and Renaissance, and was often represented in sculpture and paintings. A few examples well illustrate this. Two figured capitals in the nave of the Basilica of Ste. Madeleine at Vézelay, France show the temptations and tortures of demons on humans. *Profane Music and the Demon of Licentiousness* (Fig. 12) indicates how some types of music can lead one to sinful behavior. As the musician plays a profane tune, a demon takes hold of a woman, leading her to licentious thoughts and actions. A similar one in the same church (not shown), *Lust and the Demon of Despair*, depicts a woman who has given herself over to lusts of the flesh. The sinfulness of her actions is indicated by the snake twining upward around her legs; her agony is conveyed by her hand pulling and twisting her breast. She is losing her personal battle with tempting evil spirits, and the horrible-looking demon of despair to the left delights in torturing her. Romanesque demons (although spirit beings) are frequently shown with animal-like bodies, repulsive looking heads, snarling mouths and great tufts of hair flying upward. Works like these were meant to be revolting, in order to strengthen resolve against temptations.

In *The Devil and Luxuria* (image not available), a relief sculpture of about 1130, the Devil himself has a firm grip on a woman who has abandoned herself to the sin of lust or sexual wantonness (*luxuria*). He holds her by the wrist, while she twists and struggles to free herself from the effects of her slavery. In contrast to much Romanesque sculpture, she is depicted as a slender woman, with long-legs and shapely figure. Her long wavy hair also evokes youth and sexuality. The harmful effects of her sins are conveyed in ways indicating excruciating pain—two snakes curl up her body, around her arms, and bite her breasts, while a large toad has a biting hold on her genitals. Her head is tilted down toward her body and both arms are thrown up, expressing her horror at her condition. The Devil is shown, as always in Romanesque art as a terrifying figure. It is his terrible effects on people that are stressed, rather than his allure and attractions. His hair sticks up in curved, spiky clumps behind horns. He has a bloated belly, indicating another vice, and bony animal legs with hairy tufts or spurs and big claw feet. These gruesomely powerful images must have had a strong effect on any who entered the church here.

The temptation of Eve and Adam was the subject of a large lintel sculpture of the former north transept portal at the Cathedral of St. Lazare in Autun, France. The only part still preserved is the remarkable, large figure of *Eve* (Fig. 13), stretched horizontally across part of the original, long lintel. To the left of Eve was Adam (missing), probably of a similar length and position, facing her. Behind her was the devil, also missing, except for his claw hand, pushing down the branch with the fruit toward her grasping hand. She too is young, tall, and shapely, with long silky hair and large, seductive eyes. One hand is near her mouth, as she seems to whisper to Adam, encouraging him to eat the fruit of the Tree of Knowledge of good and evil. The existence of the devil and demons, and spiritual warfare between them and humans or God is the theme of all these works.

Today, in the post-Enlightenment modern world, the kind of spiritual warfare depicted in these works has been denied, forgotten, and scoffed at. The Devil, demons, and spirits are a joke to modernity and postmodernity. Even the concept of God is a bad joke, or rather a curse on history and humanity to radical modernist and postmodernist philosophers, and contemporary atheists like Dawkins, Dennett, Hitchens, and Harris.

But since God has determined and promised to make Israel the center of the world and Jerusalem its capital and divine place of residence, with God's own Temple, we would expect Satan, the great Adversary of God, to

Fig. 12. *Profane Music and the Demon of Licentiousness* (Demon Of
Impurity), c.1120-32. Nave capital, Church of Ste. Madelene, Vézelay, Burgundy,
France. Detail of Romanesque capital in the nave of Vézelay Basilica, depicting
the wickedness of non-sacred music. © Holly Hayes/Art History Images.

Fig. 13. *The Temptation of Eve*, c. 1130. Limestone sculpture by Gislebertus. Lintel of former north transept portal, Cathedral of St. Lazare, Autun, France. Now in the Musée Rolin, Autun, France. © Holly Hayes/Art History Images.

oppose this plan of God to his utmost, and try to defeat it. That certainly seems to describe the facts through ancient history, as well as today. God gave Satan permission to assail and test Job, who was a godly man. And he allowed Satan to discipline and punish Israel massively and painfully for her gross unfaithfulness, disobedience, and rejection of Christ. Israel was thus decimated and thrown out of her Promised Land.

Islam: the Enemy of Israel and Christianity. The present, decades-old conflict between Israel and its neighbors and their sympathisers appears agonizingly intense, threatening, and unstoppable. The hatred of Israel by millions in neighboring Islamic countries has been well documented.[46] Suicide bombers are sent in to kill indiscriminately, gunmen go in to murder, rockets are fired to kill whomever they may hit. Thousands happily celebrate in the streets when several Israelis are killed (as on March 6, 2008, with a gunman killing eight young rabbinical seminary students and wounding nine in a library in Jerusalem).[47] And recall that many thousands celebrated in the streets in several Islamic countries on 9-11-01.

A highly significant event in the history of spiritual warfare is the building of the Islamic Dome of the Rock on Temple Mount in Jerusalem in AD 691 (on what they thought was the exact spot of the much earlier Jewish Temple of God, although they mistakenly missed the exact spot). A careful study of the Koran and subsequent Islamic theology also reveals a plethora of attempts to replace and redefine the Bible (6 to 26 centuries after the Bible was written!), and set Islamic beliefs in direct opposition and conflict with the essential content of the Old and New Testaments. Prominent examples for the New Testament include: denial of the divinity of Christ; the claim that Christ was created out of dust by Allah; the claim that Jesus and his Apostles worshipped and served Allah; the claim that Jesus did not die on the cross, but ascended to be with Allah, and would return in end times as a servant of Allah, and to kill everyone, especially Jews and Christians, who refuse to serve Allah; the claim that Jesus would then institute and enforce world-wide Islamic Sharia law, and then marry, have a family, and die.[48]

The Koran and Islam directly oppose and contradict innumerable facts, meanings, and purposes of the Old and New Testaments, including the most essential ones, such as: that the Jews are the chosen people of God; that Israel is the Promised Land given to the Jews by God in everlasting covenant, with Jerusalem as the capital; that God has made enduring covenants with Israel, promising them the divine Messiah-King out of their own nation, who will rule eternally on the throne of David; that God divinely inspired the Bible and that it is inerrant. Old Testament apocalyptic prophecy from the Living God of Israel gives us a comletely different understanding of end-times in comparison to the much later claims of Muhammad, the Koran, and Islam.

Islam uses many similar elements, but reverses their meanings to favor Allah and Muslims (for example, Jesus returns to serve Allah, and kill Jews and Christians). These diametrically opposed claims tell us much about the culmination of spiritual warfare in end-times.

For nearly fourteen centuries, since their origin with Muhammad in the early seventh century, Islamic teachings have stood in stark opposition to Jews and to Christians and their beliefs. Since Israel regained nationhood in 1948 the oppositon has grown into fiery hatred and violence. Today radical Muslims and great multitudes of Muslim populations in the Middle East are either violent, avowed adversaries, intent on killing as many as possible, or simply intense haters of Jews and Christians. That hatred is focused on Jerusalem and the Promised Land of Israel, but it reaches into other parts of the world, even America. That hatred and murderous violence also extends to opposing sects of Islamic belief, with Sunnis killing Shiites, and Shiites killing Sunnis. There is also much murderous hatred for Muslims who give any kind of assistance to Jews or Americans. There have been a large number of books published during the past decade that show in considerable detail, the kind of ideology and hatred that lies at the core of radical Muslim beliefs, some of the books by former Muslims who have converted to Christianity.[49]

The most essential conflict of Islam with Christianity is the fact that Islam and the Koran deny the divinity of Jesus Christ. Since Satan's essential goal is to contradict and defeat God's work in the world and his most important teaching in the Bible, the key way to do it is to deny the divinity of Christ and his crucifixion for the salvation of humanity. So it is emphasized in the Koran and for Islam: Jesus is not "the only begotten Son of God," and triune equal of Father and Holy Spirit, as the Bible and Christian theology teach.[50] The Koran says that Allah "begetteth not," and "None is equal to Him."[51] It claims that saying Jesus Christ is the Son of God is a *lie*.[52] It is blasphemous to say that Jesus Christ is God: "They do blaspheme who declare: 'God is the Messiah, the son of Mary.'"[53] The Koran also puts a curse on everyone who believes that Christ is the Son of God.[54] To speak of a Trinity is also blasphemous.[55] Jesus was only a man, a prophet; Allah "created him from dust," like Adam (which means that Jesus will return to dust).[56] The Koran even "quotes" Jesus denying his divinity, saying "I am the servant of Allah."[57] It makes Jesus and his disciples appear like seventh-century Muslims. When Jesus asks his disciples who will help him in the work of Allah, they respond "We are Allah's helpers we believe in Allah, and do you bear witness that we are Muslims."[58] According to the Koran, Jesus did not die on the cross for our sins, and did not rise from the grave three days later. It declares that the story of Christ's death on the cross is a "monstrous falsehood."[59]

John the Apostle of Christ gave the biblical judgment about such denials of the divinity of Jesus Christ and his role as Savior: "Every spirit that acknowledges that Jesus Christ has come in the flesh is from God, but every spirit that does not acknowledge Jesus is not from God. This is the spirit of the antichrist, which you have heard is coming, and even now is in the world."[60] Citing passages from the Koran, Joel Richardson has written perceptively about "the antichrist spirit of Islam" in his 2006 book, *Antichrist; Islam's Awaited Messiah*: "The religion of Islam, more than any other religion, philosophy, or belief system, fulfills the description of the antichrist spirit. The religion of Islam makes it one of its highest priorities to very specifically deny . . . 1. That Jesus is the Christ/Messiah (The savior/deliverer of Israel and the world); 2. The Father and the Son (The Trinity or that Jesus is The Son of God); 3. That Jesus has come in the flesh (The Incarnation—that God became man)." The Muslim suggestion that Jesus is the Messiah is "just trickery," since they deny Christ the essential roles of Messiah—"Divine Priestly Savior, a Deliverer and the King of the Jews." Rather than being the true Messianic King of the Jews, "in the Islamic traditions, Jesus instead returns to lead Israel's enemies against her in battle and to kill or convert all Jews and Christians [to Islam]." Richardson says there can be no question that Islam "has been from its inception, the quintessence of the very antichrist spirit that John the apostle warned us of."[61]

The core New Testament and Christian message is that Jesus is the eternal Word of God, and the unique and eternal Son and Mediator of God to humanity,[62] and the Holy Spirit is God who indwells, regenerates, sanctifies, and guides believers. (This is not "polytheism" as the Koran and Islam assert, because God is three Persons in *One Being*.)[63] And 1 John says: "And we have seen and testify that the Father has sent his Son to be the Savior of the world. If anyone acknowledges that Jesus is the Son of God, God lives in him and he in God."[64] Jesus' purpose in coming into the world as God-man was both to expand and culminate God's revelation to humanity, and to provide the means for the salvation of all human beings through his own death for all their sins, and his triumph over death by resurrection, making possible resurrection and everlasting life for all believers.

As we have just seen, the Israelites rejected Christ as Messiah and Savior. That is the major reason the Jews were severely punished and cast out of Israel in ancient times. But there is a crucial difference with Islam. Israel was chosen as the nation of God from the time of Abraham onward, and still is. Israel was given God's everlasting covenant of the Promised Land twenty-six centuries before Muhammad and Islam. Islam's claim that Allah gave the land to Muslims is based on its own much later claims that contradict the Old and New Testaments.

Israel will also be the priviledged and paramount focus of end-times, even though it involves world-wide punishment, and great wars focused on Israel. The primary purpose and goal will be the salvation of the covenant people of God as a whole, the establishment of Christ's Millennium, and then the Eternal Kingdom of God. The Koran and Islam represent an aggressive and militant rejection of Christ's divinity. And the Koran calls for the faithful to spread Islam world-wide, with force whenever necessary. Muslims and their nations now have the opportunity to turn to the Living God through belief in Christ. In the end-times, that opportunity will become more pressing, influenced by cataclysmic demonstrations of God's actual power as he supports Israel against invasions by their enemies.

The Koran and Hadith, the two holiest books of Islam, command faithful believers in Allah to seek out unbelievers, "infidels," wherever they find them and kill them if they will not submit to belief in Islam. (Most prominent among the "infidels" and "unbelievers" are the "people of the book," the Jews and Christians.) There are numerous commands to kill in the Koran: Allah says, "I will cast terror into the hearts of those who disbelieve. Therefore strike off their heads and strike off every fingertip of them."[65] The Koran tells the killer there is no guilt for his deed because: "you did not slay them, but it was Allah who slew them, and you did not smite when you smote (the enemy), but it was Allah Who smote." Allah does this so he may test the believer and confer a good gift upon him from himself.[66] "Fight against those who (1) believe not in Allah, (2) nor in the Last Day, (3) nor forbid that which has been forbidden by Allah and His Messenger (4) and those who acknowledge not the religion of truth (i.e. Islam) among the people of the Scripture (Jews and Christians), until they pay the Jizyah [tax on non-Muslims] with willing submission, and feel themselves subdued."[67]

The true Muslim must "fight them until there is no more *Fitnah* (disbelief and polytheism: i.e. worshipping others besides Allah) and the religion (worship) will all be for Allah Alone [in the whole of the world]. But if they cease (worshipping others besides Allah), then certainly, Allah is All-Seer of what they do."[68] "Use all weapons available to defeat the Infidels: "make ready against them all you can of power, including steeds of war (tanks, planes, missiles, artillery, etc.) to threaten the enemy of Allah and your enemy, and others besides whom, you may not know but whom Allah does know. And whatever you shall spend in the Cause of Allah shall be repaid unto you, and you shall not be treated unjustly."[69] Except on sacred months "slay the idolaters wherever you find them, and take them captives and besiege them and lie in wait for them in every ambush, then if they repent and keep up prayer and pay the poor-rate, leave their way free to them; surely Allah is Forgiving, Merciful."[70]

The state of Israel was given official sanction in 1948 by the United Nations, not in terms of spiritual warfare, but as a national political right. Muslims see it as spiritual warfare against Allah and the land they claim Allah gave to the Arabs. Many Jews and Christians also see it in terms of spiritual warfare because God gave the Promised Land to the Jews by everlasting covenant 4000 years ago, and *never* promised it to Arabs or Muslims. The wars with Iraq by America and its allies in 1991 and since 2003 have not been fought as spiritual warfare—as attacks on Allah and Islam—but to oppose the aggressive military, territorial, and oil-power ambitions of Saddam Hussein. America and its allies fought the war in Afghanistan in retaliation for the 9-11 calamitous attacks on America by al Qaeda led by bin Laden. While America has not fought these wars for the reason of spiritual warfare, they actually *are* forms of spiritual warfare because Muslim's, following Islamic teachings, see it as their "religious" duty to destroy by murder, terrorism, and war, all other religious beliefs in the world, especially those of Christianity and of Jews. Because they are so heavily influenced by the teachings of the Koran and traditional Islam, millions of Muslims see these events in terms of spiritual warfare. While the prevailing American political viewpoint does not see them as spiritual warfare, they actually do represent an assault by Islam against Christianity, Israel, and the Jews.

A strong sense of their duty to hate, destroy, and kill non-Muslims, based on such teachings in the Koran, in their *madrassas*, in mosques, on TV, and by "holy men," is what drives militant Muslims and millions of Muslims who approve and support them. With such commands in the Koran to kill in order to spread the religion of Allah worldwide, and with the Koran's special focus on Jews and Christians as the key enemies, can we be surprised by the atrocities they commit? Indiscriminate killings by suicide bombers, roadside bombs, and chopping off heads are just the tip of the iceberg. In her powerful and moving book about Muslim hatred, murder, and methods of destruction, Lebanese Christian Brigitte Gabriel tells what Muslims did as they invaded the towns of Lebanon in 1975. In the town of Damour

thousands of Christians were slaughtered like sheep. The combined forces of PLO and the Muslims would enter a bomb shelter and see a mother and a father hiding with a little baby. They would tie one leg of the baby to the mother and one leg to the father and pull the parents apart, splitting the child in half. A close friend of mine became mentally disturbed after they made her slaughter her own son in a chair. They tied her to a chair, tied a knife to her hand, and, holding her hand, forced her to cut her own sixteen-year-old son's throat. After killing him they raped her two daughters in front of her. They would urinate and defecate on the altars of churches using the pages of the Bible as toilet paper before shooting and destroying the church.[71]

In a second book, *They Must Be Stopped*, Gabriel gives pages of quotations to document the fact that it is a *religious war* that radical Islam is waging, and plans to continue waging. Islam has not been "hijacked." Terrorism, killing, and suicide bombings are what pure Islam teaches.[72] Can a religion that promotes such atrocities and depravities really be a religion of God and of peace?[73]

Why do they do such things? And why did they dance in the streets and pass out candy after atrocities such as 9-11, or the murder of the eight young rabbinical students? Gabriel writes that it is "because they hate."

They hate our way of life. They hate our freedom. They hate our democracy. They hate the practice of every religion but their own. They don't just disagree. They *hate*. Not just Judaism. Not just Christianity. In various parts of the world today, Islamists are also waging terror war against Hindus, Buddhists, and all other "infidels." The imposition of Islam upon the entire world is not merely their goal. It is their religious duty. They are following the word of their holy book, the Koran, which is the guide to hatred of infidels, waging war, and victory through slaughter.[74]

How do they manage to spread hate, commit atrocities, and still persuade so many people that terrorists are themselves the victims of aggression, a war on Islam, and that Islam is a "religion of peace"? Gabriel shows that it is because of their policy of deception, lying, manipulation of the media, intimidation (and murder) of the press, and the absence of a free press in the Muslim world. She quotes several Islamic scholars and writers who say that it is not only permissable, but even *religious*, to lie if it promotes Islam. "Since the sacred goal of jihad is to make Islam 'supreme in this world,' every lie told to achieve that goal is not only permitted, but sanctified." A Saudi Arabian website (www.iad.org) promotes jihad to rule the world: "The Muslims are required to raise the banner of Jihad in order to make the Word of Allah supreme in the world."[75]

The Real God's Love. In diametric contrast to the Koranic and Islamic call for killing of unbelievers, we have seen what Jesus Christ and the New Testament call for in the Chapter Seven. Nowhere does Jesus call for hatred or persecution of non-believers, or for killing them because of their unbelief. Just the opposite: hate and anger are denounced at length by Jesus.[76] Nowhere does the Bible call for killing unbelievers to forcefully spread the gospel (although God himself at times punishes and takes the life of disbelievers who staunchly oppose his good purposes). Jesus taught that we should love not only the poor and needy, but even those who do not deserve it, those who do not love you, and those who work against you: "love your enemies, bless those who curse you, do good to those who hate you, and pray for those who spitefully use you and persecute you."[77] (But you must also defend yourself or die when they come at you with a sword or a bomb, or when they infiltrate your country with the intent of destroying it.)

God not only loves those who love Him, but also loves his enemies, and tells us to do the same. Jesus calls believers to a higher level of love for all, even their enemies: "For if you forgive men when they sin against you, your heavenly Father will also forgive you. But if you do not forgive men their sins, your Father will not forgive your sins."[78] John the Evangelist taught the new commandment of love as Jesus did: "Anyone who claims to be in the light but hates his brother is still in the darkness. Whoever loves his brother lives in the light, and there is nothing in him to make him stumble. But whoever hates his brother is in the darkness and walks around in the darkness; he does not know where he is going, because the darkness has blinded him."[79]

The Real Kingdom of God. It is important at this point to reemphasize the idea of God's sovereign control and rule over all of creation from the very beginning. This universal divine reign and providence is theologically designated as "God's universal kingdom." Geisler has written about the Kingdom of God, including this universal sense, supported by many Old and New Testament passages. Most basically, he states, "Because God is eternal, so are all of His plans. That God's rule of the universe is from the very beginning of its creation is another way of speaking about His sovereignty. His earthly reign, and particularly that of the Messiah, is one planned from all eternity." "In one sense, *everything* is in God's kingdom, for since He reigns over the entire universe and nothing is out of His control, it is appropriate to speak of everything as under His dominion."[80] "This divine reign is the foundation for all other spheres of His sovereign rule."[81]

"God's Kingdom" thus not only refers to his "all-encompassing, invisible, everlasting reign over the entire universe," but includes other aspects of God's complete plan for creation. A crucially important aspect is the future Messianic Kingdom, or Millennium, which is "a visible, earthly, political kingdom promised to Israel in which Christ, her Messiah, will reign from a throne in Jerusalem over the whole earth." In order to bring in the Messianic Kingdom God has foreordained a future Rapture and a period of Tribulation for both Jews and Gentiles.

The Rapture. The Tribulation will be an unprecedented time of trial and judgment—the outpourings of God's wrath on people for their unrelenting disbelief and disobedience, having the purpose of leading as many as possible to finally recognize Christ as the true Son of God, Savior, and Messiah. But according to pretribulation understandings of the Rapture, those who truly believe and are redeemed, will not go through the punishments of the Tribulation. This belief in the Rapture is that "the Lord himself [Jesus

Christ] will come down from heaven, with a loud command, with the voice of the archangel and with the trumpet call of God, and the dead in Christ will rise first. After that, we who are still alive and are left will be caught up together with them in the clouds to meet the Lord in the air. And so we will be with the Lord forever" (1 Thessalonians 4:16-17). Since the entire Tribulation is characterized by divine wrath and judgment, the living saved will be removed beforehand in the Rapture. And since Christ through His death for our sins bore God's wrath for every repentant believer, they "shall not come into judgment."[82] "For God did not appoint us to suffer wrath but to receive salvation through our Lord Jesus Christ".[83] Revelation 3:10 also points to a pretribulation Rapture: "Since you have kept my command to endure patiently, I will also keep you from the hour of trial that is going to come upon the whole world to test those who live on the earth."

Geisler presents extensive support for the pretribulation understanding of the Rapture.[84] Only a few points can be mentioned here: (1) the church of believers is mentioned nineteen times in the first three chapters of Revelation, but "not once during the entire Tribulation" (chapters 6-18); (2) no sign precedes the Rapture; many signs precede the Second Coming;[85] (3) only believers see Christ coming at the Rapture; all people see Him at the Second Coming;[86] (4) there is a reference to the church *in heaven* during the Tribulation, and of the church "coming down out of heaven" afterwards;[87] (5) while in heaven during the Tribulation period, believers will receive rewards for their deeds;[88] (6) references to "believers" during the Tribulation are to the 144,000 saved Jews, or to many others converted during the time;[89] (7) believers who live before the Tribulation will be kept from that trial which falls on the whole earth, and saved from God's wrath; salvation from God's wrath means deliverance from the entire Tribulation;[90] (8) the church of believers is not destined for "the time of Jacob's [Israel's] trouble," through which God works to prepare Israel to acknowledge and meet her true Messiah. "This is a time of God's wrath on unbelievers, not on believers; Christ has already borne God's wrath for us."[91]

The Tribulation. Key aspects of the coming end-times and Tribulation were foretold by Moses over thirty-five centuries ago (Deuteronomy 4:23-31)! It will come as a punishment for the sins of Israel; it will be some time after their exile among the nations, and result from the wrath of God. Because of it there will be a spiritual restoration, a return to the Lord God by Israel. It will take place in the "latter days" and will involve a fulfillment of God's covenant with Israel.[92]

Twenty-eight centuries ago Isaiah also predicted the devastating judgments to come during the future Tribulation period, and gave reasons for it: "See, the Lord is going to lay waste the earth and devastate it; he will ruin its face and scatter its inhabitants . . . . The earth will be completely laid waste and totally plundered . . . . *The earth is defiled by its people; they have disobeyed the laws, violated the statutes and broken the everlasting covenant.* Therefore a curse consumes the earth; *its people must bear their guilt.* Therefore earth's inhabitants are burned up, and very few are left . . . . No longer do they drink wine with a song; the beer is bitter to its drinkers. The ruined city lies desolate . . . . all joyful sounds are banished from the earth. The city [Jerusalem] is left in ruins, its gate is battered to pieces . . . . The earth is broken up, the earth is split asunder, the earth is violently shaken. The earth reels like a drunkard, it sways like a hut in the wind; so heavy upon it is *the guilt of its rebellion* that it falls—never to rise again."[93]

Spiritual warfare will reach a peak of deception, violence, catastrophe, warfare and massive deaths during the future seven-year period of Tribulation. These events will be worldwide, not simply local or limited. While Satan will seem to be winning the battle, God will actually be allowing his activity and using the effects of it for His own good purpose—for the final time to spread the word of God and save as many as possible; to destroy those who remain unrepentant; to remove Satan's kingdom from earth, and ultimately bring the entire world under the authority and rule of Jesus Christ the Savior and King in the subsequent Messianic Kingdom. During the Tribulation God will permit Satan to have his greatest influence and power, and to establish his kingdom throughout the earth, in its most extensive and intensive manifestations in history. But its duration will be short—limited to seven years.

Satan will operate by means of a distorted imitation and mimicry of the nature and plan of God. World rule will be established by means of an unholy, satanic "trinity" consisting of "the dragon" (Satan himself), "the beast" (the Antichrist ruler), and "the false prophet" (the spiritual adviser to the Antichrist). Satan's goal will be to replace God the Father, establish his own kingdom, and act as ultimate power and authority; the beast or Antichrist will be intended to replace Jesus Christ the Savior and Messiah; and the false prophet intended to replace the Holy Spirit. "It is Satan's best effort to thwart the plan and Kingdom program of God."[94]

However, the power of judgment rests ultimately with Jesus Christ throughout the Tribulation and the Millennium. His authority to give life and to judge had been revealed much earlier, in His life on earth when He healed a long-term invalid *by his word*—simply by telling the man to get up and walk. When the Jews found out, they persecuted Him and sought to find ways to kill Him. Jesus then told them of His life-giving power and His authority to judge given by His Father: "just as the Father raises the dead and gives them life, even so the Son gives life to whom he is pleased to give it.

Moreover, the Father judges no one, but *has entrusted all judgment to the Son . . . .* For as the Father has life in himself, so he has granted the Son to have life in himself. And he has given him authority to judge because he is the Son of Man."[95] Jesus will thus send the judgments of the Tribulation on the earth, and will rule as the authoritative King, Messiah, and Judge afterwards during the Millennium.

The many terrible judgments to be poured out upon the people of the earth during the seven years of the Tribulation will serve as punishment for unbelievers and those who rebel against God, in order to bring large numbers to repentance. They will also serve as part of final judgment for those who refuse to change. The ultimate purpose will be to subject all people, Jew and Gentile, to Jesus Christ, so that He may rule the whole earth as Messiah-King. Many will suffer terribly, and perhaps billions will die. The judgments through the seals, the trumpets, and the bowls of wrath are "preparatory to the subjugation of the nations to the authority of Christ, and to the enthronement of Christ as Ruler in the kingdom of God of heaven on earth." These judgments issue from the throne of God Himself, and will be executed by "the Lion of the tribe of Judah, the Root of David,"[96] Jesus Christ.

Jesus said of these times, "there will be great distress, unequaled from the beginning of the world until now—and never to be equaled again. If those days had not been cut short, no one would survive, but for the sake of the elect those days will be shortened."[97] But the grace of God will also reach through the earth during the Tribulation. The Gospel message of salvation through Christ and the imminent coming of the Kingdom of God will be preached by 144,000 Jews, who will be emissaries to the Gentiles, and two special "witnesses" sent as prophets to minister to the Jews.[98] Multitudes will repent and be saved by these means.

The Tribulation period will also be characterized by the rise to power of a man of great charisma and influence, identified in Revelation as the Antichrist, or the beast. He will be responsible for a seven-year peace treaty with Israel, marking the beginning of the Tribulation. The Jewish Temple will be rebuilt in Jerusalem and animal sacrifices will resume during the first half of the period. But the Antichrist's true demonic character will be increasingly revealed, and he will break the treaty in the second half of the period and turn on Israel to try to destroy her.

Both halves of the Tribulation (3½ years each) will be characterized by God's wrath, which, as Geisler writes, "persistently intensifies through-out." It will be "an unprecedented time of God's wrath."[99] The entire Tribulation will be a time of God's judgment, a time of trouble, punishment, and destruction. Dwight Pentecost gives extensive scriptural evidence that several such terms used in the Bible "describe the period in its entirety, not just a portion of it, so that the whole period bears this characterization."[100] Many passages tell us that this is the "wrath of God" being poured out, not the wrath of men, or the wrath of Satan.[101] The Tribulation period will be unique in history for this reason, and because of the extent and intensity of the terrible events.

Pentecost maintains that "the first great purpose of the tribulation is to prepare the nation of Israel for her Messiah." While there are other purposes, this is the primary one. In this sense it is known as "the time of Jacob's trouble." The Tribulation bears a special relation to Israel. It is to prepare the way for fulfillment of God's ancient Abrahamic, Palestinian, and Davidic Covenants with Israel, and the New Covenant. In order to do this Israel must endure punishment to bring about conversion, and a remnant of true believers must emerge ready for the subsequent Millennium Kingdom. "God's purpose for Israel in the Tribulation is to bring about the conversion of a multitude of Jews." A multitude of Gentiles will also endure punishment, hear the eternal gospel, and be saved during the period. "God's purpose, then, is to populate the millennial kingdom by bringing a host from among Israel and the Gentile nations to Himself."[102]

"The second great purpose of the tribulation," according to Pentecost, "is to pour out judgment on unbelieving man and nations."[103] It will be a time of final trial. Individuals and nations will be judged and destroyed because of their unrelenting godlessness, pursuit of the evil world system, and worship of the Antichrist. Despite the hardships and horrors of the Tribulation, many will refuse to change their ways and acknowledge God the Father as Lord and Jesus Christ as Savior. Since disbelievers will not be allowed to enter the righteous Millennial Kingdom, their deaths and removal will be a part of God's purpose during the Tribulation.

In the Book of Revelation, the Tribulation begins as Jesus Christ, "the Root of David" (Ch. 5), breaks, one after another, the seals of a scroll (Ch. 6). Each seal brings a new punishment. With the first seal, a rider on a white horse appears, with bow and crown, representing the rising new ruler and conqueror of the Tribulation period, the Antichrist, also later identified as the beast out of the sea (Ch. 13). "He is Satan's masterpiece and the counterfeit of all that Christ is or claims to be."[104] His acts and purposes will be the opposite of Christ the Savior and Messiah. While he appears like a victorious messiah on the white horse, bringing peace, his real legacy is lies, self-centeredness, conflict, warfare, suffering, and death: he is actually "a conqueror bent on conquest" (6:2).[105] "The Antichrist will be the ultimate expression of human lawlessness," and a "dictatorial tyrant."[106]

By breaking the first seal, Jesus Christ turns the Antichrist loose on an unrepentant, evil world, giving it the evil, punishing ruler it deserves. It will be "a form of God's wrath on rebellious Israel and the Gentiles."[107] It will include punishment, even up to death, for all who have turned away from or against the true God. But it will also include the possibility of salvation for all who will repent and turn to God in belief and trust.

During the first half the Antichrist increases his power and achieves many of his satanic objectives. He has a charismatic personality and is very clever, but thinks he is "as wise as a god," which leads him to his ultimate destruction. He is wealthy from successful business dealings.[108] He is a Gentile, and will control the last great power of Gentile world domination, a federation of nations. Through them he will eventually rule the whole world, and change laws and customs.[109] "The coming of the lawless one will be in accordance with the work of Satan displayed in all kinds of counterfeit miracles, signs and wonders, and in every sort of evil that deceives those who are perishing. They perish because they refused to love the truth and so be saved."[110] "He will cause astounding devastation and will succeed in whatever he does. He will destroy the mighty men and the holy people. He will cause deceit to prosper, and he will consider himself superior. When they feel secure, he will destroy many and take his stand against the Prince of princes [Christ]." But he will soon be destroyed by divine power.[111]

The three other apocalyptic horsemen who follow the Antichrist confirm these things. The breaking of the second seal reveals a rider with a great sword on a red horse, bringing war: "Its rider was given power to take peace from the earth and to make men slay each other." As Jesus said in Matthew 24:6-8, there will be "wars and rumors of wars . . . nation will rise against nation, and kingdom against kingdom." The third seal releases a rider on a black horse, carrying a pair of measuring scales. This rider symbolizes the bleak hopelessness of famine, poverty, and hunger that accompany war, with the scales indicating lack of means to buy scarce food.[112] Jesus also foretold the coming of these famines in Matthew 24:7. Here and earlier in the Bible, "God uses famine as an expression of His wrath against rebellious mankind."[113] The breaking of the fourth seal sets loose the rider on a pale horse, the pale greenish color of a corpse, with Hell close behind.[114] "They were given power over a fourth of the earth to kill by sword, famine and plague, and by the wild beasts of the earth" (6:8).

The exact number of deaths resulting from the breaking of the fourth seal is unknown. Neither do we know how many saints will be taken during the Rapture. But the number of deaths could be one or more billion. It "would represent the greatest destruction of human life ever recorded in history."[115] World population in 2011 is estimated at 6.9 billion.[116] The estimate for 2050 is 9 billion.[117] Every subsequent year could bring further increases. This period would be "awful beyond any words, a period without precedent in its character and extent."[118] The first four seals seem to parallel the description by Christ in Matthew 24:4-8, and thus seem to be part of "the beginning of birth pains" or "beginning of sorrows" that is the first half of the Tribulation period. This suggests that the fourth seal may take place near or at the middle of the Tribulation period,[119] and may thus be the battle of Gog and Magog described in Ezekiel 38-39.

Gog and Magog and the Possible Role of Islam. Two great wars of unprecedented carnage in end times are described at some length in the Old and New Testaments. They both appear to take place during the Tribulation period. One of them, known as the battle of Gog and Magog[120] may take place near or at the middle of the Tribulation period. Walvoord and Hitchcock, as well as Dyer and Pentecost, think it will occur during the first half, near or at the middle.[121] Pentecost gives reasons why he thinks the campaign of Gog and Magog begins at the middle and leads into Armageddon at the end, forming an ongoing campaign covering the three and one-half years ending the Tribulation.[122] While others have differing opinions about the time of the battle of Gog and Magog, it is generally agreed that the Battle of Armageddon will take place at the end of the Tribulation, and that Christ Himself at His Second Coming will conclude it.

The most striking aspect of the campaign of Gog and Magog is that most or all of the forces attacking Israel are clearly from many Islamic nations that completely surround her—to the southwest: Sudan, (biblical "Cush"), and Libya ("Put" or "Phut"); to the north and northwest: Turkey ("Meshech and Tubal," "Gomer," and "Beth Togarmah"); to the northeast: Iran ("Persia"); to the "far north" and part of the Soviet Union until 1991, the CIS states of Turkmenistan, Uzbekistan, Kazakhstan, Kyrgyzstan, Tajikistan, Azerbaijan.[123] These are all Islamic countries that could muster many millions of warriors for such a great battle. Will they be led by Russia? Several, including Pentecost, John Walvoord, John Hagee, and Grant Jeffrey think they will. Jeffrey holds that "Gog and Magog" refer to Russia, and that Meshech and Tubal are "somewhere in Russia."[124] Richardson and Dyer offer reasons why "rosh" may not refer to Russia, but that the biblical word means "chief prince," or "head," referring to "Gog," whom Richardson identifies as the Antichrist.[125] Simon Altaf's view is that "Gog" is the Anti-Messiah [Antichrist], a Turkic leader from north of Israel, probably Turkey, who is the prince of "Rosh, Meshech, and Tubal." He locates the land of Magog south of Russia and north of Israel in Asia Minor, including Afghanistan, Chechnya, Turkey, Dagestan, Girgestan, Turkmenistan, Uzbekistan, Kyrgyzstan, Tajikistan, and Azerbaijan. He thinks all these countries will be involved in the battle of Magog, but that northern Russia will not be involved.[126]

The History of Muslim Hatred and Warfare. Simon Altaf, a former Pakistani Muslim converted to Messianic Judaism, believes that the armies of Gog will all be Islamic.[127] He points out that the rampant hatred of Israel and the Jews that runs throughout Islamic nations today is not something new. It extends all the way back through history into the ancient time of Abraham and his two very different sons, Isaac and Ishmael. Isaac received his father's inheritance and more importantly, the covenant of God with Abraham continued through Isaac, not Ishmael. Ishmael's mother Hagar was an Egyptian servant of Abraham's wife, not his wife. (This predicament arose because Abraham tried to get by *his own means*, the son God had promised him.) The youthful Ishmael stood by mocking at the feast when Isaac was born. He subsequently became the father of the Arab race.

This division became determinative for history. Ishmael's frustrated loss of inheritance has, with Islam, turned into the frustration and hatred of Israel, Jews, and Christianity, and Islam's distorted mimicry of the Bible. "This hatred started with Ishmael written about in the pages of Genesis and extends all the way in history to completion of the judgments in the book of Revelation." From Isaac and Ishmael it continued into Isaac's sons, Jacob, who gained the inheritance, and Esau, who lost it. Ishmael's mother, Hagar, was Egyptian, and since Ishmael married an Egyptian woman, his descendants, the Ishmaelites, are largely Egyptian. "Esau hated Jacob because of the birthright . . . and wanted to kill Jacob . . . . Later Esau married into the Ishmaelites so the two have now become <u>one</u> family." In that way, Arab and Egyptian have family ties.[128] In Hebrews 12:16 Esau is also said to be "godless."

It was pointed out in Chapter 7 that the angel of the Lord who appeared to Hagar, also predicted that Ishmael would be "a wild donkey of a man; his hand will be against everyone and everyone's hand against him, and he will live in hostility toward all his brothers" (Genesis 16:12). Kenneth Mathews observed that this is a picture of "Ishmael as antagonist whose hostilities are indiscriminate and without restraint. Hostility toward one's 'brother' characterized the nonelect line in Genesis, beginning with Cain (4:8, 23-24); Esau, like Ishmael, is portrayed as a wild belligerent (27:39-40)." Such belligerence was repeated in Genesis 25:13-18, describing Ishmael's descendants living from Havilah to Shur near the border of Egypt: "they lived in hostility toward all their brothers."[129]

Altaf emphasizes two key biblical names referring to ancient lands now occupied by Muslims—Mount Seir and Edom. Mount Seir is south-southeast of the Dead Sea in what is now Jordan. Esau, who represents Edom and Edomites, actually lived at Mount Seir. Altaf interprets biblical references to Mount Seir and Edom as being symbolic of all the Islamic nations.[130] In this sense Ezekiel 35:3-10 tells us a great deal about Islam and major Tribulation events. In these verses the Sovereign God of Israel reveals His will to destroy these persecutors of Israel.

"Behold, O Mount Seir, I am against you; I will stretch out My hand against you, and make you most desolate; I shall lay your cities waste, And you shall be desolate. Then you shall know that I am the LORD. Because you have had an ancient hatred, and have shed the blood of the children of Israel by the power of the sword at the time of their calamity, when their iniquity came to an end, therefore, as I live, . . . I will prepare you for blood, and blood shall pursue you; since you have not hated blood, therefore blood shall pursue you. Thus I will make Mount Seir most desolate, and cut off from it the one who leaves and the one who returns. And I will fill its mountains with the slain; on your hills and in your valleys and in all your ravines those who are slain by the sword shall fall. I will make you perpetually desolate, and your cities shall be uninhabited; then you shall know that I am the LORD" (NKJV).[131]

With this understanding of Mount Seir and Edom, these verses tell us that the Arab nations, which later became Islamic, hold an ancient hatred of Israel and the Jews, and have killed many of them by the sword while they have been dispersed from their promised land. God thus promises that at some time when the dispersal is finished, and the Jews are brought home to Israel, the Islamic nations will receive God's judgment—for the blood they spilled, they will spill their own blood. Their lands will be filled with their slain, and their lands and cities made perpetually desolate. These are grim references to a great battle of the Tribulation period.

Ezekiel provides more graphic details about Gog and Magog. God Himself will use several means to bring about the defeat of this huge army, thus revealing his divine power and holiness to many nations. A great earthquake will bring devastation: "mountains will be overturned, the cliffs will crumble and every wall will fall to the ground . . . . Every man's sword will be against his brother." Judgment will also be executed by means of plague and bloodshed. Gog and all the invading troops will be inundated by torrents of rain, hailstones and burning sulfur. God will bring down fire out of the heavens on the land of Magog and the people of the coastlands. There will be so many dead that it will take seven months to bury the bodies, although many will be eaten by wild animals and birds. It will be an overwhelming defeat inflicted on Israel's enemies by God Himself. In this way God directly reveals Himself and His historical purpose to Israel and to the world: "I will display my glory among the nations, and all the nations will see the punishment I inflict and the hand I lay upon them. From that day forward the house of Israel will know that I am the LORD their God. And the nations will know that the people of Israel went into exile for their sin, because they were unfaithful to me."[132] God's stunning defeat of Gog will cause the nations to realize that they have witnessed the authority, power, and glory of the true God, and "will force Israel to acknowledge His power."[133]

Much has been written during the past decade about radical Islam, its basis in the Koran and Hadith, militant Muslim hatred of Jews, Israel, and America, and the determination to destroy Israel and spread Islam worldwide by violent means. Several of the most insightful writings have been by former Muslims converted to Christianity or Messianic Judaism. Ergun and Emir Caner tell the moving story of being raised as Muslims in Ohio by a Turkish Muslim father. The brothers were "devout Muslims." However, as they write, their "devotion was not an act of love but of fear. No Muslim has eternal security. Every Muslim fears the scales of justice, which weigh his good deeds against his bad deeds." In contrast, the Caners say, belief in Jesus Christ brings the free gift of salvation, eternal security, and eternal life. A believer in Christ is freed from fear. When Ergun was saved he was "freed from the scales of fear by grace and the atonement of Jesus Christ. The other two brothers were soon saved. In response, their father did not try to kill them, as the Hadith (9:57) requires; he simply disowned them.[134]

Mark Gabriel is a former Egyptian Muslim who was converted to Christianity at about age 35. By the time he was 12 he could quote the entire Koran by memory. He writes that "it was natural for me to grow up with a great hatred toward the Jews because it is the true attitude of Islam." "I took every opportunity to speak against them, to curse them, to spit on their gravestones." After his conversion his family also disowned him. Now he gives the good Christian advice to "hate Islam, but love Muslims." Muslims are "the victims of Islam." "It is Islam that creates all the bad attitudes and the problems."[135]

Gabriel, who has a doctorate in Islamic history and culture from Al-Azhar University in Cairo, describes the brutal and aggressive tactics of Muhammad, the founder of Islam, who received its "revelations," and who is considered "the best Muslim." He started a war with Jews at Mecca by ambushing their necessary supply caravan. He besieged the Jewish village of Qurayzah, and when they surrendered, killed all the men (800-900) by cutting their throats, and divided the money, women, and children among his soldiers. He took 20% of this "booty" for himself, selling it to buy more tools of war. Muhammad defeated another Jewish village at Khaybar, dividing large spoils, with his soldiers chanting "O victor, O victor, kill and kill." Muhammad then declared "There will never be two religions in Arabia." About a year later he vowed that "he would continue to destroy the Jewish community in Arabia and that he would clean the land from the evils of Jews and Judaism."[136] By the time of his death at 62 in AD 632, Muhammad had control of Arabia. Gabriel writes that "the Jewish community disappeared from Arabia as a result of the Muslims killing them, converting some of them, and selling them as slaves in the markets." "Muhammad taught that the Muslims would fight the Jews until the day of Resurrection . . . . So, until the Day of Resurrection comes, committed Muslims are fighting an 'unfinished battle' against the Jews." Gabriel characterizes all this as "the Arabian Holocaust."[137]

Robert Spencer briefly describes the rapid expansion of Islam, "spread by the sword." Islam surged beyond Arabia shortly after Muhammad's death in 632. Damascus fell in 635, Antioch in 636, Jerusalem in 638, Egypt in 639, Persia between 633 and 642, North Africa in 652 and 665. Sophronius, the Eastern Orthodox Patriarch of Jerusalem, handed the city over to the second Islamic Caliph Umar. He had a sense then that Jerusalem and the site of the former Temple of Solomon, the Temple Mount, would be subjected to "an abomination of desolation."[138] In Egypt, a fourth principal Christian city, Alexandria, fell in 642. An observer of the time described the massacre in Nikiou that set a pattern for Egypt: "They seized the town and slaughtered everyone they met in the street and in the churches—men, women and children, sparing nobody. Then they went to other places, pillaged and killed all the inhabitants they found."[139] By 664 raids were launched into southern Punjab (modern Pakistan). By 700 Carthage was captured, the Berbers converted, and the whole coast of North Africa brought under Muslim control. Moving eastward they pushed as far as Kabul in Afghanistan, into part of India, and battled at the borders of China by 751.

The Caner brothers tell some of the story of Islam, describing it as "a trail of blood." When the trail of blood had swept through the countries of Syria, Iraq, Persia, and Egypt, Islam turned its vision to "conquest of the known world." In 691, only 59 years after Muhammad's death, the Dome of the Rock was built on the Jewish Temple Mount in Jerusalem, to assert the superiority of Islam over Judaism. And in 715 the Great Mosque was built in Damascus, to replace the Catholic Church of St. John, and to show the superiority of Islam over Christianity.[140]

Muslims soon spilled over into the Iberian Peninsula (modern Spain, Portugal, Gibraltar), conquering most of it between 711 and 719. They were ready to surge on into Europe, making forays into France. But the great western expansion of Islam was basically halted in 732 by Charles "the Hammer" Martel at the Battle of Tours. If it had not been stopped, the history of Europe would have been very different. All of Europe, England, and then America could have been Islamic. Medieval and early modern Europe would not have been Christian. Neither the great cathedrals, the centuries of flourishing history of Catholicism and Protestantism, the art of Raphael, Michelangelo, and Rembrandt, nor the music of Bach would exist. The history of the Western world would have been Islamic. Everyone, including us now, could have been living under the tyrannical rule of Islam and its Sharia law, putting to death any who will not worship Allah. Seen in this light, the Battle of Tours was providential. Not just Charles Martel, but God the providential controller of history stopped the advance of Islam. While there were many later battles, gains, and losses, this is a major part of the story of the early spread of Islam.[141]

The Possible Role of Islam in End Times. John's vision related in Revelation 13:1-8 gives us important clues about the role of Islam in end-times, symbolically telling about the Antichrist and the ten-nation confederacy he heads during the Tribulation period. The following symbols in these verses are well known today: the dragon is Satan, the beast is the Antichrist, the ten horns are ten kings or nations led by the Antichrist during the Tribulation period, and the seven heads are seven historical empires from the ancient past up to recent times, preceding the Tribulation.[142]

1 And the dragon stood on the shore of the sea. And I saw a beast coming out of the sea. He had ten horns and seven heads, with ten crowns on his horns, and on each head a blasphemous name. 2 The beast I saw resembled a leopard, but had feet like those of a bear and a mouth like that of a lion. The dragon gave the beast his power and his throne and great authority. 3 One of the heads of the beast seemed to have had a fatal wound, but the fatal wound had been healed. The whole world was astonished and followed the beast. 4 Men worshiped the dragon because he had given authority to the beast, and they also worshiped the beast and asked, "Who is like the beast? Who can make war against him?" 5 The beast was given a mouth to utter proud words and blasphemies and to exercise his authority for forty-two months. 6 He opened his mouth to blaspheme God, and to slander his name and his dwelling place and those who live in heaven. 7 He was given power to make war against the saints and to conquer them. And he was given authority over every tribe, people, language and nation. 8 All inhabitants of the earth will worship the beast—all whose names have not been written in the book of life belonging to the Lamb that was slain from the creation of the world.

We are told in these verses that the Antichrist and the ten nations he leads, as well as the seven empires that preceded his own empire stand in a blasphemous relation to God the Father, Jesus Christ, and the Holy Spirit (1, 5). Blasphemy indicates an unremitting, radical denial of the nature and powers of God and the abuse of His name and word. Satan gives the Antichrist his power, throne, and authority (2), although it is ultimately God who has given Satan permission to do this, and given the "beast" life, breath, and opportunity to utter such blasphemies, as well as to rule the entire world for $3\frac{1}{2}$ years (the second half of the Tribulation; 5-7).

In Revelation 17:3-6 John records his vision in a desert of a prostitute riding the beast:

> 3b There I saw a woman sitting on a scarlet beast that was covered with blasphemous names and had seven heads and ten horns. 4 The woman was dressed in purple and scarlet, and was glittering with gold, precious stones and pearls. She held a golden cup in her hand, filled with abominable things and the filth of her adulteries. 5 This title was written on her forehead: MYSTERY, BABYLON THE GREAT, THE MOTHER OF PROSTITUTES, AND OF THE ABOMINATIONS OF THE EARTH. 6 I saw that the woman was drunk with the blood of the saints, the blood of those who bore testimony to Jesus.[143]

This woman, the Babylonian whore, may be a symbol of the false and blasphemous religious beliefs that have issued from the nations and empires in and around Babylonia since ancient times up to the present ("mother of prostitutes" = progenitor of false religious beliefs). She is at the core of the "mystery" of evil. "Babylon then is the symbol of apostasy and blasphemous substitution of false worship for the worship of God in Christ."[144] "Babylon" may also refer to the actual pagan city of Babylon, and possibly to a future restoration of that city as a capitol of a future Islamic Empire. The beast this religious prostitute rides is the same one with seven heads and ten horns. Throughout history such religious prostitution has taken different forms and been supported by seven major "heads" or empires. The first six are: (1) Egyptian; (2) Assyrian; (3) Babylonian; (4) Persian; (5) Greek Hellenistic; and (6) Roman.[145]

What did the sixth one, the Roman Empire, include, and when did it actually end? It was permanently divided into two portions in AD 395. As the western half centered on Rome declined and fell (395-476), the eastern half centered on Constantinople continued to grow and flourish as the Byzantine Empire, and lasted about another thousand years (c. 330/395-1453). It was based on Christianity, and served as the eastern Mediterranean bulwark of Christianity for centuries, helping to restrain Muslim expansion in Europe. "The terms Byzantine Empire ... and Eastern Roman Empire are expressions used to describe the Roman Empire of the Middle Ages centered on its capital of Constantiniople .... it was known as the 'Empire of the Greeks' to many of its western European contemporaries due to the dominance of Medieval Greek language, culture and population, it was referred to by its inhabitants simply as the *Roman Empire* (Βασιλεία ωμαίων) or *Romania* (ωμανία) and its emperors continued the unbroken succession of Roman emperors, preserving Greco-Roman legal and cultural traditions; to the Islamic world it was known primarily as (*Rûm*, 'land of the Romans')."[146]

Thus the Roman Empire in its eastern Byzantine-Christian form lasted into the mid-fifteenth century.

For centuries the Byzantine Empire "helped to shield Western Europe from early Muslim expansion, provided a stable gold currency for the Mediterranean regions, influenced the laws, political systems, and customs of much of Europe and the Middle East, and preserved much of the literary works and scientific knowledge of ancient Greece, Rome, and many other cultures."[147] The weakening and reduction of the Byzantine Empire from 1025 until its defeat by Muslims in 1453, helped open up the eastern side of Europe for Islamic conquest by Ottoman Turks. In the sense that the Roman-Byzantine Empire was conquered by the Ottoman Turks, the seventh "head" or empire would be the Islamic Ottoman Empire.

"The Ottoman Empire was, in many respects, an Islamic successor to the earlier Mediterranean empires—the Roman and Byzantine Empires."[148] Long-lasting (over six centuries) and widespread, the Islamic Ottoman Empire (1299-1923) overpowered the Byzantine Christian Empire, and reached the height of its power during the sixteenth and seventeenth centuries. It gradually declined through the next three centuries, and ended in 1923. The Caliphate was then constitutionally abolished on March 3, 1924. Extensive Islamic conquests had preceded the Ottoman Empire and led into it, from Muhammad on through the rapid expansions of the Umayyad (660-750), Fatimid (909-1171), and Abbasid Caliphates (750-1258). Thus we see, as Joel Richardson writes, "that it was the Islamic Empire culminating with the Ottoman Empire that succeeded the Roman Empire and ruled over the entire Middle East, beginning with Jerusalem for over thirteen hundred years."[149]

The nearly three-century decline and then the end of Islamic Empires and Caliphates in 1923-1924 represent a key ending. But from 1948, and especially since 1975, there has been a growing revival of Islamic militancy, expansion, and terrorism, with the expressed desire of working toward a future world-empire headed by a Caliphate.[150] In these ways such a future militant Islamic Empire fits the description in Revelation 13:3 of "one of the heads of the beast" (an empire) that "seemed to have had a fatal wound, but the fatal wound had been healed." The "fatal wound" in this sense would be the end of the Ottoman Empire and end of the Caliphate in 1923-1924. The "healed wound" would be the rise of a renewed and expanding militant Islam leading toward a world-wide Caliphate. It also seems to fit the description in Revelation 17:11—"the beast who once was, and now is not, is an eighth king. He belongs to the seven [heads = empires] and is going to his destruc-tion."[151]

Until recently the Islamic world had remained relatively dormant for several centuries. As the Caners write, "While modern people are familiar only with the defensive Islam of the last three hundred years, the religion has never forgotten the previous one thousand years of conquest in the cause of Allah. It is this traditional conquering Islam that has reemerged." For the militant Muslim, "jihad (holy war) is completed only when the entire world is placed under the submission of Allah and when his laws reign supreme . . . . War is not a sidebar of history for Islam; it is the main vehicle for religious expansion. It is the Muslim duty to bring world peace via the sword . . . . Orthodox Christians are taught to live at peace by the living and written Word of God. Muslims are taught by the Qur'an and Allah's messenger to 'fight and slay the Pagans wherever you find them' (surah 9.5)."[152]

Simon Altaf writes with a deep conviction of Islam as a false religion and of the present and future threat of radical Islam: "Fanatic Islam is the biggest threat we face in our history. Many thousands of innocent people are dead already and many more will die if we remain silent. Either the west has to do something about fanatic Islam and tell people the real truth, or fanatic Islam will do something about the west." Altaf interprets the biblical battle of Gog and Magog, predicted in Ezekiel 38-39, as World War III, brought about by a massive coalition of surrounding Islamic nations attacking modern Israel. Grant Jeffrey has a similar view.[153]

Many things today indicate that Islam will play the major role in end-time battles against Israel, and in spiritual warfare against the Living God of the Bible. Some of them are: (1) the key conflict between Israel and present-day Islam has ancient, biblical, historical roots in the split between Isaac and Ishmael, with Isaac as the miraculous, legitimate son of Abraham representing Israel and continuing the covenant inheritance line, and Ishmael as the earthly, illegitimate son[154] representing the Arabs (later, all Muslims), and being the jealous pretender to the divine inheritance; this split, conflict, and lost inheritance continued between Isaac's sons, Jacob and Esau; (2) the location of Muslim nations all around Israel in countries that were formerly parts of the empires symbolized in Nebuchadnezzar's dream, interpreted in Daniel's vision, and named in Ezekiel and Isaiah;[155] (3) the murderous hatred of Muslims for Israel, Christianity, and the Bible, and the militant quest to destroy them; (4) the intrinsic opposition of Islam to Christianity because the Koran fiercely denies the most essential teaching of the Bible—that Jesus Christ is God and Savior; (5) the building of the Islamic Dome of the Rock on the site of the Jewish Temple of God in Jerusalem, the holiest site for Israel, determined in ancient times by God, and then appropriated fifteen centuries later by Islam as its own holy site, revealing the intense spiritual warfare that underlies this conflict; (6) the Muhammad-Islamic confrontation of Hebrew-Christianity by changing the Bible to fit its opposing beliefs; (7) the increasing confrontation and assaults by militant Muslims on Israel, Jews, and Christians since 1948 and 1975, and the assaults on America as the "Great Satan"; (8) the mandate of the Koran, to spread Islam worldwide, by lies and killing wherever necessary; (9) the hundreds of millions of Muslims now in the world; (10) the much greater birth-rate of Muslims in many nations around the world, increasingly infiltrating schools, laws, and political power in Europe, England, America, and elsewhere, and the rapidly growing number of Islamic mosques and madrassas;[156] (11) the power of unlimited riches through oil; (12) the power to shut down the world's engines and economies by slowing down or cutting off the oil supply.

The Second Half of the Tribulation. This 3½ years has been characterized as "hard labor birth pains," and called "the great tribulation" because it brings increasingly severe outpourings of God's wrath.[157] It seems to include the fifth through the seventh seals, the seven trumpets, and the seven bowls that end it. At the middle of the Tribulation period, the Antichrist will break his peace treaty with Israel and begin to persecute and kill them.[158] Many Jews will flee for their lives into the wilderness. During this time 144,000 Jews will be saved to witness to the Gentiles. The Antichrist, who is "the man of lawlessness," will rule the whole world during this time. And he "will oppose and will exalt himself over everything that is called God or is worshiped, so that he sets himself up in God's temple, proclaiming himself to be God."[159] He will slander and blaspheme God and kill as many as he can of those who believe in God. His spiritual aid, the false prophet, or second beast, will enforce worship of the Antichrist, and will have power to perform "great and miraculous signs." He will also force "everyone, small and great, rich and poor, free and slave, to receive a mark on his right hand or on his forehead, so that no one could buy or sell unless he had the mark," which is 666.[160]

The Two Beasts and Worship of the Antichrist. If the beast with seven heads represents the political empires from Egypt and Assyria through Babylonia, Persia, Greece, and Rome, then the Islamic Ottoman Empire, the "Babylonian whore" ("mystery Babylon the great the mother of prostitutes and of the abominations of the earth") riding the beast must represent all the false religions those empires have carried with them that have defied the true Living God of the Bible. All those false religions have been influenced by Satan, are closely associated with him, and belong to him. Since Satan is the ultimate power behind them, we might expect him to reveal himself more directly and openly, once his agent, the Antichrist, gains total world control at the beginning of the second half of the Tribulation. This seems to explain another passage in Revelation 17:16-17:

The beast and the ten horns you saw will hate the prostitute. They will bring her to ruin and leave her naked; they will eat her flesh and burn her with fire. For God has put it into their hearts to accomplish his purpose by agreeing to give the beast their power to rule, until God's words are fulfilled.

After using religion as a deceptive lure for bringing people into his kingdom throughout history, Satan, through the Antichrist, will turn against every religion, including the Islamic religion dominating the first half of the Tribulation, and seek to destroy them. The Antichrist will establish *himself*, and thus, *Satan*, as God, requiring all people to worship only him. Men will be ordered to make an image of the first beast (the Antichrist world ruler) and to worship him. The second beast (the false prophet)

was given power to give breath to the image of the first beast, so that it could speak and cause all who refused to worship the image to be killed. He also forced everyone, small and great, rich and poor, free and slave, to receive a mark on his right hand or on his forehead, so that no one could buy or sell unless he had the mark, which is the name of the beast or the number of his name. (Revelation 13:15-17).[161]

In this context, these verses mean that all who refuse to worship the image of the Antichrist, including Muslims as well as Christians, and all other religious beliefs, will be killed, and their places of worship transformed or destroyed.

The Remaining Seals, Trumpets, and Bowls. The fifth seal gives John a vision of those souls in heaven who were martyred during the time of the first four seals of the Tribulation for their belief in the word of God and for remaining faithful to Christ. "Martyrdom in those days will be as common as it is uncommon today."[162] The fifth seal reveals that, because of the murder of these dedicated believers, God's wrath on Satan's forces on earth will be increased through the remaining seals, trumpets, and bowls.[163]

The breaking of the sixth seal brings events even more terrible—radical changes in the workings of the universe. "There was a great earthquake. The sun turned black like sackcloth made of goat hair, the whole moon turned blood red, and the stars in the sky fell to earth, as late figs drop from a fig tree when shaken by a strong wind. The sky receded like a scroll, rolling up, and every mountain and island was removed from its place"[164] (6:12-14). The lawful structure and stability of the universe seems to be unraveling, and the earth undergoing extreme changes. It will be enough to frighten anyone to death. Many will try to hide in caves and mountains, and even cry out for their death. Many of these changes must have limited extent and duration however, since further and more drastic changes in earth and universe will soon follow.

The breaking of the seventh seal introduces the next form of God's wrath during the tribulation, the trumpets (8:6-13; 9:1-20). There is silence in heaven for about half an hour, then one by one the seven angels who have trumpets come forward to blow loud blasts. These trumpet blasts reveal the increasing wrath of God against a recalcitrant world, but their purpose is still to lead people to repentance, not yet to totally destroy.

The first trumpet brings down hail and fire mixed with blood, burning up one third of trees and all green grass. With the second trumpet a third of the sea turns to blood, a third of its creatures die, and a third of ships are destroyed. The third trumpet brings a deadly "great star blazing like a torch" from space to pollute a third of rivers and springs, causing many people to die. With the fourth trumpet, one third of the sun, moon, and stars turn dark, so that one third of day and night are without light. The awful feeling is that the universe is being corrupted and shut down. Just as God had sent a corrupt and evil ruler in the Antichrist to be the kind of ruler unbelievers deserve, He is now gradually removing divine stability, structure, and goodness from created nature because they refuse to admit that God is the real power and glory behind its goodness and blessings.[165] With the tribulation period God is directing previous ways of existence toward an end, and leading toward a new beginning.

The next three trumpets bring still greater woes to the inhabitants of the earth. With the fifth trumpet a "star" falls from heaven and is given the key to "the bottomless pit" or "abyss," the abode of demons. This symbolic "star" is "none other than Satan himself."[166] When Satan unlocks the abyss, massive smoke arises, darkening the sun and moon, and out fly horrendous, surrealistic creatures, demons, in hybrid forms—human-like heads, women's hair, lion's teeth, wings, and stinging tails like scorpions. They have the power to sting and torture for five months (one of the few indications of time) only those who have rejected Christ. These people "will long to die, but death will elude them" (Revelation 9:1-11). Walvoord interprets these as images of demonic affliction and possession.[167] As God removes His goodness and blessings from creation, it is transformed into an antagonistic world of terrible pain and agony by these servants of Satan. Satan is identified as the king of these demons, and his true nature is revealed by names in Hebrew ("Abaddon") and Greek ("Apollyon"), which both mean "Destroyer." Those who follow the deceptions of Satan are now given a taste of his true character.

When the sixth angel sounds his trumpet, four "bound angels" are released at the River Euphrates to lead a great army of "two-hundred million troops." This signals preparations for the battle of Armageddon, which will be described when the sixth bowl is poured out. Today the description of these "mounted troops," with fiery death coming from their "heads and tails," seems to suggest modern warfare, perhaps with planes, helicopters, and tanks equipped with machine guns, guided missiles, and rockets (9:13-19). The result is devastating, killing another one-third of mankind. Counting this one-third plus the one-fourth killed under the fourth seal, over one-half of world population will be killed within the seven-year tribulation period. Nevertheless, the ones not killed still will not repent (20-21).

Now it is announced that when the seventh angel sounds his trumpet, God's will, as told long ago by His prophets, will be accomplished (10:7).[168] God's two special witnesses, or prophets, given miraculous powers, have been doing their work of spreading God's word for 42 months (3½ years), during the second half of the tribulation. God finally permits them to be killed, brings them back to life after 3½ days, and lifts them to heaven to be with Him as honored martyrs (11:1-11). A severe earthquake then kills 7,000 people and destroys one-tenth of Jerusalem. The terrified survivors finally begin to change, and give "glory to the God of heaven."

When the seventh angel blasts his trumpet, loud voices in heaven announce that "the kingdom of the world has become the kingdom of our Lord and of his Christ, and he will reign for ever and ever." With the end of the tribulation close at hand, angels of God pour out His final wrath on the earth from seven golden bowls. With the first bowl "ugly and painful sores" break out on the people who had "the mark of the beast and worshiped his image." Total ruin falls on the waters of the earth: with the second bowl the sea turns into blood "like that of a dead man," and every living thing in it dies. With the third, the rivers and springs turn to blood. Those who formerly shed the blood of saints and prophets are given this blood to drink as their just reward.

With the fourth bowl the sun is "given power to scorch people with fire." Their response is to curse the name of God who had control over these plagues. They still refuse to repent and glorify him. The fifth angel pours out his bowl on the throne of the beast [the Antichrist], and his kingdom is plunged into darkness. Men gnaw their tongues in agony and curse God because of their pains and sores, but they still refuse to repent.

The sixth angel pours out his bowl on the great river Euphrates, and its water dry up "to prepare the way for the kings from the East" to move against Israel. This leads into the battle of Armageddon, and "the great day of

God Almighty." Three demonic spirits go around to the rulers of the world enlisting them for a great final battle against God and the Holy Land. All of the earth's nations, with two hundred million soldiers from the east, begin to gather in the place called Armageddon. The armies of the whole world surround Jerusalem.[169]

Seven centuries ago, in the Book of Zechariah God foretold this great future battle and its outcome: "on that day, when all the nations of the earth are gathered against her, I will make Jerusalem an immovable rock for all the nations. All who try to move it will injure themselves. On that day I will strike every horse with panic and its rider with madness. I will keep a watchful eye over the house of Judah, but I will blind all the horses of the nations . . . . On that day I will make the leaders of Judah like a firepot in a woodpile, like a flaming torch among sheaves. They will consume right and left all the surrounding peoples, but Jerusalem will remain intact in her place. . . . On that day the Lord will shield those who live in Jerusalem, so that the feeblest among them will be like David, and the house of David will be like God, like the Angel of the Lord going before them. On that day I will set out to destroy all the nations that attack Jerusalem."[170]

Israel will suffer great losses, but will be preserved: "the city will be captured, the houses ransacked, and the women raped. Half of the city will go into exile, but the rest of the people will not be taken from the city." Jesus Christ will return at this time (the Second Advent), and intervene in the battle. "Then the Lord will go out and fight against those nations, as he fights in the day of battle. On that day his feet will stand on the Mount of Olives, east of Jerusalem, and the Mount of Olives will be split in two from east to west, forming a great valley, with half of the mountain moving north and half moving south . . . . On that day there will be no light, no cold or frost. It will be a unique day, without daytime or nighttime—a day known to the Lord. When evening comes, there will be light." God will demonstrate his mighty power. Fire will come down from heaven to consume the attacking nations. This divine victory signals the end of the Tribulation and the beginning of the Millennial Reign of Jesus Christ. "The Lord will be king over the whole earth. On that day there will be one Lord, and his name the only name."[171]

A strong portrayal in art of this great war between God and the armies of Satan can be seen in an illustration in the Martin Luther Bible of 1534, *Jesus Christ and the armies of heaven defeat the kings of the earth and their armies* (image unavailable). The radical opposition of the two powers is indicated by their direct confrontation from opposite sides of the picture. The billowing clouds below the armies powerfully convey the spiritual nature and extreme might of the conflict. Christ leads His army on the left:

His eyes are like blazing fire, and on his head are many crowns. He has a name written on him that no one knows but he himself. He is dressed in a robe dipped in blood, and his name is the Word of God. The armies of heaven were following him, riding on white horses and dressed in fine linen, white and clean. Out of his mouth comes a sharp sword with which to strike down the nations . . . On his robe and on his thigh he has this name written: KING OF KINGS AND LORD OF LORDS. And I saw an angel standing in the sun, who cried in a loud voice to all the birds flying in midair, "Come, gather together for the great supper of God, so that you may eat the flesh of kings, generals, and mighty men, of horses and their riders, and the flesh of all people, free and slave, small and great" (Revelation 19:12-18).

In this illustration, a dragon-like beast with seven heads and crowns is being cast down into a fiery abyss below.[172] "The rest are killed with the sword that came out of the mouth of Christ, and all the birds gorged themselves on their flesh." Their opposition to Christ is totally doomed. This Second Coming of Jesus Christ is in irresistible divine power and glory. The "sword" represents His absolute power. He destroys the resisting nations in order to establish His universal rule as rightful Judge and King of Kings.

When the seventh angel pours out his bowl, a loud voice from the throne and out of the temple says, "It is done!" Then there are flashes of lightning, rumblings, peals of thunder and an earthquake more severe than any before in history. The "great city" splits into three parts, and the cities of the nations collapse. All cities of the world collapse, along with their cultural achievements. God especially remembers Babylon the Great and pours out the fury of his wrath on her. The appearance of the entire earth is changed, including the holy land; mountains and islands can no longer be found. Huge hailstones of about a hundred pounds each fall upon men, and add to the destructive changes. As Walvoord comments, "it is a judgment compared to that of the destruction of Sodom and Gomorrah but here extending over the entire earth."[173] Many people will go through all these horrendous changes and punishments and still not admit the reality and truth of God. In the end, they only curse Him. (Revelation 16:17-20).

The End of Tribulation. The Tribulation will be a time of incomparably terrible events, suffering, deaths, and widespread destruction. It constitutes a catastrophic, but necessary ending of history as we know it. Besides the multitudes that will pass on toward their final damnation, many will be saved. The good from all this is that by its end, the world will be purged of unbelief, untruth, deception, and evil deeds, making way for the righteous Millennial Reign of Jesus Christ. Then, by the end of the

Millennium there will be a final defeat of Satan, and the resurrection and final judgment of unbelievers, to be followed by the perfect beatitude of God's Eternal Kingdom. In spite of all resistance, God's divine purpose in creation and history will at last be fully achieved. The purpose and joy of eternal life with the glorious Holy Trinity will be fully revealed in ways we cannot imagine.

Chapter Twelve

The Consummation of Creation
The Millennium and the Eternal Kingdom of God

The all-wise eternal God, who knows all things by His omniscient knowledge, makes unconditional promises based on His immutable character, plans all things by His unchangeable will, and achieves them with His omnipotent power.[1]

Because God is eternal, so are all of His plans . . . . His earthly reign, and particularly that of the Messiah, is one planned from all eternity . . . . The messianic kingdom is a visible, earthly, political kingdom promised to Israel in which Christ, her Messiah, will reign from a throne in Jerusalem over the whole earth, with His apostles and other disciples serving Him.[2]

God will do what He has said He will do, for His own glory among the nations. And what He has said He will do is fulfill the Abrahamic, Davidic, and New Covenants to a regathered, regenerated, restored nation of Israel at the second coming of Jesus Christ, and for a thousand years thereafter, prior to the eternal kingdom of God.[3]

The Physical Resurrection of Christ and His Future Return to Rule the World. The literal, bodily resurrection of Jesus Christ, His ascension, and His future return to rule the entire earth from Jerusalem in a thousand-year kingdom prior to the eternal state are indicated by many passages in the Bible. Premillennialism is the theological view that supports and develops these teachings.[4] The literal and historical-grammatical hermeneutic of premillennialism, interpreting prophetic and apocalyptic passages throughout the Bible, holds that Christ's physical Second Coming will inaugurate a visibly real, earthly Millennium Reign that is spiritual and physical, ecclesiastical and political, moral and social-economic in dimension—a real, geopolitical fulfillment of prophecy.[5] That is the understanding of the Bible supported here.

An opposing group of theological interpretations known as amillennialism holds that biblical statements of a reign of Christ in an earthly millennium are allegorical, symbolic, or "spiritual" in nature, rather than literally true. It denies a future, thousand-year physical reign of Christ on the earth,[6] and often claims instead that the millennium began at Pentecost with the church age, with Christ ruling from heaven, to return at the end of the church age in a final judgment. Amillennialism claims that the covenants of God with Abraham and David were conditional rather than unconditional and eternal, and that Old Testament promises made to Israel are being fulfilled spiritually in the church from the New Testament onward.[7] In more extreme, liberal forms of amillennialism the ideas of resurrection and final judgment for sin have even been rejected. Reinhold Niebuhr, for example, claimed that the resurrection of the body is a "myth" and not literally true. Some advocates have also denied physical resurrection bodies and a heaven with literal physical features of gold streets and gates of pearl.[8]

Another group of views, called postmillennialism, holds that Christ will not physically return to begin a literal millennium reign, but *after* a long period of spiritual, moral, and social progress and peace advanced by the church. While some hold to a literal thousand-year period, many think that "millennium" is a figurative term for an unspecified, long period of time that began in the past. Postmillennialists often teach that good will gradually triumph over evil during that period, as Christianity continually advances and the forces of Satan are defeated by the rising Kingdom of God. Both postmillennialism and amillennialism interpret much of Old Testament prophecy as allegory or symbol, rejecting consistent literal hermeneutics and dispensational understandings. Both views deny the unconditional and eternal nature of God's Old Testament covenants with Israel. Both reject consistent distinctions between Israel's covenantal future and that of the church. Premillennialism holds that both types of views do violence to the literal meanings of the covenants and many prophetic and apocalyptic Bible passages.[9] Examination of several key passages should help illuminate these issues.

Shortly before His crucifixion Jesus told his disciples, "Do not let your hearts be troubled. Trust in God; trust also in me. In my Father's house are many rooms; if it were not so, I would have told you. I am going there to prepare a place for you. And if I go and prepare a place for you, I will come back and take you to be with me that you also may be where I am" (John 14:1-3). After his resurrection Christ is described as having a touchable, physical body, but also able to pass through walls and doors. Paul emphasizes the crucial reality of the bodily resurrection of Christ and its necessity for the future resurrection of believers: "if the dead are not raised, then Christ has not been raised either. And if Christ has not been raised, your faith is futile; you are still in your sins. Then those also who have fallen asleep in Christ are lost. If only for this life we have hope in Christ, we are to be pitied more than all men" (1 Corinthians 15:16-19).

Paul continues, explaining that Christ's sacrificial death and resurrection actually make the future resurrection of human dead possible, and that Christ will return to gather true believers to Him: "Christ has indeed been raised from the dead, the firstfruits of those who have fallen asleep. For since death came through a man, the resurrection of the dead comes also through a man. For as in Adam all die, so in Christ all will be made alive. But each in his own turn: Christ, the firstfruits; then, when he comes, those who belong to him" (15:20-23). Some time before His crucifixion, Jesus had briefly indicated this to his disciples: "Before long, the world will not see me anymore, but you will see me. Because I live, you also will live" (John 14:19).

Early on the day of His resurrection Jesus appeared to Mary Magdalene outside His tomb. That same evening He suddenly appeared to His disciples inside the room where they were gathered, miraculously entering the room even though the door was locked.[10] He pointed out His physical resurrection body to them, saying, "Look at my hands and feet. It is I myself! Touch me and see; a ghost does not have flesh and bones, as you see I have." Then He ate a piece of broiled fish in their presence.[11] A week later Jesus appeared to the disciples inside a locked room again, when doubting Thomas was present. Once more He emphasized his physical body, saying to Thomas: "Put your finger here; see my hands; Reach out your hand and put it into my side. Stop doubting and believe." Jesus appeared a third time to His disciples later, by the Sea of Tiberias. They had not caught any fish until Jesus told them to cast their net on the right side of the boat. Then they pulled in a net full. When they landed on shore they saw a fire with fish already cooking on it. Then they ate fish and bread.[12]

These reports tell us, Geisler says, that Christ's resurrection body was "numerically identical to the pre-resurrection body," (meaning "indistinguishably" identical). The body that vacated the tomb is the same one that occupied it. His resurrection body had the same crucifixion scars. He ate food after His resurrection. His resurrection body consisted of flesh and bones, the same body in which He was incarnated, and in which He continually lives. The resurrection body is tangible. Geisler perceptively points out that "if there were *not* numerical identity between the pre- and post-resurrection bodies, the resurrection would have been a failure; if what died had not risen again, God would have lost the battle over death to Satan."[13] This same victory or failure would be true for human resurrection bodies.

Paul gives believers the crucial information in Philippians 3:20-21 that our own resurrection bodies will be *like that of Christ*: "the Lord Jesus Christ, who, by the power that enables him to bring everything under his control, will transform our lowly bodies so that they will be like his glorious body." And in I Corinthians 15:35-50 he compares death to sowing a seed. What is sown must die in order for the new life to arise. "The body that is sown is perishable, it is raised imperishable." Its dishonor and weakness in death are changed into glory and power. Paul calls the resurrection body a "spiritual body"; this "does not mean a nonmaterial body but, from the analogies [Paul gives], a physical one similar to the present natural body organizationally, but radically different in that it will be imperishable, glorious, and powerful, fit to live eternally with God. There is continuity, but there is also change."[14] For Geisler, these and other biblical passages indicate that the glorious resurrection body will have a radiance coming from it, "will have supernatural powers enabling it to move through space . . . perhaps through other material things," and "the ability to appear and disappear."[15]

Paul charges Timothy to "Fight the good fight of the faith. Take hold of the eternal life to which you were called when you made your good confession in the presence of many witnesses" and "keep this command without spot or blame until the appearing of our Lord Jesus Christ (1 Timothy 6:12-14). Sensing his own approaching death, Paul is confident about his real, future resurrection and eternal life when Christ *appears again*: "I have fought the good fight, I have finished the race, I have kept the faith. Now there is in store for me the crown of righteousness, which the Lord, the righteous Judge, will award to me on that day—and not only to me, but also to all who have longed for his appearing (2 Timothy 4:4-8). Paul also advises Titus, one of his converts, that God's grace brings salvation and teaches us "to live self-controlled, upright and godly lives in this present age, while we wait for the blessed hope—the glorious appearing of our great God and Savior, Jesus Christ (Titus 2:11-13). The writer of Hebrews tells us: "Just as man is destined to die once, and after that to face judgment, so Christ was sacrificed once to take away the sins of many people; and he will appear a second time, not to bear sin, but to bring salvation to those who are waiting for him" (9:27-28).

Some time after His resurrection, Christ's ascension to be with God the Father is described as literally real, and will be the same when He returns. Two angels told his disciples, "Men of Galilee, . . . why do you stand here looking into the sky? This same Jesus, who has been taken from you into heaven, will come back *in the same way* you have seen him go into heaven" (Acts 1:10-11, emphasis added).

All these verses tell us about the real, literal death and bodily resurrection of Christ, His ascension to the Father, and His future return to occur in the same manner. And they tell us that the same bodily resurrection and eternal life await all believers at the future return of Jesus Christ. By the direct way they are told, there is no possibility of them being simply "spiritualized," "symbolic," or "idealized" events that have no real, physical, bodily, or historical reality. The return of Christ is also clearly understood and told as an actual, future event.

The classic passage on Christ's return for the resurrection and Rapture of dead believers in Christ and living believers is in 1 Thessalonians 4:13-17. Only believers will see Christ then.[16] Like Geisler, Walvoord, Pentecost, Constable, and many others, the interpretation supported in this book is that many biblical statements indicate the Rapture will precede the Tribulation.[17]

Brothers, we do not want you to be ignorant about those who fall asleep, or to grieve like the rest of men, who have no hope. We believe that Jesus died and rose again and so we believe that God will bring with Jesus those who have fallen asleep in him. According to the Lord's own word, we tell you that we who are still alive, who are left till the coming of the Lord, will certainly not precede those who have fallen asleep. For the Lord himself will come down from heaven, with a loud command, with the voice of the archangel and with the trumpet call of God, and the dead in Christ will rise first. After that, we who are still alive and are left will be caught up together with them in the clouds to meet the Lord in the air. And so we will be with the Lord forever.

The Second Coming of Jesus Christ (*Parousia*, Second Advent), for everyone living to see, will occur seven years after the Rapture, at the end of the Tribulation. Christ will be "revealed from heaven in blazing fire with his powerful angels" (2 Thessalonians 1:7) Paul warns people not to believe anyone who tells them "that the day of the Lord has already come. Don't let anyone deceive you in any way, for (that day will not come) until the rebellion occurs and the man of lawlessness [The Antichrist] is revealed, the man doomed to destruction. He will oppose and will exalt himself over everything that is called God or is worshiped, so that he sets himself up in God's temple, proclaiming himself to be God" (2 Thessalonians 2:2-4).

The Biblical Basis for Christ's Return to Inaugurate a Millennial Kingdom. The essential biblical support for premillennial belief that Christ will return at a future time to establish a thousand-year kingdom rests on God's unconditional and everlasting covenants made with Israel and recorded in the Old Testament. This in turn rests on the belief that the Bible is the inerrant and authoritative word of God, and that God always keeps his word. God is Truth and the ultimate source of all truth. That God keeps His covenants and promises is affirmed over and over throughout Scripture. "God will do what He has said He will do, for His own glory among the nations. And what He has said He will do is fulfill the Abrahamic, Davidic, and New Covenants to a regathered, regenerated, restored nation of Israel at the second coming of Jesus Christ, and for a thousand years thereafter, prior to the eternal kingdom of God." These divine covenants and promises are stated in clear, literal fashion, and are understood in that way from the Old through the New Testament and into the early church period. "Old Testament promises of an earthly kingdom are not denied or redefined but confirmed by the New Testament."[18]

Dispensational premillennialism, Geisler maintains, is "the natural working out of these promises." Of first importance is that God promised by covenant with Abraham the entire land of Israel to his descendants, a great nation, and "the gifts and the calling of God *are* irrevocable" (Romans 11:29, NKJV).[19] This land-promise from God to Israel was confirmed by *oath* as *unconditional* and *eternal* by the conclusion of the Abraham narrative in Genesis, and its fulfillment is therefore certain. The Promised Land includes what is now Israel, Jordan, Lebanon, and Syria, on up to northern Iraq. This land promise is confirmed in Psalms 105:8-11 and 1 Chronicles 16:15-18 as "an everlasting covenant" and "oath" that God "remembers forever." And in the New Testament "Paul reveals his belief that the Abrahamic Covenant will be fully and literally realized in conjunction with the future restoration of national Israel."[20] Since this promise has not yet been completely fulfilled (but shows important literal and physical signs since 1948), it "must have a future literal fulfilment."[21]

A crucial second promise that God made unconditionally in covenant with David is a future, political, messianic reign on earth. In 2 Samuel 7:16 God told David, "Your house and your kingdom will endure forever before me; your throne will be established forever."[22] God confirmed this in Psalm 89:28-29: "I will maintain my love to him forever, and my covenant with him will never fail. I will establish his line forever, his throne as long as the heavens endure." God revealed his plan for a family line from David that would lead to the future reign of Jesus Christ as the Messiah. God's loyal love (*hesed*) and fidelity guarantees this geopolitical fulfillment of the Davidic covenant for Israel.

Isaiah 2:2-5 describes a wonderful future time of genuine spiritual renewal when a restored Jerusalem will be central to worship of God by all nations. Mount Zion and the LORD's temple will be paramount in the world, and "all nations will stream to it." They will come "to the house of the God of Jacob. He will teach us his ways, so that we may walk in his paths." It will be a time of peace and learning more of God. "The law will go out from Zion, the word of the LORD from Jerusalem." The LORD "will judge between the nations and will settle disputes for many peoples. They will beat their swords into plowshares and their spears into pruning hooks. Nation will not take up sword against nation, nor will they train for war anymore." John Sailhamer describes ways that this vision, while figurative in some particulars, is more narrative than poetic, and "meant to be taken literally and physically": "Isaiah is here looking forward to the physical restoration of Jerusalem and reign of the Messiah on earth in the 'last days'." The language of the vision is linked with the present earth, and does not represent the new heaven and new earth of the final eternal state. Like other prophecies of Isaiah throughout the book, this one "represents the classic depiction of the future reign of Christ"—a worldwide kingdom centered on Jerusalem, ruled by the Davidic king, with nations essentially at peace with each other and seeking knowledge of the Lord.[23] Much more of Isaiah's crucial prophecies will be discussed below.

Six passages in Jeremiah providing strong support for premillennial claims are admirably elucidated by Walter C. Kaiser, Jr. They point to the millennium as the time of God's "redemption and restoration of His people Israel," "His coming Davidic king," and His "final day of victory." Kaiser writes that these texts should be received "as the writer Jeremiah intended them to be taken under the Spirit of God about a real Israel in a real land." They show that "God will end history with a real, geopolitical Israel in the geographical territory that He announced she would have even back in the book of Genesis." They reveal that God "is in charge of history and that He is going to end it just as He planned to do from the beginning." The texts "favor a literal and unconditional fulfillment of God's promises in our kind of time and space." The Abrahamic-Davidic Covenants were "unconditional" and "unilateral, in that only God obligated Himself to keep the covenant." He did not make these great promises with all they include—the gift of the land, the Davidic king, the coming of the Messiah, and salvation—dependent on human works. His heavy judgment on Israel for her gross infidelities, her "adultery," was not his final verdict. He has always been gracious to forgive and to grant her return to Him and to the Promised Land, as these texts clearly state.[24]

Jeremiah 3:14-18 promises forgiveness and restoration of Israel despite her adultery, at a time that can only be, according to these promises and statements, an end-time period. "At that time" no one will need to speak any longer about the Ark of the Covenant as God's Throne. It "will not be missed, nor will another one be made," because Jerusalem will become "The Throne of the LORD, and all nations will gather in Jerusalem to honor the name of the LORD . . . . No longer will [the people] follow the stubbornness of their evil hearts. In those days the house of Judah will join the house of Israel, and together they will come from a northern land to the land I gave your forefathers as an inheritance." The divided nations of Israel and Judah will be fully reunited as the original twelve tribes. Kaiser emphasizes that this has "never happened since the tragic schism took place." And it will be in the specific land that God originally promised in the patriarchal and Davidic covenants. God also promises the people "shepherds after my own heart, who will lead you with knowledge and understanding." As Kaiser says, "no shepherd will completely fulfill this promise until that final Good Shepherd,"[25] Jesus Christ. All these promises match descriptions of the Millennium in other places.

In Jeremiah 16:14-21 God again emphatically promises to restore the people of Israel "to the land I gave their forefathers." This event will be seen by the people as even greater than the ancient deliverance from Egypt. God will bring "the Israelites up out of the land of the north and out of all the countries where he had banished them." But first they must pay for their unfaithfulness and evil works. They will learn, first through great suffering, and then through God's power in restoring them, that the Lord of Israel is not a worthless idol, but the real God of truth, power, and might. The Gentile nations that witness these great events will also be moved to understand. These sufferings seem to include not only the exile, Diaspora, and persecutions over many centuries, but an allusion to the Tribulation, preceding the Millennium, as primarily a time of discipline and punishment for the Jews, and secondarily for Gentile unbelievers. As Kaiser writes, such a restoration of historic land, "preceded by a time of unprecedented trouble for Israel, can fit only the premillennial scheme."[26]

In Jeremiah 23:1-8, God again promises to bring the Israelites back from all lands, and to punish those who have forced them there. The restoration to the land is again described as greater than the deliverance from Egypt. This restored remnant of Israelites will be fruitful and multiply. God will give them shepherds who will care for them and keep them from fear and terror. In these verses there is also a clear reference to the ultimate Good Shepherd, a righteous ruler of the Davidic line: God declares that "The days are coming . . . when I will raise up to David a righteous Branch, a King who will reign wisely and do what is just and right in the land. In his days Judah will be saved and Israel will live in safety. This is the name by which he will be called: The LORD Our Righteousness." Only Jesus Christ can match this description. And only premillennialism explains these as real, historical events on earth, as they are described.[27]

Jeremiah 29:10-14 speaks again of restoration of the people of Israel to their land. These verses refer directly to the end of their captivity in ancient Babylon. Babylonian supremacy and control of Israelites is accurately prophesied to end when seventy years have passed, after which God will bring the people home. But the deeper meaning of these verses reaches far beyond Babylon. In verse 14 God declares: "I will gather you from all the nations and places where I have banished you," God's unconditional covenant is with Israel as a nation. This promise again must have a future fulfillment. Individuals could and did lose out on fulfillment of these covenants in their time by turning away from God to idol-worship and wicked living. Many suffered and went to unbelieving deaths. But the disobedience of the people did not alter God's faithfulness to His covenants with Israel.

Jeremiah 30 and 31 give longer descriptions of the terrible sufferings of the Israelites before the promised restoration, and more on the restoration itself. Strong men will suffer "like a woman in labor," and every face will be "deathly pale." "How awful that day will be! None will be like it. It will be a time of trouble for Jacob [Israel], but he will be saved out of it" (30:6-7). God specifically tells them it is "because of your great guilt and many sins I have done these things to you." But He promises not to completely destroy them (30:11, 15). Jerusalem will be rebuilt and the palace will be in its proper place. Vineyards will prosper and people will dance joyfully to tambourines (31:4-5). God repeats His promise to "bring them from the land of the north and gather them from the ends of the earth . . . . a great throng will return." "They will come and shout for joy on the heights of Zion; they will rejoice in the bounty of the LORD—the grain, the new wine and the oil, the young of the flocks and herds. They will be like a well-watered garden, and they will sorrow no more . . . . 'So there is hope for your future,' declares the LORD. 'Your children will return to their own land'" (31:8, 12, 17).

Furthermore, God will bless them with the New Covenant that forgives them of all their sins through the substitutionary death of Jesus Christ, and bestow the Holy Spirit on all who are believers. This New Covenant does not abrogate the ancient covenantal promises of God to be the Lord God of Israel, build her into a great nation, and give her the Promised Land. As Charles Dyer points out, "one key element of the New Covenant is the preservation of Israel as a nation." And "ultimately the New Covenant will find its complete fulfillment during the Millennium when Israel is restored to her God." Although the church of Christian believers today enjoys the spiritual blessings of the New Covenant, its full blessings await this future millennial age when it will be universally extended to an Israel of believers.[28]

The many promises of God here in Jeremiah as well as in other places, strongly reaffirm that Israel will *always* be His chosen people, that He will restore them to their Promised Land and bless them with peace, happiness and a righteous Davidic King to lead them. How certain are these things? God makes it very clear: it is as certain as God's decrees that the sun shine by day and the moon and stars by night: "'Only if these decrees vanish from my sight,' declares the LORD, 'will the descendants of Israel ever cease to be a nation before me.' . . . 'Only if the heavens above can be measured and the foundations of the earth below be searched out will I reject all the descendants of Israel because of all they have done'" (31:35-37).

God also promised through Ezekiel (36:22-32) to bring back the people of Israel from all the nations where they were dispersed and restore them to their own land at some future time. (And we have seen, since 1948, the early stages of that restoration.) God stated that this restoration would not be because Israel deserved it, but because of His holy name and His covenantal promises. God said that at that future time there will be many transformations in the people and the land. He will cleanse them from all their impurities and idols. He will cleanse them, give them a new heart, put His Spirit in them and move them to follow His decrees and keep His laws. They will live in the land He gave their forefathers; they will be God's people, and He will be their God, as the original covenants promised. The land will then be made bountiful and there will be no famine. The fruit of the trees and the crops of the field will greatly increase. Then the people of Israel will remember and detest their previous evil ways and wicked deeds. This is clearly a statement of future millennial fulfillment, since these divine promises were not fulfilled in the postexilic period, and they were still believed to be future by New Testament writers. It cannot be the eternal state, since a Temple is promised (Ezekiel 40-48), which will not exist in the eternal Kingdom of God (Revelation 21:22). "Only premillennialism can accommodate the details of Ezekiel's many prophecies normally interpreted."[29]

The Old Testament ends, however, with Israel still expecting the messianic kingdom. Prophets looked to a future Messiah who would come to reign on David's throne over his kingdom in a reign of righteousness and justice.[30] In the New Testament, the message of the coming "kingdom of heaven," and "kingdom of God," alluding to the coming Messianic Kingdom, was preached, and offered to Israel by John the Baptist, Jesus Christ, the disciples, and others during the time of Jesus. "The kingdom John and Jesus announced was the same as the political messianic kingdom promised in the Old Testament."[31] And the kingdom the Jewish hearers expected was "a messianic reign over the earth from Jerusalem." The teachings of Jesus on the messianic kingdom of God have their basis in the Old Testament, and terms such as *son of man* and *kingdom of heaven* are linked with Daniel's messianic prophesies. There is a *literal identity* of several events in the life of Christ and Old Testament prophesies about the Messiah.[32] And Christ's message and miracles contain all the essential elements of the prophetic kingdom prophesied in the Old Testament.[33]

The Millennial Reign of Jesus Christ. It is always astonishing to realize that God has actually revealed in Scriptures, later collected in the Bible, many things about people, nations, and historical events many centuries, decades, or years before they occur! Several have been discussed in previous chapters. A great series of crucial events was foretold over seven centuries before Christ through the prophet Micah, who not only prophesied the coming of a future Messiah-Ruler, but described aspects of his future eternal reign. He correctly foretold that Bethlehem (in which both David and Jesus Christ were born) would be the birth place of the future "ruler over Israel," who is "of old, from ancient times ['days of immeasurable time']." These verses speak of a kingdom (later known as the Millennial Kingdom) in which the ruler "will stand and shepherd his flock . . . . And they will live securely, for then his greatness will reach to the ends of the earth. And he will be their peace."[34] This is the "Messiah-Ruler, who will deliver His people," "accomplish the Father's will," and "rule over the entire world." "The Ruler will destroy Israel's enemies (5:5-9)" and bring peace to Israel.[35] "He will reunite and restore the nation." Israel's catastrophic dispersion followed by a great, national regathering is figuratively foretold in Micah 5:3 by the image of a woman's labor followed by a wonderful birth.[36]

Again, over six centuries before Christ, God spoke through the prophet Jeremiah about fulfilling his covenant promise of a future Davidic king: "'The days are coming,' declared the Lord, 'when I will fulfill the gracious promise I made to the house of Israel and to the house of Judah . . . . I will make a righteous Branch sprout from David's line; he will do what is just and right in the land . . . . Judah will be saved and Jerusalem will live in safety.'"[37] A New Covenant will be in effect, which the New Testament confirms is mediated by Jesus Christ.[38] "The city of Jerusalem will be rebuilt as a Holy City that will never again be destroyed."[39] "These promises transcend anything that Israel has experienced throughout her long history. They will find their ultimate fulfillment only in the Millennial Age when the kingdom of the Messiah is established. This will be when God will fulfill the gracious promise He made to Israel and Judah."[40]

Many passages throughout the Bible point to the real, future Millennial Kingdom of Christ, and the Eternal Kingdom of God that it will usher in. Christ's Millennial Kingdom will be a real, literal, physical kingdom on earth.[41] The subsequent eternal Kingdom of God (Heaven/Paradise) will be a real global Kingdom on a New Earth with a New Heaven. Many things indicate that these successive divine kingdoms will be real, literal ones; although they will also be highly spiritual and holy, they will not be allegorical or simply spiritual (having no physical form). "Throughout the Scriptures, God repeatedly promises His followers that the goal is the coming millennial kingdom and the New Earth to follow forever."[42]

The Bible tells us that God originally created a real, literal world that was good. That world was corrupted by the entrance of sin from the time of Lucifer/Satan through Adam and Eve. Original creation's perfection was corrupted, and sin and death were inherited by the entire human race. To end with less than an actual or literally real world and kingdom would indicate a change of plan by God who is unchangeable, and some sense of defeat for the omnipotent God whose plans cannot be defeated. As Geisler states it, "God started human history by creating people in a literal Paradise with trees, plants, animals, and rivers . . . . if the Paradise lost is *not* a Paradise regained, then God will have lost the war; if physical death is not reversed by physical resurrection, then Satan obtains ultimate victory; if literal perfection is not restored, then God will have lost what He created. However, because God is immutable and omnipotent, He will reverse the curse and gain victory over the Satan-damaged creation. This He will do by a literal resurrection and by a literal earthly reign of Christ."[43] God's purpose in creation will not be defeated: what was meant to exist forever and be perfect, will be accomplished.

God predestined a divine Savior to redeem humanity from sin and lead people out of evil. The story of history is of divine salvation and redemption taking place in a world of spiritual warfare of God, his angels, and His believer-followers against Satan and his followers. That battle will reach a culmination in the end-times of history, when Christ the Messiah-Ruler will return to establish his divine Kingdom, establish holiness, peace, and justice on earth, and finally defeat Satan, evil, and death. The Kingdom of God is "the key to the true understanding of the Scriptures and God's plan for redeeming humanity from the curse of sin . . . . The kingdom of God on earth provides the spiritual key to explaining human history, from the fall of Adam and Eve, to Jesus' First Coming, and until the final appearance of Christ at the end of this age."[44]

The Book of Isaiah reveals more than any other Old Testament book about the Messiah and His future Kingdom.[45] Isaiah's prophetic ministry took place about 739-681 BC.[46] Writing over seven centuries before Christ, Isaiah accurately prophesied His birth, and many key aspects of His life! Since no man can do such things by himself, this shows that God, who plans and knows all things, spoke through Isaiah, revealing what He wanted to reveal. Isaiah wrote rhapsodically about the coming King's birth in the nation of Israel, his earthly mission, death, resurrection, and salvation, and about His future eternal reign on the Throne of David: a virgin "will give birth to a son, and will call him Immanuel" (7:14). Even before His birth God called him to be His Servant (49:1-4). He will be the "Root of Jesse" (11:1, 10; that is, a descendant of Jesse and David). "The [Holy] Spirit of the Lord will rest on him—the Spirit of wisdom and of understanding, the Spirit of counsel and of power" (11:2). He will be gentle to the weak (42:3).

He will obey the Lord and fulfill his mission (50:4-9). That mission is prophesied to be one of ministry, death, and resurrection for the salvation of mankind. He will quietly endure suffering, "led like a lamb to the slaughter," and be "cut off" (53:7-8). He will be rejected by Israel, "the Redeemer and Holy One of Israel," "despised and abhorred by the nation," "despised and rejected by men, a man of sorrows, and familiar with suffering" (49:7; 53:1-3). He will "[take] up our infirmities, [carry] our sorrows, [be] pierced for our transgressions, [and] crushed for our iniquities." "The Lord has laid on him the iniquity of us all," so that "by his wounds we are healed" (53:4-6). After death He will be resurrected: "Yet it was the Lord's will to crush him and cause him to suffer, and though the Lord makes his life a guilt offering, he will see his offspring and prolong his days, and the will of the Lord will prosper in his hand. After the suffering of his soul, he will see the light of life and be satisfied; by his knowledge my righteous servant will justify many, and he will bear their iniquities" (53:9-10). "He will then "be raised and lifted up and highly exalted" (52:13). Therefore I will give him a portion among the great, and he will divide the spoils with the strong, because he poured out his life unto death, and was numbered with the transgressors. For he bore the sin of many, and made intercession for the transgressors" (53:12).

Isaiah 61:1-2a prophesies the future coming of the Messiah, as told by the Messiah himself. It begins by identifying the three Persons of God:[47] "The [Holy] *Spirit* of the *Sovereign Lord* [Father] is on *me* [Christ the Messiah], because the Lord has anointed me to preach good news to the poor. He has sent me to bind up the brokenhearted, to proclaim freedom for the captives and release from darkness for the prisoners, to proclaim the year of the Lord's favor . . . ." Jesus himself later identified His role in the First Advent with these same verses.[48] His role in the Second Advent is then identified in 61:2b-3: to proclaim "the day of vengeance of our God." This will be the day of judgment on unbelievers, later identified as the "white-throne judgment" in Revelation 20:11-15. But he will also "comfort all who mourn, and provide for those who grieve in Zion [Israel]." Having undergone great persecutions throughout history and enduring the sufferings of the Tribulation, they will in the Millennium be filled with joy, praise, and righteousness. Christ will "bestow on them a crown of beauty instead of ashes, the oil of gladness instead of mourning, and a garment of praise instead of a spirit of despair. They will be called oaks of righteousness, a planting of the Lord for the display of his splendor" (2b-3).[49]

The Nature of the Millennium. The Millennium is to be a time of full development of righteousness for the redeemed, in the Kingdom ruled by the supremely righteous King, Jesus Christ. Satanic sources of temptation will be removed, so that inhabitants will be able to display their true character apart from such evil influences. Many saved people who survive the Tribulation will enter the Millennium in natural physical bodies. They will have many children who have unredeemed natures and must be saved or lost. They will be tested under the best conditions. For these reasons Satan and his demons will be removed from the earth immediately upon Christ's Second Coming, before the thousand-year Reign begins. Satan is the imposter king, who with his evil spirits, has been active in human history from the very beginning, lying, deceiving, and leading people, cities, and nations away from the true God. Satan has his greatest sway during the Tribulation, with his emissaries, the Antichrist and the false prophet. But he will be banished from the thousand-year Kingdom of the true King, Jesus Christ, and sealed in the bottomless pit.[50] Since Revelation 20:1-7 specifically states *six times* that the rule of Christ will be a thousand years, it should be understood as a literal number of years.

The Millennium will be a true theocracy. One faith, belief in the Triune God revealed through Israel, Jesus Christ, and the Scriptures, will be established throughout the earth.[51] Every person who enters the Millennium Reign of Christ the Messiah must be saved—a redeemed believer. As Jesus told Nicodemus, "I tell you the truth, no one can see the kingdom of God unless he is born again (John 3:3).[52] "Born again" indicates a person who, because of belief and faith in Jesus Christ as God and Savior, has received the Holy Spirit within his or her heart, and is thus renewed or redeemed. At the Second Coming of Jesus Christ there will be two judgments to determine which individuals still living at the end of the Tribulation will enter the Millennium. The Jews, the people of the nation of Israel, will evidently be judged first. Those who are saved will enter the Promised Land of the Millennium. The unsaved will be sent to their eternal punishment before the Millennium begins. Second, all living individuals of Gentile nations will be judged (the judgment of the sheep [saved] and the goats [unsaved]). Only the redeemed will enter the Millennium. The unsaved will be sent to eternal punishment.[53]

The Millennial Kingdom will be populated by the redeemed remnant of Jews, the redeemed multitude from the Gentile nations of the earth, tribulation martyrs, the resurrected and raptured saints of the church age, and Old Testament saints, who will be resurrected at this time.[54] Each person will understand spiritual matters clearly: "the eyes of those who see will no longer be closed, and the ears of those who hear will listen."[55] They will understand God's Word and speak of it in honesty and truth. There will be no conflicting religions, no propagation of falsehoods (so no Judaism that excludes Christ as Lord and Messiah, no secularism, relativism, naturalism, pragmatism, humanism, agnosticism, atheism, Buddhism, Zen, Shinto, Hinduism, Islam,

Darwinism, Marxism, Nietzscheanism, Freudianism, Modernism, Postmodernism; no Jungians, new age adherents, paganism, devil-worship, etc.). No fool will speak folly, his mind busy with evil, practicing ungodliness and spreading error concerning the Lord. No scoundrels will make up evil schemes to destroy the poor with lies (Isaiah 32:5-7).

At the beginning of the Millennium, Israel will be restored to her homeland. "In that day the Root of Jesse [Christ] will stand as a banner for the peoples; the nations will rally to him, and his place of rest will be glorious. In that day the Lord will reach out his hand a second time to reclaim the remnant that is left of his people from Assyria, from Lower Egypt, from Upper Egypt, from Cush, from Elam, from Babylonia, from Hamath and from the islands of the sea. He will raise a banner for the nations and gather the exiles of Israel; he will assemble the scattered people of Judah from the four quarters of the earth (Isaiah 11:10-12).

With the Jews back in their homeland from around the world, the land itself will be renewed, made fertile, rich with pasture and water, and the mountains and valleys will be changed. "This is what the Lord says: 'In the time of my favor I will answer you, and in the day of salvation I will help you; I will keep you and will make you to be a covenant for the people, to restore the land and to reassign its desolate inheritances, to say to the captives, "Come out," and to those in darkness, "Be free!" They will feed beside the roads and find pasture on every barren hill. They will neither hunger nor thirst, nor will the desert heat or the sun beat upon them. He who has compassion on them will guide them and lead them beside springs of water. I will turn all my mountains into roads, and my highways will be raised up. See, they will come from afar—some from the north, some from the west, some from the region of Aswan'" (Isaiah 49:8-12).

Israel "will rebuild the ancient ruins and restore the places long devastated; they will renew the ruined cities that have been devastated for generations." Israel will be so revered in the Millennium that "aliens will shepherd [their] flocks; foreigners will work [their] fields and vineyards. They "will be called priests of the Lord, [and] be named ministers of our God. [They] will feed on the wealth of nations, and in their riches [they] will boast. Instead of their shame my people will receive a double portion, and instead of disgrace they will rejoice in their inheritance; and so they will inherit a double portion in their land, and everlasting joy will be theirs" (Isaiah 61:4-7). In the Millennium God will fulfill his covenant promise of making Israel "a kingdom of priests and a holy nation."[56]

Isaiah majestically prophesies the life and work of the future Messiah from birth, to salvific mission, to Millennial Reign and Eternal Kingdom: "For to us a child is born, to us a son is given, and the government will be on his shoulders. And he will be called Wonderful Counselor, Mighty God, Everlasting Father, Prince of Peace" (9:6). Although Christ is Second Person of the Trinity, He is fully God, and will rule a just and peaceful world like a Father.[57] No human has ever accomplished this. "Of the increase of his government and peace there will be no end. He will reign on David's throne and over his kingdom, establishing and upholding it with justice and righteousness from that time on and forever. The zeal of the Lord Almighty [God the Father] will accomplish this" (9:7).

He will reign in righteousness and all other rulers under Him will rule with justice (32:1). He will rule with full divine power and authority; "with righteousness he will judge the needy, with justice he will give decisions for the poor of the earth" (11:4a). But any remaining mortals who ignore the righteous law of his Kingdom and sin will be justly dealt with: "He will strike the earth with the rod of his mouth; with the breath of his lips he will slay the wicked. Righteousness will be his belt and faithfulness the sash around his waist" (11:4b-5).

In contrast to the resurrected saints who are in eternal spiritual-physical bodies, both the living Gentile and Jewish redeemed who survive the tribulation and enter the Millennial Kingdom will be in their natural bodies. During the course of the thousand years those in their natural bodies will have multitudes of children, "born with an unredeemed, fallen, sin nature within them," and they "will need to be saved." Some will be saved, some will sin. "The outbreak of sin will be punished by immediate death:"[58] Christ the King "will rule all the nations with an iron scepter."[59] "Rebellion against the authority of the King will be immediately judged (Zechariah 14:16-19)."

In the Messiah's Kingdom there will be a new state of peace and harmony for individuals and for nations. All kingdoms of the world will be unified and remain in a state of peace and economic prosperity.[60] "The fruit of righteousness will be peace; the effect of righteousness will be quietness and confidence forever. My people will live in peaceful dwelling places, in secure homes, in undisturbed places of rest" (Isaiah 32:17-18). Christ "will judge between the nations and will settle disputes for many peoples. They will beat their swords into plowshares and their spears into pruning hooks. Nation will not take up sword against nation, nor will they train for war anymore" (2:4). "Every warrior's boot used in battle and every garment rolled in blood will be destined for burning, will be fuel for the fire" (9:5).

"For this is what the Lord says: 'I will extend peace to her [Jerusalem, Israel] like a river, and the wealth of nations like a flooding stream; you will nurse and be carried on her arm and dandled on her knees'" (Isaiah 66:12). "No longer will violence be heard in your land, nor ruin or destruction within your borders, but you will call your walls Salvation and your gates

Praise" (60:18). "He will be the sure foundation for your times, a rich store of salvation and wisdom and knowledge; the fear of the Lord is the key to this treasure" (33:6). "All your sons will be taught by the Lord, and great will be your children's peace" (54:13). "You will go out in joy and be led forth in peace; the mountains and hills will burst into song before you, and all the trees of the field will clap their hands" (55:12).

The curse placed on creation at the Fall will be removed. Nature will be transformed, losing its threatening and harmful aspects, and become more fruitful. Animals will no longer be carnivorous; they will live peacefully, without preying on each other or on humans: "In that day I will make a covenant for them with the beasts of the field and the birds of the air and the creatures that move along the ground."[61] "The wolf will live with the lamb, the leopard will lie down with the goat, the calf and the lion and the yearling together; and a little child will lead them. The cow will feed with the bear, their young will lie down together, and the lion will eat straw like the ox. The infant will play near the hole of the cobra, and the young child put his hand into the viper's nest. They will neither harm nor destroy on all my holy mountain, for the earth will be full of the knowledge of the Lord" (Isaiah 11:6-9). This removal of the curse from nature must surely also include the end of destructive events such as hurricanes, tornadoes, floods, tsunamis, earthquakes, great fires, and volcanic eruptions.

Great multitudes of people in the Millennium will already be in their eternal, spiritual-physical bodies.[62] Those who live into the Millennium in mortal bodies will live extremely long lives and continue to have children. Longevity will be restored, perhaps longer than that of Methuselah who lived 969 years in the antediluvian era. This suggests that there will be no deaths from decay, disease, or degeneration.[63] There will be no birth defects or physical and mental deformities. "The earth's population will soar." "There will be a supernatural work of preservation of life in the millennial age through the King."[64] "Never again will there be in it an infant who lives but a few days, or an old man who does not live out his years; he who dies at a hundred will be thought a mere youth; he who fails to reach a hundred will be considered accursed . . . . For as the days of a tree, so will be the days of my people; my chosen ones will long enjoy the works of their hands. They will not toil in vain or bear children doomed to misfortune; for they will be a people blessed by the Lord, they and their descendants with them. Before they call I will answer; while they are still speaking I will hear" (Isaiah 65:20-24).

Sickness will be removed from the earth during the Millennium. "No one living in Zion will say, "I am ill"; and the sins of those who dwell there will be forgiven" (Isaiah 33:24). "I will restore you to health and heal your wounds." "I will bind up the injured and strengthen the weak."[65] Death will also be largely removed, used only as a divine measure of justice for the overt sin of living mortals. However, God will destroy any who rebel against His authority: "the sleek and the strong I will destroy."[66] Although the curse of sin will be largely absent, it will not be fully removed until the end of the Millennium, when death will be completely and finally abolished.[67]

"The millennium will be the period of the full manifestation of the glory of the Lord Jesus Christ."[68] His deity, omniscience, omnipotence, and authority will be recognized worldwide. He will be worshipped as God. In Isaiah 66:18 Christ the Messiah says that He will come and "gather all nations and tongues, and they will come and see my glory." He assures Israel that He will sustain and strengthen her by His omnipotent power: "I have chosen you and have not rejected you. So do not fear, for I am with you; do not be dismayed, for I am your God. I will strengthen you and help you; I will uphold you with my righteous right hand."

Above all, holiness will be manifested during the millennial reign of the Messiah. Jesus Christ will reign in the midst of His chosen people, imparting holiness to them. "Holiness will be the great distinguishing characteristic of the Jewish people in all categories of their national life."[69] News of the Messiah's divine goodness will spread through the earth: "How beautiful on the mountains are the feet of those who bring good news, who proclaim peace, who bring good tidings, who proclaim salvation, who say to Zion, "Your God reigns" (52:7)! The will of God will be fully revealed on earth by the Messiah.[70]

In Isaiah 49:3 Christ is addressed as "Israel" by God [the Father] because, as the Messiah born in Israel, He fulfills what Israel should have done long ago—He manifests God's authority, glory, and splendor in Israel by His presence: "You are my servant, Israel, in whom I will display my splendor."[71] During the Millennium "all your people [will] be "righteous and they will possess the land forever. They are the shoot I have planted, the work of my hands, for the display of my splendor" (60:21).

The Messiah will also reach out through Israel to the Gentiles, fulfilling the Mosaic covenant promise to make Israel "a kingdom of priests and a holy nation," and making them "a light for the Gentiles."[72] "It is too small a thing for you to be my servant to restore the tribes of Jacob and bring back those of Israel I have kept. I will also make you a light for the Gentiles, that you may bring my salvation to the ends of the earth. This is what the Lord says—the Redeemer and Holy One of Israel—to him who was despised and abhorred by the nation, to the servant of rulers: 'Kings will see you and rise up, princes will see and bow down, because of the Lord, who is faithful, the Holy One of Israel, who has chosen you (Isaiah 49:6-7).'" Thus "will he sprinkle many nations, and kings will shut their mouths because of him. For what they were not told, they will see, and what they have not heard, they will understand" (52:15).

In all these ways the Millennium will serve both as the culmination and end of history, and as the necessary preparation for the Eternal Kingdom of God succeeding it. It will provide a long period of extended life for the redeemed to adapt to these new conditions of life and the holy reign of Christ. It will give the last ones born on earth the opportunity to be saved or to follow Satan. All things divinely promised will be accomplished by divine power. Death will be completely overcome by restoration of life.

Near the end of the millennium, Satan will be released from captivity in the Abyss and will go around the world deceiving people and nations. People will have one final opportunity to choose to follow God or Satan. Many will prefer the excitement, pleasure and evil of following the ways of Satan instead of worshipping God and pursuing righteousness.

The wicked and unredeemed dead will be raised at the end of the Millennium to be judged by Jesus Christ at the Great White Throne Judgment. At that time, as Jesus Christ said, "every knee will bow before me; every tongue will confess to God" and each one "will give an account of himself to God."[73] The final defeat of Satan and death will be fully actualized, and Satan and all his followers will be consigned to Hell, forever removing wickedness, temptations and deceptions.

With the end of the Millennium reign of Christ the Eternal Kingdom of God the Father will begin. 1 Corinthians 15:24-28 tells of this change: "Then the end will come, when he hands over the kingdom to God the Father after he has destroyed all dominion, authority and power. For he must reign until he has put all his enemies under his feet. The last enemy to be destroyed is death. For he 'has put everything under his feet' . . . . When he has done this, then the Son himself will be made subject to him who put everything under him, so that God may be all in all. The reign of Jesus Christ will not be completely ended with the Millennium however. Although Christ hands over the Kingdom to God the Father at the end of the Millennium, His reign continues forever, "subsumed under the Father's direct control."[74]

Heaven: The Eternal Kingdom of God. The most striking feature of the Eternal Kingdom of God is that there will be a New Heaven and a New Earth. Several Bible verses indicate this. There are three specific statements in 2 Peter 3. Verses 5-7 link destruction of the old heaven and earth with the future, end-times judgment of the ungodly: "long ago by God's word the heavens existed and the earth was formed out of water and by water. By these waters also the world of that time was deluged and destroyed. By the same word the present heavens and earth are reserved for fire, being kept for the Day of Judgment and destruction of ungodly men. Verses 10-11 are quite specific, telling of the destruction of *everything* of the old world in a roar and in fire: "the day of the Lord will come like a thief. The heavens will disappear with a roar; the elements will be destroyed by fire, and the earth and everything in it will be laid bare." And verse 12 again says: "That day will bring about the destruction of the heavens by fire, and the elements will melt in the heat." John's vision in Revelation 21:1 specifically indicates the old being replaced by the new, with a major new feature: "I saw a new heaven and a new earth, for the first heaven and the first earth had passed away, and there was no longer any sea." And 20:11 indicates that in his vision of the great white throne judgment at the end of the Millennium Reign of Christ, there was no longer any earth and sky: "Then I saw a great white throne and him who was seated on it. Earth and sky fled from his presence, and there was no place for them." Other verses seem to refer to such great changes.[75]

Walvoord has strongly supported this understanding of these verses. "The most natural interpretation of the fact that earth and heaven flee away is that the present earth and heaven are destroyed and will be replaced by the new heaven and new earth . . . . It would be difficult to find a more explicit statement than that contained here in Revelation 20:11 and in 2 Peter 3:10-11. Further, it would be most natural that the present earth and heaven, the scene of the struggle with Satan and sin, should be displaced by an entirely new order suited for eternity. The whole structure of the universe is operating on the principle of a clock that is running down. Though many billions of years would be required to accomplish this, the natural world would eventually come to a state of total inactivity if the physical laws of the universe as now understood should remain unchanged. What could be simpler than for God to create a new heaven and a new earth by divine fiat in keeping with His purposes for eternity to come?"[76]

Hugh Ross concludes that essential laws of nature, as we now know them, will no longer be in effect: (1) the second law of thermodynamics will no longer be in effect (nothing then will run down, decay, and die, as everything now does); (2) gravity, or mass, or both, as we now know them, will be absent (so that structures could be built without the present limitations imposed by gravity and mass); and (3) the present type of electromagnetic light will be replaced by the eternal light of God. The present Sun, Moon, and stars will be gone. Before God's creation of the New Heaven and New Earth, "All the stars of the heavens will be dissolved and the sky rolled up like a scroll" (Isaiah 34:4). While darkness is the dominant factor in the present world, light will have an eternal, pervasive presence then. As Ross writes, the physics of the present world will be gone, and "totally new laws will take effect."[77]

God had spoken much earlier through Isaiah of the New Heaven and New Earth: "Behold, I will create new heavens and a new earth. The former things will not be remembered, nor will they come to mind." Walvoord notes that this was spoken of in the same context as the Millennium, but that two events distantly related are often spoken of in this way in the Bible. And in Isaiah 66:10-22, which has multiple references, God spoke again of His New Eternal Kingdom and of Israel: "As the new heavens and the new earth that I make will endure before me . . . so will your name and descendants endure."

Revelation 21:1 tells us there will no longer be a sea in God's Eternal Kingdom. This is a feature distinguishing it from the Millennial Reign of Christ. During the Millennium Christ "will rule from sea to sea and from the River to the ends of the earth" (Psalm 72:8), and "the earth will be full of the knowledge of the Lord as the waters cover the sea" (Isaiah 11:9). In the present earth, the sea has associations not only of vastness and beauty, but of limitations, danger, and death. It separates people and nations, requiring dangerous voyages or flights. Many people have gone to their deaths in the sea, and by dangerous sea creatures. "Most of the earth is now covered with water, but the new earth apparently will have no bodies of water except for the river mentioned in [Revelation] 22:2."[78] John saw "the river of the water of life, as clear as crystal, flowing from the throne of God and of the Lamb [Jesus Christ] down the middle of the great street of the city. On each side of the river stood the tree of life, bearing twelve crops of fruit, yielding its fruit every month. And the leaves of the tree are for the healing of the nations."

Newness and great contrasts with the present earth and life are evident in other ways in Heaven. Most prominent is the New Jerusalem. Telling of his vision of the beautiful city, John said: "I saw the Holy City, the new Jerusalem, coming down out of heaven from God, prepared as a bride beautifully dressed for her husband. And I heard a loud voice from the throne saying, 'Now the dwelling of God is with men, and he will live with them. They will be his people, and God himself will be with them and be their God'" (21:2-3). Not only will the New Jerusalem be a fully divine creation, descending from heaven to the New Earth, but God the Father, along with Jesus Christ, will live and rule among men. Father and Son will share the rule.[79] The Holy Spirit will also be equally present, fulfilling His work. The actual plenary presence of the Trinity on Earth among men is something new, and reveals sufficient reason for a New Jerusalem and a New Earth. Newness is also confirmed by the divine proclamation from the Throne of God in verse 5: "I am making everything new!"

In John's vision, the new Holy City is so beautiful that he compares it to the most beautiful bride, glorious and shining, richly adorned for her husband. "It shone with the glory of God, and its brilliance was like that of a very precious jewel, like a jasper, clear as crystal. It had a great, high wall with twelve gates, and with twelve angels at the gates. On the gates were written the names of the twelve tribes of Israel. There were three gates on the east, three on the north, three on the south and three on the west. The wall of the city had twelve foundations, and on them were the names of the twelve apostles of the Lamb" (21:1-2; 11-14). God is not only the absolute Lord of truth, goodness, and justice, but of beauty as well. All divinely created natural beauty reflects to some degree that of God. The Eternal Holy City reveals an amazing beauty, as never seen before, far surpassing all previous beauties of earthly creations. We may for the same reasons expect something similar for the natural beauties of the New Earth.

John described more of his vision of the Holy City. It is a divinely built city of precious metals and gemstones in richly glowing and varied colors that are transparent or translucent. The descriptions suggest that these fine materials are purer than those of the present earth. While fully physical, they powerfully evoke the spiritual and immaterial: "The wall was made of jasper, and the city of pure gold, as pure as glass." While jasper occurs in red, green, and yellow colors, green is the most rare and translucent, and considered the most valuable. Will the great walls of the Eternal City be translucent green, providing a beautiful harmonic contrast with the pure, clear gold running through the entire city? The Holy City will be colossal, or better, divine in dimensions, measured at 1,342 miles in length, width, and height.[80] Apparently occupying close to two million square miles, the Holy City of Jerusalem, then, will be at least one-third the size of the entire 50 United States, and slightly larger than Argentina, the eighth largest country in the world.[81] The pure jasper walls running around the huge City will be 216 feet thick or tall, and 5,368 miles in length altogether. Outside will be the rest of the New Earth, the dimensions of which are not indicated in the Bible, but which must be much larger than now. This great City of God, by its description and dimensions, surely requires a vast New Earth.

The foundations of the city walls will be decorated with many kinds of precious stone. The first foundation is jasper, the second sapphire (the brilliant deep blue type?), the third chalcedony (white, blue, or brown?), the fourth emerald (beautiful greens), the fifth sardonyx (red, brown, and white combined), the sixth carnelian (red or reddish-brown), the seventh chrysolite (bright light green), the eighth beryl (pale rose to pale blue-green), the ninth topaz (pale, transparent pink, blue, green, or reddish yellow), the tenth chrysoprase (a unique, medium-light sea-green), the eleventh jacinth (transparent red, reddish blue, or deep purple), and the twelfth amethyst (pale to deeper purple). Just as colors and materials of the present world show

God's rich, loving, and bountiful creativity, so will the even richer materials and colors of the New Jerusalem. The twelve gates will be twelve pearls, each gate made of a single pearl. The great streets of the city will be of pure gold, like transparent glass. John saw no temple in the city, "because the Lord God Almighty and the Lamb are its temple" (21:18-22).

There is nothing inferior or degrading about the beauty of material objects such as precious metals and semi-precious stones, or flowers, or even the human body. They are some of the most beautiful works of God the Creator in the present earth, and should not be demeaned as inferior for being "physical" and "material." God Himself created all physical, material forms, and saw them as good. And Jesus Christ the Logos took on the full, material, human form along with His Eternal Spiritual Being. Walvoord thinks that the descriptions in 21:11 and 18-21 of material things, such as gold, imply that they are different, purer than those in this present earth.[82] With such beauty and perfection in the description of the New Jerusalem, we may surely expect not just the "good," but "perfect" beauty and goodness throughout the new Earth.

In the Eternal Kingdom of God human beings will live forever in spiritual-physical resurrection Bodies like that of the resurrected Jesus: Jesus Christ "will transform our lowly bodies so that they will be like his glorious body" (Philippians 3:20-21). When Jesus appeared to the disciples after His death and resurrection he showed them that His body was real, physical, and He was recognizable. He said to them: "Look at my hands and my feet. It is I myself! Touch me and see; a ghost does not have flesh and bones, as you see I have." And He ate some broiled fish in their presence. In His resurrection body Christ also walked through closed doors and disappeared from one place to reappear in another.[83] Since the redeemed are promised similar bodies, we may expect to be flesh and bone, be recognized, eat and drink, and do other things that Christ did.

The Spiritual State of America and Europe Today. In marked contrast to the teachings and beliefs discussed in this and previous chapters, many things indicate that America today is vulnerable to devastating erosion and decline from within and without. While growing greatly in population, knowledge, wealth, and power since World War II, America has clearly declined spiritually. There are still many fine Christian believers in the Creator and Lord God of the Bible, and a large number of churches, schools, and seminaries that hold to these teachings. But a *majority* of people in America now no longer knows *who God is.* Many say they believe in God, but they do not know whether God is a person or some kind of impersonal force. Many others are not even sure that there is a God, and a sizeable number are sure that there is no God. The popularity of a recent spate of atheistic books and the enthusiasm of their readers reflect this. Many people think one religion is as good as another and that any one of them can lead to eternal life. Others follow the Enlightenment view that religion is superstition and ignorance. All of this reveals a startling lack of spiritual insight, and a breathtaking ignorance. But such things are characteristic of this largely secular society.

Europe is considerably more advanced in disbelief and secularism than America. The "Age of Reason" and the "Enlightenment" in Europe gave impetus to the modern turn away from God which has been accelerating ever since. The spiritual situation in England, France, Germany, Spain, Denmark, Norway, Sweden, and some other countries is worse than that of America. While polls vary, Christian belief in many of these countries appears to range from 20% to 10%, or lower. One poll finds 16% in Britain, and 12% in both France and in Germany, with two, three, or more times that many atheists, agnostics, and various other views.[84]

While America is far more Christian than continental Europe and Britain, the proportion of Americans who believe the Bible is the authoritative word of God, and who study and uphold it in that way has grown noticeably smaller. A recent poll shows that only 36% of evangelical church members (supposedly the most dedicated) believe that their religion is the one true faith, and for mainline churches the number falls to only 12%. Of Americans with any religious affiliation 70% said they believe many religions can lead to eternal life (including 57% of evangelicals and 83% of mainline church members).[85] Such beliefs defy the Bible and classic Christian tradition that salvation and paradise come only from God the Father through Jesus Christ, and in the Holy Spirit. A survey of January 2000 showed that 62% of Americans did not believe in any absolute moral truth! [But God *is* the Absolute, eternal Truth, and provides absolute, eternal truth.] And not long after 09-11-01 the number rose to 78 %. Another survey in the Fall of 2006 showed that only about 33% of Americans under 40 held belief in any absolute truth. About 50% of this age group also indicated that morals should be based on "what is right for the person" (relativism). Early signs of this in 1931 led Bishop Fulton J. Sheen to suspect a coming era in which people would say "one-world religion is just as good as another."[86] These views indicate that American religious beliefs are "3,000 miles wide and only three inches deep."[87] They also contradict the central teaching of Jesus Christ: "I am the way and the truth and the life. No one comes to the Father except through me" (John 14:6). In a 2007 poll 41% of American adults said that when Jesus lived on earth He committed sins. (If this were true, it would make divine salvation impossible.) 57% of adults said they think Satan is not a living being but a symbol of evil (a modern, non-biblical view). For Catholics it was 64%, and for born-again Christians 46%.[88]

Many Americans hardly ever read and study the Bible and have no significant knowledge of it. As a result they have little spiritual insight and strength of conviction about important religious matters. They become spiritually blind (unable to know truth) and fall prey to false and harmful ideas and beliefs. They become like sheep who can be led by false religious teachings, by bad political, social, ethical, sexual, and religious views of popular secular culture, daytime talk shows and audience applause, or by liberal and atheistic teachers and acquaintances. The dominant, relativistic and secular society of our times becomes the overarching guide to any "truth."

The effects of modern and postmodern thought, discussed in Chapters Six through Eight, have brought forth a world very different from that of three or four centuries ago, and even notably different from that of pre-World-War-II America. Most people, however, have no real understanding of this monumental sea change. Universities, which began many centuries ago as bastions of Christianity and conservatism, are now largely ruled by secularism, liberalism, radicalism, and atheism. Baudrillard was not far wrong in saying that the new postmodern era is one of "total relativity."

Business corporations have become giant, multi-national power-houses with secular goals of production and profit, where God usually has no place. University goals and guidelines, like those of corporations, are established on liberal and relativistic concepts and purposes to promote trendy values of the politically correct, secular society. Liberal and atheistic professors crank out tens of thousands of fresh new liberals, relativists, radicals, and atheists every year. Even the U. S. government takes a leading part in this process. At every opportunity, a liberal Supreme Court and lower courts deny rights to schools and teachers to publicly read or teach the Bible and pray, to display any Christian moral teachings, or even to have a Bible on their desk. There is no problem at all, however, in teaching humanistic, anti-Christian, and atheistic philosophies such as those of Kant, Hegel, Schopenhauer, Marx, Nietzsche, Heidegger, Sartre, Adorno, Foucault, Derrida, Baudrillard, and a broad bevy of postmodernists, (which *are* "religious" in the sense that they put forward comprehensive worldviews).

"Modern" and "postmodern" philosophers, writers, artists, scientists, and others, who have increasingly rejected the God of the Bible since the Enlightenment, are the primary subject matter of present-day universities. Dominant art forms, which were 95-97% Christian in the Middle Ages, and still 65-85% Christian in the Renaissance, dropped to 50 % in the Age of Reason, then rapidly to 24% in the Enlightenment, and 10 % in the nineteenth century.[89] In the twentieth and twenty-first century the dominant art forms have become totally and completely "modern" and "postmodern," rejecting traditional belief in God and the Bible.

Government legislative branches also make laws that contradict moral principles taught in the Bible. Free sexuality, homosexuality, and abortion, sins and abominations to God the Father of all life and marriage,[90] are condoned and even promoted by government and political groups who have no interest in biblical teachings, and instead, support liberal and relativistic views, seeking to gain support and re-election by pandering to these groups. According to a recent report, the percentage of married households with children in America has dropped from 44.3 percent to 20.2 percent since 1960. "There is not one more married couple with a child today than there was 50 years ago, and the overall number of households has more than doubled since 1960." "For the first time in American history, married couples in general have dropped below 50 percent, which means that the whole concept of marriage is in question."[91] Ann Coulter notes that "various studies have shown that children raised by a single mother comprise about 70 percent of juvenile murderers, delinquents, teenaged mothers, drug abusers, dropouts, suicides and runaways. Imagine an America with 70 percent fewer of these social disorders and you will see what liberals' destruction of marriage has wrought."[92]

Natural causes and the evolution of species are the only answer allowed in universities and schools to the question of the origin of life (although with no proof), while the biblical teaching of divine creation (which is more logical and rational) is *prohibited*. There is free opportunity to teach and promote non-theistic evolution and many kinds of anti-theistic and anti-Christian beliefs such as secular pragmatism, atheistic Existentialism, neo-Marxism, Postmodernism, "deconstruction," "difference," and "simulation." Thoroughly anti-theistic modern and postmodern philosophies are freely and openly taught without protest. The Bible condemns homosexuality as unnatural and an abomination to God, but pro-homosexual views are gaining legal approval in America, and are even taught to teen and pre-teen children.[93] Anti-Christian religious views, such as Islam, are infiltrating our schools and universities, and attempting to influence American law.[94] Some universities in America have also taught and promoted worship of "the Goddess."

The proud banner of democratic freedom has been turned into a license to do or say anything at all: under the rubric of total *freedom of speech*, many films, books, and art works since 1960 or 1970 present the most bizarre, ugly, and indecent images and ideas (that are too vulgar to be reproduced in this book), and little can be done about it. Such extreme notions of freedom arise from disbelief in the Holy God, our Creator, to whom we are morally responsible. While we can hope and pray that these conditions will be reversed and set on a better course, it is presently impossible to envision.

It is extremely difficult to reverse four centuries of accelerating Modernism and Postmodernism.

The modern theory of origins and evolution of species, which posits an accidental, indifferent, purposeless world, a universe with no ground, meaning, or goal, and ending in death and extinction, has become a primary doctrine of modernity.[95]

For the genuine believer in the Living God of the Bible, these conditions are increasingly leading toward the decline and failure of the wonderful America we have known, and an increase of assaults, suffering, and sorrows.[96]Ungodly beliefs and values cannot be permanently sustained. The Bible, especially the Old Testament, shows that God controls history, countries, rulers, and empires. A nation that turns away from God does not survive. Another evil nation or false religion can be divinely influenced to destroy it, as Assyria was led to destroy Jerusalem, and as Rome was led to the second, greater destruction causing the Jewish Diaspora (as well as significant unification and growth of the Mediterranean and European lands, making the growth and spread of Christianity possible). Or it will eventually weaken and fail internally through its own spiritual blindness and corruption.

The Incompatibility of Modern and Postmodern Thought With Traditional Biblical Teachings. This book has shown ways that the triune God of the Bible and conservative Christian theology is awesomely great. He is the Supreme Being by whom the real world exists, and from whom we get our being and reality through divine creation. His eternal ideas are the basis for the forms that give structure, meaning, and purpose to the world and all created things, and make it possible for us to objectively know them. He sustains all of creation at every moment with his Being, Power, and Knowledge. Without all this there would be nothing. Instead, there would be the things late Modernism and Postmodernism say there are—no substantial reality, no universal truths, no secure knowledge, and no real purpose. All this would end in death. Expressed more exactly, there would be nothing at all. God is the unique and ultimate source of all good things in life: life itself, love, knowledge, and purpose. Without the eternal, supreme God, none of these things would exist (and their non-existence is the general position of late Modernism and Postmodernism). Divine creation is the single ultimate source of all things, including all reality, reason, knowledge, meaning and purpose. But late modern and postmodern thought and art have increasingly turned against and away from the God of the Bible and divine creation, and have, in various ways lost all these good things.

In our largely modernized and secularized society today, rapidly developing since the Age of Reason and Enlightenment, the increasing rejection of God and divine creation has brought terrible troubles with it, including the loss of the ultimate basis for universal truth, knowledge, meaning, and purpose, and a tragic final ending in death. Evidence and rational arguments in Chapters Two and Three have shown that naturalist and materialist theories of origin and evolution of one species from a different species are not only unfounded and unproven, but untrue, and rationally absurd. No genuine, factual description of the genesis of life on earth by chance and natural causes has been proven and documented. The incredibly great amounts of precise and complex information in the universe and in human cells, for example, point to the existence of a Supreme Mind as their source. Such information must come from Mind and Idea. Chance and accident cannot possibly be their source, neither can nothingness. Such complex and purposeful ideas and forms cannot evolve out of nothingness, non-mind, or lower forms of life.

If naturalist and materialist theories of origin and evolution of species were true, it would leave the world without any absolute source, ground, meaning, and purpose, as modernists and postmodernists say it is, in various ways. God would thus not be God, because there would be no divine creation, no substantial humans, and no real, objective world. God would not be God, because all things would exist in some way without him, and outside of any knowledge and power he had. God would thus be radically limited, and that is certainly not what God is. Belief in God intrinsically demands belief in divine creation. To reject divine creation, as Modernism and Postmodernism have done, is to reject God. The very notion of God requires divine creation, and creation demands the Supreme God. Only the God "I AM" can provide reliable, substantial being to creatures, and the possibility of real human knowledge of creation itself, formed according to His Ideas.

Since God created it, all creation is dependent upon him as its ultimate source, foundation, ground, and goal. The ideas, forms, and laws of all things come from God, and because they do, they unconditionally guarantee the reality of the world and the possibility of real knowledge of it, since He is eternal Being of infinite knowledge, power, and purpose. In divine creation God implants in the created world and man real substance, essence, and eternal ideas/forms, which absolutely guarantee its reality and knowability (Chapters One through Five). Divine creation also carries with it the eternal purposes and goals of God. Since God is good, He would not create all things simply to develop by chance and accident, without purpose, and to end in death and complete extinction (Chapters Nine through Twelve). These latter notions are some of the prevalent views behind modern and postmodern thought and art, because they have abandoned belief in God. And they are partially right: without God there is no guarantee of the reality of the world, apodictic truth, real purpose, and ultimate goal.

The modern and postmodern theories of the non-reality of Absolute Being, Logos, substantial contingent beings, objective reality, universal reason, meaning, and purpose emphatically show all of this. Late modern and postmodern thought and art show these things by their rejection of divine creation, and the resulting emphasis on the uncertainty, ambiguity, fragmentation, and untrustworthiness of what we think we know, and on belief that there is no real, objectively-given reason, law, purpose, morality, or meaning in the universe or in human life. Disbelief in God and divine creation even divests Modernism and Postmodernism of any basis and reason to believe in the objective reality of the world and a substantial self, as well as any universal truth, reason, knowledge, and purpose (Chapters Six, Seven, and Eight).

The most pressing choice for a person today is not between all the many competing religious, philosophical, atheistic, and other views all around us. It is between Christianity and Modernism/Postmodernism, which for four centuries has progressively and increasingly turned away from God and the Bible, upon which the Western world was founded. (I believe, like innumerable others through the centuries, that the Bible is the inspired word of God.) The result today is that God is entirely absent from modern and postmodern thought, arts, and morality, as never before in Western history. This condition is unsustainable. America's condition will further deteriorate over coming decades because of it. God is "jealous" and will not tolerate sustained unfaithfulness. Such acts bring forth terrible punishments or abandonment.

Final Words. The words of Jesus Christ close the Book of Revelation and the Bible. He identifies Himself as the "Alpha and Omega," the "Root and Offspring of David," the One who will reign in the Millennium and then forever with the Father and Holy Spirit. He says, "Behold, I am coming soon! My reward is with me, and I will give to everyone according to what he has done. I am the Alpha and the Omega, the First and the Last, the Beginning and the End. Blessed are those who wash their robes, that they may have the right to the tree of life and may go through the gates into the city. Outside are the dogs, those who practice magic arts, the sexually immoral, the murderers, the idolaters and everyone who loves and practices falsehood. I, Jesus, have sent my angel to give you this testimony for the churches. I am the Root and the Offspring of David, and the bright Morning Star. The Spirit and the bride say, 'Come!' And let him who hears say, 'Come!' Whoever is thirsty, let him come; and whoever wishes, let him take the free gift of the water of life" (Revelation 22:12-17). God the omnipotent Creator will achieve the consummation of creation. His Kingdom *will* come, and it will be wondrous to behold.

Bibliography

Ackroyd, Peter. *T. S. Eliot; A Life*. New York: Simon and Schuster,1984.

After Philosophy; End or Transformation, Edited by Kenneth Baynes, James Bohman, and Thomas McCarthy. Cambridge, Massachusetts: MIT Press, 1987.

Altaf, Simon. *World War III: Unmasking The End Time Beast*. North Miami Beach FL: YATI Publishing, 2006.

Ankerberg, John and John Weldon. *Fast Facts on Islam*. Eugene OR: Harvest House, 2001.

Ankerberg, John and Dillon Burroughs. *Middle East Meltdown*. Eugene OR: Harvest House, 2007./

Apologetics Study Bible. Nashville: Holman Bible Publishers, 2007.

Archer, Gleason L. *New International Encyclopedia of Bible Difficulties*. Grand Rapids: Zondervan, 2001.

Ariew, Roger, and Marjorie Grene. 1995. "Ideas in and Before Descartes." *Journal of The History of Ideas*. 1995: 87-88.

Aristotle. Complete Works of Aristotle. Edited by Jonathan Barnes. Princeton University Press. Vol. 1, 1971, contains: Categories and De Interpretatione, Topics, Physics, On Generation and Corruption, On the Soul; Vol. 2, 1984, contains: Metaphysics.

Armstrong, A. H. *An Introduction to Ancient Philosophy*. Totowa: Littlefield, Adams, 1981).

Armstrong, A. H., and R. A. Markus. *Christian Faith and Greek Philosophy*. New York: Sheed and Ward, c. 1960.

Arndt, William. New International Encyclopedia of Bible Difficulties. Grand Rapids: Zondervan, 2001.

Ashton, John F., ed. *On the Seventh Day; Forty Scientists and Academics Explain Why They Believe in God*. Green Forrest, AR: Master Books, 2004).

———, ed. *In Six Days; Why Fifty Scientists Choose to Believe in Creation* (Green Forrest, AR: Master Books, 2007.

Ashworth, E. J. "Descartes' Theory of Objective Reality." *The New Scholasticism* (49: 1975): 333-34.

Aquinas, Thomas. *Summa Contra Gentiles*. University of Notre Dame Press. Book I, 1991, God. Book II, 1991, Creation. Book III, 1991, Providence, Part I. Book IV, 1989, Providence, Part II; Book V, Salvation.

———. *Summa Theologica*. Translated by Fathers of the English Dominican Province. London: Burns, Oates, and Washbourne, 1920.

———. *Truth*. Translated by Robert W. Mulligan. Chicago: Regnery, 1951.

———. *An Introduction to the Metaphysics of St. Thomas Aquinas*. Translated by James F. Anderson. Washington, D. C.: Regnery, Gateway Editions, 1997.

Augustine. *The City of God*. Translated by Henry Bettenson. Harmondsworth: Penguin, 1980.

————. *Eighty-three Different Questions.* Washington, D. C.: Catholic University of America Press, 2002.

————. *On Order* (De ordine). Translated by Silvano Borruso. South Bend, Ind.: St. Augustine's Press, 2007.

————. *Retractions.* The Fathers of the Church Series. Translated by Sister M. Inez Bogan, R.S.M. Washington, D. C.: Catholic University of America Press, 1999.

Barrett, C. K. *The Gospel According to John*, 2nd edition. Philadelphia: Westminster Press, 1978.

Barrett, William. *Irrational Man.* New York: Doubleday, 1962.

————. *The Illusion of Technique.* Garden City, New York: Anchor, 1979.

Baudrillard, Jean. *Simulations.* New York: Semiotext(e), 1983.

————. *Symbolic Exchange and Death* [*L'echange symbolique et la mort*]. London: Sage, 1993.

————. *The Transparency of Evil.* London: Verso, 1993.

Baumer, Franklin L. *Modern European Thought; Continuity and Change in Ideas, 1600-1950.* New York: Macmillan, 1977.

Bavinck, Herman. *The Doctrine of God.* Grand Rapids: Baker: 1983.

Beale, G. K. *The Book of Revelation: A Commentary on the Greek Text (New International Greek Testament Commentary).* Grand Rapids: Eerdmans, 1998.

Believers Study Bible, New King James Version. Edited by W. A. Criswell. Nashville: Nelson, 1991).

Benesch, Otto. *German Painting from Dürer to Holbein. Translated by H. S. B. Harrison* Geneva: Skira/World, 1966.

Benignus, Brother. *Nature, Knowledge, and God: An Introduction to Thomistic Philosophy.* Milwaukee: Bruce, 1947.

Berkouwer, G. C. *The Providence of God.* Grand Rapids: Eerdmans, 1983.

Blake, William. *Blake Complete Writings*, ed. Geoffrey Keynes (London: Oxford University Press, 1974),

Blond, Phillip, ed. *Post-Secular Philosophy.* London and New York: Routledge, 1998.

Bloom, Harold. *The Best Poems of the English Language.* Harper Collins, 2004.

Bock, Darrell L., Kenneth L. Gentry, Robert B. Strimple, Craig A. Blessing *Three Views on the Millennium and Beyond.* Grand Rapids: Zondervan, 1999.

Bourke, Vernon J. *Augustine's View of Reality.* Villanova Press, 1964.

Bochenski, I. M. *Contemporary European Philosophy*, Translated by Donald Nicholl and Karl Aschenbrenner. Berkeley and Los Angeles: University of California Press, 1965.

Bowie, Andrew. *Schelling and Modern European Philosophy.* London: Routledge, 1993.

Bryant, Al, compiler. *Sourcebook of Poetry.* Grand Rapids: Zondervan, 1968.

Buchanan Pat. *The Death of the West; How Dying Populations and Immigrant Invasions Imperil Our Country and Civilization.* New York: St. Martin's Press, 2002.

Cahoone, Lawrence E. *The Dilemma of Modernity; Philosophy, Culture, and Anti-Culture.* Albany: State University of New York Press, 1988.

Campbell, Donald K. and Jeffrey L. Townsend. *The Coming Millennial Kingdom.* Grand Rapids: Kregel, 1997.

Caner, Ergun Mehmet and Emir Fethi Caner, *Unveiling Islam.* Grand Rapids MI: Kregel, 2002.

Caponigri, A. Robert, *A History of Western Philosophy; Philosophy from the Renaissance to the Romantic Age.* Notre Dame: University of Notre Dame Press, 1963.

Cassirer, Ernst. *Kant's Life and Thought.* Translated by James Haden. New Haven: Yale University Press, 1981.

Caton, Hiram. *The Origin of Subjectivity, An Essay on Descartes.* New Haven: Yale University Press, 1973.

Charnock, Stephen. *Discourses upon the Existence and Attributes of God.* Grand Rapids, MI: Baker, 1979.

Cheetham. Nicolas. *Universe; A Journey from Earth to the Edge of the Cosmos.* London: Quercus, 2007.

Clark, Gordon H. *Karl Barth's Theological Method.* Nutley, NJ: Presbyterian and Reformed Publishing Co., 1963.

Collins, James. *A History of Modern European Philosophy* (Milwaukee: Bruce, 1965/1954).

Columbia History of Philosophy. Edited by Richard Popkin. New York: MJF Books, 1999.

Conner, Kevin J. and Ken Malmin, *The Covenants: The Key to God's Relationship with Mankind.* Portland, Oregon: City Bible Publishing, c. 1983, revised 1997.

Craig, William Lane. "Why I Believe God Exists," In *Why I Am A Christian.* Edited by Norman L. Geisler, Paul K. Hoffman. Grand Rapids: Baker, 2006.

Culver, Robert Duncan. *Systematic Theology, Biblical and Historical.* Geanies House, Fearn, Ross-shire, England: Christian Focus Publications, 2005-06).

Damon, S. Foster. *William Blake: His Philosophy and Symbols.* Gloucester MA: Peter Smith, 1958.

Davies, Paul. *The Accidental Universe.* Cambridge: Cambridge University Press, 1982

———. *Superforce.* New York: Simon & Shuster, 1984.

———. "The Anthropic Principle," *Science Digest* 191 (October 1983): no. 10.

———. *The Cosmic Blueprint.* New York: Simon & Shuster, 1984.

Dawkins, Richard. *River Out of Eden: A Darwinian View of Life.* New York: Basic Books, 1996.

———. *The Blind Watchmaker; Why the Evidence of Evolution Reveals a Universe Without Design.* New York: Norton, 2006. Originally published 1986.

Day, Martin S. *History of English Literature 1660-1837.* New York: Doubleday, 1963.

Derrida, Jacques. "The Supplement of the Copula," in *Textual Strategies.* Edited by J. V. Harari. New York: Cornell University Press, 1979.

———. *Of Grammatology.* Baltimore: Johns Hopkins University, 1976. [*De la Grammatologie.* Paris: Minuit, 1974].

———. *Margins of Philosophy.* Translated by Alan Bass. University of Chicago Press, 1982.

Derrida, Jacques, and Maurizio Ferraris. *A Taste for the Secret.* Cambridge: Polity, 2001.

———. *Margins of Philosophy*, 22; cited in Gary Aylesworth, "Postmodernism," *Stanford Encyclopedia of Philosophy*, http://setis.library.usyd.edu.au/stanford/ entries/ Postmodernism), first published Fri. 30 Sep, 2005, p. 15.

Devitt, Michael. *Realism and Truth*. Second edition. Princeton University Press, 1997.

Duchamp. *Marcel Duchamp*. Edited by Anne D'Harnoncourt and Kynaston McShine Munich: Prestel / MoMA, 1989.

―――. *Marcel Duchamp; Work and Life*. Edited by Pontus Hulten. Cambridge, MA: MIT Press, 1993.

Dumbrell, W. J. *Covenant and Creation; A Theology of Old Testament Covenants*. Nashville: Nelson, 1984).

Dupré, Louis. *Passage to Modernity: An Essay in the Hermeneutic of Nature and Culture*. New Haven: Yale University, 1993.

Donne, The Laurel Poetry Series. New York, 1970.

Duncan, Carol. "Virility and Domination in Early 20th-Century Vanguard Painting." *Artforum* 12 (December 1973): 30-39.

Dunn, James D. G. *Christology in the Making: A New Testament Inquiry Into the Origins of the Doctrine of the Incarnation*. Grand Rapids: Eerdmans, second edition, 1996.

―――. *The Theology of Paul the Apostle*. Grand Rapids: Eerdmans, 1998.

Ehrstine, John W. *The Metaphysics of Byron*. The Hague: Mouton, 1976.

Eichrodt, W. *Theology of the Old Testament*. Westminster Press, 1967.

Ernst, Max. *The Hundred Headless Woman (La femme 100 têtes)*. Translated by Dorothea Tanning. Foreword André Breton. New York: Braziller, 1981.

―――. *Une Semaine de Bonté; A Surrealistic Novel in Collage*. New York: Dover, 1976.

Evangelical Dictionary of Biblical Theology. Edited by Walter A, Elwell. Grand Rapids: Baker, 1996.

Existentialism from Dostoevsky to Sartre. Edited by Walter Kaufmann. New York: Meridian Books, 1956.

Falckenberg, Richard. *History of Modern Philosophy From Nicolas of Cusa to the Present Time*. New York: Holt, 1997.

Ferber, Michael. *The Poetry of Shelley*. Harmondsworth and New York: Penguin, 1993.

Folger, Janet L. *The Criminalization of Christianity*. Sisters, Oregon: Multinomah, 2005.

Foucault, Michel. *Archaeology of Knowledge* [translation of *L'Archaeologie du savoir*, 1971], Vintage, 1972, 47.

―――. *The Order of Things; An Archaeology of the Human Sciences* [French: *Les Mots et les choses*, 1966]. 1970, XXII.

―――. In *Language, Counter-Memory, Practice: Selected Essays and Interviews*, ed. Donald E. Bouchard. Ithaca, N.Y.: Cornell University Press, 1977.

Frame, John M. *Apologetics to the Glory of God, An Introduction*. Phillipsburg, New Jersey, P&R Publishing, 1994.

―――. *The Doctrine of God*. Phillipsburg, New Jersey: P&R Publishing, 2002.

―――. *No Other God; A Response to Open Theism*. Phillipsburg, N.J., P & R Publishing, 2001.

Freedberg, S. J. *Painting of the High Renaissance in Rome and Florence*. Two volumes. Cambridge, Massachusetts: Harvard University Press, 1961.

Frye, Northrop. *A Study of English Romanticism*. New York: Random House, 1968.

―――. *Romanticism Reconsidered*. New York: Columbia University Press, 1963.

Gabriel, Brigitte. *Because They Hate.* New York: St. Marten's Press, 2006.

———. *They Must Be Stopped.* New York: St. Martin's Press, 2008

Gabriel, Mark A. *Islam and the Jews: The Unfinished Battle.* Charisma House, 2003.

———. *Jesus and Muhammad: Profound Differences and Surprising Similarities.* Charisma House, 2004.

———. *Islam and Terrorism: What the Quran Really Teaches About Christianity; Violence and the Goals of the Islamic Jihad.* Charisma House. 2002.

Gairdner, William D. *The Book of Absolutes; A Critique of Relativism and a Defense of Universals.* Montreal: McGill-Queen's University Press, 2008.

Gardeil, H. A. *Introduction to the Philosophy of St. Thomas Aquinas: IV, Metaphysics.* Translated by John A. Otto. London & St. Louis: Herder, 1967.

Garlick, Mark A. *The Illustrated Atlas of the Universe.* Fog City Press, 2007.

Gaskin, J. C. A. "Hume on Religion." *The Cambridge Companion to Hume*, ed. Norton Cambridge University Press, 1993

Gay, Peter. *The Enlightenment; An Interpretation* Two volumes. New York: Knopf, 1966, 1969.

Geisler, Norman L. *The Baker Encyclopedia of Christian Apologetics.* Grand Rapids: Baker, 1999.

———. *A Popular Survey of the Old Testament.* Peabody, MA: Prince Press, 2003.

———. *Systematic Theology.* Four volumes. Minneapolis, MN: Bethany House, 2002-2005.

Norman L. Geisler and Abdul Saleeb, *Answering Islam; The Crescent in the Light of the Cross.* Grand Rapids: Baker. 2000.

Geisler, Norman L. and Thomas Howe. *When Critics Ask: A Popular Handbook on Bible Difficulties.* Grand Rapids: Baker, 1992.

Geisler, Norman L., and Frank Turek. *I Don't Have Enough Faith to Be an Atheist* Crossway Books, 2004.

Gilkey, Langdon. "God, Idea of, Since 1800." *Dictionary of the History of Ideas*, Philip P. Wiener, ed. New York: Scribner, 1973-74.

Gilson, Étienne. *The Christian Philosophy of Saint Augustine.* New York: Random House, 1960.

———. *Elements of Christian Philosophy.* New York: Doubleday, 1960.

———. *God and Philosophy.* Yale University Press, second edition, 2002.

Gilson, Étienne, and Thomas Langan, *A History of Modern Philosophy, Descartes to Kant.* New York: Random House, 1963.

Gitt, Werner. *In the Beginning Was Information.* Green Forest, AZ: Master Books, 2006.

Grudem, Wayne. *Systematic Theology.* Grand Rapids: Zondervan, 2000.

Gonzales, Guillermo, and Jay W. Richards. *The Privileged Planet; How Our Place in the Cosmos is Designed for Discovery.* Washington, DC: Regnery, 2004.

Gordon, Lyndall. *T. S. Eliot; An Imperfect Life.* New York: Norton, 1998.

Green, Michael. *I Believe in Satan's Downfall.* Grand Rapids: Eerdmans, 1981.

Greenhalgh, Michael. *The Classical Tradition in Art.* New York: Harper and Row, 1978.

Greenstein, George. *The Symbiotic Universe.* New York: William Morrow, 1988.

Gribbin, John. *Companion to the Cosmos.* New York: Little, Brown, 1996.

Guarino, Thomas. "Postmodernity and Five Fundamental Theological Issues." In *Theological Studies* 57 (1996).

Haar, Michel. *Nietzsche and Metaphysics.* Translated by Michael Gendre. Albany: State University of New York Press, 1996.

Hagee, John. *Jerusalem Countdown; A Warning to the World.* Lake Maryland, Florida, 2006.

Haley, John W. *Alleged Discrepancies of the Bible.* New Kensington, PA: Whitaker House, 1992.

Hawking, Steven. [1] *The Illustrated A Brief History of Time;* [2] *The Universe in a Nutshell.* New York: Bantam Dell, 2007.

Hawking, Steven, and Roger Penrose. *The Nature of Space and Time,* The Isaac Newton Institute Series of Lectures. Princeton University Press, 1996.

Hegel, G. W. F. "The Positivity of Christianity," (1795-96) and "The Spirit of Christianity and its Fate," (1799-1800). In *Phenomenology of Spirit,* § 527-528.

Heidegger, Martin. *Being and Time.* Translated by John Macquarrie and Edward Robinson. San Francisco: Harper, 2008.

———. *Kant and the Problem of Metaphysics.* Translated by James Churchill. Bloomington: Indiana University Press, 1956.

———. "What is Metaphysics," *Existence and Being,* Translated by R. F. C. Hull and Alan Crick. Chicago: Regnery, 1967.

Helm, Paul. *The Providence of God,* Downers Grove, IL: Intervarsity Press, 1994.

Henry, Carl F. H. *God, Revelation and* Authority. Six volumes. Waco: Word Books, 1976-1983.

Hitchcock, Mark. *The Late, Great, United States; What Bible Prophecy Reveals About America's Last Days.* Colorado Springs: Multnomah Books, 2009.

Hitchens, Christopher. *god is Not Great; How Religion Poisons Everything.* New York: 12/ Hachette Book Group, 2007.

Hoitenga, Dewey I. *Faith and Reason from Plato to Plantinga; An Introduction to Reformed Epistemology.* Albany: SUNY, 1991).

Höffding, Harald. *A History of Modern Philosophy.* New York: Dover, 1958.

Holmes, Arthur F. *All Truth is God's Truth.* Grand Rapids: Eerdmans, 1977).

Honour, Hugh. *Romanticism.* New York: Harper and Row Icon, 1979.

Hooker. Richard. *The Works of that Learned and Judicious Divine, Mr. Richard Hooker.* Edited by John Keble, Rev. R. W. Church and F. Paget. New York: Burt Franklin, 1970.

Intelligent Design 101; Leading Experts Explain the Key Issues. House, H. Wayne, ed. Grand Rapids: Kregel, 2008.

Huffington, Arianna Stassinopoulos. *Picasso: Creator and Destroyer.* New York: Simon and Schuster, 1988.

Hughes, Robert. *The Shock of the New.* New York: Knopf, 1981.

Hume, David. *The Cambridge Companion to Hume.* Edited by David Fate Norton and Jacqueline Taylor. Cambridge University Press, second edition, 2008.

Hutchison, Jane Campbell. *Albrecht Dürer; A Biography.* Princeton University Press, 1990.

Jarry, Alfred. *The Ubu Plays by Alfred Jarry.* Edited by Simon Watson Taylor. New York: Grove Press, 1969.

Jaspers, Karl. *Nietzsche.* Translated by Charles Wallraff and Frederick Schmitz. Chicago: Regnery, 1966.

Jastrow, Robert. *God and the Astronomers.* New York: Norton, second edition, 2000.

Jeffrey, Grant R. *Creation: Remarkable Evidence of God's Design.* Toronto, Canada: Colorado Springs, CO: WaterBrook Press, 2003.

―――. *The Next World War: What Prophecy Reveals About Extreme Islam and the West.* Colorado Springs, CO: WaterBrook Press, 2006.

―――. *Triumphant Return: The Coming Kingdom of God.* Colorado Springs, CO: WaterBrook Press, 2001.

Jenkins, Philip. *God's Continent: Christianity, Islam, and Europe's Religious Crisis.* Oxford University Press, 2007.

Jewett, Paul K. *God, Creation, and Revelation; A Neo-Evangelical Theology.* Grand Rapids: Eerdmans, 1991.

Joost-Gaugier, Christiane L. *Raphael's Stanza della Segnatura; Meaning and Invention* Cambridge University Press, 2002.

Judovitz, Dalia. *Subjectivity and Representation in Descartes; the Origins of Modernity.* Cambridge University Press, 1988.

Kant, Immanuel. *Critique of Pure Reason.* Cambridge Edition. Edited by Paul Guyer And Allen W. Wood. Cambridge University Press, 1999.

―――. *Critique of Pure Reason.* Translated by F. Max Müller New York: Doubleday Anchor, 1966)

―――. *Practical Philosophy.* [contains the Critique of Practical Reason]. Cambridge Edition. Edited by Mary J. Gregor and Allen W. Wood. Cambridge University Press, 1999.

―――. *Critique of Judgment.* Translated by J. H. Bernard. New York: Hafner, 1972.

―――. *Critique of Judgment.* Oxford World Classics. Edited by Nicholas Walker and translated by James Creed Meredith. Oxford University press USA, 1999.

―――. *Religion within the Limits of Reason Alone.* Translated by Theodore M. Greene and Hoyt H. Hudson. New York: Harper & Row, 1960.

Karl, Frederick R. *Modern and Modernism; The Sovereignty of the Artist, 1885-1925.* NewYork: Atheneum, 1985, 84, 81, 119.

Kasper, Walter. *The God of Jesus Christ.* Crossroad Publishing Company, 1986.

Kellner, Douglas. "Jean Baudrillard." In the Stanford Encyclopedia of Philosophy (http://setis.library.usyd.edu.au/stanford/ entries/baudrillard), first published Apr. 22, 2005; revised Mar 7, 2007.

―――. *Jean Baudrillard; From Marxism to Postmodernism and Beyond.* Stanford University Press, 1989.

Kenny, Anthony. *The God of the Philosophers.* Oxford, 1979.

Kaufmann, Walter. *Goethe, Kant, and Hegel: Discovering the Mind.* Vol. I. New Brunswick: Transaction Publishers, 1995.

Krüger, Gerhard, "Die Herkunft des philosophischen Selbstwusstseins," *Logo* 22 (1933).

Larson, E. J., and L. Witham. "Scientists are still keeping the faith," *Nature* 386 (April 3, 1997.

Leighten, Patricia. *Re-Ordering the Universe; Picasso and Anarchism, 1897-1914*. Princeton, New Jersey: Princeton University Press, 1989.

Levin, Mark R. Men in Black; How the Supremee Court is Destroying America. Washington, D. C.: Regnery, 2005.

Limbaugh, David. *Persecution: How Liberals Are Waging War Against Christianity*. Harper Collins, 2004.

Lindsay, Jack. *William Blake; His Life and Work*. New York: Braziller, 1979.

Linn, Ray. *A Teacher's Introduction to Postmodernism*. Urbana, IL: National Council of Teachers of English, 1996.

Lippard, Lucy R. Editor. *Dadas on Art*. Englewood Cliffs, NJ: Prentice-Hall, 1971.

———. Editor. *Surrealists On Art*. Englewood Cliffs: Prentice Hall, 1970.

Love, Nancy S. *Marx, Nietzsche, and Modernity*. New York: Columbia University Press, 1986.

James F. Luhr, ed. *Earth* (Smithsonian Institution). New York: DK Publishing, 2003.

Malraux, Andre. *Picasso's Mask*. New York: Holt, Rinehart, & Winston, 1976.

Margenau, Henry. "Why I Am A Christian." Letter to Leadership University, www. Leaderu. com/truth/1truth16.html, p. 6.

Margenau, Henry, and Roy Abraham Varghese, eds. *Cosmos, Bios, and Theos*. La Salle, IL: Open Court, 1992.

Maritain, Jacques. *The Dream of Descartes*. Translated by Mabelle L. Andison. Port Washington: Kennikat Press, 1969.

The MacArthur Study Bible. Nashville: Nelson, Word Publishing.

McCall, Robert E. *The Reality of Substance*. Washington, D. C.: Catholic University of America Press, 1956.

McClain, Alva J. *The Greatness of the Kingdom*. Winona Lake, Ind.: BHM, 1974.

McGann, Jerome. *Fiery Dust*. University of Chicago Press, 1968.

McKinney, Richard W. A., ed. *Creation, Christ, and Culture*. Edinburgh: T & T Clark, 1976.

Megill, Allan. *Prophets of Extremity: Nietzsche, Heidegger, Foucault, Derrida*. Los Angeles: University of California Press, 1987.

Merquior. *Foucault*. University of California Press, 1985.

Meyer, Stephen C. "DNA and the Origin of Life: Information, Specification, and Explanation," in *Darwinism, Design, and Public Education* (Michigan State University Press, 2004); also available at www.discovery.org/a/2184.

Milton, John.*The Complete Poetry of John Milton*. Edited by John T. Shawcross. New York: Doubleday Anchor, 1971, revised edition.

Mondin, Battista. *St. Thomas Aquinas' Philosophy*. The Hague: Nijhoff, 1975.

———. *St. Thomas Aquinas' Philosophy in the Commentary to the Sentences*. The Hague: Martinus Nijhoff, 1975.

Morris, Leon. *The Gospel According to John, The New International Commentary on the New Testament*. Grand Rapids: Eerdmans, 1979.

Murphy, William B., Thomas C. Donlan, John S. Reidy, Francis L. B. Cunningham. *God and His Creation.* Dubuque, Iowa: Priory Press, 1958.

Nash, Ronald H., *The Light of the Mind: St. Augustine's Theory of Knowledge.* Lexington: University of Kentucky Press, 1969.

Nietzsche, Friedrich. *Beyond Good and Evil.* Translated by Walter Kaufmann. New York: Random House, Vintage, 1966.

———. *The Birth of Tragedy and The Case of Wagner.* Translated by Walter Kaufmann. New York: Random House, Vintage, 1967.

———. *The Gay Science.* Translated by Walter Kaufmann. New York: Random House, Vintage, 1974.

———. *Joyful Wisdom.* Translated by Thomas Common. New York: Ungar, 1973.

———. *Twilight of the Idols and The Anti-Christ.* Translated by R. J. Hollingdale. Harmondsworth: Penguin, 1968),

———. *The Will to Power.* Translated by Walter Kaufmann and R. J. Hollingdale. New York: Random House, Vintage, 1968.

NIV Study Bible. Edited by Kenneth Barker, Grand Rapids: Zondervan, 1985.

New Bible Dictionary. Edited by I. Howard Marshall, A. R. Millard, J. I. Packer, D. J. Wiseman. Downers Grove, IL: Intervarsity Press, Third edition. 1996.

Oden, Thomas C. *The Living God; Systematic Theology.* Vol. 1 of 3 vols. New York: Harper-Collins, 1992.

———. *The Word of Life; Systematic Theology* Vol. 2. San Francisco: HarperCollins, 1994.

Olafson, Frederick A. "Sartre, Jean-Paul." *The Encyclopedia of Philosophy,* Edited by Paul Edwards. New York: Macmillan, 1967.

Owens, Joseph. *A History of Ancient Western Philosophy.* Englewood Cliffs: Prentice-Hall, 1959.

———. *Cognition.* Houston: Center for Thomistic Studies, 1992.

Palmer, F. H. "Truth," *The New Bible Dictionary* Grand Rapids: Eerdman's, 1977.

Parker, Francis H. *The Story of Western Philosophy.* Bloomington: Indiana University Press, 1967.

———, "Traditional Reason and Modern Reason." In *Faith and Philosophy.* Edited by Alvin Plantinga. Grand Rapids: Eerdmans, 1964.

Pascal, Blaise. *Pensées.* Edited by H. S. Thayer. New York, 1965.

Pasnau, Robert and Christopher Shields. *The Philosophy of Aquinas.* Boulder, Colorado: Westview Press, 2004.

Pawlowski, Gaston de. *Voyage au pays de la quatrième dimension* [*Voyage to the Land of Fourth Dimension*]. Paris, 1912.

Pelikan, Jaroslav. *Christianity and Classical Culture.* New Haven: Yale University Press, 1993.

Pentecost, J. Dwight. *Things to Come; A Study in Biblical Eschatology.* Grand Rapids: Zondervan, 1964.

———. *Thy Kingdom Come.* Grand Rapids: Kregel, 1995.

Perotti, James L. *Heidegger on the Divine; The Thinker, The Poet and God.* Ohio University Press, 1974.

Peters, F. E. *Greek Philosophical Terms*. New York: New York University Press, 1967.

Peters, George. *The Theocratic Kingdom*, 3 vols. Grand Rapids: Kregel, 1972.

Phillips, Melanie *Londonistan*. New York: Encounter Books, 2006.

Pippin, Robert B. *Modernism as a Philosophical Problem: On the Dissatisfactions of European High Culture*. Cambridge, Mass.: Blackwell, 1991.

———. *Idealism as Modernism; Hegelian Variations*. Cambridge University Press, 1997.

Pollard, Arthur. *Richard Hooker*. London: Longmans, Green, 1966.

Postmodern Arts. Edited by Nigel Wheale. London: Routledge, 1995.

Price, David Hotchkiss. *Albrecht Dürer's Renaissance; Humanism, Reformation, and the Art of Faith*. Ann Arbor: University of Michigan Press, 2003.

Price, John. *The End of America*. Indianapolis: Christian House: 2009.

Price, Randall. *The Coming Last Days Temple*. Eugene OR: Harvest House: 1999.

Raine, Kathleen. *William Blake*. New York: Praeger, 1971.

Redner, Harry. *The Ends of Philosophy*. Totowa, New Jersey: Rowman and Allanheld. 1986).

Rees, Martin. *Universe*.(New York: DK Publishing, 2005.

Reff, Theodore. *Harlequins, Saltimbanques, Clowns, and Fools. Artforum* 10 (Oct. 1971): 30-53.

Richardson, Joel. *Antichrist; Islam's Awaited Messiah* (Enumclaw, WA: Pleasant Word/ WinePress, 2006.

Richardson, John. *A Life of Picasso*. Volume I, 1881-1906. New York: Random House, 1991.

Richardson, John. *Nietzsche's System*. New York: Oxford University Press. 1996.

Richter, Hans. *Dada Art and Anti-Art*. London: Thames and Hudson, 1965, c. 1964.

Robertson, Pat. *Courting Disaster; How the Supreme Court is Usurping the Power of Congress and the People*. Nashville: Integrity, 2004.

Rorty, Richard. *Consequences of Pragmatism: Essays, 1972-1980*. Minneapolis: University of Minnesota Press, 1982.

———. *Contingency, Irony, and Solidarity*. Cambridge University Press, 1989.

———. *Philosophy and the Mirror of Nature*. Princeton University Press, 1980.

———. *"Universality and Truth,"* in Robert B. Brandom, ed., *Rorty and his Critics* Oxford: Blackwell, 2000.

Ross, Hugh. *Creation As Science*. Colorado Springs, CO: NavPress, 2006.

———. *The Creator and the Cosmos*. Colorado Springs CO: NavPress, 2001).

———. *Why the Universe is the Way It Is*. Grand Rapids: Baker, 2008.

———. "Why I Believe in the Miracle of Divine Creation," in *Why I Am A Christian*. Edited by Norman L. Geisler and Paul K. Hoffman. Grand Rapids: Baker, 2006.

Royle, Nicholas. *Jacques Derrida*. Routledge, 2003.

Rhee, J. "Nearby Star is a Galactic Fossil", *Science Daily* (2007-05-11).

Rosenblum, Robert. *Modern Painting and the Northern Romantic Tradition; Friedrich to Rothko*. Thames & Hudson, 1978.

Rosenblum, Robert and H. W. Janson, *19th-Century Art* (New York: Abrams, 1984).

Rothman, Tony, "A 'What You See is What You Beget' Theory." Discover (May 1987).

Rubin, William. Editor. *Pablo Picasso; A Retrospective*. New York: The Museum of Modern Art, 1980.

Russell, John. *Max Ernst; Life and Work*. New York: Abrams, 1967.

Ryrie, Charles C. *What You Should Know About the Rapture*. Chicago: Moody Bible Institute, 1981.

Salter, William M. *Nietzsche the Thinker*. New York: Ungar, 1968.

Sandler, Irving. *The New York School: The Painters and Sculptors of the Fifties*. New York: Harper Icon, 1979.

Sanford, J. C. *Genetic Entropy and the Mystery of the Genome*. Lima, New York: Elim Publishing, 2005.

Scott, Nathan A. *Mirrors of Man in Existentialism*. New York: Collins, 1978.

Schacht, Richard L. "Hegel on Freedom." In *Hegel*. Edited by Alasdair MacIntyre New York: Doubleday Anchor, 1972.

Schmidt, Avin J. *The Menace of Multiculturalism; Trojan Horse in America*. Westport, Connecticut: Praeger, 1997.

Schouls, Peter A. *Descartes and the Enlightenment*, McGill-Queens Univ. Press, 1989.

———. "Descartes As Revolutionary," *Philosophia Reformata* 52 (1987).

———. *The Imposition of Method, A Study of Descartes and Locke*. Oxford, 1980.

Schroeder, Gerald L. *The Hidden Face of God*. New York: Touchstone, 2002.

Schulz, Walter. *Der Gott der Neuzeitlichen Metaphysik*. Pfullingen: Neske, 1982.

Shedd, W. G. T. *Dogmatic Theology I*. New York: Scribners, 1888 Zondervan reprint, 1969.

Sheen, Fulton J. *Philosophy of Religion; the Impact of Modern Knowledge on Religion*. New York: Appleton-Century-Crofts, 1948.

Shelley. "Preface to *Prometheus Unbound*." In *Shelley's Critical Prose*. Edited by Bruce R. McElderry, Jr. Lincoln: University of Nebraska Press, 1967.

Shoebat, Walid. *Why We Want to Kill You*. Walid@shoebat.com; Top Executive Media, 2007.

Shorrosh, Anis. *Islam Revealed: A Christian Arab's View Of Islam*. Nelson, 2001.

Showers, Renald. *Maranatha: Our Lord Come; A Definitive Study of the Rapture of the Church*. Bellmawr, NJ: Friends of Israel Gospel Ministry, 1995.

Singh, Simon. *Big Bang*. New York: Harper Collins, 2004.

Smith, Gregory Bruce. *Nietzsche, Heidegger, and the Transition to Postmodernism*. Chicago: University Press, 1996.

Smith, Ralph A. *Trinity and Reality*. Moscow, Idaho: Canon Press, 2004.

Snyder, James. *Medieval Art: Painting, Sculpture, Architecture, 4th-14th Century*. Englewood Cliffs: Prentice-Hall, 1989.

Solomon Robert C. *From Rationalism to Existentialism*. New York: Harper and Row, 1972.

Sorokin, Pitirim A. *The Crisis of Our Age*. New York: Dutton, c. 1941.

Sparrow, Giles. *Cosmos; A Field Guide*. London: Quercus, 2006.

Spencer, Robert. *Religion of Peace?: Why Christianity Is and Islam Isn't*. Washington, D. C.: Regnery, 2007.

———. *The Truth About Muhammad: Founder of the World's Most Intolerant Religion*. Regnery, 2007.

————. *The Politically Incorrect Guide to Islam (and the Crusades)*. Regnery, 2007.

Spier, J. M. *Christianity and Existentialism*. Philadelphia: Presbyterian and Reformed Publishing Co., 1961.

Edmund Spenser's Poetry. Edited by Hugh Maclean. New York: Norton, 1968.

Sproul, R. C. *Chosen by God*. Wheaton, IL: Tyndale House, 1986.

Stählin, Leonhard. *Kant, Lotze, and Ritschl: A Critical Examination*. Edinburgh: T & T Clark, 1889.

Steefel, Lawrence D. *The Position of Duchamp's Glass in the Development of His Art*. New York: Garland, 1977.

Stokes, Charlotte. "From the Edges of Floating Worlds: Meaning in Ernst's Collages." *Arts Magazine* 61 (April 1987).

Stone, Perry. *Nightmare Along Pennsylvania Avenue: Prophetic Insight into America's Role in the Coming End Times*. Lake Mary, FL: Front Line, 2010.

Strong Augustus H. *Systematic Theology*. Valley Forge: Judson Press, 1985, c. 1907.

Swinburne, Richard. *The Existence of God*. Oxford: Clarendon Press, 2004.

Tannenbaum, Leslie. *Biblical Tradition in Blake's Early Prophecies: The Great Code of Art* Princeton University Press, 1982.

Taylor, Charles. *Hegel*. Cambridge: Cambridge University Press, 1975.

Thielicke, Helmut. *The Evangelical Faith; Volume I, Prolegomena: The Relation of Theology to Modern Thought-Forms*. Grand Rapids: Eerdmans, 1974.

Thilly, Frank. *A History of Philosophy*. Third edition, revised, Ledger Wood. New York: Holt, Rinehart and Winston, 1957.

Thornton, Bruce. *Decline and Fall; Europe's Slow motion Suicide*. New York: Encounter, 2007.

Tipler, F. J. *The Physics of Immortality*. New York: Doubleday, 1994.

Tomkins, Calvin. *Duchamp, A Biography*. New York: Holt, 1996.

Unger, Merrill F. "Satan," *Evangelical Dictionary of Biblical Theology*, 973.

Van Til, Cornelius. *Christianity and Barthianism*. Nutley, New Jersey: Presbyterian and Reformed Publishing Co., 1977.

Vaughan, William. *Romantic Art*. New York: Oxford University Press, 1978.

Veatch, Henry B. *Aristotle; A Contemporary Appreciation*. Bloomington: Indiana University Press, 1974.

Vycinas, Vincent. *Earth and Gods*. The Hague: Martinus Nijhoff, 1969.

Waldman, Diane. *Roy Lichtenstein*. New York: Guggenheim Museum, 1993.

Walls, Jerry L. and Joseph R. Dongell, *Why I am not a Calvinist*. Downers Grove, IL: Intervarsity Press, 2004)

Walvoord, John F. *Major Bible Prophecies*. Grand Rapids: Zondervan, 1991.

————. *Major Bible Themes*. Grand Rapids: Zondervan, 1974.

————. *The Millennial Kingdom*. Grand Rapids: Zondervan, 1959.

————. *The Rapture Question*, Grand Rapids: Zondervan, 1979.

————. *The Revelation of Jesus Christ*. Chicago: Moody, 1989, c. 1966.

Walvoord, John F. with Mark Hitchcock, *Armageddon, Oil, and Terror* (Carol Stream, IL: Tyndal House, 2007.

Walvoord, John F. and Roy B. Zuck, eds. *The Bible Knowledge Commentary, Old Testament*. Wheaton, IL: Victor Books, 1988.

Warfield, B. B. *Studies in Tertullian and Augustine*. Westport, CT: Greenwood Press, 1970.

———. *Calvin and Augustine*. Philadelphia: Presbyterian and Reformed Pub. Co., 1956.

Ward, Peter D., and Donald Brownlee. *Rare Earth; Why Complex Life is Uncommon in the Universe*. New York: Copernicus Books, 2004.

Warlick, M. E. "Max Ernst's Alchemical Novel: 'Une Semaine de bonté'," *Art Journal* 46 (Spring 1987).

Warraq, Ibn. *What the Koran Really Says: Language, Text, and Commentary*. Prometheus Books; 2003.

———. *Why I Am Not a Muslim*. Prometheus Books; 2003. Wartenburg, Thomas E. "Hegel's Idealism: The Logic of Conceptuality." In *The Cambridge Companion to Hegel*. Edited by Frederick C. Beiser. Cambridge: University Press, 1993.

Weber, Alfred. *History of Philosophy*. Translated by Frank Thilly. New York: Scribner's, 1906, c. 1896.

Wells, Jonathan. *The Politically Incorrect Guide to Darwinism and Intelligent Design*. Washington, DC: Regnery, 2006.

Wheeler, Daniel. *Art Since Mid-Century; 1945 to the Present*. Englewood Cliffs: Prentice-Hall, 1991.

White, James R. *The Potter's Freedom*. Amityville, NY: Calvary Press, 2000.

Wiker, Benjamin and Jonathan Witt, *A Meaningful World; How the Arts and Sciences Reveal the Genius of Nature*. Downers Grove: Intervarsity Press, 2006.

Wilburn, Ralph G. *The Historical Shape of Faith*. Philadelphia: Westminster, 1966.

Wilhelmsen, Frederick D. *Man's Knowledge of Reality; An Introduction to Thomistic Epistemology*. Englewood Cliffs: Prentice-Hall, 1956.

Wittgenstein, Ludwig. *Culture and Value*. Oxford: Blackwell, 1980.

———. *Philosophical Investigations*. Translated by G. E. M. Anscombe. New York: Macmillan, 1958.

———. *Tractatus Logico-Philosophicus*. Translated by D. F. Pears and B. F. McGuinniss. New Jersey: Humanities Press, 1961.

Wolfson, Harry A. *The Philosophy of the Church Fathers: Volume I, Faith, Trinity, Incarnation*. Cambridge, MA: Harvard University Press, 1964, second edition.

Wood, Allen W. "Rational theology, moral faith, and religion." In The Cambridge Companion to Kant. Edited by Paul Guyer. Cambridge University Press, 1993.

Ye'or, Bat. *Eurabia; the Euro-Arab Axis*. Fairleigh Dickinson University Press, 2007; Young, Julian. *Nietzsche's Philosophy of Art*. Cambridge: Cambridge University Press, 1993.

Zagzebski, Linda. "Individual Essence and the Creation." *Divine and Human Action; Essays in the Metaphysics of Theism*. Edited by Thomas V. Morris. Ithaca: Cornell University Press, 1988.

Zeitlin, Irving M. *Nietzsche; A Re-examination*. Cambridge, Eng. and MA: Polity Press/Blackwell, 1994).

Glossary

A

Abraham, Abram, Abrahamic Covenant, Abraham was the first father of the Hebrew people, leaving his pagan birthplace in obedience to God. God made the first covenent with Abraham that was to continue throughout history and into the Millennium and the final Kingdom of God.

Abstract Expressionism, the first American modern art movement, during the 1940s and 50s, also international in scope. There are some similarities to Existentialism in the sense of an absence of God or any transcendent source of being, reason, or purpose, resulting in an aura of emptiness, a void, or the harsh and ugly. (Pollock, DeKooning, Still, Rothko, Motherwell, Kline).

Augustine of Hippo (354-430), a Church Father and Bishop of Hippo Regius (present-day Annaba in Algeria), a Latin-speaking philosopher and theologian, whose many writings were important and influential in subsequent Christian history. Key ideas:

rationem, rationes, "reasons," stands for the Greek term *logoi*. It emphasizes that creation is the work of divine reason and intelligence. The ideas as "certain principal forms or certain fixed and immutable reasons of things, have not been formed and hence are eternal and always in the same state of existence, and are contained in the divine intelligence." For Augustine the created universe is organized entirely on the model of the divine ideas. Its entire order, form, and productivity come from them, so that the fundamental tie linking the world to God is a relationship of similarity. Without this relationship "the universe would immediately cease to be intelligible and even to exist."

rationes aeternae, eternal reasons or ideas that serve as the principal forms or stable and unchangeable essences of things; the exemplary cause of every thing that exists, they are *the basic foundation of all created reality.*

rationes seminales, certain ideas, reasons, or forms created in nature as the "seed-like principles that exist in the nature of the world's elements. When God created the world, He embedded in creation principles that guide its development.

Aquinas, Thomas, an Italian Dominican priest, theologian, and philosopher in the tradition of scholasticism. Key ideas:

being (esse), in Aquinas' metaphysical terms, being is the reality of God—of God the Supreme Being, and the contingent reality of all beings created by God. His theory of knowledge is secondary to belief in Being and beings, act and potency, form and matter. Because God is ultimate reality and truth, all created beings are real, have real existence, and can be apprehended in knowledge. Aquinas "set being at the very core of his metaphysical system."

idea, forma (form), the Greek word *Idea* is in Latin *Forma*; "ideas" refers to the *forms* of things, existing apart from the things themselves; the world was not made by chance, but by God acting by His intellect; there must exist in the divine mind a form to the likeness of which the world was made. Since God's Ideas are eternal, so are the forms of the world He has created. An idea in God is not only "identical with His essence, but "is the principle of knowing and operating."

exemplars, God's Archetypal Ideas present in things. These Divine Archetypal Ideas reflected in things, as well as the very rational plan of their being, are called forms, as in the mind they are called ideas (and sometimes forms). Everything in the world has its form, which is the reason for its intelligibility, and makes it what it is.

B

Barthes, Roland, (1915-1980), French Structuralist and literary critic.

Baudrillard, Jean (1929-2007), French postmodern social theorist and cultural critic. See "hyperreality," "implosion," and "simulacra."

becoming, existence as flux, change; everything changes. Groundless change is all there is; the believed absence of God/Being. Nothing is universal, eternal, or everlasting.

C

Cage, John (1912-1992), American music theorist, composer, philosopher, and poet, influenced by Duchamp and Zen Buddhism. Cage thought of music as a "purposeless play" meant to "affirm life" as it is. It was not meant to find order in the chaos of life, but just to help people become more aware of the kind of life we are living (meaningless, chaotic).

Camus, Albert (1913-1960), French author, journalist, philosopher. Usually classified as an existentialist, he also has associations with absurdism (which is an aspect of Existentialism). He opposed marriage, calling it unnatural, although he married twice. Camus saw the absurd resulting from human desire for meaning in a world that could yield none (also a part of existentialism). While Camus highly valued life, he saw death as an ending putting the final stamp on meaninglessness. These views were expressed in his books, *The Myth of Sisyphus, The Stranger,* and *The Plague.*

categories, the fundamental and indivisible concepts of classic philosophical thought; they are at the same time basic features of the real. "Aristotle's ten categories are essential to natural things and to human knowledge: *substance, quality, quantity, relation, place (space), time, position, state (mode of being), activity, and passivity.*" "Together, these categories determine the concrete nature, structure, relationship, and motion of things in space and time. They assure us that "the objects of our experience exist in time and place, can be measured and counted, are related to other things, act and are acted on, have essential and accidental qualities." Aquinas' categories, are the essential divisions or highest genera of being. *Substance* is the most important of these, signifying the subject as to its essence. Substance is the subject of the accidents, the remaining nine predicaments. These understandings of being, with its transcendentals and categories, are core aspects of the realism of Thomistic metaphysics. They express his most fundamental understandings of reality.

Kant's twelve *categories* of the understanding are: quantity—*unity, plurality, totality*; quality—*reality, negation, limitation*; relation—*substance, causation, reciprocity*; modality—*possibility and impossibility, existence and non-existence, necessity and contingency*; the three *transcendental ideas* of pure reason are *self, world,* and *God*. Outside of sense experience, none of these have any guaranteed objective reality. Hegel radicalizes the subjectivity of the categories, and embeds them in dialectically developing history.

constructivism, a philosophical position that claims we should assume anything real only if we can define it in terms we already accept. Constructive reason stands in contrast to rational intuition. It is "making worlds" by the imposition of human concepts.

contingent, dependent on something or someone else for it's being, existence, form, or knowledge.

D

Dada art (c. 1912-1922), the most extreme movement in twentieth-century art, expressing great skepticism about meaning, reason, logic, rationality, and purpose in life, and reacting to this situation with absurdity, irony, and wry humor. Much of this is taken up again in broader ways by postmodern thought and art.

Darwin, Charles (1809-1882), English naturalist, evolutionist. His *On the Origin of Species* was published in 1859.

Dasein, Heidegger's term for the "essential" existence of man as "being-there"—in fundamental ways, the *opposite* of Christian theology and traditional metaphysics.

David, King (c. 1040-970 BC), the second king of Israel and an ancestor of Jesus Christ. David brought the Ark of the Covenant to Jerusalem. But the prophet Nathan told David that God would not allow him to build the temple for it. God continued the covenant line with David, promising him: "Your throne shall be established forever." That throne would culminate with Jesus Christ in the Millennium.

Dawkins, Richard (b. 1941), evolutionary biologist and atheist.

Derrida, Jacques (1930-2004), French poststructuralist and postmodern philosopher.

Descartes, René (1596-1650), French philosopher; the father of modern philosophy and the beginnings of modern subjectivism.

Devitt, Michael, (b. 1938), Australian philosopher.

difference, the skeptical postmodern theory that there are no existing formal structures in the world. There is no identity and unity, only primal *difference* (Nietzsche). "*Différance,*" *difference* and *différance* (Derrida)— different things in different forms are pervasive, with no transcendent dimension; the notion is meant to undermine traditional metaphysical concepts of being, certainty, and secure meaning. No universals or unity exist; meaning is continuously changing and "undecidable."

disjunction, in art, lack of interrelatedness; lack of correspondence or harmony.

displacement in art, removing things or images from their usual place, function, and meaning.

Donne, John (1572-1631), English poet, lawyer, and priest.

Duchamp, Marcel (1887-1968), French Dada artist.

Dürer, Albrecht (1471-1528), German Renaissance artist.

E

Elijah (9th cen. BC), biblical prophet, at the time of King Ahab and Jezebel.

Eliot, T. S. (1888-1965), American-English poet, playwright, literary critic.

epistemes (Foucault), the underlying conceptual framework that serves as the basis for the various fields of knowledge of an epoch.

Existentialism, a philosophical and arts movement during the 1930s, 40s, and 50s. The radical side rejected the reality of God's Being (Heidegger, Sartre, and Camus), instead emphasizing human existence and change (becoming). More generally in Existentialism, the universe is not divinely created with essence, reason, and purpose, and does not correspond to any rational order and plan; it is not in itself intelligible. There is no given plan or purpose. Human beings come out of nothingness, devoid of any given essence, reason, and purpose. Man is "thrown" into the world (Heidegger). We have complete freedom of will because there are no given moral laws; each person must constitute them by choices made. The absence of divine creation means that no divine Ideas determine a person's essence. One must establish his or her "essence" by choices made in life, which tragically ends in death. Thus, much emphasis was on the absurd, anxiety, and alienation. There are some similarities between these views and those of Postmodernism. Two main differences are that Postmodernism focuses centrally on language, and rejects the humanistic side of Existentialism.

Expressionism, art and literature movements, with early signs in van Gogh's paintings in the 1880s, then moving into Germany around 1905, emphasizing personal, subjective views, feelings, emotions, and the irrational. It has continued to expand through Europe and America since then, to include Abstract Expressionism, Neo-Expressionism and other forms.

F

Feyerabend, Paul (1924-1994), Austrian-born philosopher of science.

Flew, Antony (1923-2010), British philosopher of the analytic and evidentialist schools of thought; he also wrote on the philosophy of religion.

Foucault, Michel (1926-1984), postmodern French philosopher, social theorist, and historian of ideas.

fragmentation in the arts, the breaking up of forms (and meanings) into unrelated parts or areas in various ways.

G

Gabriel, Brigitte, Lebanese Christian, now living in U.S.A.

Gabriel, Mark, former Egyptian Muslim converted to Christianity.

Gay, Peter (b. 1923), German-American Professor of History.

genome, the sum total of DNA in a cell—the total of all its genetic units, including chromosomes, genes, and nucleotides.

Geisler, Norman (b. 1932), American theologian, Professor, and school founder. His four-volume *Systematic Theology* is an outstanding recent work of Evangelical theology. He has published over sixty books.

Gitt, Werner (b. 1937), German engineer and young earth creationist; he was an Engineering professor at the Physikalisch-Technische Bundesanstalt (German Federal Institute of Physics and Technology); in the 1990s he held a leadership role in the German creationist movement.

God's Eternal Being, God's identity as Eternal Unchanging Being and Lord of Creation; God's Eternal Life; without God's Being, nothing else would have being.

Goodman, Nelson (1906-1998), American phiosopher of irrealism.

Gorgias, Greek Sophist, Nihilist, c. 485-380 BC.

Grudem, Wayne (b. 1948), Protestant theologian, author.

H

Haeckel, Ernst (1834-1919), German evolutionary biologist, naturalist, and philosopher.

Hawking, Stephen (b.1942), English theoretical physicist, mathematician, and cosmologist.

Hegel, Georg Wilhelm Friedrich (1770-1831), German Idealist philosopher.

Heidegger, Martin (1889-1976), German philosopher associated with Existentialism and Phenomenology.

Henry, Carl F. H. (1913-2003), American evangelical Christian theologian, and former editor-in-chief of *Christianity Today*.

Heracleitus of Ephesus (c. 535-475 BC), pre-Socratic Greek philosopher.

Hitchens, Christopher (b, 1949), English-American author and journalist.

Hopkins, Gerard Manley (1884-1889), English poet, Roman Catholic convert, and Jesuit priest.

Hoyle, Fred (1915-2001), English astronomer and mathematician.

Hume, David (1711-1776), Scottish philosopher and historian.

Husserl, Edmund (1859-1938), Austrian philosopher and mathematician, founder of Phenomenology.

Huxley, Julian (1887-1975), English evolutionary biologist and humanist.

Huxley, Thomas Henry (1825-1895), English biologist, known as "Darwin's Bulldog"; coined the word agnostic in 1869.

hyperreality and simulation. According to Baudrillard we live in a post-modern world that is characterized by *hyperreality*. We are inundated by *simulations* in which signs and images of all kinds, including computerization, information processing, TV images, and constructed codes, replace reality as previously known. "Simulation" indicates the proliferation of signs and models in the media and throughout society to generate a new "reality" that is non-real, which he calls "hyperrealism." The explosion of such signs now dominates and controls contemporary social life and radically changes it. Simulation produces a new kind of social order and a new sense of personal identity. In Baudrillard's view this marks the end of the signifier/signified dialectic, which includes the traditional Christian metaphysical belief (e.g., Augustine, Aquinas) in the one-to-one correspondence of signs and images to real things, guaranteed by God and divine creation, and the end of such means of gaining knowledge and meaning. Signs and models today constitute "reality," even though they no longer interact with the real! "Hyperreality" indicates that distinctions between the real and unreal are blurred and lost (they "implode"). In the society of simulation and hyperrealism the experience and ground of objective, substantial reality as such disappears.

I

implosion (Baudrillard), the postmodern collapse of distinctions and boundaries that were, according to postmodern theory, important in previous eras, such as those between social classes, political parties, and genders.

Isaac, son of Abraham and Sarah in a miraculous birth. Isaac was the "seed" through whom the covenantal promise was to continue. He lived in antagonism with his brother Ishmael. He was the father of Jacob and Esau.

J

Jacob and Esau, biblical sons of Isaac and Rebekah. **Jacob's** name was symbolically changed by God to Israel, after Jacob wrestled with God in the form of a "man" or "angel." Israel thus gets its name from Jacob/Israel, an early father of his nation. The twelve tribes of Israel were descended from him and his twelve sons. Jacob also continued the line of God's covenant with the Hebrews. His wife Rachel died after giving birth to Benjamin.

Jarry, Alfred (1873-1907), French writer and absurdist.

Jezebel (fl. 9th cen. BC), the wicked pagan wife of King Ahab.

Johns, Jasper (b. 1930), American artist whose work has been labeled Neo-Dada, and has certain affinities with Rauschenberg and Postmodernism, having much sense of skepticism and uncertainty about identity and meaning relating to words and images.

Joseph, the eleventh of twelve sons of Jacob by his four wives. Joseph's mother was Rachel, who later bore Benjamin. The twelve sons became the progenitors of the twelve tribes of Israel and eventually a great nation. Joseph was sold into slavery in Egypt, but rose to power. For that reason, preordained by God, Joseph was able to save the lives of the small covenantal group around Jacob by having them come into Egypt.

K

Kuhn, Thomas, (1922-1996), American physicist, philosopher, and historian of science.

L

Laplace, Pierre-Simon, (1749-1827), French mathematician and astronomer.

Leonardo (Leonardo di ser Piero da Vinci) (1452-1519), Italian Renaissance artist, inventor, and man of all talents—a "Renaissance man."

Lichtenstein, Roy (1923-1997), American pop artist and postmodernist.

Locke, John (1632-1704), English philosopher, influential on the Enlightenment, first of the British empiricists, and Father of Liberalism.

"logocentrism" (logos-centered), derogatory name given by Derrida to the traditional emphasis on Logos in western metaphysics and the Bible.

logos, nomos, kosmos, nous, eide, ousia, arche, telos, ancient Greek concepts partly related to classic Christian thought:

> *logos*—the ordering word, law, reason underlying the changing appearances of things.

> *nomos* (law) cosmic law and order, with law treated as divine.

> *kosmos* (cosmos), the whole ordered universe; holistic order; law as a cosmic whole.

> *nous*, Plato recognized the *nous* immanent in the human soul (*psyche*), and cosmic *nous* (cosmic mind, reason) as the divine principle that orders the universe, rules everything, and leads toward the Good.

> *eidos, eide*, for Plato, the perfect, eternal Forms or Ideas that determine all existing forms, types, and categories of things (but are distinct from his creator *demiourgos* who copies them), and from cosmic *nous*, ranking still higher. The *eide*, and ultimately "the Good," are the cause of all sensible phenomena, giving them the form, order, and reality they have.

> *ousia*, substance, essence, the actual being of a thing.

401

arche, origin, beginning.

telos, the final end, goal, or *purpose* of anything, (Aristotle's "final cause").

Aristotelian Forms. For Aristotle, the universe is ruled by *Forms*, which indicate divine *Mind* (*nous*), *Ideas* (*eidè*), and *reason*. Related to Plato, and to later Christian theology, *Mind rules a real universe for a good purpose*. Aristotle found man and cosmos essentially permeated by *reason, design, structure, meaning, purpose*, and *goodness*. The same basic types of forms that determine physical nature, also determine human concepts, language and logic. Rational "categories" constitute the most fundamental forms of physical reality itself—the basic nature, structures, and patterns of all things. They also constitute the fundamental forms of language and logic, the primary subject of Aristotle's *Categories*. "The categories are the fundamental and indivisible concepts of thought; they are at the same time basic features of the real."

Lyotard, Jean-Francois (1924-1998), French postmodernist writer.

M

Margenau, Henry (1901- 1997), German-American physicist, and philosopher of science.

Maritain, Jacques (1882-1973), French Catholic philosopher; raised as a Protestant, converted to Catholicism in 1906; author of more than sixty books; helped to revive St. Thomas Aquinas in the modern world.

Marx, Karl, (1818-1883), German philosopher, revolutionary socialist, and atheist; developed the socio political theory of Marxism.

Megill, Allan, author of books on historical knowledge, modern-postmodern philosophy, and Karl Marx.

Merquior, J. G. (1941-1991), Brazilian diplomat, academic, writer, literary critic and philosopher.

metaphysics, doctrines of matters higher than the physical (classical and Christian).

Meyer, Steven C. (b. 1958), American scholar, philosopher and advocate for intelligent design. He helped found the Center for Science and Culture of the Discovery Institute, a center for the intelligent design movement.

Michelangelo (Michelangelo di Lodovico Buonarroti Simoni; 1475-1564), a Renaissance artist and one of the greatest artists of all time; sculptor, painter, architect, engineer, poet—a true "Renaissance man," perhaps greater than Leonardo because of the quality, number, and scope of his art works. Michelangelo also seems to have been a Christian, while Leonardo does not.

Milton, John (1608-1674), English poet and civil servant. He also held many unorthodox Christian theological views—rejecting the Trinity, claiming that the Son was subordinate to the Father (Arianism).

Modern thought, Modernism, the direction of thought, arts, and sciences showed some signs in the Renaissance, developed further in the seventeenth-century Age of Reason, secured its basic foundations in the eighteenth- century Enlightenment, and then continuously expanded, enlarged, and proliferated throughout the nineteenth and twentieth centuries. Romanticism (c. 1790-1830s and later) was the first major modern movement in the arts. It claimed primacy for the human self, feeling, emotion, intuition, imagination, love and sex, art, and nature, while essentially transforming or eliminating the idea of God. Modernism has been a variegated project, displaying major philosophies of empiricism, subjectivism, romanticism, rationalism, materialism, naturalism (see Ch. Three, n. 16), relativism, scientism, and evolutionism, with increasing tendencies to skepticism and nihilism (and some absurdism). A primary tendency has been to emphasize the importance of the human subject/self/ mind and its freedom or autonomy, while reducing and eventually eliminating the Being and role of God. From Descartes to Nietzsche, a period of 250 years, Modernism moved from increasing reduction of the role and necessity of God to total rejection of God/Being/Logos ("the triumph of becoming"). These ideas have spread widely in the twentieth century, and have been developed to various kinds of extremes. Modernism has thus taken a basic trajectory toward atheism (but also with some non-Christian religiosity). This atheism, already essential to Existentialism of the 1940s and 1950s, has become deeply endemic and widespread in Postmodernism. This direction should make it clear that anyone strongly conditioned by Modernism or Postmodernism, has great difficulty believing in God. And it explains why there have been numerous recent publications professing the virtues of atheism.

Moses, the great, early Hebrew leader, lawgiver, prophet, and scripture writer. He led the chosen people out of Egypt and up to the Promised Land. He continued the line of the covenant with God.

N

Niebuhr, Reinhold (1892-1971), American theologian.

Nietzsche, Friedrich (1844-1900), German philosopher, poet, philologist. His reductive, atheistic views of life and world have been extrremely influen-tial on twentieth-century modern and postmodern thought and art.

403

noumenon (pl. **noumena**; adj. **noumenal**), an existing thing-in-itself; contrast **phenomenon** (pl. **phenomena**), sense experience of a thing.

O

objective things; the world and things that actually exist as real objects outside the mind, and are not mere products or projections of a person's mind or language; they have real essence, substance, and structure. They also include God, Being, truth, beauty, purpose, form, order, laws, and patterns. Radical modern and postmodern thought tend to reject all of these as realities.

Oden, Thomas Clark (b. 1931), American United Methodist theologian and religious author.

P

Pelikan, Jaroslav (1923-2006), scholar in the history of Christianity, Christian theology and medieval intellectual history.

Pentecost, Dwight (b. 1915), Christian theologian best known for his book *Things to Come*.

Penzias, Arno (b. 1933), American physicist and Nobel laureate in physics.

Picasso, Pablo (1881-1973), Spanish artist who worked in France. The most famous artist of the modern era, and the grand master of high modern art (modern art at its apogee). He took the world apart and put it back together anyway he wanted to. He culminated the modern sense of the artist as the free, autonomous self/subject.

Plato, (c. 424-348 BC), Classsical Greek philosopher at the height of Greek culture. Plato was the first major exponent of philosophical Idealism, meaning that he believed perfect ideas to be at the basis of the reality of the world. Socrates was his teacher, Aristotle his student. Plato and Aristotle established the foundations of traditional Western philosophy, much of which Christian theologians later adapted, and modern thinkers from Nietzsche and Heidegger to Postmodernism have sought to destroy.

Postmodernism. Postmodern philosophy is one of the most radical and limiting philosophies in history, and it has been very influential in recent art and literature. It represents a sharp break with the past. It not only turns against and away from traditional Christian theology and metaphysics (e.g., the Bible, Church Fathers, Augustine, Aquinas), and against classical Greek philosophy (e.g., Plato and Aristotle), but rejects the foundational claims of previous modern philosophy as well. This is not surprising in view of the major influences on it—Nietzsche, Heidegger, and Wittgenstein. For postmodernists, language becomes the determining factor for all we think we know, and any supposed "truth." The assumption is that previous religions and philosophies are not really founded on any divine, rational, empirical, or universal grounds as theologians and philosophers have claimed, but simply arise from deceptive misuses of language, the results of which are labeled "metanarratives," "logocentrism," or simply "stories." "Metanarratives" include claims about anything beyond or above simple statements about language and life—claims such as "God," "Being," "divine creation," "logos," "universals," "truth," and "knowledge by means of "correspondences between words and things." The reason is that postmodernists treat language ("texts," images) as more essentially determinative for thought and life than the human subject/self/mind, the world, or God. God is actually dismissed from these views, and the world falls into uncertainty. Proper use of language according to postmodernists dismisses any claim to absolute or universal truth, and instead focuses on constantly changing views and attitudes [*becoming*] of people to each other and to "things" of the "world." Language merely serves useful human purposes at different times in different and changing ways [relativism, "difference," pragmatism]. According to Richard Rorty (pp. 202-4), we can never go beyond language to verify objective truth. His response to traditional views of truth is that "we should drop the topic." But since "God is truth," this means dropping God (which Rorty did).

Poststructuralism, a philosophical movement of the 1970s and later (e.g., Derrida), which has also been influential on the arts. For both Structuralism and Poststructuralism language became primary and central, replacing the human subject/self/mind and God in determining what we can and cannot know. Poststructuralism stressed language as an endless play of changing, multiple, and indeterminate meanings [constantly *becoming*]. It rejected appeal to any objective reality outside of language that could serve as an ultimate ground for linguistic meaning. Language is seen as detached from any objective world, becoming circular and self-determining. Any meaning of a word or text is by *differences* from other words or texts. Rational universals established by divine creation are thus rejected, as are rational correspondences of words to substantial things of the objective world. Poststructuralism holds many views similar to Postmodernism.

pragmatism, practical, earthly, non-metaphysical views, in extreme cases abandoning belief in God.

Purpose, goal, telos, teleology. Scripture and Christian metaphysics indicate that the reality, truth, rationality, structure, purpose, end, and knowability of all created things depend on the eternal Being of God and Ideas in the Mind, Word, and Wisdom of God. See *telos*.

Pyrrho of Elis, (c. 365-275 BC), ancient Greek skeptic.

R

Raphael (Raffaello Sanzio da Urbino; 1483-1520), Italian painter and architect. With Leonardo and Michelangelo he was one of the three greatest artists of the High Renaissance (c. 1500-1520), advancing classical style to new levels of realism, idealism, beauty, perfection, and grace.

Rauschenberg, Robert (1925-2008), American artist whose works are identified as assemblage or combines, and as Neo-Dada, as well as having several characteristics of Postmodernism. His parents were fundamentalist Christians, but he rebelled strongly against all that in his art and life. His work moved away from the seriousness and depth of Abstract Expressionism and Existentialism into a kind of postmodern skepticism, humor, and parody that made less sense, but had more jocularity. His work is characterized by difference, disjunction, and displacement.

reality, the actual being and existence of the self, the world, the universe, and ultimately, God. For Augustine and Aquinas, these realities are actual and knowable because God created the world and humans after the pattern of the divine ideas.

Rebekah, biblical wife of Isaac, and mother of Jacob and Esau.

relativism, relativistic philosophies and outlooks take little or nothing as absolute in truth, law, love, morality, or purpose. Much or everything is left to the individual person in such matters. Relativism tends to reject God in varying degrees, since God is absolute in truth, law, knowledge, power, goodness, morality, and purpose. See Ch. Six, n. 2.

Richardson, Joel, author of *The Islamic Antichrist: The Shocking Truth about the Real Nature of the Beast*; *Antichrist; Islam's Awaited Messiah*; *God's War on Terror: Islam, Prophecy and the Bible* (with Walid Shoebat).

Rimbaud, Arthur (1854-1891), French poet associated the Decadence movement of the late nineteenth-century; he was a libertine, and had a tumultous homsexual relationship with Verlaine, also a French poet.

Romanticism (c. 1790-1830), represents the beginnings of Modernism in the arts. It gave emphasis to self, imagination, feeling, emotions, and nature.

Rorty, Richard (1931-2007), American philosopher, professor, postmodernist, and pragmatist.

Ross, Hugh (b. 1945), Canadian-born astrophysicist, creationist, and author of several Christian books on the Bible, and intelligent design in the universe.

Russell, Bertrand, (1872-1970), British philosopher, logician, mathematician, historian, social critic, and a founder of analytic philosophy.

S

Sanford, J. C., geneticist, author of *Genetic Entropy and the Mystery of the Genome.*

Sandler, Irving (b. 1925), American art critic, historian, and educator.

Sarah (Sarai), biblical wife of Abraham, mother of Isaac.

Sarfati, Jonathan (b. 1964), creationist writer with a PhD in chemistry; he works for Creation Ministries International, and is the author of articles and books about creation science, favoring Young-Earth creationism.

Schopenhauer, Arthur (1788-21), German philosopher known for his pessimism and philosophy of Will.

Schroeder, Gerald L., Orthodox Jewish physicist, author, now lecturer at Aish HaTorah College of Jewish Studies; former professor of nuclear physics at MIT.

Sheen, Bishop Fulton J. (1895-1979), Christian theologian and philosopher, American archbishop of the Catholic Church.

simulacra, simulation, Baudrillard's terms for the artificial media-saturation of late capitalism: the images, signs, and models (simulacra) that, because of their omnipresence, determine individual identities, perceptions of self, rela-tion to others, and most other aspects of life (the social order of simulation).

Simpson, George G. (1902-1984), American zoologist and paleontologist.

skepticism, varying degrees of disbelief in biblical and classical metaphysical realities such as God, Being, absolute truth, spirit, substance, essence, universals, life after death, reason, meaning, and purpose (telos).

Solomon, son of David and Bathsheba; succeeded David as King of Israael; builder of the First Temple in Jerusalem.

Spearbearer, the epitome of high classical Greek art, with high levels of both naturalism and idealism.

Spenser, Edmund (1552-1599), English poet who wrote *Fowre Hymn, An Hymne of Heavenly Beautie* (1596), *Epithalamion*, and his best known epic poem, *The Faerie Queene.*

Structuralism, a philosophical movement of the 1960s and later (e.g., Barthes, Foucault). For both Structuralism and Poststructuralism language became primary, replacing the human subject/self/mind and God in determining any meaning we can know. It stressed language as a system of signs that can be "scientifically decoded." Words are said to be "arbitrary signs." They have no one-to-one link with things of the external world. Any meaning is determined by *differences* from other words. Divine ideas and universals are rejected, as are rational correspondences of words to things in the objective world.

subjectivism, the modern attempt to shift reality and truth into the human subject/self/mind, rather than attribute it to God, Being, and world; a rupture with being; in extreme forms, the world, religions, and morals, are products only of the self or subjective mind.

subjectivity, giving primary authority to subject/self/mind/idea; emphasizing personal beliefs, ideas, feelings, perceptions, judgments, and opinions, instead of the objective Creator God, world, or external laws, dogmas, teachings, authorities, or religions.

substance, the underlying, enduring nature or essence of a thing; the source of the being and unity of anything; the substance God gives in creation is *real*. Substance is primary: it constitutes the most basic nature of all things—their concrete individual reality, unity, and independence (ideas that radical modernism and Postmodernism reject).

T

Thomson, James (1700-1748), Scottish poet and playwright, known for his masterpiece *The Seasons*.

Tipler, Frank (b. 1947), American mathematical physicist and cosmologist.

U

universals, in contrast to *particulars,* denote broad or total interrelatedness or shared characteristics among things, people, ideas.

W

Warhol, Andy (1928-1987), American painter, printmaker, and filmmaker, outstanding in Pop art of the 1960s 70s and 80s.

Wells, Jonathan (b. 1942), a fellow at the Discovery Institute's Center for Science and Culture, a key center for the intelligent design movement, and at the International Society for Complexity, Information and Design, which also promotes intelligent design.

Wittgenstein, Ludwig, (1889-1951), Professor of Philosophy at Cambridge 1939 to 1947. Like subsequent Structuralism, Poststructuralism, and Postmodernism, he claimed that *language* is primary. This view is extremely skeptical and *less metaphysical* than any previous philosophy. We cannot go beyond language to know God, Being, or Logos. Such terms are thus nonsensical for Wittgenstein. The notion has become common in Poststructuralism and Postmodernism.

Endnotes

Chapter One

1. All quotations of the Bible are from *The NIV Study Bible* unless otherwise indicated.
2. Frame, *The Doctrine of God*, 202.
3. *Sourcebook of Poetry*, compiled by Al Bryant, 508.
4. Geisler and Turek, *I Don't Have Enough Faith to Be an Atheist*, 108-9; Cheetham, *Universe*, 7, 8; Gribbin, *Companion to the Cosmos*, 381.
5. Psalm 139:13-16.
6. Psalm 119:105.
7. Owens, *A History of Ancient Western Philosophy*, 198. On the central meaning and importance of Greek conceptions of Form, *kosmos*, and cosmic order, see Dupré, *Passage to Modernity*, Chapter 1.
8. Cf. Peters, *Greek Philosophical Terms*, 46-50, 108-9, 111-12, 131-38, 169-74; Parker, *The Story of Western Philosophy*, 44-111; Weber, *History of Philosophy*, 81-134; Armstrong, *An Introduction to Ancient Philosophy*; Owens, *History of Ancient Western Philosophy*, 197-249, 307-334.
9. Barrett, *Irrational Man*. A tendency from Nietzsche and Heidegger into Postmodernism has been to reverse traditional high views of theology, metaphysics, and reason, and to castigate Greek and Christian thought as the origins of centuries of illusory thought and error focused on *logos* and reason. Such views have ushered in the uncertainty and nihilism of our times.
10. See pp. 364-310. Reproduced in color in Wolfgang Fritz Volbach, *Early Christian Art*, New York, Abrams, Fig. 130. Also search the Internet, Santa Pudenziana mosaic.
11. *The Works of that Learned and Judicious Divine, Mr. Richard Hooker*, ed. Keble, vol. I, 200-202.
12. Ibid, 202-203, 207.
13. See Postmodernism in the Glossary.
14. *The Works of that Learned and Judicious Divine, Mr. Richard Hooker*, ed. Keble, vol. I, 207-208.
15. Benesch, *German Painting from Dürer to Holbein*, 83.
16. In Hutchison, *Albrecht Dürer; A Biography*, 1990), 164; on Dürer becoming a Lutheran or evangelical, see, David Hotchkiss Price, *Albrecht Dürer's Renaissance*, 226-235.
17. See Greenhalgh, *The Classical Tradition in Art*, 11-17; 93-110.
18. For a more detailed analysis of the less evident, humanistic themes and sources behind the Stanze frescoes (most likely worked out by Tommaso Inghirami, influenced by Pico della Mirandola, Cicero, and Pythagoreanism), see Joost-Gaugier, *Raphael's Stanza della Segnatura*, esp. chs. 6, 11.
19. Cf. S. J. Freedberg, *Painting of the High Renaissance in Rome and Florence*, 2 vols., vol. I, 116, 117.

[20] See *The Ubu Plays by Alfred Jarry*, ed. Simon Watson Taylor (New York: Grove Press, 1969).

[21] Reff, *Harlequins, Saltimbanques, Clowns, and Fools*, 38. 332, 363-64.

[22] In color in *Pablo Picasso; A Retrospective*, ed. William Rubin, 99; and search Pablo Picasso on the Internet.

[23] John Richardson, *A Life of Picasso*, vol. I, 1881-1906, 363.

[24] Cf. Leighten, *Re-Ordering the Universe; Picasso and Anarchism, 1897-1914*, 81. The influential roles of anarchism and Nietzscheanism in the development of Modern art, focusing on Picasso and Cubism, is the subject of Leighten's book.

[25] Ibid., 82, 83.

[26] Duncan, "Virility and Domination in Early 20th-Century Vanguard Painting," 35.

[27] John Richardson, ibid., 463, 520, n.1.

[28] Malraux, *Picasso's Mask*, 10, 11, in Huffington, *Picasso: Creator and Destroyer*, 90-1.

[29] Malraux, *Picasso's Mask*, 17; Huffington, *Picasso: Creator and Destroyer*, 90-1.

[30] Internet search for Max Ernst gives a color reproduction; so does Gaston Diehl, *Max Ernst* (New York: Crown, 1973), facing p. 28.

[31] John Russell, *Max Ernst; Life and Work* (New York: Abrams, 1967), 20, 22.

[32] Ernst, *The Hundred Headless Woman*, pp. 305, 137, 61.

[33] Ibid., 155.

[34] See Ernst, *The Hundred Headless Woman*, 27-66; Hughes, *The Shock of the New* (New York: Knopf, 1981), 248-49.

[35] Ernst, *The Hundred Headless Woman*, 291.

[36] Ernst, *Une Semaine de Bonté; A Surrealistic Novel in Collage*.

[37] Stokes, "From the Edges of Floating Worlds: Meaning in Ernst's Collages," 40.

[38] Ernst, *Une Semaine de Bonté*, 145-146, Thursday; Gen. 1:3, first day; 1:14-18, fourth day.

[39] Ibid., Chapter 2, Monday, pp. 39-68; Gen. 1:6-8, second day, p. 51 of *Une Semaine de bonté*.

[40] Ibid., 145-146, "Saturday"; cf. Gen. 1:26-31.

[41] Lucy R. Lippard, ed., *Surrealists On Art*, 127; italics added.

[42] Nietzsche, *Joyful Wisdom*, tr. Thomas Common, Book 2, paragraphs 57 and 58, pp. 96-97; emphasis added.

[43] Nietzsche, *Die Fröhliche Wissenschaft*, tr. in John Russell, *Max Ernst; Life and Work*, 50-51; emphases added.

[44] Lippard, ibid., 126-127.

[45] Cf. Warlick, "Max Ernst's Alchemical Novel: 'Une Semaine de bonté'," *Art Journal* 46 (Spring 1987), 64, 72. For a discussion of God and the nature and importance of the transcendentals [which are in effect destroyed in Ernst's work], see Étienne Gilson, *Elements of Christian Philosophy*, Chapter 6.

[46] *Edmund Spenser's Poetry*, ed. Hugh Maclean, 475-483, 485, including notes.

[47] *The Complete Poetry of John Milton*, ed. Shawcross, rev. ed., p. 354, nn. 34, 35.

[48] Arthur Pollard, *Richard Hooker*, 33.

[49] Ibid., 34.

[50] *Donne, The Laurel Poetry Series*, pp. 112-113; lines 205-218.

51 But see "Milton" in the Glossary.
52 See McGann, *Fiery Dust*, 247-55, and Bloom, *The Best Poems of the English Language*, 393-395.
53 Canto IV, CLXXVIII. CLXXXIII, CLXXXIV.
54 Bloom, *The Best Poems of the English Language*, 458-59.
55 On the interpretation of these eight verses, cf. Martin S. Day, *History of English Literature 1660-1837*, 456-57.
56 Gordon, *T. S. Eliot; An Imperfect Life*, 73, 75.
57 Ackroyd, *T. S. Eliot; A Life*, 161-63, 169, 335.

Chapter Two

1   Henry, *God, Revelation and* Authority, 6 vols, *Vol. V, God Who Stands and Stays*, 268.
2   See "The Reality and Being of World and Creator" in Chapter Four below.
3   Hugh Ross, *The Creator and the Cosmos*, 116 [italics added for emphasis].
4   Larson and Witham, "Scientists are still keeping the faith," 435-36, cited in Grant R. Jeffrey, *Creation: Remarkable Evidence of God's Design*, 20-21. And see www. religioustolereance.org/ev_publi.htm.
5   Sparrow, *Cosmos*, 212-13, with a very large two-page spread image.
6   Wikipedia, "Star". Frebel, A. et al., "Nearby Star is a Galactic Fossil," *Science Daily* (2007-05-11).
7   Richard Ellis and team at the California Institute of Technology—www.en. wikipedia.org/wiki/Timeline of the Big Bang
8   Ross, *Why the Universe is the Way It Is*, 46, 44. "13.73 ± 0.12 billion years old." "Universe," www.wikipedia.org, 1. "Age of the Universe," www.wikipedia. org. In *Why the Universe is the Way It Is*, 44, 221 n.1, Ross also indicates the age of the universe as 13.73 billion years, citing the study by E. Komatsu et al., "Five-Year Wilkinson Anisotropy Probe (WMAP) Observations: Cosmological Interpretation," *Astrophysical Journal Supplement Series* (2008). Previously suggested dates have been 14.5 and 14.9 billion years (Ross, *The Creator and the Cosmos*, 48).
9   Large color images are in Sparrow, *Cosmos, 214-15*; and Nicolas Cheetham, *Universe; A Journey from Earth to the Edge of the Cosmos*, 214-15.
10 Hawking and Penrose, *The Nature of Space and Time*, 20.
11 Ross, *The Creator and the Cosmos*, Appendix, 221-27; these points have been much shortened and simplified in this restating. Compare Ross's own wording.
12 See Sparrow, *Cosmos*, 216-17, with diagram; see also the two-page diagram of the big bang in Rees, *Universe*, 46-7, and related ones in Hawking, [1] *The Illustrated A Brief History of Time;* [2] *The Universe in a Nutshell*, [part 1] 148-49, [part 2] 168-69; Luhr, ed.(Smithsonian Institution), *Earth*, 24 ff.
13 Rees, *Universe*, 45.
14 Wiker and Witt, *A Meaningful World*, 153 citing Rees, *Just Six Numbers*, 99. Wiker and Witt's fascinating and insightful book details many ways that a fine-tuned"

universe and earth have emerged, in clear support of human life, with multiple, interrelated senses of meaning and purpose.

15 Ross, *The Creator and the Cosmos*, 27-8.

16 Margenau, "Why I Am A Christian," letter to Leadership University, www.leaderu.com/truth/1truth16.html, p. 6.

17 Davies, *Superforce*, 243. idem., *The Cosmic Blueprint*, idem., "The Anthropic Principle," *Science Digest* 191, no. 10 (October 1983), 24. Ashton, ed., *On the Seventh Day; Forty Scientists and Academics Explain Why They Believe in God;* idem., *In Six Days; Why Fifty Scientists Choose to Believe in Creation.*

18 George Greenstein, *The Symbiotic Universe* 27, quoted in Ross, *The Creator and the Cosmos*, 158.

19 Tony Rothman, "A 'What You See is What You Beget' Theory," Discover (May 1987), 99, quoted in Ross, *The Creator and the Cosmos*, 158.

20 Margenau and Varghese, *Cosmos, Bios, and Theos*, 52, quoted in Ross, *The Creator and the Cosmos*, 158-59.

21 Margenau and Varghese, *Cosmos, Bios, and Theos*, 83, quoted in Ross, *The Creator and the Cosmos*, 159.

22 Fang Li Zhi and Li Shu Xian, *Creation of the Universe*, tr. T. Kiang (Singapore: World Scientific, 1989), 173, quoted in Ross, *The Creator and the Cosmos*, 159.

23 John Noble Wilford, "Sizing Up the Cosmos: An Astronomer's Quest," *New York Times*, 12 March, 1991, B9, quoted in Ross, *The Creator and the Cosmos*, 160.

24 Tipler, F. J., *The Physics of Immortality*, preface.

25 Hawking, [1] *The Illustrated A Brief History of Time;* [2] *The Universe in a Nutshell,* [part 1] 163, emphases added. Hawking makes other statements purporting to render a Creator God unnecessary, however. And, for a brilliant man, comes up with the same ignorant question about God that Christopher Hitchens would make later: "Who created him?" (The most basic theology about God is that He is the uncreated, eternal Being.) See Ross, *The Creator and the Cosmos*, 124, 119-125.

26 "13.73 ± 0.12 billion years old," "Universe," www.wikipedia.org, 1.

27 Cheetham, *Universe*, 7-8.

28 Ross *Why the Universe is the Way It Is*, 31. Cf. Ross, *Creation As Science*, 85. Ross says there are about 10 to 50 billion trillion stars in the observable universe; Wikipedia says 70 sextillion (7×10^{22}; "Stars," n. 49: "Astronomers count the stars", BBC News [2003-07-22]; cf. Singh, *Big Bang* (New York: Harper Collins, 2004), 3.

29 Philippians 3:21; Luke 24:36-43, 20:35-36; I Corinthians 15:51-53; Geisler, *Systematic Theology*, Vol. 4, 300.

30 Wikipedia, "List of largest known stars," "List of most luminous stars," "VY Canis Majoris," and "LBV 1806-20; Sparrow, *Cosmos*, 122, 139; Garlick, *The Illustrated Atlas of the Universe*, 152; Cheetham, *Universe*, 117.

31 Sparrow, *Cosmos*, 104-5.

32 Luhr, ed., *Earth*, 25.

33 Sparrow, *Cosmos*, 104.

34 Ibid., 136; cf. Garlick, *The Illustrated Atlas of the Universe*, 155.

35 Sparrow, *Cosmos*, 148-49.

36 Ibid., 156; and see large pictures of the Milky Way, Andromeda, and Triangulum Galaxies on pp. 148-49, 162-63, 164-65.

37 In 2010 NASA's Wilkinson Microwave Anisotropy Probe (WMAP) estimated the age of the universe to be 13.75 billion years, with an uncertainty of plus or minus 110 million years. Wikipedia.org, "Age of universe," 3.

38 Jastrow, *God and the Astronomers*, 2nd ed. (New York: Norton, 2000), 10-11.

39 Hugh Ross, "Why I Believe in the Miracle of Divine Creation," in *Why I Am A Christian*, ed. Geisler and Hoffman (Grand Rapids, Baker Books, 2006), 136-37; and see Sparrow, *Cosmos*, 156-57, 175, 194-99.

40 Sparrow, *Cosmos*, 204-05.

41 Ibid., 204-05, 189, 212; Cheetham, *Universe*, 212.

42 Sparrow, *Cosmos*, 208, with a reproduction of the map; larger map in Cheetham, *Universe*, 206-07; cf. Mark A. Garlick, *The Illustrated Atlas of the Universe*, 194-95.

43 Sparrow, *Cosmos*, 206-07.

44 Ross, "Why I Believe in the Miracle of Divine Creation," 136-37; and see also the two-page diagram of the big bang in Rees, *Universe*, 46-7, and related ones in Hawking, [1] *The Illustrated A Brief History of Time;* [2] *The Universe in a Nutshell*, [part 1] 148-49, [part 2] 168-69.

45 See the computer simulations of dark matter in Sparrow, *Cosmos*, 210-11, and Cheetham, *Universe*, 216-17.

46 Gribbin, *Companion to the Cosmos*, 104-5; cf. Sparrow, *Cosmos*, 210-11; Hawking, [1] *The Illustrated A Brief History of Time;* [2] *The Universe in a Nutshell*, [part 2] 203.

47 Ross, *Why the Universe is the Way It Is*, 33-4, 37.

48 Ibid., 33-35, 37.

49 Ibid.

50 Ibid., 39; "Dark Energy," wikipedia.org, 2.

51 The data in this paragraph is based on Ross, *Why the Universe is the Way It Is*, 37 (with chart), 23, 33, 36-38; and on "Universe," "Dark Energy," and "Dark Matter," wikipedia.org. Ross cites the work of D. N. Spergal et al., "Three-Year Wilkinson Microwave Anisotropy Probe (WMAP) Observations: Implications for Cosmology," *Astrophysical Journal Supplement Series 170* (June 10, 2007), 377-408; E. Komatsu et al., "Five-Year Wilkinson Microwave Anisotropy Probe (WMAP) Observations: Cosmological Interpretation," (preprint, National Aeronautics and Space Administration, 2008).

52 "Dark Energy," wikipedia.org, 2.

53 Ross, *Why the Universe is the Way It Is*, 39-40, citing Lawrence Krauss, *Quintessence: The Mystery of the Missing Mass* (New York: Basic, 2000), 103-5; Krauss, "The End of the Age Problem and the Case for a Cosmological Constant Revisited," *Astrophysical Journal 501* (July 10, 1998), 461, 465.

54 Ross, *Why the Universe is the Way It Is*, 40, with citations.

55 "Dark Matter," and "Universe," wikipedia.org.

56 Ross, *Why the Universe is the Way It Is*, 35-8.

57 Ibid.

58 Ross, *The Creator and the Cosmos*, 43-4.

59   A test was made of the typing monkey theory by Plymouth University in England in 2002. A computer was left in the cage of six macaque monkeys. Besides the gibberish of endlessly repeated letters they pounded out, the monkeys urinated and defecated all over the keyboard, and tried to bash it in with a stone. (Oh well, no doubt a million monkeys could have done a better job.) Reported in Wiker and Witt, *A Meaningful World*, 31-2.

60   Hoyle's comment is in an unpublished University of Cardiff preprint entitled "The Universe: Some Past and Present Reflections," cited in Wiker and Witt, ibid., 155, and in Paul Davies, *The Accidental Universe* (Cambridge: Cambridge University Press, 1982), 118.

61   Ross, *The Creator and the Cosmos*, 176.

62   Ibid.

63   Ross, *Why the Universe is the Way It Is*, 48-50.

64   Cf. Garlick, *The Illustrated Atlas of the Universe*, 116; and see the short explanation of the thermonuclear process on p. 117.

65   Wiker and Witt, ibid., 159-60, 164, citing Gonzales and Richards, *The Privileged Planet; How Our Place in the Cosmos is Designed for Discovery*, 66.

66   Ross, *The Creator and the Cosmos*, 178-79.

67   Ibid., 180.

68   Hawking, [1] *The Illustrated A Brief History of Time;* [2] *The Universe in a Nutshell*, [part 2], 88, 90.

69   Hawking, ibid., [part 2], 96-98.

70   Ross, *The Creator and the Cosmos*, 45, 46, 53, 56. Dark energy and the cosmologi-cal constant. Dark energy is thought to be a form of energy that permeates all of space and tends to increase the rate of expansion of the universe. "Dark energy is the most accepted theory to explain recent observations and experiments that the universe appears to be expanding at an accelerating rate. In the standard model of cosmology, dark energy currently accounts for 73% of the total mass-energy of the universe. Two proposed forms for dark energy are the cosmological constant, a *constant* energy density filling space homogeneously, and scalar fields such as quintessence or moduli, *dynamic* quantities whose energy density can vary in time and space. Contributions from scalar fields that are constant in space are usually also included in the cosmological constant. The cosmological constant is physically equivalent to vacuum energy. Scalar fields which do change in space can be difficult to distinguish from a cosmological constant because the change may be extremely slow." Wikipedia, "Dark Energy." With references to: P. J. E. Peebles and Bharat Ratra (2003), "The cosmological constant and dark energy". *Reviews of Modern Physics* 75 (2): 559-606; Sean Carroll (2001). "The cosmological constant". *Living Reviews in Relativity* 4. http://relativity. livingreviews.org/ Articles/lrr-2001-1/ index.html. Retrieved 2006-09-28

71   These quotations and list of ten anthropic principles were drawn from Ross's Internet site, www.reasons.org in July 2007, search: "Anthropic Principle," "Design and the Anthropic Principle."

72   Ross, *The Creator and the Cosmos*, 36.

73   Ibid., 180.

74   Calculated layer sizes, temperatures, and densities vary somewhat according to the source; approximate sizes here are derived from Charles C. Plummer, David McGeary, and Diane H. Carlson, *Physical* Geology, ninth edition (New York: McGraw Hill, 2003), 417; temperatures and densities are taken from Luhr, ed., *Earth*, 54-57; and some information is derived from the Internet at pubs.usgs.gov/gip/ dynamic/dynamic.html.

75   Luhr, ed., *Earth*, 82-85.

76   Ibid., 10.

77   Ibid., 58, 59, 108-109.

78   See a fuller explanation of these processes in Ward and Brownlee, *Rare Earth*, 195-202, esp. 201.

79   Ibid., 202-04.

80   Ibid., 204-06; and see diagram on p. 202.

81   Ibid., 207, 208-09.

82   Ibid., 209-12.

83   Ibid., 212-13.

84   See "Periodic Table" at www.wikipedia.org.

85   This discussion of elements and the periodic table is much indebted to Wiker and Witt, *A Meaningful World*, 135, much of Chapter 5, "The Periodic Table," and Chapter 6, "A Cosmic Home."

86   Wiker and Witt, ibid., 136-37.

87   Ibid.

88   Ibid., 138-40.

89   Ibid., 140-41.

90   Ibid., 127.

91   Ibid., 147, Chapter 5.

92   Margenau and Varghese, ed., *Cosmos, Bios, and Theos* 57, 59, 61, 63.

93   Phillip Blond, ed., *Post-Secular Philosophy*, 7.

Chapter Three

1   Approximately 30,000 genes—Gerald L. Schroeder, *Hidden Face of God*, 190. "20,000-40,000 protein encoding genes (estimates greatly vary, . . . 1.5 billion nucelotides"-- Sanford, *Genetic Entropy and the Mystery of the Genome*, 38. "Early estimates of the number of human genes that used expressed sequence tag data put it at 50,000-100,000. Following the sequencing of the human genome and other genomes, it has been found that rather few genes (~20,000 in human, mouse and fly, ~13,000 in roundworm, >46,000 in rice) encode all the proteins in an organism."—Wikipedia, "Genes," 6.2.

2   Sanford, *Genetic Entropy*, 1, 4.

3   Ibid., 2-3.

4   Ibid., 3-4; cf. Schroeder, *Hidden Face of God*, 190, 196.

5   Ibid., 2.

6   "There are between 50 and 75 trillion cells in the human body." – Wikipedia, "Cells, human." Cf. Schroeder, *Hidden Face of God*, 189. Sanford, *Genetic Entropy*, 4.

7   Schroeder, *Hidden Face of God*, 193-94, 63. Much of the information in the next three paragraphs about cells, DNA, and RNA is indebted to Schroeder's vivid descriptions. However, my essential interpretation fully traces these marvelous structures of information, to the Wisdom, Logos, and Ideas of the Creator God of the Old and New Testaments and traditional theology securely based on them, and does not involve the kabala, which Schroeder makes use of in his interpretation.

8   Ibid., 62, 189.

9   Ibid., 189, 62.

10   Ibid., 194-95.

11   Ibid., 191, 195.

12   Gitt, *In the Beginning Was Information*, 92-3.

13   Schroeder, *Hidden Face of God*, 60, 192, 189, 67; Luhr, ed., *Earth*, 27-29.

14   The description in this and the next two paragraphs of the process involved in creation of a protein by a cell is closely based on Schroeder, *Hidden Face of God*, 196-200. For more details see those pages.

15   This chapter and the next one have more to say about this issue. And see Wells, *The Politically Incorrect Guide to Darwinism and Intelligent Design*. Wells' Chs. Two and Three, expose much of the falsity and fakery of evolutionary claims. Also see Wells, *Icons of Evolution*.

16   Naturalist and materialist claims that go beyond the legitimate bounds of science have no authority as science, or claim as actual fact. Some of these claims, indicated in Chapters One, Two, and Three also stand in opposition to another, polar side of modernism that centers on the self. Both philosophies reject the God of the Bible and turn to nature, matter or the self as primal ultimates. Instead of working from an accumulation of smaller facts up to an ultimate (which is impossible), they work from an ultimate hypothesis downward. When such philosophies are taken into the sciences, the result is "scientism," which steps beyond the proper bounds of the sciences. Naturalism and materialism are a major side of modernism, standing in polar opposition to the subjective pole that will be given fuller study in Chapters Six, Seven, and Eight. These poles can be identified as "subject vs. object"; "subjectivism vs. naturalism, materialism"; "self vs. world"; "arts vs. sciences." Since both poles tend to deny the Absolute God of the Bible as a principle, neither has any ultimate and unifying ground, only philosophical *theory*. There is also a split, a gap, between the two poles that is characteristic of modernity. It is a gap and polar oppositon resulting from rejection of the unifying Being, Truth, and Authority of God.

17   Wiker and Witt, *A Meaningful World*, 201.

18   Ibid.

19   Ibid., 210.

20   Hubert P. Yockey, "A Calculation of the Probability of Spontaneous Biogenesis by Information Theory," *Journal of the Theoretical Biology* 67 (1977): 385; cited in Wiker and Witt, *A Meaningful World*, 210.

21   Wiker and Witt, *A Meaningful World*. The authors provide a lengthy tracing of materialistic notions of a "warm little pond" and "prebiotic soup" as the proper

setting and condition for the origin and evolution of living cells. They present arguments and evidence that leave such views, still prevalent today, with no substantial support, 198-219.

22   Ibid., 210-11.

23   The following description of mitosis, brief as it is, is also based on Schroeder's much fuller and more detailed treatment in *Hidden Face of God*, 201-210.

24   Schroeder, ibid., 206-7.

25   Ibid., 207, 208-9, 210.

26   See Chapters Four and Five.

27   *Philosophia Christi* 6, no. 2 (2004); http://www.biola.edu/antonyflew. There is some controversy about whether Flew actually turned to deism (related to his time of mental decline); see Wikipedia, "Flew, Antony."

28   Wiker and Witt, *A Meaningful World*, 201.

29   *Handbook of Evangelical Theologians*, Elwell, ed., 445-46.

30   Gitt, *In the Beginning Was Information*, 50-3.

31   Ibid., 58-9.

32   Ibid., 60-70.

33   Ibid., 71-74.

34   Ibid., 74-81.

35   Dawkins, *River Out of Eden: A Darwinian View of Life*, 96.

36   Gitt, *In the Beginning Was Information*, 80-2, cf. 106; bold type added for emphasis.

37   Ibid., 98. Bold type added for emphasis.

38   Ibid., 112.

39   Sanford, *Genetic Entropy*, Chapter 1, esp. 4-8.

40   Dawkins, *The Blind Watchmaker*, 9.

41   Sanford, *Genetic Entropy*, 8-13.

42   See more specific detail in Sanford, *Genetic Entropy*, Chs. 2 & 3, esp. 22-27, 29-32. Citations include: P. J. Gerrish and R. Lenski, 1998, The fate of competing beneficial mutations in an asexual population, Genetica 102/103: 127-144; Bataillon, 2000; S. F. Elena et al, 1998, Distribution of fitness effects caused by random insertion mutations in E. coli, Genetica 102/103:349-358; M. Kimura, 1979, Model of effective neutral mutations in which selective restraint is incorporated, PNAS 76:3440-3444.

43   Sanford, *Genetic Entropy*, Chapter 4, esp. 47-51, 63.

44   Ibid., 48-9, 52-5, citing J. F. Crow and M. Kimura, An Introduction to Population Genetics Theory (NY: Harper and Row, 1970), 249.

45   Sanford, *Genetic Entropy*, 100-1, and all of Chapter 6.

46   Ibid., Chapter 9, esp. 123-5, 139.

47   Ibid., Appendix 4, 189-93.

48   Wells, *The Politically Incorrect Guide to Darwinism and Intelligent Design*, 49-55, 58-9, 223 n.12; citing Lynn Margulis and Dorion Sagan, *Acquiring Genomes: A Theory of the Origins of Species* (New York: Basic Books, 2002), 32; and Alan Linton, "Scant Search for the Maker." *Times Higher Education Supplement*, April 20, 2001, Book Section, 29.

49   Phillip Johnson writes, "Natural Selection's great deficiency is that it cannot create new biological information." *Intelligent Design 101*, House, General Editor, 31. This book is an excellent introduction to the recent discoveries and issues of Intelligent Design experts.

50   Wells, *The Politically Incorrect Guide to Darwinism and Intelligent Design*, 25-29. See Haeckel's embryo drawings on p. 26. Compare them with more accurate ones on p. 29.

51   Huxley, *Evolution After Darwin*, ed. Sol Tex, vol. 3 (Chicago: University of Chicago Press, 1960), in "The Centennial Celebration of *The Origin of Species*"; *Intelligent Design 101*, 155; Wells, *The Politically Incorrect Guide to Darwinism and Intelligent Design*.

52   Meyer, "DNA and the Origin of Life."

53   Meyer, Ibid., Meyer's quotation (page 224) of Bernd-Olaf Kuppers, *Information and the Origin of Life* (Cambridge: MIT Press, 1990), 170-72.

54   Meyer, ibid., 224-5,

55   Ibid., 225-27.

56   Ibid., 227-30.

57   Ibid., 237; Meyer provides more evidence and reasoning concerning complexity, specificity, and biological information on pages 233-39, and in subsequent parts of the paper—much more than can be indicated here.

58   Ibid., 239-44.

59   Ibid., 243.

60   Ibid., 244-45.

61   Ibid., 245-46; C. de Duve, *Blueprint for a Cell: The Nature and Origin of Life* (Burlington, N>C.: Neil Patterson, 1991), 187.

62   Meyer, "DNA and the Origin of Life, 245-46; T. Dobzhansky, "Discussion of G. Schramm's Paper," in *The Origins of Prebiological Systems and of Their Molecular Matrices*, ed. S. W. Fox (New York: Academic Press, 1965), 310.

63   Dawkins, *The Blind Watchmaker*, 47-49; Kuppers, "On the Prior Probability."

64   Meyer, "DNA and the Origin of Life, 247-48.

65   Meyer, ibid., 246, with reference notes 77-79 to von Neumann, Pennisi, Wigner, Landsberg, and Morowitz.

66   Meyer, "DNA and the Origin of Life, 248-49.

67   Ibid., 250-51.

68   Ibid., 251-52.

69   Ibid., 254; Meyer gives eight more pages of arguments against other naturalist origin-of-life scenarios.

70   Ibid., 262-63, and see Meyer's notes 120-122.

71   *The Believers Study Bible, New King James Version*, note to Romans 1:19.

72   Frame, *Apologetics to the Glory of God*, 7-8, 11, 20. 22.

Chapter Four

1   Culver, *Systematic Theology, Biblical and Historical*, 127.

2   Discussed in this chapter, and see p. 238.

3   Craig, "Why I Believe God Exists," 68.

4   Craig, ibid.

5   Geisler, *Systematic Theology, Vol. Two*, 56; Étienne Gilson, *God and Philosophy*, Chapter 1.

6   Craig, "Why I Believe God Exists," 68-70.

7   Craig, ibid., 70-1; Craig's arguments, only very briefly indicated here, are more fully developed in his text. J. L. Mackie, *Times Literary Supplement* (5 February 1982): 126; Steven Hawking and Roger Penrose, *The Nature of Space and Time*, 20.

8   Craig, "Why I Believe God Exists," 71-3.

9   Geisler discusses these attributes at some length in *Systematic Theology, Vol. Two*. They are also developed by Oden in *The Living God; Systematic Theology, Vol. I*.

10   Pelikan, *Christianity and Classical Culture*, 213.

11   *The Believers Study Bible*, notes for Exodus 3:14 and Genesis 2:4.

12   *Ibid. The Columbia History of Philosophy*, 712.

13   Pelikan, *Christianity and Classical Culture*; with references to Gregorius Nazianzenus *Orationes*, 30:18, *Sources Chretiennes* (Paris: Cerf, 1940-).

14   Geisler, *Systematic Theology, Vol. Two*, 32.

15   Ibid., 35-6.

16   Ibid., 17-8.

17   Walvoord and Zuck, *The Bible Knowledge Commentary, Old Testament*, 112.

18   Frame, *The Doctrine of God*, 351, and all of Part One.

19   Pelikan, *Christianity and Classical Culture*, 3-4.

20   Ibid., 213-14, with references to Gregorius Nazianzenus *Orationes* 31.23, and Gregorius Nyssenus *Contra Eunomium*, 3.8.32.

21   Cf. *The Believers Study Bible*, note to verse 8:58.

22   Geisler, *Systematic Theology, Vol. Two*, 32.

23   *The Believers Study Bible*.

24   Geisler, *Systematic Theology, Vol. Two*, 30-1, 35, 56.

25   Aquinas, *Summa Theologica*, 1a.3.1.

26   *The Believers Study Bible*, emphases added; Geisler, *Systematic Theology, Vol. Two*, 31.

27   Frame, *The Doctrine of God*, 227, 221, 224, 230.

28   Frame, *Apologetics to the Glory of God*, 34-5 ff. *The Doctrine of God*, 229-30.

29   Oden, *The Living God, Vol. I*, 47-49; with reference to Aquinas, *Summa Theologica*, I, Q4, 5, 12, 1, pp. 20ff., 48 ff.

30   Oden, *The Living God*, 48-9, with reference to Aquinas, *Summa Theologica*, I, Q2, 1, pp. 11 ff.; *Summa Contra Gentiles*, 1.13, pp. 85 ff.

31   Oden, *The Living God*, 53-8, with numerous references to the Bible, Church Fathers, and theologians.

32   Geisler, *Systematic Theology, Vol. Two*, Chapter 11, 254-261.

33   Oden, *The Living God*, 64-6, with numerous references.

34   Geisler, *Systematic Theology, Vol. Two*, 181-82 ff. (emphasis added); with numerous quotations from the Bible, Church Fathers, and theologians.

35   Bavinck, *The Doctrine of God*, 183.

36   Geisler, *Systematic Theology, Vol. Two*, 213; Oden, *The Living God*, 71.

37 Bavinck, *The Doctrine of God*, 197.

38 Geisler, *Systematic Theology, Vol. Two*, 503, 507 and all of Chapter 21.

39 Cf., Geisler, ibid., 503-4.

40 Cf., Geisler, ibid., 503-7.

41 Frame, *The Doctrine of God*, 289, 288, 40, 278; Frame's three other modes of divine preservation pertain to historical redemption, covenant, and eternal salvation.

42 Bavinck, *The Doctrine of God*, 256.

43 Job, 28:20-27; Proverbs, 8:22-23 f., *The Believers Study Bible; New King James Version*, 854-855; Proverbs, 3:19-20, *The NIV Study Bible*.

44 Leon Morris, *The Gospel According to John*, 123.

45 A. F. Walls, "Logos," *The Evangelical Dictionary of Theology*, 646.

46 See Dunn, *Christology in the Making*. Wolfson, *Philosophy of the Church Fathers: Vol. I*. Snyder, *Medieval Art*.

47 Henry, *God, Revelation and Authority*, vol., I, 43; cf. V, 67, 334-36.

48 Ibid., III, 205; see Henry's strong discussion of the meanings of Logos in his "Thesis Nine: "The mediating agent in all divine revelation is the Eternal Logos—preexistent, incarnate, and now glorified," III, 164-247; other volumes develop points of this exposition further, esp., vol. V, Chapters 17-20, on God's Mind, divine Reason, Logos, and human knowledge; and I, 280-395 on the related topic of the religious a priori.

49 Henry, *God, Revelation and Authority*, I, 43.

50 Sheen, *Philosophy of Religion*, 167.

51 Bavinck, *The Doctrine of God*, 197-99.

52 Ibid., 199.

53 Sheen, *Philosophy of Religion*, 167-68; Aquinas, *Sum. Theol*. Part I, q. 44, a. 3; I, q. 15, aa. 1, 2, 3; I, 14, qq. 4, 8; I, q. 34, aa. 2, 3; *Contra Gentiles*, III, 20.

54 Rom. 8:3, cf. Gal. 4:4; Col. 1:15; Col. 1:16, I Cor. 8:6; Col. 1:17, cf. Heb. 1:3; I Cor. 1:30, 24, 2:7.

55 John 1:18, 14, 1-4, 9, 8:12, NIV.

56 Jewett, *God, Creation, and Revelation*, 489, 490.

57 Wolfson, *Philosophy of the Church Fathers*, 280-82; Augustine, *On Order*, I, 11, 32 (PL 32, 993); *Retractions*, I, 3, 2; emphases added.

58 Augustine, *Eighty-three Different Questions*, 46. 1-2; Bourke, *Augustine's View of Reality*, 55-9; Kenny, *The God of the Philosophers*, 16.

59 Wolfson, *Philosophy of the Church Fathers*, 280-82; Augustine, *On Order*, I, 11, 32 (PL 32, 993); idem., *Retractions*, I, 3, 2. Plato's later writings seem to move closer to later Christian teachings in these respects: see Timaeus 28-30 on the creator, the "father," creation, goodness of creation, soul, intelligence, order, intelligible ideas, and providence; and "the whole," in which "the original of the universe contains in itself all intelligible beings." In the Laws, 716c, Plato writes of God as "the measure of all things" (*The Collected Dialogues of Plato*, ed. Edith Hamilton, Huntington Cairns But any attempts to find in Plato a transcendent mind (*nous*) or God to contain the ideas are ultimately ruled out (Peters, *Greek Philosophical Terms*, 134, 131-139; 47-51.)

60 Wolfson, *Philosophy of the Church Fathers*, 282; Augustine, *City of God*, XII, 26; cf. *Eighty-Three Different Questions*, 46, 2; Boland, ibid., 41.

61 Wolfson, *Philosophy of the Church Fathers*, 282-83 ff.; Augustine, *Eighty-Three Different Questions*, 46, 2.

62 Gilson, *The Christian Philosophy of Saint Augustine*, 210.

63 Aquinas, *Summa Theologica, Part I*, q. 8, a. 1.

64 Ibid., I, q. 14, a. 4; q. 34, aa. 2, 3; single quotation marks substituted for italics.

65 Ibid., Part I, q. 14, a. 8; q. 15, aa. 1, 2; q. 44, a. 3; Augustine, *Eighty-Three Different Questions*, 46; also see Aquinas, *Truth*, vol. I, esp. qq. 3, 4, 2.

66 Mondin, *St. Thomas Aquinas' Philosophy*, 56.

67 Ibid., 43, 46, 47, 48, 50, 51; Aquinas, II Sent. d. 1; Brother Benignus, *Nature, Knowledge, and God: An Introduction to Thomistic Philosophy*, 370, 337-69.

68 Benignus, *Nature, Knowledge, and God*, 358-59, 362, 370-71; Gardeil, *Introduction to the Philosophy of St. Thomas Aquinas: IV*, Chapter 4. To the transcendentals of the one, true, and good, modern authors add the "beautiful."

69 Gardeil, *Introduction to the Philosophy of St. Thomas Aquinas*, Chapters 4-5; Benignus, *Nature, Knowledge, and God*, 362-63. Aquinas's nine other predicaments, the accidents, essentially the same as Aristotle's categories, are **quantity, quality, relation, activity (action), passivity (passion), place, time, situation or position (*situs*), and possession (*habitus*)**; cf. note 73.

70 Zagzebski, "Individual Essence and the Creation," *Divine and Human Action; Essays in the Metaphysics of Theism*, ed. Morris, 135-36; Aquinas, *De veritate*, q. 2, a. 4, ad 6.

71 Zagzebski, "Individual Essence and the Creation," 119, 120, 129-30, 142-43.

72 Baumer, *Modern European Thought; Continuity and Change in Ideas, 1600-1950*, Part V, Chapter 1.

73 Ibid., Table of Contents, 414, 439.

Chapter Five

1 Frame, *The Doctrine of God*, 231.

2 Fulton J. Sheen, *Philosophy of Religion*, 168-169.

3 Aquinas, *Sum. Theol.*, Part I, q. 16, a. 3, a. 5; cf. *Contra Gentiles*, Book I, 45, 60, 61; Etienne Gilson, *Elements of Christian Philosophy*, 152-53.

4 Strong, *Systematic Theology*, 260-61.

5 Frame, *The Doctrine of God*, 231.

6 Ibid., 475-79.

7 *The Believers Study Bible; New King James Version*, note to John 14:6.

8 Ibid., note to John 14:16.

9 Grudem, *Systematic Theology*, 74.

10 Ibid., 83.

11 Geisler, *Systematic Theology, Vol. One*, 236, 248.

12 See the notes for these biblical verses in both the NIV and NKJV Study Bibles. For longer, more detailed treatments of the divine authority and infallibility of Scripture, see, Geisler, *Systematic Theology*, Vol. One, Chapters 13-29; and Grudem, *Systematic Theology*, Chapters 2-8.

[13] Geisler, *Systematic Theology, Vol. One*, 245.

[14] Grudem, *Systematic Theology*, 83-4.

[15] Ibid., 119-20.

[16] Compare translations and notes for these verses in the NIV and NKJV Study Bibles.

[17] Grudem, *Systematic Theology*, 84.

[18] Ibid., 278-79. On "problem texts," see Geisler and Howe, *When Critics Ask*; Archer, *Encyclopedia of Bible Difficulties*; Arndt, New International Encyclopedia of Bible Difficulties; Haley, *Alleged Discrepancies of the Bible*.

[19] John Murray, *Principles of Conduct* (Grand Rapids: Eerdmans, 1957), 123, quoted in Frame, *The Doctrine of God*, 476.

[20] The expression is Augustine's and earlier Church Fathers; used as book title by Holmes, *All Truth is God's Truth*.

[21] I Corinthians. 3:19; 1:20; cf. Dunn, *The Theology of Paul the Apostle*, 73-5, 82-3.

[22] Cf. Oden, *The Word of Life; Systematic Theology*, 69-74, 199-205, with ref. to T. W. Manson, *Studies in the Gospels and Epistles*, 118; Barrett, *The Gospel According to John*, 27-66, esp. 34-41, 39; Dunn, *Christology in the Making*, 163-250; McKinney, ed., *Creation, Christ, and Culture*, Chapters 3-4.

[23] Thilly, *A History of Philosophy*, 103, 99-103; *Aristotle's Categories and De Interpretatione*, 4, 1b25-2a4; *Aristotle's Topics, Books I and VIII*, I.9, 103b20-25; cf. note 72.

[24] Veatch, *Aristotle; A Contemporary Appreciation*, 80-89; cf. Wilhelmsen, *Man's Knowledge of Reality; An Introduction to Thomistic Epistemology*.

[25] Weber, *History of Philosophy*, 81-134; 108; Aristotle, *Physics* II, 194b, 190b; *Metaphysics*, 1010a, 1013a, 1036a, 1050b, 1084b; *On the Soul*, III, 431b-432a; II, 412a; *On Generation and Corruption*, II, 335b; cf. Veatch, ibid.

[26] Thilly, *A History of Philosophy*, 103.

[27] Armstrong and Markus, *Christian Faith and Greek Philosophy*, 2, 7.

[28] Barrett, *The Gospel According to John*, 12; cf. *"logos," "nous,"* in Peters, *Greek Philosophical Terms*; Owens, *History of Ancient Western Philosophy*; Armstrong, *Introduction to Ancient Philosophy*; Armstrong and Markus, *Christian Faith and Greek Philosophy*; Thilly, *A History of Philosophy*; Weber, *History of Philosophy*.

[29] C. K. Barrett, *The Gospel According to John*, 12-13.

[30] Carl F. H. Henry, *God, Revelation and Authority*, III, 167-68.

[31] Ibid., V, 336.

[32] Ibid., V, 355, with ref. to Spier, *Christianity and Existentialism*, 125).

[33] Ibid. V, 355, quoting W. T. Conner, *Revelation and God: An Introduction to Christian Doctrine* (Nashville: Broadman Press, 1936), 62.

[34] Henry, *God, Revelation and Authority*, III, 192.

[35] Ibid., V, 334, 335, 336, 337, 383; William Temple, *Basic Convictions* (New York: Harper, 1936), 54.

[36] Henry, *God, Revelation and Authority*, V, 383.

[37] Ibid., V, 338, 383.

[38] Ibid., III, 165, quoting Gordon H. Clark, *Karl Barth's Theological Method* (Nutley, NJ: Presbyterian and Reformed Publishing Co., 1963), 112.

[39] Henry, *God, Revelation and Authority*, III, 167-68, 171, emphasis added.

40 Sheen, *Philosophy of Religion*, 168-169; refs. to Aquinas, *Sum. Theol.*, Part I, q. 14, a. 8, ad. 3; I, q. 16, a. 5; I, q. 104, a. 3; *Contra Gentiles*, Book III, 47; cf. Wilhelmsen, *Man's Knowledge of Reality*.

41 In addition to Sheen, *Philosophy of Religion*, see Henry, *God, Revelation and Authority*, I, 323-343; B. Warfield, *Studies in Tertullian and Augustine*; Hoitenga, *Faith and Reason from Plato to Plantinga;* Etienne Gilson and Thomas Langan, *A History of Modern Philosophy*; Murphy, Donlan, Reidy, Cunningham, *God and His Creation*, 436-38.

42 Henry, *God, Revelation and Authority*, I, 325-26.

43 Augustine, *Eighty-Three Different Questions*, 46, 1-2; Nash, *The Light of the Mind: St. Augustine's Theory of Knowledge*, 6.

44 Nash, *The Light of the Mind*, 6-7, viii.

45 Ibid., emphasis added.

46 Ibid., 76-77.

47 Ibid., 77-8, 81-4.

48 Ibid., 111, quoting B. B. Warfield, *Calvin and Augustine*, 397.

49 Aquinas, *The Commentary to the Sentences*, II, d. 12. q. 1, a. 3 ad 5m; Battista Mondin, *St. Thomas Aquinas' Philosophy* (The Hague: Nijhoff, 1975), 27.

50 Mondin, *St. Thomas Aquinas' Philosophy*, 28-9; Gardeil, *Introduction to the Philosophy of St. Thomas Aquinas, IV. Metaphysics*, 135-37.

51 Mondin, *St. Thomas Aquinas' Philosophy*, 28-9; St. Thomas Aquinas, *Truth*, tr. Robert W. Mulligan, I Sent. d. 19, q. 5, a. 1; Gardeil, *Introduction to the Philosophy of St. Thomas Aquinas*, emphases added.

52 This slightly modified translation from Aquinas's *Truth* (*De Veritate*), 1, 1, is derived from those in *An Introduction to the Metaphysics of St. Thomas Aquinas*, tr. James F. Anderson, 61, and Aquinas, *Truth*, tr. Robert W. Mulligan, vol. I, 6-7.

53 Mondin, *St. Thomas Aquinas' Philosophy*, 28-9, and Aquinas, *Truth*, tr. Robert W. Mulligan, I Sent. d. 19, q. 5, a. 1.

54 Gardeil, *Introduction to the Philosophy of St. Thomas Aquinas*, 61; cf. Mondin, *St. Thomas Aquinas' Philosophy*, 28-9, and Aquinas, I Sent. d. 19, q. 5, a. 1.

55 Benignus, *Nature, Knowledge, and God*, 375-76; Aquinas, Sum. Theol., I, 16, 6, c; De Veritate, I, 8, c.

56 Benignus, *Nature, Knowledge, and God*, Part II, Ch. XI, esp. 232-33, 215, 228-35, emphases added. These points are more fully explained in this Chapter of Benignus's book, which is a clear introduction to Thomistic thought.

57 Aquinas, III Sent., d. 33, q. 1, a. 3, sol. 3; I Sent., d. 19, q. 5, a. 1; Mondin, *St. Thomas Aquinas' Philosophy*, 30-1.

58 For understandings of the historical and theological significance of this difference, see Henry, *God, Revelation and Authority*, I, 36, 78, 86-88, 280-88, 321-347, and Nash, *The Light of the Mind*, 94-111.

59 Gardeil, *Introduction to the Philosophy of St. Thomas Aquinas*, 26-27.

60 Henry, *God, Revelation and Authority*, III, 169, quoting Francis Parker, "Traditional Reason and Modern Reason," 41, 46. Cf. Parker, *The Story of Western Philosophy*.

61 Henry, *God, Revelation and Authority*, quoting Parker, "Traditional Reason and Modern Reason," 46, 41, 47.

[62] II Tim. 3:7, NKJV.

[63] John 14:6; F. H. Palmer, "Truth," *The New Bible Dictionary*, 3rd ed., 1301.

[64] Strong, *Systematic Theology*, 311.

Chapter Six

[1] William Barrett, *The Illusion of Technique*, 126.

[2] A survey of January 2000 showed that 62% of Americans did not believe in any absolute moral truth. And not long after 09-11-01 the number rose to 78 %. Another survey in the Fall of 2006 showed that only about 33% of Americans under 40 held belief in any absolute truth. About 50 % of this age group also indicated that morals should be based on "what is right for the person" (George Barna surveys: January 2000, November 26, 2001, and October 31, 2006, at www.barna.org). For an excellent treatment of modern relativism, see William D. Gairdner, *The Book of Absolutes; A Critique of Relativism and a Defense of Universals.*

[3] The growing contrasts of modern thought and art with biblical and traditional Christian teachings can best be understood by comparing them with Christian and classical metaphysics. Compare the increasingly extreme views of modern and postmodern ones treated in Chapters Six, Seven, and Eight with Christian and classical ones in Chapters Four and Five on topics such as God's Being, Wisdom, Logos, divine creation, divine structuring of creation, and the reality of substances, essences, universals, reason, truth, and knowledge.

[4] See the excellent historical analysis by Baumer, *Modern European Thought, 1600-1950.*

[5] Richard Swinburne, *The Existence of God* (Oxford: Clarendon Press, 2004), 2.

[6] Peter A. Schouls, *Descartes and the Enlightenment*, 3-8, 13, 63; 77-127, passim; "Descartes As Revolutionary," 4-23; *The Imposition of Method, A Study of Descartes and Locke*, emphasis added.

[7] As indicated in Chapters One, Two, and Three, naturalist and materialist claims that go beyond the legitimate bounds of science have no authority as science, or claim as actual fact. Some of these claims also stand in opposition to another, polar side of modernism that centers on the self. Both philosophies reject the God of the Bible and turn to nature, matter, or the self as primal ultimates. Instead of working from an accumulation of smaller facts up to an ultimate (which is impossible), they work from an ultimate hypothesis downward. When such philosophies are taken into the sciences, the result is "scientism," which steps beyond the proper bounds of the sciences. Naturalism and materialism are a major side of modernism, standing in polar opposition to the subjective pole of modernity that begins with Descartes (Chapters Six, Seven, and Eight). These poles can be identified as "subject vs. object"; "subjectivism vs. naturalism, materialism"; "self vs. world"; "arts vs. sciences." Since both modern poles tend to reject the Absolute God of the Bible as a first principle, neither has any ultimate and unifying ground, only philosophical *theory*. There is also a split, a gap, between the two poles that is characteristic of modernity (beginning

with Descartes). It is a gap and polar oppositon resulting from rejection of the unifying Being, Truth, and Authority of God as first principle.

8   Maritain, *The Dream of Descartes*, 170-72. E. J. Ashworth, "Descartes' Theory of Objective Reality," 333-34: "In postulating "an isolated mind contemplating its own contents in order to reach out beyond them," Descartes certainly "cannot assume that his ideas, or he himself, need a cause. They are there and no more can be said."

9   See Caton, *The Origin of Subjectivity*, 1973), 10-20, esp. 12, passim; Dalia Judovitz, *Subjectivity and Representation in Descartes; the Origins of Modernity*, 32-34, 71, 76-77, 93- 97, 119-26, 150-52, 161, 174-78, 180-82, passim.

10 Schouls, *Descartes and the Enlightenment*, 60.

11 Caton, *The Origin of Subjectivity*, 124-25, 11, quoting Gerhard Krüger, "Die Herkunft des philosophischen Selbstwusstseins," 246.

12 Schouls, *Descartes and the Enlightenment*, 60-62; Pascal, *Pensées*, Section 2, no. 77, p. 26; Maritain, *The Dream of Descartes*, 44. Fordiscussion at length of Descartes's arguments concerning a veracious or deceiver God or demon, relative to reason, see Caton, *The Origin of Subjectivity*, Chapter 4, and p. 116.

13 Maritain, *The Dream of Descartes*, 170-72, 176, emphasis added.

14 Ibid.

15 Roger Ariew and Marjorie Grene, "Ideas in and Before Descartes," *Journal of the History of Ideas* (1995): 87-88. Compare the Christian use of "idea" on p.111-12.

16 Ibid., 93, 97, 100, 95, 98, 103.

17 Ibid., 101, 104, 105, 95, 106.

18 Barrett, *Irrational Man*, 202, 203, 216, 232-33; Idem. *The Illusion of Technique*, 126, 127, 128, 121-25. And see Cahoone, *The Dilemma of Modernity*, 17-174, passim. Robert E. McCall, *The Reality of Substance*, 3-18, 48-54.

19 Maritain, *The Dream of Descartes*, 177, 182.

20 Gay, *The Enlightenment*, II, 171, 168, 174.

21 These concepts draw on the writings of Schouls: *Descartes and the Enlightenment*; "Descartes As Revolutionary," 4-23; Gilson and Langan, *Modern Philosophy, Descartes to Kant*; and the writings of Caton, Judovitz, William Barrett, and Maritain, listed above.

22 Gay, *The Enlightenment*, II, 171, 172.

23 Diderot quoted in Baumer, *Modern European Thought*, 152; Diderot, art. *Encyclopédie*; Rev. 1:8;

24 Baumer, *Modern European Thought, 1600-1950*, 160.

25 Thilly, *A History of Philosophy*, 376.

26 Hume, *A Treatise of Human Nature*, bk. 1, pt. 1, sec. 7; pt. 2, sec. 7; pt. 3, sec. 7.

27 Thilly, *A History of Philosophy*, 374-5, 376; cf. McCall, *The Reality of Substance*, 7-12.

28 Hume, *A Treatise of Human Nature*, bk. 1, pt. 4, sec. 2, emphases added; cf. McCall, ibid., 10-11. If reason is attributed only to the human mind, as it increasingly was through the seventeenth and eighteenth centuries, it is obvious that reason and nature become "enemies." But such an attribution is only an unprovable assertion, and is rejected by Christian thought and doctrine.

29 Ibid., bk. 1, pt. 4, secs. 2, 5, 6; cf. McCall, *The Reality of Substance*, 11.

30 McCall, *The Reality of Substance*, 12. Hume, *A Treatise of Human Nature*, bk. I, pt. 4, sec. 5.

31 Gaskin, "Hume on religion," *The Cambridge Companion to Hume*, ed. Norton, 318-22; cf. 18, 20-1. Gaskin adds that because of Hume's view of the "limitations of human understanding" and his own caution regarding the question of the being and nature of God, he was "unable to advocate straightforward atheism," and Gaskin has characterized Hume's "emasculated concession to the proposition 'there is a god'" as an "attenuated deism," which left "no more than a dim possibility that some non-providential god exists." See also Rausch, "Hume, David," *Evangelical Dictionary of Theology*, 536.

32 Gay, *The Enlightenment*, I, 401, 417-19.

33 Solomon, *From Rationalism to Existentialism*, 7.

34 Pippin, *Modernism as a Philosophical Problem*, 12, 10, 46-61. Cf. his *Idealism as Modernism*, 5, 7, 216, 24; and see other sections on Kant, German Idealism, and the central issues of autonomy, freedom, and self-determination in these books.

35 Pippin, *Modernism as a Philosophical Problem*, 47.

36 Thielicke, *The Evangelical Faith; Volume I*, 34.

37 Van Til, *Christianity and Barthianism*, 247-48.

38 Stählin, *Kant, Lotze, and Ritschl*, 80-81.

39 Wilburn, *The Historical Shape of Faith*, 70.

40 Kasper, *The God of Jesus Christ* (New York: Crossroad, 1986), 21-22; cf. Kaufmann, *Goethe, Kant, and Hegel*, 88.

41 Kant, *Critique of Pure Reason*, tr. Müller, A 670-71 B 698-99, pp. 439-40 third and fourth italics added for emphasis; cf. Kant, *Critique of Pure Reason*, tr. and ed. Guyer and Wood, pp. 605-6; and esp. A619-20: B647-48.

42 *Critique of Pure Reason*, tr. Müller, A 685 B 713, pp. 447-48.

43 Henry, *God, Revelation and Authority*, V, 30; Stählin, *Kant, Lotze, and Ritschl*, 25, 275.

44 Gilkey, "God, Idea of, Since 1800," *Dictionary of the History of Ideas*. II, 357; cf. Kasper, *The God of Jesus Christ*, 16-46.

45 Cassirer, *Kant's Life and Thought*, 212-13, 264-65. Kant; *Critique of Pure Reason*, tr. Müller,. A510/B538; A582/B 610 f. Kant, "The Existence of God as a Postulate of Pure Practical Reason," *Critique of Practical Reason*, (V, 136) (Ak. V, 124). Kant, *Critique of Judgment*, tr. J. H. Bernard, secs. 87, 88).

46 Wood, *Kant's Rational Theology* (Ithaca: Cornell, 1978), 16. Idem, *"Traditional Theology, moral faith, and Religion,"* In *The Cambridge Companion to Kant*, 396 ff.

47 *Religion within the Limits of Reason Alone*, tr. Greene and Hudson, 54-128. Falckenberg, *History of Modern Philosophy*, 395-96. Höffding, *History of Modern Philosophy*, II, 100-3.

48 Kaufmann, *Goethe, Kant, and Hegel*, 87-90.

49 Henry, *God, Revelation and Authority*, vol. I, 353; 344-63, emphases added.

50 Parker, *The Story of Western Philosophy*, 270-71, emphasis added; *Critique of Pure Reason*, tr. Müller, Preface to the Second Edition, xxxiii; cf. Joseph Owens, *Cognition*, 9: "Taking the lead given by Hume's tenet that the notion of causality

was imposed upon objects by the knower, the German philosopher extended this viewpoint to all the universal and necessary aspects found in experience."

51 For Kant's revolutionary restriction of the forms and categories to subjective human sensibility and understanding, see the *Critique of Pure Reason*, especially B146-51; A 125-28; B 164-68; A 248-60 B 304-315; A 146-47 B 186-87; A 30-2 B46-8; A 46-9 B 64-7; B xxvi-xxvii (for more citations and related quotations concerning the various forms and categories, see the Introduction and Index to the *Critique of Pure Reason*, tr. and ed. Guyer and Wood. But Kant himself was at times ambiguous and self-contradictory relative to his own foundations.

52 Thielicke, *The Evangelical Faith; Volume I*, 49-53, 51, emphases added.

53 Rosenblum and Janson, *19ᵗʰ-Century Art*, 59-60. "Arch-non-conformist," Honour, *Romanticism*, 286.

54 Frye, *A Study of English Romanticism*, 42 et. seq. Tannenbaum, *Biblical Tradition in Blake's Early Prophecies*, 201-224; Rosenblum, *Modern Painting and the Northern Romantic Tradition*, 42.

55 Damon, *William Blake*, 116.

56 Tannenbaum, *Biblical Tradition in Blake's Early Prophecies*, 201-204, 206, 210; this book is one of the best, detailed sources on Blake's revision, inversion, and satire of the Bible.

57 Kathleen Raine, *William Blake* (New York: Praeger, 1971), 78, 156.

58 Vaughan, *Romantic Art*, 73; Damon, *William Blake*, 213.

59 Vaughan, *Romantic Art*.

60 *The Marriage of Heaven and Hell*, in *Blake Complete Writings*, ed. Keynes.

61 Lindsay, *William Blake*, xiv. Lindsay gives a good, overall interpretation and analysis of Blake's work and thought, more comprehensive and balanced than some more specialized works.

62 See Frye, *A Study of English Romanticism*. esp. 13-14, 87-89. The book as a whole analyzes the sweeping changes brought by the "imaginative revolution" of Romanticism (p. 15) although Frye interprets it from a perspective sympathetic with Romanticism, and discusses it in terms of a shift in "mythological" views. See also his *Romanticism Reconsidered*, 16-19; and see Ferber, *The Poetry of Shelley*, esp. 13, 15-19, 52-3, 56-7, 59-60, 61-3, 82-3, 85, 87, 89; McGann, *Fiery Dust*, esp. 247-55.

63 The points on Shelley in this and the previous paragraph are based on the analysis by Frye in *A Study of English Romanticism*, esp. pp. 100-101, 13-15, 20. See also Ferber, *The Poetry of Shelley*, esp. 13, 15-19, 52-3, 56-7, 59-60, 61-3, 82-3, 85, 87, 89.

64 Cf. Ferber, *The Poetry of Shelley*, 83-85, 87, 69, 56; Shelley, "Preface to *Prometheus Unbound*," *Shelley's Critical Prose*, 64; *Queen Mab*, IV.210.

65 "Preface to *Prometheus Unbound*," ibid., 66.

66 The material on Byron's opposition to key Christian doctrines is derived from McGann, *Fiery Dust*, 247-55, which draws on, among other things, *His Very Self and Voice*, ed. Ernest J. Lovell, Jr., New York, 1954, 437, 446-47, 568-69; cf. Ehrstine, *The Metaphysics of Byron*, 1-14, passim.

67 McGann, *Fiery Dust*, 250-51.

68 Ibid.

69 Ibid., 249, 251, 252-53; *The Works of Lord Byron: Letters and Journals*, ed. Roland E. Prothero, 6 vols., London, 1898-1901, 6:38-39.

70 McGann, *Fiery Dust*, 260-61.

71 A short, penetrating analysis of Hegel's complex thought is given in Caponigri, *History of Western Philosophy*, III, 518-72. On *Geist*, will, freedom, and *Begriff*, see Schacht, "Hegel on Freedom," in *Hegel*, ed. MacIntyre, esp. 289, 304-5. On *Begriff* and history, see Pippin, *Idealism as Modernism*, 76-78. Wartenburg, "Hegel's Idealism," 102-3.

72 Caponigri, *History of Western Philosophy*, III, 565, 533.

73 Cf. Taylor, *Hegel*, 56-60, 207-11; Hegel, "The Positivity of Christianity" (1795-96), and "The Spirit of Christianity and its Fate" (1799-1800), in *Early Theological Writings, G. W. F. Hegel*. Cf. Hegel, *Phenomenology of Spirit*, § 527-528.

74 Bowie, *Schelling*, 1-3. On the end of metaphysics also see Pippin, *Idealism as Modernism*, 52-53, and Redner, *Ends of Philosophy*, chs. 2-4.

75 Zeitlin, *Nietzsche*, back cover and p. vii.

76 Karl, *Modern and Modernism*, 84, 81, 119.

77 E.g., Megill, *Prophets of Extremity*, 1.

78 *Gay Science*, tr. Kaufmann, sect. 110, p. 169.

79 *Twilight of the Idols and The Anti-Christ*, tr. Hollingdale, Foreword, 21.

80 Collins, *History of Modern European Philosophy*, 787; Collins gives a good short analysis of Nietzsche's philosophy, 774-808.

81 Redner, *The Ends of Philosophy*, 3, 28 n 8, 11-13, 48-49, 106-107, 250, 303.

82 *The Will to Power*, sec. 200.

83 *Twilight of the Idols and The Anti-Christ*, sec. 27, p. 139.

84 *The Will to Power*, sec. 1, pp. 158-252.

85 Zeitlin, *Nietzsche; A Re-examination*, 4.

86 Barrett, *Irrational Man*, 203-4.

87 Jaspers, quoting Nietzsche, in *Nietzsche*, 242.

88 For a good discussion of the nature of this nihilism and how Nietzsche felt it, see Küng, *Does God Exist?*, 387-94; cf. the discussion by Pippin, "'Nihilism Stands at the Door': Nietzsche," ch. 4 in *Modernism as a Philosophical Problem*.

89 Collins, *History of Modern European Philosophy*, 786.

90 *Twilight of the Idols and the Antichrist*, IV, sec. four, p. 37; VII, sec. 8, p. 54.

91 *Ibid.*, sec. 18, p. 128.

92 Ibid., secs. 62, 61, 15, pp. 184-187, 125.

93 Ibid., sec. 49, p. 165; cf. *The Will to Power*, sec. 169; cf. Haar, *Nietzsche and Metaphysics*, 133, 138.

94 *Twilight of the Idols*, IV, section 2, 5, pp. 36, 37-38.

95 Haar, *Nietzsche and Metaphysics*, 4, cf. 2-3; 34-5, 83-111.

96 Ibid., sec. 109, p. 168; cf. Zeitlin, ibid., 5-6.

97 Collins, ibid., 789, 790; cf. Richardson, *Nietzsche's System*, 20, 21, 17: will to power is "most basically applied not to people but to 'drives' or 'forces', simpler units which Nietzsche sometimes even calls 'points' and 'power quanta.' . . . . Nietzsche takes the units of will to power to be deeply diverse in their types,

differentiated by their distinctive efforts or tendencies." "Things 'really are' will to power and really do have whatever structural features this implies, whereas all their other properties are true of them only relative to some perspective." But the "structural features" of will to power are the structureless opposites of traditional theological and metaphysical structures of cosmos and things of the world—no God or Being; no creating, guiding, and governing divine or cosmic Mind; no mediating, structuring, revealing, and saving Logos; no sustaining, guiding, and empowering Holy Spirit; and no substance, essence, unity, identity, rationality, self, soul, world, things, stable end goal; and no eternal or enduring truth, beauty, or goodness, etc.

98 See Chapter 5 above.

99 Haar, *Nietzsche and Metaphysics*, 5, 7; Nietzsche, *Beyond Good and Evil*, sec. 186; *On the Genealogy of Morals*, Second Essay, sec. 12; *The Will to Power*, secs. 874, 715; Kröner's Taschenausgabe, 2 vols. (Stuttgart: Kröner Verlag, 1956), II, sec. 874; cf. Richardson, *Nietzsche's System*, esp. Chapter 1.

100 Collins, *History of Modern European Philosophy*, 800.

101 *On the Genealogy of Morals; Ecce Homo*, p. 335; cf. *The Will to Power*, section 1052.

102 *The Birth of Tragedy*, tr. Kaufmann, sec. 25, p. 143; sec. 1, p. 36, 37.

103 Kaufmann, *Nietzsche; Philosopher, Psychologist, Antichrist*, 128, 129.

104 The expression is used by Baumer to characterize twentieth-century culture from about the end of World War I onward: *Modern European Thought*, Part V, Chapter 1, esp. p. 402.

105 Ibid., 381.

106 Collins, *History of Modern European Philosophy*, 785; cf. Richardson, *Nietzsche's System*, Chapter 2.

107 *Twilight of the Idols*, sec. 4.2, p. 36.

108 *The Will to Power*, sec. 567.

109 *Beyond Good and Evil*, sec. 12; cf. *Twilight of the Idols*, IV, sec. 2, p. 36: "the lie of unity, the lie of materiality, of substance, of duration"; cf. Young, *Nietzsche's Philosophy of Art*, 63.

110 *The Will to Power*, secs. 616, 604, 634, 556, 555, 558, 560, 545; first, second, third, fifth, and sixth emphases added; cf. Salter, *Nietzsche the Thinker*, 182-201; and Love, *Marx, Nietzsche, and Modernity*, 47-49.

111 *The Will to Power*, sec. 1067; Nietzsche's view of "the world" as Dionysian force and Will to Power seems to be most directly and fully stated here.

112 Smith, *Nietzsche, Heidegger, and the Transition to Postmodernism*, ibid., 101-2, 132, emphasis added; bracket material added.

113 Ibid., 130.

114 Baumer, *Modern European Thought*, 402-4.

115 Ibid., 410-15.

Chapter Seven

1 Luciano Berio, in *Marcel Duchamp; Work and Life*, ed. Hulten, Cambridge, MA: MIT Press, 1993, 21.

2   Early twentieth-century modern art and thought (from about 1900 through 1950, and later) is very diverse and complex. Since the subject is far too large to deal with in one chapter, I have chosen to discuss four of the most extreme or radical expressions, Dada, Duchamp, Heidegger, and Wittgenstein. These four have also turned out to be some of the strongest influences on art and thought of the later twentieth-century and up to the present (indicated in Chapter Eight). The views of two other major modern artists, Picasso and Ernst, are described in Chapter One.

3   The growing contrasts of modern thought and art with biblical and traditional Christian teachings can best be understood by comparing them with Christian and classical metaphysics. Compare the increasingly extreme views of modern and postmodern ones treated in Chapters Six, Seven, and Eight with Christian and classical ones in Chapters Four and Five on topics such as God's Being, Wisdom, Logos, divine creation, divine structuring of creation, and the reality of substances, essences, universals, reason, truth, and knowledge.

4   Steefel, *The Position of Duchamp's Glass*, 34.

5   Richter, *Dada Art and Anti-Art*, 87.

6   Steefel, *The Position of Duchamp's Glass*, 52, 53-54.

7   Ibid., 35.

8   Gaston de Pawlowski, *Voyage au pays de la quatrième dimension* (Paris, 1912; *Voyage to the Land of Fourth Dimension*); W. Rubin, *Dada, Surrealism, and Their Heritage*, 17.

9   Ibid.

10 Lippard, ed., *Dadas on Art*, 8-9.

11 Color reproduction in *Marcel Duchamp*, ed. Anne D'Harnoncourt and Kynaston McShine (Munich: Prestel / MoMA, 1989), facing p. 128.

12 *"Elle a chaud au cul!"* ("She has a hot a_ _!").

13 www:mirriam-webster.com/dictionary/nihilism. Cf. American Heritage Dictionary.

14 Color reproduction in *Marcel Duchamp; Work and Life*, ed. Hulten, 79.

15 Luciano Berio, in *Marcel Duchamp; Work and Life*, ed. Hulten, 21.

16 Tomkins, *Duchamp*, 122.

17 E. g., Perotti, *Heidegger on the Divine*, 4; Vycinas, *Earth and Gods*, 317; Barrett, *Irrational Man*, 209.

18 Vycinas, *Earth and Gods*, 317.

19 Perotti, *Heidegger on the Divine*, 31-32.

20 Ibid., 56, 57.

21 Heidegger, "The Way Back into the Ground of Metaphysics," *Existentialism from Dostoevsky to Sartre*, 209; Perotti, *Heidegger on the Divine*, 56-57, 70 n7.

22 Perotti, *Heidegger on the Divine*, Chapter 4: "Overcoming Metaphysics and Theology."

23 Cf. Vycinas, *Earth and Gods*, 10; for a longer discussion of Heidegger's "destruction" of metaphysics, see Redner, *The Ends of Philosophy*, 123-133.

24 Vycinas, *Earth and Gods*, 42, n. 46; emphases added.

25 Perotti, *Heidegger on the Divine*, 56, 70 n. 4;

26 Ibid., 62; Heidegger, *Kant and the Problem of Metaphysics*, Translated by James Churchill, 13.

27 Perotti, ibid., 65; emphasis added.

28 Cf. Vycinas, *Earth and Gods*, 316.

29 Perotti, *Heidegger on the Divine*, 61, 62; Heidegger, *An Introduction to Metaphysics*, 6, 1.

30 Ibid., 56.

31 Ibid., 58.

32 Ibid., 63, 56; emphasis added.

33 Redner, *The Ends of Philosophy*, 5.

34 *After Philosophy; End or Transformation.*

35 Heidegger's inversion is somewhat similar to Hegel's. For Heidegger, "Being" arises out of human existence, rather than human existence being created and grounded by God the Supreme Being. For Hegel, mankind actualizes and produces the full, comprehensive reality of Spirit, Being, or God (Geist) by progressively evolving and realizing "adequate concepts" throughout history. The difference is that Hegel's philosophy apotheosizes spirit, mind, Idea, and reason, while Heidegger's deflates reason and elevates human existence, thrown out of nothingness. Heidegger's philosophy lacks the remaining transcendence of Hegel's.

36 Heidegger. *Being and Time*, 42.

37 Scott. Mirrors *of Man in Existentialism*, 115, 102.

38 Bochenski, *Contemporary European Philosophy*, 1965, 171; cf. Heidegger, "What is Metaphysics," in *Existence and Being*, 337-349.

39 Olafson, "Sartre, Jean-Paul," in *Encyclopedia of Philosophy*, ed. Edwards, VII, 291.

40 Barrett, *Irrational Man*, 226.

41 Ibid., 346. Heidegger here quotes Hegel, "The Science of Logic," I, WW III, 74; emphasis added.

42 Cf. Perotti, *Heidegger on the Divine*, 16; cf. Heidegger, "What is Metaphysics," 339, 347.

43 Vycinas, *Earth and Gods*, 107; cf. 102-109.

44 Schulz, *Der Gott der Neuzeitlichen Metaphysik*, 44.

45 Cf. "What is Metaphysics," 339.

46 Perotti, *Heidegger on the Divine*, 35; emphases added.

47 Vycinas, *Earth and Gods*, 3; key works by Heidegger are *Being and Time*, and "What is Metaphysics?"

48 Baumer, *Modern European Thought*, 436.

49 Heidegger, *Being and Time*, p. 431.

50 Scott, *Mirrors of Man in Existentialism*, 100.

51 Perotti, *Heidegger on the Divine*, 34; *Being and Time* (*Sein und Zeit*, 1927; *The Question of Being* (*Zur Seinsfrage*, 1955); *Letter on Humanism* (*Brief über den Humanismus*, 1949).

52 Baumer, *Modern European Thought*, 21; also see Pt. V, Chapter 1, "The Triumph of Becoming."

53 Perotti, *Heidegger on the Divine*, 34, 35-36.

54   See *Being and Time*, e.g., H. 237-52, 182-92, 342-45, 382-87, 326-32, 379, 387-97, 405-46.

55   *Being and Time*, p. 233, emphasis added.

56   Thomas Guarino, "Postmodernity and Five Fundamental Theological Issues," *Theological Studies* 57 (1996), 655-56, 661.

57   Perotti, *Heidegger on the Divine*, 31-32.

58   Vycinas, *Earth and Gods*, 25.

59   See Perotti, ibid., 29-32.

60   Quoted in Barrett, *Irrational Man*, 206; emphasis added.

61   Perotti, *Heidegger on the Divine*, 77-80; Heidegger, *Introduction to Metaphysics*; "What is Philosophy," *Vorträge und Aufsätze*, Teil II.

62   Heidegger, however, tries to make the case that "Being," "as contrasted with becoming, is permanence, permanent presence. Contrasted with appearance, it is appearing, manifest presence." See *An Introduction to Metaphysics*, 106-113; 156-159.

63   Redner, *Ends of Philosophy*, 217-237.

64   Ibid., 235.

65   Wittgenstein, *Tractatus Logico-Philosophicus*, tr. Pears and McGuinniss, pp. 3-4; secs. 6.42, 6.53-54; Redner, *Ends of Philosophy*, 187.

66   Wittgenstein, *Philosophical Investigations*, remark 309, p. 103; remark 120, p. 49; p. 226; Redner, *Ends of Philosophy*, 235; Linn, *A Teacher's Introduction to Postmodernism*, xv, 21-27.

67   Redner, *Ends of Philosophy*, 233-36.

68   Ibid., 234; Diels, *Fragmente der Vorsokratiker*, 76B, 553-4.

69   Redner, *Ends of Philosophy*, 234-36.

70   See Fergus Kerr, "Metaphysics and Magic: Wittgenstein's Kink," *Post-Secular Philosophy*, Blond, ed., 240-57, esp. 250-57, on which much of this paragraph is based; cf. Wittgenstein, *Culture and Value*. 33.

Chapter Eight

1   Baudrillard, *Transparency of Evil*, London: Verso, 1993, 11, 14, 15, 16.

2   See these terms in the Glossary.

3   The growing contrasts of modern thought and art with biblical and traditional Christian teachings can best be understood by comparing them with Christian and classical metaphysics. Compare the increasingly extreme views of modernism and Postmodernism treated in Chapters Six, Seven, and Eight with Christian and classical beliefs in Chapters Four and Five on topics such as God's Being, Wisdom, Logos, spirit, divine creation, divine structuring of creation, and the reality of substances, essences, universals, reason, truth, and knowledge. And see the Glossary.

4   Rorty, *Consequences of Pragmatism*, 1982, x-xx; idem, *Philosophy and the Mirror of Nature*; cf. Linn, *A Teacher's Introduction to Postmodernism*, 29-30.

5   Rorty, *Consequences of Pragmatism*, x-xx; idem, *Contingency, Irony, and Solidarity*, 80; Linn, *A Teacher's Introduction to Postmodernism*, xv, 28-29, 30-35.

6   Rorty, *Philosophy and the Mirror of Nature*.

7   Rorty, "Does Academic Freedom Have Philosophical Presuppositions?" *Academe* 80.6 (December): 56; Linn, *A Teacher's Introduction to Postmodernism*, 31.

8   Rorty, *Consequences of Pragmatism*, xiii-xiv.

9   Rorty, *Contingency, Irony, and Solidarity*, xv, 79-80; cf. Linn, *A Teacher's Introduction to Postmodernism*, 33-34, 36-37.

10 Rorty, "Universality and Truth," in Robert B. Brandom, ed., *Rorty and his Critics* (Oxford: Blackwell, 2000), 21-22.

11 See Structuralism in the Glossary.

12 Devitt, *Realism and Truth*, 235-36, viii-ix, 8, 249, and Chapters 9, 14. For the anti-Realism and "worldmaking" of Nelson Goodman, see his *Ways of World-making* (Indianapolis: Hackett, 1978; for other anti-Realists, see Devitt's bibliography.

13 Sandler, *The New York School*, 164-179.

14 A large number of pictures of Rauschenberg's art in color (including *Odalisk* and *Monogram*) can be seen on the Internet. Search Robert Rauschenberg at Yahoo, then click on robert rauschenberg paintings (then go to p. 10).

15 *Postmodern Arts*, ed. Nigel Wheale (London: Routledge, 1995), 44.

16 Cf. Sandler, *The New York School*, 140-144.

17 Merquior, *Foucault*, 148.

18 Ibid.

19 Guarino, "Postmodernity and Five Fundamental Theological Issues," esp. 655-56, 661.

20 Foucault, The Order of Things; An Archaeology of the Human Sciences; cf. Merquior, *Foucault*, 36-37.

21 Merquior, *Foucault*, 42, 41.

22 Foucault, *Archaeology of Knowledge*, 203.

23 Megill, *Prophets of Extremity*, 1985), 223.

24 Foucault, *L'Archaeologie du savoir*, 65;.*Archaeology of Knowledge*, 47.

25 Megill, *Prophets of Extremity*, 223-24.

26 Ibid., 231.

27 Ibid. 228; Peface to the second edition of Nietzsche's *The Gay Science*.

28 *Postmodern Arts*, ed. Nigel Wheale, 44.

29 Megill, *Prophets of Extremity*, 232-36.

30 Foucault, in *Language, Counter-Memory, Practice: Selected Essays and Interviews*, ed. Donald E. Bouchard (Ithaca, N.Y.: Cornell University Press, 1977), 160.

31 Megill, *Prophets of Extremity*, 233, 238-39.

32 Ibid., 224-25.

33 Redner, Ends of Philosophy, 296-98.

34 Derrida, "The Supplement of the Copula," 84; cf. Redner, *Ends of Philosophy*, 297.

35 Derrida, "The Supplement of the Copula,"83.

36 "Il n'y a pas de hors-texte," *Of Grammatology* (1976), 158; *De la Grammatologie* (Paris: Minuit, 1974), 227; cf. Megill, *Prophets of Extremity*, 266.

37 Cf. Megill, *Prophets of Extremity*, 269.

38 "I Have a Taste for the Secret," in Derrida and Maurizio Ferraris, *A Taste for the Secret*, 88; cited in Royle, *Jacques Derrida*, 7.

39   John 3:15-16; Acts 13:48; Romans 5:21, 6:23; Titus 1:2, 3:7; all of I John.

40   Cf. Royle, *Jacques Derrida*, 5.

41   John 1:1, "In the beginning was the Word [Greek, *logos*], and the Word was with God, and the Word was God." See Morris, *The Gospel According to John*, 72-87, 115-125. See Logos in the Glossary.

42   Derrida, *Margins of Philosophy*, 22; cited in Aylesworth, "Postmodernism," Stanford Encyclopedia of Philosophy, 15.

43   "Afterword: Toward an Ethic of Discussion," in *Limited Inc* (Evanston, IL: Northwestern University Press, 1988), 116; cf. Royle, *Jacques Derrida*, 5.

44   Redner, *Ends of Philosophy*, 259-260, 266.

45   Megill, *Prophets of Extremity*, 260-61.

46   See the informative 28-page article by Kellner, "Jean Baudrillard," in the online Stanford Encyclopedia of Philosophy, pp. 2-3.

47   Baudrillard, *The Consumer Society*, 1998, 190, 198; Kellner, "Jean Baudrillard," 3-5.

48   Kellner, "Jean Baudrillard," 6-8; Baudrillard, Review of Geroges Bataille's *Complete Works*, 1976, pp. 57, 60.

49   Kellner, "Jean Baudrillard," p. 10.

50   *Symbolic Exchange and Death*, 8; Kellner, "Jean Baudrillard," pp. 9-10; emphasis added.

51   Kellner, "Jean Baudrillard," 10.

52   Kellner, "Jean Baudrillard," 11, 12; idem., *Jean Baudrillard; From Marxism to Postmodernism and Beyond* (Stanford University Press, 1989), 63.

53   Baudrillard, *Symbolic Exchange and Death*, 125 [*L'echange symbolique et la mort*], Paris: Gallimard, 1976, 18.

54   Kellner, *Jean Baudrillard; From Marxism to Postmodernism and Beyond*, 63, emphases added.

55   Kellner, "Jean Baudrillard," Stanford Encyclopedia of Philosophy, p. 11.

56   Cf. Kellner, *Jean Baudrillard; From Marxism to Postmodernism and Beyond*, 60-64, 77, 80; Baudrillard, *Simulations*, 1983, 83-93, 96, 100-104, 111; idem., *L'echange symbolique et la mort*, 18-23.

57   Kellner, "Jean Baudrillard," Stanford Encyclopedia of Philosophy, p. 14-15.

58   Ibid., 16.

59   Baudrillard, *The Transparency of Evil*, 5-7.

60   Ibid., 8-10.

61   Ibid., 11, 14, 15, 16; bold type added for emphasis.

62   A large number of pictures of Lichtenstein's paintings in color can be seen on the Internet. Search Roy Lichtenstein at Yahoo, then click on roy lichtenstein paintings, or roy lichtenstein paintings new york. Also see a large selection of reproductions in Waldman, *Roy Lichtenstein*.

63   For much more about these meanings see Waldman, *Roy Lichtenstein*.

64   Ibid., 119.

65   Ibid., Figs. 101, 104, 105.

66   Ibid, 131.

67   Ibid., 137.

68 Ibid., Figs. 162, 164.

69 Ibid., 211.

70 Ibid., Figs. 170 and 173.

71 Waldman, *Roy Lichtenstein*, 355.

72 Ibid.

73 Kellner, ibid., 11, 12; idem., *Jean Baudrillard; From Marxism to Postmodernism and Beyond* (Stanford University Press, 1989), 63.

74 See the following books and make up our own mind: *Art Now*, ed. Uta Grosenick and Burkhard Riemschneider, Taschen, 2005; and *Art Now*, vol. 2, ed. Uta Grosenick, Taschen, 2006; Brandon Taylor, *Contemporary Art; Art Since 1970*, Upper Saddle River, NJ: Pearson/PrenticeHall, 2005); Eleanor Heartney, *Postmodernism*, Cambridge University Press, 2002; Linda Weintraub, Arthur Danto, Thomas McEvilley, *Art on and Over the Edge: Searching for Art's Meaning in Contemporary Society 1970s-1990s*, Litchfield, CT: Art Insights, Inc., 1996; David Hopkins, *After Modern Art 1945-2000*, Oxford University Press, 2000; *American Art Now*, Edward Lucie Smith, New York: William Morrow, 1985;. Klaus Honnef, *Contemporary Art*, Taschen, 1988.

75 On the Internet, search "David Salle" to find dozens of his paintings in color.

76 Both can be seen in color on the Internet.

77 www:moma.org, David Salle, "Muscular Paper." Accessed June 19, 2011.

78 Ibid.

79 For example, *His Brain*, 1984; *Saltimbanques*, 1986; *Gericault's Arm*, 1985; *Clean Glasses*, 1985; *Dual Aspect Picture*, 1986; *Before No Walk*, 1982. Scores of Salle's paintings can be seen in color on the Internet. Search David Salle at Yahoo, then click on David Salle Artist—Image Results.

80 Several examples can be seen in Honnef, *Contemporary Art*; Jonathan Fineberg, *Art Since 1940; Strategies of Being*, Prentice Hall, 1995; Art Now, Vol 2; and see the art works of David Salle, Jeff Koons, Eric Fischl, Lucian Freud, Cindy Sherman, Robert Arneson, Gladys Nilsson, Jim Nutt, Robert Mapplethorpe, Judy Chicago, Vito Acconci, Jenny Saville, Delmas Howe, Paul Georges, Rob Scholte, Ron Mueck, Lucie McKenzie, Lynn Randolph, Vanessa Beecroft, Thomas Ruff.

81 See "Carolee Schneemann" at wikipedia.org.

82 Ibid.; Robert C. Morgan., "Carolee Schneemann: The Politics of Eroticism," *Art Journal* 56, Winter 1997, 97-100; Carolee Schneemann, "The Obscene Body/Politic," *Art Journal* 50, Winter 1991), 28-35; Nancy Princenthal, "The arrogance of pleasure—body art, Carolee Schneemann," *Art in America*, October 1997.

83 Daniel Wheeler, *Art Since Mid-Century*, 317.

84 Heartney, *Postmodernism, 30*.

85 Megill, *Prophets of Extremity*, 1985), 223.

86 See text above on Foucault, pp. 207-210.

87 Wheeler, *Art Since Mid-Century*.

88 Weintraub, Danto, McEvilley, *Art on and Over the Edge*, 200.

89 Ibid., 202-3.

[90] Ibid., 201-2.
[91] A search on the Internet for "Jeff Koons" yields several sites with a large number of pictures of his works in color, e.g., "Jeff Koons Sculpture," showing "Puppy."
[92] "Jeff Koons," www.wikipedia.org, biographical dictionary.
[93] Weintraub, Linda. *Art on the Edge and Over*, 202-3; "Jeff Koons," www.wikipedia.org.
[94] Cf. *Postmodern Arts*, ed. Wheale, 43.

Chapter Nine

[1]   Frame, *The Doctrine of God*, 220.
[2]   Hitchens, *god is Not Great*, 17.
[3]   Ibid., 22-7.
[4]   Ibid., 64-5.
[5]   The quality and importance of the metaphysics of Augustine and Aquinas have been suggested above in Chapters IV and V, with numerous references given. What Hitchens says about them addresses none of the issues, and is so petty and prejudiced that it is hardly worth comment. Also see Robert Pasnau and Christopher Shields, *The Philosophy of Aquinas* (Boulder, Colorado: Westview Press, 2004).
[6]   Hitchens, *god is Not Great*, 64, 68.
[7]   Peter Gay, *The Enlightenment; An Interpretation* 2 vols. (New York: Knopf, 1966, 1969), II, 168.
[8]   Hitchens, *god is Not Great*, 70-71.
[9]   Geisler, *Systematic Theology*, Vol. Three (Minneapolis, MN: Bethany House, 2004), 111.
[10] Ibid., II, 367-69, 378 with biblical quotations.
[11] Ibid., Vol. Three, 87.
[12] Ibid., *Vol. Two*, 369.
[13] Ibid., Vol. Three, 86-7.
[14] Ibid., *Vol. Two*, 367-70, 378
[15] Frame, *The Doctrine of God*, 416.
[16] Ibid.
[17] Ibid., 229-30.
[18] Ibid., 402, 404, 406.
[19] Ibid., 410.
[20] Ibid., 416-19; Matthew 5:44; Ephesians 2:3; Romans 2:4.
[21] Ibid., 428; Acts 15:10-11; Romans 3:21-4; Galatians 2:21; Ephesians 2:8-9; II Timothy 1:9.
[22] Ibid., 437-41; Deuteronomy 6:5; Matthew 22:37; Ezekiel 16:8; Malachi 2:14; Hosea 1:3; Ezekiel 16; Ephesians. 5:22-33.
[23] Ibid., 608-11.
[24] Geisler, *Systematic Theology*, Vol. Two, 123.
[25] Ibid., 166.
[26] Frame, *The Doctrine of God*, 409.

27   *Why I Am Not a Christian*, 1927.

28   Bertrand Russell, "A Free Man's Worship," in *Mysticism and Logic*, London: Longman's, Green, 1950, 47. See also the views of George G. Simpson, Ernst Haeckel, Thomas Henry Huxley, Nietzsche, Duchamp, Heidegger, Julian Huxley, Christopher Hitchens, and Richard Dawkins on pp. 79, 85-6, 88, 93-4, 173-83, 186-93, 193-206, 246-48.

29   Similarly stated in Mark 12:29-31 and Luke 10:27-28.

30   *The MacArthur Study Bible*, note for Matthew 5:38.

31   *The NIV Study Bible*, note for Exodus 21:23-25.

32   *The MacArthur Study Bible*, note for Luke 6:29-35.

33   *The Apologetics Study Bible* (Nashville: Holman Bible Publishers, 2007): "Who Are You to Judge Others," p. 1417, and note for Matthew 7:1-2.

34   On God's sovereignty and providence, see Geisler, *Systematic Theology*, Vol. Two, Chs. 23-24; Frame's *The Doctrine of God*, Chs. 2-7, and 14; Grudem, *Systematic Theology*, Chapter 16.

35   Frame, *The Doctrine of God*, 276.

36   Ibid., 50-3, 47-102.

37   Ibid., 52; Proverbs 16:33; Jonah 1:7; Acts 1:23-26; Exodus 21:13; Judges 9:53; I Kings 22:34.

38   Geisler, *Systematic Theology*, Vol. Two, 537, 540-41, 543.

39   Grudem, *Systematic Theology*, 317, 315-50; Frame, *The Doctrine of God*, Chs. 3-5.

40   Frame, *The Doctrine of God*, 52; *Evangelical Dictionary of Biblical Theology*, 405; Matthew 5: 45; 6:26; chs. 8-10; 10:1, 29-30; 12:40; 16:21; 17:1-5, 9, 14-18, 22-23, 27; 18:20 (space); 28:20 (time); 19:28; 20:18-19, 34; 21:33-44; 24; John 9:1-41; 11:1-44.

41   Frame, *The Doctrine of God*, 59; and *No Other God*, 61-2.

42   Ibid.; Genesis 4:1, 25; 18:13-14; 25:21-23; 29:31-30:2; 30:17, 23-24; Deuteronomy. 10:22; Ruth 4:13; Psalms. 113:9; 127::3-5.

43   Cf. Romans 8:29-30; 9:23; I Corinthians 2:7; Ephesians 2:10.

44   Matthew 1:1-16.

45   For fuller treatment of the biblical covenants, see J. Conner and Malmin, *The Covenants*; W. J. Dumbrell, *Covenant and Creation*.

46   Genesis 17:4-5; *Evangelical Dictionary of Theology*, Walter A, Elwell, ed. (Grand Rapids: Baker, 1987, c. 1984), 6.

47   Genesis 16, and notes for 16:2 and 2:24 in *The Believer's Study Bible, NKJV Version*. Centuries later, David, also a man of great faith, and covenant, also violated God's basic ordinance for marriage, committed adultery, and was responsible for the death of the woman's husband. Thus, both men listed most prominently in the human ancestry of Christ, committed adultery. God forgave both of their sins, although both were punished.

48   The "angel of the Lord" speaks with the authority of God, and is addressed as God by Hagar; see the notes to Genesis 16:7 in *The Believer's Study Bible, NKJV Version, The NIV Study Bible*; and cf. Frame, *The Doctrine of God*, 633-34, and Kenneth A. Mathews, *The New American Commentary: Genesis 11:27-50:26* (Nashville: B & H Publishing, 2005), 188-89.

49 Mathews, ibid., 191.

50 Genesis 17:1-22; Mathews, ibid., 193.

51 There is some uncertainty and disagreement about a number of dates in the history of the Hebrew people. Dates used in this and the next two chapters are based on traditional and biblical ones indicated in the following sources: Walvoord and Zuck, *The Bible Knowledge Commentary, Old Testament* (which has some discussion of the differences in dating); Geisler, *A Popular Survey of the Old Testament*; *The NIV Study Bible* (which often gives possible alternatives).

52 Walvoord and Zuck, The *Bible Knowledge Commentary, Old Testament*, 109-110; Exodus 1:22, 2:9.

53 Genesis 36-47; Frame, *The Doctrine of God*, 54; *The Bible Knowledge Commentary, Old Testament*, 86-95.

54 Walvoord and Zuck, *The Bible Knowledge Commentary, Old Testament*, 89; a second view is that Ramesses II was the Pharaoh of the exodus in 1290 B.C. See the discussion by John D. Hannah, 104-5. Cf. The *NIV Study Bible* introduction to Exodus.

55 See the discussion of "heart," "hardening of the heart," and God's changing of minds and wills in Frame, *The Doctrine of God*, 62-3, 65-9, 135, 142; and in Grudem, *Systematic Theology*, 322-27.

56 Exodus 5-12; *The Bible Knowledge Commentary, Old Testament*, 118-29.

57 Exodus 9:16.

58 Exodus 10:16-17, 20, 28; 11.

59 Exodus 3:21-22; repeated in 12:35-36.

60 1 Samuel 22:6-19; Dumbrell, *Covenant and Creation*, 144.

61 Conner and Malmin, *The Covenants*, 58-62; Dumbrell, *Covenant and Creation*, 150-51.

62 Genesis 17:6, 16; 35:11; 49:8-12; Deuteronomy 17:14-20.

63 Matthew 1:1-16; Genesis 17:6-7, 16; 35:11; Psalms 2:6-7; 89:3-4, 34-37; 110; 2 Samuel Chapters 2, 5-7; Eugene H. Merrill, "2 Samuel" in Walvoord and Zuck, *The Bible Knowledge Commentary, Old Testament*, 464; Conner and Malmin, *The Covenants*, 58-62; Dumbrell, *Covenant and Creation*, 150-51, and Chapter 5.

64 Grudem, ibid., 328-29.

65 Grudem discusses these translations in *Systematic Theology*, 326. The same translation of Isaiah 45:7 was used by W. G. T. Shedd in *Dogmatic Theology*, 405-12, and Shedd is supportively quoted in Culver, *Systematic Theology*, 2005-06), 139.

66 Frame, *The Doctrine of God*, 175; full discussion, 160-182.

67 Acts 2:23; 4:27-28; Romans 8:29-30; 9:23; I Corinthians 2:7; Ephesians 1:5, 11; 2:10.

68 Frame, *The Doctrine of God*, 170.

69 Ibid. 161, italics added for emphasis; Gen. 3:17-19; Rom. 8:22, 19.

70 Geisler, *Chosen But Free*, 62; *Systematic Theology*, Vol. Three, 120.

71 Geisler, *Systematic Theology*, Vol. Three, 148; *Chosen But Free*, 42.

Chapter Ten

1 Geisler, *Systematic Theology*, Vol. Two, 537.

2   See the detailed treatment of covenants in Geisler, *Systematic Theology*, Vol. Four, 499-546, and his analysis and criticism of traditional and modified covenant theological interpretations, ibid., 430-36, 500, 542; for possible biblical references to creation of the universe and the creation of Adam and Eve involving "covenant," see Jeremiah 33:19-22; Hosea 6:7. Also see Gerard van Groningen, "Covenant," *Evangelical Dictionary of Biblical Theology*, 125-26; Genesis 1-2; Conner and Malmin, *The Covenants*, 18; Frame, *The Doctrine of God*, 30-35, 102.

3   Isaiah 14:12-15; Ezekiel 28:11-19; Luke 10:18; Ephesians 2:2; Jude 6; 2 Peter 2:4; Revelation 12: 9; 20:10; John 12:31-32; compare passages and notes of the NKJV and NIV Study Bibles; Grudem, *Systematic Theology*, 412-33; Geisler, *Systematic Theology*, Vol. II, 496-98.

4   Cf. Geisler, *Systematic Theology*, Vol. Three, Chapter Three, 130, 128, 87. Geisler says that "human free choice involves self-determinism (to be the efficient cause of our own choices) but also the ability to do other than good (that is, evil)." And this sense of human freedom "is for the purpose of being tested" (pp. 87). On free choice and free will he says: "free choice was the virtually unanimous view of the Fathers up to the time of the Reformation." With some exceptions, notably Luther, Calvin, strong Calvinism, "it has continued to be the consistent view since the time of the Reformation." Examples are on pp. 94-98.

5   Geisler, *Systematic Theology*, Vol. Three, 160. And, "if evil is not permitted, it cannot be defeated." (158).

6   John 8:44.

7   See Frame, *The Doctrine of God*, 125; and Frame, "Without a Supreme Being, Everything is Permitted," *Free Inquiry* 16 (spring 1996): 4-7.

8   Ephesians 1:4-6, 11; 2 Timothy 1:9; Acts 2:23; 4:27-28; Romans 9:23, 29-30; Frame, *The Doctrine of God*, 70-71, 86-87.

9   Romans 3:22-24.

10 See note 2.

11 Romans 5:18; 12-20; cf. Geisler, *Systematic Theology*, Vol. Three, 17-44; Frame, *The Doctrine of God*, 102.

12 Genesis 2:15-17.

13 Conner and Malmin, *The Covenants*, 17; Romans 5:12-14; 1 Corinthians 15:45-49; Geisler, *Systematic Theology*, Vol. Three, Chapters 1, 3-5; Grudem, *Systematic Theology*, 490-504; Strong, *Systematic Theology*, 573-664.

14 B. A. Demarest, "Fall of Man," *Evangelical Dictionary of Theology*, 404.

15 Genesis 3; Hosea 6:7; Romans 5:12-21; 1 Timothy 2:13-15; 1 John 3:4; Conner and Malmin, *The Covenants*, 17.

16 Deuteronomy 32:4; 2 Samuel 22:31; Matthew 5:48.

17 Geisler, *Systematic Theology*, Vol. Three, 17.

18 Hosea 2:18; Isaiah 9:6-7; 11:6-9; 33:24; 65:20-24; Jeremiah 30:17; Ezekiel 34:16; Geisler, *Systematic Theology*, Vol. Four, 564; Pentecost, *Things to Come*, 489, with several biblical references; see "The Nature of the Millennium" in Chapter Twelve below.

19 Acts 2:23; 4:27-28; Ephesians 1:4-6, 11; 2:10; Romans 8:29-30; 1 Corinthians 2:1-8; 1 John 2:2; 4:10; Matthew 1:1-16.

20 Grudem, *Systematic Theology*, 495-96.

21 Psalm 51:1-5, *The NIV Study Bible*, with text note.

22 Grudem, *Systematic Theology*, 496.

23 Psalm 58:3, translated in Grudem, *Systematic Theology*.

24 Ephesians 2:1-3; Grudem, *Systematic Theology*.

25 Cf. Grudem, ibid., 497, 657-65.

26 Geisler, *Systematic Theology*, Vol. Three, 120, 126, 146, 147-50, and all of Chapter Five.

27 John 6:44; cf. Hebrews 11:6; 1 Corinthians 2:14; 15:5; Romans 8:8.

28 See note 26.

29 Ibid., 130, citing 2 Corinthians 4:4; Jeremiah 17:9; Romans 1:21:32; Ephesians 2:1-3; Romans 3:10-18.

30 See the arguments against extreme Calvinism and Arminianism in Geisler, *Chosen But Free*, second edition; and those against aspects of Calvinism in Walls and Dongell, *Why I am not a Calvinist*. Recent arguments for Calvinism are in White, *The Potter's Freedom*, and Sproul, *Chosen by God*.

31 Geisler, *Chosen But Free*, 98.

32 Ibid., 53, 54-55; Walvoord, *Major Bible Themes*, Grand Rapids: Zondervan, 1974, 233; cf. Geisler, *Systematic Theology*, Vol. Three, Chapter Three.

33 Geisler, *Chosen But Free*, 42; Charnock, *Discourses upon the Existence and Attributes of God*, 450; Westminster Confession of Faith, 1646, 9.1; and 5.2: "Although in relation to the foreknowledge and decree of God, the first cause, all things come to pass immutably and infallibly, yet, by the same providence, he ordereth them to fall out according to the nature of second causes, either necessarily, freely, or contingently."

34 Geisler, ibid., 53, 47, 88, 51.

35 Ibid., 26.

36 Ibid.

37 God said to Adam, "You are free to eat from any tree in the garden; but you must not eat from the tree of the knowledge of good and evil, for when you eat of it you will surely die" (Genesis 2:16-17).

38 Emphases added; cf. Geisler, ibid., 72-73, 78-79, 200 ff.

39 See Geisler, ibid., 69, 72, 74, 79; John 3:16; Acts 16:31; Romans 5:1.

40 Geisler, ibid., 191, 188-99, emphases added; John 3:16, 18; 6:29; 11:40; 12:36; Acts 5:31; 16:31, 41; 17:30; 20:21; Ephesians 2:8-9; Philippians 1:29; 3:8-9; 1 Corinthians 4:7; 7:25; 12:8-9; John 6:44-45; Romans 12:3; 10:17; 1 Peter 1:21; 2 Peter 1:1; 1 Thessalonians 1:4-6; Luke 13:3; Hebrews 11:6.

41 cf. Geisler, ibid., 72-73, 78-79, 200 ff.

42 "Or do you not know that wrongdoers will not inherit the kingdom of God? Do not be deceived: Neither the sexually immoral nor idolaters nor adulterers nor men who have sex with men will inherit the kingdom of God." (1 Corinthians 6:9, NIV); cf. Lev. 18, Rom. 1:18-32, I Cor., 6:9-20, I Tim. 1:8-11.

43 www:pewforum.org "U. S. Religious Landscape Survey," "Full Reports."

[44] Romans 1:19-21; 2:14-15.

[45] Romans 3:9-18; 7:18-20; 8:6-8; Titus 1:10-16; Ephesians 4:18-19; John 8:34; Frame, *The Doctrine of God*, 130-31; Grudem, *Systematic Theology*, 497.

[46] Romans 8:8; 9:15-21; 1 Corinthians 2:14; John 6:44; 15:5; Hebrews 11:6; Grudem, *Systematic Theology*, 497-98.

[47] 2 Timothy 3:14-16; Romans 1:16; Isaiah 55:11; 1 Thessalonians 1:5; 1 John 2:5; Acts 19:16-20; 1 Corinthians 2:1-5.

[48] 1 Corinthians 2:14; Romans 8:6-11; 1 John 3:24; 5:6.

[49] There is some uncertainty and disagreement about a number of dates in the history of the Hebrew people. Dates used in this and the next chapter are based on traditional and biblical ones indicated in the following sources: Walvoord and Zuck, *The Bible Knowledge Commentary, Old Testament* (which has some discussion of the differences in dating; and provides biblical evidence for some dates); Norman L. Geisler, *A Popular Survey of the Old Testament* (Peabody, MA: Prince Press, 2003); *The NIV Study Bible* (which often gives possible alternatives).

[50] Thomas L Constable, "1 Kings," in *The Bible Knowledge Commentary, Old Testament*, 485.

[51] Conner and Malmin, *The Covenants*, esp. Chapter 9, "The New Covenant."

[52] *The NIV Study Bible*, note to Exodus 20:5.

[53] Ibid., Exodus 22:20, and notes to 32:6, 7, 9; Campbell, "Joshua," *The Bible Knowledge Commentary, Old Testament*, 338.

[54] Deuteronomy 2:31-34; Numbers21:1-3.

[55] Deuteronomy 3:3-7; Numbers21:33-34.

[56] Archer, Gleason L. *A Survey of Old Testament Introduction* (Chicago: Moody Press, 1961, 2007), 247.

[57] Joshua 2:9-21.

[58] Joshua 3-4; Campbell, "Joshua," *The Bible Knowledge Commentary, Old Testament*, 332-36.

[59] Campbell, "Joshua," *The Bible Knowledge Commentary, Old Testament*, 336-38; Joshua 5; Deuteronomy 10:16; 30:1-18.

[60] Campbell, "Joshua," ibid., 338; Joshua 5:1-12.

[61] Joshua 5:13-15; cf. Campbell, "Joshua," *The Bible Knowledge Commentary, Old Testament*, 339; *The NIV Study Bible*, note to Joshua 5:13; Frame, *The Doctrine of God*, 633-34, 637, 638.

[62] Joshua 6.

[63] Joshua 7; Campbell, "Joshua," ibid., 341-44.

[64] All of 1 John; 1 John 5:7; and see Chapters Four and Five above; Frame, *The Doctrine of God*, 619-735; "Trinity," *Evangelical Dictionary of Theology*; Smith, *Trinity and Reality*.

[65] Geisler, "Islam," *The Baker Encyclopedia of Christian Apologetics* (Grand Rapids: Baker, 1999), 368, 97.

[66] *The New King James Study Bible*: Matthew 3:17, 11:27; 17:5; John 1:14, 18; 3:16, 18; Acts 13:33; Hebrews 1:5; 5:5; 11:17; 1 John 4:9; 5:1, 9-12.

67 The Koran, tr. N.J. Dawood (New York: Penguin, 2006, c. 1956), Sura 112, p. 434; and quoted in Geisler, "Islam," *The Baker Encyclopedia of Christian Apologetics*, 369.

68 The Koran, tr. Dawood, Sura 37, p. 316; cf. Sura 38, p. 317, Sura 2, p. 21; Sura 78, p. 81.

69 Ibid., Sura 4, p. 78.

70 Ibid., Sura 5, p. 81, 84.

71 Ibid., Sura 5, p.87.

72 Ibid., Suras 43, p. 346; 4, p.78; 19, p.26.

73 Ibid., Sura 4, p.76.

74 Geisler, "Islam," *The Baker Encyclopedia of Christian Apologetics*, 368-69; Geisler and Saleeb, *Answering Islam*, 2000, 9.

75 John 8:44; Matthew 4:8-9; Isaiah 14:12-17; Daniel 10:12-13; Ephesians 6:12; 2:1-3; 2 Corinthians 4:3-4; cf. Green, *I Believe in Satan's Downfall*, 28, 49-50.

76 Green, *I Believe in Satan's Downfall*, 49-50; Ps. 106:36-39; John 8:44.

77 Caner and Caner, *Unveiling Islam*, 63; winner of the Gold Medallion Book Award; see a slightly fuller discussion of Muhammad and "the demonic and anti-biblical revelations that began in the Cave of Hira" in Joel Richardson, *Antichrist; Islam's Awaited Messiah*, 120, 115-120.

78 1 Timothy 1:5-6.

79 Frame, *Apologetics to the Glory of God*, 38n, 54, 121n, 213.

80 See "Moshiach: the Messiah," and "The Nature of G-d" at Judaism 101, www:jewfac.org/toc/htm. In contrast to mainstream Judaism (Orthodox, Conservative, and Reform), Messianic Judaism does profess belief in Jesus Christ as divine Messiah and Savior, see "Judaism," "Messianic Judaism," and "Judaism's View of Jesus" at www:wikipedia.org.

81 www.religionfacts.com/buddhism/beliefs/atheism/htm.

82 John 8:14-47; *The NIV Study Bible*, and partly from the translation in Grudem, *Systematic Theology*, 421-22.

83 Grudem, *Systematic Theology*, 415, with the additional quotation of John 10:10.

84 See Chapter 6 on "Counterfeit Religion" in Michael Green, *I Believe in Satan's Downfall* (Grand Rapids: Eerdmans, 1981), 148-194, dealing with such phenomena as the Unification Church, counterfeit political religion, Fascism, Marxism, Maoism, Transcendental Meditation, and Hinduism.

85 Green, *I Believe in Satan's Downfall*, 34, 55.

86 Ibid., 18-23, and Chapter 5, "The Fascination of the Occult," 112-147.

87 Matthew 4:1-11; Mark 1:13, 1:21-2:1-12; 3:22-24.

88 Matthew 10:1, 8; Mark 3:15, 16:17.

89 Green, *I Believe in Satan's Downfall*, 28.

90 Ibid.

91 Daniel 10:13-20; 1 Thessalonians 2:2-18, John 8:44, 59.

92 Green, *I Believe in Satan's Downfall*.

93 Merrill F. Unger, *What Demons Can Do To Saints* (Chicago: Moody Press, 1991), 14-15.

94   Green, ibid., 49-50; Acts 26:18; Unger, "Satan," *Evangelical Dictionary of Biblical Theology*, 973.

95   Judges 8:29-9:57; Walvoord and Zuck, *The Bible Knowledge Commentary, Old Testament*, 396-99.

96   1 Samuel 10-14; 16:14, 22; 18:10-11; 19:9-10; 28:7-14; 31; Walvoord and Zuck, *The Bible Knowledge Commentary, Old Testament*, 441-455.

97   I Kings 18:1-4.

98   I Kings 16:29-18:46; Deuteronomy 12:13-15; *The Bible Knowledge Commentary, Old Testament*, 525-27.

99   I Kings 22:1-38.

100 2 Kings 9.

Chapter Eleven

1   Many examples have been given in previous chapters, especially Chapters 7 and 8. For more on this subject see: Geisler, *Systematic Theology, Vol. Two*, Chapters 24, 25; Frame, *The Doctrine of God*, 243-45, 274-88, 769-80; Grudem, *Systematic Theology*, 315-354; Helm, *The Providence of God*; Berkouwer, *The Providence of God*; Eichrodt, *Theology of the Old Testament*, vol. 2, Chapter 17; Walvoord, *Major Bible Prophecies*.

2   These points were developed more fully in Chapter Eight.

3   For a clear analysis of methods of interpretation of biblical prophecy relating to literalism, symbolism, allegory, and metaphor, see Pentecost, *Things to Come*, Section One.

4   Cf. Acts 1:7; Matthew 24:22; Luke 12:40.

5   Geisler, *Systematic Theology, Vol. Four*, 530-37.

6   Ibid., 530, 536; more points of difference are discussed on pp. 530-45.

7   Ibid.,532, 534. Promise of the Holy Land: Genesis 13:14-15; cf. 15:7-21; 17:1-8; 26:3-5; 30:10-12. Reign of descendant of David: 2 Samuel 7:12ff.; Psalm 89:24-37; Isaiah 2:3. Geisler shows that these and other biblical texts reveal eschatological events of Israel's future, and refute claims of replacement theology (or realized eschatology) and progressive dispensationalists.

8   Matthew 1:1-16.

9   Geisler, *Systematic Theology, Vol. Four*, 535.

10   Ibid., 534-35; Chapter 16; Matthew 3:2; Zechariah 14:4; Revelation 1:7.

11   Geisler, *Systematic Theology, Vol. Four*, 535; Chapter 8; Vol. One; Chapter 26; Vol. Two, appendix 1.

12   Geisler, *Systematic Theology, Vol. Four*, 536.

13   Romans 11:1-10 and note on 11:7.

14   Geisler, *Systematic Theology, Vol. Four*, 536; Romans 11:25: "Israel has experienced a hardening in part until the full number of the Gentiles has come in."

15   Pentecost, *Things to Come*, 193.

16   Paraphrase of Geisler, *Systematic Theology, Vol. Four*, 537; for more on these attri-butes of God, see Geisler, *ibid.*, Chapter 1; and Vol. 1, Chapters 1, 4, 7-9, 17, 23.

[17] Geisler, *Systematic Theology, Vol. Four*, 536; Romans 11, esp. 25-29; NIV: "All Israel will be saved."

[18] Deuteronomy 26:18-19.

[19] Romans 3:1-2.

[20] Romans 9:4-5.

[21] Romans 11, NIV: "All Israel will be saved" (all who will believe).

[22] Geisler, *Systematic Theology, Vol. Four*, 544; Deuteronomy 10:15; 26:19; Romans 3:1-2; 9:4-5; Isaiah 2:2-3; 45:14.

[23] Isaiah 2:1-3; 45:14.

[24] Ezekiel 5:5.

[25] Zechariah 2:8.

[26] 2 Samuel 6:12-17.

[27] 2 Chronicles 7:16; emphasis added.

[28] Jeremiah 3:17.

[29] Zechariah 8:3.

[30] 2 Chronicles 7:17-22.

[31] 1 Kings 11:1-8, 33; Walvoord and Zuck, *The Bible Knowledge Commentary, Old Testament*, 508.

[32] 2 Kings 17.

[33] 2 Kings 21:1-6; 23:4-7, 10-11.

[34] 2 Kings 21:11-13.

[35] 2 Kings 23:26-27.

[36] 2 Kings 24:8-14.

[37] Jeremiah 27:4-7; Walvoord and Zuck, *The Bible Knowledge Commentary, Old Testament*, 1126-1127.

[38] Jeremiah 32;28-29 et seq.

[39] 2 Kings 25:1-17, and entire Chapter; Jeremiah 52.

[40] Daniel 9:24.

[41] Randall Price, *The Coming Last Days Temple*, 75; Daniel 8:23-25; 11:21-35; 7:24-26; 9:24-27; 11:36-45.

[42] Price, *The Coming Last Days Temple*, 76.

[43] Deuteronomy 28:49-57.

[44] Josephus (c. AD 37-100), *The Jewish Wars* (c. 75 AD).

[45] Matthew 24:2.

[46] Many books and several Internet sites of the past decade or so clearly document Koranic and Islamic hatred of Israel and Jews and the goal to destroy them. See: Walid Shoebat, *Why We Want to Kill You*; Joel Richardson, *Antichrist; Islam's Awaited Messiah*; Brigitte Gabriel, *Because They Hate*; idem., *They Must Be Stopped*; Robert Spencer, *Religion of Peace?: Why Christianity Is and Islam Isn't*; idem., *The Truth About Muhammad: Founder of the World's Most Intolerant Religion*; idem., *The Politically Incorrect Guide to Islam*; Caner and Caner, *Unveiling Islam*; idem., *More Than a Prophet: An Insider's Response to Muslim Beliefs About Jesus and Christianity*; Mark A. Gabriel, *Islam and the Jews: The Unfinished Battle*; idem., *Jesus and Muhammad: Profound Differences and Surprising Similarities*; idem, *Islam and Terrorism: What the Quran Really Teaches About Christianity, Violence and the Goals of Islamic Jihad*; P.

David Gaubatz and Paul Sperry, *Muslim Mafia: Inside the Secret Underworld that's Conspiring to Islamize America*; Ibn Warraq, *Why I Am Not a Muslim*; idem., *What the Koran Really Says*; Anis Shorrosh, *Islam Revealed A Christian Arab's View Of Islam*; Simon Altaf, *World War III: Unmasking The End Time Beast*; John Ankerberg and John Weldon, *Fast Facts on Islam*; John Ankerberg and Dillon Burroughs, *Middle East Meltdown*.

47 See the Washington Post for 03-06-08 and 03-07-08.

48 See Joel Richardson, *Antichrist; Islam's Awaited Messiah*, esp. Chapters 5-6.

49 See note 46.

50 *The New King James Study Bible*: Matthew 3:17, 11:27; 17:5; John 1:14, 18; 3:16, 18; Acts 13:33; Hebrews 1:5; 5:5; 11:17; 1 John 4:9; 5:1, 9-12.

51 The Koran [Quran, Qur'an], tr. N.J. Dawood (New York: Penguin, 2006, c. 1956), Surah (Chapter) 112:1-4; cf. yusufali (Yusuf Ali) translation at www:TheQuran. com; quoted in Geisler, "Islam," *The Baker Encyclopedia of Christian Apologetics*, 369.

52 The Koran, tr. Dawood, Surah 37:149-152; cf. yusufali translation at www: TheQuran.com; cf. Surah 38, p. 317, Surah 2, p. 21; Surah 78, p. 81; cf. Caner and Caner, *Unveiling Islam*, 219.

53 Ibid., Surah 5, p. 81, 84.

54 The Quran (Koran), Surah 9:30, yusufali translation at www:TheQuran.com.

55 The Koran, tr. Dawood, Surah 5:72-73; cf. yusufali translation at www: TheQuran.com.

56 Ibid., Surah 3:59; cf. yusufali translation at www:TheQuran.com.

57 Ibid., Surahs 43:59; 4:171-173, cf. yusufali translation at www:TheQuran.com; 19:30, 35; cf. Caner and Caner, *Unveiling Islam*, 218.

58 Surah 3:52-53, yusufali translation at www:TheQuran.com; cf. Caner and Caner, *Unveiling Islam*, 215; see more in this book by the Caners (two Muslim brothers converted to Christianity) on Christ as viewed by the Koran and Islamic scholars.

59 Ibid., Surah 4:157-8; cf. yusufali translation at www:TheQuran.com; cf. Joel Richardson, *Antichrist; Islam's Awaited Messiah*, esp. Chapter 6.

60 I John 4:1-3.

61 Richardson, *Antichrist; Islam's Awaited Messiah*, 122-23, 128.

62 John 1:1-15; 1 Timothy 2:5; Hebrews 1:3; 8:6; 9:15; 12:24; Revelation 19:13; Matthew 4:3, 6; 8:29; 14:23; 27:43, 54; Mark 1:1; 3:11; 15:39; Luke 1:35; 4:3, 9, 41; 22:70; John 1:34, 49; 5:25; 11:27; 19:17; 20:31; Acts 9:20; Romans 1:4; 2Corinthians 1:19; Galatians 2:20; Hebrews 4:14; 6:6; 7:3; 10:29; 1 John 3:8; 4:15; 5:1, 5, 10; 12-13, 20; Revelation 2:18.

63 The Westminster Confession II.III: "In the unity of the Godhead there be three Persons of one substance, power, and eternity: God the Father, God the Son, and God the Holy Ghost. The Father is of none, neither begotten nor proceeding; the Son is eternally begotten of the Father; the Holy Ghost eternally proceeding from the Father and the Son." For more theological explication, see for example, Frame, *The Doctrine of God*, 619-735; Geisler, *Systematic Theology, Vol. Two*, 269-312; Grudem, *Systematic Theology*, 226-261.

64 I John 4:14-15.

65 Koran, Surah 8:12, Shakir translation.

66 Koran, Surah 8:17, Shakir and Pickthal translations.

67 This verse, At-Tawba 29, "abrogates" (meaning it abolishes the authority of) Surah 8:61, which was originally "inspired" in the Koran, and replaces it (Al-Hilali translation).

68 Koran, Surah 8:39, Shakir translation.

69 Koran, Surah 8:61, Al-Hilali translation.

70 This verse, At-Tawba 5, "abrogates" (abolishes) Surah 8:72.

71 Brigitte Gabriel, in *Because They Hate* (35) idicates that Islamic teachings can be used to nurture murderers, rapists, and the depraved.

72 In *They Must Be Stopped*, Gabriel gives specific evidence that "we are in a religious war" (p. 58, and all of Chapter 3). "It is not yet politically correct to talk about a religious war. But this is exactly what we are facing: a religious war declared by devout Muslims" (70). And "Going forward we must realize that the portent behind the terrorist attacks is the purest form of what the Prophet Mohammed created. It's not radical Islam. It's what Islam is at its core" (71). In her Chapter 4 Gabriel details 26 points of an Islamic 100-year plan to take over the world. This is one of the best books available for revealing the dangerous nature and threat of "core" or "pure Islam," which religiously follows Muhammad and the Koran, and is not simply "radical" or "hijacked."

73 See the informative discussion of Islamic hatred and atrocities against Jews and Christians, based on sources in the Koran, in Joel Richardson, *Antichrist; Islam's Awaited Messiah*, Chs.13, 12, 14; Shoebat, *Why We Want to Kill You*.

74 Gabriel, *Because They Hate*, 145; cf. Shoebat, *Why We Want to Kill You*.

75 Gabriel, *Because They Hate*, 150, 149, 105-114; www.iad.org, "Why Do We Pray?" Gabriel states that "Yasser Arafat was the father of modern terrorism" (93), but as late as 2008 we saw former President Carter placing a wreath honoring Arafat at his grave.

76 See Chapter Seven, and Matthew 5-7; 22:37-40; Romans 13:9-10; I John 2:11.

77 Matthew 5:44.

78 Matthew 6:14-15.

79 1 John 2:9-11.

80 Geisler, *Systematic Theology*, Vol. Four, 464; for full-length studies of the meaning of God's Kingdom, see the classic work on the subject by George Peters, *The Theocratic Kingdom*; McClain, *The Greatness of the Kingdom*; Pentecost, *Things to Come*, 9-15, Chapter 28; idem., *Thy Kingdom Come*.

81 Geisler, *Systematic Theology*, *Vol. Four*, 460-61; cf. vol. 2, Chapter 4 and Part 4; Matthew 25:34.

82 Norman B. Harrison, *The End* (Minneapolis, MN: Harrison Service, 1941), 120, quoted in Pentecost, *Things to Come*, 195; see the extensive supporting material here in Pentecost and on pp. 233-36.

83 1 Thessalonians 5:9.

84 Geisler, *Systematic Theology*, *Vol. Four*, 612-635; cf. Pentecost, *Things to Come*, 233-36; Walvoord, *The Millennial Kingdom*, 240-255; idem., *The Rapture Question*, esp.

191-99 For further explanations and arguments against other interpretations of rapture and tribulation (preterism, partial rapture; midtribulation rapture, pre-wrath view, and posttribulationism), see Geisler, ibid., 635-55; Pentecost, *ibid.*, Chs. X-XIII.

85 Geisler, *Systematic Theology, Vol. Four,* 623; 1 Thessalonians 5:1-3; Matthew 24:3-30.

86 Geisler, *Systematic Theology, Vol. Four,* 1 Thessalonians 4:17, Revelation 1:7.

87 Geisler, *Systematic Theology, Vol. Four,* 612-635; Revelation 13:6; 12:12; 13:8, 14.

88 Geisler, *Systematic Theology, Vol. Four,* 618; 2 Corinthians 5:10; Revelation 22:12; 1 Corinthians 3:11-15.

89 Geisler, *Systematic Theology, Vol. Four,* 614-15.

90 Geisler, *Systematic Theology, Vol. Four,* 615-16; Revelation 3:10; 1 Thessalonians 4:16-17; Pentecost, *Things to Come,* 195, 233-36; Ryrie, *What You Should Know About the Rapture.*

91 Geisler, *Systematic Theology, Vol. Four,* 617; Jeremiah 30:7; Daniel 9:24; Zechariah 12:6; Romans 11:25; Romans 8:1-2; 2 Corinthians 5:21.

92 Geisler, *Systematic Theology, Vol. Four,* 597-98; The King James translation for verse 30a is: "When thou art in tribulation, and all these things are come upon thee, even in the latter days . . . ." "Latter days" usually refers to the Tribulation period. Cf. Pentecost, *Things to Come,* 351.

93 Isaiah 24:1-20, emphases added.

94 Pentecost, *Thy Kingdom Come,* 309, 303.

95 John 1-30; 20-22; 26-27; emphasis added. Since Jesus is the only Person of the Trinity to be born into a human family, He is called the "Son of Man." He is also the "Son of God" from eternity. And He is the "King" and "Messiah" who will rule forever. Since He is fully God and fully man, Jesus has been justly given the right to judge mankind.

96 Pentecost, *Thy Kingdom Come,* 300; Revelation 5:5; cf. Isaiah 11:1; 2 Samuel 7:16; Psalm 89:3.

97 Matthew 24:21-22.

98 Revelation 7, 11; Pentecost, *Thy Kingdom Come,* 311-13.

99 Geisler, *Systematic Theology, Vol. Four,* 615-16.

100 Pentecost, *Things to Come,* 195, 233-36, with citations: **wrath**—Rev. 6:16-17; 11:18; 14:19; 15:1, 7; 16:1; 19:1; 1 Thess. 1:9-10; 5:9; Zeph. 1:15, 18; **judgment**—Rev. 14:7; 15:4; 16:5-7; 19:2; **indignation**—Isa. 26:20-21; 34:1-3; **punishment**—Isa. 24:20-21; **hour of trial**—Jer. 30:7; **destruction**—Joel 1:15; **darkness**—Joel 2:2; Zeph. 1:14-18; Amos 5:18.

101 Pentecost, *Things to Come,* 235-36, with several passages quoted.

102 Ibid., 237-38.

103 Ibid., 238-39; Revelation 3:10; 14:6-11; 13:11-18; 6:10-17.

104 Walvoord, *The Revelation of Jesus Christ,* 126-127. Due to the shortness of this chapter, the interpretations offered must be very brief. Extensive supporting argument, quotations, and comparisons of contrasting views cannot be given. For each interpretation, the reader is encouraged to consult further the works and passages cited.

[105] Compare the very revealing parallel descriptions by Jesus in Matthew 24:4-31.

[106] Showers, *Maranatha: Our Lord Come*, 106, 109; additional important material is included in Showers, 104-9.

[107] Ibid., 113.

[108] Ezekiel 28:1-10.

[109] Revelation 13:1 and 17:15 indicates that he came from the "sea." "Sea" in the Bible often symbolizes Gentile nations. See Daniel 7:7-8; 20, 24; 8:24; Revelation 13:8; 17:9-12; Pentecost, *Thy Kingdom Come*, 304.

[110] 2 Thessalonians 2:9-10; context, 2:3-12.

[111] Daniel 8:23-27, a reference to Antiochus IV, 2nd cen. B.C., but even more so to the Antichrist who will be a similar, but even stronger emissary of Satan.

[112] Cf. Walvoord, *The Revelation of Jesus Christ*, 129; Showers, ibid., 113-14.

[113] Showers, *Maranatha: Our Lord Come*, 114 ff.; Jeremiah 21:5-7, 9; 42:17-18, 22; 44:8, 11:3; Ezekiel 5:11-17; 7:3, 8, 14-15.

[114] Walvoord, *The Revelation of Jesus Christ*, 130.

[115] Ibid., 131.

[116] www.census.gov/main/www/popclock.html.

[117] www.wikipedia.com, "World Population."

[118] Walvoord, *The Revelation of Jesus Christ*, 131.

[119] The timing of tribulation events is not specifically defined in the Bible. Christ says in Matthew 24:7-8 that "nation will rise against nation, and kingdom against kingdom," that "there will be famines and earthquakes in various places," and that "all these are the beginning of birth pains." Geisler thinks that this "beginning of birth pains" appears to be the first half of the Tribulation (3½ years) with "hard-labor birth pains" in the second half. Thus, the first four seals appear to take place during the first half, with the fourth one at the middle. "If this is correct, then the fifth, sixth, and seventh seals of Revelation 6, as well as the bowls that follow, will be the last half of the Tribulation" (*Systematic Theology, Vol. Four*, 602; cf. 610-11). The sixth trumpet must be very near the end of the second half, since with the blast of the seventh trumpet, loud voices in heaven say, "The kingdom of the world has become the kingdom of our Lord and of his Christ, and he will reign for ever and ever." And since the seven bowls issue from the seventh trumpet and mark the end of the Tribulation period, they surely must occur rapidly very near the end. Not many suggestions are given in the Bible about the timing of the seals, trumpets, and bowls within the seven-year Tribulation period, and interpretations vary considerably. Pentecost suggests that the seals are during the first half, the trumpets during and ending the second, and the bowls immediately afterwards (*Thy Kingdom Come*, 300-01). Cf. Walvoord, *The Revelation of Jesus Christ*, 132. There are several other views.

[120] Ezekiel 38-39. A third great battle, involving "the nations in the four corners of the earth—Gog and Magog" occurs at the end of the Millennium. Revelation 20:8-9.

[121] Walvoord with Hitchcock, *Armageddon, Oil, and Terror*, 97, 113; Pentecost, *Things to Come*, 342-55; Charles H. Dyer, "Ezekiel," *The Bible Knowledge Commentary, Old*

Testament, 1300; Grant Jeffrey, in *The Next World War*, 146-49, thinks it will occur before the signing of a peace treaty with Israel and the Tribulation.

[122]   Pentecost, ibid., 352.

[123]   Ezekiel 38:1-6 ff.; Joel Richardson, *Antichrist: Islam's Awaited Messiah*, 99-110. Richardson has a good, recent discussion identifying modern nations listed by biblical names in Ezekiel. An important further question is whether "the many nations with you" of Ezekiel 38:6 also include Syria, Lebanon, Iraq, Afghanistan, and Pakistan; Grant Jeffrey, citing Psalms 83:4-8, lists Syria, Lebanon, and Iraq, along with Jordan and Iran, in *The Next World War*, 12-13. Walvoord, Hitchcock, Jeffrey, and Dyer add Ethiopia (which Richardson apparently does not), Walvoord and Hitchcock, *Armageddon, Oil, and Terror*, 87-95; see the map in Dyer, "Ezekiel," *The Bible Knowledge Commentary, Old Testament*, 1124.

[124]   Jeffrey, *The Next World War*, 139-42, 12-15, 18, and all of Chapter 12; John Hagee, *Jerusalem Countdown; A Warning to the World* (2006), 102-05.

[125]   Richardson, ibid., 103-4; Ezekiel 38:1, 2; 39:1; Dyer, "Ezekiel," *The Bible Knowledge Commentary, Old Testament*, 1299.

[126]   Simon Altaf, *World War III*, 62, 340.

[127]   Ibid., 62, 340, 35-36, 203, 215-18, 322-326, 376.

[128]   Ibid., 36, 35.

[129]   Kenneth A. Mathews, *The New American Commentary: Genesis 11:27-50:26* (Nashville: B & H Publishing, 2005), 191, cf. 188-89, 191.

[130]   Altaf, ibid., 36, 187. On the land and descendants of Esau, see Genesis 36.

[131]   Cf. Ralph Stice, *From 9-11 to 666* (Nashville, TN: ACW Press, 2005), 72: "The prophet Obediah tells us that the final conflict over Mount Zion will be between the houses of Jacob, representing Israel, and Esau, representing Edom ...." Obediah 1: "'The house of Jacob will be a fire and the house of Joseph a flame; the house of Esau will be stubble, and they will set it on fire and consume it. There will be no survivors from the house of Esau.' The LORD has spoken."

[132]   Ezekiel 38:18-23; 39:6-22.

[133]   Dyer, "Ezekiel," *The Bible Knowledge Commentary, Old Testament*, 1302.

[134]   Ergun and Emir Caner, *Unveiling Islam* (Grand Rapids, MI: Kregel, 2002) 17-19. The third brother is Erdem Caner.

[135]   Mark A. Gabriel, *The Unfinished Battle; Islam and the Jews* (Lake Mary, FL: Front Line, 2003), xiii, xvii.

[136]   Gabriel, ibid., 115, 107-17; citing Ibn Kathir, *The Beginning and the End*; cf. Caner and Caner, *Unveiling Islam*, Chapter 2.

[137]   Gabriel, ibid.; Koran, Surah 5:64; Gabriel also points out several incorrect statements in the liberal writing of Karen Armstrong, including: Muhammad didn't have "any hostility toward Jews in general, but only towards the three rebel tribes", that "the Quran does not sanction warfare", and that "Muhammad never asked Jews or Christians to accept Islam unless they particularly wished to do so, because they had received perfectly valid revelations of their own" (115; cf. xvi & 221 nn1-3; 39 & 222 n3; 52 & 223 n1, and 54 & 223 n3). Gabriel

says: "I am amazed at how people in the West misrepresent Islam in the name of tolerance" (xvi).

138 Robert Spencer, *The Politically Incorrect Guide to Islam (and the Crusades)* (Washington, DC: Regnery, 2005, 108. Five Bible verses speak of an "abomination that causes desolation": Daniel 9:27; 11:31; 12:11; Matthew 24:15; Mark 13:14.

139 From Bat Ye'or, *The Decline of Eastern Christianity Under Islam*, 271-72; quoted in Spencer, *The Politically Incorrect Guide to Islam*, 109-110.

140 Ergun and Emir Caner, *Unveiling Islam*, 68-71.

141 There is not enough space here to go into the complexities, the massacres and brutalities of the Crusades, and the expansion and decline of the Muslim Ottoman Empire.

142 Ten horns: Daniel 7:7, 20, 24; Revelation 12:3; 13:2; 17:7, 12, 16. Seven heads: Revelation: 12:3; 13:2; 17:3, 7, 9. Cf. Richardson, *Antichrist; Islam's Awaited Messiah*, 110-14.

143 See the illuminating analysis of these and other verses in Roland L. Back and Michael A. H. Back, *What is the Antichrist-Islam Connection?*162-190.

144 Walvoord, "Revelation," *The Bible Knowledge Commentary, New Testament*, ed. Walvoord and Zuck, 971, 970.

145 Richardson, *ibid.*, 110-11.

146 wikipedia.org, "Byzantine Empire," 1; see the articles and maps at wikipedia on the Roman, Byzantine, and Ottoman Empires.

147 Wikipedia.org, "Ottoman Empire," 1.

148 Ibid

149 Richardson, *Antichrist; Islam's Awaited Messiah*, 113.

150 Brigitte Gabriel, *Because They Hate*; Richardson, *Antichrist; Islam's Awaited Messiah*; Altaf, *World War III*.

151 I tend to agree with those who now point toward an end-time Islamic Empire or Caliphate led by a Muslim Antichrist, rather than a European Union or Confederacy. Those who interpret the future empire as Islamic include: Joel Richardson, Ralph Stice, Roland and Michael Back, and Simon Altaf. Those who have supported an interpretation of a European Union or Confederacy include John Walvoord, Mark Hitchcock, John Hagee.

152 Caner and Caner, *Unveiling Islam*, 70, 77-78, 174.

153 Altaf, *World War III*, 374 and Chapters 1-5; Jeffrey, *The Next World War*, Introduction, Chapters 1, 12.

154 Even though a social custom of the time considered Abraham's progeny by Hagar the Egyptian maid legitimate, by God's own creation law of marriage in Genesis, Ishmael was illegitimate. And by doing what he did to father Ishmael, Abraham showed some lack of faith to wait for God to fulfill his promise, which He did in the miraculous birth of Isaac several years after Ishmael's birth.

155 Daniel 2:29-45. Ezekiel 38:1-7; Isaiah 11:10-16; 43:3; 45:14. See Joel Richardson, *Antichrist: Islam's Awaited Messiah*, 99-110.

156 See note 46, especially Brigitte Gabriel, *They Must Be Stopped*, and *Because They Hate*. Also see Ye'or, *Eurabia; the Euro-Arab Axis*. Fairleigh Dickinson University Press, 2007); Phillips, *Londonistan*, 2006.

157 Matthew 24:21; Geisler, *Systematic Theology*, *Vol. Four*, 602.

158 Daniel 9:24-27.

159 Daniel 9:26-27; "And on a wing of the temple he will set up an abomination that causes desolation, until the end that is decreed is poured out on him" (v. 27).

160 2 Thessalonians 2:8-12; Revelation 13; Geisler, *Systematic Theology*, *Vol. Four*, 610.

161 See Revelation 14:9, 11; 15:2; 16:2; 17:16-17; 19:20; 20:4. And compare Walvoord, *The Revelation of Jesus Christ*, on these passages; "With the rise of the first beast to a place of worldwide dominion, the apostate church is destroyed according to Revelation 17:16, and the worship of the whole world is directed to the beast out of the sea" . . . the image "becomes the center of the false worship of the world ruler" (205, 207); cf. Pentecost, *Things to Come*, 333-34.

162 Walvoord, *The Revelation of Jesus Christ*, 134.

163 Showers, ibid., 118-19.

164 While some have interpreted this and other end-times events symbolically or figuratively, I agree with Walvoord that there are good reasons for understanding this one in some literal sense (ibid., 136-37). The question is, exactly what literal sense? Beyond its indication of great changes in the universe, it seems impossible to define these events precisely. There are particular questions concerning stars and their great distances from the Earth. The total number of stars in the universe has been recently estimated at fifty billion trillion (see Chapter 2). Since stars are largely hydrogen and helium, and there are billions and billions of stars larger than the earth, how could they fall to the earth, and earth survive, as it does? Furthermore, by the subsequent third and fourth trumpets of Revelation there are still stars in the heavens. If some literal meaning is meant, perhaps these "stars" could be small fragments of some burned out and exploded stars, or of other exploded heavenly bodies, such as meteorites or asteroids. The explosion of a giant star (supernova) can cause an expanding shell of "dust" and gas mixed with interstellar matter (supernova remnant). Aging stars that have burned out the hydrogen fuel at their core (red giants) expand until the outer layer explodes, shooting clouds of "dust" and gas (nebula) into space (Cf. Sparrow, *Cosmos*, 104-5, 221.)

165 Cf. Walvoord, *The Revelation of Jesus Christ*, 156-57; cf. Romans 1:21-22.

166 Walvoord, *The Revelation of Jesus Christ*, 159; 158-164; Luke 8:31.

167 Walvoord, *The Revelation of Jesus Christ*, 160-164.

168 Pentecost interprets this as marking the end of the tribulation and the beginning of a 45-day period in which the bowls will quickly be poured out just before the second advent of Christ. Others interpret the bowls as falling in the closing months or weeks of the tribulation. The Bible is not definitive about this.

169 Revelation 16:12-16. Geisler, *Systematic Theology*, *Vol. Four*, 607-8; Pentecost, *Things to Come*, 340-55.

170 Zechariah 12:3-4, 7-9.

171 Zechariah 14:4-9.

172 This image of the beast with seven heads and crowns suggests similar images in Revelation 12:3, 13:2, and 17:3-7. It may be a composite, symbolic image, referring to the successive evil empires of history, culminating in the evil world empire led by the Antichrist during the Tribulation, as well as to the Antichrist himself, and to Satan, who is the evil power behind all of them.

173 Cf. Walvoord, *The Revelation of Jesus Christ*, 240-42.

Chapter Twelve

1   Geisler, *Systematic Theology, Vol. Four*, 564.
2   Ibid., 460-61.
3   Townsend, in *The Coming Millennial Kingdom*, ed. Campbell and Townsend, 271.
4   For excellent theological support of premillennialism see Campbell and Townsend, *The Coming Millennial Kingdom*; Walvoord, *The Millennial Kingdom*; Pentecost, *Things to Come*; Geisler, *Systematic Theology, Vol. Four*, 547-595, 459-546.
5   Geisler, *Systematic Theology Vol. Four*, Chapter 13, "The Interpretation of Prophecy," p. 465, 478, citing McClain, *The Greatness of the Kingdom*, 66-85.
6   A highly rated recent statement of amillennial interpretation is: Beale, *The Book of Revelation*, 1998.
7   See the critique of amillennialism in Geisler, *Systematic Theology, Vol. Four*, 548-49.
8   See the critique of amillennialism in Walvoord, *The Millennial Kingdom*, 106-07, et. seq.; Niebuhr, "Beyond Tragedy," in *Contemporary Religious Thought*, ed. Thomas S. Kepler, 373, 380.
9   For analyses and critiques of amillennialism and postmillennialism, and comparisons with premillennialism, see Geisler, *Systematic Theology, Vol. Four*, 547-58; Walvoord, *The Millennial Kingdom*, Chapters II-IX; esp. pp. 105-10, 33-36; Bock, et.al., *Three Views on the Millennium and Beyond*; wikipedia.org: "premillennialism," "amillennialism," "postmillennialism."
10 John 20.
11 Luke 24:39, 42-43.
12 John 20-21.
13 Geisler, *Systematic Theology, Vol. Four*, 269, and n. 63.
14 The NIV Study Bible, I Corinthians 15:35-50 and note to 15:42-44.
15 Geisler, *Systematic Theology, Vol. Four*, 271; with references to Luke 14:31, Acts 1:10-11, and John 20:19.
16 Geisler, ibid., 623; with references to 1 Thessalonians 4:17, Revelation 1:7.
17 Walvoord, *The Millennial Kingdom*, 240-255; idem., *The Rapture Question*, esp. 191-99; Geisler, *Systematic Theology, Vol. Four*, 612-635; cf. Pentecost, *Things to Come*, 233-36; Thomas L. Constable, "1 Thessalonians," *The Bible Knowledge Commentary, New Testament*, ed. Walvoord and Zuck, 703-05; for further explanations and arguments against other interpretations of rapture and tribulation (preterism, partial rapture; midtribulation rapture, pre-wrath view, and posttribulationism), see Geisler, ibid., 635-55; Pentecost, *Things to Come*, Chapters X-XIII.

18   Campbell & Townsend, *The Coming Millennial Kingdom*, 271. This scholarly book backs up these claims with detailed studies of covenants, promises, and related claims throughout the Bible.

19   Geisler, *Systematic Theology, Vol. Four*, 554, and 555-558.

20   Robert B. Chisholm, Jr., in Campbell & Townsend, *The Coming Millennial Kingdom*, 52-54.

21   Geisler, *Systematic Theology, Vol. Four*, 554-58, 532, 534; promise of the Holy Land: Genesis 13:14-15; cf. 15:7-21; 17:1-8; 26:3-5; 30:10-12; reign of descendant of David: 2 Samuel 7:12ff.; Psalm 89:24-37; Isaiah 2:3. Geisler shows that these and other biblical texts reveal eschatological events of Israel's future, and refute claims of replacement theology (or realized eschatology) and progressive dispensationalists. See detailed studies of these covenants and promises in Campbell & Townsend, *The Coming Millennial Kingdom*, esp. pp. 47-54; more, confirming passages are listed on pp. 52-3 (Leviticus 26; Deuteronomy 4:25-31; Hosea 1:10, Micah 7:11-20; and Zechariah 7:14, 8:4-8).

22   2 Samuel 7:11-16; Psalm 89:20-37.

23   Campbell & Townsend, *The Coming Millennial Kingdom*, 95-6, 98; 264-65; cf. other visions of Isaiah in 11:1-16; 60; 61:3-62:12; 66.

24   Kaiser, in *The Coming Millennial Kingdom*, 103-05.

25   Ibid., 106-7.

26   Ibid., 108.

27   Cf. Kaiser, ibid., 108-10.

28   See the excellent commentary by Charles Dyer in "Jeremiah," *The Bible Knowledge Commentary, Old Testament*, ed. Walvoord and Zuck, 1171-72.

29   Townsend, in *The Coming Millennial Kingdom*, 266; cf. 134, 119-133.

30   Isaiah 9:6-7; 16:5.

31   Geisler, *Systematic Theology, Vol. Four*, 555, citing McClain, *The Greatness of the Kingdom*, Chapter 21.

32   Geisler, *Systematic Theology, Vol. Four*, discussed in detail below.

33   Ibid.

34   Micah 5:1-5; John A. Martin, "Micah," *The Bible Knowledge Commentary, Old Testament*, 1475, 1486.

35   Martin, "Micah," *The Bible Knowledge Commentary, Old Testament*, 1486-87.

36   Ibid.

37   Jeremiah 33:14-16 ff; Charles H. Dyer, "Jeremiah," *The Bible Knowledge Commentary, Old Testament*, 1125-26, 1176.

38   Jeremiah 31:31-34; Luke 22:20; 1 Corinthians 11:24-26; Hebrews 8-9 (directly linked with Jeremiah); 12:24.

39   Dyer, "Jeremiah," *The Bible Knowledge Commentary, Old Testament*, 1176; Jeremiah 31:38-40.

40   Dyer, "Jeremiah," ibid.

41   See the overwhelming evidence collected in the classic work on the subject by Peters, *The Theocratic Kingdom*, 3 vols.; McClain, *The Greatness of the Kingdom*; Pentecost, *Things to Come*, 9-15, Chapter 28; idem., *Thy Kingdom Come*; Geisler,

Systematic Theology vol. 4, Chapter 16; Grant R. Jeffrey, *Triumphant Return: The Coming Kingdom of God,* 145-59.

[42] Cf. Jeffrey, *Triumphant Return: The Coming Kingdom of God,* 146-148. They are not allegorical kingdoms as taught by Origin, Augustine, and much medieval theology. For more, consult works listed in note 41. Numerous examples will also be given below.

[43] Geisler, *Systematic Theology, Vol. Four,* 565.

[44] Jeffrey, *Triumphant Return: The Coming Kingdom of God,* 146; and note 8.

[45] Martin, "Isaiah," *The Bible Knowledge Commentary, Old Testament,* 1029.

[46] Ibid. The following prophetic descriptions of the Messiah in Isaiah are listed by Martin, 1049.

[47] Ibid., 1115-16. Hebrew for Messiah, *"masiah,"* means "the Anointed One," and Christ (*christos,* from *chrio,* 'to anoint') is the Greek equivalent of *masiah,"* ibid.

[48] Luke 4:18-19. John Martin writes, "Apparently Isaiah assumed that the messianic Child, Jesus Christ, would establish His reign in one Advent, that when the Child grew up He would rule in triumph. Like the other prophets, Isaiah was not aware of the great time gap between Messiah's *two* Advents." Martin, "Isaiah," *The Bible Knowledge Commentary, Old Testament,* 1053-54; cf. 1 Peter 1:10-12, and Martin's comments on Isaiah 61:1-2, 1115-16. If this was Isaiah's understanding, it must have been because of what God chose to reveal and not to reveal to him.

[49] Ibid., 1116.

[50] Revelation 20:1-3; Pentecost, *Things to Come,* 477; 2 Corinthians 4:4.

[51] Cf. Geisler, *Systematic Theology, Vol. Four,* 562.

[52] Pentecost, *Things to Come,* 420; and see Matthew 18:3, 25:30, 46; Ezekiel 20:37-38; Jeremiah 31:33-34; Zechariah 13:9; Charles H. Dyer, "Ezekiel," *The Bible Knowledge Commentary, Old Testament,* ed. Walvoord and Zuck, 1300.

[53] Pentecost, *Things to Come,* 412-22, with scripture citations; Matthew 25:31-41; Geisler, *Systematic Theology, Vol. Four,* 560-61.

[54] Pentecost, *Thy Kingdom Come,* 311-15; Revelation 7:1-17; 11:1-12; 12:14-16; Daniel 12:2; Isaiah 26:19-20; Hebrews 12:22-24.

[55] Isaiah 32:3-4; John A. Martin, "Isaiah," *The Bible Knowledge Commentary, Old Testament,* 1082.

[56] Exodus 19:5-6.

[57] Martin, "Isaiah," *The Bible Knowledge Commentary, Old Testament,* 1053.

[58] Cf. Pentecost, *Thy Kingdom Come,* 316-17, and Geisler, *Systematic Theology, Vol. Four,* 559-60.

[59] Revelation 12:5.

[60] Pentecost, *Things to Come,* 487-88.

[61] Hosea 2:18.

[62] See Paul's description of the new, incorruptible body in I Corinthians 15:35-57.

[63] Geisler, *Systematic Theology, Vol. Four,* 564.

[64] Pentecost, *Things to Come,* 489, with several biblical references.

[65] Jeremiah 30:17; Ezekiel 34:16; Pentecost ibid.

66   Pentecost, *Things to Come*, 489; Ezekiel 34:16.

67   Martin, "Isaiah," *The Bible Knowledge Commentary, Old Testament*, 1057; Revelation 20:14.

68   Pentecost, *Things to Come*, 480-81.

69   Ibid., 485.

70   Ibid., 481; Matthew 6:10.

71   Martin, "Isaiah," *The Bible Knowledge Commentary, Old Testament*, 1103, 1049.

72   Exodus 19:5-6; Isaiah 49:6.

73   Romans 14:11-12.

74   Geisler, *Systematic Theology, Vol. Four*, 574.

75   Matthew 24:35; Mark 13:31; Luke 16:17; 21:33.

76   Walvoord, *The Revelation of Jesus Christ*, 305-6.

77   Ross, *Why the Universe is the Way It Is*, 196-98. If gravity, or mass, or both, as we now know them, are to be absent, apparently a very different kind of mass would exist to constitute the physical dimensions of the Kingdom and the everlasting spiritual-physical bodies of saints; "some kind of spatial dimensionality (or its equivalent) must exist in the new creation."

78   Walvoord, *The Revelation of Jesus Christ*, 311, 312; cf. Ezekiel 47:10-20; 48:28 Zechariah 9:10; 14:8.

79   Walvoord, *The Revelation of Jesus Christ*, 315, 316. Revelation 21:3, 5-6, 13; 1:8.

80   Revelation 21:15-21; Walvoord, *The Revelation of Jesus Christ*, 323-24.

81   1342 x 1342 = 1,800,964 square miles; wikipedia.org: "List of countries and outlying territories by total area."

82   Walvoord, *The Revelation of Jesus Christ*, 320.

83   Luke 24:30-43; Mark 16:9-14.

84   (1) www.religionstatistics.net; (2) Harris poll, "Religious Views and Beliefs Vary Greatly by Country, According to the Latest Financial Times/Harris Poll," December 20, 2006.

85   www:pewforum.org "U. S. Religious Landscape Survey," "Full Reports."

86   Fulton J. Sheen, "*A Plea for Intolerance*," 1931.

87   Michael Lindsay, Rice University sociologist of religion, in "Religious Americans embrace many paths to eternal life—even if their denominations don't," by Eric Gorsci, AP June 23, 2008.

88   www:barna.org, 2007 poll.

89   Sorokin, *The Crisis of Our Age*. New York: Dutton, c. 1941, 45. I have rounded off Sorokin's decimal points to the nearest whole number.

90   "Or do you not know that wrongdoers will not inherit the kingdom of God? Do not be deceived: Neither the sexually immoral nor idolaters nor adulterers nor men who have sex with men will inherit the kingdom of God." (1 Corinthians 6:9, NIV); cf. Lev. 18, Rom. 1:18-32, I Cor., 6:9-20, I Tim. 1:8-11.

91   Peter Francese, "The Amazing Decline of the Iconic Household," quoted in "18 Signs The Collapse Of Society Is Accelerating." Internet article accessed June 15, 2011.

92   "Casey Anthony—Single Mom of the Year!" by Ann Coulter, in Human Events, July 6, 2011.

93   See note 90 above. "You shall not lie with a male as with a woman. It *is* an abomination" (Leviticus 18:20, New King James Version). "For even their women exchanged the natural use for what is against nature. Likewise also the men, leaving the natural use of the woman, burned in their lust for one another, men with men committing what is shameful, and receiving in themselves the penalty of their error which was due" (Romans 1:26-27, New King James Version).

94   See the disturbing accounts given in Brigitte Gabriel, *They Must Be Stopped*, Chs. 4-5.

95   See the views of Bertrand Russell, George G. Simpson, Ernst Haeckel, Thomas Henry Huxley, Nietzsche, Duchamp, Heidegger, Julian Huxley, Christopher Hitchens, and Richard Dawkins on pp. 79, 85-6, 88, 93-4, 173-83, 186-93, 193-206, 246-48.

96   On the degradation, decline, and possible end of America, see: John Price, *The End of America*. Perry Stone, *Nightmare Along Pennsylvania Avenue*. Mark Hitchcock, *The Late, Great, United States*. Mark Steyn, *After America: Get Ready for Armageddon*; Mark Steyn, *America Alone: the End of the World As We Know It*. Dennis McCallum, *The Death of Truth*. Alvin J. Schmidt, *The Menace of Multiculturalism*. David Limbaugh, *Persecution: How Liberals Are Waging War Against Christianity*. Mark R. Levin, *Men in Black; How the Supremee Court is Destroying America*. Pat Buchanan, *The Death of the West; How Dying Populations and Immigrant Invasions Imperil Our Country and Civilization*. Pat Robertson, *Courting Disaster; How the Supreme Court is Usurping the Power of Congress and the People*. Janet L. Folger, *The Criminalization of Christianity*. Avin J. Schmidt, *The Menace of Multiculturalism*. On the steep decline of Europe, see: Claire Berlinski, *Menace in Europe; Why the Cotinent's Crisis Is America's Too*. Tony Blankley, *The West's Last Chance*. Bruce Thornton, *Decline and Fall; Europe's Slow motion Suicide*. Philip Jenkins, God's Continent: Christianity, Islam, and Europe's Religious Crisis.

27124334R00271

Printed in Great Britain
by Amazon